"Financial crises and stock market crashes are all over financial history. These episodes have already been described in great detail and yet they keep surprising us. This new book deals with the underlying problem: the inherent difficulty of equity valuation. Poitras describes the development of approaches to valuing equity securities from ancient times until the crash of 1929. I am glad to recommend this book to anybody who wants to better understand financial markets."

—*Abe de Jong, Erasmus University, the Netherlands*

"Poitras provides what is by far the most comprehensive and best documented contribution on the topic of the historical foundations of modern equity valuation."

—*Stephen Buser, Professor Emeritus, Ohio State University, USA*

Equity Capital

Capitalism is historically pervasive. Despite attempts through the centuries to suppress or control private ownership of commercial assets, production and trade for profit has survived and, ultimately, flourished. Against this backdrop, accounting provides a fundamental insight: The 'value' of physical and intangible capital assets that are used in production is identical to the sum of the debt liabilities and equity capital that are used to finance those assets. In modern times, this appears as the balance sheet relationship. In determining the 'value' of items on the balance sheet, equity capital appears as a residual, calculated as the difference between the 'value' of assets and liabilities. Through the centuries, the organization of capitalist activities has changed considerably, dramatically impacting the methods used to value, trade and organize equity capital. To reflect these changes, this book is divided into four parts that roughly correspond to major historical changes in equity capital organization.

The first part examines the rudimentary commercial ventures that characterized trading for profit from ancient times until the contributions of the medieval scholastics who affirmed the moral value of equity capital.

The second part deals with the evolution of equity capital organization used in seaborne trade of the medieval and Renaissance Italian city states and in the early colonization ventures of western European powers and ends with the emergence in the market for tradeable equity capital shares during the 17th century.

The third part begins with the 1719–1720 Mississippi scheme and the South Sea bubble in northern Europe and covers the transition from joint-stock companies to limited liability corporations with autonomous shares in England, America and France during the 19th century. This part ends with a fundamental transition in the social conception of equity capital from a concern with equity capital organization to the problem of determining value.

The final part is concerned with the evolving valuation and management of equity capital from the 1920s to the present. This period includes the substantive improvement in corporate accounting methods for publicly traded shares engendered by the Great Depression. This has facilitated the use of 'value investing' techniques and the conflicting emergence of portfolio management methods of modern finance.

Equity Capital is aimed at providing material relevant for academic presentations of the organization and valuation of equity capital, and it is targeted at researchers, academics, students and professionals alike.

Geoffrey Poitras is a Professor of Finance at Simon Fraser University in Canada.

Routledge International Studies in Business History
Series Editors: Jeffrey Fear and Christina Lubinski

Equity Capital

From Ancient Partnerships to
Modern Exchange Traded Funds

Geoffrey Poitras

Routledge
Taylor & Francis Group

NEW YORK AND LONDON

First published 2016
by Routledge
711 Third Avenue, New York, NY 10017

and by Routledge
2 Park Square, Milton Park, Abingdon, Oxon OX14 4RN

Routledge is an imprint of the Taylor & Francis Group, an informa business

© 2016 Taylor & Francis

Library of Congress Cataloging-in-Publication Data
Names: Poitras, Geoffrey, 1954– author.
Title: Equity capital : from ancient partnerships to modern exchange traded funds / by Geoffrey Poitras.
Description: First Edition. | New York : Routledge, 2016. | Series: Routledge international studies in business history ; 32 | Includes bibliographical references and index.
Identifiers: LCCN 2015041551 | ISBN 9781138819931 (hardback : alk. paper) | ISBN 9781315744070 (ebook)
Subjects: LCSH: Stocks—History. | Stock exchanges—History. | Finance—History. | Investments—Law and legislation.
Classification: LCC HG4661 .P65 2016 | DDC 332/.0415—dc23
LC record available at http://lccn.loc.gov/2015041551

ISBN: 978-1-138-81993-1 (hbk)
ISBN: 978-1-315-74407-0 (ebk)

Typeset in Sabon
by Apex CoVantage, LLC

Printed and bound in the United States of America by Publishers Graphics, LLC on sustainably sourced paper.

Contents

PART IV
Conceiving Modern Equity Capital 373

Preface

This book contains many echoes of projects stretching back over two decades. The research time line begins with a project on medieval finance I started while a faculty member at the National University of Singapore in the early 1990s and continues, over many different projects, to the present with a research paper on the trading of shares in the Roman *societates publicanorum* started while visiting the *Università degli studi di Bergamo* in Bergamo, Italy, in 2013. Those familiar with my previous books will find that I reworked and incorporated significant material from many of those efforts—in particular, *The Early History of Financial Economics* (2000), *Security Analysis and Investment Strategy* (2005) and *Valuation of Equity Securities* (2011). I borrowed lesser amounts of material from my edited books, *Pioneers of Financial Economics* (2006, vol.1 and 2007, vol.2) and *Handbook of Research on Stock Market Globalization* (2012). Given concerns expressed in this book on the expanding modern usage of equity derivatives, hedge funds, programmed trading and cash market short selling, there are also small parts of *Risk Management, Speculation and Derivative Securities* (2002) that have migrated to this effort.

As initially conceived, the historical time line for this study of equity capital organization and valuation was to span from antiquity to the end of the Renaissance. This is a period and topic of interest to me, but not too many others. It seems that those who are interested in equity capital organization and valuation want a more recent time line, and those who are interested in that time period are not too interested in how equity capital was organized and profit was determined. At the wise direction of the Routledge editorial staff, I decided to extend the time line to the present. Given the number of historical studies examining topics related to equity capital in this extended time period, there was a considerable amount of research to assemble. The length of the bibliography is evidence of the research effort needed. In contrast to my previous book projects, there is a strong element of dissent about the wealth and income distribution implications of the organization, valuation and taxation of modern equity capital. On the landscape of the intellectual attention space, this book identifies the greatest general threat to economic democracy, not from the limited liability corporation with autonomous shares, but from the failure of an archaic income-based taxation system to deal with the implications of commercial globalization and the associated untaxed and tax-deferred equity capital wealth accumulation.

This history of equity capital is roughly divided into two parts. The earlier part deals with the evolution of equity capital organization, from the partnerships of ancient times to the joint-stock companies of the 18th century. The rudimentary character of commercial activity over this period often involved single voyages or sojourns, with profits distributed at the end of the venture. As a consequence, the valuation of equity capital shares is an uneventful division of profit (or loss) and return of capital (if any). When joint stock organization was used, there was often a public or foreign policy objective in granting a charter with limited term; so even when transferable shares were available, the valuation problem cannot be disentangled from the organizational context. The 19th century marks a turning point from a focus on equity capital organization to equity security valuation. It was during this century that the general limited liability corporation with tradeable autonomous shares emerged. As Ireland et al. (1987) and others detailed, this involved a separation of the 'corporation' from its members, allowing the creation of an 'autonomous share'. Because this share is tradeable, the equity security valuation problem takes center stage during the last part of the historical time line.

Those familiar with my previous books, especially *The Early History of Financial Economics, 1478–1776* (2000), *Risk Management, Speculation and Derivative Securities* (2002) and *Valuation of Equity Securities* (2011), may be concerned that this effort will be a source of more examples of the creeping incursion of typographical and editing errors in modern academic texts. For the sometimes annoying typos in my previous books, I apologize. Though there are no guarantees in life, rest assured that Herculean effort has been made to keep bugs out. As with my previous books, the website at www.sfu.ca/~poitras will have a listing of the typos and other errors that have been uncovered since publication. (In addition to containing errata lists for my previous books, the website has a wealth of material on other subjects.) This book has benefited considerably from the comments of anonymous and not-so-anonymous reviewers on preliminary drafts of this text and other efforts. The risk of omission is such that I provide a global thank you to all who have participated in a review or refereeing process. Feedback and discussion from numerous students and colleagues over the years has also had a significant impact on the topic coverage. At Routledge, I would like to give special thanks to Laura Stearns, David Varley, Brianna Ascher and the production crew. Without their excellent efforts and patience, this book would not have survived to see the light of day.

Prologue

CAPITAL, amongst merchants, bankers, and traders, signifies the sum of money which individuals bring to make up the common stock of a partnership, when it is first formed. It is also said of the stock which a merchant at first puts into trade, for his account. It signifies likewise the fund of a trading company or corporation, in which sense the word stock is generally added to it. Thus we say, the capital stock of the bank, &c. The word capital is opposed to that of profit or gain, though the profit often increases the capital, and becomes itself part of the capital, when joined with the former.

Excerpt from Universal Dictionary of Trade and Commerce, *trans. from French edition by J. Savary (1657–1715) with "Large Additions and Improvements" by* Malachy Postlethwayt (1755)[1]

Capitalism is historically pervasive. Despite attempts through the centuries to suppress or control the private ownership of commercial assets, production and trade for profit has survived and, ultimately, flourished. At the core of the modern capitalist economy are markets where parties to a transaction determine the prices at which capital assets, goods and services are exchanged and profit is generated. In turn, profit and the ability to price debt and equity capital drive the process of capital accumulation that is central to the modern capitalist economy. Against this backdrop, accounting provides a fundamental insight: The 'value' of physical and intangible capital assets that are used in production is identical to the sum of the debt liabilities and equity capital that are used to finance those assets. In modern times, this appears as the balance sheet relationship. In determining the 'value' of items on the balance sheet, equity capital appears as a residual, calculated as the difference between the 'value' of assets and liabilities.[2] Recognizing the potentially complicated implications, calculations and estimations involved, this book addresses two essential historical questions: How was equity capital organized? And, how was the 'value' of equity capital determined?

Historically, how the value of equity capital was determined depends on the context arising from the various financial, social, political and legal roles played by equity capital. As such, it is difficult to overcome philosophical and historical differences over the definition of value. Because 'value' for equity capital involves an *ex ante* variable—expected future 'profit', somehow defined—it is typically unobserved at the time of valuation. With the rising of autonomous exchange traded shares of limited liability corporations, it was possible to value equity capital using the price of a common stock or other equity capital security observed in the financial markets. This 'efficient markets' interpretation of value lacks relevance to equity capital valuation for the rudimentary corporations, co-partnerships, joint-stock companies and partnerships of earlier times. In contrast to the modern efficient markets approach that equates 'market price' with the 'intrinsic value' of a publicly traded equity capital share, modern 'fundamental analysis' assumes that the market price does not necessarily capture the 'intrinsic value' of a publicly traded equity security. At any point in time, the market price may be above or below the intrinsic value, creating opportunities for profitable trading of 'mis-priced' equity capital claims.

Such modern financial definitions of 'value' lack historical relevance to the social, moral and political 'intrinsic value' of equity capital. Through the centuries, the organization of commercial activities has changed considerably, impacting the choice between debt and equity capital in the financing of commercial assets. In turn, there is an underlying social and political tension in this choice, reflected in the rules governing the use of equity capital at a given point in time. Even the use of equity capital by rudimentary partnerships of ancient times was dependent on the ability of the state and ruling class to control commercial activity and compel the use of debt finance. Abuses largely associated with consumption loans contributed to the medieval scholastics morally condemning much debt financing of commercial assets, affirming the moral 'value' of equity capital. Centuries later, the speculative manias of 1719–1720 in northern Europe led to a century-long restriction on the joint-stock organization of equity capital. Legislative actions during the 19th century that produced widespread introduction of 'general' limited liability and incorporation for equity capital organization were the result of political debate that reflects themes in the profound social changes that have overtaken modern society.

To capture the changing value of equity capital over time, this book is divided into four parts that roughly correspond to major historical changes in the organization of equity capital. Following an introductory section on etymology and legal concepts, the first part of the book deals with the rudimentary commercial organizations that characterized trading for profit from ancient times until the canon law contributions by the medieval scholastics. The general geographical area covered is the Middle East, the Mediterranean countries and northern Europe. Equity capital and the *ius fraternitalis* of the partnership were symbiotic during this period, with the extent of empire being a determinant of usage. An important theme is the evolving use of equity capital in long-distance trade. Especially in Roman times, commercial ventures were often slave-run, funded by household capital using *peculium*, negating the use of *societas* (Roman partnership) to obtain equity capital in many commercial ventures (see Abatino et al. 2011). Despite fanciful claims to the contrary by Badian (1972), Malmendier (2009) and others, equity capital in ancient and medieval times was more than difficult to trade. In medieval times, the scholastic analysis of *societas*, usury and risk provides fundamental insights into the moral 'value' of equity capital.

The second part deals with the role of equity capital in the age of European colonization up to the emergence of the market for joint-stock shares in northern Europe. This part covers the transition from the medieval *commenda* partnerships to the regulated companies and joint-stock companies of the 16th and 17th centuries. The requisite development of accounting and commercial arithmetic needed to sustain this evolution is detailed. A seminal event during this period was the commencement of rudimentary exchange trading of Dutch East India Company joint-stock shares. This trade was facilitated by specific items included in the corporate charter related to share transferability. The emergence and expansion of organized trading of shares required various legal changes that impacted equity capital organization (Gelderblom and Jonker 2004; Gelderblom et al. 2011; Gelderblom 2013). Propelled by the Glorious Revolution of 1688, transmission of Dutch trading practices into England led to creative legal methods being used to circumvent restrictions on the formation of English joint-stock companies without royal charters or acts of Parliament (MacLeod 1986; Harris 2000; Murphy 2009a).

The third part narrows the geography to examine the use of equity capital starting from the fascinating 1719–1720 market manias associated with the Mississippi scheme in France and the South Sea bubble in England. These events led to severe restrictions on use of the joint-stock company to raise equity capital for financing commercial assets. These restrictions lasted into the 19th century. In the UK, the US and, to a lesser extent, France, the 19th century saw profound legal changes associated with the widespread introduction of limited liability and incorporation and the subsequent development of global markets for trading 'autonomous' equity capital shares (Ireland 1996). During this period, 'owners' of commercial ventures supplying equity capital became increasingly separated from day-to-day operations. In turn, these changes fuelled the ability to trade and financially value such 'autonomous' equity capital shares, leading to the emergence of a global stock market, centered on exchanges in London, Paris and New York. The political debate surrounding the requisite legislative changes captures fundamental issues associated with the use and organization of equity capital. The associated social and political issues still have echoes in modern times.

Equity capital organized as limited liability corporations with autonomous shares emerged in the 19th century and flourished in the 20th century. As a consequence, the fourth and final part commences with the valuation of equity capital at the beginning of the 20th century and ends with the social history of 'fiduciary capitalism' and the implications of the 'slow motion' crash of equity capital markets in 2008–2009. This period featured the emergence of 'scientific' portfolio diversification using a hodgepodge of equity capital funds. This completed the divorce of equity capital providers from control of the commercial assets that are being funded, an issue Berle and Means identified early in the 20th century. This period also included the Depression-era reforms to equity capital markets that ushered in the modern era of 'fundamental valuation' for equity securities, which relies heavily on the accounting information provided in the regulatory filings of publicly traded companies. Fuelled by technological revolutions associated with radio, television, the computer and wireless communication, the modern era has witnessed changes in the institutional structure of equity security markets associated with: (a) exchange demutualization and consolidation; (b) the introduction of hedge funds and exchange-traded funds; (c) the expansion of online trading; and (d) the growth of equity derivative markets. Although the discussion concentrates on developments in the largest and most liquid equity capital market in the US, the geographical scope in the fourth part is necessarily global.

In addition to detailing the accounting, legal, financial and social history relevant to the evolution of equity capital organization and valuation, this book has other objectives. Despite decades of enhanced regulation, 'scientific' study and attempts at financial 'education', modern equity capital markets continue to be subject to boom and bust cycles that, at times, seriously disrupt the wealth creation process that is central to the modern capitalist economy. In addition, the concentration of wealth in the hands of equity capitalists associated with the capture of the economic gains from technological change has dramatically impacted the social and political landscape of the early 21st century. Modern political institutions have been increasingly incapable of adapting to the threats that such wealth inequities pose for the social fabric, not to mention long-term economic stability. Documenting the 'value' of equity capital in earlier times uncovers a variety of simpler commercial situations that provide useful guidance in understanding the associated 'intrinsic value' of modern equity capital.

Throughout history, social and political tension has surrounded the use of 'debt' or equity capital in the financing of commercial ventures. Much of the modern scholarship on early financial history, such as the influential work of Grief (1989) and Kessler and Temin (2007), focuses on apolitical abstract economic problems of agency and moral hazard in early commercial relationships, especially in external trade. Various contractual methods are identified for resolving agency problems—for example, kinship in the metals trade in Old Assyria; religious affiliation for Maghribi traders; limited liability for *en commandite* co-partnerships. This considerable literature largely ignores the social and political context associated with the organization of equity capital at a given point in time, if only because timeless agency and moral hazard problems are common to either debt or equity financing. Accurate contextualization of equity capital cannot ignore the role of political, social and other factors arising from the organization and use of debt or equity financing for commercial ventures.

The upshot is that this book speaks to a wider audience than scholars of financial history. Equity market practitioners will find subtle connections between valuation methods used in the 19th and early 20th centuries and the methods employed in modern equity security markets. For this audience, the discussion will, hopefully, be entertaining and 'profitable'. Students of social, legal, accounting and financial history will find a new perspective on the evolution of commercial activity in general and the 'virtuous' role of equity capital in particular. There is a 'newness' that comes from moving beyond the exploration of agency and moral hazard problems in commercial contracting that have consumed studies on early financial history. The focus on 'equity capital' provides an alternative approach to the almost universal adoption of physical 'capital' as the relevant variable for historical analysis, as reflected in popular contributions by Piketty (2014) and De Soto (2000). In this book, the 'tent' is large enough to encompass the histories of accounting, economics, finance and law. The largely non-technical discussion will, hopefully, provide the general public with a comprehensive source on the history of equity capital, in the process identifying fundamental social, political and economic issues that are still relevant in modern times.

NOTES

1 Howard (1932, pp.243–4) provides a brief biography of Jacques Savary. Among other accomplishments, Savary was the most active member of the Council of Reform and is credited with so much of the authorship of the Ordinance of 1673 that the commercial code therein contained was commonly known as the "Code Savary."

2 Bernstein (1993, p.6) provides useful examples of the modern presentation of 'equity' and 'equity capital': "The equity interest in an enterprise is the supplier of its basic risk capital. The capital is exposed to all the risks of ownership and provides a cushion or shield for the preferred and loan capital that is senior to it. Since the equity interest is entitled to distributions only after the claims of senior securities have been met, it is referred to as the *residual* interest". Similarly, chapter 8, titled "Analysis of Stockholders' Equity", examines topics such as "The Distinction between Liability and Equity Instruments", "Classification of Capital Stock" and the calculation of "Book Value per Share".

Part I

Equity Capital Prior to Joint-Stock Companies

1 Etymology and Legal Concepts

> Capital has been so variously defined, that it may be doubtful whether it have any generally received meaning.
>
> Nassau Senior (1790–1864)

A THE MODERN EMERGENCE OF 'EQUITY CAPITAL'

Early Problems of Definition

References to 'equities', 'equity capital', 'equity securities' and the like are relatively recent in historical terms. Until the 20th century, there was considerable lack of clarity in definitions of 'capital', and references to 'equity' in relation to 'capital' were concerned with application of the 'law of equity' to legal situations involving owners of the 'capital stock'. Fundamental disagreements about the definition of 'capital' are captured in the academic debate between Böhm-Bawerk (1891) and Irving Fisher (1896, 1904) about the relation between 'capital' and 'interest'. Fisher (1896, p.510) described the problems of definition at that time: "What Senior wrote half a century ago is far truer to-day: 'Capital has been so variously defined, that it may be doubtful whether it have any generally received meaning.'" Fetter (1900, 1907) provided a helpful review of the debate. The modern usage of 'equity' and 'equity capital' emerged haphazardly from this debate, providing some clarity to the confusing collection of definitions. The evolution of the accounting profession and the expanded usage of accounting terminology also contributed to this clarification.[1]

It is only near the end of the chronology for this book that the conventional modern use of 'equity capital' terminology emerged. This is not to imply that the 'essence' of equity capital was not recognized prior to this time; quite the contrary. Rather, there was a somewhat confusing collection of terms that badly needed improvement. An early contribution by Mortimer (1761, p.5) reported the confusing use of 'stock' to refer to both 'public debt' issues and company 'shares', especially those of the public companies. Mortimer does recognize the correct usage: "The word STOCK, in its proper signification, means, that capital in merchandise, or money, which a certain number of proprietors have agreed to be the foundation for carrying on an united commerce, to the equal interest and advantage of each party concerned, in proportion to the sum or share contributed by each." In effect, at least as early as Mortimer (1761), the correct terminology for 'equity capital' was 'stock'. To allay confusion, it became conventional to refer to 'stocks and shares', where 'shares' made explicit reference to equity capital.

In particular, up to the beginning of the 20th century it was conventional to refer to 'stocks and shares', where 'stocks' was a general term that could refer to either debt or equity and 'shares' made reference to equity capital. For example, Withers (1910, p.5) observed: "Stocks and shares, as dealt in on the Stock Exchanges of the world, fall into two main classes. They represent either (1) the debts of Governments, municipalities and other public bodies, or (2) the debts and capitals of joint stock companies". For further clarity, Withers (1910, p.361) provided the following definition in a glossary: "Stock in a general sense means any kind of security dealt in on the Stock Exchange; more particularly a form of debt or capital which is divisible into, and transferable in, odd and varying amounts, and is always registered or inscribed". Until the 20th century, it was trading in 'loan stock', rather than 'shares' in 'joint-stock companies', that constituted the bulk of trading on 'stock exchanges'.

Traditional Usage of 'Capital'

In contrast to the absence of references to 'equity', there was an abundance of references to 'capital'. Fisher (1896, 1904, 1906) recognized significant differences between economists, "business men" and bookkeepers in the definition of 'capital' employed. Dewing (1919) expanded this list to include legal definitions and, perhaps confusingly, identifies the origins of the definition of 'capital' with the Greek philosopher Xenophon (430–354 BC) where "capital was that from which profit may be obtained". Dewing (1953, p.50) also makes an astute observation referring to the use of 'capital' by businessmen: "the accepted meaning of a term by men who have the most occasion to use it invariably finds its way into legal and economic literature". This appears to have been the case with 'equity', though diffusion of this terminology was slow and haphazard. For example, examining the differing usage of 'capital' in economics and accounting, Fetter (1937) made no reference to 'equity'. Initial usage of 'equity' by academics was primarily by those with an immediate connection to the business world.

The confusion and gradual evolution for the meaning of 'equity' in relation to 'capital stock' and 'surplus' in the legal and accounting spheres was captured by Deinzer (1935, pp.334–5). While economists speak of capital "as indicating those material instruments which are concretely used in the production of goods", when referring to the same capital goods the accountant refers to "goods used in a particular business enterprise". In contrast, there is "no uniformity of meaning by the courts of the several states. The property owned and used by the corporation in carrying on its business may be designated by the term capital stock". In some states, capital stock legally referred "to a specific fund of property", making a distinction between 'capital stock' and 'surplus'. In such situations, the terms "capital and capital stock are sometimes used synonymously or interchangeably". Deinzer (p.337) recognized difficulty with the fund approach and observed: "capital stock may be defined as an equity or interest of stockholders in the totality of business property owned by a corporation. The economic values of assets are expressed in terms of money; from the sum of such money values is subtracted the total of liabilities; the resultant amount expresses the money value of stockholders' interest in the totality of assets. The value of this residuum may or may not be the amount of the capital stock."

In one sense, 'capital' can be interpreted as a shortened version of 'equity capital' in the modern sense. Dewing (1953, p.55) reflects this approach: "The capital stock of a corporation always represents, legally, a contract whereby the corporation, as separate from its owners, acknowledges the conditions under which it accepts capital delivered to it by its owners or proprietors". However, the plethora of definitions for capital made this connection opaque. For example, most economists and some businessmen identify 'capital' with the assets side of the balance sheets, especially those assets directly connected to 'production', leading to the specification of 'fixed capital' and 'variable capital'. "All economists make this distinction" (Braudel 1982, p.242). Some initial clarification in the definition of 'equity capital' was obtained by referring to 'common stock' (e.g., Mitchell 1910, 1916), which was often shortened in American sources to 'stock'. With this transition, the traditional definition of 'stock' that encompasses debt securities passed into history, and 'common stock' and 'stock' became conventional references for equity capital.

The gradual adoption of 'equity' terminology in academic studies was propelled by Smith (1924), where the "common stock theory" was proposed (e.g., Harold 1934; Siegel 1998). The prominent economist Irving Fisher was an active proponent of the common stock theory, which maintained the return on an actively managed portfolio of common stocks would outperform bond returns over a long investment horizon. As president of the Investment Managers Company, E. L. Smith was intimately connected to the financial markets. The liberal use of 'equities', 'equity investment' and the like in Smith (1927) reflects the common usage of this terminology among finance practitioners involved in the trading of equity securities. While May (1939) reflects the general acceptance of 'equity capital' in academic studies, 'common stock' was the preferred terminology prior to World War II. Reference to 'equity' was absent from academic studies associated with W.C. Mitchell and the institutional school of economists, where reference to 'common stock' was used (e.g., Macaulay 1938).

In addition to evolution of accounting standards, there were other practical reasons initiating reference to equity capital. The limitations of using 'common stock' to define equity capital were captured by Fisher (1930b), who referenced "equity securities", explicitly recognizing that there were other types of equity capital than just common stock—for example, convertible bonds and warrants. This recognition reflected the dramatic evolution in the equity securities traded in financial markets during the 1920s. In contrast, the influential Graham and Dodd (1934) used an accounting approach to define "Equity" as "Book Value". In keeping with this accounting practice, preferred stock is not identified as an 'equity' security; this reference to book value connects 'equity' only with

Table 1.1 Example of Early 20th-Century Balance Sheet

BABCOCK & WILCOX LIMITED

Balance Sheet, 31st December, 1909.

Dr.

To CREDITORS:—
	£	s.	d.		£	s.	d.
Sundry Creditors	148,763	6	1				
Dividends unclaimed ...	1,142	0	0				
Reserve for estimated further Expenditure on orders invoiced, fall in value of Investments, &c	139,847	3	1		289,752	9	2

To CAPITAL:—
Authorized and Issued.
	£	s.	d.		£	s.	d.
100,000—6 per cent. Cumulative Preference Shares of £1 each, fully paid	100,000	0	0				
830,000—Ordinary Shares of £1 each, fully paid ...	830,000	0	0				
930,000 Shares					930,000	0	0

					£	s.	d.
To RESERVE FUND					500,000	0	0
To DIVIDEND EQUALIZATION FUND					195,000	0	0
To PROFIT AND LOSS ACCOUNT:—							
Balance brought forward	43,278	19	9				
Profit for the year ending 31st December, 1909 ...	360,003	15	0		403,282	14	9

Cr.

	£	s.	d.
By CASH AT BANKERS on Deposit, and Current Accounts, and in Hand London, Glasgow, and Branches ...	325,669	0	1
By INVESTMENTS AT COST	552,303	0	3
By BILLS RECEIVABLE	20,306	6	9
By DEBTORS	558,266	0	0
By EXPENDITURE ON ORDERS NOT INVOICED	61,020	0	1
By STOCK OF MERCHANDISE, AND WORK IN PROGRESS	288,312	14	6
By FREEHOLD LAND AND LEASEHOLD PROPERTY, PLANT, BUILDINGS, PATENTS, AND SHARES IN ASSOCIATED COMPANIES, including additions for the year ending 31st December, 1909	442,758	2	3

Deduct—

Interim Dividends
paid 11th
October, 1909
On Preference
   Shares ...   £ 3,000 0 0
On Ordinary
   Shares ...   66,400 0 0

          69,400 0 0

          333,882 14 9

          £2,248,635 3 11

          £2,248,635 3 11

Source: Balance Sheet (UK) from Withers (1910)

common stock, as the value of preferred stock is deducted to arrive at book value.[2] Propelled by the profound changes in securities laws that gave credence to the regular filing of accurate accounting information by publicly traded companies, references to the 'capital account' gradually were replaced by references to the 'equity account' in standard accounting discussions. The extent of current accounting practices regarding 'equity' calculation are reflected in the 'Statement of Shareholder Equity' that is prepared for the securities filings of publicly traded companies.

B   BASIC CHARACTERISTICS OF EQUITY CAPITAL

Accounting Definitions

In modern usage, reference to 'capital' can be identified with the balance sheet relationship where **Assets = Liabilities + Equity**. In this context, **Assets** represent the physical 'capital', variable 'capital' and, possibly, the intangible 'capital' that generate the net cash flows for the firm or individual.[3] In turn, the Assets are financed with a combination of debt obligations (**Liabilities**) and equity capital (**Equity**). For a modern corporation, this distinction between the sources of financial 'capital' given by the right-hand side of the balance sheet is well defined. Legally, debt 'capital' is a contractual obligation defined by the indenture or similar contract, while equity capital depends on the specifics of the ownership structure and the legal environment provided by the corporation law and other statutes. Many modern commercial operations have a large and permanent stock of physical assets, financed by the pooling of equity capital from a large number of 'owners'. Such operations are typically organized as limited liability corporations, for which modern corporation law provides essential characteristics of the legal environment. When the equity capital is traded on public markets, securities laws also assume importance.

Modern colloquial usage of 'equity' often belies the conceptual meaning of 'equity capital'. For the modern household balance sheet: **Assets − Liabilities = Net Worth**. If only a specific asset is of interest, then **Asset Value − Debt Secured by Asset = Net Asset Value**. In colloquial usage, 'equity' is used to reference both Net Worth (household equity) and Net Asset Value. For example, a homeowner will refer to the 'equity' in a residential property as the market value of the property minus the unpaid balance on the mortgage. However, in a more technical sense, **Equity Capital** is conceptually applicable only for commercial situations where profit and loss is shared. In other words, 'equity' requires sharing of profit and loss, which is not relevant to the single entity household or sole proprietorship. For this reason, **Net Worth** is the appropriate technical reference for household capital and wealth. Similarly, equity capital involves joint asset ownership and requires some method of management and organization. Net asset value may enter the calculation of the value of equity capital, but net worth does not sufficiently capture basic characteristics of equity capital.

Table 1.2 Inter-war, Pre-SEC US Balance Sheet

CALCULATION OF BOOK VALUE OF UNITED STATES STEEL COMMON ON
DECEMBER 31, 1932
CONDENSED BALANCE SHEET DECEMBER 31, 1932 (*in millions*)

Assets			Liabilities		
1	Property Investment Account (less depreciation)	$1,651	7	Common Stock	$870
			8	Preferred Stock	360
2	Mining Royalties	69	9	Premium on Common Stock	81
3	Deferred Charges[1]	2	10	Bonded Debt	96
4	Miscellaneous Investments	19	11	Mining Royalty Notes	19
			12	Installment Deposits . . .	2
5	General Reserve Fund Assets	20	13	Current Liabilities . . .	47
6	Current Assets	398	14	Contingency and Other Reserves . . .	37
			15	Insurance Reserves . . .	46
			16	Appropriated Surplus	270
			17	Undivided Surplus . . .	329
		$2,159			$2,159

Tangible assets	$2,159,000,000
Less: All liabilities ahead of common (Sum of items 8, 10, 11, 12, and 13)	524,000,000
Accumulated dividends on preferred stock	4,504,000
Net assets for common stock	1,630,496,000
Book value per share (on 8,700,000 shares).	$187.40

Source: Balance Sheet (US) from Graham and Dodd (1934)

[1] Considerable argument could be staged over the question whether Deferred Charges are intangible or tangible assets, but as the amount involved is almost always small, the matter has no practical importance. It is more convenient, of course, to include the Deferred Charges with the other assets. Standard Statistics Company, Inc., however, rules them out.

Ancient Instances of Equity Capital

In ancient times, commercial operations requiring equity capital, being relatively simple, were typically organized as some form of partnership. For this reason, it is difficult to compare them to modern equity capital organization. In particular, the fundamental modern distinction between household and commercial balance sheets was often blurred in earlier times. This distinction between household and commercial wealth has a long history, going back at least as far as Xenophon's *Okonomikos* (ca. 380 BC), in which 'capital' is "what a man possesses outside of his own household" (Dewing 1953, p.45). As a consequence, a basic characteristic of equity capital is that two or more 'merchants' are involved in a commercial venture where profit and loss are shared 'equitably'. In addition, in the long-distance trade so important to the early history of equity capital, many early partnerships were formed only for a single venture. The accumulation and permanence of modern equity capital in commercial ventures is one point of sharp demarcation between early and modern equity capital organization.

An important historical example of the need to identify the household as the source of capital is the Roman *peculium*, where the head of the household (*pater familias*) would make a loan of 'capital' to a slave or other agent for use in a particular commercial activity, such as the manufacture of textiles or the rearing and grazing of animals. All profits from the commercial venture would, under Roman law, be the property of the master. However, if the master did not participate in the management of the commercial venture, the extent of liability would be limited to the initial amount of the *peculium* plus any payments of profit from the venture made over time. At the end of the commercial venture, the capital and accumulated profit retained in the enterprise would be returned to the master. Various sources indicate financing using *peculium* was the conventional legal structure used in commercial ventures in the Roman Empire. In contrast, equity capital was associated with commercial ventures using the Roman form of partnership organization, the *societas*.

Following Hansmann et al. (2006), the *peculium* exhibited "complete owner shielding (limited liability) but no entity shielding at all". Similar to modern corporate limited liability, complete owner shielding means that, under typical conditions where the master did not engage in management of the commercial venture, losses to the owner from the venture were limited. Creditors of the 'entity' would only have claims against the slave or other agent and the *peculium* assets. However, the master's financial and social status would impact the ability of the *peculium* to enter contracts and secure loans on favorable terms. This follows because, in the event that the master went into bankruptcy, assets held by the *peculium* were attachable by the creditors of the master (i.e., there was no entity shielding). In addition, unlike modern limited liability corporations, the *peculium* featured a single owner who, in many situations, obtained the *peculium* funding by borrowing against or pledging landed property. Can funds advanced to the *peculium* be classified as 'equity capital'? Such a question illustrates the quandary of applying modern concepts to the ancient world.

While the capital used in the *peculium* had some characteristics of modern 'equity capital', it does not fit the conventional modern criteria unless the source of funds was commercial—for example, from profit generated by the activities of the *peculium*—and did not originate from the household balance sheet. Commercial ventures in the ancient world involving equity capital were conventionally organized as partnerships. Ventures involved in long-distance trade tailored the partnership organization to the needs of those ventures. As such, an essential feature of 'equity capital'—the sharing of profit, possibly negative, among the shareholders in a commercial venture—is reflected in Roman law of *societas*, which codified partnership practices from ancient times (Gaius, *Elements* Book 3, Sec.150): "If no agreement has been made as to the division of profit and loss, it must be in equal shares. If the shares are expressed in the event of profit but not in the event of loss, the loss must be divided in the same proportions as the profit." A *peculium* lacks this essential characteristic, as profit is not strictly shared, but is the property of the master.

What Is Equity Capital?

Equity capital originates when merchants combine together in a commercial venture with the objective of making profit. This characteristic of equity capital is inconsistent with sole proprietorships and not-for-profit ventures. There is no sharing of profit in these arrangements, though a sole proprietor can have 'net worth' in a business that can be 'valued', just as a not-for-profit can have 'net worth' in a residential building that can be 'valued'. A more complicated case is the capital used in state and state-sponsored enterprises. In most cases, financing of such ventures also does not technically qualify as equity capital. However, consider the construction of a bridge by a partnership between a government and a construction contractor. In partnership with the contractor, the cost of construction and toll revenues from the completed bridge are shared according to some formula set out in the partnership agreement. This could be an equity capital arrangement. In other words, it is possible for governments and other entities to qualify as a 'merchant' in a commercial venture financed using equity capital as long as essential features, such as sharing of profit and loss, are present.

The alternative to using equity capital in financing commercial ventures is to issue debt. Unlike in an equity capital arrangement, in a loan transaction the risk of commercial losses falls on the borrower. As such, the incidence of risk is another basic characteristic separating equity capital from debt. Over time, the extent of liability for losses evolved considerably, and partnership contracts were used that had characteristics associated with debt. One variation of the 'sea loan'—also known as a bottomry loan or transmarine loan—limited the investor's risk and fixed the amount of payment the investor would receive at the end of the loan. Given the sometimes severe restrictions on lending at interest in ancient and medieval times, much attention was given to determining whether such transactions were usurious, as generally maintained by the medieval Schoolmen, or 'licit usury', as concluded by the Roman jurists. The licit medieval *commenda* contract limited the investor's risk and fixed the 'shares' of profit. Limited liability and the ability to incorporate represent essential features that alter the character of equity capital and facilitate exchange trading of equity capital shares (e.g., Halpern et al. 1980; Forbes 1986).

In addition to having 'sufficient' sharing of risk, the timing and type of payment can be used to distinguish equity capital from debt. In exchange for the borrower assuming the commercial risk, the providers of loan capital agree to the amount of interest payments. Failure to make interest payments or to return loan principal at the end of the agreement carries severe sanction.

Equity capital requires a sharing of losses as well as profits. Modern preferred stock is a hybrid that offers a regular payment not depending on the amount of positive profit. As with common stock, failure to make a preferred stock dividend payment does not have the severe bankruptcy sanction associated with defaulting on a debt payment. Like common stock, preferred stock usually does not have a fixed maturity date, and the amount of equity capital that can be raised using preferred stock is determined by the corporate charter or partnership agreement. In contrast to common stock, preferred stock has little, if any, voting rights associated with ownership. Significantly, while having the debt-like feature of no profit and loss sharing, preferred stock is reported in modern accounting as part of the equity account due to the lack of a bankruptcy implication in the event a scheduled preferred dividend payment is not made.

Against this backdrop, the essential characteristic that differentiates equity capital from loan capital is the participation in the profit and loss that can arise in a commercial venture, where the organization of this participation can be structured by agreement. From the rudimentary partnerships of ancient times, the various forms for such agreements include: the Roman *societas;* the *commenda* and the *compagnia* of the Middle Ages and the Renaissance; the various forms of the joint-stock company from the 16th to the 19th century; and, ultimately, the limited liability corporation, with autonomous exchange-traded shares. In contrast, the requirement to make payment of principal and interest on a loan is independent of the success of the commercial venture. This particular distinction between debt and equity capital was especially important in early times. For example, in the ancient societies of Mesopotamia, consumption loan transactions were often made with default in mind in order to acquire the bonded labor and, possibly, the land of the borrower. As a consequence, the legal and social environment for debt capital differed substantively from that for equity capital.

Identification of equity capital in early history is complicated by the frequent confluence of the household and commercial balance sheets. In addition, families with political power were sometimes able to structure favorable commercial relationships that acted to shield personal wealth. For example, Frank (1927, p.275) observed about the timocratic Roman civilization: "Roman history does not point to a single effective leader trained in business". The use of slaves and children *in potestate* endowed with *peculium* to conduct commercial ventures limited the liability of wealthy Romans not involved in managing the business. Especially in ancient times, family relationships, religion and kinship played a key role in the structure of merchant networks essential to the external trade and colonization that generated numerous commercial opportunities for equity capital investors. Miskimin (1975, p.116) captured the ethos of two or more merchants combining equity capital in a commercial venture where the profit, possibly negative, was shared 'equally': "Even during the most dismal and bleak centuries . . . long-distance trade was undertaken by those intrepid adventurers who were prepared to risk the dangers of the sea or overland travel in search of great rewards afar, which were kept at high levels by the very dangers that turned away the fainthearted."

C   THE ETYMOLOGY OF 'EQUITY' AND 'CAPITAL'

Early Definitions of Capital

Despite the voluminous definitions of 'capital' in numerous sources, the etymologies provided for 'capital' are not consistent. For example, Fetter (1937, p.5) provided the following etymology for capital:

> 'Capital' . . . made its first appearance in medieval Latin as an adjective *capitalis* (from *caput*, head) modifying the word *pars*, to designate the principal sum of a money loan. The principal part of a loan was contrasted with the 'usury'—later called interest—the payment made to the lender in addition to the return of the sum lent. This usage, unknown to classical Latin, had become common by the thirteenth century and possibly had begun as early as 1100 A.D., in the first chartered towns of Europe.

In contrast to the literal etymology of Fetter, Dewing further hypothesized that 'head' refers to the use of the head or visage of important persons on coins dating as far back as 555 BC. Dewing (1953, p.45) makes a direct connection between capital and wealth in ancient times:

> Wealth in the days of Greece and Rome consisted of specific material things—land, houses, ships, slaves, tools and coins. Consequently, when the Roman merchant of the time of Augustus wished to gather together a hoard of wealth, other than land, that would occupy a small compass, he would corral a mass of coins; and most of these coins, especially the Roman gold coins, bore a head. It was his capital, his reserve of material resources. Thus the Roman concept of capital, as a reserve of hoarded wealth, passed to the commercial cities of Medieval Italy—thence to England and western Europe.

The Latin root *capitalis* thus sustains an origin for 'capital' in Roman times not necessarily connected to 'the principal sum of a money loan'.

While the actual word 'capital' has a Latin root, the concept of capital had a much earlier beginning. As with other aspects of ancient history, careful attention to context, translation and interpretation of a limited number of surviving sources is required in order to provide an accurate impression of the historical situation. Consider the translated quote from Dewing (1953) from the Greek philosopher Xenophon (430–354 BC) where "capital was that from which profit may be obtained". By comparison, the Loeb Classical Library translation of Xenophon's *Oeconomicus* gives this translation: "wealth is that from which a man can derive profit". The surrounding discussion in the text is concerned with the relationship between 'profit', productive 'property' and 'wealth'. Direct connection of 'capital' to funds used to finance a commercial enterprise is lacking. Dewing (1953, p.44) traced the first use of 'capital' "in anything resembling its current usage" to the English trading companies, noting especially the East India Company records of 1614. Without sufficient context, even this less ambitious historical reference gets caught up in the confusion surrounding the various modern definitions of 'capital'.

Perhaps Braudel (1982, pp.232–3) provided the most accurate etymology:

> *Capitale* (a Late Latin word based on *caput* = head) emerged in the twelfth to thirteenth centuries in the sense of funds, stock of merchandise, sum of money or money carrying interest. It was not at first defined with any rigour, as the discussions of the time centred primarily on interest and usury . . . Italy, the forerunner of modernity in this respect, was at the centre of such discussions. It was here that the word was first coined, made familiar and to some extent matured. It appears incontestably in 1211 and is found from 1283 in the sense of the capital assets of a trading firm. In the fourteenth century, it is to be found practically everywhere: in Giovanni Villani, in Boccaccio, in Donato Velluti. On 10 February 1399, Francesco di Marco Datini wrote from Prato to one of his correspondents: 'Of course, if you buy velvet or woollen cloth, I want you to take out an insurance on the capital (*il chapitale*) and on the profit [to be made]; after that, do as you please'. The word, and the reality it stood for appears in the sermons of St Bernardino of Siena (1380–1444), '. . . *quamdam seminalem rationem lucrosi quam communiter capitale vocamus*', 'the prolific cause of wealth we commonly call capital'.

Based on this, it appears that Dewing's claim of an origin for 'capital' in its modern sense in the records of English trading companies is misplaced. The selection of medieval Italy, also obscured by Fetter, seems consistent with the historical record. Primary sources as early as the Genoese notarial records of the 11th century identify more sophisticated commercial development in the Italian city states compared with the rest of Europe. Various Italian mercantile and other records use the word in a more-or-less modern sense, providing further support for Braudel's historical etymology.

From Adam Smith and Karl Marx to Modern Definitions

Focus on historical roots can obscure the philosophical evolution of 'capital' as a concept in a broader social or legal or financial or economic theory. With Marx (*Capital,* vol. III), there is an alienation of physical capital from control of commercial operations: "the abolition of capital as private property within the confines of the capitalist mode of production itself". As Henderson (1986, p.126) observed: "The profit income received in the form of dividends by the money capitalist is an income derived from mere property ownership and not from any value-creating function performed by such [equity] capitalists, who are superfluous to the value-creating processes of production". This 'alienation' is a decidedly different view of the 'capital' than the 'agency costs' associated with the separation of joint-stock capital ownership from control of commercial operation initially identified by Adam Smith and pioneered in the 20th century by Berle and Means. These two historical perspectives on 'capital'—which are central to modern perspectives on 'capital' and 'capitalism'—are separated by the fundamental transition of equity capital organization permitted by general registration for limited liability corporations during the 19th century.

The conceptual difference between the 'capital' of Smith and that of Marx is apparent in modern scholarship. Marx is an important part of an intellectual tradition searching for the inexorable 'laws of capitalism'. As Acemoglu and Robinson (2015, p.3) observed: "Economists have long been drawn to the ambitious quest of discovering the general laws of capitalism. David Ricardo, for example, predicted that capital accumulation would terminate in economic stagnation and inequality as a greater and greater share of national income accrued to landowners. Karl Marx followed him by forecasting the inevitable immiseration of the proletariat." The contemporary popularity of this intellectual tradition is reflected in the surprisingly widespread popularity in both the academic and popular media of "Thomas Piketty's (2014) tome, *Capital in the 21st Century*, [which] emulates Marx in his title, his style of exposition, and his critique of the capitalist system. Piketty is after general laws that will demystify our modern economy and elucidate the inherent problems of the system—and point to solutions" (Acemoglu and Robinson 2015, p.3). In this tradition, capital and capitalism are intimately connected.

Piketty is ultimately concerned with "putting distribution back at the heart of economics". An important part of the argument supporting Piketty (2014) is use of 'empirical data' to demonstrate the rate of return on capital exceeds the growth rate of the economy, resulting in an increasing inequality of wealth within and across countries. Such arguments depend fundamentally on a particular definition of 'capital'. While a claim that the rate of return on capital exceeds the growth rate of the economy implies a physical definition of 'capital', Piketty (2015, p.70) claimed that any definition of capital depends on the historical context:

> Capital is not an immutable concept: it reflects the state of development and prevailing social relations of each society . . . The boundary between what private individuals can and cannot own has evolved considerably over time and around the world, as the extreme case of slavery indicates. The same is true of property in the atmosphere, the sea, mountains, historical monuments, and knowledge. Certain private interests would like to own these things, and sometimes they justify this desire on grounds of efficiency rather than mere self-interest. But there is no guarantee that this desire coincides with the general interest.

This definition seems to reference an association between capital and ownership of property. In contrast, in *The Mystery of Capital* De Soto (2000) argued that 'dead capital' associated with inadequate claims to title for physical assets such as land and houses prevents entrepreneurs in developing countries from accessing 'active capital' needed to fund commercial ventures.

Written at the end of the 19th century, after the emergence of the limited liability corporation with autonomous shares, *Capital* III perceived an 'alienation of capital' that Smith could not foresee. As Henderson (1986, p.127) observed, one facet of 'finance capitalism' was "a matter of alienation, the owning capitalist estranged from his capital, the functioning capitalist replaced by managers who exploit the workers for the benefit of others who are superfluous to the production process". Whereas Smith perceived significant agency costs associated with a separation of management and ownership in joint-stock companies, Marx observed a more developed stage of equity capital organization, where separation of ownership from control of the production process generates surplus value. The pervasive character of the associated 'alienation of capital' was an essential element in the Marxian thesis about the 'laws of capitalism'. In modern times, diverse notions of 'capital' and 'capitalism' have led to the 'varieties of capitalism' approach that informs the two-volume effort by Neal and Williamson (2014) that aims to trace the historical evolution of 'capitalisms' from ancient to modern times.

The Connection between Equity and Capital

Given this background, the relevant etymology for 'equity capital' revolves around the problematic meaning for 'equity'. Fortier (2005, p.3) observed that "equity taxes simple notions of etymology". Similarly, Falcón y Tella (2008, p.13) called the word 'equity' "an ambiguous term." Falcón y Tella argued that the historical approach is "indispensable" in understanding the concept of equity and identified several distinct historical periods. The earliest period in the etymology of 'equity' is represented by the Greek *epieikeia,* a concept found in the writings of Aristotle, especially *Nichomachean Ethics,* and Plato (e.g., *The Republic*). For Aristotle, equity had a positive tone, while for Plato the tone was negative. In both cases, 'equity' translated roughly as 'correction of the generic law to suit the specific case' (p.15). The notion of equity evolved for Plato. Initially (in *The Republic*), Plato maintained that failures in the general laws could be adjusted by the wise and prudent statesman, who would stand above the law and was able to make 'equitable' adjustments in specific cases. The difficulties in identifying a wise and prudent ruler eventually led Plato to seek general laws to which even the ruler was subservient. In this case, equity claims reflected negatively on the perfection of law and the art of politics.

Applying to the 'justice of a specific case', *epieikeia* involves 'correcting generic law to suit a specific case'. The Greek root word for *epieikeia* is *epieikes,* which means reasonable or moderate. Applied to the law, numerous Greek philosophers used *epieikeia* to distinguish between the justice of a specific case and the abstract ideal justice which a system of laws aims to obtain. Greek philosophers generally differed as to whether *epieikeia* was a positive or negative concept, with significantly different implications for the conduct of legal affairs. For Plato and others seeking an ideal 'rule of law', *epieikeia* was an imperfection, a deviation from the ideal. To them, the 'rule of law' was supreme, and judges were to be severely restricted in exercising judgment in the application of laws. In contrast, for Aristotle *epieikeia* was a 'correction' of the law that, in specific cases, seeks a 'more just' outcome than the 'rule of law'. By the Middle Ages, Thomas Aquinas and other scholastics captured the subsequent adoption of 'equity' in canon law associated with the Aristotelean concept of *epieikeia*.

In modern times, it is the positive Aristotelean *epieikeia* that is the accepted version.

Epieikeia is so deeply rooted in Aristotelean philosophy that some translators resist the temptation to translate the word as 'equity', preferring to leave *epieikeia* untranslated. While Plato viewed *epieikeia* in the technical context of applying a law to a specific case, Aristotle elevated *epieikeia* to the status of 'virtue', providing a fundamental connection to his theory of ethics. This debate over the interpretation of *epieikeia* took place at a time when Greek society was governed by the harsh laws and customs of ancient times. For example, Aristotle identified difficulties with applying the Greek law that a foreigner climbing the city walls was to be sentenced to death. Designed to punish attacking enemies, the law would require putting to death an individual climbing the wall for less nefarious reasons, such as to enter without paying an entry toll. Ancient Greek society tended toward strict application of the 'rule of law', which would have the person put to death, whatever the specifics of the case. Aristotle was arguing against such actions, allowing for virtuous intervention in specific cases.

The etymology of 'equity' capital in modern commercial usage combines Aristotelean and Roman roots. Aristotle's influence on Aquinas and other scholastics' interpretation of equity provided a system of equity based on "plain justice and good faith" (Kerr 1929, p.355) that was the foundation for subsequent development of the law merchant, used for centuries by merchants to settle disputes. "Etymologically, . . . as its first meaning, *'aequitas'* seems to refer to equality, and in legal terms means that law has as an end the awarding of equal protection to equal interests . . . the law must be the same for all individuals" (Falcón y Tella 2008, p.23). This interpretation fits with the Commutative vs. Distributive Justice identified by Malynes (1622):[4]

> *Justice* is administered, which is *Distributive* and *Commutative*. The *Commutative* part includeth *Traffick*, which is the sole peaceable instrument to in rich kingdomes and common-weales, by the means of *Equalitie* and *Equitie*, performed especially by the *Law Merchant* by reason of her stabilitie.

It is tempting to extend *epieikeia* to interpret 'equity capital' as 'virtuous', as in Islamic finance or medieval scholasticism, an interpretation that is relevant to distributive justice. In seeking to apply *epieikeia* to problems of commutative justice, medieval scholastics also developed canon law doctrines concerning usury and risk that were not favourable to debt-financed commercial transactions.

D   EQUITY CAPITAL AND CONCEPTS OF LAW

Types of Law

The legal history of equity capital includes: the early law codes of Sumer and Babylonia; the Roman law of partnership (*societas*) and 'sea loans' (*foenus nauticum*); the medieval and Renaissance *commenda* and *compagnia* contracts; the canon law and 'law merchant'; the regulated and joint stock chartered companies of the 16th to 18th centuries; and the modern law of incorporation and limited liability. Concepts of law appear again and again as essential elements in the history of equity capital. This begs a fundamental question: How does the law impact the organization and valuation of equity capital? For example, medieval scholastic doctrine and the associated canon law was profoundly concerned with the moral 'value' of equity capital. As Noonan (1957, p.21) stated: "A firm belief in the rationality, immutability and universality of law is at the heart of the scholastic approach to all moral problems." Yet, canon law and scholastic doctrine evolved to accommodate commercial developments. Strong canon law restrictions on payment of interest were gradually relaxed to admit 'moral' exceptions to the usury sanctions.

For purposes of discussing history related to financing, conduct and organization of commercial ventures, three general types of law can be identified: divine law, positive or civil law and natural law. In Jewish and Christian traditions, divine law originates with the Bible. However, interpretation of scripture is complicated. St Paul's Epistle to the Romans (Romans 1–16) provides a useful example. St Paul recognizes the commandments of the Old Testament, divine law as revealed to the Jews and to be accepted by Christians. He also recognizes the divine law revealed in the New Testament, which incorporates and advances the divine law of the Old Testament, and recognizes law that extends beyond divine law and applies to all individuals, whether Christian, Jew, Gentile or pagan. This law, which is an interpretation of natural law, imposes "natural moral duties" (Noonan 1957, p.21) required to maintain civil society. Canon law evolved as a collection of laws providing scholastic interpretation of the divine law contained in the scriptures.

Natural law is difficult to define precisely. Discussion of natural law can be found in the writings of Greek philosophers, such as Aristotle, and was explicitly developed in Roman law. Natural law is immutable. "The natural law may not be dispensed from by any human authority. It binds all men. Its first principles are innate, though experience is necessary for their application or development. Sometimes the natural law is considered in its subjective principles, and then it is identified with reason itself; sometimes it is considered in its objective content then it is identified with what is taught by reason" (p.23). Natural law applies to fundamental issues, such as the rules governing union of the sexes, the birth and raising of children and the proper treatment of neighbours. Because divine law also speaks to these issues, medieval canonists did not formally distinguish between divine law and natural law. By the 18th century, natural law philosophy had largely superseded scholasticism.

Unlike natural and divine law, civil or positive law is more changeable and does differ across time and location. In modern times, 'civil' or positive law encompasses a range of legal areas such as criminal law, constitutional law and the civil tort law. In addition to governing commercial relationships, civil law is responsible for maintaining social order and, by design, must recognize that virtue is sometimes a difficult objective to achieve. Vices may be permitted, if these do not conflict with the social order. Civil law is made by governments or by local custom and, as a result, can be adapted to conform to changing social and commercial norms. Despite these qualifications, there are limits to the types of civil laws that can be imposed. In particular, natural law is the measure of civil law. For example, natural law dictates that criminals must be punished. Civil law establishes the precise punishment that will be applied. As demonstrated repeatedly over the centuries, civil laws that violate natural law are unreasonable and can lead to the breakdown of social order.

Significantly, natural law and divine law do not provide precise guidance on numerous issues of importance to civil law. The institution of private property is a case in point. Is private property protected under natural law? The answer to this question is at the root of many fundamental political, social and economic questions, and it has been an essential feature in the evolution of equity capital. Capitalist societies maintain that reason dictates private property is required for social peace and the encouragement of industry. Hence, private property rights are derived from natural law, although the specific form of private property rights have to be determined by civil law. In turn, private property rights play a central role in determining the use of equity capital in commercial ventures. For example, in scholastic doctrine, usury is considered a form of theft, violating the property rights of the individual who is required to make these unjust payments. As such, the scholastic usury doctrine applies equally to rich and poor, providing substantial impetus to the use of equity capital in financing commercial ventures during the Middle Ages.

De Roover (1944, p.185) directly addressed the impact of the scholastic usury doctrine and arrived at a forceful opinion:

> The usury prohibition should be taken more seriously than it usually is. One should not assume that the canonist doctrine on usury was merely a topic for academic discussion among theologians. The opposite is true: the usury prohibition had a tremendous influence on business practices all through the Middle Ages, the Renaissance, the Reformation period, and even down to the French Revolution. Since the taking of interest was ruled out, such a practice had to be concealed by resorting to various subterfuges, which the merchants justified by all kinds of sophisticated and fallacious arguments.

That interest was paid in commercial transactions during the Renaissance and Reformation is not disputable. What is of topical interest are the techniques and arguments that were used to structure licit interest-bearing transactions. Understanding of these techniques and arguments requires discussion of how the scholastic usury doctrine evolved and the permitted exceptions to this doctrine, such as *cambium* and *census* and, especially, the *societas*. In this vein, the legal history of commercial law is distinct from criminal and constitutional law. For much of early history, legal mechanisms for resolving commercial disputes were separate from the courts that decided criminal and constitutional matters. Merchant custom, somehow defined, tended to determine the legal outcome of a commercial dispute, independent of the locale where the dispute was being settled. However, at least since Bewes (1923), there has been scholarly debate surrounding the extent to which merchant law represented a 'transnational law' independent of local legal constraints.

Roman Law Origins

Compared to modern limited liability corporations, the legal environment for organizing and valuing equity capital is different when the ownership structure is a *societas* or partnership, an essential form of business organization throughout ancient and early history. The influence of the Roman *societas* on the subsequent centuries of equity capital organization has been profound. The extent and duration of the Roman Empire, combined with the careful codification of Roman laws, provided the legal foundation for the financing of subsequent commercial activities, especially in long-distance trade. Yet, it is well known the Romans adopted and adapted commercial laws of countries they conquered, such as Greece. For example, the Greek sea loan described by Demosthenes (384–322 BC) has the essential legal features of the Roman *foenus nauticum*. Modern knowledge of Roman law comes from the *Corpus Juris Civilis* prepared under the instruction of the Eastern Roman Emperor Justinian I (482?–565). In turn, the Roman law of Justinian was a foundational influence for later European laws governing commercial organization.

While the corpus of modern corporation law evolved over the centuries, it was not until the 19th century that the limited liability corporation started to take modern form. In contrast, the origins of the 'law' surrounding partnerships predate recorded history. The rudimentary character of most commercial operations in the agrarian societies of antiquity did not require the permanent equity capital stock needed by modern corporations with publicly traded common stock. In many situations, the value of equity capital was directly related to the profit from a particular venture. For example, equity capital from an individual merchant or partnership of merchants would be used to purchase goods to be carried by sea or land to another location, where the goods would, hopefully, arrive in good order and be sold by a travelling partner or an agent. At the end of the venture, profits and return on capital would be distributed in shares determined by the specific arrangements for the transactions. Especially in ancient times, kinship, military, political and religious affiliations determined the structure of equity partnerships.

The modern organization of equity capital depends fundamentally on the properties of limited liability, incorporation and autonomous shares. While today there are a wide variety of legal forms of equity capital organization, such as the traditional partnership, the limited liability company and the limited liability partnership (e.g., Guinnane et al. 2007; Ribstein and Sargent 1997), the combined legal characteristics of limited liability and corporate status have proved to be the most expedient for public trading of equity securities, an essential feature of the modern equity capital landscape. Recognizing that there is a much longer historical time line for the evolution of these legal characteristics than for equity capital organization, the tipping point for the widespread introduction of limited liability and corporate status for commercial ventures can be traced to debates that took place during the 19th century.

Having the most influential market for trading equity capital during this period, debates in the UK have particular significance. Alternative forms of equity capital organization employed elsewhere, such as the French *société en commandite simple*, were considered in these debates but not widely adopted in practice.

Limited liability, incorporation and market trading of equity securities are fundamental to the modern equity capital landscape. This situation begs the following questions: When did trading in equity capital 'shares' in a commercial venture begin? How does limited liability and incorporation facilitate this trade? Many conditions need to be satisfied before a 'share' in a commercial venture can be 'traded'. The precise conditions depend on the legal type of business organization. For various reasons, a 'share' in a private partnership is more than difficult to trade than a 'share' in an exchange-traded, limited liability corporation. Recently, claims for ancient 'trading' of equity capital shares in commercial ventures have been made for the *societates publicanorum* of the Roman Republic, where corporate or joint stock organization is also claimed (e.g., Badian 1972; Malmendier 2009). Such fanciful claims suffer a number of defects. In addition to conceptual difficulties with the rationale and commercial basis for such trading, there is an underlying confusion about the organization of equity capital as 'corporate' or joint stock. Neither the joint-stock nor the corporate claim has a sound basis in the commercial context of the Roman economy, because the Roman Republic had not developed sufficient legal foundation to sustain such forms of organization.

Legal and economic historians have long recognized differences between joint-stock and 'corporate' organization (e.g., Poitras 2000, pp.267–72). For example, Kessler and Temin (2007, p.318) recognized this distinction in making the following claim about the *societates publicanorum*: "There is evidence showing that at least some Roman companies functioned similarly to the joint-stock companies of the English and the Dutch in the sixteenth and seventeenth centuries". This could implicitly reference the appearance of a market for trading in shares of the *VOC* (Dutch East India Company), a joint-stock company, that commenced in 1602. However, the claim for share trading in the 16th and 17th centuries is muted. This predates the historical emergence of 'autonomous' shares of private, commercial limited liability 'corporations' during the 19th century (e.g., Taylor 2006; Blair 2003; Ireland 1996). There is a legal and historical distinction between a 16th-to-17th-century 'joint-stock company'—chartered with a public purpose and a separate 'corporate' identity but with liability determined more in the fashion of partnerships—and a 19th-century 'corporation'—with both limited liability for shareholders and a separate 'corporate' identity—that is often obscured. For example, Verboven (2002, p.23) confounded this difference: "The legal concept of the 'corporation' as a private enterprise with limited liability dates from the Early Modern period and was intended to facilitate long distance maritime trade, the Elizabethan 'East India Company' (1600) being the first of its kind."[5]

Any capital association can be loosely defined as a 'company' or, where business involving the state is involved, a 'state enterprise'. Such terms are generic and are not indicative of the organizational structure of the company. For example, the 15th-to-17th-century English 'Company of Merchant Adventurers' was a regulated company with 'shares' that were typically acquired by birthright and apprenticeship.[6] At times, some English regulated companies admitted all those willing to pay a fee (e.g., the Levant Company). Business organization in general, and the concepts of limited liability and incorporation in particular, have had a long development. The Roman state (*Senatus populusque Romanus*) and, especially, the *municipia*, evolved as legal public entities separate from individual citizens. From this point, determining the status in Roman private law of corporate entities with "juristic personality" is "a vast and deep problem" (Daube 1944, p.128; 1943; Duff 1938).

Some private arrangements that had achieved a level of corporate status during the late Republic were *collegia, universitates* and *sodalicia*. In the general case of a *societas*, Verboven (2002, p.277) observed:

> Roman *societas* was fundamentally different from modern corporations or trade companies, which are characterized by their corporate capacity. Outsiders doing business with *socii* could in no way acquire claims on or incur obligations toward the *societas* as such because the *societas* as a legal entity did not exist.

Against this backdrop, *societates publicanorum* with 'corporate' personality independent of the *socii* were established. This 'corporate' personality originated by extending the public personality of the *populus Romanus*; the activities of the *societates publicanorum* were predominately public, not private, duties—that is, tax farmers were contractors providing essential revenues for the state, and public works contractors were building essential infrastructure. Beyond this, there is no evidence that the *societates publicanorum* had a 'private' corporate personality independent of that extended by the *populus Romanus*. This is an essential issue for the claim of trading in shares.

The *Societates Publicanorum*

The specific organizational details we have of the *societates publicanorum* are scant. Despite a paucity of details, Balsdon (1962, pp.135–6) provided a conventional modern description of a *societas publicanorum* that can be found in earlier secondary sources, including Deloume (1890) and Kniep (1896):

> The only tax-farming company (*societas*) at Rome of whose organization we have a detailed description is the company which farmed the '*scriptura et sex publica*' of Sicily; it had a Chairman (*Manceps*), a Managing Director (*Magister*), a Board of Directors (*Decumani*), and there were Shareholders (*Socii*). In the province the staff of this as of all tax-farming companies consisted of a Local Manager (*Pro Magistro*) and of minor officials (*Qui operas dabant*).

The 'primary sources' for this detailed description are scattered and numerous (e.g., Poitras and Geranio 2016) and are insufficient to support the description given; artful interpretation has taken place. Basing inferences about the organization of the *societas publicanorum* involved in Sicilian tax farming described by Cicero (*In Verrum II*) seems somewhat incongruent given that recognition of the *Lex Hieronica* meant contracts for the tithe (*decumae*) were auctioned in Sicily, not Rome. The *scriptura* and the lucrative *portoria* were auctioned in Rome, though Scramuzza (1937) indicated only one, possibly, two *societates* were farming those taxes. Traditional Sicilian methods of *decumae* collection attract modern attention because of claims the Romans adopted this practice in other conquered territories. Sherwin-White (1977) and Cotton (1986) demonstrated the organization of tax farming in Anatolia was also dependent on local traditions, given the discretionary authority of the governors (e.g., Rauh 1989a, b).

A 'trade' of a 'share in a *societas publicanorum*' (*partes*) was an inherently legal operation. The rights and obligations associated with ownership of a share had to be legally defined; the transfer of ownership legally recorded; an accurate legal receipt provided for funds exchanged. Perhaps verbal agreements with witnesses involving only *familiares* and *amicii* were used? In any event, certain legal details relevant to the claims of share trading attracted attention from Roman jurists and are captured in the *Institutes* of Gaius (Gordon and Robinson 1988) and the *Digest* of the emperor Justinian (Watson 1985). It is well known that these sources originated from legal decisions well after the end of the Republic and also suffer, to varying degrees, from philological difficulties. In addition, legal sources are not always indicative of actual commercial activities. However, to ignore these sources for such reasons presumes an absence of reliable continuity in key features of Roman commercial law.[7]

Given this, many sections are relevant: *Institutes*[III, 148–52] and *Digest* [17,2] on the organization of partnerships; *Digest*[3,4] on actions for and against corporate bodies; *Digest*[39,4] on actions against tax farmers; *Digest*[50,10] on public works; *Digest*[19,2] on lease and hire; *Digest*[6,3] on actions for *vectigalian*; *Digest*[10,3] on actions dividing common property; and, *Digest*[50,11] on markets. If claims of share trading are correct, the absence of legal interpretations in the *Institutes* and *Digest* directly relevant to disputes on the 'trading' of shares is, presumably, because this was a practice only during the (late?) Republic and, for some reason, received no interest from the jurists of the Empire. This seems highly unlikely.

With these provisos, the most significant legal description of the *societas publicanorum* is found in *Digest*[3,4,1], where private 'corporate bodies' are described as follows:

> Partnerships, *collegia* and bodies of this sort may not be formed by everybody at will; for this right is restricted by statute, *senatus consulta,* and imperial *constitutiones*. In a few cases only are bodies of this sort permitted. For example, partners in tax farming, gold mines, silver mines and saltworks are allowed to form corporations . . . Those permitted to form a corporate body consisting of a *collegium* or partnership or specifically one or the other of these have the right on the pattern of the state to have common property, a common treasury, and an attorney or syndic through whom, as in a state, what should be transacted and done in common is transacted and done.

Significantly, there is considerable debate over the textual validity of this "corrupted" source (Daube 1944, p.126). In addition to 'bad Latin'—the source is identified as Gaius, 'Commentary on the Provincial Edict', Book 3, not the more influential *Institutes*—the reference to imperial *constitutiones* involves a method of organizing these activities appearing during the Empire.

Given such qualifications, *Digest*[3,4,1] can be claimed as support for the position of Verboven (2002, p.278) and others:

> In some exceptional cases a *societas* was granted corporate capacity by a law, a senatorial decree or (later) an imperial *constitutio*. The most famous example is the large *societas vectigalium* formed to collect taxes on behalf of the state. Under the Republic, they were no doubt the only 'incorporated' *societates*.

The precise meaning of 'incorporated' in this case is elusive. Property held in common is a feature of partnerships that can be found in the origins of Roman law (*societas ercto non cito*). Common property 'on the pattern of the state' indicates that a partner does not have the traditional right to bring an *actio pro socio* to dissolve the partnership (*Institutes* III, 151). Similarly, this *societas* survives the death of a *socius* (*Institutes* III, 152). As such, the *societates publicanorum* had a 'corporate' identity separate from the *socii*. This was exceptional in the Roman law of *societas* at the time of the late Republic and provides indirect support for a limited claim of share trading—for example, if a partner dies, a 'share' may become available for sale. However, the 'corporate' features granted were only those necessary to ensure that the essential state activities of revenue collection and public works construction were not disrupted.

The two other features of the *societates publicanorum* described by Gaius as 'on the pattern of the state' are harder to clarify. For the *municipia,* having a common treasury was essential for the provision of common services and maintenance of public works. In the Greek and Roman eras, the 'treasury' was typically a building of importance, reflecting the independent corporate status of a *municipium* or city state. Having a common treasury in the sense of the *collegia* that, say, emerged among soldiers during the early Empire often meant a common fund that would be used to pay burial expense and, possibly, provide a rudimentary form of 'social insurance' (e.g., Lewin 2003). The need for a *societas publicanorum* to have a 'common treasury' is likely related to the *publicani* providing essential funds for provincial administration and, where appropriate, making payments in Rome. The 'common treasury' would provide a fixed location where tax collection business of the *societas* could be conducted and revenues collected and disbursed. If the *publicani* employed municipal authorities in the Asian provinces to collect taxes within their scope of influence, then the 'common treasury' of the local authorities could be used to collect state revenues and disburse funds to the Roman administration for purposes such as provisioning the troops and compensating a variety of officials on the governor's staff. *Digest*[3,4,7.1] suggests a common treasury of a *societas publicanorum* would also provide a legal method for those "put to some expense" in collecting taxes or erecting public works to seek redress without having to take action against *socii* individually.

The final feature identified by Gaius—having an attorney or syndic act in the common interest—implicitly requires some method for the *socii* to select and replace such an individual. This feature also extends the traditional limited liability of a *socius* in, say, a *peculium* beyond initial funds invested (plus any profit earned) if not directly involved in the management of the venture (e.g., *Digest*[17,2,25]). Further detail on the liability of the *socii* is provided in *Digest*[39,4,1]: "If a tax farmer or his *familia* takes anything by force in the name of the public revenue and it is not returned, I will grant a *judicium* against them". It is observed that '*familia*' in this context includes all *familiares* who work for the tax farmer collecting *vectigalia*. This includes slaves owned by the tax farmer, freedmen and slaves belonging to others. *Digest*[39,4,6] provides detail on liability when tax farmers act in concert: "If a number of tax farmers has been involved in making an illegal exaction . . . all shall pay their share and anything that one cannot pay will be exacted from another." Finally, *Digest* [39,4,9.4] observed that "Where partners in *vectigal*-collection administer their shares of the contract separately, one of them can legally petition to have the share of another who is of doubtful solvency transferred to himself".

Digest[39,4] and other sections demonstrate that *socii* in the *societates publicanorum* did not have the limited liability of a modern corporation. Most legal actions were taken against a *socius,* not the *societas.* Those *familiares* responsible for the collection of taxes were responsible to the *socius* and not the *societas.* Even when acting in concert, the liability was individual and would be shared according to the partnership agreement. Because partners could 'administer shares separately', the role of the syndic or attorney acting in the common interest was, again, likely related to conducting tax-farming business in multiple locations—for example, in Rome and the Asian province associated with the contract—and the need to disburse funds for Roman administration. This allowed the syndic or attorney to act in place of a *socius* who was in another location or was otherwise unavailable.

Is the associated liability of the *socii* consistent with the broader liability of a shareholder in a 16th-to-18th-century joint-stock company? Such a comparison is complicated due to differences in the commercial context between late Republic tax farming and long-distance seaborne trade of the early joint-stock companies. The presence of an attorney or syndic, somehow selected, creates a liability for the *socii* similar to that of shareholders in the VOC with respect to the assembly of 'Seventeen Masters' (e.g., Poitras 2000, p.273). However, resources of the *societas* used to collect taxes were owned individually, unlike the joint-stock companies where ships, cargoes, outposts and the like were owned by the company. On balance, the equity capital organization of the *societas publicanorum* was decidedly ancient Roman in character.

NOTES

1 Modern accounting standards issued by accounting entities such as the Financial Accounting Standards Board (US) and the International Accounting Standards Board are replete with references to 'equity'. For example, in 1990 the

FASB issued a discussion memorandum, "Distinguishing between Liability and Equity Instruments and Accounting for Instruments with Characteristics of Both", to clarify issues associated with the increasing appearance of 'hybrid' equity (debt) securities with debt (equity) features.

2 Another illustration of the accounting differences between preferred and common stock is that declared but unpaid dividends on cumulative preferred stock is classified as a liability while unpaid dividends on common stock do not have such accounting treatment.

3 This is a notional approach aiming to provide a connection with historical notions of 'capital'. In accounting practice, there are numerous other items also included on the assets side of the balance sheet, such as goodwill and accounts receivable, that do not qualify as either physical or intangible assets.

4 Corrective or criminal justice could also be added to this list of justice concepts. However, Malynes (1622) was only concerned with detailing the 'law merchant' associated with rules of commercial relationships that were international in character. Disputes were generally settled by reference to the 'laws of equity'. Depending on the time period, such disputes over the value of individual shares of 'equity capital' could be adjudicated by civil authorities, religious bodies or a council of merchants.

5 As evidence, consider that the charter of the East Indies Company contains a list of 200 named individuals and the requirement that "they, at their own Adventures, Costs, and Charges" are required to satisfy the following: "[The] Company of Merchants of London, Trading into the East-Indies, and their Successors, that, in any Time of Restraint, Six good Ships and Six good Pinnaces, well furnished with Ordnance, and other Munition for their Defence, and Five Hundred Mariners, English Men, to guide and sail in the same Six Ships and Six Pinnaces, at all Times, during the said Term of Fifteen Years, shall quietly be permitted and suffered to depart, and go in the said Voyages." This is not consistent with limited liability, as there is a distinct possibility of calls for shareholders to provide more capital (beyond the amount of the initial investment). The early joint-stock companies often made additional calls on shareholders. As for separate corporate identity, the charter is clear: "they and every of [the 200 named individuals] from henceforth be, and shall be one Body Corporate and Politick, in Deed and in Name, by the Name of The Governor and Company of Merchants of London, Trading into the East- Indies."

6 Though the origins of the Company can be found in the 13th century and remnants of the company survived into the 19th century, the key charter was obtained in the 15th century. This began a period of prominence for the Company, which lasted until the Glorious Revolution at the end of the 17th century.

7 Reliance on the *Digest* and *Institutes* is complicated, because Roman law evolved over time and because and the period from the Grachan law (*Lex Sempronia Agraria*) to the end of the Republic was an especially active period of legal change and evolution. It is well known that the dating of legal opinions listed in the *Digest* is not transparent. The *Institutes*, likely written during the early Empire and largely concerned with Roman 'old private law', lacks detail on specific issues associated with the *societates publicanorum*.

2 Equity Shares in Antiquity

locupletare amicos umquam suos destitit, mittere in negotium, dare partis
(he never ceased enriching his friends, sending them upon commissions, bestowing shares upon them)

Pro C. Rabiro Postumo [2.4]

eripuerisne partes illo tempore carissimas partim a Caesare, partim a publicanis?
(Did you not at the same time filch shares when they were at their highest, in part from Caesar, in part from the tax-farmers themselves?)

Pro Vatinium testem interrogatio [12.29]

Cicero (106–43 BC)

A EQUITY CAPITAL AND 'MARKETLESS' TRADING

Trade, Markets and Money

The study of commercial life in antiquity is hampered by the limited and fragmented evidence available. Business activities following the introduction of the printing press in the 15th century are captured in a substantial number of notarial records, merchant archives, toll registers, company records, price *courants*, records of legal proceedings and the like. In contrast, information about Roman, Greek, Egyptian, Phoenician, Babylonian, Sumerian, Assyrian and other ancient civilizations survives in a relatively small number of sources. While archaeology has been able to fill in some gaps, "the general inadequacies of the evidence accentuate the role of conceptualization in historical research" (Bang 2008, p.3). The only sources available deal with a small slice of ancient history and cannot provide enough detail to construct an accurate historical record. In addition, many sources deal only with a particular non-commercial activity (e.g., military campaigns, classical literature, criminal law, royal edicts), leaving no trace of many aspects of ancient commercial life. Careful examination and scrutiny of sources has to be supplemented by 'artful' interpretation. "Sources are . . . not self-explanatory. They must be interpreted to bring us to the ancient reality" (Bang 2008, p.3).

In modern times, the difficulty of determining specifics of commercial activities in the ancient world is reflected in the ongoing debate over the extent of 'the market economy'. This debate features ideologically charged questions such as 'Was a market economy present at the beginnings of civilization?' Seeking a reflection of modern times in ancient societies, Temin (2001, 2004, 2006), Malmendier (2009) and other economic historians "have gone their own way in creating models that describe how early civilizations might have developed if it had followed the lines of modern individualism at the outset" (Hudson et al. 2002,

Figure 2.1   Stele for Code of Hammurabi in the Louvre

p.19). Ancient historians, anthropologists and sociologists often find alternative explanations of the available sources. For example, an early contribution by Weber (1896/1909) argued that ancient Mesopotamian irrigation systems required continuous supervision, giving rise to complex bureaucratic structures that employed bonded and forced labor on an immense scale. The upshot was an ancient world characterized by despotic states dominating economic life, what Dale (2013) identified as "hydraulic-bureaucratic official-states". In this interpretation of ancient life, there was limited scope for a 'market economy' and the associated use of equity capital in commercial ventures.

Understanding the context of economic life and commercial activity is essential to identifying methods of organizing and valuing equity capital in the ancient world. Polanyi (1957) provided insight into the problem by identifying three essential commercial institutions: trade, markets and money. For Polanyi, trade in ancient Mesopotamia was "marketless", though the precise meaning of this claim requires considerable clarification (e.g., Dale 2013; Cangiani 2011; McCloskey 1997; Silver 1983). In modern times, all three institutions have merged into the market system. Economic historians "tend to assume that the same triadic nexus applied in earlier epochs, and to assume markets to have been the generative and coordinating instance, with trade conceived of as a movement of goods through markets, facilitated by money as a means of exchange" (Dale 2013, p.160). Polanyi and other economic anthropologists, however, such as Finley (1973, 1981), view trade, markets and money as discrete elements that need to be examined independently.[1] Avoiding the argument about economic development based on consideration of the three essential institutions in the ancient world, the 'triadic nexus' still provides helpful structure to interpret the use of equity capital in the ancient world (e.g., Oka and Kusimba 2008).

To see the importance of equity capital in the structure of ancient trade and commercial activity, consider some basic characteristics. For Polanyi, trade was a method of acquiring goods that were not available locally. Goods could be traded for in various ways, not just the price-driven mutually beneficial exchange of the market. As such, market trade was "geared toward making a profit" and was well suited to the use of monetized accounting. However, there was also 'administered trade', in which prices "were fixed largely by custom, statute, or proclamation, and perhaps should not generally be called prices at all" (Polanyi 1966, p.xix).[2] Instead of variable prices for services being set in markets, 'prices' for many important economic activities in the agrarian societies of Old Babylonia and other parts of Mesopotamia were set by fiat, supporting the view advanced by Polanyi (1957) that there was 'marketless trade'. Similarly, in ancient societies money could serve different functions than in a monetized market economy. For example, commodity 'money' of ancient times such as barley could serve as 'currency' in the payment of tribute or taxes with little or no use as a store of value or medium of exchange. This begs questions such as 'What were the methods used to organize and value equity capital in ancient times? Were equity capital shares transferable, and, if so, could the monetary value of equity capital fluctuate? What methods of contracting and accounting were employed?'

In the search for marketless trading in the ancient world, Polanyi (1977, p.124) observed:

> [A] market mechanism is beyond the most nimble spade. While it may be comparatively easy to locate an open space where, sometime in the past, crowds were wont to meet and exchange goods, it is much less easy to ascertain whether, as a result of their behaviour, exchange rates were fluctuating and, if so, whether the supply of goods offered was changing in response to the . . . up or down movement of those rates.

Unfortunately for any examination of 'ancient times' that seeks 'general explanations', ancient historians have gradually come to recognize the extensive commercial diversity of ancient societies and the sometimes dramatic evolution and devolution in commercial practices and laws that took place over time within the same society. It is not surprising that economic historians such as Rostovtseff, Temin and Malmendier, pondering the character of economic activity in

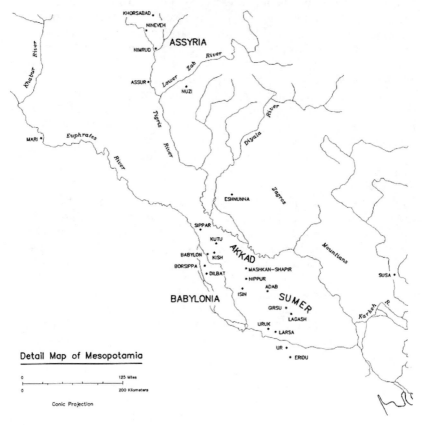

Figure 2.2   Bronze Age Mesopotamia City States

Source: Oriental Institute, University of Chicago

ancient times, seek answers predominately in the Greek and, especially, Roman civilizations. Yet, even Polanyi recognized the emergence of widespread monetized market-driven trade in Greek times, possibly earlier. By Greek times, rudiments of the 'law merchant' governing rules of conduct in commercial practice had evolved, reflecting a level of 'generality' in international trading that was relatively sophisticated in terms of monetized valuation and accounting accuracy.

The historical importance of Roman law governing the usage, organization and valuation of equity capital is difficult to understate. Roman law played a fundamental role in the development of commercial law throughout Europe and, via the mechanisms of colonization, throughout the modern world. Yet, despite numerous sources evidencing Roman civilization, the character of trade and markets in Roman times is not completely clear. That significant bulk trade in goods extended throughout the Roman Empire is well established, if only from archaeological evidence. The works of Cicero and others provide some account of the workings of the *publicani* in tax farming and public works construction. What is often overlooked in the search for evidence of markets, money and trade is the fact that Roman commercial law evolved from laws and customs going back millennia, to a time when a large segment of commercial activity was not purely monetary in character. In turn, relevant laws were shaped by commercial activity of the time and did not evolve in a linear fashion, either temporally or geographically.

The Bronze Age Law Codes in Sumer and Babylon[3]

The earliest form of record-keeping, called cuneiform script, is thought to have begun in Sumer, in southern Mesopotamia, during the 4th millennium BC. It consisted of using a wedge-shaped stylus to make impressions on wet clay tablets (see Figure 2.3). Because many cuneiform documents originated as commercial contracts, especially 'loans' associated with agricultural production, we have considerable information about the evolution of commercial practices throughout ancient Mesopotamia. Accurate interpretation of these documents—which is where the history of equity capital begins—requires understanding of another artefact: the law codes of the various city states that characterized the region.

The law codes of ancient Sumer and Babylonia reflect the symbiotic relationship between the legal codes that have survived from ancient times and the character of trade that is likely associated with such codes. In modern times, the Code of Hammurabi (ca. 1780 BC) of Old Babylonia is the best-known illustration of such law codes (Kent 1903). However, the code of Lipit-Ishtar, ruler of the Sumerian kingdom of Isin, preceded the Code of Hammurabi by as much as 175 years (Steele 1947, p.159). Because laws of this era required the use of written contracts for common commercial activities, a great many cuneiform tablets related to these activities were produced, many of which remain to be interpreted.[4]

Only fragments of the Isin law code survive. However, based on those fragments, there were laws relating to the use of boats, possibly relevant to the

Figure 2.3 Sumerian Cuneiform Tablet, A 'River Loan' of Silver, British Museum Collection

conduct of trade. There were also laws dealing with slaveship, servitude, and feudal obligations. Steele (1947) estimated there were only a little over a hundred laws in the complete Lipit-Ishtar code, compared to over 250 laws in the Code of Hammurabi. Steele (1947, p.162) concludes: "In general, there appears to have been considerable revision of the individual laws and probably even some rearrangement of the laws within the larger groups during the interval between Lipit-Ishtar and Hammurabi. A majority of the extant Sumerian laws, however, find either close parallels or at least analogues in the Babylonian code." The increase in the number of laws likely reflects the increased sophistication of commercial activity by Hammurabi's time.

Unfortunately for our study, sections of the Code of Hammurabi that almost certainly relate to commercial activities and equity capital in particular have been obliterated. However, combining archaeological evidence from 'loan' documents with the laws that have survived gives us a somewhat clear picture of commercial activities. For example, Laws 45 and 46 identify the difference between debt (rental lease) and equity capital transactions in agricultural production:

> 45. If a man rent his field for tillage for a fixed rental, and receive the rent of his field, but bad weather come and destroy the harvest, the injury falls upon the tiller of the soil.
> 46. If he do not receive a fixed rental for his field, but lets it on half or third shares of the harvest, the grain on the field shall be divided proportionately between the tiller and the owner.

It appears that landowners were able to take a debt or equity position in the production of grain for the upcoming harvest. However, the situation may have been considerably more complicated. Significantly, Law 46 does establish there were legally defined half or third shares associated with dividing the returns to such agrarian ventures between the source of the equity capital and the laborer, providing some insight into the structure and scope of transactions in which rudimentary pricing mechanisms might have been used. In this vein, it becomes essential to make a distinction between commercial activity within a given state and trade between different states.

Given the agrarian character of economic life in ancient times, many laws deal with agricultural situations. Following two such laws:

> Law 64. If any one hand over his garden to a gardener to work, the gardener shall pay to its owner two-thirds of the produce of the garden, for so long as he has it in possession, and the other third shall he keep.
> Law 65. If the gardener do not work in the garden and the product fall off, the gardener shall pay in proportion to other neighboring gardens.

there is then the unfortunate gap in the Hammurabi law code created by obliterated sections of the stele. The code restarts with the following, dealing with trade to other areas:[5]

> 100. .... interest for the money, as much as he has received, he shall give a note therefor, and on the day, when they settle, pay to the merchant.
> 101. If there are no mercantile arrangements in the place whither he went, he shall leave the entire amount of money which he received with the broker to give to the merchant.
> 102. If a merchant entrust money to an agent (broker) for some investment, and the broker suffer a loss in the place to which he goes, he shall make good the capital to the merchant.
> 103. If, while on the journey, an enemy take away from him anything that he had, the broker shall swear by God and be free of obligation.

104. If a merchant give an agent corn, wool, oil, or any other goods to transport, the agent shall give a receipt for the amount, and compensate the merchant therefor. Then he shall obtain a receipt from the merchant for the money that he gives the merchant.

Modern analysis of such laws has revealed the difficulties of translation, context and interpretation. In particular, commercial practice in ancient Sumer up to the Ur III period indicates a high degree of state control, in which 'merchants' (*damgar* in Sumerian) were likely functionaries of the city-temple under the direction of a palace official. The contrast with Old Babylonia of the early second millennium is striking (Van de Mieroop 2002, p.69):

> It is remarkable how the bias of our documentation has shifted from the previous Ur III period. While the 21st century [BC] textual record derives almost exclusively from central institutions, the temples and palaces of the early second millennium are poorly documented as compared to the private citizenry. The large majority of tablets from both licit and illicit excavations were found in the domestic quarter of the cities.

Due to the growth and size of Old Babylonia: "The central institutions 'privatized' many of their services . . . Private individuals acted as intermediaries between institutions and the citizenry, collecting dues, issuing payments and organizing the collection and distribution of resources". This context was favorable to profitable investment of private equity capital in commercial enterprise, leading, ultimately, to an equity capital valuation problem when, say, ventures were completed or where probate was involved. Such situations were managed by the extensive use of written contracts, including some partnership contracts.

B   THE OLD ASSYRIAN EXTERNAL TRADING NETWORK

Merchants of Mesopotamia

The change in context across time and geography in Bronze Age Mesopotamia is reflected in the use of *tamkārum* for 'merchant' in Babylonian, which is consistent with the same usage in Old Assyria.[6] While there was a *gal damgar* (chief trader) in ancient Sumer, there were more layers in the process of extending credit to merchants marketing the largely perishable agricultural surplus generated by the Babylonian state. This change in reference reflects the rise of *kārum* (Veenhof 2010, p.42):

> In the Babylonia of the early second millennium BC a system emerged which allowed groups of merchants from various trading cities to settle in other cities, occasionally even—presumably on the basis of political agreements— in those of neighboring territorial states. These merchants were usually concentrated and often lived together with the local traders in a special area,

called *kārum*, "quay, harbor," where they conducted their business in the interest of themselves, their mother-city, and their host city.

Key elements in the commercial activity of 'merchants' were the extent of state control of agricultural production and the importance of trade beyond the borders of the state. In the first and second centuries of the second millennium BC, the borders of the Babylonian state did not extend to the Assyrian territory to the north: "during the first centuries of the second millennium BC . . . trade was the preferred, most efficient, and presumably also the cheapest way of obtaining the materials essential for its highly developed and urbanized culture" (p.41). In particular, the merchants of Assur in Old Assyria traded with Babylonians for wool, textiles, grains and slaves. These were exchanged for tin, copper, silver and other goods obtained through a network of Assyrian trading colonies, of which the important colony of Kanesh in Anatolia has proved a rich source of cuneiform documents.[7]

It is evident from the law codes and numerous cuneiform tablets that there were 'merchants' who invested equity capital in both agrarian production and commercial trade. It is also evident that there was considerable diversity in the specific role of 'merchants' across the various civilizations of Bronze Age Mesopotamia. While Law 46 of the Hammurabi code and other laws indicate that there were conventions surrounding distribution of returns to equity shares in Old Babylonia, rules for equity valuation appear to have considerable flexibility, in which written contracts played a crucial role. While it is the "loan document [that] is probably the most commonly preserved record from ancient Mesopotamia, and the Old Babylonian period (c. 2000 to 1595 BC) is especially rich in such records" (Van de Mieroop 2002, p.163), interpretation of such documents is complicated by the use of the same general contract format for different commercial situations. Without sufficient context, such as why the document was preserved, the tendency is to interpret a given tablet as a 'loan'. It was not until Neo-Babylonian times (626–539 BC) that contracts typically contained accurate dating and identification of the individuals involved, using a three-part name (person's name, father's name, family name), substantively increasing our ability to put documents in context.

While it is difficult to isolate many generalities regarding commercial activity across the millennia of the diverse civilizations of ancient Mesopotamia, it is still essential to distinguish between production within a given area of political control and trade between different areas. It is generally accepted among ancient historians that domestic agricultural production involved the use of debt-bondage contracting similar to the *nexum* contracts of the early Roman Republic, abolished by the *Lex Poetelia Papiria* in 326 BC (e.g., Finley 1981; Skaist 1994; Steinkeller 2002). Such 'loans', which comprise the bulk of surviving tablets from Old Babylonia, were made 'in kind' by wealthy landowners advancing goods to sharecroppers and subsistence farmers. The objective of the 'loan' was typically not to make interest but to obtain the labor and, possibly, the land of the debtor. In the event of default, debtors would make payment by providing bonded labor (either their own or a family member's) for a period of time. Money loans of silver for commercial purposes, such as payment for goods obtained in external trade, were not common and typically earned a customary 20%.

The extent of control by the political, religious and military structures of the palace-temple organization over the societal wealth used in agricultural production was fundamental in determining the role played by 'merchants' in commercial ventures. For example, in Ur III the state controlled the bulk of agricultural production—that is, "during Ur III times, all arable land belonged to the state, meaning, consequently, that there was no outright ownership of such holdings . . . all arable land available in Ur III took the form of either 'temple estates' or subsistence land, the latter category also including the holdings of the royal family" (Steinkeller 2002, p.115). This situation is substantively different from that in Old Babylonia, where the extent of state ownership and direct control was significantly less and 'loans' were extended to merchants to market the agricultural surplus both domestically and externally. The situation was even more different in Assyria, especially in the Old Assyrian period, in which Assur served

Figure 2.4 Bronze Age Statue of Nannar, Sumerian Moon God

as the hub for a network of trading colonies (e.g. Larsen 1976, 1977; Veenhof 1997, 2010). In this case, state control was muted, and merchants played an important role in state activities.[8]

The Bronze Age was characterized by the spread and adoption of metallurgy required to produce bronze, a combination of mostly copper and some tin[9], which is significantly stronger than unalloyed copper. Bronze was used to produce weapons, agricultural implements, luxury goods such as statutes and the like. Though copper is relatively plentiful in the earth's crust, the acquisition of copper that had already been smelted, as well as tin and especially silver, was an important feature of the external trade of Babylonia and other states of the alluvial plain of southern Mesopotamia. In this trade, silver played an essential role as a medium of exchange and unit of account. Wool, woolen textiles and grains were exchanged for silver that was used to acquire copper, tin, lapis lazuli and other high-value items. More importantly, delivery of silver was the required method of settling the 'loan' that financed the initial allocation of goods involved in the external trade.

Ancient historians do not know with certainty where the tin and silver that Bronze Age Mesopotamians traded for came from. Of these two, tin has remained the more elusive (e.g., Dayton 1971; Stech and Pigott 1986; Muhly 1973; Amzallag 2009). From the perspective of equity capital organization, mining ventures are particularly important due to the possible need to maintain a permanent stock of physical assets. In cases where the mineral source is on the surface—for example, in alluvial deposits—it is possible for ore to be obtained without significant capital resources. However, where the ore body extends below the surface and some type of shaft mining is required, a 'permanent' equity capital investment could be needed (e.g., Richardson 1976). In addition, the impetus for a 'permanent' equity capital stock can arise in the smelting of ore in furnaces (not crucibles) and the establishment and maintenance of the external trading network to distribute processed ore to population centers. In turn, a long-lived physical capital stock is fundamental to the transition of equity capital organization beyond individual commercial ventures where there is distribution of profits and return of equity capital at the end of each journey or harvest cycle.[10]

The Trading Network of Assur

In the absence of detailed information on the organization of ventures for mining tin and silver, attention turns to the external trading networks needed to acquire high-value goods. Due to impressive efforts by ancient historians and archaeologists such as Larsen (1976, 1977), Veenhof (1997, 2010), Dercksen (1996), and Byrne (2003), we have gained substantial insight into the workings of the remarkably "modern" network of external trading colonies of Old Assyria in the first two centuries of the second millennium BC. Unlike in Babylonia and Sumer farther south on the alluvial plain, the more abundant rainfall and ecology of Old Assyria meant significantly less reliance on the 'bureaucratic, hydraulic oligarchies' of their southern neighbors. As a consequence, there was substantially less state control over both agricultural production and geography. Treaties, rather than military might, were commonly used to support trade between cities. The economic and trading center of Old Assyria was the city of Assur. Veenhof (2010) describes the Assur of this period:

> Assur was not an "imperial" city, with a strong military and a ruling elite supported and supplied by a large productive territory and with income from subjected fringe areas. Its commercial presence in Anatolia and the trade routes through northern Mesopotamia had not been enforced, and could not be backed, by military power, but were based on mutual commercial interests, sealed by treaties.

Unfortunately, the archaeological evidence on the trading networks of Assur comes primarily from Anatolia, where 23 colonies (*kārum*) and 15 trading stations (*wabartum*) have been identified. That there was trading by merchants from Assur with other important trading centers in Mesopotamia such as Mari, Susa and locations in Elam seems necessary, but archaeological evidence is scant.[11]

Absent commercial ventures that require a permanent capital stock, equity capital is invested in single ventures associated with the harvest cycle or the transport and marketing of goods, either domestically or externally. In such cases, equity capital organization is relatively simple. Equity capital shares are generally non-transferable (i.e., illiquid), and valuation is determined at the end of the venture by the return of capital and distribution of shares in the profit from the venture, as determined in the initial contract. However, in Old Babylonia, there was little need for private equity capital to market goods domestically and, in most cases, externally. The state would 'loan' the goods to the merchant,

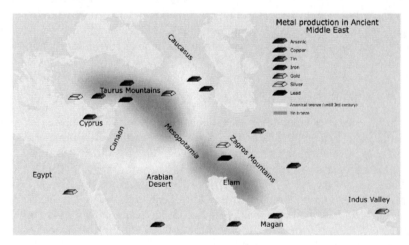

Figure 2.5 A map showing the major sites of metal production in the Ancient Near East, including Egypt, Asia Minor, Mesopotamia, Persia, and the Indus Valley Civilization

Source: van der Crabben (2012) from http://www.ancient.eu/image/350/

requiring the payment of silver at a later date after the sale of the goods. Domestically, merchants would often 'loan' these goods to sharecroppers and subsistence farmers. 'Profit' from such ventures would appear as loan 'interest' and would not have a direct equity capital component. As is common in agrarian economies, considerable capital investment was directed to land ownership. Given the often complicated social issues surrounding land ownership, in cases where equity capital was employed, valuation was driven by the annual profit from the agricultural production cycle.

The situation changed dramatically where external trading involved a permanent network of colonies, as in ancient Assur.[12] Building on contributions by Larsen and others surrounding the substantial archaeological finds at Kanesh, the most important Old Assyrian *kārum* in Anatolia, Veenhof (2010, p.55) identified an important equity capital element:

> The main and probably most successful traders in Kanesh were usually involved in many transactions, at times also together with partners, and many in addition carried out commission sales and purchases for relatives, friends, and women in Assur. Most of these traders had become more independent by having become managers of a "joint-stock fund" (called *naruqqum*, "money bag"), usually set up in Assur. This phenomenon appeared for the first time around 1900 BC and seems to have been an Old Assyrian invention that went beyond individual partnerships and cooperation in a joint caravan. The arrangement, rather similar to that of the early medieval *compagnia*, meant enlisting a number (usually about a dozen) of investors (*ummiānum*, "financiers"), who supplied capital rated in gold, usually in all ca. 30 kilos, ideally consisting of shares of 1 or 2 kilos of gold each. It was entrusted to a trader (the *tractator*), usually for ca. ten years, for the generally formulated purpose of "carrying out trade." The contract contained stipulations on a final settlement of accounts, on paying dividends, on the division of the expected profit, and on fines for premature withdrawal of capital (meant to secure the duration of the business). Investors or shareholders mostly lived in Assur, but successful traders in Anatolia too invested in funds managed by others, perhaps also as a way of sharing commercial risks. In such cases a contract would have to be drawn up in Anatolia that obliged the *tractator* "to book in Assur *x* gold in his joint stock fund in the investor's name." Among the investors we find members of the *tractator*'s family, but also business relations and others, probably a kind of "merchant-bankers," and other rich citizens, who aimed at fairly safe, long-term investments.

Larsen (1977, p.123) made a significant connection between practices of the Old Assyrian traders and those of Jewish merchants documented in the Geniza archive, an important documentary record that commences in the 9th century AD and has been an important primary source on the commercial activities of a network of Jewish traders in the Middle Ages:

> For the Geniza material Goitein has made the observation that "at least one-half of the international trade was based on informal business cooperation

which could last for a lifetime and even for several generations" and it is therefore not at all surprising that in the similar Old Assyrian system we have not one example of a real partnership contract.

While detailed contracts laying out precise terms and conditions of enduring business 'partnerships' have not survived, Larsen was able to report details of a *naruqqu* contract (p.124):

> Landsberger has published the one known *naruqqu*-contract, a tablet which is now in the museum in Kayseri. It starts with a list of personal names, each connected with a sum of gold, i.e., the names of the investors and the size of their investments. At the beginning two lines are missing, and it can be seen from the rest of the text that the two names must have been connected with a total investment of 6 minas of gold; five men are noted for 2 minas each, four for 1½ mina, two for 1 mina, and one person is booked for 2½ minas. At the end of this list we find the name of the man who was entrusted with this *naruqqum*, a certain Amur-Igtar, and he is credited with an investment of no less than four minas of gold. The main body of the text continues as follows:

>> In all: 30 minas of gold, the *naruqqum* of Amur-Igtar. Reckoned from the eponymy Susaja he will conduct trade for twelve years. Of the profit he will enjoy (lit. "eat") one-third. He will be responsible (lit. "stand") for one-third. He who receives his money back before the completion of his term must take the silver at the exchange-rate 4:1 for gold and silver. He will not receive any of the profit.

After this follows a list of seven witnesses, the first one being the *laputtd'um*-official.

Based on additional archaeological evidence, Veenhof (2010) reported that

> The few contracts we have of the setting up of a joint-stock fund do mention the names of the investors, some of whom are family and business relations of the trader, but others are unknown and some are registered anonymously as *tamkārum*, probably again in order to enable the transfer of shares, e.g. in cases of disputed ownership or in connection with the division of an inheritance.

The fascinating evidence that there may have been trading in *naruqqum* shares, unfortunately, does not also provide detail about the methods used to price the equity capital or the goods involved in such transactions.[13]

An important theme in the early history of equity capital concerns the role of kinship and family relationships. The impersonal character of modern equity markets results in a traded 'price' that is mutually agreeable to both buyer and seller of the equity capital claim. The same is not necessarily the case where kinship and family bonds are involved. Pricing and trading of specific shares could reflect a host of additional factors beyond the 'fair value' of the actual shares. This difficulty is compounded in ancient markets where scant evidence surrounding specific trades is typical. In this vein, Veenhof (2010, pp.56–7) provided the following useful summary of archaeological and other evidence uncovered in Kanesh:

> A "Kanesh trader" was supposed to invest his own money in his business, but its size and costs made investments, thus financing by others, necessary. This could be achieved in three different ways, perhaps in part by the same persons in different roles. Money could in the first place be obtained in the form of interest bearing long-term loans or commercial credit granted *in natura*, which for those who supplied them were fairly risk-free and yielded a substantial interest of 30% per year. More important, however, was a second possibility . . . the acquisition of capital in the form of a "joint-stock fund" (*naruqqum*, "money bag") supplied by investors, among whom we meet male (rarely also female) members of the *tractator's* family, and others, rich and commercially interested citizens who aimed at fairly long-term investments with safe returns and a good chance of a share in the profit. Because many traders managed to create such funds, some investors and traders had "shares" in several of them, which could be inherited and sold; such investments, to quote Larsen, "crisscrossed the entire community" and made them "a factor in the creation of social cohesion." Finally, there were also merchants who acted (perhaps it was their specialization) as moneylenders, who supplied commercial loans, when traders experienced temporal shortages of cash, due to delayed caravans, arrears of commission agents, or special expenses (e.g. the purchase of a house).

The extent of family and kinship bonds is detailed further (p.58):

> Relations and cooperation between traders in Kanesh and merchants in Assur were frequently based on family ties, not rarely through several generations, and "Kanesh traders" could enjoy the support and advice of fathers, brothers, or uncles in Assur. They could also figure as their representatives in business and legal matters and in contacts with the city administration, and could provide help to overcome a financial crisis, e.g., by soft loans or acting as guarantors. But Larsen has recently shown that "family firms" as formal institutions did not exist; no "family" occurs as a creditor or debtor and ownership of funds—apart from formal partnerships—was basically individual. After the death of a *pater familias* and the division of the inheritance, his sons carried on independently, even in separate houses in the same colony. This development was perhaps stimulated by the fact that each son acquired his own "joint-stock fund" or inherited part of his father's shares in one, although we occasionally observe that the sons continued to work with their father's business relations, partners, or agents.

There is ample evidence that Kanesh traders from Assur intermarried with the local population, for a variety of reasons, and were able to maintain trading

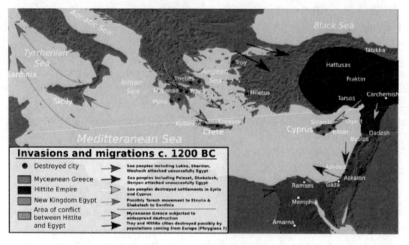

Figure 2.6   Bronze Age Collapse Map, 1250–1150 BC

activities well past the decline in influence of ancient Assur during the second and subsequent centuries of the second millennium BC.

C   FROM THE BRONZE AGE COLLAPSE TO THE ROMAN REPUBLIC

Traversing the Bronze Age Collapse

The commercial law of Bronze Age Mesopotamia relevant to equity capital depended fundamentally on the legal concept of partnership and the use of written contracts. Specific practices and terminology differed across time and geography. For example, the *naruqqu* contract used in the external trading networks of ancient Assur does not appear in the evidence from Old Babylonia or Sumer of that time. Similarly, there is diminishing evidence of the contract in ancient Assur following the collapse of the external trading networks with the expansion of the Babylonian empire in Mesopotamia and the Hittite empire in Anatolia. From this, there is considerable distance to travel to the precisely codified Roman partnership law of *societas,* an important benchmark in the legal history of equity capital organization. In addition to the *societas,* the evolution of maritime law captured in the *Corpus Iuris Civilis* of Justinian details the *foenus nauticum* that impacted legal practices in civil law jurisdictions from the Middle Ages to modern times.[14] The contractual structure of 'sea loans'—also known as bottomry loans or transmarine loans—and the often high returns associated with external seaborne trade raise fundamental issues regarding whether and when these so-called loans—*foenus*—were, *de facto,* equity capital transactions.

If the roots of Roman commercial and maritime law relevant to equity capital are to be found in the practices of earlier civilizations, the chronology of such transfer has to traverse the Collapse of the Bronze Age civilizations that commenced around the end of the 13th century BC, often dated 1206–1150 BC. The Collapse severely impacted the Mycenaean kingdom in the eastern Mediterranean, the Minoan civilization in Crete and the Hittite empire in Anatolia and Syria following invasions by the mysterious 'Sea Peoples'. Archaeological evidence reveals destruction of many important trading sites during the Collapse. In turn, the period following the Collapse signals the beginning of an era involving struggles between empires and the subsequent transition of much external trade. This encouraged private merchants into domestic trade activities, significantly changing the commercial context for private merchants who had previously sought profit in external trade. In the emerging era of empires, political or military connections and debt capital assumed greater importance in commercial trade, such as the manufacture of textiles and the transport of goods.

There was a long period from which we have a paucity of details about the use of equity capital, only partly due to the destruction of possible archaeological evidence by invaders. For various reasons, merchants of the important Mediterranean civilizations following the Bronze Age Collapse, unlike merchants of ancient Mesopotamia, did not keep meticulous records. For example, in Hellenic Greece, following traditions inherited from ancient Egypt, verbal contracts using witnesses, instead of detailed written contracts, were common in many domestic commercial transactions.

A more compelling example of a lack of evidence about commercial activity is provided by the seemingly mythical Phoenicians. Despite being credited with the introduction of an alphabet and writing system that has descended to modern times as the Greco-Roman alphabet, what is known about Phoenicia comes largely from sources attached to other civilizations, including some references in the Old Testament.[15] Operating at a time when the power of empires was weakened, using advanced seafaring technology and heavily involved in external trade, the possibilities for profitable ventures using private equity capital seem compelling. Unfortunately, the little direct evidence that remains suggests an alternative course.

It is likely that the failure of certain types of archaeological evidence to survive from ancient Phoenicia is due to the use of timber for construction and religious statutory, combined with the likely use of leather (parchment or vellum) and papyrus for writing. The methods and media used to record commercial transactions contributed to a general absence of surviving commercial records across civilizations from the Bronze Age Collapse to the Middle Ages. Unlike the clay tablets and stylus common in Mesopotamia, papyrus and especially leather were costly to produce and, in the case of papyrus, significantly less durable. This meant that conventional merchant transactions either used less durable methods of recording business transactions or relied on verbal contracts with witnesses. Records on parchment or papyrus were reserved for more socially important items, such as religious text or the writings of philosophers and statesmen. Over time, considerable effort has been given to recovering, translating and preserving such writings as the works of the Greek philosophers, such as Demosthenes, or the writings of Roman politicians, such as Cicero.

Despite the impact on business records of non-durable writing medium, some written evidence of commercial activity has survived from Egyptian, Greek and Roman times. This is not the case with Phoenicia. Important Phoenician trading sites such as Carthage and Tyre suffered considerable destruction at various times in history. These limitations to uncovering positive archaeological evidence have been compounded by the disproportionate attention given to regions south of Phoenicia associated with biblical history and the negative view of Phoenicians in several sections of the Bible.[16] This general lack of positive evidence about Phoenicia following the Bronze Age Collapse is unfortunate (e.g., Boyes 2012). The collapse of inter-regional trade for part of the 11th century BC was not total. Though the old Phoenician city of Byblos was sacked by invaders, the most important Phoenician trading city at the time of the Old Testament was Tyre, which was spared.[17] The speed with which the revival of inter-regional trade took place "indicates its dependence on what had gone before, and especially in the areas associated with maritime trade. . . . The area which recovered most rapidly was the southern Levant (Philistia and Phoenicia), linked both to Cyprus and now also to the incense-producing areas of southern Arabia, via the west Arabian coast route. This southern Levantine focus was the core region of expansion at the start of the first millennium" (Sherratt and Sherratt 1993, p.364).

Much of what is known about Phoenicia is based on the recovery of artifacts, especially pottery, at trading sites. Combined with other positive archaeological evidence, the extension of the Phoenician seaborne trading network from the Bronze Age Collapse to the middle of the first millennium BC likely included

Figure 2.7   The ancient city of Tyre, taken from the isthmus. Coloured lithograph by Louis Haghe after David Roberts, 1843

the Levant, Cyprus, Egypt, Sicily, Northern Africa (especially Carthage), Sardinia, the Mediterranean coast of Spain and, possibly, the Canary Islands and Ireland. Various sections of the Old Testament make reference to Phoenicians (Canaanites), such as the reference to 'Tarshish merchants' in Ezekiel 27:12. Oppenheim (1967) argued the Phoenician trading network also extended into Mesopotamia via caravans. Phoenicians' dependence on mutually beneficial trade with other cultures, typically relying on trading posts instead of colonies, is well established. In contrast, the emergence of Greek seafaring following the Collapse relied more on colonization and encompassed the trading areas of the

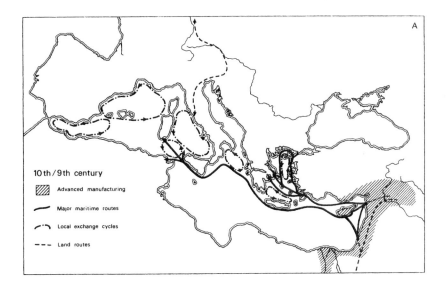

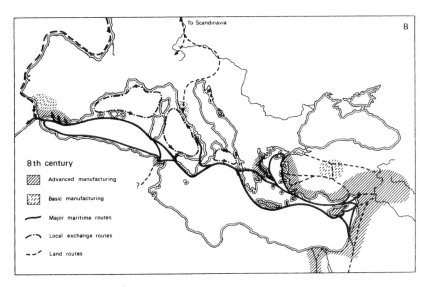

Figure 2.8   (Continued)

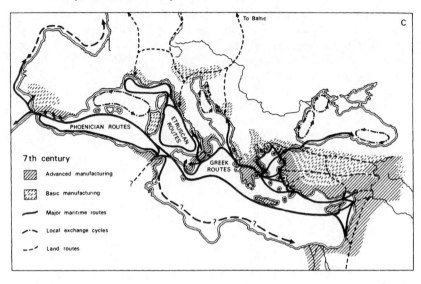

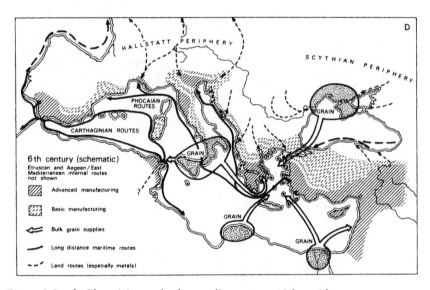

Figure 2.8a–d   Phoenician and other trading routes, 10th to 6th century BC

Source: Sheratt and Sheratt (1993, pp.372–3)

pre-Hellenic Minoan and Mycenaean civilizations in the Aegean and parts of Italy (e.g., Boardman 2001).

The place of Phoenicia in the period leading up to the Roman Republic was described by Bikai et al. (1993, p.24) as follows:

At the end of the Bronze Age, ca. 1200 BC, the decline of both Mycenaean Greece and of Egypt created a power vacuum in the eastern Mediterranean.

Assyria, Persia, and classical Greece would not be major forces for some centuries to come. During the intervening years, the first centuries of the Iron Age, a center of activity developed that would lay the basis for much of later history, and that center was Phoenicia.

The geographical proximity of Phoenicia with trading centers in Anatolia, and the expansion of the Neo-Assyrian empire westward during this period, suggests a possible adoption of trading practices associated with the Old Assyrian colonial network. However, the archaeological evidence indicates the contrary (e.g., Sherratt and Sherratt 1993; Boardman 2001). The limited evidence available is insufficient to determine the Phoenicians' methods of financing external seaborne trade. Was it similar to the previous use of contracts by the Bronze Age seafarers from Ur in Sumer and Ugarit on the Mediterranean coast of southern Anatolia? Subsequently, the Greeks and later the Romans used sea 'loans' in which a source of capital was the wealthy landed or military classes that controlled political power and were able to extract relatively generous terms.

The Sea Loan (*Foenus Nauticum*)

The financing of long-distance trade is a complicated commercial transaction that evolved considerably over time. The sea loan or *foenus nauticum* contract used in the Roman Empire is described in *Digest* [22,2,1]: "A 'transmarine' loan consists of money carried abroad. If it is spent where lent, it is not 'transmarine'. But are goods bought with the money in the same position? It depends on whether they

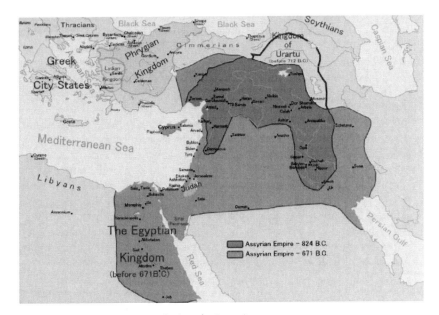

Figure 2.9   Assyrian Empire during the Iron Age

are carried at the lender's peril".[18] *Digest*[22,2,3] further details: "The risk of a transmarine loan is on the creditor from the day on which it is signed". While actual contracts from Greek and Roman times have not survived, considerable information has been gleaned from the writings of Demosthenes (384–322 BC)— for example, *Against Dionysodorus*. This source identifies common Greek practice with interest-bearing sea loans made to ship owners to finance the purchase of cargo for transport and sale in a foreign port. While it is often claimed that Roman contracting methods for financing long-distance trade were adapted from the Greek sea loan, it is also possible that a *societas* of labor and capital with some sharing of profit was also used. An important, if unrecognized, difference between these two methods of financing is that the sea loan involved a formal contract and the *societas* was formed and sustained by mutual agreement, "the *ius fraternitatis* which was intrinsic to the *societas*" (Pryor 1977, p.17).

In determining the meaning of 'usury', medieval scholastics struggled with the classification of sea loan as illicit 'usury' or a special form of licit *societas*. In more modern history, the transaction has typically been sweepingly classified as debt financing when considerable variation in contracting is apparent, over time and locale. Reference to transactions involved in financing long-distance trade as 'loans' has long standing (e.g., Emerigon 1811). Ziskind (1974, p.134) described the conventional view of the transactions as follows:

> In ordinary loans, if money was loaned to buy income property, and the buildings purchased with the borrowed money burned down, the lender's right to demand repayment was in no way diminished, or if a man borrowed money and purchased slaves with the hope that the slaves' productive capacity would generate income to pay off the loan, but the slaves ran away, again, the lender could still demand his money. Not so the bottomry loan. Although the specific terms of the contract varied from place to place and from one people and epoch to another, generally speaking, the transaction operated in the following manner: A shipowner or lessee of a ship would borrow a sum of money to either repair or outfit a ship or to acquire cargo for a one-way or round trip voyage. The loan was secured by hypothecating the ship, the cargo, or both. The obligation to repay the loan became due within a specified time-usually twenty days after the ship and cargo safely arrived at the destination stipulated in the contract. If the security became lost at sea due to pirates, storms, or some other disaster in which there was no evidence of negligence or criminal or fraudulent intent on the part of the borrower, then the obligation to repay the lender with respect to both the principal and the interest was automatically canceled. If the cargo was partially lost, repayment of the loan was usually on a *pro rata* or *ad valorem* basis. It also must be understood that the application of the money is seldom referred to in the Graeco-Roman documents—only that a ship or cargo was being hypothecated, and the loan will be repaid upon the safe arrival of the ship.

This interpretation identifies some fundamental elements of the sea loan: the borrower was a ship owner or lessee, responsible for the loss of the mode of transport; the borrower pledged collateral to ensure satisfactory completion of the contract; and the lender's funds were at risk in the event of shipwreck or loss of cargo. The interpretation also implicitly has the borrower bearing the commercial risk of being unable to sell the cargo profitably. Given the lender's general inability to be present when the goods were sold, such an allocation of this risk was commercially sensible. However, the risk of monitoring profit generated by the sale of goods varied. In particular, it is well known that long-distance trade in ancient times often involved inter-generational associations of merchants in different geographical locations (e.g., Goitein 1964, p.319). In addition, there was the practice of having a travelling partner or agent accompany the goods. Both of these features change the risk profile for the investor.

A fundamental characteristic of an equity capital financing is the sharing of uncertain profit or loss from a commercial venture. Such sharing of profit and loss is difficult when the investor is unable to adequately monitor the purchase, sale and transport of goods. There are a number of avenues to manage such commercial risks. Based on evidence in the Cairo Geniza, Goitein (p.316) concluded: "the Mediterranean and Indian trade, as revealed by the Cairo Geniza, was largely based not upon cash benefits or legal guarantees, but on the human qualities of mutual trust and friendship". In addition to using merchant networks to manage risks, the Romans were known to have a travelling partner accompany goods on the voyage. It is also possible that modern interpretations have been confused by the translation and interpretation of 'interest' in ancient sources. Given that a higher rate of 'interest' could be charged on a sea loan than a conventional loan, a sharing of profit based on the maximum expected profit from the venture could be determined before the voyage. Prior to Justinian imposing a maximum interest rate on sea loans, 'interest' rates could vary widely. Does an 'interest' rate of, say, 50% reflect a division of expected profit or a risk-adjusted interest rate on a commercial loan?

In a partnership, failure of the venture can result in complete loss of equity capital and, possibly, even further losses. In a venture financed with a 'loan', the profit or loss from the venture falls on the borrower, and, in return, the debt holder is only entitled to 'interest', possibly zero, plus return of principal. In the event of default, the creditor could claim the security pledged against the loan. By locating liability for loss at sea with the creditor, the sea loan differed from a conventional commercial loan. The characteristics of this risk of loss impact the interpretation of financing long-distance trade as debt or equity capital. Though external trade was essential in ancient civilizations, there was a substantive difference in the commercial risks of caravans, river barges and seagoing vessels as a mode of transport. The evidence from the *Digest* on the use of sea loans is applicable to a period of the Roman Empire in which, by the end of the Republic, the risks of piracy had been largely suppressed. There was also considerable political and commercial control in the far-flung regions of the empire. If risk of loss is high and ability to monitor is low, is the commercial rationale for the use of a 'loan' rather than a 'partnership' undermined?

In the financing of long-distance trade, did the *societas* of labor and capital and the *foenus nauticum* differ substantively in the sharing of profit and loss? Unlike a conventional *societas*, the investor in a sea loan did not share in the commercial risk associated with generating profit from the sale of goods abroad. In the sea loan, the investor was also not responsible for the conduct of business and was not liable for agreements made by the borrower. However, the Roman *societas* was a flexible arrangement that allowed for considerable variation. Adjustment of shares in the profit and loss was permitted by agreement. Payment of a fixed 'share' was permissible. As long as the *societas* was not leonine, each partner could be fully responsible for certain losses. Given this, the key feature separating a *societas* of labor and capital from the *foenus nauticum* was the binding nature of the contract. A *societas* was held together by mutual agreement. The withdrawal or death of one partner ends the *societas*. The *foenus nauticum* had no such right of withdrawal. The contract was formal and binding.

The modern and widely held interpretation of financing long-distance trade in ancient times is reflected in Ziskind (1974, p.134) speaking about the Roman sea 'loan': "the *faenus nauticum* may be considered not as a loan per se but as a kind of maritime insurance in which the money advanced to the shipper served as an indemnity against possible loss, and if no loss occurred, the lender could expect repayment at an amount in excess of the customary or statutory interest rates set for ordinary loans." This common interpretation reflects the modern 'bottomry' loan onto ancient practice. A modern bottomry 'loan' is conceived as a combination of a loan and an insurance policy. The difference between the return on a bottomry 'loan' and, say, a loan of silver in a commercial venture is due to the charging of an insurance premium. In this interpretation, little attention is paid to fundamental context, especially: (a) the details of the parties involved in the contracts; (b) the difficulties of the voyage; (c) the relationship between the size of the 'interest' on the bottomry loan, the customary return on a commercial loan and the typical profit on an equity capital investment in an onshore business; (d) the medium used to effect delivery (e.g., payment in goods or silver); (e) the amount and type of collateral pledged to ensure return of principal; and (f) the maximum profit that could be earned.

Sea Loans in Earlier Times

An important theme in the history of equity capital is how the financing of long-distance trade changed over time. An early work by Oppenheim (1954) provides some essential context on financing during the dynasty of Larsa (ca. 1961–1674 BC) in Ur of the Old Babylonian period. During this time, there was extensive state control over the largely agrarian domestic economic activity, with merchants engaged in domestic trade often working as agents of the state. In contrast, different financing methods arose in the specialized seaborne trade with Telmun (also referred to as Dilmun), an important trading center on the western shore of the Persian Gulf. Telmun was especially important for trade in copper ingots that likely originated in mines in the area of modern-day Oman. It is also likely that goods from the Indus River civilizations and other far-flung regions could be obtained in Telmun. The voyage was likely undertaken in vessels made primarily from reeds and tar. In addition to specialized seafaring skills and considerable courage, the voyagers would require reliable contacts or agents in Telmun to locate and exchange goods. Special arrangements would be warranted for such ventures.

Oppenheim provides the text of a surviving bottomry 'loan' contract for the seafarers of Ur (p.8):

> The exact nature of the business transactions typically performed in Telmun is unequivocally stated in UET V 367: "2 mina of silver (the value of) : 5 gur of oil (and of) 30 garments for an expedition to Telmun to buy (there) copper, (as the) capital for a partnership, L. and N. have borrowed from U. After safe termination of the voyage, he (the creditor) will not recognize commercial losses (incurred by the debtor) . . . they (the debtors) have agreed to satisfy U. (the creditor) with 4 mina of copper for each shekel of silver as a just [price (?)]".

This contract has two non-standard features for a loan: The 'creditor' cannot hold the 'debtor' responsible for commercial losses that prevent repayment, presumably associated with shipwreck, loss or spoilage of cargo and the like; and the 'creditor' could only demand payment with the 'safe termination of the voyage' when, presumably, the 'debtors' would realize profit from the venture. In addition, there does not appear to be any collateral pledged to secure the 'loan'. Oppenheim (1954, p.9) also reports a transaction in which 'shares' in an seafaring venture were traded, though the mechanism for determining price is not provided. Given all these features, is it more appropriate to refer to this Ur text as a bottomry 'partnership'? Is equitable 'sharing of profit and loss' consistent with the agreement of a fixed payment upon successful completion? Does it matter that the ownership of the boat is not stated?

Over time and geography, the bottomry arrangement varied. Ziskind (1974, p.138) reports a bottomry 'loan' from Ugarit just prior to the Collapse:

> Under the terms of this transaction, the Byblian king borrowed a large sum of money from the king of Ugarit, with an undisclosed quantity of ships valued at 540 heavy silver shekels pledged as security and an additional 50 shekels borrowed against the cargo. Whether these 590 shekels, at least 540 of them of the heavy type, corresponded to the exact amount of the principal is uncertain. It was customary among the Greeks that the value of the hypothecated property be equal to twice the principal in round trip voyages.

Together with Tyre and Sidon, Byblos was one of the important cities of Phoenicia. At this time, Ugarit and the Phoenicians were on good terms. The pledge of security in this arrangement and the presence of kings as parties to the contract changes the context considerably compared to the Ur III contract. Unlike the practice in Ur, Greece and Rome, in which private merchants were involved, in Ugarit of this time, and apparently also in Phoenicia, trade was a royal matter. It is possible, even likely, that the 'creditor' in the Ur text is a royal agent and the bottomry 'partnership' is closer to an agreement by the state—the creditor—to purchase from seafaring merchants copper for future delivery, with an advance payment of silver to ensure delivery was made. Given the positions of 'creditor' and 'debtor' and the type of transaction, in such a case there would be no need for collateral.

Lack of details makes it difficult to determine the context of bottomry transactions in the period up to and including the Collapse. Information improves significantly as time progressed. For example, the bottomry arrangement of Ur can be compared with the text of a *harranu* partnership contract from private archives of Neo-Babylonian times (Wunsch 2002, p.238):

> Dar 134: "12 minas (of silver of current quality with a mark) of A (are) at the debit of B for a *harranu* venture. Of whatever he (B) achieves (lit. works) with these 12 minas, B will give a half share to A. B must not pursue (lit. go) another *harranu* venture apart from this one (. . .) B guarantees for this capital amount [of 12 minas of silver]. B is in charge of the *harranu* business. 5 witnesses, scribe. Babylon 5/viii/4 Dar (Nov. 8, 512 BC).

In the *harranu* partnership between merchants, the working partner guaranteed the equity capital principal that the other non-working partner had advanced to start the venture. Both partners split any profit, but one partner was responsible if the venture failed. There was also an absence of collateral to ensure the return of principal in the event the venture failed. The close connection with the bottomry 'partnership' of Ur is more than apparent.

Context, translation and interpretation of texts from ancient Mesopotamia face significant challenges. In terms of relevance to modern times, Greek maritime practices had substantial subsequent impact on the more formalized Roman practice: "the Romans were not the sea-faring people that the Greeks, Phoenicians, or Ugaritians were. The Roman maritime law was probably an appropriate adaptation of the laws and usages of the various sea-faring peoples the Romans had come to know or conquer" (Ziskind 1974, p.135). An early work by Finley (1953, p.259) described the bottomry 'loan' in Greece, where more precise information about the context of the arrangements was easier to obtain, as follows:

> In the fourth century B.C., from which our information about bottomry comes, a set pattern can be seen. The loans rarely, if ever, exceeded 2,000 drachmas; they were made for the duration of the voyage (weeks or months, no more); the articles of agreement were detailed and always in writing; interest rates were high, even an annual figure of 100 per cent was not unheard of; all the risks of the voyage, though not of economic failure, were borne by the lender, who held the ship or cargo or both as security for prompt repayment once the vessel was safely back in the harbor of Athens.

The use of written contracts in a commercial venture was not characteristic of Greek commerce, much of which was associated with land holdings. Hellenist

Greece tended to follow the commercial practice of ancient Egyptians, in which verbal agreements and witnesses were typically used. As for the return on bottomry transactions: "Land-secured loans, in contrast, averaged only a little less than the maximum for bottomry and frequently ran to far larger sums. They were often arranged verbally and without interest. When interest was charged, the rate was roughly 10 to 18 per cent". Land-secured loans were usually not for productive purposes, though such loans were made, but rather for consumption purposes – for example, to secure a dowry or to support 'elaborate expenditures'.

For bottomry transactions of the ancient Greeks, some actual 'interest rate' estimates are available. Circa 350 BC, Demosthenes gave accounts of a cargo of a thousand wine casks to be transported in a large oared vessel. When interest rates for regular loans were 12%–18% without insurance, an 'interest rate' of 22½% was charged on the sea loan, with provision for a further increase to 30% if the return voyage was delayed. Such numbers reflect a dramatic change in context compared to earlier times. By the fourth century BC seaborne trade was increasingly reliable due to improved maritime technology, such as larger ship size and better design. Larger oared vessels were more seaworthy and much more difficult to attack, deterring piracy. There was also increased knowledge of sea lanes and ability to plot courses using the stars, reducing the chance of shipwreck. Bottomry arrangements in both Greek and Roman times usually stipulated that the lender had the right to place on board the ship an employee, called a *kermakolouthos* in Greek times, whose job was to see that the lender's interests were not criminally subverted, further increasing the probability that the stated 'interest' would be paid.

Roman Sea Loans

One feature of a bottomry transaction that qualifies it as a 'loan' is the fixed return on the capital provided. Nearing the end of the Roman Empire, the change in commercial context associated with bottomry arrangements was such that the 'profit' from the transaction had become similar to that for money loans. "Before Justinian, the interest rate for ordinary loans was limited at twelve per cent with no limit for maritime loans. In 528 A.D., the interest ceiling was lowered and maritime loans were limited at twelve per cent" (Ziskind 1974, p.134). Kessler and Temin (2007, pp.323–4) documented the use of bottomry arrangements by private merchants in the massive Roman wheat market and identified the use of detailed written receipts (in triplicate) and sealed samples sent with each shipment as a method of reducing losses due to substitution of inferior grain. The extent of seaborne trading required to sustain Rome's demand for wheat, metals and other commodities created various opportunities to 'manage' the risks associated with seaborne trade.

Given the lack of surviving primary sources, precisely how commercial risks of seaborne trade were managed in Roman times is difficult to determine. One often-quoted source is Plutarch's *Cato Maior* [21.6–21.7]. For example, Kessler and Temin (2007, p.318) implicitly referenced this source when claiming:

"Cato's famous statement that he would take a one-fiftieth share in a *societas* that operated 50 ships . . . Verboven insist[s] . . . that 'Cato and the 50 traders simply joined hands to minimize the risks involved in the overseas merchant venture. When the journey was over and Cato's loan to finance the venture repaid, the *societas* would automatically be ended' ".[19] Written during the early Empire, Plutarch's *Cato Maior* [21.6–21.7], states (B. Perrin 1914, trans.):

> [Cato] used to loan money also in the most disreputable of all ways, namely, on ships, and his method was as follows. He required his borrowers to form a large company, and when there were fifty partners and as many ships for his security, he took one share in the company himself, and was represented by Quintio, a freedman of his, who accompanied his clients in all their ventures. In this way his entire security was not imperilled, but only a small part of it, and his profits were large.

Malmendier (2009, p.1089) referenced *Cato Maior* in making the fanciful claim that shares in the *societates publicanorum* were traded:

> Plutarch quotes Cato with the expectation that his readers in the early Roman Empire would understand his boasting. In other words, educated Romans knew about the possibility of buying shares in the *societates publicanorum*.

One problem with the interpretation that this source supports claims of Roman share trading involves timing. Plutarch was discussing the consul and censor Marcus Porcius Cato (*Maior*, the Elder) (234–149 BC), while primary sources on trading of shares are silent until the time of Cicero and Cato the Younger, great-grandson of Cato the Elder, about a century later (Nelson 1950). In addition, the commercial context is different. As a condition for a loan from Cato, borrowers in a sea loan were required to form a partnership in which Cato participated. This is substantively different, in both a legal and a commercial sense, from the tax farming and public works activities associated with the *societates publicanorum* of the late Republic. The source does reveal that senators, consuls and others of high Roman office during the middle Republic did conduct business through others, Quintio the freedman in the case at hand. As for share trading, despite philological issues with the ancient Greek text for 'he took one share in the company', there is no supporting evidence in this source for share trading.

Another problem with this interpretation is that the Cato commercial context being proposed is confusing. A 'share' in a partnership was being purchased, presumably by payment of equity capital at the creation of the partnership, while a 'loan' was being made to members of the partnership. The apparent stability and reduced payment size to the contributor of capital in a sea loan is a result of the substantially lower risk of a zero payout than for those supplying labour. However, there are essential equity capital features of the ancient sea loan transaction. Similar to the Neo-Babylonian partnership, there were Greek and Roman contracts in which one partner would provide financing for the

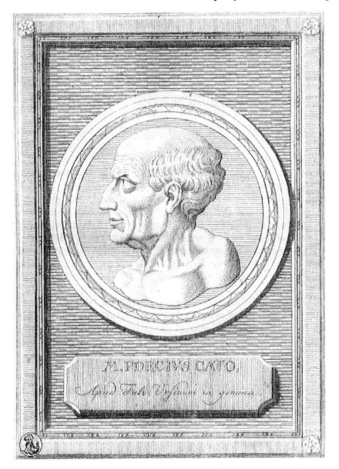

Figure 2.10 Marcus Porcius Cato (234–149 BC) a.k.a. Cato the Elder

trading venture, while the other partner would do the work, with a predetermined sharing of the profits upon completion of the venture. However, in such
cases, the lender's personal liability would no longer be limited to the amount
on loan. At least since Weber (1891), the peculiar characteristics of ancient capitalism have been recognized and explored; "political capitalism" (Love 1991)
in the Roman Empire. Aside from some direct state-sponsored trade, such as
the *annona,* tasked to supply wheat for about 15% of the population of Rome,
there was almost complete domination of sea loan transactions by *equites.* Only
a few wealthy freemen and clandestine senators, acting through *familiares,* participated, attesting to the importance of politics in the commercial affairs of the
Empire.[20]

The evolution of the bottomry arrangement illustrates the difficulties of
classifying the source of commercial financing as debt liability or equity capital partnership. One debt-like feature of a bottomry arrangement is the fixed

payment to the creditor. The 'creditor' does not share in the profit beyond what is stated. Yet, modern equity security markets feature fixed coupon preferred stocks that have a set dividend. In this case, it is the inability to force default in the event a dividend payment is not made that determines the classification as equity capital. Translated to the ancient bottomry arrangement, in which the stated return could be 100% or more, not including possible additional gains due to favorable exchange, the return stated in the contract may have been based on an estimated value for a share in the expected profit from the venture. In effect, the equity valuation problem is solved by making a two-state expected value calculation, in which the return in one state is zero and in the other state is the payment specified in the contract. This sharing arrangement would be preferable to one in which an accurate accounting of the profit upon safe arrival in harbor has to be determined based on transactions in a foreign market that could not be observed and would be hard to monitor.

Another characteristic of the bottomry contract, similar to secured debt liabilities, is the addition of collateral conditions in bottomry contracts going back at least to Bronze Age Ugarit. Such conditions were conventional by Greek and Roman times. However, this condition was aimed more at obtaining the agreed payment from profit upon safe return than at ensuring repayment of principal if the venture failed, as was the case in a conventional debt contract. As evidenced by the maritime law in the *Corpus Iuris Civilis* of Justinian (AD 482–565), in addition to the *foenus nauticum,* the ancient Roman jurists discussed such problems as shipwreck, cargo liability, jettison, salvage, and injuries, all relevant to the need to obtain collateral. Another aspect of the sea loan contract that does not qualify as a 'loan' is that the stated 'interest' was afforded separate treatment from customary land- or money-based interest rates. Unfortunately, the absence of commercial records from Old Testament, Greek and Roman times often reflects the attitude of Aristotle (*Politics,* Book I, ch. 11, sec. 5), in which discussing "the various forms of acquisition . . . minutely and in detail might be useful for practical purposes; but to dwell long upon them would be in poor taste". Similar attitudes appear in the New Testament, such as Matthew 21:12, with Jesus throwing out the 'money lenders'.

D　*PECULIUM* AND ROMAN LAW OF *SOCIETAS* (PARTNERSHIP)

What Is *Peculium*?

As Pryor (1977) demonstrated, whether bottomry arrangements were, *de facto,* a special type of partnership designed to deal with the hazards of seaborne trade is difficult to determine precisely. Over time, Roman legal notions associated with the *foenus nauticum* and *societas* evolved into the Italian *commenda* and *compagnia* arrangements of the Middle Ages and the Renaissance, which had subtly different features designed to satisfy requirements of medieval canon and civil law. In combination with bottomry arrangements, it was the Roman *societas* that evolved into the modern concept of equity capital in partnerships employed in legal systems of Europe and, through the colonization process, throughout the world (e.g., Poitras 2000; Musacchio and Turner 2013). However, given the reliance of Roman law on the concept of the individual and the family (*familia*), Roman commercial law did not develop a framework for business organization applicable to the permanent private equity capital stock associated with modern limited liability corporations. While subsequent evolution of the *commenda* and *compagnia* forms of business organization did significantly impact the later organization of equity capital, the widespread use of *peculium* contributed to commercial capital's continued entanglement with the household balance sheet in Roman times (e.g., Abatino et al. 2011).

Interpretation of the role of *societas* in Roman commercial activity requires considerable context. Hansmann et al. (2006, p.1358) described the widespread use of *peculium* in slave-run commercial ventures during the Empire as follows:[21]

> Slaveholding was extensive in ancient Rome, and it was to their slaves that Roman families frequently delegated the responsibility for managing commercial activity. This arrangement was congenial to Roman social mores, under which trade was considered demeaning. Moreover, Rome's slaves often exhibited commercial talent, in part because they frequently were captured in colonial wars with societies such as Greece in which commercial activity was less discreditable. It was common practice for a master to provide his slave (or sometimes his own son) with a set of assets, termed a *peculium*, for use in a business venture. The *peculium*, plus any profits it generated, formally remained the property of the master. The master benefited from the arrangement either by receiving regular payments from the slave, or by offering manumission as a reward for efforts by the slave that grew the *peculium*'s assets. Unlike the *societas*, the *peculium* business exhibited a degree of asset partitioning. Although default on *peculium* debt enabled creditors of the *peculium* enterprise to sue the slave's master, the master's liability was capped at the value of the *peculium* (plus any distributions he had received from it) so long as he had not participated in its management.

The use of *peculium* combined with the rules surrounding the *familia* and the *pater familias* (p.1357):

> the Roman family [was] both large and, from a creditor's view, robust. The family had an indefinitely long life span, remaining intact over multiple generations. Moreover, those persons to whom a family member evading creditors would be most inclined to pass his assets—close relatives, and especially descendants—were themselves part of the same entity and thus also liable for the same debts. The wealth of a single, prosperous Roman family was apparently sufficient to finance the typical commercial firm, thus reducing the need for multi-owner enterprise forms such as the partnership.

As such, a modern connection to the *societas* needs to recognize the significant differences in commercial context arising in Roman times.

The Roman Law of *Societas*

Interpretation and context for commercial legal structures in Roman times need "at least in part to [account for] Rome's reliance on other forms of organization for most business activity. Chief among these alternatives were the family and the *peculium*" (Hansmann et al. 2006, p.1357). Given this, Roman law formally permitted at least two legal structures where merchants could combine together in a commercial venture: the *societas* and the *collegium*. However, while a *collegium* could have a corporate personality, uses for *collegia* were limited to certain social or public activities, such as the organization of fraternal orders for soldiers, and lack relevance to the equity capital used in most commercial ventures. In contrast, a *societas* could be formed for a wide range of commercial and social activities, to be determined by the partners (*socii*). The length of a *societas* was flexible. It could be formed for limited duration (*vel ad tempus vel ex tempore*) or in perpetuity (*in perpetuum*). Malmendier (2009) traced the perpetual *societas* to the ancient custom of *consortium ercto non cito* (partnership by undivided inheritance), in which heirs to an estate decide to administer the inheritance jointly rather than distributing it among the testates. Given the ancient history of partnerships, this begs an archaeological question: Is the Roman treatment of partnership consistent with the treatment of 'family and kinship' partnerships and the disposition of estates in Old Assyria and Babylonia?

In commercial practice, the *societas* had no legal personality in a 'corporate' sense. Partners were responsible for the liabilities of the commercial venture and had the rights to the profits and return of capital as set out in the partnership agreement. As Hansmann et al. (2006, p.1356) observed, beyond this point there is little connection to modern partnerships:

> The simplest ancient Roman commercial form was the *societas*, a term often translated as "partnership" because it referred to an agreement among Roman citizens to share an enterprise's profits and losses. Beyond joint enterprise, however, the *societas* had little in common with the modern partnership form. For one thing, the *societas* lacked mutual agency; each partner had to endorse a contract to be bound by it. Partners also did not stand behind one another's obligations: the default rule of liability when they cosigned a debt was *pro rata* rather than joint and several. More generally, Roman law made no distinction between the obligations and assets of the *societas* and those of its members, precluding the rules of weak asset partitioning that characterize the modern partnership.

A *societas* was formed by simple consent, *consensus* or *affectio societatis*, with each *socius* (partner) making a contribution to the venture that could involve: financial (money) investment; the provision of skills and labor—in long-distance trade during the Republic this was often associated with the contribution of the captain or traveling partner; or in-kind capital such as goods, rights or claims. This has reflections in modern venture (equity) capital 'start-ups', where a corporation is formed with 'shares' distributed to the venture capitalists providing financial backing and further shares given to the commercial functionaries involved in running the business. Unless otherwise stated in the partnership agreement, differences in the form and amount of 'equity' capital were permissible. In anticipation of the triple contract employed in medieval times, the partnership could also permit differential sharing of profit and loss, with the possibility that a given partner could be exempted from sharing any loss. However, a partnership where a partner was totally excluded from profits (*societas leonina*) was not permitted.

Following Buckland (1963), four main technical forms of Roman *societas* can be identified: (a) the *societas omnium bonorum*, in which the current and future property of partners became common property of all *socii*; (b) the *societas omnium bonorum quae ex quaestu veniunt*, the default commercial format, in which the property covered by the partnership was limited to that acquired for the purpose of the *societas*; (c) the *societas alicuius negotiationis*, probably the most common form of *societas*, in which the partnership was limited to profit and losses for a specific commercial venture; and (d) the *societas unius rei*, applicable to execution of a single transaction, which might not be commercial. Methods of dissolving a *societas* were: (a) *ex voluntate*, where either all *socii* agreed to dissolve or a single partner unilaterally withdrew; (b) *ex personis*, due to the death or *capitis deminutio* of a *socius*; (c) *ex rebus*, where the goal of the *societas* was accomplished or the agreed term of the partnership had expired, typical of bottomry arrangements; and (d) *ex actione*, where one *socius* initiated a suit against one or more of the other *socii* (*actio pro socio*).

Trading of Shares in the *Societates Publicanorum*?

It is conventional to observe that contractual design features of the *societas* worked against development of a group of merchants combining in commercial ventures with a permanent equity capital stock. In particular, a *societas* did not have a legal identify separate from that of the partners. If the partnership was not limited to a specific commercial venture, it was difficult for profit to be distributed over time, instead of at the end of the *societas*. Without the ability to sell and transfer shares, equity capital would be locked in, deterring the development of longer term commercial ventures. Malmendier (2009) and others observed that neither the classical Roman jurists of the Republic or Justinian jurists of the *Corpus Iuris Civilis* were able to construct the legal foundation for a contract that encouraged commercial organizations with a permanent equity capital stock. One "remarkable exception" to this case claimed by Malmendier, Badian and others was the *societas publicanorum*, the partnership of state franchisees. Consistent with the diminishing economic role of the *publicani* and use of the *societas publicanorum* during the Empire, the *Corpus Iuris Civilis* of Justinian only recognized the *societas vectigalium*, the partnership of tax collectors. This has some overlap with the tax-farming activities associated with the *societas publicanorum* of the late Republic, which covered a wider range of activities.[22]

Significantly, it is claimed that the *societaes publicanorum* of the Roman Republic developed a form of public trading in shares. While playing a fundamental role in tax farming (i.e., bidding on contracts for collection of taxes in specific parts of the conquered territories), the *publicani* were also involved in contracts for the construction and repair of major public works, billeting and supplying of the armies, and working the Spanish mines.[23] Beyond this, there is far from complete agreement among historians. By some accounts (e.g., Rostovtzeff 1957; Malmendier 2009), by the time of Cicero and Julius Caesar, public trading in such shares was conducted at the Forum, in Rome near the temple of Castor. In 59 BC, it is claimed, Cicero provided a description of the trading in such shares (see the quote at the beginning of the section); the *societas* office or individuals already owners of shares were sources for obtaining shares; and it was common practice to trade 'unregistered' shares where purchasers did not become *socii*; both Caesar and Cassius were reported to have done so, presumably to evade the political fallout in the Senate associated with the perception of self-dealing.

Though the roots of the *publicani* stretch to the beginnings of the Roman civilization, the influence of the *societates publicanorum* was greatest during the middle and late stages of the Republic. Under the Empire, the state moved to assume direct control of tax collection. Around 150 BC, the Greek historian Polybius recounted the following about the Roman Republic (Chancellor 1999, p.5) in *Rise of the Roman Empire*:

> All over Italy an immense number of contracts, far too numerous to specify, are awarded by the censors for the construction and repair of public buildings, and besides for the collection of revenues from navigable rivers, harbours, gardens, mines, lands—in a word every transaction which comes under the control of the Roman government is farmed out to contractors. All these activities are carried on by the people, and there is scarcely a soul, one might, say, who does not have some interest in these contracts and the profits which are derived from them.

A Greek aristocrat held as hostage for 16 years in Rome, Polybius examined the growth of the Roman Republic with the aim of aiding Greeks to understand how Rome managed to rise to dominate the region. By the middle of the first century BC, immense tax-farming opportunities were available at auction in Rome and certain provinces, primarily five-year contracts for tax collection in Asia. Arguing for state support of the often abusive tax collection practices of the *publicani*, Cicero observed: "financial confidence and the whole monetary system based on the Forum here at Rome is bound up with and depends upon these Asian investments". In 61 BC, when the *publicani* significantly overbid for the Asian tax-farming contract, Cicero argued successfully in the Senate for releasing the *publicani* from this contractual obligation. The subsequent transition from the Republic to the Empire led to devolution in the role of the *publicani*.

While it is tempting to trace the origins of equity capital trading and, by implication, valuation to the *societates publicanorum*, the historical record is insufficient to sustain such fanciful claims. There is no specific evidence concerning either pricing or trading practices. It is claimed that the *publicani* had

Figure 2.11   Bust of Marcus Tullius Cicero (106–43BC), *Musei Capitolini*, Rome

some elements of modern corporations, with ownership divided into shares (*partes*) with operational control by *magistri* who constituted a board of directors headed by the *manceps* (e.g., Badian 1972). However, Roman law was focused on the individual and had difficulties recognizing rights and duties for associations of individuals outside the *familia*. Following Malmendier (2009), the *publicani* were able to attain the appearance of continuous legal status that extended beyond the period for a particular contract because of the connection with Roman financial administration. In effect, the *publicani* "may be considered as vocational corporations but not as bodies derived from private law. Rather they appeared as political bodies that included social relationships of private law". Legally, contracts were entered into with the *manceps*, not with the *societas*. The specific listing of *socii* on contracts was only relevant to determining the collateral required to ensure fulfillment of the contract.

Though little can be said directly about the extent of trading in *publicani* equity claims, further background on the rigidity of the wealth-determined

Roman social structure is helpful. Duncan-Jones (1982, p.2) observed the rigidity that was formalized by Augustus during the early stages of the Empire: "The Roman state was firmly oligarchic and timocratic. The ownership of wealth was the essential prerequisite for all the high statuses of public life . . . Entry to the Senate, the body of knights (*equites*), the judiciary, and the local town council was in each case controlled by a property qualification . . . The formal structure of civilian wealth qualifications represented ratios of 1:2:4:12 . . . the senator [must have] three times the wealth of the knight." As is common with ancient history, it is difficult to determine the precise degree of rigidity in the *de facto* wealth classifications, especially between the periods of the Roman Republic and Empire. Nicolet (1966, 1974) indicated that, during the late Republic, wealthy *equites* who were the *publicani* were also often involved as moneylenders and merchants, though only a relatively small percentage of *equites* were involved in the public contracts. Recognizing that the *equites* roughly corresponded to the officer class, throughout Roman history building activity by the standing army during times of peace was commonplace. The *publicani* provided an expedient method of organizing such activities and compensating those involved. The organizational skills of past and present army officers were also well suited to the control and direction of large numbers of slaves involved in public works projects.

When the collection of tax-farming revenues was transferred to provincial officials following the reforms of Augustus, the role of the *equites* and the *societates publicanorum* in the tax-collection process changed significantly. Following Hansmann et al. (2006, p.1364):

> When Rome transformed itself from a republic into an empire in the first century B.C., the wealth and influence of the *publicani* drew jealous attention from the emperors, who ordered the state to take over much of the construction of public works. The *publicani* persisted for a time as tax collectors, but repeated clampdowns eliminated them from even this role by the end of the second century A.D.

Instead of being tax-collection contractors with the potential to generate profit from this activity, the role of the military in tax collection within the provinces devolved into managing any fallout from the often aggressive methods used by local tax collectors. Similarly, the role of the military in public construction projects during the Empire was diminished due to the increasing demands from foreign campaigns and sustaining control in conquered territories. While the army was, at times, available for public work construction during the Republic, such opportunities were diminished under the Empire. The organization of such activities was more rigidly controlled, with profits captured by the politically connected families and managed through the *peculium*.

In the unlikely event that senators such as Caesar and Cassius did trade unregistered shares during the Republic, it may have been more for political reasons than for profit. Returns to bottomry loans were likely to be more attractive than *publicani* shares (e.g., Kessler and Temin 2007). As such, the equity capital value of *publicani* shares had a significant political element, unlike modern equity capital. Available evidence indicates that senators' wealth was based on income from large landed agricultural estates with income from loans or 'usury' of not more than 5%–10% (Duncan-Jones 1982, pp.17–32). Recognizing the substantial difficulties in trading registered shares, in the period leading up to a contract auction it is possible that the Forum was used as a trading venue for those *equites* seeking to purchase a share, and possibly a senator or two and some freemen seeking to trade shares through proxies. However, it is inaccurate to depict such trading as "an immense stock exchange where monetary speculation of every kind was going on" (Cunningham 1913, p.164) or that "crowds of men bought and sold shares and bonds of tax-farming companies, various goods for cash and on credit, farms and estates in Italy and in the provinces, houses and shops in Rome and elsewhere, ships and storehouses, slaves and cattle" (Rostovtzeff 1957, p.31).

Following Chancellor (1999, p.4), the Roman comic playwright Plautus was probably more accurate in describing the Forum as a collection of "whores, shopkeepers, moneylenders, and wealthy men." Polybius's observation about the widespread use of *publicani* contracting in the Roman Republic is consistent with an efficient oligarchic contracting method for determining compensation for the construction of public works and the collection of taxes. Such methods of organizing state tax collection and public duties have roots in Bronze Age Babylonia. The prevalence of 'loans' to members of the military for internal and external commercial ventures is well documented in Neo-Babylonia. As such, the ancient record provides little support for the position of Malmendier (2009, p.1007): "I propose that, contrary to widespread belief, the earliest predecessor of the modern business corporation was not the English East India Company nor the medieval *commenda* but the Roman *societas publicanorum* (i.e., the 'society of government leaseholders')." Insofar as the modern corporation requires a permanent stock of equity capital with transferable shares, those seeking ancient origins of modern corporate organization are advised to examine the colonial trading networks and "'joint-stock fund' (*naruqqum*, 'money bag')" of ancient Assur (Veenhof 2010, p.57).[24]

As with empire expansion in ancient Mesopotamia, the expansion of the Roman Empire led to the internalization of what had been external trade, with a resulting diminution of ventures involving private equity capital in the regions controlled by the Empire. In the post-Actium period, the search for the use of non-household equity capital in commercial ventures in which merchants combined in partnerships shifted to external trade—with regions around the Indian Ocean, with China and with regions of Africa. Following Rathbone (2000) and Fitzpatrick (2011, p.34), this dramatic change in context was because the Roman Empire:

> continually appropriated the wealth of the Mediterranean basin in its own treasury and citizenry through the mechanism of empire. Conquests were obviously profitable, with the massive influx of gold and silver after the Punic Wars; the conquests of Spain and Greece; and the conquests of Egypt, Jerusalem, Parthia, and Dacia producing astronomical inflows of gold and

silver that profoundly affected the Roman economy. It has been estimated that the treasure that Augustus brought back from Egypt saw interest rates drop 60%, and Caesar's plunder from Gaul resulted in a sharp slump in the price of gold. Key assets such as gold and silver mines throughout the empire were also crucial here, directly contributing to the income of the Roman state.

Where trade within the Empire could be carried on by agents ultimately responsible to Rome, trade outside the Empire required specialized knowledge and connections in the various ports of call. In the ancient world, this is the realm of equity capital (e.g., Nadri 2007).

NOTES

1 Temin (2006, p.133) observed: "Previous generations of ancient historians divided into 'modernists', who followed Marx as applied to ancient history by Rostovtzeff (1958), and 'primitivists', who followed Polanyi as applied to ancient history by Finley (1973). Ancient historians today universally argue that these positions are outmoded and counterproductive, but they frequently lapse into one position or the other when pushed." While technically correct regarding the too-general primitivist-versus-modernist distinction, substantive elements of Polanyi's and Finley's arguments about ancient society still receive considerable support, e.g., Greene (2011). For example, Steinkeller (2002, p.111) observed: "Finley's explanation of *nexum* as a voluntary bondage arrangement resulting from an unpaid loan has received broad acceptance among classicists, most emphatically by the British scholar Cornell".

2 Following about 100 laws dealing with family relationships, the treatment of slaves, the conduct of physicians and selling of family into slavery to settle debts, the Code of Hammurabi has about 50 laws like the following:

> 270. If he hire a young animal for threshing, the hire is ten ka of corn.
> 271. If any one hire oxen, cart and driver, he shall pay one hundred and eighty ka of corn per day.
> 272. If any one hire a cart alone, he shall pay forty ka of corn per day.
> 273. If any one hire a day laborer, he shall pay him from the New Year until the fifth month (April to August, when days are long and the work hard) six gerahs in money per day; from the sixth month to the end of the year he shall give him five gerahs per day.
> 274. If any one hire a skilled artisan, he shall pay as wages of the . . . five gerahs, as wages of the potter five gerahs, of a tailor five gerahs, of . . . gerahs, . . . of a ropemaker four gerahs, of . . . gerahs, of a mason . . . gerahs per day.
> 275. If any one hire a ferryboat, he shall pay three gerahs in money per day.
> 276. If he hire a freight-boat, he shall pay two and one-half gerahs per day.
> 277. If any one hire a ship of sixty gur, he shall pay one-sixth of a shekel in money as its hire per day.

3 Dates for important periods in Bronze Age Mesopotamia can only be roughly defined. It is conventional to subdivide the Bronze Age into the Early (3300–2100 BC), Middle (2100–1550) and Late (1550–1200) periods. The Early

Bronze Age in Mesopotamia begins with the empire of Sargon (2350–2330) of Akkad (2350–2200 BC), which ends with the sack of Akkad and the rise of Sumer (2100–2000 BC), ending with the dynasty of Ur III. This is followed by the Old Babylonian period (2000–1600 BC), which includes the Isin-Larsa period (2000–1800 BC) and the reign of Hammurabi (1792–1750 BC). In the north of Mesopotamia, the Old Assyrian period begins around 1900 BC with the Middle Assyrian period commencing with the reign of Ashur-uballit I (1365–1330 BC) and ends with the Bronze Age Collapse. The Late Bronze Age is characterized by the emergence of Kassite rule in Babylon (1531–ca. 1155 BC) following the sack of Babylon by the Hittites in 1595 BC. This period also corresponds with the rise of Assyria. In the Near East and eastern Mediterranean, the Bronze Age Collapse is often dated 1206–1150 BC. This period is associated with the collapse of the Mycenaean kingdom in the Mediterranean and the collapse of the Hittite Empire in Anatolia and Syria in the face of technological advances in iron working, possibly originating in what is modern Bulgaria and Romania. If diffusionist arguments are not accepted, Cyprus is another possible locale. During the Iron Age, there was the subsequent rise of the Neo-Assyrian Empire (934–609 BC) and the associated Neo-Babylonian period (626–539 BC), a rich source of cuneiform documents from both temples and private archives of "prosperous businessmen . . . [though] the surviving evidence of business operations is often limited to records . . . mainly in the form of property titles" (Wunsch 2002, p.222).

4   Given the fragmentary character of the evidence, archaeologists of the ancient world are sensitive to the possibility of 'negative' and 'positive' bias in interpreting sources. More precisely, the absence of any evidence of a particular activity (negative outcome) does not necessarily imply that such activities were not present. Similarly, given the presence of a particular type of evidence (positive outcome), such as loan documents or land titles, it does not necessarily follow that the activities associated with such evidence was widespread or common. Speaking about loan documents from Old Babylonia, Van de Mieroop (2002, p.163) observed: "In order to investigate these documents from an economic point of view, it is necessary to focus on their context rather than their form . . . For private individuals this is usually only feasible when these texts are found in their archival context, unfortunately a rare occurrence".

5   Any presentation of the cuneiform writings for the Code of Hammurabi has to deal with the difficulty of translation of cuneiform script. In addition, in some modern presentations 'laws' are bundled together. For example, Laws 102 and 103 can be combined as "If a merchant lent money to a trader for benefit, and he saw a loss where he went, he shall pay back the principal of the money to the merchant. If, when he went on the road, an enemy made him give up what he was carrying, the trader shall so affirm by God and then shall go free" (Lewin 2003, p.16). The presentation of the Code of Hammurabi used here follows a translation of L.W. King and is consistent with the format used by many archaeologists.

6   There are differing conventions about referencing Old Assyria, with some sources foregoing reference to Assyria, instead referring only to ancient Assur, the main city in Old Assyria. This convention recognizes that the first and second centuries of the second millennium BC—the period when the commercial Assyrian trade centered at Assur reached its zenith—was a time before the emergence of the Assyrian Empire of the late Bronze Age. The era of ancient Assur or Old Assyria was characterized by trade agreements with a network of trading centers in Anatolia and possibly other areas.

7   The merchants of ancient Assur established this network by making treaties between Assur and the state authorities in the different colony locations. There

is evidence that some treaties required a death penalty for trading with Babylonians. For example: "A treaty concluded with a town near the Euphrates, in the area where one enters Anatolia proper, stipulates that the local ruler is forbidden to let Babylonian traders enter his town and, if they do, has to seize and extradite them to the Assyrians to be killed" (Veenhof 2010, p.51). In this fashion, Babylonian traders would be obligated to go to Assur, or vice versa, instead of trading directly with the relevant locations where the Assyrians were obtaining goods. Veenhof (2010, p.44) made the following observations about *kārum* trading: "This so-called '*kārum*-system' was very important for trade and for exploiting the economic potential of the cities and their countryside and even for trade across some territorial boundaries. But, as far as the evidence now available goes, it never developed, not even in powerful states such as Babylon, Larsa, or Mari, into a real 'colonial system', that is a more or less coherent network of traders settled in market-cities and emporia abroad serving the economic interests of a particular empire. What we are rather dealing with here were in essence commercial arrangements that facilitated regional, inter-city trade, in some cases also across territorial boundaries, by groups of merchants from various cities operating in, and from, other cities, preferably capitals and strategically located emporia and market towns. While these merchants were thus important for palaces and rulers in supplying them with required goods or converting their mostly agricultural surpluses—tasks also performed by local traders and occasionally by officials of the palace sent out on particular commissions—they were basically private entrepreneurs."

8 Regarding the positive evidence: "In the case of Assur nearly all our extensive written documentation (nearly 25.000 cuneiform texts, less than half of which are accessible) consists of the archives of ca. eighty Assyrian traders who had settled in *kārum* Kanesh (excavated since 1948), while Assur itself has yielded very little data, also archaeologically" (Veenhof 2010, p.47).

9 The metallurgy associated with production of bronze in ancient times is discussed in Amzallag (2009), Yener et al. (1993), Muhly (1973) and various other sources. An important feature of the technology of metallurgy is the transition from crucibles to open furnace smelting.

10 Even this relatively simple method of equity capital valuation can be complicated. For example, in some Old Assyrian contracts the equity capital would be paid in 'gold' and the return of equity would be valued in 'silver', where the exchange ratio in the contract would be twice the market rate, producing a 100% return to the contributors of equity capital before the 'profit' was distributed.

11 The area of Elam and its important trading center Susa are likely sources of Bronze Age tin. The amount of tin was considerable, so there may have been many small mines from which the tin was aggregated for trading in a central location; and, more likely, there were a small number of large mines sourcing the tin. There is also some evidence of tin having been mined in Afghanistan during this period. Afghanistan was also an important source of lapis lazuli, a cherished semi-precious stone. It is known that Elam was an important trading center for lapis lazuli. The connection with significant Bronze Age tin trading in Elam is only suggestive. Whether merchants from Assur established *kārum* in Elam, and vice versa, is not yet known.

12 Motives for the Anatolian authorities permitting these colonies are provided by Veenhof (2010, p.47): "These settlements had been established on the basis of treaties (called "oaths") concluded between the Assyrian authorities and many local rulers, who allowed the Assyrians to settle, travel, and do business in the various Anatolian 'countries' in exchange for the right to levy taxes on

imported tin (ca. 3%), textiles (5%), and a preempt part (10%) of the latter. These treaties in combination with the efficient colonial organization, commercial skills, good transport and information facilities, agency and representation, and the administrative support of the mother-city of Assur stood at the basis of Assyrian commercial success."

13 Veenhof (2010, p.56) reported the following: "A remarkable feature was that the shares invested gold at an exchange rate of gold:silver = 4:1, while the real rate was 8:1. This means that after the term stipulated the investor would in any case get 200% of his investment back, augmented, if the business had been successful, by one third of the profit." While this claim was not supported by documenting the primary evidence, the possibility of being able to pay in equity capital using gold and receiving return of capital and share of profit in silver has fascinating implications.

14 Justinian (482–565 AD) was emperor of the eastern Roman Empire from 527 to 565. Ziskind (1974) described the Roman maritime law that evolved into the *Corpus* of Justinian: "The sea loan was only one aspect of maritime law the *Corpus* touched upon. The ancient Roman jurists also discussed such problems as shipwreck, cargo liability, jettison, salvage, and injuries. That these subjects should be of interest at all to the Roman jurists is most striking when one considers that the Romans were not the sea-faring people that the Greeks, Phoenicians, or Ugaritians were. The Roman maritime law was probably an appropriate adaptation of the laws and usages of the various sea-faring peoples the Romans had come to know or conquer."

15 Bikai et al. (1990, p.24) observed: "until the late 1960s, the Phoenicians were known mainly from chance finds, from a few excavations at their colonies around the Mediterranean like Carthage and Motya, off the coast of Sicily, and from what had been written about them by classical and biblical authors, hostile witnesses at best. In the 20 years since, there has been great progress, particularly at sites in the western Mediterranean. That progress was marked by a major exhibition in Venice in 1988 . . . which brought together hundreds of Phoenician objects for the first time." The increasing availability of positive evidence provides a benchmark to identify previous finds that were not known to be Phoenician because of the absence of comparable objects.

16 Noting that Phoenicians were likely descended from Semitic tribes, some scholars even suggest an anti-Semitic bias in the lack of searches for positive evidence (e.g., Bikai et al. 1990, p.23), though the credibility of such statements is questionable.

17 There is considerable debate about the extent of the destruction the Sea Peoples inflicted on the Phoenicians (e.g., Gilboa 2005). On this issue, the views of Boardman (2001, p.34) are germane: "We know a lot more about antiquity now than we did fifty years ago, without necessarily understanding it any better". The descriptions of Phoenician history from the late Bronze Age to the early Iron Age are based on very limited archaeological data. The views presented here reflect the loosely held but far from unanimous consensus currently proposed.

18 Given the absence of business records from Roman times, it is difficult to determine how widely used was the sea loan versus *societas* in the organization of maritime trade. Items in the *Digest* are a difficult source; because the *Digest* was prepared during the latter stages of the Empire, it lacks connection with earlier developments. However, the *Digest* lists only nine rulings on sea loans, compared to eighty-four on partnerships. Restrictions on the allowable interest in sea loans during the Empire indicate that a considerable amount of maritime trade was 'controllable' and the perils were lower than in early

periods. Possibly there was some change in the organization of capital needed for maritime ventures around this time.

19 A number of personages are referred to as 'Cato', including Marcus Porcius Cato (234–149 BC), 'Cato the Elder' and Marcus Porcius Cato Uticensis (95–46 BC), 'Cato the Younger' or 'Cato of Utica'. There is also Dionysius Cato, an anonymous author of the *Distichs of Cato* from the 3rd or 4th century AD, thought to be possibly Cato the Elder or Cato the Younger. The *Distichs* became an important work in the Middle Ages for the study of Latin. Both Cato the Younger, a contemporary of Cicero, and Cato the Elder are featured in the *Lives* by Plutarch. Cato the Younger played an important role in the defense of the Republic against the machinations of Caesar. The quote is from the *Lives* of Cato the Elder (XXI) and, as such, refers to commercial arrangements during the middle Republic.

20 The *Lex Claudia* of 218 BC restricted the commercial activity of senators and their sons, a Stoic view that such activity was incompatible with senatorial status. Senators were prohibited from owning ships of greater capacity than 300 *amphorae* (about 7 tonnes), so that they could not conduct the large-scale seaborne transportation associated with bottomry arrangements. As a consequence, the wealthiest individuals in Roman society, the senators, usually operated in such ventures clandestinely—for example, through proxies or agents. Under Augustus (30 BC–14 AD) there was a transition of tax collection from the *equites*-dominated *publicani* to regional governors, causing a transition of *equites* activity to private moneylending and equity capital investments. Consistent with the views of Aristotle and the New Testament, the rationale for the *Lex Claudia* was that obtaining wealth through commercial activities was a lower-class activity. The highest Romans were expected to derive wealth from landholding, government service, and profits from military expansion of the Empire.

21 Despite apparent similarities, the *peculium* differs significantly from the *naruqqum* 'joint-stock' fund of Old Assyria. These differences highlight the character of modern 'equity capital'. Both involve the advancement of capital for a commercial venture. However, the *naruqqum* involves combining the equity capital of different merchants, while the *peculium* is an extension of the *familia*. In effect, the *peculium* had a single owner, the household, entitled to all profits but with limited liability when not directly involved in managing the venture. In the *naruqqum*, profits were shared *pro rata* among the partners. In modern economic terms, the *peculium* is associated with household equity and the *naruqqum* with equity of a firm. Searching for the historical roots of modern equity capital involves a search for firm, not household, equity.

22 As in Bronze Age Babylonia, tax collection was not done by the state but rather contracted, usually to 'merchants' in Babylonia and *equites* in Roman times. Roman partnership law established more permanence for the *societas publicanorum* to allow for the long time periods involved in tax farming.

23 Because aggregate production was primarily agrarian, the bulk goods trade was important in ancient markets. While the movement of higher-value goods by land was the basis of the caravan travel, waterborne transport was the mainstay for moving grain, pottery, wine, oil and other bulky commodities needed to sustain urban centers. Even as late as the Roman Empire, the huge number of grain ships bringing supplies from Egypt and Africa to Rome have left hardly any trace in the archaeological record. As such, the organization of this trade could have been closer to the bottomry loans common in Greek seaborne trade. However, a document from the second century AD, the Muziris Papyrus, provides evidence of political capitalism dominating such trade.

(Muziris was a port city in what is now the Indian state of Kerala.) This interpretation is consistent with the need to have political influence to ease the burden of onerous customs duties and other charges that were common in the Roman Empire, especially after the collapse of the Republic.

24 In general, the search for 'first instances' of a particular form of business organization in the historical record ignores the importance of context and, where relevant, translation and interpretation. Where the ancient world is involved, lack of evidence and the potential bias in interpretation posed by evidence that is available also assume importance. Modern forms of business organization are the result of evolution in commercial practices over the millennia of recorded history. This evolution has been uneven, both temporally and geographically. As a consequence, it is possible to isolate certain features of modern practice, find what appears to be a striking reflection in the commercial practice of some past society, and claim a 'first instance'. Such a 'static' comparative exercise ignores the 'dynamic' of evolving commercial practice. For example, was Malmendier (2009) correct in finding a reflection of modern limited liability corporate organization in the Roman *publicani*? Available evidence has Cicero appealing to the Senate to have the terms of a *publicani* contract renegotiated because the *publicani* had bid too high a 'price' for an important tax-farming agreement. This seems to indicate that 'limited liability' was not inherent in the *publicani* arrangement. Similarly, the role of the *manceps* appears to be similar to that of a *tractator*, placing the *publicani* closer to organizational formats found in ancient Mesopotamia than the modern corporate form.

3   *Societas,* Usury and Risk

And Jesus went into the temple of God, and cast out all them that
sold and bought in the temple, and overthrew the tables of the moneychangers, and the seats of them that sold doves.

(Matthew 21:12, King James version)

Business is in itself an evil, for it turns men from seeking true rest,
which is God.

(Saint Augustine, AD 354–430)

A   MERCHANTS AND SCHOLASTICS

The Schoolmen and Scholasticism

In modern times, the value of equity capital is typically expressed in monetary terms. In contrast, in medieval and Renaissance times it was the 'moral'
value of equity capital that was of concern. Details appear in the evolution of
scholastic doctrine on contracts involving partnership, usury, exchange and
risk. Despite some claims to the contrary, the Church Schoolmen, the authors
of scholastic doctrine, did not have commercial motivations.[1] Nor did the
Schoolmen have much experience with the day-to-day workings of commercial and financial markets, even though the importance of the Church as an
economic institution in those times did involve substantial financial and commercial dealings. Rather, the Schoolmen were scholars, steeped in the tradition
of medieval Christianity, founders of the first universities and instructors in
the abbey schools across Europe. The search for justice, not profit, was the
primary motivation of scholastic doctrine. In turn, until well into the 18th century, the Schoolmen did have a fundamental role, both directly and indirectly,
in shaping civil laws that governed commercial activities and financial markets.

The Schoolmen were careful, even ponderous, in arriving at positions on
specific issues. In the process of formulating doctrine relating to commercial
matters, the Schoolmen developed a body of knowledge loosely categorized as
'scholastic economics' (e.g., de Roover 1955; Schumpeter 1954, ch.2; Monsalve
2014a). The role of scholastic economics in the evolution of equity capital organization and valuation is often unappreciated and misunderstood. Important

historians of economic thought, such as Schumpeter and de Roover, found roots of modern economics in the scholastic doctrines, Adam Smith's views on monopoly being a case in point (de Roover 1951). Though study of scholastic doctrine has been experiencing a recent revival, the conventional approach in modern times is to ignore contributions of the Schoolmen and to trace the pre-Smithian roots of economics to the mercantilists.[2] This is of relevance because issues surrounding the morality of commercial activities connected with the use of equity capital, such as the morality of trading with asymmetric information, are examined and, to some extent, resolved.

Scholasticism emerged and flourished in the Church schools and universities in the period from Charlemagne (8th century) to the Reformation (16th century), with a waning influence lasting into the 18th century. What followed the ponderous casuistry of the scholastics is less well defined. There has been considerable debate about whether mercantilism of the 15th to 18th century qualifies as an 'ism'—that is, "a theory governed by an inner harmony and advocated or applied in a particular time or phase of development" (Heaton 1937, p.393). Was there a coherent economic approach that could be associated with mercantilism? Heckscher (1931) attempted to answer this question in the affirmative, identifying five unifying themes. However, Heaton (1937), Johnson (1937) and, more recently, Blanc and Desmedt (2014) ably demonstrated that this is a slippery slope. Hecksher (1936, 1955) recognized that numerous qualifications are required to obtain some semblance of a coherent notion of 'mercantilism'. Perhaps the most successful efforts at distilling certain common elements have drawn primarily on the English mercantilist contributions (e.g., Viner 1937; Schumpeter 1954).

Even if it is not possible to identify a fully coherent doctrine of mercantilism, certain distinct features relevant to equity capital organization and valuation can be identified in the musings of the various merchant writers of the 15th to 18th centuries. One particular feature is the underlying moral approach of the mercantilists, an approach that is in stark contrast to the moral approach of the scholastics. De Roover (1951, pp.323–5) identified this point in a comparison of the mercantilist contributions to those of the Schoolmen:

> the Doctors were moralists, their main preoccupation was with social justice and general welfare . . . The mercantilists, too, professed to further the cause of the commonweal; however, their declarations in this respect should not always be taken at their face value. All too often they serve as a screen for private interests . . .
>
> In contrast to scholastic economics, mercantilism was amoral. The later mercantilists were interested in a large population and full employment only because they thought such conditions would stimulate trade and increase the economic power of the state. Usury was no longer considered a voracious monster . . . Trade has no soul and the individual did not count: why should mercantilists be disturbed by moral issues?

This contrast in moral orientation between the scholastics and mercantilists is reflected in the evolution of equity capital in the commercial activities of this historical period.

The roots of the modern approach to equity capital are firmly planted in the mercantilist camp, if only because many of the early contributions were from merchants engaged in trade, finance and other commercial ventures. The explicit reference to 'merchants' is intentional. The licit use of *societas* created an intimate connection between equity capital in a venture and those involved in running the venture. The modern situation, in which much equity capital is sourced from individuals with no direct connection to the business, was far in the future. The scholastics struggled with situations in which a provider of capital was not directly involved in the venture and sought to limit liability for loss in lieu of taking a fixed payment from profit. This concern typically involves 'the sterility of money' in scholastic doctrine, a position adapted from Aristotle and accepted by Saint Thomas Aquinas. The precise interpretation of this doctrine varied significantly over time, with arguments for exceptions becoming increasingly prevalent and, ultimately, accepted.

Moral issues, such as those surrounding the payment of interest on loans, were not an essential element in the requisite financial calculations of the 'merchants'. As far as civil law permitted, this was the case, both before and after the Reformation. In contrast, Adam Smith, the acknowledged founder of modern economics, was a professor of moral philosophy. Smith's attack on mercantilist ideas was engaged at various levels. That many of these ideas were a natural progression from the ideas of the Schoolmen is not surprising. What is somewhat surprising is that the connection is not more commonly recognized and developed. One essential connection is the concern with moral issues. Drawing on the arguments developed in the *Theory of Moral Sentiments*, Smith was able to construct a moral basis that is somewhat at odds with the modern approach to equity capital organization. Though Smith had little to say on the valuation and trading of equity capital, he did express views on the joint-stock form of organization.

At best, Adam Smith is a minor figure in the history of intellectual contributions on equity capital, with views that, though morally justified, are largely incongruent with later historical development of limited liability and incorporation. Most of the 'mercantilists' with surviving contributions were merchants and reckoning masters operating at the core of financial markets, seeking to use the policy instruments available to the emerging nation states to expand trade and increase wealth. Given the social and religious restrictions on debt financing during the times when scholastic doctrine was influential, much of this wealth appears as equity capital. Recognizing that mercantilism is, perhaps, most effectively identified with the public views of prominent merchants, this places mercantilism squarely in the 'amoral' domain. Though many of these early contributors were almost certainly devout in their private lives, profit was the discipline of the financial markets. This mercantilist genealogy is in contrast to the moral philosophy that was a systemic part of the doctrines of both the Schoolmen and Adam Smith.

Scholasticism has an approach to the organization and valuation of equity capital that contrasts starkly with the modern approach, in which pricing of equity securities requires an assessment of the expected rate of return and the level of risk posed by the equity capital investment. By seeking to influence the

Figure 3.1 Jesus Expelling the Moneylenders from the Temple (1725), Giovanni Pannini (1691–1765), *Museo Thyssen-Bornemisza*, Madrid

legal framework within which markets operated, scholastic doctrine played an essential role in determining the types and format of contracts used in commercial practice. Similarly, the assessment and allocation of risk within a partnership also fell within the scope of scholastic doctrine, affecting how business financing was structured. The prevalence of the *commenda* and *societas maris* in the Italian seaborne trade in the Mediterranean during the medieval and Renaissance period attests to this influence. Though major progress comes well after the peak of scholastic influence, scholastic doctrine also affected the role of insurance in business dealing and the emergence of joint-stock companies. This influence, and the moral issues that were discussed, have discernable echoes in modern times.

Scholastic Economics

The recent interest in scholastic economics is a revival of interest during the 1940s and 1950s, when Schumpeter (1954), de Roover (1955) and others attempted to "rescue the Schoolmen from intellectual exile" (Kirshner 1974, p.19) by changing the conventional perception of scholastic economics. The main thrust of the argument was that the roots of classical economics were derived from the Schoolmen and not from mercantilists, physiocrats and 18th-century free-trade writers. In turn, scholastic economics was not a medieval doctrine due solely to Thomas Aquinas but, rather, an evolving school of thought that reached an apex with the works of the Spanish Jesuit Luis Molina (1535–1600) and the Belgian Jesuit Leonard Lessius (1554–1623), building on the contributions of the school of Salamanca founded by Francisco de Vitoria (1480–1546), (e.g.

Grice-Hutchinson 1952). By focusing on the modern relevance of these later scholastics, the recent revival goes well beyond the initial efforts of the likes of de Roover and Schumpeter (e.g., Decock 2009; Monsalve 2014a,b), where the central concern was more historical than with demonstrating modern relevance.

The earlier revisionists aimed to change the prevailing view that the 'science' of political economy begins with Adam Smith. While admitting that it is "improbable that Adam Smith went back to the ponderous treatises of the Doctors" (de Roover 1951, p.302), substantive connections were made between Smith and the writings of the jurists and natural law philosophers Hugo Grotius (1583–1645), a Dutchman, and Samuel Pufendorf (1622–1694), a German. Though Grotius and Pufendorf were not scholastics, the influence of scholasticism on natural law philosophy is systemic. Not only do scholasticism and natural law philosophy share an Aristotelean foundation, many scholastic arguments were readily adopted and adapted by natural law philosophers. In this fashion, many fundamental elements of scholastic economics, such as the aversion to monopoly, are reflected in the writings of Adam Smith and other classical economists.

Much of the revisionist argument is aimed at scholastic views on 'value': value in use versus value in exchange and, especially, just price. Regarding the notions of 'just price' and utility as a source of value, there was general agreement among the revisionists. Monsalve (2014b) provided a useful overview of the interpretation of 'just price'. However, on the central usury question, the revisionists were not in agreement. On the subject of usury, Schumpeter (1954) and Dempsey (1948) both argued forcefully that scholastic doctrine was a major advance in interest theory (e.g., Melitz 1971). In contrast, de Roover (1955, p.173) felt the "great weakness of scholastic economics was the usury doctrine". The most detailed scholarly study of the scholastic usury doctrine identifies various shortcomings of the usury doctrine but eventually concludes that "the theory is formally perfect" (Noonan 1957, p.360). The apparent casuistry reflected in many scholastic writings on usury is better understood by considering that the Schoolmen were products of the Church school and university educational system. Subjects of relevance to commercial ventures were an academic sideshow compared to subjects of ethics and law. Commercial questions were typically addressed in the context of evaluating civil contracts involved in specific transactions. This approach was consistent with the tradition of Roman law, an essential component of the scholastic tradition.

Following de Roover (1955, p.307): "What the Doctors of the Middle Ages were really interested in was to determine the rules of justice governing social relations." While charity was an important element of scholastic tradition, it was justice that governed scholastic thinking. Two forms of justice are identified: distributive justice and commutative justice. Distributive justice related to the distribution of wealth and income. Scholasticism perceived a natural order in which every individual was to receive according to their station in life. Though there was an element of communalism in scholastic thought, the distinction between private and public property was accepted as part of natural law. Substantial variation in the distribution of wealth and income was permitted, providing such variation was 'just', or in accordance with the scholastic perception of morality, ethics and the law. Differences in the social structure across societies were also accepted, meaning that scholasticism permitted variations in the types of distribution consistent with justice.

Commutative justice deals with the rules governing relations between individuals. Of central importance to the organization and valuation of equity capital, rules of commutative justice govern the exchange process and the buying and selling of goods. The concepts of 'just price' and usury relate primarily to the "equality of objects given in exchange" (Noonan 1957, p.31). Issues of justice apply as much to the rich as to the poor. As such, the exchange process is a test of honesty, the question of charity is largely irrelevant. Commutative justice is closely related to the perception of property rights and the acceptance of profit. Scholastics acknowledged the acceptability of both property rights and profits. However, certain types of profits, such as those earned from usury, were not acceptable. In the words of Saint Bernadine: "All usury is profit, but not all profit is usury."

In the rudimentary markets of medieval times, the demands on scholastic economics were relatively uncomplicated. Questions about just price and usury were often simple. For example, Böhm-Bawerk (1914) and others argued that the bulk of loans in ancient and medieval times were of the consumption variety, usually involving a rich lender and a poor borrower. In these circumstances, on grounds of both charity and commutative justice, charging of interest would arguably be unjust. Whether this is a valid motivation for early scholastic usury notions depends on whether the empirical observation is correct. In medieval times, the state was often a sizeable net borrower—for example, for funding Crusades—and the Church was often a large lender.[3] Hence, there may have been a decidedly more complex economic and political interaction underlying medieval financial markets, and, as such, the consumption loan rationalization for medieval scholastic usury doctrine may be too simple.

In any case, as markets evolved following the Dark Ages, contracts became more complicated and a much wider variety of circumstances were encountered. The difficulties of sorting out a just relationship were not always clear to the Schoolmen, whose education and training did not always provide the type of commercial knowledge required to make reasoned determinations. By the 16th century, the conceptual problem of identifying specific transactions that were usurious was almost insurmountable for the Schoolmen. An important scholastic of the Salamanca School, Domingo de Soto (1504–1560), wrote in 1553: "this matter of exchange, although sufficiently abstruse by itself, becomes each day more complicated because of the new tricks invented by the merchants (to avoid the usury restrictions) and more obscure because of the conflicting opinions advanced by the doctors" (see de Roover 1956, p.257). Monsalve (2014b) detailed the evolution of scholastic usury doctrine: "while the issues, methods, and purposes of scholastic thought remained the same, there was also an analytical evolution to bring the essence of the doctrine more in line with economic reality evolved."

In a controversial and stimulating attack, Ekelund et al. (1996) questioned the whole approach of attributing intellectual validity to scholastic doctrine, instead seeing scholastic doctrine as largely the result of the 'corporate' Roman

Catholic Church seeking to legitimize various economic activities. Specifically, the "Church functioned as a franchise monopoly that enjoyed certain economies of scale but that continually faced the dual problems of enforcement and entry control . . . (the) Church surpassed many modern-day corporations in its size, complexity and sophistication". The conclusion reached by Ekelund et al. is startling: "It is our view that historians of economic thought have tended to over-intellectualize the doctrine on usury, which is the one aspect of the Church's complex regulatory framework that has typically drawn the most attention" (p.128).

In effect, Ekelund et al. argued that Church doctrines concerned with financial activities were largely the outcome of a rent-seeking process. This argument is not limited to the usury doctrine but extends, for example, to the doctrine of just price. To what extent can Ekelund et al. be accused of 'under-intellectualizing' the content of scholastic doctrine? The immense size of the Church from the Dark Ages to the Reformation dictates that it was deeply involved in economic and financial activities.[4] The Church could not avoid establishing doctrines in those areas in which it had a beneficial interest. However, it is a leap of faith to conclude that, because there was a beneficial Church interest, scholastic doctrine was designed to maximize the potential rents from that beneficial interest. In addition, the Church as an institution did not participate directly in licit commercial activities financed with equity capital, which raises some obvious questions about the Church as a rent-seeking entity. However, well before the time of Luther, important members of the clergy participated in various commercial activities.

Ekelund et al. (1996) are not alone in proposing a 'new' rent-seeking interpretation of scholastic doctrine. Monsalve (2014a, p.216) provided the following summary:

> the seminal rent-seeking model of the Roman Catholic Church by Ekelund, Herbert, and Tollison (1989), the Social Welfare approach by Glaeser [and Scheinkman] (1998), the linkage of usury prohibitions to pooling and charity by Reed [and Bekar] (2003), and the barrier to entry explanation by Koyama (2010) all stressed in some way the vested-interest dimension of the usury prohibition. A common feature in these new approaches is the emphasis placed on the concept of "*homo-oeconomicus*" rationality (utility maximization) over justice and moral concerns. These evolutionary approaches seem to shrink the moral dimension of scholastic economy, which would appear as an *ex post* attempt to legitimize the particular doctrinal position of the Roman Catholic Church on this matter without seeing much merit in its logical reasoning.

Following Noonan (1957), those seeking an interpretation of scholastic doctrine in "the possibility of benevolence, the ideal of mutual benefits via a just and free exchange, the social responsibility of individuals to others, and the instrumental use of money and wealth to satisfy human necessities" included Langholm (1979, 1998), Lapidus (1991), Decock (2009) and Monsalve (2014a,b).

B   SCHOLASTIC DOCTRINE ON *SOCIETAS* AND SEA LOANS

Financing Trade in the Middle Ages

Much modern attention to scholasticism focuses on the usury doctrine. As a consequence, there is the modern perception that the medieval Schoolmen worked against commercial interests by restricting the availability of credit. However, this interpretation only deals with contracts deemed illicit by the Schoolmen. "By itself the prohibition applied to the loan contract seems to bar effectively any profit from pecuniary investment, any practical development of commercial credit, any capitalistic management of finance. But this isolated view is seriously misleading" (Noonan 1957, p.133). It is also necessary to consider the investment outlets that were considered lawful—that is, the *societas*, the "one great and universal form of licit investment in commerce throughout medieval Europe." The same notions of central importance to finding contracts that are illicit usury also arise in determining whether contracts were licit. These notions are as follows: ownership of the item loaned during the period of the loan; the incidence of various types of risk associated with owning the item; and the sterility of money.

A central feature of scholastic casuistry was the problem of determining whether a particular commercial activity was licit or illicit. Though some scholastics did hold contrary views, the scholastic model for a licit investment contract was the Roman *societas* of the *Digest*[17, 2] and *Institutes*[III]: 'a union of two or more persons combining money or skill for the purpose of making profit'. In practice, the numerous forms that a *societas* could take created a range of conceptual problems. For example: "In the theoretical treatment of the *societas*, is the usury theory's identification of the use and ownership of money maintained? Is money consistently considered as sterile? Is risk successfully used as a criterion of ownership?" (Noonan 1957, p.133). To see the difficulties, consider a partnership of labour and capital in which one partner invests only money and the other only the skill and labour involved in the commercial activity. In such an arrangement, the Roman *societas* could allow the investing partner to be freed from the risk of loss beyond initial capital invested and for there to be unequal shares of the profit. The similarity to an illicit usurious loan is apparent, especially if the payment from profit to the investing partner was a fixed amount instead of a percentage of profit.

The Schoolmen's handling of the sea loan poses a variation of these complications. While similar in *de facto* design to a partnership, both Roman law and scholastic doctrine made "sharp discrimination" between a sea 'loan' and a partnership. However, Roman law considered the sea loan to be licit usury, as the scholastics struggled with medieval forms of the contract. The essential issue revolved around the amount of risk needed for the investor to avoid the sanction of usury.[5] As Noonan (1957, pp.137–8) recognized, the key decretal of Gregory IX (Pope from 1227 to 1241), *Naviganti*, reads: "One lending a certain quantity of money to one sailing or going to a fair, in order to receive something beyond the capital for this that he takes upon himself the peril, is to be thought a usurer."[6] Noonan (1957, p.138) proceeded to make the following strong claim: "If the implication of the apparent meaning of *Naviganti* were worked out, one would be forced to conclude that every investment of money at a profit with another person would be usury, whatever form the investment took. *Naviganti* would seem to strangle commerce at its roots." Such a claim, which is reflected in other early sources, such as Coulton (1921) and O'Brien (1920), requires closer examination.

Interpreting the evolution of scholastic doctrine on the financing of external trade during the Middle Ages needs to consider actual commercial practice and the timing of religious canons and papal decrees. The two early papal instructions that have attracted modern interest are the canon *Per vestras,* issued by Pope Innocent III (1160?–1216, Pope 1198–1216) on the disposition of a dowry, and the decretal *Naviganti* by Gregory IX (Pope 1227–1241). The 13th century was a period of organizing, compiling and disseminating the position of the Church on a wide range of issues. *Naviganti* is part of the *Decretales Gregorii IX* appearing in 1234 when Pope Gregory IX commissioned Raymund of Peñafort, a Dominican, to prepare a collection of nearly 2,000 decretals. These dates are significant ecclesiastic benchmarks that can be compared with the historical record on commercial activity, a record that is informed and influenced by Genoese notarial records, the earliest surviving of which are by the notary Giovanni Scriba ('John the Scribe'), covering 1154–1164. The continuous records for 1190–1192 of the important notary Guglielmo Cassinese are particularly fruitful.

The Genoese Notarial Records

As de Roover (1940, p.41) observed: "Chance has preserved earlier and more complete notarial records for Genoa than for any other European city". Notaries in Genoa and other Italian city states drew up the contracts for parties to a variety of commercial ventures and agreements. In Genoa, the notaries were public officials of the commune. To facilitate business, notaries were usually stationed in the meeting places of merchants. The sailing of a ship or a convoy to Syria or another locale would generate many contracts in a single day. It was also possible for a notary to draw up a contract in the home or place of business of a merchant party to the contract. Transactions were written down by the notary, with copies given to the parties involved in the contract and the original filed in the municipal archives. Information gleaned from the valuable Cassinese source about merchant activities in Genoa was summarized by de Roover (1940, pp.43–4). The importance of equity capital transactions in Genoese commercial ventures is apparent:

> Cassinese was busiest in the spring and autumn when fleets of ships were getting ready to sail for Levantine or North African ports. But there was trade with Sardinia, Sicily, Marseilles, and Barcelona all the year around. The arrival of a caravan of merchants coming from the fairs of Champagne also kept Cassinese and other notaries busy for several days at a time.

Information about the organization of equity capital in long-distance trade in medieval Genoa provided by the notarial records, in general, and the Cassinese records, in particular, provides a fascinating description of those 'equity capitalists' involved in financing trading ventures (pp.43–4):

> Each April and September Cassinese was busy from early morning until late at night drawing up contracts relating to the overseas trade. Ships were preparing to sail for Constantinople, Tunis, Bougie, or Ceuta. All the traveling merchants who were going on a voyage were being entrusted with goods or money belonging to persons in almost every class of society in Genoa: the cloth dealers were giving them the expensive Flemish and French cloths which they had recently purchased on credit and some of the cheaper Milanese fustians which, because of their strength and durability, were in demand among the Moslems; the wealthy importers gave them goods or, more frequently, money; professional men, nobles, clerics, widows, guardians of orphans, small artisans and shopkeepers, even sailors were handing over funds to the traders, according to the notary's records.

While many of those involved in supplying the equity capital in the Genoese long-distance seaborne trade were at least partly involved in related commercial activities, there is ample evidence of the beginnings of joint-stock organization in which large numbers of investors not directly involved in the trade combine capital.

One feature of later joint-stock organization not apparent in the Genoese notarial records is the lack of permanence in the equity capital stock. This is reflected in the contract format employed in the long-distance seaborne trade of Genoa described by de Roover:

> All this was done by means of commercial contracts, usually in the form of a temporary partnership, which was to last only for the duration of the round-trip voyage. Whether a merchant was entrusting the overseas trader with thousands of pounds in cash or goods or whether someone was risking his hard-earned savings of a few pounds, the contract of partnership would be the same, that is to say, one of two forms would be used in either instance. If the stay-at-home partner or partners entrusted the traveling partner with a stated sum—large or small—in money or wares and the latter contributed only his services, then the contract would provide that the former was to receive back his capital and two-thirds of the profits at the end of the venture. This form of partnership was called a *commenda*—Cassinese drew up hundreds of them. If the traveling partner contributed some funds as well as his services, another form, called a *societas maris*, was used. The usual terms of the *societas* contract were that the traveling partner contributed one-third of the capital and received one-half of the profits, the other half going to the stay-at-home partner who contributed two-thirds of the funds. This form is even commoner in Cassinese's records than the *commenda*.

Within this general contractual framework, there was considerable variation. Notarial records, municipal statutes and the like from other Italian city states confirm such variation. For example, Byrne (1916, p.135) recognized factors influencing contractual choice:

> The precarious conditions under which maritime commerce was conducted in the twelfth century, the dangers to be encountered through piracy, the losses so constantly incurred by the attacks of commercial rivals in the more or less continuous warfare among the maritime cities of the western Mediterranean, prevented individuals of means from engaging in trade over-seas solely on their own capital and initiative. The result was the development of associations and partnerships of various sorts, which divided the risk and at the same time allowed the use of a greater amount of capital; thereby the opportunities for profits were greatly increased.

Trading activities of the medieval Genoese were primarily concerned with seafaring ventures. Travel to the fairs with goods imported to Genoa was typically in the hands of other peoples, such as the Lombards. Within this context, contractual choice evolved to reflect the changing commercial landscape (e.g., p.139):

> By the middle of the [12th] century a certain degree of stability in the Syrian trade had been achieved; the principal centers of trade in Syria were in the hands of the Crusaders; the Genoese were established in Syria as colonists; commercial conditions within Syria were fairly well understood by certain Genoese merchants. A few therefore felt so assured of the continued prosperity of their commercial relations with Syria as to form *societates*, not for a single voyage alone, but for trade over a period of years, or for a succession of voyages.

Such are the rudiments of the earliest forms of the 'permanent' capital stock feature of joint-stock organization. With the growth of both long-distance trade

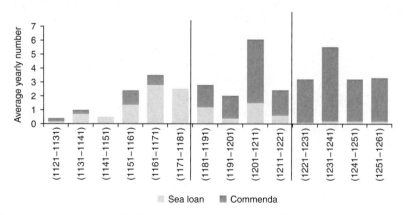

Figure 3.2 Documented Sea Loans and Commenda Contracts and Their Distribution over Time in Venice

Source: Gonzalez de Lara (2008), p.253

and the associated stock of merchant capital obtained from this trade, Hoover (1926) detailed how creative Genoese merchants evolved sea loan contracts designed to evade the usury restriction. Given that this evolution was coincident with *Naviganti*, it is possible this decretal was aimed at the contractual development of a medieval sea loan. However, Gonzalez de Lara (2002, 2008) documented the dissimilar transition from sea loans to *commenda* in Venice around this time, so that explanation requires more consideration.

Contractual Choice in Long-Distance Trade

Considerable confusion appears in modern interpretations of the influence that religion had on medieval and Renaissance commercial activity. The Church was not proactive in commercial matters. Rather, good Christian merchants would be compelled to seek moral guidance about proper conduct in business affairs. Wide variation in commercial risks encouraged variation in contractual design across time and location. Seeking institutional generalities to explain contract selection and the method of organizing long-distance trade, Greif (1991, 1994, 2012) compared (Christian) Genoese commercial organization as revealed in selected notarial records with the activities of the (Jewish) 'Maghribi' traders captured in the Cairo Geniza. In an attempt to apply modern economic theory to the historical record, Greif (2012, p.445) claimed:

> a multilateral reputation mechanism was particularly important among the eleventh-century (Jewish) Maghribis traders who operated in the Muslim Mediterranean. The related institution, a 'coalition', deterred opportunism in bilateral agency relations based on a credible threat of losing future profitable relations in the traders' broader community. In contrast, legal enforcement and a bilateral reputation mechanism were particularly important among the Genoese. Cultural distinctions—collectivism among the Maghribis and individualism among the Genoese—contributed to this distinction and the associated cultural beliefs influenced subsequent institutional, organizational, and contractual developments. In Europe, these developments included the legal and organizational changes that facilitated impersonal exchange and thus market expansion.

Gonzalez de Lara (2001, 2008) extended this approach to identify Venetian commercial success during this period with "public-order, reputation-based" institutions that contrast with the "combined public coercion with private reputation" institutions in Genoa.

More than two decades after this historical adaptation of the institutional economics pioneered by North (1981, 1990) appeared, considerable debate still surrounded this approach (e.g., Clark 2007; Edwards and Ogilvie 2012). Clark (2007, p.727) described the general argument as follows:

> Greif argues . . . that the institutions that allow long distance trade are complex and difficult to create, and will not emerge naturally from a minimum of social order . . . Long distance trade, had collapsed in the Dark Ages

from 500 AD to 900 AD. The path to modern growth, a tortuous and difficult one, was through the creation of institutions that supported trade.

At one level, this begs the traditional question that is raised about the institutional approach to historical interpretation: 'Did the institutions create the trade in medieval Europe, or did trade possibilities create their own institutions?' Such questions seek to understand and explain the subsequent rise of Western European colonization and global commercial dominance. In turn, this will, hopefully, provide guidance about the institutional structures that are 'best' for the commercial success of modern emerging economies. The historical dynamics of equity capital do not enter this discussion. Big-picture conclusions are based on a narrow foundation of historical evidence. Acrimonious debates over accurate interpretation of primary sources, such as Edwards and Ogilvie (2012) versus Greif (2012), are a predictable conclusion.

The roots of contractual choice in long-distance trade are ancient. In addition to the commercial characteristics of a particular venture, such as the risk of loss due to piracy, the control, distribution and aggregate amount of capital available for investment is relevant. In turn, this capital supply is impacted by past and present profitability of such ventures. A key failing of the institutional approach proposed by North, Greif and others is the lack of attention to the influence that size and ownership of the capital stock have on political, social, military and religious developments at a point in time and over time. Inevitably, there is considerable intersection between those in political control and the owners of sizeable capital. *Ceteris parabus*, owners of a large stock of aggregate capital, seek to preserve that capital, inducing preference for the safer fixed, if lower, return on a debt contract. This requires legal and other institutions to facilitate enforcement of such contracts. Similarly, the higher, riskier return on equity capital in a *societas* requires social attitudes sufficient to sustain the *ius fraternitatis* required for the contract enforcement of this method of financing. Against this backdrop, political and military elements were important influences on the risk and profitability of the long-distance trade of the medieval and Renaissance Italian city states.

Despite indignant claims to the contrary (e.g., Greif 2012, p.447), it is not possible to evade the problem of 'sample selection bias' in medieval primary sources. The issue is more subtle than commonly recognized. For example, subtle bias was recognized by de Roover (1941, p.87):

> Since there are thousands of partnership agreements in the extant cartularies of medieval Genoese notaries, we are well informed about all the legal aspects of such contracts, but we know little about the way in which these partnerships actually carried on their business, because hardly any accounting records of the twelfth century have survived.

As a consequence, detailed accounting information about profitability of a long-distance trading venture associated with a specific notarial record is unavailable. As late as the 15th century, detailed information about profitability of trade with the Levant is still sketchy (e.g., Ashtor 1975). Without such information, it is not possible to determine precisely whether, say, the stated 'interest rate' on a sea loan is actually an efficient method of dealing with the problem of determining the return to a 'share' in an equity capital financing of long-distance trade. Passive investors have difficulty monitoring the various revenues, expenses and possible loss of principal in a long-distance trading venture. Determining a 'share' *ex ante*, expressed as a percentage return on invested capital, could be based on an estimate of expected profitability of the venture based on past experience. Alternatively, a given 'sea loan' contract may be a subterfuge to pay interest, unrelated to the direct financing of long-distance trade. Without more accounts and accounting for the underlying commercial venture, it is difficult to classify a particular contract.

The Impact of the Crusades

In addition to unavailable or incomplete accounting information about the profitability of medieval commercial ventures, there is the subtle influence of historical timing. The availability of Genoese notarial records occurs after the Second Crusade (1147–1149), providing direct insight on contract usage only for the Third (1189–1192) and Fourth (1202–1204) Crusades. The Crusades are key historical events, for a host of reasons. The mobilizing and movement of large numbers of people, animals and material associated with the First and Second Crusades generated profitable opportunities for merchants of the Italian city states in supplying and, in some cases, transporting crusaders by sea.[7] However, such gains paled in comparison with the opening up of trade with Syria, the Levant and, after the Fourth Crusade, Egypt. As Day (1981, p.160) observed: "To understand economic conditions in the Levant as they relate to the crusading states and to the Italian cities, close attention needs to be paid to the commercial arrangements which Genoa, Pisa, and Venice had made for themselves in the various Levantine emporia". The commercial importance of access to trading routes with the East is difficult to underestimate.

The relevant history surrounding key events of the various Crusades still attracts modern attention and some debate (e.g., Fotheringham 1910; Queller and Day 1976; Day 1981; Tyerman 1995). The basic history informs that, until the First Crusade (1095–1099), access by Italian merchants to the goods carried along the one of three major trading routes to the East was through the great emporium of Constantinople. At the time of the First Crusade, this Greek capital received most of the goods from the East via sea, either from Antioch or Muslim Alexandria. With the successes of the First Crusade, other locales for trade with the East—especially Antioch, Tyre and Acre—were opened to Italian traders, a significant development for the Genoese, as this reduced the importance of Constantinople, where the Venetians had long-standing privileged status. Venice had a quarter in Constantinople and free trade throughout the greater part of the Byzantine Empire since 1084 as a reward for its naval support against the Norman Robert Guiscard (1015?–1085) invading Byzantine territory. The sporadic and, sometimes, tragic Genoese experiences in Constantinople were not the foundation of wealth that location provided to the Venetians.

Against this backdrop, it is difficult to draw strong conclusions about the relationship between the 'institutions' in a specific Mediterranean locale and the contract choice used in equity capital organization during the medieval and Renaissance period. Differing geography and shifting political fortunes underpinned the commercial characteristics of long-distance trade for the Genoese, Pisans and Venetians. By the middle of the 12th century, the buildup of capital from the profits of the Byzantine trade, combined with the security of trade on Adriatic routes, created opportunities for Venetian capitalists to seek the safer fixed return provided by a sea loan. In contrast, the shifting fortunes of potentially very profitable long-distance trade to Syria required the Genoese to use

Figure 3.3   St. Thomas Aquinas (1225–74) by Carlo Crivelli (1435?–1495?), National Gallery, London

contracts with a sharing of profit on these routes to account for the significant commercial uncertainties. The opening of Egyptian trade to Pisa, Venice and Genoa, especially the lucrative trade through Alexandria, in the 1170s altered the commercial landscape in the Mediterranean by providing cheaper access to Eastern goods than in Constantinople. While notarial records provide a fascinating picture, the changing commercial landscape of long-distance trade makes for inconclusive inferences about institutional influences of, say, contract choice.

All this history had passed by the time that Saint Thomas Aquinas (1225–1274) produced the definitive contribution to scholastic doctrine, the *Summa Theologica*. Written from 1265 to 1274, the following influential statement on the *societas* is provided:

> He who commits his money to a merchant or an artificer by way of partnership doth not transfer the ownership [*dominium*] of the money to him, but it remaineth his own; so that the merchant tradeth therewith, or the artisan worketh therewith, at the lender's peril; therefore the lender can lawfully demand his share in the accruing gain as in a thing which is his own. (*Summa Theologica* II-II:9:7:8:2)

Noonan (1957, p.145) observed: "This doctrine . . . makes the incidence of risk the key [to ownership], ignores *Naviganti*, and implicitly denies the sterility of money. It will be the standard defense of the *societas* for the next two hundred years". Insofar as a 'share' can be expressed as a fixed return on invested capital, instead of a fixed share of total profit, the scholastic doctrine on *societas* in the *Summa* could arguably provide a rationale for a sea loan.

C SCHOLASTIC DOCTRINE ON USURY AND EXCHANGE

Types of Credit Transactions

The use of credit is prehistoric, predating the use of coinage and, possibly, the use of barter. Even in the most rudimentary societies, three basic types of credit transactions can be identified: (1) loans where no direct repayment is expected, effectively gifts that may or may not have an implied *quid pro quo*; (2) loans where repayment involves the return of the loaned article in the same condition as when it was borrowed; and (3) loans at interest where, in addition to the return of the loaned article, repayment includes an amount to compensate the lender for the use of the article. There is evidence of all three types of loan transactions in ancient societies. For example, early languages, such as Sumerian and Egyptian, contain words for 'interest'. Unfortunately, there also appears to have been those who used the payment of interest as a pretext to exploit their neighbours. As a consequence, ancient societies developed laws regulating the payment of interest.

Much of ancient literature and law is concerned with condemnation or restriction of interest. Where interest was permitted, a maximum allowable rate was usually specified. Legal restrictions on the payment of interest can be found, for example, under the Mosaic Code, in which it was forbidden for Jews to lend at interest to other Jews but not to strangers. Another example is provided by the Code of Hammurabi, which recognized loans at interest and fixed a maximum interest rate that was higher on loans of grain than for loans of silver. Attempts to charge higher rates through subterfuge cancelled the debt. Allowances were provided for cases where the debtor could not make full repayment. As such, the distinction between funding of commercial ventures via a loan or equity capital can be found at the beginnings of civilization.

There were sensible reasons for the practice of restricting interest payments. The accumulation of capital and the associated use of credit in the production process was quite limited in ancient markets. Loans between individuals were often for consumption purposes, involving a poor debtor and a rich creditor. Where possible, the 'state' would seek to conduct business using loans.

Recognizing some influence from Aristotle, the scholastic position on interest was primarily and selectively gathered from Roman law. The legal framework for the early part of Roman history was influenced by the ancient struggle between subsistence farmers (*plebians*) and wealthy lenders (*patricians*) (Maloney 1971, p.88):

> Romans, like Greeks, regarded loans at interest as a fact of life. But what was an element in the general prosperity of Greece brought misery and revolt to Rome. Whereas in Greece loans at interest served primarily to finance commercial enterprises, in Rome they served to supply the daily expenses of small farmers, to satisfy previous debts and to pay tribute. The plight of the debtor was tragic in the first centuries of the Republic because of the unscrupulous practices of the ruling patricians. As late as 326BC creditors had power over the person of the debtor, whom they could sell or even put to death if he failed to satisfy them.

ARISTOTLE ON INTEREST AND USURY

In the *Politics* (III, 23) Aristotle observed:

> Of the two sorts of money-making one . . . is a part of household management, the other is retail trade: the former is necessary and honourable, the latter a kind of exchange which is justly censured; for it is unnatural, and a mode by which men gain from one another. The most hated sort, and with the greatest reason, is usury, which makes a gain out of money itself, and not from the natural use of it. For money was intended to be used in exchange, but not to increase at interest. And this term usury, which means the birth of money from money, is applied to the breeding of money, because the offspring resembles the parent. Wherefore of all modes of making money this is the most unnatural.

Though information about the first centuries of Roman civilization are scant and available sources come from later contributors, such as Tacitus (AD 56–120) and Livy (59? BC–AD 12), it is apparent that the struggles between plebians and patricians produced a string of legal restrictions on the activities of lenders. Such restrictions appear in the Twelve Tablets (451–450 BC); the eighth tablet states: "no person shall practice usury at a rate of more than one-twelfth". Resistance to interest payments reached an apex with the *Lex Genucia*, 322 BC, in which lending at interest was forbidden between Roman citizens. This restriction was later extended to *socii* and to provincials (Böhm-Bawerk 1914). As Maloney (1971, pp.90–1) observed: "The law seems to have had little lasting practical effect". Given the fragmentary details about early Roman history, it is still apparent that "the laws concerning interest-taking were generally not obeyed, as was the case with the *Lex Genucia*. The legal rate of interest was regarded more as a minimum than a maximum . . . Legal prohibitions could easily be eluded."

To quote Homer and Sylla (1991, p.46):

> These early centuries of Roman history have left . . . little evidence of organized financial activity or credit other than personal debt secured by real estate. Large banking firms were unknown. The state, however, encouraged foreign traders to come to the city, and for their convenience it rented out money booths in the forum. The bankers were called by the Greek name '*trapezit*' and probably were mainly Greeks, as they were later in Cicero's day. They were trusted with large sums, lent money at interest, paid interest on deposits, changed money, bought and sold as agents, and later kept agents in the provinces and issued foreign drafts.

Over time, Roman law on interest evolved considerably. By the first century BC, Rome had emerged as the financial centre of the ancient world. Various legal conditions had developed under which the taking of interest between Romans was permitted (e.g., Temin 2004). However, even where the payment of interest was permitted by the Romans, only simple interest was allowed. Even though compound interest was recognized and prohibited (Lewin 1970), the payment of compound interest was permitted if the contracting process was properly structured. Malynes, in the *Lex Mercatoria*, addressed this point directly:

> The Romans and Grecians made a difference . . . according to the law of *Justinian*. But the taking of one in the month was most usual, because Merchants were the most lenders. And this twelve *pro centum* is to be understood also to be Interest upon Interest, wherein equity is to be observed: for this twelve pounds being delivered out again unto another, is *pro rata* as beneficial as the £100 principal. Albeit in the case of damage, when matters between men are grown litigious, and depending in suits, then the courts of Equity will account the whole time of forbearance of the money, according to years past, without any Interest upon Interest.

Hence, while compound interest was not permitted by law, by using a sequence of contracts compound interest could be paid.

Doctrine on Usury[8]

Roman law was selectively used by the early scholastics to develop the foundations of the usury doctrine. By the end of the Roman Empire, there were sophisticated laws concerning contracts. Loan contracts were characterized according to whether ownership of the good being loaned was transferred during the period of the loan. In a *commodatum* the use of a good was freely transferred but ownership resided with the lender. Two developments on the *commodatum* were: (1) the *locatio,* in which free transfer was replaced with a charge for lending the good; and (2) the *foenus,* in which a premium was charged for the loan. These contracts were deemed licit because ownership, and the associated possibility of loss, resided with the lender. Hence, the lender was permitted to impose charges beyond the return of the original goods.

In a *mutuum,* the ownership of the good was temporarily transferred during the period of the loan. Ownership permitted the borrower use of the good, even to consume the good, so long as the same quality and quantity of good was returned at the end of the loan. Hence, the *mutuum* applied to the case of fungibles, or goods that were measured using number, weight or measure. A *mutuum* would not apply to the loan of a commodity with special characteristics, such as a horse or a house. However, under scholastic doctrine, a *mutuum* did apply to the loan of money. 'Money is sterile'. This position had significant implications for financial transactions.[9] Because ownership of the good in a *mutuum* resided with the borrower during the period of the loan, the borrower assumed the peril of ownership. It was not considered licit to impose a charge above the return of the goods in kind.

More precisely, under canon law *interisse* (from the Latin verb 'to be lost')[10] was acceptable, while *usura* (from the Latin noun 'use') was not. Compensation could be charged for a *mutuum* loan only if it was a reimbursement for a loss or expense; no net gains were permitted (see, for example, Dempsey 1948). However, this strict interpretation of a *mutuum* was not workable in practice. Various conditions arose where it was reasonable to require payment on a *mutuum* beyond the return of the original fungible good.[11] This led to the development of the scholastic doctrine of *extrinsic titles*, conditions where payment on a *mutuum* beyond the return of the goods in kind was permitted. While many different types of extrinsic titles were permitted, three were particularly important: *lucrum cessans, damnum emergens* and *poena conventionalis.*

IMPORTANT OLD TESTAMENT PASSAGES ON USURY

'If thou lend money to any of my people that is poor by thee, though shalt not be to him as a usurer, neither shalt though lay upon him usury' (Exodus 22:25).

'Lord, who shall abide in thy tabernacle? . . . He that putteth not out his money to usury, nor taketh reward against the innocent' (Psalm 15).

'And if thy brother be waxen poor, and fallen in decay with thee . . . yea, though he be a stranger or a sojourner . . . Take thou no usury of him, or increase . . . Thou shalt not give him thy money upon usury, nor lend him thy victuals for increase' (Leviticus 25:35–7).

'He that hath not given forth upon usury, neither hath taken any increase . . . he is just' (Ezekiel 18:8–9).

'Thou shalt not lend upon usury to thy brother; usury of money, usury of victuals, usury of anything that is lent upon usury: Unto a stranger thou mayest lend upon usury; but unto thy brother thou shalt not lend upon usury' (Deuteronomy 24: 19–20).

The *poena*, or penalty, was chronologically the first widely used extrinsic title invoked to legitimize payments on loans beyond the return of principal. *Poena* is *interesse* in the strict Roman meaning: It is a penalty that is imposed as compensation for a delay in payment of principal. However, instead of waiting until the actual damages due to delay in payment can be determined, *poena* is agreed upon in advance and the penalty specified in the loan contract. Hence, licit loan contracts could be written with the implicit understanding that the borrower would delay payment the requisite number of days beyond the due date required to incur the *poena* condition. Principal plus penalty would *de facto* be the same as a loan at interest, albeit not subject to the sanctions of canon law.

Poena was acceptable to the early scholastics because the basic concept of a loan as a gratuitous transaction was retained. Both *lucrum cessans*, 'profit ceasing', and *damnum emergens*, 'loss occurring', represent substantive changes to this position. Both of these forms of extrinsic title require that a return be paid on a loan that is not due to any fault of the borrower. As a consequence, these extrinsic titles are much closer to the modern-day concept of interest. Up to around 1250, the leading scholastic writers did not recognize the licitness of these two forms of extrinsic titles as a basis for receiving payment beyond the return of principal. The period between 1250 and 1400 witnessed some arguments made in favour of the two extrinsic titles, but, by 1400, the majority of scholastic opinion was still against (Noonan 1957, ch. V).

NEW TESTAMENT PASSAGES RELATED TO USURY

'And Jesus went into the temple of God, and cast out all them that sold and bought in the temple, and overthrew the tables of the moneychangers . . . And said unto them, it is written, my house shall be called the house of prayer; but ye have made it a den of thieves' (Matthew 21: 12–13).

'And if you lend to them of whom ye hope to receive, what thanks have ye? for sinners also lend to sinners to receive as much again. But love ye your enemies, and do good, and lend, hoping for nothing again' (Luke 6: 34–5).

'For the love of money is the root of all evil' (Timothy 6: 10).
'He that is greedy of gain troubleth his own home; but he that hath gifts shall live' (Proverbs 15: 27).

Around 1400, payments on the forced government loans imposed by the Italian city states, the *mons*, had become a source of considerable controversy. Though such loans had a history stretching back over a century or more, by 1400 the size of these loans had grown to be multiples of the Italian city states' abilities to finance the repayment of principal on such loans out of tax revenues. This undermined the traditional *census* justification for such loans, based on a direct connection of the loans to specific tax revenues. The controversy centred on the annual payments that were made on the forced loans. The governments of the city states were careful to identify the form of such payments in a manner that was seemingly consistent with scholastic doctrine. The *mons* statutes of Florence, for example, stated that the payments were made as 'gift and interest' to the holders of shares in the *mons*. The obligation of the state to make regular payments was explicitly denied.

The difficulty that payments on the *mons* posed for the scholastic defenders was the absence of a traditional argument supporting such payments. Those opposed to payments argued that, as *poena* (penalty) was the only accepted justification for payments due from the beginning of a loan, the payments were usurious. The final result of the controversy was that the defenders were able to gain general acceptance of *damnum emergens* as a licit extrinsic title, with considerable progress being made on the licitness of *lucrum cessans*. By the time of the *Treviso*, scholastic writers such as Saint Bernadine (1380–1444) had established general theoretical grounds for *lucrum cessans*, though contracts such as fictitious exchange were still not considered acceptable. Despite this change in scholastic doctrine, during the 16th century extrinsic titles were much less important sources of justification for interest payments than the *census*; the triple contract; and, using implicit interest available in foreign exchange transactions, the bill of exchange.

Noonan (1957, p.20) summarized scholastic doctrine on usury by identifying common elements: 'the nature of law; the rightness of private property; the character of justice; the nature of profit; the place of intention in human acts; and the difference between public and private sinners'.[12]

Opinion on the Scholastic Usury Doctrine in the 18th Century

By the 18th century, the scholastic usury doctrine had only limited influence in civil law. Payment of interest on loans of money was permitted throughout most of Europe.[13] Remnants of the scholastic usury doctrine survived in the civil law statutes requiring a legal maximum interest rate on loans. Recognizing that states were almost invariably large debtors, the legal maximum interest rates may have been more due to concerns about state finances than for religious considerations. Despite this decline, scholastic usury doctrine still received some attention from financial economists, such as Cantillon, and the later scholastics, such as Ferdinando Galiani (1728–1787) (e.g., de Roover 1955, p.334). However, this attention was invariably critical and aimed at pointing out the limitations and inconsistencies in the doctrine.

Cantillon (1755, pp.205–11) was particularly critical of the usury doctrine. Cantillon explicitly recognized that there are often valid economic reasons for lenders to charge high rates of interest: "a Money Lender will prefer to lend 1000 ounces of silver to a Hatmaker at 20 per cent. interest rather than to lend 1000 ounces to 1000 water-carriers at 500 per cent. interest". Elements such as risk and solvency of the borrower play a fundamental role in determining the rate of interest. Even in situations where loans were made at high interest rates, such as 430% per annum to "Market-women at Paris . . . there are few Lenders who make a fortune from such high interest". With Cantillon, analysis of the payment of interest had evolved from the scholastic concern with natural law and commutative justice to an economic analysis of the reasons why a specific rate of interest was charged.

Cantillon explicitly recognizes the implications of his reasoning for the usury doctrine developed by the scholastics or, in Cantillon's words, 'the casuists':

The Casuists, who seem hardly suitable people to judge the nature of Interest and matters of Trade, have invented a term, *damnum emergens*, by whose aid they consent to tolerate these high rates of interest; and rather than upset the custom and convenience of Society, they have agreed and allowed to those who lend at great risk to exact in proportion a high rate of interest: and this without limit, for they would be hard put to it to find any certain limit since the business depends in reality on the fears of the Lenders and the needs of the Borrowers.

Maritime Merchants are praised when they can make a profit on their Adventures, even though it be 10,000 per cent.; and whatever Profit wholesale Merchants may make or stipulate for in selling on long credit produce or Merchandise to smaller retail Merchants, I have not heard the Casuists make it a crime. They are or seem to be a little more scrupulous about loans in hard cash though it is essentially the same thing. Yet they tolerate even these loans by a distinction, *lucrum cessans*, which they have invented. I understand this to mean that a Man who has been in the habit of making his money bring in 500 per cent. in his trade may demand this profit when he lends it to another. Nothing is more amusing than the multitude of Laws and Canons made in every age on the subject of Interest and Money, always by Wiseacres who were hardly acquainted with Trade and always without effect.

The dramatic erosion in the level of social concern over usury is evident from a comparison of Cantillon's views with the writings of Malynes a century earlier.

By the time of *Wealth of Nations*, there was little social relevance to the scholastic doctrine for the analysis of interest payments. In *Wealth of Nations*, Adam Smith (1776, p.339) launched a now-familiar assault on the notion that prohibitions on interest payments are socially beneficial:

> In some countries the interest of money has been prohibited by law. But as something can every-where be made by the use of money, something ought every-where to be paid for the use of it. This regulation, instead of preventing, has been found to increase the evil of usury; the debtor being obliged to pay, not only for the use of money, but for the risk which his creditor runs by accepting a compensation for that use. He is obliged, if one may say so, to insure his creditor from the penalties for usury.

In turn, Smith argues that laws which fix a legal maximum which is "fixed below the lowest market rate" are not substantively different than total prohibitions. Similar arguments by Charles de Moulin (1500–1566) more than two centuries earlier had exposed the author to persecution for heresy. In contrast, Smith's observations attracted little controversy.

If Adam Smith rejected the scholastic usury doctrine, then what is the precise connection between Smith and the scholastics? Were Smith's views a natural progression from the scholastics, as indicated by de Roover, Schumpeter and others, or was Smith something much different? Such questions are not easy to resolve. Smith was definitely concerned with commutative and natural justice and with natural law themes (e.g., Young and Gordon 1996). In this regard, Smith's views were a coherent progression from the scholastics. On certain specific issues, Smith held views that were closely aligned with the Schoolmen. For example, Smith's approach to monopoly could be fairly characterized as a development on scholastic notions (e.g., de Roover 1951). Yet, Smith did not embrace the body of scholastic doctrine. Rather, he evolved a new framework, based on the central scholastic concerns of distributive and commutative justice. As such, there are elements of the scholastics in Smith's writings. However, Smith was too far removed from the medieval concerns of scholasticism. Smith was a product of his times, and those times were much different than those of the Schoolmen.

Doctrine on Exchange

Medieval scholastic doctrine directly on *cambium* or exchange is relatively sparse, though related contributions on 'just price' are numerous. There was no direct Roman law on the subject that was directly applicable, and the early canon laws and decretals, such as the *Naviganti*, did not deal with *cambium* directly. The first scholastic writings relating directly to the exchange transactions associated with banking activities at the fairs deemed such activities usurious. However, by the time of the *Treviso*, the majority of scholastic writers favoured the general licitness of *cambium per litteras*, the bill of exchange, at least as it applied in genuine exchange transactions. There was disapproval of dry exchange (*cambium siccum*) and fictitious exchange (*cambium ad Venetias*) transactions, which used bills of exchange to structure transactions that were arguably disguised loans.

The bill of exchange was, *de facto*, an important financial market mechanism for the payment of interest at a time when such payments were deemed unacceptable by the Schoolmen. Merchants were able to disguise interest payments in bill of exchange transactions because there was both a time and an exchange element in the transaction. The bill of exchange separated, in both time and place, the initial delivery of one currency from the repayment of the other currency (e.g., de Roover 1944). This time element created the opportunity for an interest payment, in a given currency, to be disguised in the process of exchange and re-exchange. Though there was some degree of risk in the exchange rate applicable to the re-exchange transaction being uncertain at the time the initial bill of exchange was initiated, the payment of interest was facilitated by the market practice of systematically quoting exchange rates in one centre at a premium (or discount) of the par for the exchange rate with the other centre.

Though some writers, such as Thomas Wilson (1525–1581) in *A Discourse Upon Usury* (1572), explicitly objected that the bill exchange transaction was usurious, the primary canonists accepted the merchants' stated view that the bill of exchange was an inherently risky transaction. Due to this risk, interest was not assured and the transaction was not usurious (de Roover 1944, pp.198–9):

> The canonists accepted this theory . . . that the exchange contract was not a *mutuum* or a loan of money for certain gain and hence did not fall under the scope of the usury prohibition. According to them, the exchange contract was either a permutation of monies (*permutatio praesentis pecuniae cum absenti*) or a contract of purchase and sale (*emptio venditio*). They failed to see that dealings in time or usance bills necessarily involved the extension of credit. The canonists did not realize the dual nature of merchants' exchange.

Only where the merchant attempted to eliminate the inherent riskiness of the re-exchange transaction, as in dry or fictitious exchange, did the canonists object.

Despite the scholastic usury doctrine, the financial markets were able to design securities that enabled the payment of interest. The bill of exchange was a key financial security for the payment of short-term interest. It was the backbone of the international money market. The payment of interest for long-term borrowings was enabled by the scholastic doctrine on the *census*. The *census* contract does not appear in Roman law and is almost certainly the outcome of feudal economic relations. More precisely: "A *census* is an obligation to pay an annual return from fruitful property" (Noonan 1957, p.155). The *census* was the most common contract used both for investment in land and for state credit. The popularity of this form of contract was probably related to the medieval ban on *mutuum* loans.

Initially, the *census* was an exchange of money for an agreement to pay a certain quantity of produce, such as grain, for a number of years in the future. Other than the difference in the timing of the settlement and delivery, this type of transaction did not differ from a typical exchange. As long as the *census* was done at a just price, the transaction was licit. As markets and trade evolved, a 'new' *census* agreement also evolved to include transactions in which the 'payment from fruitful property' was made in cash, instead of goods. By the middle of the 15th century, the sale of both 'old' and 'new' *census* was widespread. The state sold *census* on available revenue sources, from monopolies, tax revenues and state lands. Both the landed nobility and peasants sold *census* on their possessions. Even workmen sold *census*, secured by their future labour.

To the modern reader, the distinction between a new *census* contract and a usurious loan is subtle, at best. Instead of the exchange of money for 'fruitful goods' embodied in the old *census* contract, the new *census* contract involved a current payment of money by the lender in exchange for an agreement by the borrower to make a sequence of regular future payments of money. How did this differ from a regular loan? A credible answer to this question was a quandary for the Schoolmen as well. Much of the scholastic discussion concentrated on identifying practical distinctions between a usurious loan and a *census*. For some types of *census*, such as the old or 'real' *census*, the distinctions were obvious. Being dependent on the returns generated from real estate, this *census* was similar to a loan secured by a mortgage. However, the return paid on this *census* "was set directly by the estimated productivity of the (real estate) base" (p.159).

Some other types of *census* were more difficult to distinguish from a loan than the real *census*. A life *census*, depending on the length of the life for either the lender or the borrower, was distinct from a loan in having the element of life-contingent risk. Both the personal *census* and the temporary *census* were less transparent cases. Payments on a personal *census* depended on the labour services of the issuer, which differs from a loan in the restriction that the issuer be an income-producer. A temporary *census* ran for a fixed number of years and required fixed annual payments. This was very similar to a loan. An additional feature that made the *census* distinguishable from a loan was the treatment of redemption. The *census* contract could be non-redeemable or redeemable at the option of the buyer, the seller or both. A temporary, personal *census* having fixed payments that were redeemable at the option of the buyer was dangerously close to the case of a usurious demand loan.

Decisions of the Schoolmen about the *census* were organized according to the arguments about the different possible types. There was little debate about a perpetual, real *census*. This type of contract was licit. The personal *census* met general opposition. More importantly, government credit contracts, effectively government bonds, were generally approved. The terms of redemption also attracted attention: 'the *census* might be redeemable, or redeemable only at the option of the buyer or only at the option of the seller, or it might be redeemable by either'. Noonan (p.164) observed that on various other forms of the *census* contract "The overall impression from (a) survey of authors is one of considerable confusion".

Just Price and the Merchant of Rhodes

Though largely ignored in modern times, the influence that *De officiis* of Cicero had on scholastic doctrine and natural law philosophy is difficult to underestimate. The second printed book, after the Gutenberg Bible, by the 17th century *De officiis* was widely used in European universities as a standard text on morals, an essential part of the core curriculum. Important European natural law philosophers, such as Grotius and Pufendorf, drew heavily on *De officiis*. Echoes of *De officiis* pervade the work of John Locke. In the 'Merchant of Rhodes', *De officiis* considers a moral problem that is of profound philosophical importance to the organization and valuation of equity capital. Decock (2009, p.59) described the story as follows:

> A decent merchant (*vir bonus et sapiens*) is shipping grain from Alexandria to the island of Rhodes, where prices have raced up and people are dying from starvation (*in Rhodiorum inopia et fame*). At the same time, he knows for sure that many more grain dealers are setting forth to Rhodes, and will be arriving there in the near future. The qualm of conscience he faces is whether or not he is obliged to tell the wretched citizenry of the boost in supply coming soon, thereby giving up on making huge profits. It should be noted that Cicero explicitly confronts us with a seller who is distinctly sincere and who wonders if it is in accordance with the principles of decency (*honestas*) to conceal his information to buyers who, in their turn, are explicitly said to be in a desperate position.

The implications for determining the morality of trading in an environment with asymmetric information are apparent. While morality of the conventional trade in goods is the proximate concern, the problem is systemically related to the subsequent trade in equity capital shares of joint-stock companies and modern limited liability corporations. As part of the more general problem of determining the just price, this problem still has considerable modern relevance—for example, 'why is insider trading illegal?'.

In *De officiis*[III, xii-xiii, 50–58] Cicero joined the discussion of the 'Merchant of Rhodes' with a situation in which the seller of a house fails to declare known defects to an unsuspecting purchaser (Loeb edition, Miller 1913). In these two cases, the sellers do not make fraudulent claims but are silent about the information they possess. The moral issues are surveyed in a debate between "Diogenes of Babylonia, a great and highly esteemed Stoic, [who] consistently holds one view; his pupil Antipater, a most profound scholar, [who] holds another." Diogenes argues for the seller keeping silent, while Antipater favours the seller revealing the information. Having presented the two sides of the moral debate, Cicero concludes:

> I must give my decision in these two cases; for I did not propound them merely to raise the questions, but to offer a solution. I think, then, that it was the duty of that grain-dealer not to keep back the facts from the Rhodians, and of this vendor of the house to deal in the same way with

his purchaser. The fact is that merely holding one's peace about a thing does not constitute concealment, but concealment consists in trying for your own profit to keep others from finding out something that you know, when it is for their interest to know it. And who fails to discern what manner of concealment that is and what sort of person would be guilty of it? At all events he would be no candid or sincere or straightforward or upright or honest man, but rather one who is shifty, sly, artful, shrewd, underhand, cunning, one grown old in fraud and subtlety. Is it not inexpedient to subject oneself to all these terms of reproach and many more besides?

Decock (2009) recognized the initial position of Cicero and, after a brief reference to Aquinas, proceeded to discuss the later scholastics, especially Leonardus Lessius (1554–1623), who was a Jesuit moral theologian from the Spanish-ruled Southern Netherlands, and Ludovicus Molina (1535–1600), who was a Spanish Jesuit and author of the controversial *Concordia liberi Arbitrii* (1588). The time line includes the sack of Antwerp in 1576 and the subsequent beginnings of Amsterdam as the commercial capital of Europe.

Seeking to recognize the contributions of Lessius and the state of scholastic doctrine at the beginning of the 17th century, Decock (2009) presumed an audience familiar with the position of Aquinas. While identifying two earlier 16th-century scholastics who took a contrary position on the Merchant of Rhodes, the waypoint in the evolution of scholastic doctrine provided by Aquinas is unstated. In considering sins committed in buying and selling (SS Q[77] Para. ½-D), Aquinas maintained a general position not too distant from Lessius and Molina:

[T]rading, considered in itself, has a certain debasement attaching thereto, in so far as, by its very nature, it does not imply a virtuous or necessary end. Nevertheless gain which is the end of trading, though not implying, by its nature, anything virtuous or necessary, does not, in itself, connote anything sinful or contrary to virtue: wherefore nothing prevents gain from being directed to some necessary or even virtuous end, and thus trading becomes lawful. Thus, for instance, a man may intend the moderate gain which he seeks to acquire by trading for the upkeep of his household, or for the assistance of the needy: or again, a man may take to trade for some public advantage, for instance, lest his country lack the necessaries of life, and seek gain, not as an end, but as payment for his labor.

Aquinas also maintained: "It is altogether sinful to have recourse to deceit in order to sell a thing for more than its just price, because this is to deceive one's neighbor so as to injure him." With this background, it is more apparent how far scholastic doctrine had progressed, especially in clarifying notions of just price and, more importantly, in demonstrating how late scholasticism "heralds in the end of the 'ethics of fraternity' believed to underlie the scholastic paradigm" (Decock 2009, p.75).

IMPORTANT BIBLICAL AND *DE OFFICIIS* PASSAGES ON EXCHANGE

Deut. 25:13,14: "Thou shalt not have divers weights in thy bag, a greater and a less: neither shall there be in thy house a greater bushel and a less," and further on (Dt. 25:16): "For the Lord . . . abhorreth him that doth these things, and He hateth all injustice."

Prov. 20:14: "It's no good, it's no good!" says the buyer—then goes off and boasts about the purchase.

Matt. 7:12: So in everything, do to others what you would have them do to you, for this sums up the Law and the Prophets.

Matt. 21:12: Jesus entered the temple courts and drove out all who were buying and selling there. He overturned the tables of the money changers and the benches of those selling doves.

In the *Summa* Aquinas interpreted this as: "He that buys a thing in order that he may sell it, entire and unchanged, at a profit, is the trader who is cast out of God's temple."

2 Tim. 2:4: No one serving as a soldier gets entangled in civilian affairs, but rather tries to please his commanding officer. Aquinas applied this to trading by clerics: "No man being a soldier to God entangleth himself with secular businesses."

De Offic. iii, 15: "Contracts should be entirely free from double-dealing: the seller must not impose upon the bidder, nor the buyer upon one that bids against him."

De Offic. iii, 11: "It is manifestly a rule of justice that a good man should not depart from the truth, nor inflict an unjust injury on anyone, nor have any connection with fraud."

D SCHOLASTIC DOCTRINE ON GAMBLING AND RISK

Scholastic Views on Gambling

Modern social attitudes toward gambling are confusing. There is an explicit, if diminishing, aversion to certain forms of gambling, as reflected in various state or provincial laws prohibiting slot machines, while at the same time there is an acceptance of other forms, such as state/provincial lotteries or the coin toss at the start of a game. These modern customs and laws have a long history. This history is intertwined with intellectual progress on the mechanics of gambling practices. During the 17th century, gambling played "a primary, though not necessarily unique, impetus for developments in probability" (Bellhouse 1988, p.65). In turn, this intellectual progress diffused only slowly into customs and laws surrounding gambling. Society at large struggled with the implications that probability theory had for previously held beliefs.[14]

The probabilistic basis for many modern laws on gambling can be traced to the 16th- and early 17th-century writings by Protestant sects such as the French

---

IMPORTANT BIBLICAL PASSAGES ON GAMBLING

"the land shall be divided by lot: according to the tribes of their fathers they shall inherit. According to the lot shall possession thereof be divided between few and many" (Numbers 26:55–6).

"Therefore Saul said unto the Lord God of Israel, Give a perfect *lot*. And Saul and Jonathan were taken: but the people escaped. And Saul said, Cast *lots* between me and Jonathan my son. And Jonathan was taken" (I Samuel: 41–2).

"The lot causeth contentions to cease, and parteth between the mighty" (Proverbs 18:18).

"The lot is cast into the lap; but the whole disposing thereof *is* of the Lord" (Proverbs 16:33).

"And they prayed, and said, Thou, Lord, which knowest the hearts of all *men*, shew whether of these two thou hast chosen . . . And they gave forth their lots; and the lots fell upon Matthias; and he was number with the seven Apostles" (Acts 1:24,26).

"And they crucified him, and parted his garments, casting lots: that it might be fulfilled which was spoken by the prophet, They parted my garments among them, and upon my vesture did they cast lots" (Matthew 27:35).

Calvinists and English Puritans. The traditional views of the Roman Catholic Church on gambling were much less rigid. The rigid Puritan anti-gambling position required a more precise analysis of the probabilistic events associated with gambling activities. Thomas Gataker (1574–1654) and other, later, Puritan writers argued forcefully that it was not possible to sustain the early Puritan view that "all randomized outcomes are determined by God", leading to the conclusion that gambling constituted a form of blasphemy as it undermined the "singular and extraordinary providence of God which controls a purely contingent event" (Ames 1629, quoted in Bellhouse 1988).

Gambling presented a somewhat puzzling problem for the scholastics, because gambling relies on a chance event, while, at the same time, the influence of God is all pervasive. This led Saint Thomas Aquinas to a relatively sophisticated conclusion: "the ultimate reason why some things happen contingently is not because their proximate causes are contingent, but because God has willed them to happen contingently, and therefore has prepared contingent causes from them". Aquinas offers little direct guidance on gambling other than to forbid the practice in specific cases, such as "winning at the expense of minors and those out of their minds, who have no power to alienate their property; or out of sheer greed to induce someone to gamble; or again, to win by cheating".

Unlike usury, on which the Bible provides explicit guidance, the treatment of gambling is more obscure.[15] Gambling, in the form of 'divination by lots', seems to be recommended by the Bible as the desired mechanism for determining God's will in situations where the desirable outcome is uncertain. For example, lots are used in deciding whether Saul or Jonathan is to be 'taken' in

I Samuel 14:41. However, divination by lot is not applicable as a rationale for all forms of gambling activity. Aquinas provided some guidance about the types of actions that could be determined through divination by lot. By Gataker's time, the casuistry surrounding the issue was considerable. For example, Bellhouse (p.70) observed:

> Gataker (1619) . . . makes an interesting argument against Divine intervention in randomized events using proof by contradiction. He notes that in repeated trials it is unlikely that the same outcome will always recur. He argues that if the lot is used to find God's purpose and the outcome of the lot is variable then God must be fickle; but God is not fickle and hence God must not determine the outcome.

Gataker's views on probabilistic outcomes eventually came to be accepted. By the end of the 17th century, the practice of divination by lot had been ended by all but a few extreme Christian sects.

Scholastic doctrine did make a distinction between gambling outcomes, determined by randomizers, and the related notion of risk. The concept of risk or 'peril' was inherited from Roman law and explicitly recognized in scholastic doctrine. For example, risk is fundamental to the concept of *mutuum*. Because the ownership of the good is transferred to the borrower, the risk of ownership is also transferred. This makes the charging of interest illicit. In the case of temporary transfers involving non-fungibles such as houses or horses, the risk of ownership during the period of ownership still resides with the lender. As such, the incidence of risk on a loan is an important element in deciding whether the loan is licit (Noonan 1957, pp.40–1). The trading of risk, in the form of insurance, was permissible so long as the object was not to circumvent other restrictions, such as the usury doctrine. Nelli (1972) dated the first modern-style 'insurance' contract with a premium payment to a 1343 Genoese contract.

The admission of insurance as a valid contract led to one of the more interesting rationalizations for interest payments: the triple contract. This contract involved the merging of the *societas* with insurance. The *societas*, or partnership, being a central feature of Roman commercial relationships, the concept of the triple contract was adopted without substantive changes by scholastic doctrine. In Roman law, a *societas* was "the union by two or more persons of their money or skill for a common purpose, usually profit" (Noonan 1957, p.134). The triple contract involved the insurance of a partner's profit, in exchange for any returns above that insured level. In effect, the triple contract was, in terms of cash flows, indistinguishable from an interest-bearing security, either a short-term deposit or a long-term bond.

The Christian aversion to gambling extended naturally to speculation in financial markets. The *windhandel* trade in 17th-century Dutch commodity and security markets led to a series of pamphlets on the subject that are reflective of the state of liberal Christian thinking on this issue (De Marchi and Harrison 1994, p.56):

Calvinist *predikanten* (preachers) held that gain is not in itself to be refused; rather it may be honest or 'foul'. The labourer is worthy of his hire; and since trade undergirds the Republic's well-being, so the honest merchant too should enjoy a reward for his risk and trouble. Net profit indeed— something over and above a reward for risk and trouble—is also not unacceptable, so long as it does not arise through damage done to another, is put to good use, and is not an expression of avarice.

In this view, the Calvinists could cite general Church doctrine, based on biblical passages relating to 'overprofit', such as Ezekiel 18:9, 18:13. What remained was to sort out whether a specific activity was acceptable.

Despite a generally liberal attitude to profit, Dutch Calvinists writing on the acceptability of the 17th-century *windhandel* trade were decidedly negative. These views were reflected in repeated legislative attempts to ban the trade:

> it is no accident that the official ordinances prohibiting short selling themselves argue in effect that the guiding rule espoused by the preachers—no harm to others—was invariably broken by the share traders. Starting with the first, in 1610, the ordinances repeat the arguments initially adduced by the VOC directors: *windhandel* harms the reputation of the company, makes a mockery of the state, and disadvantages widows and orphans and any who cannot sit out a period of low prices. Even if share trading had the dubious status of gambling, what caused the practice to incur moral censure was, over and above that, (1) the ruin that often ensued for losers, especially those who allowed themselves to become leveraged beyond their means; (2) the shady tricks employed; (3) the strong sense (which necessarily held true for option trades) that in all such dealings one party must lose; and (4) the idea that the short seller must fervently pray for prices to go against the buyer.

The difficulty of interpreting and extending scholastic doctrine to the progressive evolution of trading in financial markets was not limited to the *windhandel* trade.[16]

The Evolution of Scholastic Doctrine

Scholastic doctrine was the product of an intellectual approach to science and philosophy stretching back to Aristotle. Scholasticism was not static; it underwent considerable evolution in the centuries following the contributions of Saint Thomas Aquinas. Important contributions still appear as late as the 17th century, such as those originating with the School of Salamanca in Spain (de Roover 1955, p.316):

> In economics, the scholastic doctrine reaches its full maturity in the monumental works of Cardinals Juan de Lugo (1583–1660) and Giambattista de Luca (1613–1683) . . . Despite an impressive array of scholarship, their

works ill conceal the fact that the Doctors had exhausted the possibilities of their method and that further progress no longer depended upon more elaboration and refinement, but upon a complete renewal of the analytical apparatus.

For whatever reason, scholasticism was unable to cope with the profound advances in experimental sciences that started with the Renaissance. Though scholastic doctrine still had a strong hold over social attitudes, particularly in southern European countries such as Spain, France and Italy, by the 17th century the battered intellectual framework had largely lost its credibility.

The influence of scholasticism over social and intellectual life changed at different rates throughout Europe. For example, contracts explicitly permitting interest, up to some legal maximum, were legalized in England and Holland during the 16th century, though such contracts were not legally permitted until the mid-18th century in Italy and 1789 in France. The Catholic Church did not formally abandon the usury doctrine until 1830. Similarly in intellectual life (p.317):

> On the continent of Europe, and to a lesser extent in England, the dying Aristotelian system kept its hold on the universities, which thus become asylums for old fogies and citadels of bigoted pedantry. Learning deserted this musty environment and found a haven in the academies and in the salons of the eighteenth century.

In England, there was considerable intellectual progress from the time of Thomas Wilson, who criticized the interest embedded in the bill of exchange transaction, to that of Gerard de Malynes (1583–1623).

Who was Gerard de Malynes? As with many individuals in the early history of financial economics, many personal details of Malynes's life are either sketchy or unknown. That Malynes was both a mercantilist and a prolific writer is well known. Malynes's *Consuetudo vel Lex Mercatoria or the Ancient Law Merchant* (1st ed. 1622) and *A Treatise of the Canker of England's Common Wealth* (1601) are, perhaps, the works that attract the most modern attention. De Roover (1974, pp.350–1) explained why Malynes is of interest in the context of scholastic doctrine:

> Of all mercantilists, Malynes is perhaps the one who was influenced the most by Scholastic doctrines. This influence is not so much in evidence in his polemical pamphlets on foreign exchange—although one finds it there, too—as in his great work, *Consuetudo vel Lex Mercatoria*. That Malynes, more than any other economic writer of his time, represents the transition from Scholasticism to mercantilism is not a debatable statement. The supporting evidence is so overwhelming that there is little room for doubt.

As such, Malynes's writings are an excellent reflection of the social acceptance of scholastic doctrine in the merchant community of the early 17th century.

Much like Richard Witt, Gerard de Malynes is an enigma. Both his name and origins are uncertain. Though Malynes claimed in *Lex Mercatoria* that his ancestors were from Lancastershire, based on historical detective work, de Roover (pp.347–8) concludes:

> there is no doubt that he was a Fleming born in Antwerp who emigrated to England either for religious reasons or for business purposes, perhaps as a factor of Antwerp merchants trading with England . . . The decisive proof . . . that Gerard de Malynes hailed from the Low Countries rests on the fact that, in English records of the 1580s and 1590s, he is consistently listed among the aliens residing in the City and Suburbs of London. He was a member of the 'Dutch' church.

There were good reasons why Malynes would seek to disguise his true identity. Perhaps the most compelling was his desire to acquire political influence. This is reflected in his changing his name in his published work from Gerard de Malynes, for 1603 and prior, to Gerard Malynes, in those articles published after 1603; the time period that coincides with the most influential of Malynes's writings.

Based on the name originally chosen following emigration to England, Gerard de Malynes seems most likely to have been from Malynes, "a rather important town located halfway between Antwerp and Brussels". Yet again, there is evidence to indicate that Malynes's real name was Gerard van Mechelen, a member of an aldermanic family from Antwerp. This would seem to be supported from an examination of Malynes's known acquaintances and business associates in London. In his business dealings, Malynes "did not enjoy an untarnished reputation inasmuch as he involved himself in some shady business deals and highly speculative ventures that did not always turn out as expected". After a close examination of the historical evidence, de Roover (p.349) concluded: "Malynes, while he proclaimed himself in his writings to be a worshipper of free trade (the expression then used for free competition), was in actual fact a projector of the worst kind and a monopolist who sought only his own advantage".

These personal shortcomings of Malynes were matched by his positive scholarly contributions. "However disreputable and cunning as a businessman, Malynes was a scholar of sorts and a devotee of good literature. He was quite a learned man, perhaps the most learned of all the mercantilists" (p.349). Judging from the content of *Lex Mercatoria*, this learning included a healthy exposure to scholastic doctrine. Malynes was definitely familiar with the works of various recent predecessors, such as 'Doctor Wilson'. As such, the contents of the *Lex Mercatoria* can be taken as an important reflection of the stature and acceptance of the usury doctrine within the English merchant community, circa 1622.

The bulk of the discussion of usury in *Lex Mercatoria* is contained in the second part, chapters 10–16. The titles of these chapters are indicative of the coverage: Ch. 10, Of the lawes and prohibitions against usurie; Ch. 11, Of usurie politicke, and moneys delivered at interest; Ch. 12, Of intollerable Usurie, and Lombards; Ch. 13, Of *Mons pietatis*, or Banks of charitie; Ch. 14, Of the true calculation of moneys at interest; Ch. 15, Of usurious Contracts; Ch. 16, Of lawfull Bargaines and Contracts. Relative to other topics, the coverage given to usury is considerable. Referencing the many 'authors which have written against usurie in all ages', Malynes clearly identifies usury with 'biting' (Malynes 1622, p.325):

> Usurie in the Hebrew tongue is called Biting, of this word *Neshech*, which is nothing else but a kind of biting, as a dog useth to bite or gnaw upon a bone, so that he that biteth not doth not commit Usurie; for Usurie is none other thing than biting, as I said of the verie Entimologie and proper nature of the word, otherwise it cannot be called *Neshech*, as the Hebricians say.

The contrast between Thomas Wilson and Malynes is apparent.

NOTES

1 Reference to the 'Schoolmen' is generic. The category of individuals involved is quite broad, including both canonists and theologians: 'The distinction between a scholastic canonist and a scholastic theologian may seem trifling. Each was a servant of the Church; each was guided by the teaching of the Gospel, the natural law and the canons. Yet the observer will note differences in their approach . . . The canonists were concerned mainly with solutions valid for the external forum of the Church; they were concentrating on the administration of the law. The theologians were focussing mainly on the confessional. Moreover, the canonists, fitting their commentaries to specific canons, made no comprehensive effort to reconcile the canons or to produce a synthesis. The theologians were at once more systematic, more logical, and often more severe' (Noonan 1957, p.48).
2 Included in this revival are Decock (2009), Hamouda and Price (1997), Langholm (1998), Monsalve (2014a,b), van Houdt (1998), Reed and Bekar (2003), and Vivenza (2004).
3 Following Homer and Sylla (1991), this was also true in the ancient markets of countries such as Greece.
4 Ekelund et al. (1996, p.8) reported the following: 'Before the year 900 AD, the Church directly owned approximately one-third of all cultivated land in western Europe, including 31 percent of such land in Italy, 35 percent in Germany, and 44 percent in northern France.'
5 This is a simplification. Discussion among the later scholastics revolved around two forms of contractual risk: an 'intrinsic' risk associated with the goods, and an 'extrinsic' risk associated with the transaction. In a commercial loan, the risk passes from the lender to the borrower because the borrower is responsible for the success or failure of the venture. In a sea loan, this risk is split because the goods are at the lender's risk during transport. Recognition of 'extrinsic' risk allowed the later scholastics to justify the widespread practice of lending at interest.
6 In a fascinating conjecture, Coulton (1921) claimed there was an error by a scribe responsible for preparing the original text. The Latin text reads:

"Naviganti vel eunti ad nundinas certam mutuans pecuniae quantitatem pro eo, quod in se periculum, recepturus aliquid ultra sortem, usurarius est censendus" (Decretales V:19:19).

7   The situation for the Third Crusade was much different. For example, Madden (1993, p.441) reported: "the over-estimation by the Franks of the amount of transport and provisions they required for their expedition to the Holy Land, which put them in hopeless debt to Venice, and the Venetians in dire economic straits". In comparing the Third Crusades with previous Crusades, Tyerman (1995) observed: in "the period before the Third Crusade, . . . what we call 'the Crusades' in fact covered a fragmented series of military and religious activities that lacked coherence: general expeditions (only one between 1101 and 1188); private armed and unarmed pilgrimages, not all of which can be proved to have been undertaken in response to specific or general papal authorization; the interest of settlers in the east, such as Fulcher of Chartres or even William of Tyre, to create a process of constant reinforcement; and the birth and growth of the military orders. Each activity was distinct in motive, appeal and implementation, with nobody seriously trying to incorporate these diverse strands into one institution, theory, or even name."

8   Despite the academic attention given to the scholastic usury doctrine, the underlying importance of the financial transactions involved requires discussion. In this vein, (Noonan 1957, p.249) observed: 'Throughout the sixteenth century, the triple contract and the personal *census* are more important than interest titles.'

9   The position that 'money is sterile' is usually attributed to Aquinas, who likely derived this view from Aristotle.

10   Noonan (1957, pp.105–6) traced the origins of the use of the word *interesse*. The word originates from the Roman law regarding *quod interest*, 'that which is the difference', which applies to the payment a delinquent party to a contract is required to pay to the damaged party. The concept extends beyond the narrow notion of payment on a loan to incorporate damages due on any contract—for example, a partnership—due to the default or delinquency of one of the parties. The term is taken up in the writings of the 12th-century Bolognese school. Use of the term is commonplace after 1220.

11   Nelli (1972) and others observed that sea loans were often described in notarial records as *mutuum nauticum*, instead of the Roman description as *foenus nauticum*, to provide a basis for not identifying such transactions with usury.

12   Various interpretations of canon law permitted interest to be paid on state loans, partnerships, and the census. Interest was also disguised in monetary exchange transactions combined with credit, which took the form of bills of exchange. The interest derived from partnerships led to the development of interest on bank deposits and, starting around 1485 (Noonan 1957), to the 'triple contract', an 'insured' partnership with a fixed rate of return. The interaction between the growth of commercial activity and social acceptance of interest payments is an essential element in the evolution of security pricing theories. For example, consider the emphasis on problems of dividing the shares from partnerships. Earlier in history, prohibitions against usury had a significant impact on the recognition and valuation of interest payments (e.g., Noonan 1957; Daston 1988, ch. 1). As well as being a primary source of funds for business enterprises, because income received from partnerships was considered licit under canon law, the partnership was also used as a method of disguising interest payments in order to avoid the usury prohibition.

13   Smith (1776, p.339) stated: 'In some countries the interest of money has been prohibited by law.' The context of this quote implies that these laws were in place circa 1776, but it is possible that Smith had in mind prior historical

situations where interest had been prohibited in European countries. If not, then Smith was likely alluding to 'Mahometan nations' or Mohammedan or Muslim countries, where 'the law prohibits interest altogether' (p.96).

14 The level of confusion surrounding gambling during early history is reflected in the usage of the word 'lot': "In their writings on gambling and divination the Puritans often use the words 'lot' and 'lottery'. Their usage of these words is similar to some modern usages but differs slightly from the most common usage. By 'lot' the Puritan writers mean any randomizer such as cards or dice; by 'lottery' they mean any outcome determined by randomization" (Bellhouse 1988, p.67). Prior to Gataker, Puritan writers did not typically distinguish between pure gambling using purely random devices (such as dice) and gambling, which involved a combination of skill and chance.

15 Numerous sources attempt to trace the various biblical references—for example, Ashton (1899).

16 Forward trading in commodities posed another problem for scholastic doctrine. In addition to coming under many of the same criticisms aimed at the dishonest practices of the *windhandel* trade, forward trade posed additional doctrinal problems (e.g., Ekelund et al. 1996, pp.126–7).

Part II

From *Commenda* to Joint-Stock Company

4 The Evolution of Accounting and Commercial Arithmetic

> Three merchants have invested their money in a partnership . . . Piero put in 112 ducats, Polo 200 ducats and Zuanne 142 ducats. At the end of a certain period they found that they had gained 563 ducats. Required is to know how much falls to each man so that no one shall be cheated.
>
> *Treviso Arithmetic* (1478)

A ACCOUNTING, COMMERCIAL ARITHMETIC AND BUSINESS EDUCATION

The Origins of Modern Accounting

If the origins of partnership, trade and credit are prehistoric, predating the use of coinage, then the history of bookkeeping has a similar lineage. Even in the rudimentary barter economies of prehistory, some method of recording what and how much was spent or sold or accumulated or distributed or lent to what person is essential. Mattessich (1987, p.71) reported archaeological evidence from the Middle East in layers from the 8th to 3rd millennium BC indicating a developed method of accounting prior to the development of cuneiform script, the first written language. The accounting system employed "simple (and later complex) *clay tokens* of various shapes . . . aggregated in *hollow clay receptacles or envelopes* (and later *sealed string systems*) to represent symbolically assets and economic transactions". Given the limited amount of primary evidence from the civilizations of antiquity, it is still evident that sophisticated methods of accounting were available at the beginning of recorded history and that the demands of accounting contributed to the development of cuneiform writing (e.g., Crawford 1950; Garbutt 1984; Ezzamel and Hoskin 2002; Vollmers 2009).

Despite early evidence of accounting practices, evidence for the use of accounting to determine profit for equity capital shares in a partnership or in support of management control of a commercial venture is elusive. What is in evidence is the use of possibly sophisticated accounting in administrative control of the early empires. For example, Vollmers (2009) examined the cuneiform Persepolis Fortification tablets from the Achaemenid Empire of Persia under

Darius I (ca. 549–486 BC). In addition to receipts for transactions, there were accounting balances for specific grain handlers at the temple storehouse. The role of accounting in the Roman Empire, which is apparent in many primary sources, has been detailed in Murray (1930) and Oldroyd (1995). Murray (1930, p.128) observed, with some hyperbole:

> The great internal trade of the Romans and their extensive foreign commerce involved elaborate systems of accounts and accounting. Correspondence and commercial documents were required just as now. Book-keepers and accountants, clerks, managers, brokers, and commercial travelers were all employed as they are to-day. Lawyers of many kinds were as prominent in commercial affairs as they are now, and professional accountants, valuers, and other experts were as commonly resorted to as now in adjusting intricate business transactions, in settling disputed questions, and in winding up and distributing insolvent estates.

The *Digest* of Justinian is replete with instances where some method of accounting is either strongly implied or directly required.

In the face of such obvious evidence of ancient accounting systems, the traditional modern approach to accounting history begins the narrative with double-entry bookkeeping (e.g., de Roover 1956; Yamey 1980, 2005; Carruthers and Nelson 1991; Cushing 1989). This is apparently intentional. While recognizing that there were accounting systems prior to double-entry (e.g., Nobes and Abdullah 2001), modern accounting history is still haunted by the ghosts of Werner Sombart (1863–1941) and Max Weber (1864–1920). Most (1976, p.23) provided the following description of Sombart:

> Sombart saw the invention of double-entry bookkeeping as a device for rendering objective the concept of capital . . . The idea of capital was divorced from all want-satisfying objectives or motivations of the people who took part in the development of the firm, and this led directly to the formulation of economic rationalism: *Quod non est in libris non est in mundo.* By this means, production and distribution were reduced to calculations, which meant that the tools of mathematics could be used to plan saving and investment and to further the growth of capitalism.

In *Der moderne Kapitalismus* (1902) Sombart was effusive in proposing a central position for double-entry in the development of modern capitalism. For example, Sombart quotes J.W. von Goethe (1749–1832) from *Wilhelm Meister's Apprenticeship* (1795): "What advantages does the Merchant derive from Book-keeping by double-entry? It is amongst the finest inventions of the human mind." Similarly, there is the strong claim by Sombart that double-entry bookkeeping (quoted in Most 1976, pp.23–4):

> must be compared to the knowledge which scientists have built up since the sixteenth century concerning relationships in the physical world. Double-entry

bookkeeping came from the same spirit which produced the systems of Galileo and Newton and the subject matter of modern physics and chemistry. By the same means, it organizes perceptions into a system, and one can characterize it as the first Cosmos constructed purely on the basis of mechanistic thought. Double-entry bookkeeping captures for us the essence of an economic or capitalistic world by the same means that later the great scientists used to construct the solar system and the corpuscles of the blood. Without too much difficulty, we can recognize in double-entry book keeping the ideas of gravitation, of the circulation of the blood, and of the conservation of matter. And even on a purely aesthetic plane we cannot regard double-entry bookkeeping without wonder and astonishment as one of the most artistic representations of the fantastic spiritual richness of European man.

Though the *magnum opus* of Sombart receives little attention in present times, the themes were continued in the influential work of Weber and Schumpeter.

Sombart was part of an intellectual tradition, similar to that of Marx and Engels, seeking to explain the broad scope of European economic progress in general and capitalism in particular. Sombart divided the development of capitalism into three stages: early capitalism, which ended before the Industrial Revolution; high capitalism, which began circa 1760; and, finally, late capitalism, beginning with World War I. A close collaborator with Sombart, Weber further developed these notions into the influential *The Protestant Ethic and the Spirit of Capitalism* and *Economy and Society*. Written in German from 1904 to 1905, the text of the *Protestant Ethic* was originally translated into English in 1930 by Talcott Parsons (1902–1979). Though more restrained, Weber took a similar tack to Sombart: "The most general presupposition for the existence of this present-day capitalism is that of rational capital accounting as the norm for all large industrial undertakings which are concerned with provision for everyday wants" (Weber [1927] 1981, p.276). As Carruthers and Espeland (1991, pp.32–3) observed: "Weber considered double-entry bookkeeping the most highly developed form of accounting".

This is not meant to imply that Sombart and Weber held similar views. As Robertson and Funnell (2012, p.343) recognized, Sombart took a more rigid interpretation than Weber, requiring that "the modern capitalist mentality associated with commercial capitalism depended on both the prior existence of double-entry bookkeeping to measure profit and the desire (spirit) to use this technology to make rational business decisions". In contrast, Weber took a more agnostic view on double-entry bookkeeping, seeing it as "not as an essential requirement for the development of modern capitalism but as mainly a technology that facilitated rational capitalist action" which "rests on the expectation of profit by the utilization of peaceful opportunities for exchange" (Weber 1958, p.17). As Weber ([1927], 1981, p.275) observed, a rational capitalist business entity determines its "income yielding power by calculation according to the methods of modern bookkeeping and the striking of a balance". Unlike Sombart, Weber was more careful about the historical record, less inclined to hyperbole and, as a consequence, closer to capturing an accurate picture of the historical relationship between double-entry and the development of capitalism.

Religion, Capitalism and Double-Entry Bookkeeping

Despite being criticized, even pilloried, from various quarters, the search for connections between religion, capitalism and double-entry bookkeeping initiated by Sombart survives to the present. After a fashion, Schumpeter (1950, p.123) was a proponent of the traditional connections: "Capitalism develops rationality and . . . exalts the monetary unit—not itself a creation of capitalism—into a unit of account. That is to say, capitalist practice turns the unit of money into a tool of rational cost-profit calculations, of which the towering monument is double-entry book-keeping." In contrast, at least since Yamey (1964) and Winjum (1971) debated the historical legitimacy of the influence and use of double-entry in early capitalism, accounting historians have increasingly questioned the traditional interpretation that double-entry was central to the transition to capitalism. For example, Robertson and Funnell (2012) examined the first two decades of the *VOC* (Dutch East India Company) and found that "at no time during the period covered by the first charter (1602–1623) of the Dutch East-India Company, or thereafter, did the domestic operations of the Company use this form of bookkeeping across all chambers. This meant that the investors did not have the necessary information that would have allowed them to calculate the return on their investments."

Identification of the actual path taken by the accounting activities of the merchants of early capitalism requires an accurate definition of double-entry bookkeeping. Though the need for definition was recognized as early as Winjum (1971), Derks (2008, p.188) still emphasized that "When trying to define [double-entry bookkeeping], we arrive directly at the core of the debate." More precisely, Winjum (1971, p.334) observed:

> To some, double entry merely refers to a system in which the only criterion is the equality of debits and credits. At an opposite extreme, double entry refers to a system of record keeping in which real and nominal accounts are integrated within a coordinated and internally consistent structure capable of simultaneously producing reports on both the accounting entity's progress and its status. These calculations are assumed to take place at fixed periodic intervals. At least four definitions of double entry fall within these two extremes. (1) A bookkeeping system constantly in equilibrium in which the only criterion is the equality of debits and credits.
>
> (2) The addition of a capital account to the first system.
>
> (3) The use of nominal accounts (revenues, expenses, ventures, etc.) in addition to the capital account of system 2, but an irregular closing of these accounts to capital. Under this system, there is no periodic calculation of net income.
>
> (4) The same as system 3 except for the periodic closing of nominal accounts to capital and the annual calculation of net income.

There is ample evidence that (4) was not common practice among the merchants of early capitalism. Periodic closing of accounts was not common practice until the 18th century, perhaps later in some locales. In many actual commercial situations, 'venture accounting' sufficed for merchants in long-distance trade to engage in 'rational' business decisions without the use of double-entry. However, as commercial operations increased in complexity and the amount of permanent 'capital' demanded required larger numbers of investors, the benefits of double-entry increased.

It is not surprising that accounting historians find fault with technical features of the Sombart-Weber interpretation of double-entry bookkeeping. Neither Sombart nor Weber was an accountant. Continuing modern interest in the relationship between religion, capitalism and double-entry is not seriously damaged, because the historical record does not precisely correspond to the substance of the argument. At one level, the substance is semantic. For Sombart, "capitalism" requires a notion of 'capital', and this is provided by 'double-entry bookkeeping'. At this level, the argument is that (Carruthers and Espeland 1991, p.36):

> changes in accounting practices had important cognitive consequences. According to Sombart, the central idea of capital itself was engendered by double-entry bookkeeping. Double-entry bookkeeping created new categories for classifying and evaluating business transactions. It was a technique that helped to organize and make sense of the business world. Consequently, the relationship between accounting and behavior was not a unilateral one: double-entry bookkeeping was devised to account for business transactions, but once established, it altered those transactions by changing the way businessmen interpreted and understood them.

At this level, it is not necessary for there to be a formal equivalence with the double-entry process. It is the numerical preparation of 'the accounts' that can be examined by partners or shareholders that has the rhetorical value. This requires a 'rational' method of preparing the accounts and, though there are alternatives, double-entry is well suited to the demands of large-scale business where management is separated from the owners (i.e., the equity capitalists).

The historical implications of double-entry bookkeeping for 'equity capital' valuation and organization are immediate and profound. These implications extend beyond the ability to determine a numerical value for 'equity capital' using the capital account, though this calculation is significant in providing a specific form to the concept of capital. In addition: "The use of an integrated system of interrelated accounts made it possible for the entrepreneur to pursue profits rationally. Rationalization could now be based on a rigorous calculation. Present economic status could be readily determined and rational plans for future operations could be developed" (Winjum 1971, p.336). The rationalization process was facilitated by the ability of double-entry to provide an orderly and systematic record of a firm's commercial activities. This process of rationalization and systemization was essential to the emergence and growth of joint-stock companies, where separation of ownership and management was necessary. This required some method of alleviating the depersonalization that accompanied the combination of equity capital from a large number of shareholders.

The Relevance of Commercial Arithmetic

What is the relevance of medieval and Renaissance commercial arithmetic to the history of equity capital organization and valuation? This question can be approached from many directions. Commercial arithmetics from the 15th century, such as the *Treviso Arithmetic* and the *Libro de Abacho,* echo the level of basic training required to manage the commercial ventures of that time. Societal restrictions on debt financing, and the rudimentary character of commercial ventures, resulted in widespread use of partnerships financed with equity capital. The problems provided in commercial arithmetics used in the reckoning schools reflect the variety of commercial situations to be encountered by young men apprenticing with the reckoning master. In some cases, commercial arithmetics such as Chuquet's *Triparty* reflect the level of mathematical sophistication used in the central financial markets. As such, the commercial arithmetics also reflect the character of the underlying business, where profit was being generated using equity capital. Some commercial arithmetics are contained in larger works, especially the *Summa de arithmetica, geometria. Proportioni et proportionalita* (Venice 1494) by Fra Luca Pacioli (1445–1517) and the *Mathematica Hypomnemata* (1608) by Simon Stevin, which also contain an essential early element in the evolution toward modern accounting: double-entry bookkeeping.

Due to the prevalence of closely held partnerships at the time of the *Summa,* it was difficult and usually unnecessary to transfer equity capital. The beginning of a market for impersonal trading of autonomous equity capital shares was still some centuries ahead. While scholastic doctrine dictated how financing of commercial ventures *ought* to be done, the early commercial arithmetics are reflections of the actual, if rudimentary, methods used in commercial practice. Some commercial arithmetics were influenced by the scholastic Church school educational process, with the commercial arithmetic being part of a larger study that also featured the theoretical aspects of arithmetic, algebra and geometry, which were the substance of mathematical training in the abbey schools and early universities. Other commercial arithmetics were wholly practical, designed only for use in reckoning schools and commercial practice. From the time of the Renaissance, the important commercial arithmetics were primarily algorisms, though the older abacus methods were still popular in some locales until well into the 16th century. A few of these algorisms provided significant advances in mathematics, such as the introduction of the decimal system by Simon Stevin.

The association of business schools with universities is a relatively modern development. Traditionally, universities and Church schools used a curriculum that had a scholarly emphasis on the humanities. Continuing a tradition stretching back to the Greek philosophers, use-oriented subjects, such as engineering, applied mathematics and business studies, were of secondary importance. Starting in the 16th century, this neglect of practical subjects at the expense of humanist pursuits, combined with the use of Latin in university instruction, was increasingly questioned by scholars such as Petrus Ramus at the University of Paris. Though there was considerable resistance from the largely Church-dominated academic leadership, there was a gradual trend toward acceptance of teaching in the vernacular and of use-oriented subjects, as evidenced by the

Figure 4.1 A 1535 woodcut print showing a father apprenticing his son to a reckoning master

Source: Swetz (1987, Figure I.3).
Note: This picture was used in Petrarch's *Mirror of Consolation* to illustrate the duties of a just guardian.

establishment in 1600 of the Dutch Mathematical School, associated with the University of Leiden. This trend continued during the 17th century, with dramatic intellectual advances in astronomy, mathematics, physics, engineering and other use-oriented subjects.

Despite the post-17th-century trend toward giving increased academic importance to use-oriented subjects, adequate business education was still difficult, if not impossible in some areas, to obtain within the universities and Church school system. Those desiring a detailed commercial education, such as merchant apprentices, were obliged to attend other institutions, such as the reckoning schools or their successors. Reckoning schools, where reckoning masters accepted students for private tuition or conducted formal group classes, appeared in Italy prior to the 14th century and spread to northern Europe along the trade routes. Students came, typically, from merchant families, usually following a grammar school education. Braudel (1982, p.408) provided a useful description of the education and apprenticeship system:

Secular education had been organized in Florence from the fourteenth century. According to Villani, 8000 to 10,000 children (at a time when the city's population was under 100,000) were learning to read in primary school (*a botteghuzza*). It was to the *botteghuzza* kept by the grammar-master Matteo, '*al piè del ponte a Santa Trinità*', that the young Niccolò Machiavelli was brought in May 1476 to learn to study in the abridged

Figure 4.2   A woodcut from the title page of Adam Riese's *Rechenbach* (1529)

Source: Adapted from Swetz (1987).

Note: The theme of the woodcut is concerned with the controversy between algorists and abacists, which was quite heated at the time that Riese was writing.

version of Donatus's grammar (known as *Donatello*). Of these eight to ten thousand children, 1000 to 1200 went on to the high school, specially for merchant apprentices. Here a boy remained until his fifteenth year, studying arithmetic *(algorismo)* and accountancy *(abbaco)*. After this 'technical' education, he was already able to keep the registers for accounts we can inspect today, which reliably recorded details for sales on credit, commission, compensatory payments between different centres, or the distribution of profits among the partners in companies.

The reckoning school was essential in the training of merchant apprentices. The reckoning master also acted as a consultant on various types of often complicated problems involving commercial calculations. Such consultants in important commercial centres, such as Chuquet in Lyons, reflected the best in mathematical skill of the age.

Together with bookkeeping, commercial arithmetic was an essential component of the reckoning school curriculum. Following the introduction and adoption of the printing press in the second half of the 15th century, texts in the vernacular on commercial arithmetic which reckoning masters used in their classrooms began to be published and circulated. Though ultimately derived from the more mathematically sophisticated *Liber abaci* (1202) by Fibonacci, such early efforts were almost always exclusively practical, early versions of the modern business school textbooks. The reckoning school as an institution evolved over time, as did the Church schools and universities, where the curriculum gradually admitted the study of practical arts and sciences. This evolution occurred to suit the profound changes in business practices that took place during the 16th and 17th centuries. For example, the increasing importance of bookkeeping and accounting led to increasing emphasis on that subject in the reckoning school curriculum.

The reckoning school, as an institution, was also adapted to suit the particular characteristics of the countries into which it was transplanted. In England and Scotland, the reckoning school evolved into the commercial academies and 'writing schools' that were the backbone of commercial education during the 17th and 18th centuries. By the late 17th century, instruction in handwriting had risen to a level of importance equal to that of instruction in commercial arithmetic and accounting. The English writing master had come to replace the reckoning master as the purveyor of commercial education. The traditional reckoning master, a specialist in the 'arte of numbers', was now more of a consulting specialist. Compared with the 15th and 16th centuries, by the 18th century the gap between reckoning school education and the knowledge of the consulting specialists was substantial; only the most capable of the writing masters, such as James Dodson (1705–1757), were able to make the transition to consulting specialist.

B   *THE TREVISO ARITHMETIC*, LIBRO DE ABACHO *AND* SUMMA

Medieval and Renaissance Accounting

Given the considerable emphasis on the historical importance of double-entry bookkeeping, it is not surprising that accounting methods employed prior to the introduction of double-entry have received much less attention. This lack of attention is compounded by the absence of account books and other evidence concerning the accounting activities of medieval and Renaissance commercial ventures. This lack of primary evidence is even more acute for Roman times, as the use of wax tablets and verbal contracts has left almost no trace of accounting practices. From as late as the 12th and 13th centuries, from which we begin to have the notarial records of the Italian city states, there is still an absence of accounting information. "Since there are thousands of partnership agreements in the extant cartularies of medieval Genoese notaries, we are well informed about the legal aspects of such contracts, but we know little about the way in which these partnerships actually carried on their business, because hardly any accounting records of the twelfth century have survived" (de Roover 1941, p.87). Constructing an accurate historical record is difficult when only fragments and inferences from later practices are the only primary evidence available.

The absence of direct primary evidence makes historical inference difficult, but not impossible. However, modern historical research is not immune from the desire for a 'scientific', evidence-based approach. The presence of thousands of 12th- and 13th-century partnership agreements in the Genoese notarial cartularies provide primary evidence about legal arrangements. Except in rare instances, the accounting associated with these partnerships is unavailable. Dutiful modern historians have proceeded to explore the available primary evidence, developing elaborate theories to explain the forms of legal contracting observed in 'the data' (e.g., Greif 1994; Gonzalez de Lara 2008). In this process, the connection between the commercial context, the legal contract employed and the methods of accounting available can be lost. The Genoese were able to raise large sums of equity capital to finance highly complicated, risky and usually very profitable ventures to Syria using rudimentary accounting systems and an adaption of the ancient Roman *societas*. Surely these venturers were 'rational capitalists'?

The choice of legal contract selected for a commercial venture is systemically related to the methods of accounting available. In turn, the ability to collect data impacts the selection of a particular accounting method. As late as the 16th century, Posthumus (1953), Funnell and Robertson (2011) and others have demonstrated Hanseatic accounting was primarily concerned with "the need to enable a settlement between partners at the conclusion of a business venture." Using partnership arrangements similar to those in medieval Genoa, "Hanseatic businesses did not have a common capital but instead were loose associations of businessmen in which no partner could exercise formal control over the actions of other partners" (Robertson and Funnell 2012, p.343). This is historically important, because north German commercial practices had a significant influence on Dutch practices, at this time, due to substantial trade relationships. As the Dutch republic is widely credited as the 'cradle of early capitalism', this implies that double-entry bookkeeping, in the sense where a capital account is central, "was neither possible nor desirable and any notion of accounting for an entity as a whole by means of a centralised accounting system was entirely foreign to both the 16th century north Germans and the Dutch" (p.343).

Few have done more to bring light to the early history of accounting than Raymond de Roover (1904–1972). Recognizing there was an origin for double-entry well before Pacioli, de Roover (1940, p.45) observed:

> The keeping of accounts by the overseas trader of all the money and goods he received from scores of different persons, of the goods he brought back, and the profits on each transaction entailed considerable bookkeeping. It is not surprising that double-entry bookkeeping developed first in Genoa.

This position on the primacy of Genoa and the reference to 'overseas' trader de Roover attributes to the influential early 20th-century Italian accounting historian Fabio Besta, a position that de Roover later found to be misplaced (de Roover 1955, p.405):

> On the authority of Besta and his students it was thought . . . that double-entry bookkeeping originated in Genoa around 1340 and spread from there

to other Italian trading centers, such as Milan, Florence, and Venice . . . this hypothesis has been completely shattered and replaced by a much more complicated and more confused picture. It is now doubtful whether double-entry bookkeeping was born in Genoa; Florence is henceforth a serious contender to the Genoese claims, but it is even more likely that double entry was developed almost simultaneously by the merchants of several Italian cities who had been searching for a system that would minimize errors, facilitate control, and give them a comprehensive view of the financial state of their business.

Not only were questions asked about the primacy of Genoa, the emphasis on the 'form' of the accounts was gradually shifting to the use of accounting as a system and as a tool for management and control. In determining whether a given ledger or account book qualifies as double-entry, de Roover (1955) suggested the criterion: "At the end, do we have a real balance showing the owners' equity and the composition of assets and liabilities? Only if the answer is affirmative, is one justified in speaking without hesitation of books kept in double entry."

Another facet of the traditional interpretation of the origin of double-entry concerns the role of the "overseas trader". Early instances in which surviving merchant accounts are complex enough to qualify as 'double-entry' are associated with firms not primarily involved in 'overseas' trade. Consider the Giovanno Farolfi & Company ledger of 1299–1300 examined by Lee (1977). This was a substantial firm of Florentine merchants, with head office at Nîmes in the Languedoc. The surviving ledger, from a Florentine archive, is for a branch of the firm at Salon, a town in the independent county of Provence, about 45 miles from Nîmes. The activities of the firm revealed by the ledger are considerable. At Salon, the firm was engaged in the wholesale trade of wheat, barley, oats, olive oil, wine, wool, and yarn. The firm also did business in cloth and was engaged in lending at interest. There was a sizeable number of customers and suppliers. This level of activity, by a group of Florentine merchants operating in France, is indicative of an ongoing commercial venture complex enough to employ some form of double-entry accounting. In contrast, the accounts of an 'overseas trader' using contracts covering a single voyage seem simple.

Before dismissing the overseas trader from 12th-century Genoa as having insufficiently complex business dealings to require a complex method of accounting, such as double-entry, consider that larger passive merchant 'investors' were also almost certainly engaged in a range of business dealings, including travel to the fairs or doing business with those who were. However, no record survives to confirm this suspicion, illustrating again how the availability of primary evidence determines the historical record. With the emergence of the Medici bank in Florence and the Bank of St. George in Genoa around the turn of the 15th century, detailed accounting records for complex commercial operations involving sizeable numbers of debit and credit operations in different geographical locations using different monetary units become available. In the case of the Medici, there was even a *libri segreti* that contained a confidential statement of the capital account only available to the partners. It is more than evident that some form of double-entry bookkeeping was well established before Pacioli's *Summa*.

The Impact of the Printing Press

The 'invention' of the printing press in Europe around the middle of the 15th century by Johannes Gutenberg (1398–1468) is a watershed historical event. How much Gutenberg knew about the block printing process with movable type that had been used in East Asia since the 11th century for wood blocks and the 14th century for metal blocks is unknown. In any case, Gutenberg would have been familiar with various medieval and Renaissance technological advances potentially useful in printing, such as the screw press and movable type. Gutenberg, a goldsmith by trade, was able to combine previous innovations to create a process for mass printing that revolutionized European society. Before Gutenberg, the bulk of texts available had been scholarly works handwritten in Latin. The rapid spread of printing technology in Europe facilitated many popular books written in the vernacular. The spread of ideas and the encouragement of literacy contributed to the Reformation and the gradual demise of scholasticism.

Significantly, some of the first printed books were merchant manuals and accounting treatises. Though the printing press originated in Germany, the following table (Table 4.1) captures the key role Italians played in the early printing revolution.

While Italy was the centre for European commercial education, by the time of the printing of the *Treviso Arithmetic* in 1478 there were numerous commercial centres outside of Italy where reckoning masters, or algorists, were in increasing demand. Lyons was one such centre, where a flourishing spice market contributed to the success of the Lyons fairs following the royal protection provided to the fairs by Louis XI in the 1460s. It was in Lyons where Nicolas Chuquet, a master algorist, worked and by 1484 completed a series of handwritten manuscripts referred to as *Triparty* (*Triparty en la science des nombres*). While *Triparty* is arguably the most significant theoretical contribution among

Table 4.1   Establishment of Printing Centers

	Before 1471	1471–1480	Total to 1480	1481–1490	1491–1500	Total at 1500
Northern Italy	2	33	35	9	5	49
Rest of Italy	2	3	5	4	0	9
Germany*	7	28	35	20	11	66
Switzerland	2	3	5	8	2	15
Iberia	1	6	7	14	9	30
France	1	8	9	11	12	32
England	0	4	4	0	0	4
Scandinavia	0	0	0	4	2	6
Eastern Europe	0	4	4	3	3	10
Total	15	89	104	73	44	221

Source: E. Eisenstein, *The Printing Revolution in Early Modern Europe,* Cambridge University Press, 1983, pp.14–5.

* Includes present-day Austria and Benelux

the early commercial arithmetics, other commercial arithmetics, in manuscript form, also had emerged in various cities in the time between Fibonacci's *Liber abaci* and the *Treviso Arithmetic*.

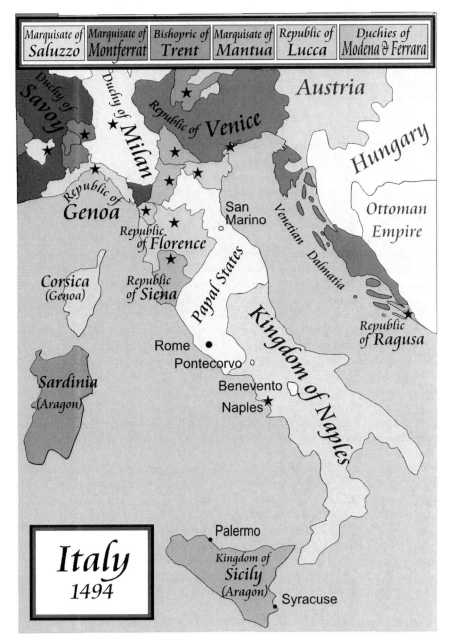

| Marquisate of Saluzzo | Marquisate of Montferrat | Bishopric of Trent | Marquisate of Mantua | Republic of Lucca | Duchies of Modena & Ferrara |

Figure 4.3 Wikicommons, https://commons.wikimedia.org/wiki/File:Italy_1494_v2.png

The *Treviso Arithmetic* (1478) is not a particularly memorable book from the standpoint of high theory. The primary relevance of the book is that it is the first known printed book on commercial arithmetic and, more generally, on mathematics. As such, the book almost certainly provides a snapshot of the teachings that an unnamed *maestri d'abbaco* gave to the students of his reckoning school. The book is untitled and draws its name from being an arithmetic published in Treviso, a town in the Venetian republic. Treviso was a town of some economic importance, being located on the main trade route linking Venice with northern and central European centres such as Vienna and the German cities. Economic activity in Treviso was sufficiently robust that, as early as 1372, the town was capable of supporting a *maestri d'abbaco* (Swetz 1987, ch. 1).

The significance of the *Treviso* to the history of equity capital lies more with what the book represents than with what it contains. The *Treviso* was the first printed mathematics book, though there were other potential candidates for this honour with considerably greater scholastic interest, such as the works of Euclid, representing a 'profitable' application of early printing technology. The book was written by some anonymous reckoning master—possibly not the master who requisitioned the printing—intended as a self-study *practica* for those involved in commercial trades and as an instructional reckoning school text. It is written in the Venetian dialect, not in Latin, which was the language of scholarly instruction in medieval and Renaissance universities. As such, the *Treviso* represents the importance and advanced development that Venetian commercial education and the subject of commercial arithmetic had achieved by the latter part of the fifteenth century. The *Treviso* also represents the beginning of Italian commercial notions being disseminated to other areas of Europe, contributing to the gradual appearance of vernacular printed editions of commercial arithmetic and bookkeeping texts throughout northern Europe.

The contents of the *Treviso Arithmetic* were translated to English by noted mathematics historian David Eugene Smith in 1907, with the text of the translation given, in full, by Swetz (1987). There is no title page, table of contents or index. The original folio has 62 double pages, and the text is not broken into chapters. After a brief discussion of numbers, the *Treviso* proceeds to discuss addition, subtraction, multiplication and division, with illustrations often involving monetary units, which complicates the discussion but is a necessary feature of commercial arithmetic. This consumes approximately half of the text. Starting on the 30th folio page, the rule of three is examined and treated with numerous examples. This consumes the next 28 pages of text. The absence of decimal fractions meant worked solutions involving complicated fractions. After a brief examination of computing calculations, the *Treviso* concludes with a listing of practical rules useful in mercantile calculations—for example, "Note that to make pounds of ounces, divide the ounces by 12".

The *Treviso Arithmetic* was not a popular book. The book appears to have had only one edition, and copies of the book today are extremely rare. Much more successful than the *Treviso Arithmetic* was the *Libro de Abacho* by Pietro Borgo (or Borghi), which first appeared in 1484 and went into no less than 16 printed editions, with the last edition appearing in 1577. D. Smith (1926, p.49) called the *Libro de Abacho* the "First Great Commercial Arithmetic" and recognized that a "book so valued as to go through at least sixteen editions in a century must have had and evidently did have a great influence on the work of later generations". The original and later editions of the book were published in Venice, and the book was written in the Venetian dialect. Little is known of the author other than what is on the title page: his name and the appellation "*da venetia*", Pietro Borgo of Venice. Unlike scholarly tomes, the *Treviso Arithmetic*, the *Libro de Abacho* and similar efforts treated only the subject of commercial arithmetic, leaving aside other important commercial subjects such as bookkeeping and writing.

The *Libro de Abacho* is an unabashedly practical commercial arithmetic, stating explicitly that the types of theoretical numbers that were of interest to the Greeks and Boethius were to be discarded and only those of use in commercial applications were to be examined. The text follows the general approach of Fibonacci's *Liber abaci* by starting with a discussion on the reading and writing of numbers and then proceeding to cover multiplication, division, addition and then subtraction, in that order. In contrast, the *Treviso Arithmetic* is strikingly modern in covering the arithmetic operations by proceeding from addition to subtraction to multiplication and then division. Both books proceed to deal with fractions and the rule of three, essential for calculations involving currency exchange and barter. Both books end with a substantial number of practical

Figure 4.4 Fra Luca Pacioli (1447?–1517) by unknown artist (1495), *Museo e Gallerie di Capodimonte in Napoli* (Italy)

problems, with worked solutions provided. In both books, there is no substantive discussion of accounting and bookkeeping methods, indicating these topics were likely of a nature to be treated in more advanced courses.

Even though the *Libro de Abacho* may have been the most important *practica* in the period from the late 15th to the end of the 16th century, it is little more than a curiosity to modern researchers. The accessibility of printing to commercial education marked by the publication of the *Treviso Arithmetic* led to a surge of mathematics works printed in Italy. From 1480 to 1490, at least 63 mathematical works were printed in Italy alone (D. Smith 1958, v.1, p.41), rising to 214 by 1500 and 1,527 by 1600 (D. Smith 1958, v.1, p.249). Of all the commercial and mathematical texts produced during this period, one text still receives considerable attention from modern researchers: the *Summa de Arithmetica, Geometria, Proportioni et Proportionalita* (1494) by Fra Luca Paciolo (1445–1523?), also known as Luca Pacioli (Paccioli), Lucas Patiolus, Luca Paciuolo, Luca Paciuolo de Borgo san Sepulcro (D. Smith 1970, p.54) and Fra Luca di Borgo, the name that he took upon entering the Franciscan order (Figure 4.4). The text is commonly referred to as the *Summa*.

In the history of accounting, the most important claim to priority associated with Pacioli and the *Summa* is that the *Summa* was the first printed treatise containing a treatment of double-entry accounting. Given the relevance of accounting in the history of equity capital organization and valuation, the *Summa* has a symbolic role. The bookkeeping part of the *Summa*, which is composed of 36 chapters and is entitled 'Of Reckonings and Writings' (*De computis et scripturis*), had a profound influence on accounting practice. In the 100 years following its original publication, the bookkeeping part of the *Summa* was translated into at least five languages. The 1543 English translation by Hugh Oldcastle, a London reckoning master, is the oldest known treatise on accounting in English. Until approximately the 19th century, the 'method of Venice' dominated accounting education and practice. When modern accounting historians refer to the *Summa,* it is in such terms as follows: "The treatise by Pacioli has been the foundation upon which practically all subsequent writings concerning double entry bookkeeping have been predicated" (Green 1930, p.41).[1]

Unlike the *Treviso Arithmetic* and the *Libro de Abacho,* which had purely commercial education in mind, the *Summa* was written in the manner of the *Liber abaci* and other scholastic tracts. However, unlike the *Liber abaci,* which was written in Latin, the *Summa* was written in the Venetian dialect. The text of the *Summa* covers five topics (Chatfield 1974, ch. 4): algebra and arithmetic; the use of these subjects in business; bookkeeping; money and exchange; and pure and applied geometry. Though the book was published in Venice in 1494, it appears as though much of the text was written about seven years earlier, when Fra Luca was at Perugia. The primary purpose of the *Summa* was not to give instruction in bookkeeping, the subject for which it is most famous in modern times. Rather, the objective was to summarize the mathematical knowledge available at the time. While the book does contain some previously unpublished work by Pacioli, among historians of mathematics and statistics it is generally maintained that the *Summa* is "a remarkable compilation with almost no originality" (D. Smith 1958, v.1, p.252). In *'De computis et scripturis'* (16th century), Pacioli referred to the Italian double-entry bookkeeping system as "long established" (Murray 1930, p.167).

Biographies of individuals living in Renaissance Italy are often difficult to obtain. The modern practice of writing laudatory biographies or self-promoting autobiographies was uncommon. Life was usually absorbed in the service of Church and state. For individuals such as Pietro Borgo, writing to further the interests of *mei signori Merchandanti Venetiani* was sufficient reward. Though sketchy in parts, with some disagreement on specific points in the available sources (e.g., Green 1930; David 1962; Chatfield 1974), in contrast to other contributors in this period, much of Pacioli's life is quite traceable. Little is known of Pacioli's early life, other than that he was born about 1445 at *Borgo Sancti Sepulchri* in the province of Arezzo in Tuscany. He apparently received a Church school education from the Franciscan friars and may have received some instruction and academic influence from a fellow townsman, Pietro Franceschi (1410?–1492), an artist who also produced a respectable work on geometry (D. Smith 1958, v.1, p.251).

Around the age of 20, Pacioli travelled to Venice and became a tutor in mathematics to the three sons of the wealthy merchant Ser Rompiasi. Pacioli's six years in this position were spent in the study of mathematics and, just prior to his leaving for Rome in 1471, he completed writing an algebra text that was never published. Because of the need to provide instruction to the sons of merchants, it is likely that he became well acquainted with commercial arithmetic and bookkeeping during this period. Upon arriving in Rome, Pacioli entered the Minorite order of the Franciscans, taking the name Fra Luca di Borgo. Whether Pacioli undertook becoming a Franciscan for purely religious reasons is unknown. However, in Renaissance Italy, becoming a Franciscan was a desirable means of both obtaining university education and securing employment as a teacher in Church schools and universities (Chatfield 1974, p.44). The Franciscans also played a key role in establishing in 1495 the *monte di pieta* in Florence to provide a pool of funds for the poor to obtain small consumption loans.

The next period of Pacioli's life was taken up with travel, teaching and education. The actual route of his travels is unknown, though there were extensive excursions in Italy and possibly in the Orient. He held a teaching position in Perugia for a number of years starting from 1475 and another position in Zara in Dalmatia in 1481. By this time, he had gained recognition as a superior lecturer in mathematics, and in 1482 he received the honour of being called to Rome to serve as a mathematics lecturer. Having traveled extensively and earning the equivalent of a doctorate, Pacioli returned to Perugia in 1486 or 1487 and commenced writing the bulk of the text for the *Summa*. Over the next eight years, Pacioli taught mathematics in Naples, Pisa, Venice and finally Urbino as well as giving public lectures in Rome and Venice. It was in Urbino that he completed the text of the *Summa*, as evidenced by the dedication to the Duke of Urbino.

The last third of Pacioli's life, which followed the publication of the *Summa,* involved more travel, teaching and writing. From 1496 to 1499, Pacioli was a professor of mathematics at Milan, where he held a position in the court of Duke Ludovico Sforza il Moro (Lewis the Moor). It was in Milan that Pacioli met Leonardo da Vinci, who was said to spend evenings "telling stories to ladies of the court and joining in their pastimes and games" (David 1962, p.36). Pacioli and da Vinci become acquainted to the point where da Vinci produced figures for a text that Pacioli was writing on geometry, *De diuina proportione.* D. Smith (1958, v.1, p.254) claims that Pacioli borrowed much of the material for this book from Franceschi. After holding positions in Pisa, Rome, Florence, and Venice, in 1510 he returned to his birthplace to head the Monastery of San Sepulcro. Details of his death are uncertain, but Pacioli was apparently alive in 1523 when the second edition of the *Summa* was published.

Plagiarism

Aside from the reverence given to the *Summa* in accounting, modern opinion on the contribution made by Pacioli with the *Summa* is decidedly negative. Numerous sources express an overt indignation about the degree of plagiarism contained in the text. David (1962, p.37) stated that "Fra Luca was not a great mathematician and his importance lies in the fact that he summarized the mathematical learning that was then common". David observed that the *Liber abaci* is incorporated almost in its entirety. Recognizing material that had been borrowed from Euclid, Ptolemy, Fibonacci and Boethius, among others, D. Smith (1958, v.1, p.252) stated that Pacioli in the *Summa* "borrowed freely from other sources, often without giving the slightest credit". D. Smith also observed that Pacioli was "a careless writer, so much so that Cardano has a chapter devoted to errors in his book" and that his summary of Euclid was "poor". Boyer (1968, p.307) stated that the *Summa* "was more influential than original" and that Pacioli "borrowed freely" from the technical commercial arithmetics and bookkeeping manuals of the time.

There is a sharp contrast between the similar opinions expressed by historians of mathematics and the dissimilar opinions in accounting. For example, Chatfield (1974, p.45) stated that "the *Summa* was unsurpassed for 100 years even by imitators who wrote with Pacioli's text in hand . . . Pacioli was most remarkable for his possession of qualities which are common enough in themselves but are hardly ever found together in the same mind". Green (1930, p.40) was almost apologetic in stating, "There is no evidence that Pacioli laid claim to having originated the method of double entry bookkeeping. He specifically stated that he followed the method which was then utilized in Venice." Green (p.41) was also unambiguous in stating that "The treatise by Pacioli has been the foundation upon which practically all subsequent writings concerning double entry bookkeeping have been predicated." Such strong claims seem to confound accounting theory and accounting practice.

Unlike the uniformly negative opinions of Pacioli derived from mathematicians, there is not complete agreement among accountants. For example, de

Roover (1956, p.178) stated that: "in the fifteenth century, the practice of the counting-house was far ahead of the rather simple system described in the early treatises, including the first and most celebrated one, by . . . Luca Pacioli". Elsewhere, de Roover claimed that much of the bookkeeping material in the *Summa* was "more or less reworked' from a manuscript of another author circulating in the reckoning schools of Venice around that time. While recognizing the importance of the *Summa* in the development of accounting, Brown (1905, p.120) did not agree about the importance of the *Summa* in spreading knowledge of accounting to the masses. Rather, "Pacioli uses no examples, and without the assistance of these the art can hardly be acquired by a novice. Pacioli addresses himself to experts."

Given this, are later references to 'the Italian method' that appear in bookkeeping treatises throughout Europe on preparing accounts necessarily referencing the *Summa*? For example, Malynes (1622, ch.xx) observed: "The manner of keeping accounts by Debitor or Creditor, was first devised in Italy upon very good considerations." Murray (1930, p.180) observed: "Pacioli's treatise was to a large extent theoretical. He laid down rules and showed how they were to be carried out, but gave no examples of actual business transactions." As the '*De computis et scripturis*' is contained in the much larger *Summa*, it seems more likely that printed works aimed at commercial education, dealing exclusively with bookkeeping, and produced in the period following the *Summa* were responsible for the 'heavy lifting' of transmitting the 'Italian method' throughout Europe. Murray (p.179) identified two Italian teachers who provided instruction in bookkeeping and writing—Giovanni Tagliente and Domenico Manzoni—who also produced popular printed books on bookkeeping in 1525 and 1540. Both books had a practical focus and, as such, were better suited to the transmission of accounting concepts. "Manzoni intended that his book should be entirely practical. and sufficient for self instruction, and that it should embrace all the affairs of ordinary life" (p.181). In keeping with the use of separate books for different topics in commercial education, Tagliente also produced a book on writing and Manzoni on commercial arithmetic.

The dating of the Manzoni and Tagliente efforts on bookkeeping can be compared with the first printed texts appearing in Germany. Murray (p.193) identified an arithmetic teacher in Vienna, Heinrich Schreiber, as producing the first printed book in German in 1518, in which bookkeeping is treated in the fifth of six chapters. Further editions of the text were published in 1535, 1544 and 1572. Murray (1930, p.197) observed: "Schreiber's book was written twenty-four years after that of Pacioli, and he may have been acquainted with it, but he borrowed nothing from it, and it rather seems to be an independent production, based upon the current practice of the day." The approach to bookkeeping used by Schreiber was adopted in a text by Johann Gotlieb, a burgess of Nuremberg, a text that was initially printed in 1531 with further editions in 1546 and 1592. It was only with an anonymous bookkeeping treatise published in Nuremberg in 1541 that a German text "largely compiled from those of Pacioli and Manzoni" first appeared (p.201).

C   THE PROGRESS OF COMMERCIAL ARITHMETIC AND ACCOUNTING

Chuquet's *Triparty*

The general scope of the early printed texts on commercial arithmetic and accounting has been sketched. The pedagogical tradition of many commercial arithmetics and bookkeeping texts was distinct from the humanities and classical mathematics that were the core curriculum at the Church schools and universities. Renaissance commercial needs required vernacular texts oriented to explaining the calculations required and to record increasingly complicated commercial transactions. Many of the European commercial arithmetics were similar in form to the *Treviso Arithmetic* and the *Libro de Abacho*. Bookkeeping texts were progressively more like the single-subject efforts of Manzoni than the *Summa* of mathematical knowledge prepared by Pacioli. Texts were written in the vernacular and designed for use by merchants or in reckoning schools; effectively these commercial arithmetics and bookkeeping texts functioned as early business school textbooks. These books did not contribute significantly to theoretical developments in mathematics but, rather, reflected the business practices of the time.

Related to the purely commercial arithmetics were texts that incorporated a commercial arithmetic into a broader mathematical framework. These books were closer to the scholastic tradition that considered arithmetic as one of the arts. A commercial arithmetic was included as part of a text that also dealt with subjects such as geometry, number theory in the tradition of Boethius and algebra. These texts, while less accessible to a merchant audience, do capture the progress in commercial arithmetic. Certain texts, such as Nicolas Chuquet's *Triparty en la science des nombres* (1484), contain significant contributions to other areas of mathematics—algebra, in the case of *Triparty*. By implication, such texts are also relevant to issues at hand if the quality of the author signals that the commercial arithmetic contained in these works was likely the best available at that time.

Compared to Pacioli, almost nothing is known about Nicolas Chuquet (1440?–1500). The date and place of his birth are unknown, though it is possible he was born in Paris. Information from tax registers indicates that he started working in Lyons, France, in 1480 as an *escripvain*, literally a copyist or writing master. Lyons at this time was an important commercial centre. It was also a banking centre and was developing a printing industry. In this environment, an *escripvain* performed the role of copying various commercial and legal documents. In this capacity, it is likely that Chuquet came into frequent contact with the sizeable Italian community of Lyons, members of which were actively involved in economic affairs.

In addition to requiring such *escripvains* for the writing and witnessing of contracts, Lyons was a place where the math skills of an advanced reckoning master would be in demand. By 1485, the tax registers of Lyons listed Chuquet as an algorist, indicating that his mathematical skill had been recognized and he had progressed to where he was working as a reckoning master. The quality of mathematics contained in *Triparty* clearly indicate that mathematical skill and advanced knowledge of mathematics in general and commercial arithmetic in particular had spread well beyond the confines of Italy by the time that mass produced printed texts first appeared. We can only guess as to the sources that influenced Chuquet. It is possible that he visited Italy, and there is strong evidence that he was familiar with important Italian mathematical texts of the time.

The immediate impact of Nicolas Chuquet's *Triparty* on the development of commercial arithmetic is difficult to assess. Because the handwritten manuscript was not published until Aristide Marre resurrected it in 1880 (Flegg et al. 1985), it is unlikely that *Triparty* had any direct influence. Writing outside Italy, Chuquet had little apparent influence on the study of commercial arithmetic in Italy, which was the centre of reckoning school education at that time. Modern mathematical opinion maintains that the bulk of the commercial arithmetic contained in *Triparty* was "fairly conventional" (Flegg et al. 1985, p.24); however, *Triparty* is important for its explicit recognition and treatment of compound interest and for the use of the 'rule of first terms' in dealing with interest calculations (Benoit 1988). In the history of mathematics, *Triparty* is recognized for important insights in algebra, with the proviso that the text on algebra was so advanced for its time that it was neglected. As a reckoning master, Chuquet certainly passed on his insights to his students, and it was through this avenue that his impact was made.

Though there are few references to Chuquet's work by 16th-century mathematicians, substantial portions of his *Triparty* manuscript were incorporated wholesale into the 1520 publication, *Larismethique nouellement composee*, of Estienne de la Roche, probably a former student of Chuquet. As a contribution to algebra, Marre considered *Larismethique* to be "vastly inferior" to *Triparty*, though much of Chuquet's contribution to algebra can be ascertained from this printed text. *Larismethique* did have an impact as a commercial arithmetic. According to D. Smith (1958, v.1, p.313): "Perhaps no other French arithmetic of the 16th century gives a better view of the methods of computation and commercial applications of the subject." Even though France was not a leading commercial nation in the 16th century, Lyons was of Continental importance as a commercial and banking centre. To quote de Roover (1949, p.108), around the middle of the 16th century "the principle banking centres in Europe were Antwerp, Lyons, Genoa and the fairs of Castille". The importance of Lyons as a banking centre almost certainly contributed to the emergence of the Lyons school of commercial arithmetic. In addition to Chuquet and de la Roche, the Lyons school included Jacques Peletier (1517–1582) and Jean Trenchant (1525–?). *L'Arithmetique* (1558,1566), published in Lyons by Trenchant, is noteworthy in providing tables needed for compound interest calculations (Lewin 1970).

As the 16th century progressed, social attitudes toward payment of interest slowly evolved, and this was reflected in the commercial arithmetics. In a detailed examination of 14 French commercial arithmetics written during the 16th century, all published in French, Davis (1960, pp.22–4) found 10 explain the method of computing compound interest, with 4 of those criticizing the practice but still providing an explanation to be in accord with regular business practice. The earliest of the texts examined by Davis (1960) was written by two monks—one Spanish and one French—and published in 1515. This text gives an uncritical explanation of compound interest: "Here follows another rule for lending money, by which the profit or interest earns as well as the principal." During the 16th century, numerous contributions to commercial arithmetic appeared throughout Europe. These works were usually written in the native tongue, though works in Latin were still produced. With some refinements, the content of the vernacular texts typically corresponded with what was contained in Borghi, while the Latin texts continued to feature a commercial arithmetic as part of a wider study of arithmetic.

Divergent Paths

During the 16th century, increasing sophistication of commercial ventures found practical printed texts in the vernacular increasingly focusing on either commercial arithmetic or bookkeeping. In Germany, where commerce was active, Jacob Köbel (1470–1533) and Adam Riese (1489–1559) published the first editions of their influential German-language commercial arithmetics in 1514 and 1518. Köbel's most influential arithmetic, *Rechenbiechlin*, went into 22 editions during the 16th century, while Riese's book has been characterized as "one of the most popular textbooks of the century", consistent with the view that Riese was the "greatest of all the *Rechenmeisters*" of the century (D. Smith 1958, v.1, p.337). German commercial arithmetic of this period was concerned with progressing from the older abacus methods, based on counters and Roman numerals, to written calculation using pen and Hindu-Arabic numerals. Riese is recognized as the most influential writer in this movement. As a mathematician, he also made contributions to algebra. While Heinrich Schreiber and Johanes Gotlieb also referred to themselves as '*Rechenmeisters*', this reference obscures the increasing specialization of function in commercial education.

Compared to Germany, England was less commercially developed at this time, and this is reflected in the development of commercial arithmetic. The first substantive English contribution to commercial arithmetic in the century appeared in Latin in 1522 by Cuthbert Tonstall, a non-mathematician remembered more for his diplomatic and ecclesiastical contributions. This work lacked originality but was useful in summarizing the approach used in the Italian commercial arithmetics. Tonstall undoubtedly acquired the relevant background during his time spent at Padua while acquiring his doctor of laws. In any event, Tonstall's work is more of historical interest. Being a Latin text, the book lacked popularity as a commercial arithmetic.

The first English-language commercial arithmetic with any influence was Robert Recorde's (1510–1558) *The Ground of Artes* (1542), which covers both abacus and Hindu-Arabic calculation methods. This book went into 18 editions by the end of the century, with a further 11 editions in the 17th century. Unlike Tonstall, Recorde was a mathematician, arguably "just about the only mathematician of any stature in England throughout the [16th] century" (Boyer 1968, p.317). In addition to his popular commercial arithmetic, Recorde is recognized by historians of mathematics for making contributions to both astronomy and geometry.

The only other popular English commercial arithmetic to appear during the 16th century was *The Well Spring of Sciences* (1562) by Humphrey Baker. Much as with Borghi, little is known of Baker. We know that he was a Londoner and that he died after 1587. Judging from the contents of his book, it is likely that Baker was an English reckoning master reproducing material used in his daily work and, possibly, his reckoning school classes. The book borrows liberally from Recorde and follows the approach of using a combination of abacus and Hindu-Arabic approaches. One clue as to the motivation for the book is contained in the author's preface, which indicates that the book "was written to meet the criticism of continental scholars on the backward state of [commercial arithmetic] in England" (D. Smith 1958, v.1, p.321).

In contrast to the uptake of Recorde's influential commercial arithmetic, the appearance of printed accounting texts in English was slow. "The earliest English writer on book-keeping was Hugh Oldcastle, schoolmaster in Mark Lane, London, who published, apparently anonymously" a text in 1543. Oldcastle's contribution is significant, as it "formed the foundation of an enlarged work by John Mellis, published in 1588" (Murray 1930, p.219). Mellis explicitly acknowledged a scholarly debt to Oldcastle. Another anonymous work appeared in 1547 that "seems to be an English translation of Ympyn", a reference to a text from 1543 by Jan Ympyn Christoffels, a merchant from Antwerp, who translated an Italian original by Paulo de Biancy. In turn, this text was based on a combination of the bookkeeping section of the *Summa* and the text by Tagliente. The publication in 1553 and 1569 of two works on bookkeeping following the Italian method by James Peele, a "practizer and teacher" of bookkeeping, reflects an enhanced specialization in English commercial education toward the end of the 16th century.

The Low Countries, comprising what is now Belgium, the Netherlands and Luxembourg, have a diverse collection of 16th-century texts on commercial arithmetic and bookkeeping. Consistent with an advanced stage of commercial development that had been achieved in Antwerp and, following the sack of Antwerp in 1576, in Amsterdam and Rotterdam, there were a large number of 'vernacular' commercial arithmetics. As much of the merchant populace was multilingual, printed texts in the vernacular could include a range of French, Italian and German commercial arithmetics and bookkeeping works. In addition to arithmetics emanating from France, some Dutch and Flemish authors elected to publish in French. The list of authors includes Valentin Menher, a reckoning master, whose three or four arithmetics, published in the second half of the century, "occupied the same position in the Netherlands that Borghi's did in Italy and Recorde's did in England" (D. Smith 1958, v.1, p.342).

In addition to works in French, the Low Countries produced arithmetics in Latin, including an important and popular work by Gemma Frisius (1508–1555), the "most influential of the various Dutch mathematicians of [the] century", also known as Gemma Regnier. Frisius is second only to Simon Stevin in importance among 16th-century Low Country mathematicians. Compared to

England, the merchant class in the Low Countries had a firmer grasp of Latin (due to wider religious education), allowing greater accessibility to the *Arithmeticae Practicae Methodus Facilus* (1540). As expected from a mathematician writing in Latin, the book examines both theoretical and commercial topics. The popularity of the arithmetic is evidenced by the 59 editions of the book published in the 16th century, with several more in the 17th century.

As for books in the Dutch vernacular, the first printed commercial arithmetic appeared in 1508, initially printed by Thomas Vander Noot, with an enlarged version appearing in 1510, printed by Willem Vorsterman. Part of the 1508 arithmetic appears in a 1527 printing by Jan Severz. The English translation of the 1508 title, "The way of learning to calculate according to the true art of Algorisms in whole and broken numbers", suggests that the contents are a commercial arithmetic. The 1510 version is enlarged to include a section on the abacus arithmetic topic of reckoning with counters. Only two other Dutch

Figure 4.5   Simon Stevin (1548–1620), Flemish mathematician"

arithmetics are known to have been printed in the first half of the 16th century: an untitled 1532 printing by Christianus van Varenbraken, also a commercial arithmetic, and a 1537 arithmetic by Gielis Vanden Hoecke, 'On the Noble Art of Arithmetic'. Little is known about either of the authors (Kool 1988).

Nearing the end of the 16th century, the most important contributions to both commercial arithmetic and bookkeeping originating from the Low Countries were from Simon Stevin. Important sources are found in Flemish, Latin and French. For example, an important commercial arithmetic was contained in a section of an arithmetic published originally in Flemish and republished in the same year in French. The historical importance of *La Pratique d'Arithmetique* (1585) as a commercial arithmetic is due at least as much to the reputation of its author, Simon Stevin, as to the contents of the text. However, the commercial arithmetic is only one part of a larger text that is devoted primarily to theoretical arithmetic. The contribution of the other parts of the arithmetic, in particular to the development of decimal fractions, is more noteworthy. Of particular historical importance, the topic of interest calculations is given a long chapter, "with excellent tables for facilitating its calculation" (Murray 1930, p.215).

Simon Stevin and Leiden

Simon Stevin (1548–1620) was born in Bruges and, at a young age, was placed in a merchant's office in Antwerp. Stevin probably gained a useful exposure to commercial practice during the brief period he was in this position, following which he travelled extensively to countries such as Prussia, Poland and Norway. Upon his return, Stevin embarked on a successful public service career that was to include such positions as Surveyor of Taxes at Bruges, Inspector of the Dikes, Quartermaster General of the Dutch army and Chief Inspector of Public Works. Stevin provides an excellent example of the Dutch practice of inducing individuals with the strongest intellectual abilities into careers in public service. Jan de Witt and Jan Hudde provide other 17th-century examples of this practice (e.g., Poitras 2000, ch.6).

Stevin is, perhaps, most legitimately remembered for his contributions to engineering mathematics, especially in the fields of hydrostatics and dynamics. He is also credited with inventing a practical canal lock and a sail-carriage and writing an important treatise on fortification. In theoretical mathematics, he is recognized for making substantive contributions to the development of symbolic algebra, such as being the first systematic user of decimal fractions and in extending this notion to fractional powers. In physics, Stevin produced a 1586 report, in Flemish, describing an experiment where two spheres of lead, one sphere ten times the weight of the other, were dropped from a height of 30 feet. Stevin's observation that the sounds of the spheres striking the ground appeared to be simultaneous predates a similar observation by Galileo.

Stevin had the personal misfortune of having to live during a period of hostilities between the Catholic Spanish crown and the Protestant Dutch Republic. In this dispute, Stevin took a public position squarely in line with the Protestant party of Mauritz, the Prince of Orange and, for a time, Stevin acted as tutor to the prince. One of Stevin's significant academic contributions was to write up the course of instruction that he gave to the prince. The result was the *Hypomnemata Mathematica* (1605, 1608) ('Mathematical Traditions'), a work in two volumes, with the Latin edition of the second volume being written by Stevin and published in 1605 and the first Latin volume being published in 1608 (being a translation into Latin by Willebrond Snellius, a professor of mathematics at Leiden, from an original Flemish text by Stevin). This translation of *Hypomnemata Mathematica* contains *De Apologistica Principum ratiocinio Italico*, "by far the most important work on bookkeeping published in the Netherlands, at this period" (Murray 1930, p.212).

The text of the *Hypomnemata Mathematica* was constructed primarily to provide an overview of mathematics. However, in Part II of the second volume, Stevin produced *De Apologistica Principum Ratocino Italico,* which roughly translates as 'Account-keeping for Princes after the Italian manner'. This treatise has been recognized as a key contribution to the history of double-entry bookkeeping, albeit not wholly successful in its application of double-entry to public accounts. To quote Brown (1905, p.136):

> At the close of the sixteenth and the commencement of the 17th century there stands a figure that fitly represents the transition from the old order to the new in book-keeping. Simon Stevin ranks with Pacioli in this respect that he is a man of general learning who has not thought it beneath his dignity to compose a treatise on book-keeping.

As Holland was to be the 'training school' of many English merchants, the impact of the accounting standards established by Stevin extends far beyond the time and place of his writings.

Judging from the substance of his contributions, it is not difficult to recognize that Stevin was oriented to practical applications of mathematics. He saw little value in studies concerned with the more speculative and theoretical aspects of mathematics. This approach was not novel to Stevin but was representative of a school of thought associated with Petrus Ramus, who advanced the view that much of what was taught in universities was overly complicated, too abstract and too theoretical. Intellectual study had to be focused on concrete, simple and practically oriented problems. For the study of mathematics, this meant that mathematical methods should focus on solving the problems of navigators, merchants, engineers and surveyors (Van Berkel 1988, p.157). This was clearly the orientation that Stevin chose as the focus for his mathematical contributions.

Needless to say, Ramism was unpopular among the humanist leaders who dominated the university system of Stevin's era. These leaders were comfortable with "the social and intellectual barriers between the theoretical science inside the university and the practical arts outside" (p.158). Circa 1600, the humanist-dominated university leadership typically judged mathematics with the contempt that was associated with the crafts. Yet, there was a pressing need for solutions to various mathematical problems that arose in military, engineering and commercial situations. This inherent social demand created a strong foundation for the spread of Ramism among progressive academics. An interesting connection between a major proponent of Ramism and the practical social need for mathematical training arose with the creation of the Dutch Mathematical School at Leiden in 1600. By the mid-17th century, this institution played a key role in developing future Dutch leaders.

The Dutch Mathematical School was initially designed as a school for military engineers. Because it was founded by Mauritz, the Prince of Orange, it is not surprising that Simon Stevin was chosen to design the curriculum and draw up the statutes for the new school. The school was to be affiliated with but not part of the University of Leiden. The affiliation was physical, with the school being housed in a university building. Members of the school were permitted access to the university library. Faced with the creation of the Dutch Mathematical School, the directors of the University of Leiden were obliged to legitimize the role of practical mathematics in the university curriculum and to give adequate recognition to faculty teaching practical mathematics, such as the overt Ramist Rudolf Snellius. As such, the creation of the Dutch Mathematical School marks the beginning of a mathematical tradition that was soon to include Frans van Schooten (1615–1660) and his students Christian Huygens, Jan de Witt and Jan Hudde.

Among all these scholarly and practical achievements, Stevin took time to prepare in Flemish the little-known *Verrechning van Domeine* in 1604, which provides "ingenious devices" associated with internal control. Recognizing that Stevin began his career "as a book-keeper and cashier in Antwerp", it is not surprising to find Stevin advising Prince Mauritz on the application of mercantile bookkeeping principles to the management of state accounts. Emphasis on the importance of double-entry bookkeeping in historical accounts ignores the practical need for internal control and audit. In the context of military administration, Lee (1971, p.157) identified three devices from the 1604 text:

> (1) Payrolls should be sent direct to the auditors for immediate verification by them. (2) The cook should report independently to the auditors on the number of meals served by him to the troops; Stevin advocated the use of a budgeted cost per meal to ensure no fraud or error was occurring in the cookhouse. (3) Arrears of rent should be reported monthly to the general treasurer for suitable action . . . Stevin was the first advocate of control accounts for debtors, creditors, etc.

In effect, Stevin recognized that actual management of increasingly complex commercial organization could not rely on double-entry and external auditors alone. The human element required equally sophisticated methods of internal audit and control.

The Ready Reckoner

Simon Stevin's contributions mark a crossroads in the development of accounting and commercial arithmetic. By the early 17th century, the leading mathematical theorists had progressed markedly beyond the elementary concerns of practical commercial arithmetic, the keeping of accounts and the teaching of writing. The era of Descartes, Fermat, Pascal, Leibnitz, Halley and Newton was about to begin. Reckoning masters were no longer cutting-edge mathematicians. To be sure, with the emergence of probability theory in the late 17th century, mathematicians were drawn back to specific commercial problems, such as the pricing of aleatory contracts. However, after Stevin, those making substantive contributions in commercial arithmetic were no longer those responsible for making path-breaking contributions to mathematics. During the 17th century, progress in commercial arithmetic was largely in form, such as the adoption of decimal notation. By the end of the 17th century, the subject of commercial arithmetic was not much different than that in use in the mid-20th century (D. Smith 1958, v.1, p.444).

As the extent and sophistication of mercantile activity increased, specialization of function emerged. By the late 16th and early 17th centuries, the major commercial centres appear to have had individuals specializing in compound interest calculations. In London, one such individual was Richard Witt, author of *Arithmeticall Questions* (1613). The full title of the text reveals its contents: "Arithmeticall Questions, touching The Buying or Exchange of Annuities; Taking of Leases for Fines, or yearly Rent; Purchase of Fee-Simples; Dealing for present or future Possessions; and other Bargaines and Accounts, wherein allowance for disbursing or forebearance of money is intended; Briefly resolved, by means of certain Breviats." The term 'breviats' is synonymous with 'tables'. The material contained in the book is so difficult that it would not have been practical to use as a text at a commercial academy. Hence, it would appear that Witt was an early 17th-century version of an actuary, conveying his specialized knowledge to his peers.

Other than the reference on the title page to 'R.W. of London, practitioner in the Arte of Numbers', little is known about Richard Witt. The introduction to the second edition of *Arithmeticall Questions* (1634), produced by Thomas Fisher, provides the information that Richard Witt was dead in 1634 and that 'the Book almost forgot and out of use'. Murray (1930, pp.296–8) considered the book to be a 'ready reckoner', "a book of completed calculations of various kinds, generally a Table of Products . . . in use in shops and counting-houses, and commercial establishments of all kinds". As the book does contain much more in the way of explanation and worked problems, this characterization reflects the level of commercial sophistication achieved by English commerce by the middle of the 17th century. Lewin (1970, p.130) captured this view, claiming that Witt "was probably the first to produce a practical text-book on the subject [of compound interest], with an extensive range of tables which readers could apply to their own problems". The inclusion of numerous worked problems supports the use of the book in commercial education.

Murray's classification of the *Arithmeticall Questions* as a ready reckoner is also used to characterize other English works of that time that provided interest tables as part of a more extensive discussion of other matters, such as Thomas Clay's *Chronological discourse of the well ordering, disposing and governing of an honourable estate or revenue . . . together with certain Briefe, easie and necessary Tables of Interest and Rents forborne; and also the Valuation of Leases* (1618, with further editions in 1619 and 1624). Clay also produced *The Treasurers Almanacke, or the Money Master* (1624, 2nd ed.), which also contained interest tables. Throughout the 17th century, various other sources appeared in England and other countries that contained detailed compound or simple interest tables, such as William Purser's *Compound Interest and Annuities* (1634), Johan Coutreels' *L'arithmetique de Jean Coutreels d'Anvers* (1626) and William Leybourn's *A Platform for Purchasers, a Guide for Builders, a Mate for Measurers* (1685).

William Leybourn (1626–1700), a printer who went on to become a teacher of mathematics, is credited with producing the original 'work which is the foundation of the Ready Reckoner of to-day; the author had a fancy for outlandish names and styled his book *Panarothmologia* and published it in London in 1693' (Murray 1930, p.300). Leybourn's book proved to be popular, in some cases even indispensable, and went into numerous editions, the last being in 1808. The term 'Ready Reckoner' is due to Daniel Fenning, an English schoolmaster, who published *The Ready Reckoner, or Traders' most useful Assistant* (1757), a book that went into numerous further editions. The term 'ready reckoner' appears in the title of numerous subsequent books. The title was so popular that it replaced the obscure *Panarothmologia* in the later editions of that book. Fenning produced numerous schoolbooks in his time, including *The Schoolmasters' most useful Companion* (1765), which has a section on bookkeeping.

NOTE

1 In addition to the section on bookkeeping, the *Summa* has been recognized for a minor contribution to the history of statistics. There is one example from the *Summa*, concerned with dividing the stakes from a game of chance that terminates prior to completion, that captures the essence of the 'problem of points', a topic of fundamental importance in the history of statistics (e.g., David 1962, p.37): 'A and B are playing a fair game of *balla*. They agree to continue until one has won six rounds. The game actually stops when A has won five and B three. How should the stakes be divided?' Unfortunately, Pacioli's solution provided to the stated 'problem of points' is incorrect (5:3 instead of the correct solution of 7:1), which substantively undermines his importance in that subject. It is unlikely that Pacioli recognized the probabilistic implications of the problem.

5 Characteristics of Early Joint-Stock Companies

> Behold, then, the true form and worth of forraign trade, which is, the great revenue of the king, the honor of the kingdom, the noble profession of the merchant, the school of our arts, the supply of our wants, the employment of our poor, the improvement of our lands, the nurcery of our mariners, the walls of our kingdom, the means of our treasure, the sinnews of our wars, the terror of our enemies.
>
> Thomas Mun, *England's Treasure by Forraign Trade*
> (London, 1669)

A *COMMENDA, COMPAGNIA* AND THE SEA LOAN

Details of Contract Choice

The financing of long-distance trade is an essential part of the early history of the joint-stock form of equity capital organization. Starting in the 15th century, long-distance seaborne trade provided conditions needed for the formation of significant early instances in which equity capital was organized as 'joint stock'. This method of organizing equity capital evolved somewhat haphazardly from partnership arrangements such as the *commenda*. The earliest joint-stock ventures were little more than large co-partnerships with some agreeable method of managing the venture and determining the method of sharing profit or loss. The risks to equity capital and the amount of financing needed to fund commercial ventures during the age of European colonization provided essential conditions for the formation of early joint-stock companies. Corporate charters, traded shares and other features evolved gradually to meet the sometimes conflicting needs of monarchs and merchants. Modern scholarship has given little attention to the role of equity capital in the political and, especially, the social role of equity capitalists during the period. In particular, the pursuit of profit guided much of the human trafficking that underpinned the profitability of long-distance seaborne trade from the 15th to the 18th century.

The basic organization of financing for long-distance trade had passive investors providing goods or money to facilitate the trade, while active 'partners' transported and sold the goods abroad, usually also procuring items for the return trip. Due to the significant risk to principal, traditional methods of debt financing were usually not practical. Passive investors providing equity financing were typically not present when goods were being transported and sold, making it difficult to determine the amount of profit generated. Certain features of the traditional partnership method of organizing equity capital financing created difficulties, especially sharing of liability and determining the amount of profit to be shared. As a consequence, financing of long-distance trade both before and after the emergence of joint-stock companies employed contracting methods that were tailored to the specifics of the commercial context. Modern references to 'sea loans', 'trans-marine loans' and 'bottomry loans' often inappropriately identify such contracts as debt financing, when the essence of the commercial context has key features of a partnership between the passive investor and the traveling 'partner' (e.g., Gonzalez de Lara 2002).

"A contract in which one party invested his labor and the other invested his capital was an eminently practical means of financing commerce" (Pryor 1977, p.5). The use of such contracts is ancient (e.g., Perdicas 1939). At a given point in time, the commercial fundamentals determining the contractual arrangement used in long-distance trade depended on: (a) details of the parties involved in the contracts; (b) the difficulties of the voyage and risk of losing cargo; (c) the ownership and type of transport vehicle—for example, ship or caravan; (d) the location and medium used to effect delivery—for example, payment in goods or silver; (e) the amount and type of collateral, if any, pledged to ensure return of principal; (f) the risk of commercial losses trading and purchasing goods; and (g) the maximum profit that could be earned. In addition, there may be social and political considerations in contract choice, such as civil and canon law restrictions on the payment of interest. At any time and place, a variety of contract types could be in use. For example, both the *commenda* and the sea loan were in used in Genoa and Venice at the time of the Crusades. In addition, contracts could be and were written to avoid the appearance of usury. The practice of settlement in a foreign location using foreign monetary units was often used for this purpose.

Given this, the 'rational' passive investor in a sea loan considered the temporal relationship between the promised 'interest' on the 'loan' (adjusted for the risk of loss from 'acts of God or pirates') and the more certain 'interest' on a local commercial loan. Making reference to modern bottomry loans, the return on the sea loan was conventionally decomposed into 'interest' plus an 'insurance premium' to compensate for the risk of loss during transport. In contrast, the 'rational' passive investor in a *commenda* compared the typical profit on an equity capital investment in an on-shore partnership with that from a long-distance trading venture. Each of these had distinct liability implications for the passive investor. In the sea loan, the investor had risk during transport but did not bear the commercial risk of selling and buying the goods during the venture. In a *commenda*, this additional risk was assumed in exchange for a fixed share of profits. This arrangement raised substantive accounting issues associated with determining actual revenue and expenses. As such, the emergence of long-distance trade during the Middle Ages is an important historical waypoint in the evolution of modern accounting systems that are essential to the management and control of limited liability corporations.

How could the passive investor manage the difficulties of monitoring both expenses and revenues from a long-distance trading venture? Greif (2012, p.445) and followers sought an answer in "bilateral agency relations based on a credible threat of losing future profitable relations in the traders' broader community" for the Maghribi traders and "legal enforcement and a bilateral reputation mechanism [that] were particularly important among the Genoese". Gonzalez de Lara (2001, 2008) extended this approach to identify Venetian commercial success during this period with "public-order, reputation-based" institutions that contrast with the "combined public coercion with private reputation" institutions in Genoa. This abstract argument is used to explain the evolution in use from the sea loan to the *commenda* in Venice from the 11th to the 14th century. Such hyper-modern explanations implicitly assume the depersonalization of markets that proponents claim the contracting mechanisms facilitated. Legal contract form is taken at face value, and essential elements of commercial, political and social context are inadequately recognized.

Despite the presence of "thousands of partnership agreements in the extant cartularies of medieval Genoese notaries . . . we know little about the way in which these partnerships actually carried on their business" (de Roover 1941, p.87). This begs obvious, if unrecognized, questions: Why have almost no accounting records survived from this period, while volumes of notarial records have survived? Does this imply that the commercial and social context permitted only rudimentary accounting methods to be used or that the method of recording and retaining accounting records prevented these records from being preserved? What role did the *ius fraternitatis,* an essential feature of the Roman *societas*, play in contract choice and in the methods of payment and settlement used in the contract? What role was played by social monitoring in the off-shore quarters for foreign merchants that were essential to the execution of long-distance trade? Was contract choice influenced by the level and change in risk of the commercial venture, such as following the destruction of the Italian quarter in Constantinople in 1082 (Fotheringham 1910)?

Regarding 'depersonalization' and contract choice, it is difficult for modern observers—even those steeped in medieval and Renaissance history—to escape the 'individualized' mindset. Kinship, plus an almost filial attachment to the city state and a pious dedication to Christianity, underpinned the spirit of *ius fraternitatis* that circumvented the need for detailed accounting. In addition, there was a "moral community" among Christians that, while changing over time and place, provided for 'rules of conduct' between different political jurisdictions (Nader 2002, p.402). Given this, the historical record of commercial activities during the medieval and Renaissance periods is informed by notarial protests, giving the appearance to modern observers of the need for contract enforcement mechanisms when, it seems, almost all contracts were successfully executed and completed on the basis of honour and trust. Strong conclusions based on the form of contract, such as sea loan versus *commenda,* generally ignore the possibility that the form of the contract could be disguising the commercial context. The well-documented evidence of various machinations used by medieval and Renaissance merchants to avoid the sanction of usury suggest that disguised motivations may also have impacted contract design and selection in long-distance trade.

To illustrate issues surrounding disguised motivations in contract design, consider a sea loan. This contract typically had a fixed 'interest' payment, giving the appearance of a conventional loan. However, the amount of this fixed 'interest' payment may not have been related to a commercial loan but, rather, have been with reference to the expected 'profit' from an equity capital share (not the insurance premium plus interest on a commercial loan). Such a method of setting a return to equity capital is one feasible method of dealing with the difficulties of rudimentary accounting used to determine the *ex post* division of profit at the completion of the venture. The use of 'expected profit' to determine the 'fixed' return on a 'sea loan' involves a sharing of the commercial risk beyond the risk of loss at sea. Such an *ex ante* method of determining partnership shares provides incentives to the travelling partner to do better than expected in the sale and purchase of goods off-shore. Hence, the formal presence of a fixed return on 'sea loan' may be based on 'expected profit', not 'interest'.

Hoover (1926, p.505) reported late 12th-century interest rates on sea loans in Genoa:

> The interest rate to Syria was usually about fifty per cent. To Sicily the rate was customarily between twenty-five and thirty per cent, to North Africa from twenty to thirty per cent, and to Sardinia or Corsica from ten to twenty per cent, with a similar rate to the sea towns of southern France and the small Italian ports near Genoa.

Absent information about the *commenda* profit rate for similar voyages, appropriately adjusted for instances of 'God and piracy', it is difficult to determine whether these 'interest rates' are estimates of the actual return on *commenda* 'shares' after appropriate adjustment for the expenses of the travelling partner. As medieval markets became more 'impersonal' with the growth of seaborne commercial ventures, such contracts would eliminate problems of over-reporting expenses and under-reporting revenues by the travelling 'partner'. Alternatively, sea loans in which commercial risks were comparatively low, such as voyages to southern France or Sardinia, could be used as a contractual vehicle to evade usury restrictions. It is difficult to make definitive statements about the use of debt or equity capital financing based on the surviving notarial records of partnership contracts.

The *Commenda* Contract

The revival of Mediterranean and European trade coincident with the First Crusade (1095–1099) witnessed the 'appearance' of the *commenda* contract in the maritime Italian city states: Venice, Amalfi, Pisa and, especially, Genoa. Prior to this time, there is limited availability of primary sources with detail about the contracts used in organizing European long-distance trade. Given the erratic commercial environment of the Dark Ages, this is unsurprising. However, despite the situation in Europe, substantial commercial trade continued in the Islamic Mediterranean, across the Indian Ocean and in some parts of the traditional silk routes to the East. Building on the work of Goitein, Udovitch and others, supplemented with interpretations of Islamic and Jewish legal and religious texts, there is information about the organization of equity capital in the regions where merchants of the Italian city states came to access the riches of trading with the East. These sources reveal close similarities between the *commenda* and contracts used in the long-distance trade of the Muslims (*qirād*), the Byzantines (*chreokoinōnia*) and the Jews (*'isqa*). However, it difficult to escape the conclusion that contractual developments in the Italian maritime city states were also heavily influenced by the Roman *societas* (e.g., Pryor 1977).

The earlier availability of Genoese notarial records has established a case for selection of Genoa over Venice and other Italian city states for the lead in commercial innovation during this period. At one level, this reveals the impact of a subtle difference in social context identified by Byrne (1916, p.129):

> The Venetian merchants, members of a political unit of superior organization, were forced by their political concept to subordinate their individual enterprises to the good of the republic. The Genoese merchants, members of a commune continually torn by factions as was no other Italian city in the Middle Ages, politically inapt, were by this very defect enabled to pursue their individual courses more freely. The result was apparently a higher development not only of individual enterprise, but of a collective superiority in the technique of trade, in the formation of commercial organizations in the twelfth century, in the establishment of shares in the public debt of the thirteenth, in the double entry book-keeping of the fourteenth, in insurance and banking in the formation of joint-stock-companies.

Modern interest in the *commenda* to finance trade from Genoa and other Italian maritime states is influenced by the survival of detailed notarial records from the 12th century. Following scholarly examination of the Cairo Geniza by Udovitch (1970) and Goitein (1955, 1960, 1964), considerable, if misplaced, effort has been dedicated to establishing religious influences on the origins of the *commenda* (e.g., Ackerman-Lieberman 2011; Cohen 2013).

The nomenclature used to describe the contract in notarial and other records differed within and across locales. Given this, the general structure of the *commenda* was described by Pryor (1977, pp.6–7) as follows:

1 A sedentary investor, generally known as a *commendator*, delivered capital into the possession of a travelling associate, generally known as a *tractator*.
2 The *tractator* might or might not add capital of his own to that of the *commendator*. If he did not, the contract is referred to by modern historians as a unilateral *commenda* since the capital was supplied by one party only. If he did invest some additional capital, it was usually a half of that contributed by the *commendator* and modern historians refer to the contract as a bilateral *commenda* since both parties supplied capital.

The following conditions usually applied:

3 The *commendator* might give certain directions concerning the management of the enterprise to be undertaken by the *tractator*.
4 The *tractator* took the capital away with him, generally overseas, and put it to work in some way.
5 On expiration of the time or voyages specified in the agreement made between the parties, the *tractator* returned to the home port to render account and divide the proceeds with the *commendator*. Under certain circumstances, or by agreement with the *commendator*, the *tractator* could remit the proceeds without returning to the home port himself.
6 After allowing for expenses incurred and deducting the capital originally contributed by either or both parties, profit or loss was divided according to a ratio agreed upon in the original contract. Generally, and in the archetypal case, in a unilateral *commenda* the *commendator* received 3/4 of any profit and bore all liability for loss while the *tractator* received 1/4 of any profit and bore no liability for loss of capital. He lost the value of his labor of course. In a bilateral *commenda* any profit was usually divided 1/2–1/2 while the *commendator* bore 2/3 of any loss and the *tractator* 1/3.

Pryor was careful to observe (p.7): "This is the archetypal division of profit and loss for both forms of the *commenda* as found in the statutes and most contracts from ports such as Genoa, Venice, Amalfi, Marseilles, and Barcelona. There were, of course, many variations. At Dubrovnik, for example, the 3/4–1/4 division of profit for the unilateral *commenda* was not the rule at all."

Given this background, there was considerable variation across time and location in the nomenclature used in notarys' records, municipal statutes and the like to describe the *commenda* contract. Closer examination of this nomenclature reveals a fascinating cognitive connection between the contractual practices of medieval Italian maritime city states and common commercial terms used in modern times. Pryor revealed the earliest connections (p.13):

Because the *commenda* was a development of the customary law of commerce rather than of juridical science, the earliest extant sources referring to it are notarial acts and municipal statutes. It is first referred to in 976 in its Venetian form of *collegantia* and the first extant notarial act for a *collegantia* contract dates from 1073. Of the municipal statutes referring to *commendae* whose date can be fixed with certainty, the oldest is the Pisan *Constitutum Usus* of 1156.

This is not to say that '*commenda*' was a common term in municipal statutes and notarial records. On the contrary (p.10):

Amongst the municipal statutes, the *Constitutum Usus* of Pisa used *compagnia* for the unilateral *commenda* and *societas* for the bilateral, but only the one generic term *societas* when discussing provisions of the law applying equally to both forms of *commenda*. Venetian legislation used the name *collegantia* [*colegantiam*] and Amalfitan legislation the name *societas maris* for both forms of *commenda*. The statutes of Pera, Genoa, and Marseilles treated *accomendationes* (Marseilles—*commande*) and *societates* together without differentiating between them in any way.

The modern use of *commenda* to refer to this contractual form in English terminology was likely borrowed from French.[1] More significant, the English use of 'company' is descended from the use of *compagnia* in certain Italian city states to refer to one form of a *commenda* contract.

The Municipal Statutes and the *Ius Commune*

In addition to the wealth of notarial records starting from around the middle of the 12th century, the municipal statutes of the Italian city states provide information about the workings of commercial ventures in medieval and Renaissance times. Unfortunately, accurate interpretation of these sources requires considerable knowledge of the political and legal specifics in each of the Italian city states. For example, Stern (2004, p.209) recognized: "The Venetian [legal] system was unique and can only be properly studied, understood, and evaluated in the context of the systems of the city-states surrounding it." In particular, unlike other Italian city states, Venice did not follow the *ius commune*: "the combination of Roman and canon law that formed the basis of legal principles in Italy, and to some extent all of Europe, from 1100 to 1800". Not applicable to England, where there was a separate 'common law', the *ius commune* served as the 'common law' in countries that subsequently became civil law countries, such as France and Germany. Rather, "Venice avoided the adoption of *ius commune* . . . in order to fashion law to its own purposes, both in the lack of adoption of Roman law and in the adoption of a system partially grounded in discretion" (p.210).

In medieval and Renaissance Venice, the aristocracy controlled the courts and the legal process. The policing and administrative bodies were staffed by nobility. For purposes of interpreting the municipal statutes, this is significant because of the composition of the Venetian aristocracy (p.211):

> The aristocracy in Venice was formed from the union of the nobility involved in the Byzantine government and the *Exarchate*, and the long-distance, wealthy merchants who often traded with Byzantium. These two groups had everything in common and coagulated into a political group (or class) that could carry forward its agenda. Venetians had no feudal aristocracy to split the upper class, they were not reliant on their guild system, rather on international trade.

As a consequence, the interests of Venetian merchants who were involved in long-distance trade, especially with the Byzantine Empire, would almost certainly be addressed in the municipal statutes of Venice, providing insight into the commercial context surrounding the use of *commenda* contracts. However, the statutes are not a completely satisfactory primary source, for a number of reasons. One reason has to do with timing. As the opening lines of the statutes indicate, the statutes of Venice (*Usus Venetorum*) were the beginnings of a formalization of Venetian customs and law: *Incipiunt usus Venetorum; similiter et leges costitunt* ("Here begin the Venetian customs; and also here stand the laws"). The *Usus Venetorum* initially appeared in 1204, with amendments and the addition of chapters continuing until 1236. This places the appearance of the Venetian statutes circa the Fourth Crusade.

The statutes of the Venetian commune appeared over a half century into the commune period (1143–1297). There are 74 chapters, haphazardly prepared, dealing with a range of matters, including the boundaries between ecclesiastical and secular jurisdiction, rules of inheritance and the rights of widows and foreigners. Chapter 30 gives primacy to the *colleganza/commenda* contract over Venetian custom in the long-distance trade of the Venetians (Gasparini 2014):

> **30. If somebody shall receive goods from another as a *colleganza*.**
> If someone shall receive goods from another as *colleganza* and shall write a contract, the text of the contract must be abided: and coming to the agreed term, the *debitor* shall give account to the *creditor* of the *colleganza*.

This gives force of Venetian law to the requirement that an accurate accounting be given under the terms agreed upon in the contract. Pryor (1977, p.14) attributed the use of *debitor* and *creditor* to describe the parties to the contract to "the close historical relationship of Venice . . . with Byzantium, the overtones of debt (*chreos*) recognized in the Byzantine *chreokoinonia* may have been inherited in the conception of the *commenda* held at Venice". However, the reference to '*debitor*' and '*creditor*' as parties to the contract may be referencing the accounting process and not characterizing the underlying contract as a 'debt'.

Despite the statute, the difficulty of accurate accounting at settlement was acute enough that an amendment of 1229 was even more explicit (Gasparini 2014):

> **16. About those who received the goods of another in *colleganza*.**
> We declare that from now on it must be observed that anyone who received or held goods in *colleganza* shall give a detailed report to his creditor about how he invested and sold, and how he came to miss [anything] from what he received in *colleganza*. And if the *creditor* shall wish, he [= the *debitor*] shall be bound to corroborate by oath all these things which he shall have reported in detail in Court, except those who suffered a shipwreck or robbery. About those, we want that the ancient custom be followed.

The implication here is that the Venetians did adhere to 'ancient custom' in many aspects of long-distance trade. In 1233, a further amendment was added (Gasparini 2014):

2. About the payment of a *colleganza*.

Moreover we order that, if anyone in front of the judges, according to custom, shall offer a sum of money by reason of a *colleganza*, declaring that he is unable to give a different or better account to his counterpart, it shall be in the discretion of the judges whether he [the counterpart] must accept it or not.

The aim of this amendment was clearly to curb litigation surrounding final contract settlement. Such litigation could arise for various reasons. For example, there is a chapter dedicated to "One who accepts goods from another without witnesses". However, based on previous chapters and amendments in the *Usus Venetorum* on the *colleganza*, poor, sloppy or absent accounting was likely the source of most disputes. In a medieval world where writing was a skill and illiteracy was common, disputes over accounts in long-distance trade seem inevitable.

In contrast to Venice, Florence did have a feudal aristocracy to split the upper class. In addition, Florence was not a maritime state, and the reliance on the wool and other industries gave much greater strength to the medieval guilds. As a consequence, Florence developed methods of equity capital organization distinct from the *commenda* and the 'sea loan'. Contrary to the conventional view that contracts used in long-distance trade were the origin of the joint-stock form of equity capital organization, the extended partnerships of Renaissance Florence possess some essential characteristics of joint-stock companies and, as such, represent a distinct evolution from the ancient partnership arrangements common in long-distance trade. The use of *compagnia* to describe important Florentine trading and banking firms, such as the *Compagnia dei Bardi*, reinforce the later English use of 'company'. Braudel (1982, p.436) observed:

> In the end, the large firms of the inland Italian cities were far more important individually than those of the seaports, where firms were numerous but mostly small and short-lived. Away from the sea, some concentration was necessary. Federigo Melis contrasts the 12 individual enterprises of the Spinola family in Genoa for instance, with the 20 partners and 40 *dipendenti* of the single firm of Cerchi in Florence in about 1250.
>
> These large units were in fact both the means and the consequence of the entry of Lucca, Pistoia, Siena and lastly Florence, to the major currents of trade, where one would not originally have expected to find them. They virtually forced their way in and were excelling in the 'sectors' open to them . . . The *compagnia* was not, in short, an accidental discovery made by the landlocked towns, but a means of action developed as necessity arose.

In addition, the growth of Florentine merchant banking propelled the evolution of double-entry bookkeeping. While there are hints of double-entry in scattered fragments from earlier times, there is ample evidence of double-entry in the vast Medici and Datini archives, which hold "the largest collections of business letters to survive before the sixteenth century" (Padgett and McLean 2011, p.1). The 1427 tax census is another rich source of primary evidence on commercial ventures.

Commercial development in Florence occurred somewhat later than in the important maritime states. As late as 1427, well after the Ciompi revolt of 1378, Renaissance Florence had only 37,246 residents (p.19). Being a follower of the *ius commune,* Roman law was present in the first Florentine statute compilations. However, the first municipal statutes of Florence, The Ordinances of Justice of Florence (1293/1295), had a decidedly more political objective. The title of the first chapter of the ordinances is revealing: "Chapter 1. On the Union, Oath, and Agreement of the Guilds expressed in this Ordinance". While the Venetians were holding the Serrata of 1297, which effectively created a "hereditary oligarchy" (Stern 2004, p.212), the Ordinances of Justice solidified the political control of Florence by the guilds: "An upper merchant class rejected the lawless and private-minded feudal magnates to join instead with the guildsmen of the middle guilds". The result was: "a government in which the upper class merchants along with representatives from other classes ruled and the lawless magnates were excluded for the public good" (p.213).

The explicit public identification and discrimination against the aristocratic 'magnates' contained in the municipal statutes is a reflection of the complex and unique history of Renaissance Florence (e.g., Klapisch-Zuber 1997). Documents from this period provide so much political and social detail that it is difficult to assess the impact of specific historical events on commercial developments. Against this backdrop, there is a "precarious discrepancy . . . between the rich archival sources and the scant historiography" on Florentine commercial ventures (Goldthwaite 2009, pp.409–10). Those searching for connections between politics and commercial innovation have ample grist for the mill. The availability of the Datini and Medici archives starting in the 14th century directs attention to the Ciompi revolt of 1378, which "fused economic, social, and political networks into a new socially open oligarchic-republican elite that remade not only commercial markets but also political factions and kinship."

Of these two archives, the earliest is the almost complete collection provided by Francesco di Marco Datini (1335?–1410) covering 1366–1410, with detailed double-entry (minus the *libri secreti*) after 1390, when Datini undertook a major expansion of his business. After a merchant apprenticeship in Prato, in 1358 Datini moved to Avignon, the seat of papal government at that time, to begin a career as merchant trader (Padgett and McLean 2006, pp.1474–5). The archive indicates Datini was a successful trader of goods and was not involved in the business of banking for the papal authorities that involved some larger Florentine bankers. Datini's decision to leave Avignon for Prato in 1382 and then Florence in 1386 captures the subtle influence of political change on the Renaissance merchant. "When Francesco di Marco decided to move to Florence and establish himself there, his decision was partly due to the fact that the city had just come under the rule of a few powerful families—rich bankers, merchants, and professional men—whose laws he thought likely to be favorable to trade" (Origo 1957, p.78).

Figure 5.1   Map of Tuscany with Florence (*Firenze*) and Prato at the Time of Leonardo da Vinci

Source: http://leonardodavinci.stanford.edu

It is tempting to claim that the equity capital organization Datini employed to deal with the growth of his business after 1390 was seminal, in some sense. This is unlikely. Rather, Datini reflects the methods of management and control that the most successful inland trading merchants and merchant bankers of the Renaissance employed. Padgett and McLean (2006, p.1476) identified the organizational features that Datini employed to construct and control commercial expansion and achieve diversification:

1   legally distinct partnerships with branch managers (or the owner) in each location;
2   separate sets of account books for each branch;

3 diversification of companies into multiple industries;
4 a "holding company" arrangement, in which Datini's Florentine partnership owned parts of other partnerships;
5 centralized oversight of branches through vast numbers of business letters between Datini and his branch partners and through regular meetings between Datini and his branch partners;
6 double-entry bookkeeping in bilateral format; and
7 current accounts both among partnership-system companies and with major trading partners (de Roover 1974, pp.144–9).

Though the archive is less complete, various contributions by de Roover demonstrate a similar organizational structure was employed by the Medici Bank. "The organizational structure of the Datini system scaled up easily to the larger size of the Medici bank." Ultimately, though creative and sophisticated, this 'extended partnership' model retained numerous features of the individual partnership contract and does not provide a direct historical avenue to the emergence of the joint-stock company.

Italian Influence on the Age of Colonization

The progression of equity capital organization for long-distance trading ventures during the 15th and 16th centuries is often obscured in modern sources (e.g., Boardman 2001; Blanc and Desmedt 2014). The most significant ventures during this period originated in the Iberian Peninsula—initially in Portugal then, later, in Spain. This contributes, at least partly, to the limited availability and other difficulties of the primary sources. There was also a complicated and changing political situation in the Italian city states of Genoa and, to a lesser extent, Florence—where the bulk of Italian merchants operating in Spanish trading centers originated—that needs to be integrated with developments in the states of Castile, Aragon and Portugal on the Iberian Peninsula. The historical narrative of the period is often fascinated with details of the great voyages of European discovery and the opening of a sea route from Europe to the Orient. Financial details of these and lesser-known long-distance seaborne trading ventures have emerged slowly, the result of many painstaking contributions by historians working in several different languages; Italian, Spanish and Portuguese documents have yielded sufficient detail to construct the basic character of the equity capital arrangements.

Two essential elements of the early voyages of European discovery, trade and colonization have been understated in the traditional historical narrative: (1) the key role played by equity capital, especially that provided by merchants of Italian origin, in financing the pursuit of profit by merchants and sovereigns; and (2) the reliance on slave trading to achieve profitability for many, but not all, ventures. The most famous of the early voyages, that by Christopher Columbus in 1492, was governed by the *Santa Fé Capitulations*, a partnership contract between Columbus and the Spanish monarchs: "Because all the parties conceived of [the first voyage of Columbus to America] as a commercial venture, the *Santa Fé Capitulations* are mostly devoted to specifying what and how much each partner would invest and how the profits would be divided" (Nader 2002, p.409). The Italian merchants operating in Seville—the Genoese Francesco Pinelli and Giannotto Berardi—loaned funds to Ferdinand II of Aragon and Isabella I of Castile to enable to the Genoese mariner Christopher Columbus to sail in search of a westward sea route to the Orient. Seeking a westward route to the Orient, Columbus optimistically agreed the sovereigns would receive "nine-tenths of the precious goods— specifically pearls, precious stones, gold, silver and spices—brought back from the Indies, and Columbus would receive one tenth" (p.409). When such treasures did not emerge, Columbus resorted to the only feasible source of profit: slave trading.

Because the Church possessed extensive political and economic authority, the moral value of equity capital during this period cannot be ignored (e.g., Nader 2002). Starting in 1500, 'traditional justifications for enslaving conquered people' disguised the role of equity capitalists in pursuing the slave trade in the 'new territories', involving American and Canarian subjects, despite prohibitions by the Church and the Spanish crown. However, the demands of colonization in the Americas and the inability to adapt the local populus to the arduous manual tasks needed to produce cash crops created an irresistible opportunity for slave traders from all the seafaring nations of western Europe during the 16th century. "The royal prohibition began the Spanish struggle for justice"; as a consequence, "Genoese and Florentine merchants resident in Spain were deeply implicated in the Castilian slave trade" (pp.401–2). Though the Portuguese and Spanish crowns jealously guarded their monopoly on such trade with territories in the 'New World'—farming the slaving monopoly to merchants in Iberia not inhibited by moral concerns—the history of this period is replete with instances of seaborne conflict, privateers and pirates associated with French, English and Dutch interlopers in this trade.

It is conventional to start the narrative of the early voyages of European discovery with the capture of Ceuta by the Portuguese in 1415: "it is generally assumed that in Portugal the period of the great discoveries begins with Henry the Navigator, who took the lead after the conquest of Ceuta, in 1415. As for Spain, it is even frequently stated that nothing of importance occurred before the first voyage of Columbus in 1492" (Verlinden 1953, p.203). Various sources demonstrate this narrative is misleading. Italians' pervasive influence in the long-distance seaborne trade from the Iberian Peninsula—starting in the 12th century with the Genoese and the Pisans appearing in Catalonia—needs to be identified. The symbiotic character of Catalan and Genoese interests in long-distance trade was reflected in Sicily (Dauverd 2006, p.46):

> By the time the Aragonese crown acquired Sicily in 1282, both Catalans and Genoese were firmly established in the island . . . Working in tandem, their commercial alliance started in the Middle Ages and continued during the Renaissance. The Genoese-Catalan mercantile entente in the Kingdom of Sicily was both lasting and beneficial because each community needed the other.

Table 5.1 Genoese Trade with African Ports 1155–1164*

	Eastern cities				Western cities			
	Bougia	Tunis	Tripoli	Gabes	Ceuta	Garbo	Saleh	Barbaria
1155		5						
1156	200							
1157	148	234	72					
1158	106	1						
1150	109							
1160	773	60	66		355			
1161	225			88	744			4
1162	41	66			214	16	50	53
1163	409	227			150	296	340	
1164	518		4		220	100		
	2,529	802	142	88	1,683	412	390	57

Total (1155–1159) 875 *lire*

Total (1160–1164) 2,686 *lire*   Total (1160–1164) 2,542 *lire*

Source: Krueger (1933, p.380)

* It is quite impossible to give an accurate account or estimate of this trade. Fragmentary sources missing dates, indefinite statements like *tot, tantum, de rebus* as to amounts, and the omission of destinations cut any estimates of extent and volume down to a minimum. However, in spite of all deficiencies, the sums that do remain have value in themselves in that they show that a trade existed, and a trade that was quite flourishing. These tables shows the relative importance of these cities. The amounts are given in Genoese *lire*.

Table 5.2 Genoese Trade with African Ports 1179–1200

	Western cities					Eastern cities			
	Ceuta	Garbo	Oran	Barbaria	Tlemsen	Bougia	Tunis	Tripoli	Africa
1179	995		33		33	149			
1182	2,255					364	250		
1184	1,357	377				444	222		
1186	2,331	10	5			380	583		
1190		86							
1191	7,250	3,210	430	177		2,544	1,901	466	210
1192	673	330	668			1,191			
1195							110		110
1197	1,731		98			109	26		
1198	1,177	108		62		323	20		
1200	1,703			80		645	20		
	18,472	4,121	1,234	319	33	6,147	3,132	466	320

Total for western cities: 24,179 *lire*;   for eastern cities: 10,165 *lire*

Source: Krueger (1933, p.383).

When the Portuguese arrived in Ceuta in 1415, there was already a well-established Genoese trading presence, a *fondaco*, according to the records of the early Genoese notaries, that stretches back at least to the 12th century (Verlinden 1953, p.205). In turn, the subsequent Portuguese voyages of discovery would not have been possible without considerable previous progress in which the Italians were centrally involved.

Often lost in the historical fascination with the Crusades are the related developments in the western Mediterranean. The Crusades were more than a struggle to recapture the Holy Land; the Crusades were part of a larger conflict between Christian and Muslim spheres for control of territory throughout the Mediterranean and the Levant. In the western Mediterranean, the Genoese played an important role in the conflicts. Moorish control in the Iberian Peninsula commenced in the 8th century. "In 935 the city of Genoa . . . was attacked by a Saracen fleet from Africa, and Genoese churches and buildings were robbed and sacked by Arab bands" (Krueger 1933, p.377). Similar attacks were made on Pisa in the early 11th century. "In 1092 or 1093 the Genoese, aided by the Pisans and Christian princes of Spain, made an unsuccessful attack upon Tortosa [in Spain], then in Saracen hands." This period of hostilities led eventually to a treaty in 1161, initiating a period of peace with Muslim North Africa and allowing Genoese merchants to extend seaborne trading ventures to Morocco (see tables 5.1 and 5.2).

The age of European 'discovery' began inauspiciously when: "In 1162 and 1163, a ship must have passed from the Mediterranean into the Atlantic bound for the district of Garbo and the city of Saleh [Salé]", the capital of the Almohade kingdom (p.381). Such early voyages revealed the difficulties of using large ships designed for Mediterranean trade in the more difficult seafaring environment of the Atlantic. Especially after 1179, trade to Ceuta and beyond increased Genoese knowledge of the trade routes across the Sahara and, most likely, brought Genoese sailors into contact with Muslim and other seafarers who ventured along the African coast beyond Ceuta. As the 12th century progressed, Genoese trade with Ceuta increased in importance beyond that involved in the northern traffic to the medieval fairs. Goods from the Levant, Alexandria and the north were increasingly shipped westward: "Instead of selling . . . Levantine wares to some other African investor, [Genoese traders] sent them to Africa [directly], and so [were] in a position to receive a much larger profit than otherwise". The use of the *societas maris* and *accomendatio* in equity capital financing for this trade is captured in the records of the Genoese notaries.

As revealed in the notarial records, Genoese trade with Northern Africa differed significantly from the more established Levant trade (p.382):

> the African trade and market in the middle of the [12th] century was a business endeavor for the small and average merchant, whose small investments did not present an appreciable total; the unusual commercial privileges and monopolies which the great Genoese families held in the East and which encouraged greater investments and gave larger profits were lacking in the West.

The expansion of Italian seaborne trading routes in the western Mediterranean was not limited to North Africa: "Pisans and Genoese appear in Catalonia at the beginning of the twelfth century. They draw Spain and Portugal into the sphere of the 'international' trade of the time. Everywhere along the shores of the Iberian peninsula they create centers for an activity marked by long-distance maritime trade". When Seville was retaken by Christians in 1248, "Genoa immediately is granted far reaching privileges . . . [The] Genoese *barrio* in Seville during the thirteenth and fourteenth centuries is the foremost center of activity in the Iberian peninsula for the subjects of the Ligurian Republic. A great many Genoese tradesmen are also settled there. The Genoese are even so numerous that they are able to play a part in the conflicts in which Castile is involved and above all in the wars on the sea" (Verlinden 1953, pp.200–1).

If the age of European 'discovery' begins with the first voyages beyond Ceuta into the Atlantic, the age of colonization begins with the 'discovery' of the Canary Islands between 1325 and 1339 by Lanzarotto Malocello, who "was a Genoese acquainted with the Pessagno and had probably traded with them to England". This trade to England was an element in the 14th- and 15th-century Italian convoy ventures that circumvented the land routes for moving goods from Italy to the markets of northern Europe. The connection with the Pessagno reflects the systemic involvement of the Genoese in expansionary activities of the Iberians (p.204):

> In 1317 King Diniz of Portugal had introduced into his country the Geno-ese merchant family of the Pessagno and since then a series of its members held, during nearly two centuries, the highest positions in the Portuguese navy. Such admirals were not only in command of the fleet; they also built ships and were concerned with trade and exploration.

From this point, the age of colonization was systemically related to European monarchs' dependence on the financial, political and military support of merchants driven by the pursuit of profit. The subsequent development of the economic policies identified as 'mercantilism' by Adam Smith and later critics typically fail to recognize these non-economic aspects.

While the equity capital organizations of the long-distance seaborne ventures of the Genoese and other Italian merchants were based on the *societas maris* and *commenda*, the involvement of monarchs in the age of colonization witnessed a change in traditional financing arrangements. With the discovery of the Canary archipelago:

> From this time, Portugal, Castile, and Aragon were interested in the Canary archipelago. It was made a rule to promise feudal concessions to those who intended to discover and take possession of new territory. The same practice had long been a habit in Italian colonial procedure, especially among the Genoese . . . The expeditions to the Canary Islands went on during the whole fourteenth century, and gradually other archipelagos were explored and colonized with the same methods.

In the Canaries, colonization involved "a long-established European tradition that tolerated enslaving non-Christian war captives" (Nader 2002, p.401).

The early Portuguese voyages were financed by the Crown, usually by borrowing and farming state revenues which asserted monopoly rights over trade. Adventurers were servants of the Crown, receiving titles and land grants for services rendered to the Crown. The name of Vasco de Gama still resonates in modern times due to the previous efforts of the little-known Portuguese merchant Fernão Gomes and the Genoese merchant family of the Pessagno (Verlinden 1953, p.204). The opening of the seaborne trade route to the Orient altered the situation in Africa, where Portugal had maintained 'first-mover' status (Williamson 1927, pp.34–5):

> Portugal, her most enterprising leaders pushing on to wealth and power in the East, had reduced her African activities to a system which had become rather stagnant by the middle of the sixteenth century. In the north she conducted the foreign trade of Morocco, but made no pretence to conquest or suzerainty over the Moslem princes of that country. From the Senegal down to the Congo she did claim political jurisdiction over the coast. Her authority was more nominal than real. At Elmira on the Gold Coast, and perhaps at two or three other places, there were fortifications and Portugese garrisons. Elsewhere, in river-mouths and negro settlements offering good trade, there were Portugese factors and a few priests. But in general the occupation was so thin as to be invisible. The Portugese claimed the negro chiefs were Christians and vassals of the crown, yet it is certain from their observed behaviour that the claim was fictitious. More effective was the Portugese exploitation of trade. The commerce of the African conquests was a royal monopoly, shares of which for given places, commodities and times, were farmed to capitalists who paid a fixed sum and made what they could of the bargain. One of the most important of these farms was that of the slave trade. The chief place of sale was in the Spanish colonies of the West, and the Spanish slave-dealers, having no African property of their own, had to obtain their supplies from groups of Portugese undertakers. The Portugese crown maintained this monopoly system with strictness, allowing no African trading to the unprivileged among its own subjects; buts its enforcement against foreigners rested upon the assumption that Portugal had the power as well as the right to debar them.

The ancient practice of farming state revenues to well-connected equity capitalists contributed to 16th-century Portugal's inability to protect its African trade from English, French and Dutch interlopers.

B   THE EMERGENCE OF JOINT-STOCK COMPANIES[2]

What Is a Joint-Stock Company?

The origins of the joint-stock company have been a topic of scholarly debate for decades, if not centuries (e.g., Schmitthoff 1939; Kim 2011; Kryiazis and

Metaxus 2011). The introduction of legislation impacting joint-stock companies in England during the first half of the 19th century stimulated much interest (e.g., Wordsworth 1845). Recognizing that many of the early northern European 'joint-stock' companies of the 16th and 17th centuries originated in long-distance seaborne trade, in which the capital requirements of the venture required a large number of 'partners' to combine equity capital, the search for 'origins' has led some to suggest the equity capital organization used in the long-distance seaborne trade and the banking ventures of medieval and Renaissance Italy. The early Pisan use of *compagnia* to describe a form of the *commenda* suggests such a connection. Others reject such a connection and, where the English case is involved, find: "The development of the joint-stock company in England is characterized by a singular continuity. An unbroken line leads from the guild to the regulated company, and thence to the joint-stock form" (Schmitthoff 1939, p.79).

To trace the evolution of the joint-stock form of equity capital organization, it is helpful to distinguish between several types of joint-stock companies that had appeared in England by the passage of the Joint Stock Companies Act (1844) (Todd 1932, p.49): (i) unincorporated and unregistered; (ii) incorporated by Royal charter; (iii) incorporated by private act of Parliament; (iv) formed using privileges conferred upon by Letters Patent; (v) incorporated by registration under the Companies Act. This list omits joint-stock companies operating under 'provisional agreements' while seeking approval under one of (ii)–(v) but is otherwise in agreement with Wordsworth (1845). Though closely connected, the limited liability feature, introduced in the Limited Liability Act (1855) and by amending the Joint Stock Companies Act (1844/1856), is an additional legal feature that a joint-stock 'company' can possess. In modern times, a joint-stock company incorporated with limited liability by registration is referred to as a 'corporation'. However, in England issues surrounding the creation of incorporated 'joint-stock companies' were debated separately from those of allowing general limited liability as a feature of incorporation (e.g., Bryer 1997).

Given this, any search for the 'origin' of the joint-stock company will, ultimately, be futile. The most that can be done is to identify specific 'joint-stock company' features and to seek a previous historical instance in which a particular feature was observed. The first feature identified by Wordsworth (1845) is the distinction between "private partnerships" and "public companies, where a great number of persons are concerned, and the stock is divided into a great number of shares, the object of the undertaking being of an important nature, and often embracing public as well as private interests or benefits." As Taylor (2006, pp.3–4) observed, the transition from partnerships to joint-stock organization required a fundamental change in social attitudes toward 'public companies':

> [incorporated] companies were not an invention of the nineteenth century. Since medieval times, the state had delegated corporate powers to favoured subjects for public purposes, usually religious, educational or municipal . . . From the sixteenth century, corporate powers began to be extended to profit-making concerns. These were mostly overseas trading

companies, which in addition to the privileges of incorporation, were also granted monopoly trading rights . . . The creation of profit-making corporations with monopolies attracted controversy at an early stage: were these institutions really serving the public interest, or were they the by-product of cash-strapped monarchs selling privileges to the highest bidder?

Prior to the legal legitimacy provided by the Joint Stock Companies Act (1844), justification for the delegation of state powers, either by the monarch or by the legislature, depended on merchants applying for incorporation to "prove that their projects were in the public interest."

Observing that joint-stock companies could be unincorporated and unregistered implies incorporation is not a necessary feature of joint-stock organization. The description by Wordsworth (1845, p.2) is revealing:

> Unincorporated companies and associations differ in no material respect as to their general powers, rights, duties, interests, and responsibilities, from mere private partnerships, except that the business thereof is usually carried on by directors, or trustees, or other officers acting for the proprietors or shareholders, and they usually extend to some enterprise in which the public have an ultimate concern.

Similarly: "in unincorporated companies the shareholders are personally responsible in their individual capacities for all acts of the officers and company, in the same manner and to the same extent as private partners are . . . members of unincorporated partnerships . . . may be answerable for the debts of the firm, to use a recent expression of the Lord Chancellor 'even to their last shilling'."
However, in the period between the Glorious Revolution and the passage of the Bubble Act, the unincorporated joint-stock company did have a method of organization that was assumed to be legal. This method involved using deeds of settlement to create trusts, managed by trustees, holding the property of the shareholders. In this fashion, the 'company' acted through trustees "rather than as a mass of individuals, approximating the corporation's ability to sue and be sued in its own name" (Taylor 2006, p.4). In some cases, the deeds allowed shares to be freely transferred and allowed for limited liability, though this feature was disputable in law.

The rudimentary unincorporated and unregistered joint-stock company was eliminated in England by the Joint Stock Companies Act (1844), which required companies with more than 25 shareholders to register. The act also required "Every partnership with a capital divided into shares, transferable without the express consent of all the co-partners" to register as a corporate joint-stock company. From the perspective of equity capital valuation, this is a profound development: Companies with tradeable shares had to incorporate. The subsequent addition of limited liability to the mix established the framework of equity capital organization needed to sustain modern exchange trading. However, while requiring incorporation, the Joint Stock Companies Act gave those registering new companies scope to choose limited liability.

Medieval Corporations and Other Precursors

Joint-stock companies represented a gradual evolution from the partnerships, medieval corporations (e.g., guilds) and regulated companies that had previously characterized equity capital organization. The early history of joint-stock companies is structured around individual companies with a well-defined public purpose. It was not until the second half of the 17th century when economic and legal changes had progressed to the point where the start of a 'general movement' away from partnership and toward joint-stock organization can be detected. It was not until the second half of the 19th century that the evolution of the joint-stock company into the limited liability corporation with autonomous, exchange traded shares was completed. Though there were some significant continental European developments, such as the early introduction of the Dutch East India and West India Companies in Holland, the thrust of the general movement toward 'commercial capital associations with corporate character and tradeable shares' appears in England following the Glorious Revolution of 1688 (e.g., Macleod 1986; Murphy 2009).

Much of medieval business organization was structured around municipal regulation. For example, the regulation of guilds, taxation of goods, and the production of coinage were largely municipal. Craft industries bound to local markets protected by municipal guild regulation did not require much capital, and the capital that was invested was not subject to much risk. The need for pooling of equity capital was muted. Trading enterprises, particularly those

Figure 5.2 Syndics of the Clothmakers' Guild (1662) by Rembrandt van Rijn (1606–1669) in the *Rijkmuseum*, Amsterdam

involved in long-distance seaborne trade and certain types of mining and metal manufacture, were different. The amount of equity capital required was larger, the risks were often substantial and, in the case of seaborne trade, the equity capital was tied up at least for the duration of the expedition and subsequent sale of goods. A related situation arose in large-scale mining, where there was also a sizeable capital stock required, with attendant risks and a long investment period. It was with these two types of commercial ventures that the first instances of commercial joint-stock ventures arose. However, for cash-starved monarchs of the 16th century, regulated companies sometimes had certain political advantages over joint-stock companies.

Hecksher (1955, v.1, p.392) characterized joint-stock companies as being 'capital associations of a corporate character'. This somewhat obtuse characterization distinguishes the joint-stock company from the partnership, a non-corporative capital association, and from corporate associations either not bound together by capital, such as the guilds, or where the capital was not common, as in the regulated companies. Using Hecksher's definition, the first capital associations of a corporate character arguably did not arise in commercial ventures but, rather, were an outcome of the organization of public credit in the Italian city states, especially Genoa. Two types of such organizations can be identified (e.g., Hecksher 1955, v.1, p.334; Braudel 1982, p.440). One type, the *maone (mahone)*, was associated with groups of individuals combining to outfit a military expedition, in exchange for a share in the profits of the expedition. As colonization was sometimes involved, the *maone* could become involved in colonial administration, as with the island of Chios following colonization successfully undertaken by Giustiniani in 1346, marking a period of 'light' rule by Genoese families lasting until 1566.

The other type of early Italian capital association of a corporate character, the *compere*, arose from organization of state creditors. Braudel (1982, p.440) observed: "The *compere* were state loans, divided in *loca* or *luoghi*, secured against the revenues of the *Dominante*." While less active than the *maone*, these organizations secured control over city state revenue sources in order to ensure the security of payments on debt capital that had been lent to the state. Having control over state credit permitted the *compere* to be a conduit for further lending to the state. In some cases, this financial importance permitted the *compere* to secure special privileges. One important *compera* found in Genoa was the *compere* that, similar to the *maone*, secured the privilege of establishing the famous bank, the *Casa di San Giorgio* (Bank of Saint George), in 1408. The perpetual 'bonds' issued by the Bank of Saint George were (from 1419) the variable dividend *luoghi*, one of the most stable and noteworthy securities of the 16th and 17th centuries. The variable, not fixed, payment and transferability of the *luoghi* gives these capital associations some, though not all, essential features of joint-stock shares. However, when the additional banking activities of the *Casa* are taken into account, the picture is less clear.

There is a lack of agreement about where the joint-stock form of business organization originated: "can these *compere* and *maone* really be described as joint stock companies? Scholars are divided over this" (Braudel 1982, p.440).

Hecksher (1955, v.1, p.355) made a clear statement of one position on this point:

It is usually considered, in the literature on the subject, that the *compere* were no joint stock companies but altogether non-commercial associations like, for example, the Board of Foreign Bondholders in the late 19th century. The economic correspondence between the *compere* and several of the most famous companies at the end of the 17th and the beginning of the 18th century is, however, complete almost down to the smallest detail. Both the Bank of England, the English South Sea Company, John Law's French Mississippi Company, as well as other well-known institutions of this period, were originally associations of capitalists who obtained the right to pursue various kinds of trade in return for making fresh loans to the state, or for taking over old ones. The Bank of England, in fact, had precisely the same function as made the *Casa di S. Giorgio* famous. The correspondence here is obvious. The only doubtful point is whether the origin of the more recent of these organizations can be attributed directly or indirectly to the influences of the earlier ones.

This authoritative statement calls into question the often-expressed modern view that joint-stock companies were developed during the 16th and 17th centuries to meet the requirements of long-distance seaborne trade (e.g., Kindleberger 1993, p.191; Clough and Rapp 1975, p.152). Details of other aspects relevant to joint-stock organization, such as the degree of separation between ownership and control and whether shares were transferable and could be exchange-traded, do not attract attention.

The view that joint-stock organization arose due to the requirements of long-distance seaborne trade is understandable. By the 16th century, maritime partnerships had evolved to the point where it was common for individual voyages to involve a large number of co-owners who divided the cost of the ship and its cargo. Examples of these arrangements were the *loca navis* in the Mediterranean—a *commenda* where the ship and cargo was divided into shares (Martinelli 1977, p.56)—and the Dutch *rederij* and German *reederei* in the North Sea. A typical arrangement would have one partner responsible for sailing the ship and selling the cargo while the other partners contributed capital and goods and shared in the profit or loss according to their contribution. In some cases, partnership shares in a *loca navis* were transferable. However, because such partnerships were generally dissolved after the voyage was completed, there was no permanent equity capital stock undermining the need for share trading. This begs the question: Is a permanent equity capital stock an essential feature of joint-stock organization?

Using a different perspective, it is apparent that a permanent stock of equity capital did not require joint-stock organization. To see this, consider another precursor of the joint-stock company, the enlarged family partnerships of which the Fuggers of Augsburg from the 16th and 17th centuries are an example (Parker 1974, p.554). The Fugger partnerships featured a permanent capital stock, the *corpo*, that was advanced by the family partners. Shareholders in the *corpo* participated in the profit and loss of the company. Additions to capital, the *sopracorpo*, were raised either from partners or from outsiders, through the use of deposits with an insured return. Under the scholastic treatment of the triple contract, interest was permitted on these deposits. Payments on all *sopra-corpo* deposits were made before any payments were made to the *corpo*. While similar to the use of common stock and bonds used by the modern corporation, this form of business arrangement was still a family partnership, not a corporate entity with transferability of shares.

The importance of corporate status to the evolution of equity capital organization during the 16th century was captured by Harris (2000, p.39):

> In the second half of the sixteenth century and during the seventeenth century, the corporation, a familiar legal conception, increasingly began to be used for a new purpose. Employed since medieval times for ecclesiastical, municipal, educational and other public and semipublic purposes, the corporation or, as it was often called at that time, the body corporate or body politic, was increasingly used for profit-oriented organization of business. There had been other, earlier, business associations such as guilds, but these had considerable social elements, and served as fellowships or brotherhoods which controlled and ritualized whole aspects of their members' lives.

The 16th century marks the gradual emergence of the joint-stock company in northern Europe to accommodate the demands for equity capital for funding voyages to the far-flung regions that were progressively opened up to competitive trade during this period. While the corporate structure of a regulated company was suited to travel by Dutch merchants trading to the Baltic or English merchants trading to Calais and Antwerp, the capital requirements, associated commercial risks and length of voyage were larger and longer for voyages to new frontiers in West Africa, the Levant, Russia, North America and the Orient.

Early English Companies

English and Dutch joint-stock companies emerged during the 16th and 17th centuries to deal with the need for larger stocks of equity capital to be invested in risky ventures for long holding periods.[3] For a variety of geographical, political and social reasons, developments in Holland did not parallel those in England. Harris (p.39) described the situation in England as follows:

> Prior to the sixteenth century, a number of groups of merchants such as the Merchants of the Staple and the early Merchant Adventurers traded with nearby continental ports, but these were associations of individuals with no formal legal basis, neither incorporation nor even a royal franchising charter. The novelty of the sixteenth-century corporation lay in the combination of specific business purposes with a formal corporate form of organization and the fact that many of these new corporations reached beyond Western Europe.

Distinguishing these early joint-stock corporations from regulated companies is revealing. Both types of companies were incorporated during the 16th century, with the Merchant Adventurers—a regulated company—being the first to receive a charter in 1505. Charters were not permanent, being granted only for a number of years, and were subject to a possibly contentious renewal process.

Continuing a tradition reaching back to the Dark Ages, granting of charters, licences, letters patent, deeds to land and the like was an important source of revenue for the English crown. By generating payments before, during and after the Crown granted a charter, the chartering of for-profit corporations could be lucrative at a time when 'no taxation without representation' was a politically important consideration for the absolute monarchy. In addition to bullion, payments could be made as loans of goods in kind. The companies would also help cover the Crown's expenses, such as maintaining embassies and fortifications overseas (e.g., p.42). In some cases, a more important motivation for the granting of corporate charters was to assist in the ongoing international conflict and competition that characterized Western Europe during this period. The potential profitability of ventures to the newly opened seaborne trading areas in the Americas, West Africa and the Orient created social urgency to rally national resources to assist in furthering 'English interests'. Leaders in both the mercantile and political establishments were important motivators and contributors of equity capital to the early joint-stock ventures. Queen Elizabeth I herself took a share in some of the slave-trading voyages by John Hawkins to Guinea in the 1560s and contributed ships to these ventures.

Only some of the early joint-stock ventures were able to secure charters conferring corporate status. In most cases of incorporation charters granted by the Crown, a monopoly on trade to some geographical area was conveyed. Over time, interloping on the monopoly privilege could legally occur for a range of reasons, such as explicit provisions in charters and special permits issued by the Crown (Hecksher 1955, v.1, p.407). Especially under James I, the sale of further privileges to favored merchants of the Crown allowed interlopers to infringe on a monopoly privilege. This led to a decline in value of this royal privilege and to the Statute of Monopolies in 1623. The legal rationale for this statute was that only an act of Parliament could confer certain privileges. Harris (p.46) described the context as follows:

> The Statute of Monopolies of 1623 was passed during one of the peaks of the long conflict between the early Stuarts and the Parliament and common-law judges. The original aim of the Statute of Monopolies, as designed by the dismissed Chief Justice of King's Bench, Edward Coke, was to deprive the King of his power to freely sell new monopolies. The passage of the statute was intended to block an alternative source of income and force the King to turn to Parliament for permission to raise more taxes.

Unfortunately, the statute had numerous loopholes that allowed Charles I to continue the practice of granting monopolies, usually in the form of incorporation. This exacerbated long-standing disputes with Parliament and contributed to the beginning of the Civil War.

Despite being over a century old, the three-volume work by Scott (1910,1912) is still the essential secondary source on English joint-stock companies before 1720. Scott (1910, p.15) provided the following insight into the emergence of the joint-stock company in England:

> The appearance of the fully constituted joint-stock company [in England] was the product of two different lines of development . . . on the one side, there were the diverse forms of medieval partnership; and, on the other, the organization of corporate activity, which originated in the gild. The former practice effected a synthesis of the capital, owned by a few persons, but the undertaking, started in this manner, was temporary in its nature, and no lasting plans could be made for its continuance. Moreover, should events require the utilization of considerable resources, it would be necessary to introduce a large number of partners, and the medieval *societas* had not a sufficiently elaborate organization for the government of an extended membership. Yet the necessary system had been developed in the gild-merchant and the early regulated companies, and it only required the stimulus of a suitable occasion to graft the company organization on to the partnership.

With this background, Scott identified the initial emergence of the joint-stock company in England (p.15):

> The precise date, at which this union [of medieval partnership and gild corporation] was effected in England, was conditioned by a number of circumstances connected with the religious, social and industrial condition of the country. The progress of maritime discovery was extending foreign trade at the commencement of the sixteenth century, and it was in this branch of commerce that capital was of most importance. But the attitude of the Church to capital was on the whole not a progressive one . . . In England, in many respects, the Reformation, in liberating capital from the position it had occupied under the Church, forced this country to work out the corporate organization of capital independently.

Though there may have been precursors of the joint-stock company in Renaissance Italy, Scott correctly recognized that a range of religious, social, geographical and political factors played an essential role in the emergence of the early English joint-stock companies. For example, Oldland (2010) documented the finances of the early Tudor merchants.

Though primary sources on the early English joint-stock companies are markedly better than those from Renaissance Italy, the historical record is still conditioned by sources that have survived. In particular, Scott claimed the first two joint-stock ventures in long-distance trade were formed in 1553: one for trade with Africa, the Guinea Adventurers; and one with an original title of "The mysterie and companie of Merchants adventurers for the discoverie of regions, dominions, islands and places unknown" that came to be known as the Russia or Muscovy Company. Of these, the Russia Company is identified by Scott (1910, p.17) as being "the first English joint-stock company of importance" due to "some corporate character and fixed methods of procedure in the conduct of business". More precisely, the Russia Company was the first venture to later obtain a charter conferring corporate character with a governance structure similar to that of a regulated company. "At first there was to be one governor, and this position was to be held by Sebastian Cabot for life" (p.20). Such was the character of the separation of ownership and control in the early joint-stock companies.

The separation of ownership and control in the modern limited liability corporation with autonomous, exchange tradeable shares requires complex accounting methods, especially internal and external audit procedures. Though evidence for such procedures stretches back to antiquity, the commercial and legal context is decidedly different. Accounting historians conventionally identify the 20th century with the introduction of 'managerial internal audit'—in which the internal audit was integral to the management process and more than just 'policing' of financial and compliance items (e.g., Brink and Witt 1982; Flesher 1977). Only the most adventurous accounting historians seek roots in the 19th century, such as Boockholdt (1983) for American railways and Spraakman (2001) for the Hudson's Bay Company. In contrast, economic and financial historians detail various aspects of "agency problems" in the early joint-stock companies and the various methods developed to deal with such problems. For example, Carlos and Nicholas (1990) identified contracting methods and hiring practices as effective mechanisms used by the Hudson's Bay Company in the early 18th century. Chartered in 1670, the Hudson's Bay Company had headquarters in London, with outputs along Hudson's Bay bartering goods in exchange for furs, a challenging environment for both external and internal audit.

In focusing on the procedural elements of managerial internal audit, accounting historians fail to establish a useful connection to the earlier methods of dealing with agency problems. For the early joint-stock companies, Carlos and Nicholas observed: "Two features of the external environment are important in determining profitability: the cost effectiveness of monitoring, and the ease with which managers may engage in private trade. Both of these factors differed widely among the chartered companies and may help explain differing company successes" (p.859). In particular, the governance structure of the Russia Company generated "very numerous complaints of the almost complete failure of the governor and assistants . . . to exercise control over its factors in Russia" (Scott 1910, p.68). While drunkenness and shirking were problems, trading commodities on one's own account at the expense of the company was usually the most serious problem. Losses arising from the 'private trade' of managers, factors or agents operating in the foreign market were a concern for shareholders in all the early joint-stock companies organized for long-distance trade. However, while effective administrative mechanisms for audit and control in the Russia Company were weak or absent, the Hudson's Bay Company did have some success. Unlike the Hudson's Bay Company, the Russia Company also served an essential national service in providing gunpowder, timber, cordage and pitch on favorable terms that were essential to Elizabeth I and later English monarchs. This may have created a commercial environment less restrictive to private trade.

Both of the early ventures of 1553 were involved in opening up long-distance trade to new territories and were started on mercantile speculation, without a royal charter. Only the Russia Company was able to secure a royal charter in 1555, granting a monopoly on trade with Russia and any other territories to be secured by the company's adventures. The Russia Company received preferential treatment from the Russian czar and an open willingness to engage in trade. This affected the organization of English joint-stock ventures later in the 16th century. Given the exclusive privileges contained in the Russia Company charter of 1555, the 'Northwest Company'—the Colleagues of the Fellowship for the Discovery of the Northwest Passage—had to obtain a license from the Privy Council to permit Martin Frobisher to sail with two small ships and a pinnace in search of a northwest passage to the Orient in 1576. Though unsuccessful in finding either a route or trading opportunities, the potential for a gold mine discovered in 'Baffin Land' was enough to have the assets and liabilities of the first voyage transferred to the second voyage, subject to conditions.

The Northwest Company is of interest for several reasons. In particular, none of the four voyages that took to sea between 1576 and 1583 was able to return a profit, and the company was wound up with equity capital losses for the adventurers. The company did not obtain a charter, though plans were drawn up for incorporation with similar governance structure to the Russia Company. Perhaps this did not happen because it was an added expense in a venture that was not generating profit. More importantly, detailed records of the venture have survived, enabling identification of the 'adventurers' who supplied equity capital (including Sir Thomas Gresham), the amount of capital subscribed and rules governing share ownership. Except in the case of death of an adventurer, shares were not transferable, but each voyage required additional subscriptions which enabled new adventurers seeking shares to join the venture; thus, there were 18 adventurers for the first voyage and 41 for the second. In addition, the process of funding the second, third and fourth voyages involved rolling the paid-in equity capital plus addition for losses into subsequent voyages, thereby creating a type of permanent equity capital stock. Whether this 'permanence' would have happened if any voyage was profitable, when there would have been a return of equity capital and distribution of profits, is unclear.

The Levant Company, also known as the Turkey Company, represents yet another set of circumstances influencing the early English joint-stock companies. Unlike trading ventures to newly discovered regions in North America and Guinea, English trade to the Levant and other areas of the Mediterranean did not commence in the 16th century. Cawston and Keane (1896, p.67) reported:

> [The] first feeble attempts [of the English] to trade in [the Mediterranean] date from about the year 1413, when it is recorded that 'a company of London merchants laded several ships with much wool and other merchandise to the value of £24,000 towards the western parts of Morocco. But some Genoese ships, emulous of this commerce, made prize of those London ships outward bound, and carried them into Genoa. Whereupon King Henry IV grants the sufferers reprisals on the ships and merchandise of the Genoese wherever they can find them.'

Whether this early venture was organized as a joint-stock company is unknown, though the amount of capital raised suggests such a possibility. In the 15th century, commercial trade in the Mediterranean was dominated by the Italian city states. With a history of commercial trade stretching back to antiquity, there were a host of competitors in this potentially lucrative trading arena. Cawston and Keane observed somewhat obscurely: " 'letters of marque and reprisals on the bodies and goods' of powerful rivals could little avail in the hands of skippers unsupported by the prestige and resources of a corporate body" (p.67). Precisely how corporate status would assist in such ventures is unclear. Perhaps corporate status granted by a royal charter would provide the venture with a basis for military support from the Crown?

The historical record for ventures to the Mediterranean and the Levant is somewhat jumbled from this early 15th-century venture until a charter was obtained from Elizabeth I in 1581 for "The Governour and Companie of Marchantes of the Levant". Information about the period before the charter draws heavily on: (a) the 20-volume Latin source *Foedera, Conventiones, Litteræ, et cujuscunque generis Acta Publica inter Reges Angliæ et alios etc.* [Treaties, Agreements, Letters and Public Acts made between the Kings of England and others etc.] prepared by Thomas Rymer, the royal historiographer, and published between 1704 and 1713; and (b) the 14-volume work by Richard Hakluyt, *The Principal Navigations, Voyages, Traffiques and Discoveries of the English Nation,* published between 1598 and 1600 (Hakluyt 1885). Use of these sources requires some artful interpretation. While there is evidence of trade to the Levant "carried on at intervals" between the beginning and middle of the 16th century, it was Queen Elizabeth who gave the primary impetus to the creation of the Levant Company, initially sending an agent in 1579 to procure permission from the Sultan "for English merchants to resort freely to the Levant on the same footing as other nations" (Cawston and Keane 1896, p.68).

Having granted in the 1581 charter a monopoly on trade to the region for seven years, "Elizabeth either invested or lent as much as £40,000 [of the initial subscribed capital of £80,000], and her contribution came out of the treasure taken from the Spaniards by Drake, a portion of which had been given to the Crown" (Scott 1910, p.84). The initial company charter was granted to four named individuals—Sir Edward Osborn, Thomas Smith, Richard Staper, and William Garret: "Her Majesty therefore grants unto those four merchants and to such other Englishmen, not exceeding twelve in number, as the said Sir E. Osborn and Staper shall appoint to be joined to them and their factors, servants and deputies, for the space of seven years to trade to Turkey". Despite risks from Barbary pirates, the Spanish control of Gibraltar and a burdensome import duty, the company was "highly profitable". The restrictions on company membership led to calls to expand the list to include those previously engaged in the trade in Venice and elsewhere in the region. While the charter was renewed with some delay in 1592, Scott (p.88) indicated: "In March 1599 the trade was on a joint-stock basis, but in June 1600 a list was drawn up which shows that it was then a regulated body".

Attempts to characterize any of these early exercises in joint-stock ownership as seminal events in the history of equity capital organization would be incorrect. The Russia Company had initial difficulties and had to resort to calls on shareholders to the point where, in 1564, the original £25 subscription had been increased to £200. While, from this date, the company was able to carry on profitable trade until the end of the century, it was converted to an "ad hoc" joint-stock company in 1586 and to a regulated company in 1622. The Guinea Company can only generously be considered a joint-stock company, as it engaged in the practice of raising separate subscriptions for each voyage, making complete disbursements of capital upon return of the ships and sale of cargo. The instability in trade with Africa had companies being formed and dissolved until a joint-stock company with a permanent capital stock and a strong charter—the Royal African Company—was established in 1672, after the Restoration. Even this company converted to a regulated company in 1750 (Hecksher 1955, v.1, p.375).

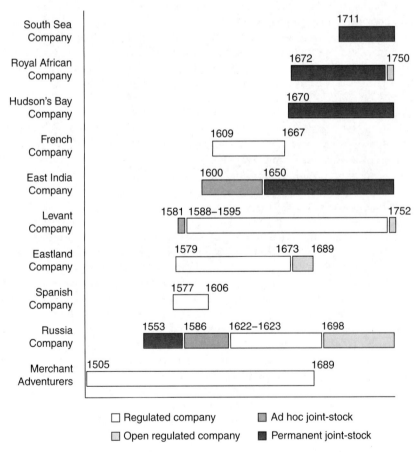

Figure 5.3 Organizational Transformation of Major English Trading Companies, 1505–1760

Source: Harris (2000, p.52)

Much modern discussion surrounding the early English joint-stock companies considers only the arena of long-distance trade, e.g., Carlos and Nicholas (1996). Scott (1910, p.383) hinted at an earlier origin in the mining sector. A patent granted by Henry VII in 1485 identifies the "governors of the Mines Royal" being constituted, amalgamating the earlier system of "grant[ing] the privilege of discovering and working the Royal Mines within a certain district to some patentee for a limited period". Two of the earliest joint-stock companies not engaged in long-distance trade—the Company of the Mines Royal and the Mineral and Battery Company—both originated in mining. Both companies were granted charters in 1568, though both had conducted business for some years before that date. The Mines Royal was involved in silver and copper mining and manufacture, while the Mineral and Battery Company was involved in a range of mining and metallurgical activities including the mining of zinc ore, the manufacturing of brass and the milling of iron. The share ownership of both of these companies reflected a strong German influence. Heckscher observed that "it is very probable that these companies were influenced by the numerous and well-developed capital associations in German mining".

From the *Bulletin of the Business Historical Society* (Jan. 1929, pp.7–8):

WE ARE indebted to Mr. E. A. S. Clarke, Secretary of the American Iron and Steel Institute, for calling our attention to an article in the 1901 *Transactions of the British Institute* which places the oldest joint-stock enterprise in the world at Domnarfvet, Sweden. It is the Stora Kopparbergs (Great Copper Mountain) Mining Company, deriving its name from the celebrated copper mine at Falun, where one of its plants is located. In 1896, the Company celebrated its 550th anniversary, dating from its oldest charter; and a deed for the transfer of shares in the Company dated 1288 is still in existence in the State archives.

The experience of the early English mining joint-stocks, and the Italian connection with English merchants involved in early joint-stock companies, reinforces the view that the roots of this form of business organization can be found in the experiences of various countries. These experiences range from the early Italian organizations, such as the *Casa di San Giorgio*, to the permanent capital associations of the wealthy continental European family partnerships, to the business relationships developed for long-distance trade. It is not surprising that the first English joint-stock companies retained some features common to other forms of business organization, such as the partnership and regulated companies. However, with the emergence of the Dutch and British East India Companies, the joint-stock form of business organization permitted a seminal transformation in commercial practice. This change was the beginning of exchange trading of company shares. This activity, a central feature of the modern limited liability corporation, did not emerge until much later than the chartered corporation. Similarly, limited liability in the modern sense was also not present.

Though the early joint-stock companies represented an important evolution in commercial finance, there were still significant differences between these early companies and the modern, publicly traded corporation (Baskin 1988, pp.201–2):

> The first British trading companies combined features that today would be associated with both partnerships and public corporations. As in a partnership, "most of the earlier companies probably began by being exclusive, in the sense that shares were sold amongst persons known to each other" (Scott 1910). Also, as in a partnership, the number of shares was fixed and liability was unlimited: investors were subject to calls whenever the firm needed additional capital. On the other hand, as in a modern corporation, managerial ranks distinct from ownership arose (that is, although recruitment appears to have been limited to current shareholders, the degree of management control exercised by a partner was not necessarily equal to the percentage of ownership, but became increasingly related to issues of knowledge, interest and ability). Tradable shares were an early development, and of course they came to play a crucial role in the growth of corporate finance. But these shares were originally intended only to facilitate exchange among known business associates and not to create securities to be sold on public exchanges (which in fact did not exist when the idea of shares was conceived).

At a more abstract level, the successful evolution of joint-stock shares depended on transferability, which, in turn, depended on methods of handling the

Figure 5.4   Slave Market (1910) by Otto Pilny (1836–1936), one of a series on this theme

asymmetric information problems for passive shareholders surrounding the evaluation of company performance. Once the joint-stock company developed a permanent capital stock, such that assets were retained in the company after the end of a specific venture such as a voyage, this imposed considerable demands on the accounting systems used (e.g., Yamey 1949).

John Hawkins and the Early English Slave Trade

Following the tradition of Scott (1910), much of the history surrounding the evolution of English equity capital organization during the 16th and 17th centuries focuses on 'institutional' issues such as the adoption by the joint-stock companies of corporate governance methods employed by the regulated companies and the guilds. Details of the charter, the number of shareholders, the amount of equity capital subscribed and the like have been painstakingly reported for various companies. Modern treatments have further abstracted the history to concerns about the early chartered companies being "efficient transactors or rent-seeking monopolists" (Jones and Ville 1996) and "agency problems in the early chartered companies" (Carlos and Nicholas 1990). The relevance of political, religious, geographical, social and, most importantly, moral influences has been largely forgotten. In cases where the social basis of commercial expansion during this period is specifically examined (e.g., Brenner 1972), the history is constructed around a comparison of the Merchant Adventurers, a regulated company, and the comparable joint-stock ventures involved in long-distance trading: the Russia Company, the Levant Company and the East India Company. Sordid details of other early English joint-stock companies are conveniently ignored.

Even careful scholar Harris (2000, p.43) maintained that "long distance trade to the outlying frontiers of Europe and to other continents, only entered by English traders during this period, was initially organized into joint-stock corporations. The first of these was the Russia Company (also known as the Muscovy Company) founded in 1553 and chartered in 1555". In only recognizing the Russia Company, Harris only included the evolution of the joint-stock company from the regulated company. The contribution from the medieval partnership identified by Scott was forgotten. It seems likely that commercial ventures involved in the line of development from the medieval partnership preceded the Russia Company, but records are too scant to permit a definitive conclusion. Scott (1912, p.3) provided some context:

> In a communication of the Sieur de Guerchy to the Duc de Praslin, dated February 24th, 1767, the origin of the Africa company is traced back to 1536. The allusion seems to be to three voyages undertaken by William Hawkins, father of Sir John Hawkins, to Africa and Brazil . . . There is no information to show whether these expeditions were at the sole charge of William Hawkins, or whether, although he owned the ship, others entered into partnership with him . . . In 1540 divers wealthy merchants of Southampton were engaged in the African trade and this expedition may be taken as the first syndicate or company for this venture.

It is now recognized that William Hawkins undertook voyages in 1530, 1531, 1532 and 1540, progressively extending trading activities to the west coast of Africa and Brazil. The reference to 1536 by the Sieur de Guerchy may be a reference to Hawkins' suggestion "to Cromwell that the King should finance him on further voyages of this kind and should take a share of the profits through the customs, but the proposal does not seem to have been adopted" (Bindoff 1982).

With this in mind, accurate "social history" for the early chartered companies cannot ignore the commercial ventures of John Hawkins (1532–1595), the second son of William Hawkins (1495?–1554?) and second cousin of Francis Drake (1540?–1596). Pollitt (1973, p.29) identified essential social context for the early slaving voyages:

> it is in the syndicates that supported the ventures, the hazy figures in London who had the gold to make them possible, rather than in smoking cannon, sinking ships and Hawkins's cries of treachery that the significance of England's first experience with slaving is to be found. Who were these men who were willing to risk large sums on such risky ventures? What were their motives? Did they have any idea of the possible impact of their investments?

Details of the financing for the early voyages and other commercial activities of William Hawkins are scarce. What is known is that, by the time the voyages were undertaken, William Hawkins was established as an important merchant in Plymouth, "exporting large quantities of tin and cloth to the Continent and importing goods from France, Spain and the Mediterranean". Over time, he became the most important merchant in Plymouth, being elected to Parliament in 1539. The outbreak of war with France in 1540 discouraged further peaceful seaborne trading ventures, and William Hawkins turned to the lucrative trade of outfitting the privateers who preyed on French trade.

The early English joint-stock companies were not homogeneous in character. In cases where a royal charter and a monopoly on trade were obtained, specific features of corporate status were conferred that varied according to the wording of the charter. However, some form of public benefit was required to obtain a charter, in addition to the political connections and equity capital needed to influence the granting process. Charters would typically restrict the number of company members, list the names of some or all of those involved, and provide details of the governance structure. Joint-stock companies involved in long-distance trade formed without a charter, such as the voyages of John Hawkins, were substantively different (p.27): "The most striking feature of those slaving voyages is that they were supported by unlicensed, joint-stock organizations, attracting increasingly wealthy and powerful backers as the profit potential of the enterprises became apparent". If the initial venture was profitable, the return of capital and division of profit at the end of a voyage meant such ventures relied on company members rolling distributions into the next voyage to obtain a semblance of a permanent capital stock. In the method of equitable sharing of profit and loss, such ventures were some-what more of a capital association than the *commenda* or *societas maris*, even though the ad hoc character of governance did not rise to the level of 'corporate personality'.

The time frame for the three slaving voyages of John Hawkins begins in 1562: "when Hawkins was inspired . . . to secure modest financial backing for a voyage from England to Africa, from there to America and finally back to England on the famous triangle run inaugurated by his father" (p.27). Fortunately, some details of this voyage have survived:

> The first voyage in 1562 was a relatively minuscule affair, led by John Hawkins himself, organized and equipped by his elder brother William, and financed by a small combine of London business men and middle-range government officials.

While the full list of equity capital investors for each of the voyages is not available, it is known that, for the first voyage, "London merchants who took shares were Sir Lionel Duckett and Sir Thomas Lodge, while the bureaucrats were Benjamin Gonson, Sir William Winter and Mister Bromfield." Despite the loss of two ships loaded with hides to the Spanish, 'the venture proved to be a financial success and the profits secured explain in large part the impressive membership of the syndicate which supported the second voyage', which was mounted in 1564. "Indeed, the syndication for the 1564 voyage reveals a group dramatically larger than before" (p.28). The financial success of the 1564 voyage led to the formation of a third, and last, syndicate for a voyage in 1567, which "was simply a complete disaster". Though no records survive as to the exact distribution of profit and loss among the investors of the three voyages, it was estimated that the return on equity capital invested in the three voyages combined was between 40% and 60% (Scott 1910, pp.41–3).

The Composition of the Investor Syndicates

The three slaving voyages of John Hawkins capture essential elements separating the various forms of joint-stock company appearing in the 16th and 17th centuries. Consistent with mercantilist objectives generated by competition between emerging monarch-led nation states, one feature of many joint-stock and regulated companies was the granting of a charter to pursue commercial activities with a public purpose. Unlike the Russia Company and the Levant Company, trade to West Africa in the 16th century did not have the approval of a head of state in the area such as a czar or sultan. Chartering an English company for trade to areas within West Africa would conflict with the interests of the Portuguese and could lead to the interdicting of English ships at sea. In the case of transport and sale of slaves in the West Indies: "Politically its consequences were momentous. The Spaniards guarded the trade to their Western possessions and more especially the Royal monopoly of importing slaves" (Scott 1912, vol.2, p.9).[4] Despite Queen

Elizabeth's likely participation as an investor in the second and third voyages, the Hawkins voyages did not have the formal recognition associated with a royal charter. As Pollitt (1973, p.39) observed: "aside from the profit motive there was a strong possibility that the trade was being used by the Crown as an instrument of its policies, through the collusion of government officials and merchants."

Having assumed the crown from her half-sister Mary in 1558, Elizabeth I (1533–1603) relied almost all through her reign on the advice of Sir William Cecil (1520–1598). The connection between Cecil and his "good friend and faithful ally", Benjamin Gonson (1525–1577), reveals "the link between the diverse elements which supported the slaving voyages". For, as Pollitt observed, "it is in the syndicates that supported the ventures, the hazy figures in London who had the gold to make them possible, rather than in smoking cannon, sinking ships and Hawkins's cries of treachery that the significance of England's first experience with slaving is to be found" (pp.29–30). In particular, the slaving syndicates consisted of two groups, one of 'merchants' and one of 'government officials': "Numerically the groups were roughly equal, but the government officials were far superior in apparent national power and influence. The merchants, however, . . . were in their own right influential men of considerable stature". As such, the composition of the equity capital syndicates that funded Hawkins' slaving voyages speaks profoundly about the connection between national policy, equity capital and the ruling class in 16th-century England.

Pollitt detailed what was known about the merchants, bureaucrats and Court officials involved in the first voyage (pp.27–8):

> The first voyage in 1562 was a relatively miniscule affair, led by John Hawkins himself, organized and equipped by his elder brother William, and financed by a small combine of London businessmen and middle-range government officials. The London merchants who took shares were Sir Lionel Duckett and Sir Thomas Lodge, while the bureaucrats were Benjamin Gonson, Sir William Winter and a Mister Bromfield. The original list indicates that there were other investors as well, but they have not been identified from the available sources.

The profitability of the first voyage led to a dramatic evolution for the second:

> Indeed, the syndication for the 1564 voyage reveals a group dramatically larger and more powerful than before. With the possible exceptions of Lodge and Duckett, all of the first group were included in the second, but there was a marked influx of London businessmen and high Court officials as well. The new London merchants included Sir William Garrard, Sir William Chester, Edward Castlyn and probably Castlyn's partner, Anthony Hickman. If the Spanish Ambassador is to be believed, the ubiquitous Italian, Benedict Spinola, who had extensive business interests in England, was also a subscriber. The Court officials

were Lord Clinton and Saye, who was the Lord Admiral, Sir William Cecil, the Queen's principal advisor, Lord Robert Dudley, who was created Earl of Leicester in 1564, and the Earl of Pembroke. Even Queen Elizabeth herself is listed as one of the adventurers in the most reliable source.

There is evidence that the significant profit obtained from the second voyage led to much of the syndicate from the second voyage taking shares in the disastrous third and final voyage, together with some new investors.

The merchants were a diverse group, with different geographical roots. However, the "great common tie of these merchants is the city and its economy, for all of them began their business lives as members of the various Livery Companies. It was in this traditional form of enterprise that they made fortunes which enabled them to invest in and become leaders of the novel joint-stock forms of organization that appeared during the middle decades of the century" (p.30). Only Lodge was not involved in the cloth trade, having risen to an important position in the Grocer's Company. Given that such members of the Hawkins equity capital syndicates were successful and important members of regulated companies, taking a leading role in an early and risky joint-stock venture seems incongruent (p.31):

> Exactly how the merchants became involved in limited liability companies is a difficult question, but they all did to the extent of risking their entire fortunes. Lodge is a good case in point. For twenty years he operated successfully as an archetypal London grocer and wool merchant; then suddenly in the 1550s he began investing in the new Russian trade, first taking shares in the Muscovy Company. Within a decade he became so active and invested so heavily that he emerged as governor of the company. By 1555 he expanded his interests in the opposite geographic direction, engaging in the Barbary trade, which apparently led him eventually to invest in the embryonic Guinea trade to West Africa.

There were other merchants in the Hawkins syndicate who were even more deeply involved in the emerging 16th-century English joint-stock companies. Several of the merchants involved were also important political figures. In particular, Lodge, Duckett, Chester, Gerrard and Heyward all served as Lord Mayor of London, with some also serving in Parliament. Among others, Lodge was an influential advisor to Queen Elizabeth.

Of the second group of investors (p.34):

> the Crown officials, must be sub-divided into sections of bureaucrats and Councillors to determine the true construction of the syndicates. Of these two subgroups the smallest and least powerful was that of the bureaucrats, but it was vitally important to the formation of the slaving companies. It consisted of Benjamin Gonson, Sir William Winter and William Bromfield. Because of their administrative positions, mercantile backgrounds and

close contacts with the Crown policy makers, they formed a keystone upon which the Hawkins syndicates were built. They were, quite simply, the link between the diverse elements which supported the slaving ventures.

Of the bureaucrats, the most significant was Benjamin Gonson, "a good friend and faithful ally" of Sir William Cecil. As such, "Benjamin Gonson was not only the undisputed head of a major government department, but also a wealthy merchant and valuable ally of Queen Elizabeth's principal advisor" (p.35). Continuing the work of his father, Gonson's bureaucratic career was intimately tied to the Admiralty and stretched back to Henry VIII. In contrast to the bureaucrats:

> Little needs to be said about the Councillor sub-group of the Crown officials. The power and prestige of Sir William Cecil during Elizabeth's reign is common knowledge. William Herbert, first Earl of Pembroke, was nearly equal in stature to Cecil in the 1560s. He was described in the preceding decade by the Venetian Ambassador as "the chief personage in England," and his involvement in the slave trade seems to have distressed the Spanish more than that of any other investor. Robert Dudley, Earl of Leicester, was probably less influential than Cecil or Pembroke, but he is certainly too well known to require a listing of his offices and evaluation of his power. Lord Clinton and Saye, later Earl of Lincoln, was Lord Admiral and a Privy Councillor to both Mary and Elizabeth, a lifelong friend of Cecil, and has been too long ignored by historians. He was the first high government official to involve himself in the African trade by lending Royal Navy ships to the Guinea adventurers in the 1550s, and it is hardly surprising that he emerged as prominent in the slaving syndicates. Together, these men constitute as powerful a group as could have been brought together for any purpose in the early years of Elizabeth's reign.

Pollitt made the following insightful observation about the social and political aspects of the early English joint-stock companies (p.40):

> what [the Hawkins voyages] and numerous joint-stock ventures may have accomplished was to mingle the merchant and official classes in a profit-oriented melting pot. This did not, of course, make England a classless society, but it did help to frustrate the emergence of a "Hidalgo spirit," the legendary fatal flaw of Spain. It furthermore kept channels of communication open between at least part of the ruling nobility and the business classes, and made the government sensitive to a degree matched only by the Dutch to the aims and aspirations of the business community.

Though the historical context is decidedly different, similar comments apply to the connection between prominent equity capitalists and 'the ruling nobility' in modern society.

EQUITY CAPITAL IN THE 'NEW WORLD'

Super (1979, pp.269–70) detailed the equity capital organization used by the merchants of Quito in the Spanish American colonies in the 16th century.

Merchants in 16th-century Quito organized their ventures in ways similar to merchants in other parts of the Spanish New World. A few acted independently, using their own capital to buy and distribute goods. Through careful use of powers of attorney, promissory notes, and letters of credit, individuals could manage extensive financial enterprises. Few traders acted alone, however, because of the capital requirements of long-distance trade. They usually assumed the responsibility for organizing ventures, then recruited capital from different investors, all without the formal agreement to a partnership. Profits for the investor were usually set at a percentage of the investment or a percentage of the total profits of the investment. Agreements of this type covered most commercial needs, from buying and selling to carrying gold and performing specific services. Commercial needs that were regular features of trade eventually had set percentage costs. The carrying of gold to Panama, for example, usually cost 7% of the value of the gold. Another form of commercial organization was the company (*compania*). Companies were not restricted to trade, but they were used more frequently in trade than in other endeavors. From the first days of colonization, companies had aided Europeans' commercial objectives. Quito companies had their origins in the *commenda* and *societas* agreements that were so important to the commercial life of the Mediterranean. Instead of using the terms *commenda* and *societas*, Spaniards adopted the comprehensive term *compania* for their New World endeavors. The organization of companies was straightforward. Two or more individuals contributed capital or labor (at times a combination) to a specific venture for an agreed length of time. Almost invariably, partners divided profits equally after the return of the principal. Several other conditions were made a part of the contracts, all of them designed to ensure that the partners fulfilled their responsibilities.

C   THE CREATION OF THE DUTCH EAST INDIA COMPANY (*VOC*)

Early Dutch Companies

Building on results from much earlier studies (e.g., van Dillen 1935), knowledge about Dutch equity capital arrangements in the 16th and 17th centuries has been substantially improved by recent contributions of Oscar Gelderblom, Joost Jonker, Abe de Jong and others. The 16th- and 17th-century development of the joint-stock company in the Low Countries differs from the English experience. Political, geographical and religious considerations played a significant role in this divergence. The economic and financial importance of Antwerp until later in the 16th century would seem to favour an earlier development of joint-stock arrangements than occurred in Amsterdam. However, geographical, political and military developments subverted this outcome:

> In 1581 the seven United Provinces of the Netherlands declared their independence of Spain. As the intrepid Dutch sailors ventured out from their homeland they met not only the ships of their old master, Philip II, but those of the Portuguese as well. Since the government of Portugal had just fallen into the hands of Philip II the Dutch ships could expect no more consideration from Portuguese than from Spanish vessels. Notwithstanding the manifest dangers the prospects of obtaining the coveted products of the Portuguese colonies inspired the Dutch to such a great extent that in 1595 Bernard Ereckson sailed to the west coast of Africa, at that time usually called Guinea (Zook 1919, p.136).

The freeing of Dutch commercial interests from the control of the Spanish crown meant that previously forbidden areas, especially in America and Africa, were now open to those willing to run the gamut of risks. Longer round-trip voyages; competition from English and French interlopers in the Spanish and Portuguese spheres of influence; and risks from pirates, privateers and foreign forces combined to compel the use of alternatives to the traditional '*commenda*'-based methods of organizing equity capital.

As Gelderblom et al. (2011, p.34) observed, the 1580s marked a turning point in the scope of Dutch commercial activities and the associated organization of equity capital:

> Until the 1580s merchants in Holland had largely concentrated on trade between the Baltic and France, Spain, and Portugal. This trade was organized by individual merchants, small family partnerships, and shipping companies or *partenrederijen*. It is tempting to view these shipping companies as a distinct legal entity, but the term *partenrederij* is a nineteenth-century invention. The underlying contract was a partnership with a specific purpose, in this case the exploitation of a ship, and particular only in the arithmetical division of shares (½, 1/4, 1/8, etc.). The accounts of shipping companies were settled after a specific trip or after a trading season, following which participants were free to reinvest or not. As with all specific-purpose partnerships, the partners were jointly and severally liable for debts related to the purpose of the company, with one key exception. Any loss of cargo would be spread over all freight owners, while a total loss of the ship would free all shipping partners from any remaining claims on the company.

Partnership arrangements used by the Dutch in the Baltic trade were strikingly similar to the *commenda* arrangements used by the medieval and Renaissance Italian seafarers. However, the seaborne trade to Africa, America and Asia posed decidedly larger and more complicated risks than the traditional Dutch Baltic trade. In addition, the Dutch commercial ventures originated from an aggregation of provinces requiring political leadership to bind the various provincial interests to achieve a common goal. This process was part of a much larger political and social struggle for Dutch autonomy from Spanish Hapsburg rule. This struggle commenced in 1572 when Holland and Zeeland broke from direct Spanish rule.

The importance of the *VOC* to the evolution of equity capital organization has diverted modern attention from other 16th- and 17th-century Dutch commercial ventures, especially in West Africa and, to a lesser extent, the Americas. The West African trade reveals the importance of geography in the development of equity capital organization (Gelderblom et al. 2011, p.35):

> Following the fall of Antwerp in 1585, Amsterdam emerged as the new long-distance trade centre in the Low Countries. Antwerp merchants migrated north and continued their trade with Russia, the Levant, and Africa from the Dutch port. The Russia trade continued to be dominated by Antwerp firms, and the earliest voyages to Genoa and Venice in the 1590s were also organized by Flemish companies. Merchants in the long-distance trade were mostly left to their own devices, but to support the Levant trade the government sometimes supplied arms to individual ships, and it negotiated commercial privileges with the Ottoman sultan. The same was true for the Atlantic world. The early sugar expeditions to the Canaries, Madeira, and Brazil and the first voyages to West Africa were run by special-purpose partnerships, and the salt trade to the coast of Venezuela was done by shipping companies.

The record of these early Dutch overseas ventures is unlike the French, in which " 'much of the seventeenth century French traffic is missing' . . . A large part of France's slave trading was then clandestine, conducted by interlopers challenging royal monopoly companies" (Geggus 2001, p.120). In comparison, the Dutch evidence indicates equity capital organization somewhat similar to that used in the English expeditions of John Hawkins, albeit without direct royal involvement (Gegus 2001, p.120):

> Between 1593 and 1598 at least 30 ships sailed to West Africa from Amsterdam, Enkhuizen, Hoorn, Rotterdam, Middelburg, and Delft . . . Surviving accounts reveal that investments in the African trade were typically made for one voyage, with the capital raised in advance and spent on the ship, its equipment, crew, armament, and merchandise . . . A small number of partners coordinated the expedition, for which they received a small fee. Upon the return of the ship the same men notified the other participants, sold the cargo and sometimes also the ship, and distributed the proceeds among all their fellow investors.

As Riemersma (1950, p.35) observed about this period: "merchant associations with a government charter occupied a relatively minor position in Dutch trade as a whole. While English traders became to a large extent incorporated into large associations with exclusive rights, the bulk of Dutch trade remained in the hands of an immense plurality of small firms and partnerships, operating without any explicit sanction from the state".

In addition to competition from French and English interlopers, the early Dutch voyages to West Africa revealed considerable information about the potential opportunities to 'despoil' "the Portuguese [who] had long occupied the trading points along the coast, and had erected forts and factories wherever it seemed advisable for the purpose of defense and trade" (Zook 1919, p.35). In turn, it was early Dutch trade with Africa that instituted changes to the organization of equity capital that fostered the development of the VOC (Gelderblom et al. 2011, p.35):

> The early success of these early African companies quickly raised concerns about increasing competition. In 1598 the eight companies then trading between Amsterdam and Africa decided to merge into a General Guinea Company so as to avoid competition, as director Jacques de Velaer explained to shareholder Daniël van der Meulen. The new company maintained the governance structure of the previous companies and organized single voyages only. These ventures were all private enterprises, with little or no government involvement. The various companies sailing to Africa armed their own ships and sailed in convoy whenever possible; government support was initially limited to naval escorts in European waters for incoming and outgoing ships.

Similar to later incentives provided for the formation of the VOC, until 1598 the companies were exempted from the customs duties that were levied by the admiralty boards that ran the navy. The merging of the companies signaled that a regular trade and profit was sufficient enough that contributions through customs duties could be levied. From this point, trade to West Africa became connected to the colonization activities of the Dutch in the West Indies and America. "The Dutch realized that the African trade was indispensable to their West India colonies as a means of supplying slave labor. Hostilities, therefore, continued against the Portuguese who still had possession of the principal part of the African trade" (Zook 1919, p.137).

Following the pattern used in the organization of the VOC, the Dutch government relied on commercial interests, supplemented by support from the state, to spearhead national objectives in colonization and empire expansion. In 1611, the Dutch made a treaty with a native African prince and gained Mauree, in modern-day Ghana. In 1612, Fort Nassau was erected at this site. In 1617, Dutch merchants bought the island of Goree at Cape Verde from local natives, and four years later, in 1621, the Dutch West India Company was formed. The charter for this company included the West Indies, New Amsterdam and the west coast of Africa. In 1625, government support for this venture resulted in the Dutch making a "vigorous attempt" to capture the main Portuguese African stronghold at St. George d'Elmina, a location in the Gold Coast that had been under Portuguese control since 1481. In this effort the Dutch were unsuccessful. However, in 1637 Prince Mauritz of Nassau, accompanied by 1,200 fighting men, succeeded in capturing this important Portuguese trading base.

Recalling that the history of 16th- and 17th-century joint-stock companies in England followed a zigzag path between joint-stock and regulated company organization, a similar pattern is observed with one of the two emerging and important Dutch joint-stock trading companies. In 1638, the Dutch West India Company abandoned its trading monopoly. As with the English joint-stock companies that converted to regulated companies, such as the Levant Company, the directors of the Dutch West India Company felt that sharing the expenses and risks associated with trade by opening up the protected areas to other merchants and collecting fees for trading in those locations would be a more cost-effective way of managing the considerable expenses associated with the Dutch colonial expansion in the Americas and West Africa. With the passage of the Articles and Conditions in 1638 and the Freedoms and Exemptions in 1640, the Dutch West India Company allowed merchants of all friendly nations to trade in the relevant jurisdictions under Dutch control, subject to a 10% import duty, a 15% export duty and the restriction that all merchants had to hire West India Company ships to carry merchandise.

The Dutch East India Company (VOC)

As Gelderblom et al. (2012) observed, the Dutch East India Company (VOC) has achieved almost mythic status among those searching for 'institutional innovation' that led to the 'modern corporation':

> The intercontinental trading companies set up by the British and Dutch around 1600 are generally considered key institutional innovations because of their corporate form . . . They pioneered features which later became textbook characteristics of modern corporations: a permanent capital, legal personhood, separation of ownership and management, limited liability for shareholders and for directors, and tradable shares.

Leaving aside the difficulties of claiming share 'trading' for the English companies, the basis of this claim is stated as follows (Gelderblom et al. 2012):

> The success of these trading companies in spearheading European colonization is generally associated with the competitive edge lent by their particular corporate form, which in turn counts as an example of the superiority of Western legal traditions over those in China or the Islamic world . . . The new corporate features are usually seen as purposeful adaptations of existing legal forms to the challenges of Europe's overseas trade with Asia, notably the large amounts of capital required, the long duration of voyages, and the increased risks along the way . . . They are also regarded as closely related to each other, a logical set making up a winning formula. This interpretation rests heavily on work by legal scholars seeking to unearth the roots of concepts such as limited liability and legal personhood.

Significantly, Gelderblom et al. correctly recognized the difficulties with such claims:

> There are two major problems with [this interpretation]. First, for a long time the dominant British and Dutch companies faced identical challenges,

but differed in their adoption of the associated legal solutions. By the early 1620s the Dutch East India Company [(*VOC*)] . . . possessed transferable shares, a permanent capital, and limited liability for owners and managers . . . This contrasts with the English East India Company (EIC, founded in 1600), which introduced similar features only during the 1650s . . . Second, while this particular lag may relate to political factors, notably the need for limited government . . . the time it took for the *VOC* to assemble various features shows that they did not form a coherent logical set from the start, but instead emerged one-by-one in response to particular circumstances, not the general challenges associated with the Asian trade. The company had transferable shares and limited liability for shareholders from the outset, but obtained a permanent capital only in 1612 and limited liability for directors in 1623.

While this is an insightful recognition of the importance of historical context, there is inadequate recognition that the EIC did not develop exchange-traded shares until the end of the 17th century (why?). This interpretation also omits the importance of 'public purpose' in the chartering of the *VOC* and related English joint-stock ventures. Following a practice common in the early trading and colonization efforts of the Iberian states, commercial interests often spearheaded such developments. The symbiosis of commercial interests and national foreign policy objectives cannot be ignored. Finally, the need to renew the charter after 10 years and provide a settling of accounts at that time (how?) is another decidedly 'non-modern' feature of *VOC* equity capital organization.

That the earliest exchange trading in joint-stock shares originated in Amsterdam is a credit to the ingenuity and commercial acumen of the Dutch merchants of that era. Yet, the creation of the primary vehicle for the emergence of exchange trading of joint-stock shares, the 'Dutch East India' company, was due as much to statesmanship as entrepreneurial initiative. The *VOC* emerged shortly after the creation of the purely private *Compagnie van Verre*, for the purpose of engaging in the Dutch East India trade. There followed quickly the creation of at least 10 similar companies, centered in different Dutch provinces, particularly Holland and Zeeland. Collectively these early companies were known as the *voor-compangnieen*. The competition among these companies proved to be "violent and not exclusively commercial" (Hecksher 1955, v.1, p.356). In 1602, the States General, under the leadership of the Dutch statesman Johan van Oldenbarnevelt (1547–1619), was able to unify these various companies into the *Vereenigde Oostindische Compagnie* (*VOC*), commonly known as the Dutch East India Company.

The negotiations leading up to the creation of the *VOC* indicate that a variety of possible organizations were considered (Hecksher 1955, v.1, p.360). While having sufficient legal and organizational structure to facilitate the emergence of trading in company shares, the final product was uniquely Dutch, though numerous elements were similar to English joint-stock companies. Consistent with mercantilist objectives behind the English joint-stock trading companies, there was the element of monopoly on trade granted by state charter to further national interests. To facilitate the creation of the *VOC*, the company charter passed by the States General granted a monopoly on the India trade for a period of 21 years, conceived as a succession of ventures, with an initial term that was to be 10 years. Even though another provision of the charter provided conditions for the shareholders to demand the return of capital with interest, in 1612 this provision was declared void by the company's governors and a decree issued that shares were to be cashed in through open sale on the Amsterdam exchange.

Permanence of the equity capital stock is an essential prerequisite for exchange trading of shares (e.g., Blair 2003). The reluctance of the company to permit the withdrawal of capital is understandable. The need to make large fixed investments involving expenditures on troops, making fortifications, and paying gratuities to gain agreements with foreign princes meant that a large portion of initial capital investment was not readily recoverable. As Gelderblom et al. (2012) documented, ships sent to 'India' were often seconded there for long periods of time (see Table 5.3). However, the process by which an article of the charter was voided does reflect how much the internal organization of the VOC differed from the English counterparts. The administration of the company was not unified but, rather, contained six chambers organized on local lines. This roughly reflected the composition of the *voor-compangnieen*, with the Amsterdam chamber being the most important, followed by Zeeland. Elaborate arrangements provided for the sharing of costs and profits among the chambers. Needless to say, such a system was administratively chaotic.

The administrative problem created by the six chambers was countered by the almost absolute authority of the governors of the company, organized in a common assembly known as the 'Seventeen Masters'. In turn, the VOC charter ceded authority over the 'Seventeen Masters' to the Estates General and not shareholders (Gelderblom et al. 2011). With one vote from any smaller chamber, the strength of the Amsterdam chamber was strong enough to control the assembly. Within this framework, shareholders had no effective influence: "no statement of accounts was made by the management during the whole of the company's existence. Dividends were paid entirely at the arbitrary pleasure of the governors and on one occasion they even openly threatened to withhold payments altogether if shareholders showed themselves refractory towards their 'lords and masters'" (Hecksher 1955, v.1, p.366). Similar to the 16th- and 17th-century English joint-stock companies, the company maintained strong links with the government. Within the governors of the company appear a variety of important public officials, both municipal and from the States General.

Following the creation of the VOC, other joint-stock ventures were introduced, but only one, the Dutch West India Company, chartered in 1621, met with prolonged success, though there was also some trade in shares of a smaller insurance company. The East and West India Companies were anomalies within the fabric of Dutch commercial success of the 17th and 18th centuries. Even the success of the West India Company required considerable government involvement, with half the capital coming from the government and considerable government pressure being used to raise the other half from private sources. Unlike the VOC, which engaged in political and military efforts solely for commercial objectives, the West India Company was chartered with state objectives in mind. The charter granted more authority to the States General, and military functions

Table 5.3   Overview of VOC Voyages 1602–1613

Ships departed from the Republic	92
Lost on outbound voyage	–3
Arrived in Asia	89
Stayed in Asia	–66
Returned to Republic	23
Returned to Republic	23
Lost on inbound voyage	–1
Too late to observe	–1
Arrived in Republic without stay in Asia	21
Stayed in Asia	66
Lost in warfare	–7
Lost due to shipwreck	–9
Broken up	–2
Other reasons for not returning	–17
Lost on inbound voyage	–4
Lost in Asia or inbound voyage	–39
Too late to observe	–5
Arrived in the Republic after stay in Asia	22

Probability of not arriving in Asia = 3/92 = 3.26%

Probability of not arriving in Republic when no stay in Asia 1/(23–1) = 4.55%

Probability of not arriving in Republic when stay in Asia 39/(66–5) = 63.93%

Statistics on arrival in Republic without stay in Asia (21 observations minus 2 missing observations)

Average 669.84 days

Standard deviation: 209.62 days

Minimum: 246 days

Statistics on arrival in Republic with stay in Asia (22 observations)

Average 1270.41 days

Standard deviation: 245.39 days

Minimum: 941 days

Source: Gelderblom et al. (2012)

Note: The other reasons for not returning are that ship stays in Asia permanently (8 ships), out of sight (2 ships), unknown (7 ships). Stayed in Asia is defined as ships having a duration of stay in Asia of more than one year.

were more in evidence. Perhaps for these reasons, of the only two Dutch company shares regularly traded on the Amsterdam exchange, West India Company shares were always far less important.

Gelderblom et al. (2011, 2012) provided numerous significant observations about the financing of the company, directors and shareholders in the VOC.

In particular, almost from the beginning of shares being exchange traded, a market value was established that shareholders could use to secure financing, such as for making a subscription payment. VOC shares were preferred collateral compared to municipal and government annuities. Another significant observation concerned the method of using short-term debt to finance voyages with long-horizon payback. Instead of obtaining more long-term financing, the company extinguished short-term debts using cash flow from returning ships. (Shades of Antonio the merchant in Shakespeare's *Merchant of Venice!*) However, this created problems for the smaller chambers and impacted the VOC's ability to expand. "The dependency on circulating capital for finance thus formed a serious check on operations, let alone on expansion. Yet expansion was what the company needed" (Gelderblom et al. 2012, p.11). Similarly, "the directors' personal credit provided a vital ingredient to the early expeditions. They paid for supplies from their own purse and charged interest on these advances, or else obtained them with suppliers' credit" (Gelderblom et al. 2011, p.37).

In addition to methods of financing the VOC, Gelderblom et al. (2011, pp.39–40) discussed the terms set out in the charter to permit transferability of shares. Holland, a small country, faced considerable commercial, military and political difficulties in mustering resources to confront the Portuguese and other countries in seaborne trade with Asia. Unlike with more traditional seaborne routes to the Baltic and West Africa, the need for equity capital of long duration was paramount. Given that the initial contract was for 10 years, precise terms describing the process for transferring shares needed to be included in the charter to obtain the needed funds.

> Shareholders in the VOC received the right to have their money back on the presentation of full accounts for the first ten-year period in 1612 (article 7). These terms were not fundamentally different from the four-year turnover time of earlier expeditions to Asia, only longer. The longer timespan was probably the reason for defining a share transfer procedure, though the speed with which share trading developed after the VOC's launch suggests that a demand for easy transferability of shares had manifested itself before.

As for the specific terms that were included in the VOC charter dealing with the transfer of shares: "Two articles defined exit rights. In addition to the right to sell shares stipulated in the preamble to the subscription register, shareholders were given a general exit right after the 1612 accounts (No. 7), while as we have seen the shareholders in the 1602 expedition could opt out (No. 9)."

Appendix: Charter of the English 'East India Company' (1600)

The text of the Royal Charter granted by Queen Elizabeth to the East India Company is available at: http://www.sdstate.edu/projectsouthasia/loader.cfm?cs Module=security/getfile&PageID=857407. This company was only a pale precursor of the British East India Company (BEIC)—the United Company of Merchants of England Trading to the East Indies—which was formed in 1708 by merging the East India Company with a rival. The BEIC was a cornerstone in the British Empire and played a critical role in many historical events—including the Great Bengal Famine (1770), the Boston Tea Party (1773), the First (1839–1842) and Second (1856–1860) Opium Wars and the Indian Rebellion of 1857. The BEIC is a classic example of the connection between national foreign policy objectives and joint-stock companies formed with royal charter subject to renewal. It was private armies controlled by the BEIC that led to British control over much of India in the early 19th century. The government effectively nationalized much of the BEIC with the Government of India Act (1858), though the company continued with reduced power and influence until the East India Stock Dividend Redemption Act (1873), which resulted in the winding up of the company.

The text of the East India Company charter (1600), in the fashion of legal documents of the era, was written over a number of pages without paragraphing. This renders the text difficult to read. Despite this barrier, there is considerable substance in the document. The beginning of the text names the 200-plus individuals that "shall be one Body Corporate and Politick, in Deed and in Name, by the Name of The Governor and Company of Merchants of London, Trading into the East-Indies". The intertwining of national and company objectives is specified as "they, at their own Adventures, Costs, and Charges, as well for the Honour of this our Realm of England, as for the Increase of our Navigation, and Advancement of Trade of Merchandize, within our said Realms and the Dominions of the same, might adventure and set forth one or more Voyages, with convenient Number of Ships and Pinnaces, by way of Traffic and Merchandize to the East-Indies, in the Countries and Parts of Asia and Africa, and to as many of the Islands, Ports and Cities, Towns and Places, thereabouts, as where Trade and Traffic may by all likelihood be discovered, established or had". The first governor of the company, "Thomas Smith, Alderman of London", is named, as are important committee members. Rules for company governance and much more are detailed.

NOTES

1 The use of *commenda* is not standard, especially where the contract used in one specific locale is of interest. For example, Martinelli (1977), who examined early records by John the Scribe in Genoa, referenced the *accomandatio* and the *societas maris* and did not refer to the *commenda*. The *tractator* and *commendator* were referred to as *accomandatario* and *accomandante*. The use of *commenda* was popularized by Udovitch.

2 A number of sources make reference to joint-stock companies appearing as early as Roman times, being used in the financing of public projects and tax farming. More precisely, companies of *equites* ('knights') were used for collecting taxes, especially in Asian provinces, and in public works construction. However, while these early associations may have had some basic characteristics of the later joint-stock companies, such as a form of corporate personality, other features such as negotiability and transferability of shares were not present.

3 Bosher (1988, 1995) discussed the corresponding situation in France around this time.

4 It was not until 1672 that Charles II granted a charter of incorporation to the Royal African Company. The charter "included a monopoly on the slave trade between West Africa and the West Indies. [The Company] flourished for a while, experiencing its heyday in the 1680s, when it accounted for more than two-thirds of the slave deliveries to the Indies. Yet it declined rapidly after the Glorious Revolution as it could not get parliamentary ratification of its royal monopoly" (Harris 2000, p.49).

6 The Early Markets for Trading in Shares

> The man who is interested in nothing but 'facts' forgets sometimes that religious, social and political ideals are among the most real and insistent facts in history, which must be frankly faced, even if they are finally to be explained away.
>
> Coulton (1921, p.67)

A THE ORIGINS OF EXCHANGE TRADING

Exchange Trading of Goods

The rudiments of modern exchange trading in equity capital shares emerged during the 17th century. Yet, there are subtle and not-so-subtle differences between modern common shares and the joint-stock shares of the 16th to 18th centuries. A number of differences arise from the form of business organization. Modern corporations operate within a different legal structure than applied to the early joint-stock companies. The early methods of joint-stock company formation, such as by chartering and subscription, and the applicable law of limited liability were substantively different than in modern times (Shannon 1931; Baskin and Miranti 1997; Gelderblom 2013). Another important difference arises because many of the most important English joint-stock companies and some of those in Europe were chartered with monopoly privileges over some activity in exchange for using the paid-in share capital to later purchase government debt. This made the cash flows and risk characteristics of these joint stocks different from those of modern common shares.

The origin of exchange trading of equity capital claims can be found in the goods market. Commercial goods transactions in early markets often involved a rudimentary sale agreement structured as a forward contract with option features. The contract could vary from loosely structured to formal and notarized. Unstated terms and conditions of such agreements were often governed by merchant convention (e.g., Malynes 1622; Peri 1638). For example, because trading on samples was common in 16th- and 17th-century goods markets, an agreement for a future sale would typically have a provision that would permit the purchaser to refuse delivery if the delivered goods were found to be of inadequate quality when compared to the original sample. As reflected in notarial protests stretching back to antiquity, disagreement over what constituted satisfactory delivery was common.[1] Contracting practices in the goods market were also employed in the early trading of 'stocks'. The history of stock market globalization demonstrates the importance of recognizing the connection between cash market trading and the corresponding use of forward sale contracts to facilitate such trade.

Following van der Wee (1977) and Gelderblom and Jonker (2005), the first instance in which a contingent claim was unbundled and traded as a separate security on an exchange was the transferable 'to arrive' commodity contracts traded on the Antwerp exchange during the 16th century. This development signifies the depth of liquidity and degree of trading sophistication associated with commodity transactions at a time when commercial sales typically employed either outright cash sales or, where trading on samples was involved, non-transferable forward contracts with multiple delivery dates. Similar to modern OTC (over-the-counter) derivative transactions, these contracts were executed as private deals between two signatories, usually employing *escripen*, notaries and "scriveners" to formalize the contract. As Malynes (1622, p.126) observed, if a broker was involved, a verbal contact could be used:[2]

> Verbal contracts are made between party and party, or by means of Brokers or Mediators, and that only by word without writing. Such are the daily buying and selling of commodities either for ready money, or payable at some dates of payment, wherein the mediation of a Broker is most necessary: For as it would be troublesome to use Scrivners in every bargain; so is it commodious to use the means of Brokers, the commodities are not only bought and sold with more credit and reputation, but all controversies which do arise by misadventure or otherwise are sooner determined, and a sworn Broker is taken as a double witness, if he do produce his book, with a *Memorandum* of the bargain, as the same was agreed between both parties, whereby many variances are reconciled, and differences (like to fall out) are prevented.

This brief discussion on the use of brokers in commodities transactions follows a longer discussion by Malynes (1622, pp.124–6) regarding the use of "notarial contracts" in the trading business of the regulated company of "Merchant Adventurers", where the systemic use of forward sale contracts in their commercial transactions is apparent.[3] In modern vernacular, the contracts that Malynes described for the sale of English cloth goods arranged on the English bourse in Antwerp, the Bruges bourse and other important commercial centers were structured as non-transferable forward sale contracts with option features.

Since the 17th century, share trading has been increasingly associated with 'stock exchanges', which requires 'exchange' to be defined. As painfully apparent in the modern difficulties confronting the SEC (US Securities and Exchange Commission) since Reg ATS was contemplated in 1997 (see Poitras 2012, ch.12), this is not as easy as might be expected. Many conventional and technical definitions for an "exchange" are possible (e.g., Lee 1998, pp.322–3). Almost all modern academic definitions identify an exchange with a physical location or building. This creates problems when, say, the 'exchange' is in cyberspace. The Securities Exchange Act (1934; amended 2010) currently identifies an exchange as follows:

> The term "exchange" means any organization, association, or group of persons, whether incorporated or unincorporated, which constitutes, maintains, or provides a market place or facilities for bringing together purchasers and sellers of securities or for otherwise performing with respect to securities the functions commonly performed by a stock exchange as that term is generally understood, and includes the market place and the market facilities maintained by such exchange.

This expands the location of an exchange to be a 'market place' with 'facilities' which:

> includes its premises, tangible or intangible property whether on the premises or not, any right to the use of such premises or property or any service thereof for the purpose of effecting or reporting a transaction on an exchange (including, among other things, any system of communication to or from the exchange, by ticker or otherwise. . .).

Significantly, while recognizing the technological evolution of segmented exchanges into a market system of trading platforms, this definition does not detail "the functions commonly performed by a stock exchange as that term is generally understood".

The history of the stock market illustrates the relevance of accurately identifying stock exchange functions. Some general definitions treat 'bourse' and 'exchange' as synonyms; an example is provided by Ehrenberg (1928, p.54):

> A bourse or exchange is an assembly meeting at frequent intervals, usually daily, consisting of the merchants and other persons, who meet for the purpose of dealing without exhibiting, delivering or paying for their goods at the same time.

This definition identifies essential characteristics that apply to 'bourse' and 'exchange', but in doing so ignores features that can be used to distinguish 'bourse trading' and 'exchange trading'. The definition is sufficient to distinguish an exchange from, say, a marketplace selling produce and is preferable to definitions that identify an exchange only as a physical location where buyers and sellers meet to trade goods.[4] However, this commonly used general definition fails to identify characteristics of an 'exchange' that facilitate "speculative exchange trading". Characteristics associated with contracts, clearing and settlement procedures can be identified to make a distinction between centralized 'exchange' trading in a single building and decentralized bourse trading that takes place in multiple venues in a specific geographical location.

Given this, the impact of exchange-trading techniques on the historical evolution of the stock market can be more readily identified. In particular, speculative exchange trading of a transferable security contract needs to be distinguished from a situation where a buyer and seller meet at, say, the Royal Exchange and agree to a forward sale of goods with a contract then drawn up by a 'scrivner'. In this situation, it is the goods that are being traded, not the forward contract. Speculative exchange trading requires transferability and an exchange-clearing mechanism to settle positions. In turn, transferability requires standardized contract terms and relatively homogeneous deliverable commodity. A transaction where merchants meet at the Royal Exchange and agree to a non-transferable forward contract with multiple delivery dates would correspond, in modern terms, to an OTC commodity swap transaction. There is no exchange-clearing mechanism for the transaction. The merchants that are party and counter-party to the trade are responsible for completion. As such, a technical distinction is being made that corresponds to the modern difference between trading derivative securities on exchanges or OTC. In addition to the clearing mechanism, there can be significant variation in the character of exchange speculation due to settlement practices – that is, between cash settlement and 'settlement by account'.

The beginning of purely speculative exchange trading occurs when the parties involved in the completion of the trade are different from those initiating the trade. This requires a traded contract to be created for which there is no intention of completing the underlying goods transaction; in effect, the seller may not have possession of the goods and the buyer may not intend to take delivery. In this case, a contract is created for which there is no resulting delivery of goods. This requires a clearing method for determining and settling gains and losses on contracts. Various conditions are required for such trading to occur. The evolution was gradual, not dramatic, and depended on a range of informal restrictions on those participating in the trade. Recognizing that initial trade was in the bulk commodities of herring, whale oil and wheat—commodities that required special warehousing, grading and handling facilities—initial trade was associated with brokers and dealers directly involved in the bulk commodity trade willing to execute 'to arrive' forward contracts for which there were no associated goods transactions, seeking to offset the position prior to delivery or, if necessary, cover the position in the spot market upon the fleet's arrival. Given the vagaries of market liquidity, in the event the contract could not be transferred, both parties to the contract needed to be able to complete delivery.

From Fairs to Bourse Trading

The evolution of exchange trading techniques for bulk commodities revolved around two important elements: (1) enhanced securitization of the transactions; and (2) the emergence of speculative trading. Both of these developments were closely connected with the increasing concentration of commercial activity, initially at the large medieval market fairs and, later, on the bourses and exchanges. Securitization of bulk commodity transactions was facilitated by extending trading methods that had been in use for centuries in the market for bills of exchange.[5] Prior to the emergence of joint-stock companies, bills of exchange and related contracts were the primary methods of raising capital for trading ventures during this period. By implication, the early markets in bills of exchange were the precursors of modern stock markets. By the 16th century, the central role of bills of exchange in financing domestic and international trade was associated with the prevalence of partnerships to structure firm governance. The seasonality of the commodity businesses that dominated commercial trading and the 'localized' character of international trade did not require permanency in firm capital structure, which the joint-stock company facilitated in the following century.

In addition to being centers of trade in goods, the medieval fairs were financial events. The fairs, such as those at Champagne, featured well-organized money markets conducting manual foreign-exchange transactions and substantial dealings in bills of exchange (de Roover 1954, p.204).[6] Because the larger fairs involved transactions between merchants from many different regions, it was not practical to settle all transactions using manual exchange of coin. This was a primary impetus for dealings on credit, as de Roover (1949, p.110) observed:[7]

> Today banks discount the trade acceptances or the promissory notes of merchants who are in need of credit. Such a procedure was ruled out as long as contracts involving the payment of interest were unenforceable at law. It is true that usury laws could be circumvented by various subterfuges. However, the easiest method for securing short-term credit was for merchants to "take up" money by exchange and not at interest. The result of this practice was that commercial credit was tied to the exchange. This point, although obvious, is so fundamental that its importance should be stressed . . . the credit system rested on the exchanges.

As such, methods for clearing and settlement of bill of exchange transactions were fundamental to the smooth operation of the international commercial and financial system.

Though the precise origin of the practice is unknown, 'arbitration of exchange' first developed during the Middle Ages. Around the time of the First Crusade (1095–1099), Genoa had emerged as a major sea power and important trading centre. The Genoa fairs had become important economic and financial events that attracted traders from around the Mediterranean. To deal with the problems of reconciling transactions using different coinages and units of account, a forum for arbitrating exchange rates was introduced. On the third day of each fair at Genoa, a representative body composed of recognized merchant bankers would assemble and determine the exchange rates that would prevail for that fair. The process involved each banker suggesting an exchange rate, and, after some discussion, a voting process would determine the exchange rates that would apply at that fair. Similar practices were adopted at other important fairs later in the Middle Ages. At Lyons, for example, Florentine, Genoese and Lucca bankers would meet separately to determine rates, with the average of these group rates becoming the official rate. These rates would then apply to bill transactions and other business conducted at the fair. Rates typically stayed constant between fairs in a particular location, providing the opportunity for arbitraging of exchange rates across fairs in different locations.

The actual clearing process differed from fair to fair (Parker 1974, p.546). At the Lyons fairs, clearing involved the participation of all merchants attending the fair. At other fairs, such as the fairs of Besançon or Medina del Campo, clearing was controlled by a restricted group of merchant-bankers who were responsible for setting exchange rates and for handling the book-transfers between the accounts of merchants at the various clearing member banks. Ehrenberg (1928, p.284) described the clearing process used in Lyons as follows:[8]

> Before the merchants attended the fair they entered in their 'market book' . . . all the payments due from or to them in the fair. At the beginning of the fair these payments books were compared with one another. In the case of every entry found correct the person from whom the payment was due made a mark which was taken as a binding recognition of the debt; later he had to sign his whole name. The bill—for, generally speaking, there was no question of anything but bills—was *accepted* in this way. If an item was not recognized, the owner of the book would write by it 'S.P.' (*sous protest*).
>
> After the acceptance of the old bills there followed the new business with foreign markets, which originated wither at the preceding fair or as the result of the acceptance, or otherwise. Here we meet for the first time a peculiar arrangement, the settlement of an official average price for each species of bill, the so-called Conto . . .
>
> [T]he Conto in Lyons was done as follows: The bill dealers met on a certain day and formed a circle (*Faire la Ronde*); the Consul of the Florentines then asked the dealers of the different nations in turn what they thought the price ought to be. The answers were noted and an average taken. This was the official rate for bills which was noted in the bulletins . . . and sent abroad. The dealers themselves were naturally not bound by this, their business was left free to bargaining. Yet the Conto at the beginning had some meaning for the market itself, as previously many transactions had been concluded at the average rate which had not yet been settled . . .
>
> The payment proper closed the fair. It was affected chiefly by *viremant de parties, giro* or *scontro*, as follows: Two persons were commissioned to collect and compare . . . all the fair books. They then canceled the payments against one another, and only paid the balances in cash . . . The fair payments at Lyons owe their form to the Florentines, a fact which is clearly shown by the development of the Lyons Bourse.

Various features of the clearing process at Lyons not only were adapted for use at other important fairs but also had an impact on the methods later employed on the Lyons bourse. The method of offset used in the end-of-fair settling process was later reflected in the *rescontre* system adopted to settle exchange trading of shares in 17th-century Amsterdam and 18th-century England.[9]

The Lyons fairs first assumed importance in the 1460s due to the explicit mercantilist policies of Louis XI. As early as 1419, various French kings had granted privileges to merchants doing business in Lyons in an attempt to counteract the success of the fairs held in Geneva. These privileges included freedom to engage in various financial transactions, such as manual exchange of coin and dealing in bills of exchange, activities that were tightly regulated elsewhere in France. Even more than the economic benefits associated with the commodities trade, the French monarchs were motivated by the gains associated with the financial dealings of the fairs. By the 15th century, substantial capital could be raised at important fairs such as those of Geneva. This capital was essential to securing financing for the military adventures in which European monarchs were almost continually engaged. The extension of commercial liberties beyond the time period of the fairs contributed significantly to the emergence of bourse trading. As early as the end of the 13th century, the dukes of Brabant encouraged the growth of Antwerp by granting privileges to alien merchants visiting the city (van Houtte 1966), such as not requiring that local brokers be used to transact commodity business. Such merchants trading in Bruges, the northern centre of European commerce during the 14th century, were required to use local brokers.

While the medieval fairs were an important step in the growth of trade and payments, by the late 15th century economic activity was outgrowing the restrictions of the fixed fair dates. A network of international merchants had established permanent offices and warehouses throughout the key commercial centres of Europe. To support the associated trading activities, sizeable communities of foreign merchants were established. These changes meant that liquidity was sufficient to support trading throughout the year. This growth sustained the creation of bourse trading in various cities, designed to facilitate dealings in both physical and financial commodities. The bourses were, effectively, meeting places for merchants of various countries to transact financial and commodities business. The use of the term 'bourse' (beurs) is indicative of the historical development, the term being taken from a square in Bruges, named for an inn on the square owned at one time by the van Beurs family, where the Florentines, Genoese and Venetians had their consular houses. This inn was a popular meeting place for foreign merchants. Though exchange trading of free-standing derivative securities was yet to come, some essential characteristics of exchange trading are discernible at the beginnings of the bourses: a self-regulating collection of merchants—both brokers and dealers—meeting for the mutual gain of enhanced liquidity. For the early bourses, access to credit and foreign-exchange facilities were integral.

Bourse trading was a major improvement over trading at medieval fairs and local markets for at least two reasons. First, trading at the fairs was restricted to specific time periods. While initially useful as a method of concentrating mercantile activity, the growth of trade soon surpassed the narrow time windows provided by the individual fairs. Bourse trading involved both financial transactions and trading in goods. For the medieval fairs, these two activities were complementary. Commercial trade in goods generated financial transactions, activities that were facilitated by the concentrated activity of the fair. Yet, as evidenced in the activities of merchant bankers in centres such as Bruges (e.g., de Roover 1948), there were other reasons for financial activity independent of goods trading, especially trading in bills of exchange for investment and market-making purposes. These financial activities formed the basis of an element of bourse trading that can be traced back to the Middle Ages in southern Europe, starting in the trading centers of Italy. By the 14th century, financial bourse trading could be found in certain northern European centers, most importantly Bruges (Ehrenberg 1928, p.55):

> in the trading cities of Italy, [bourse trading] arose from the business which developed at the banks of the money-changers native to the city, when the notaries likewise had stalls in the open air . . . there arose . . . the character-istics of the exchange business as early as the fourteenth century . . . In the countries north of the Alps bill business . . . developed in closest connection with the factories of the Italians. The streets and market places where they lived, and more especially where they had their consular houses or Loggias, were the localities where the bourse business first developed.

Bruges was geographically well situated to have the first significant bourse trading in northern Europe. The opening of trade routes through the Strait of Gibraltar contributed to the decline of fairs along the land trade routes, such as the Champagne fairs. In addition, the Hansards developed important seaborne trade from northern Europe. This growth in seaborne traffic contributed to the rise of Bruges as "the greatest market of Christendom in the fourteenth century" (van Houtte 1966, p.37).

In addition to being a major seaport, Bruges was the locale for one of the five fairs of Flanders. Bruges's importance peaked in the mid-1300s, with the comparatively faster growth of commercial markets and bourses in other centres being due to two primary local factors: (1) the silting of the waterway connecting Bruges to the ocean and (2) the various restrictions imposed by Bruges on foreign merchants trading there. The international growth of trade meant that Portuguese, Spanish, South German and Italian merchants had sufficient reason to establish permanent colonies in locales such as Bruges and Antwerp, where, before, these merchants sojourned to the fairs. The freedoms granted to alien merchants also played a key role in determining where bourse trading was concentrated.[10] From the beginnings of bourse trading there was competition between geographical venues for business.

A second factor favouring bourse trading was that fairs required goods to be transported to the fair for inspection in order to conclude specific transactions. The goods were then transported to another district to be sold. As trade expanded, factors such as acceptable levels of standardization and the growth of mutual merchant confidence allowed goods transactions to be made without actual inspection of goods at the time the sale was completed. In turn, bourses and exchanges were located close to the center of the underlying bulk goods trade. Such factors significantly reduced transactions, transport and other costs. By providing enhanced liquidity and cheaper execution, bourse trading was an essential impetus to the emergence of speculation in commodities, which, ultimately, progressed into speculative exchange trading of derivative securities on stocks and shares.

The Antwerp Exchange

Though the transition from discrete trading intervals at the medieval fairs to the regularity of bourse trading was gradual, the 16th century did provide a transition period: At the beginning of the century, the fairs still played an important role in providing fixed dates and locations at which concentrations of liquid capital were assembled; by the end of the century, general economic activity was such that bourse and exchange trading predominated. During the century, the emergence of exchange trading in Antwerp and Lyons was especially important, though by the end of the century both of these centers were in decline. Of the two, Antwerp was initially more important for trade in commodities, while Lyons was initially more important for trade in bills of exchange. In 1531, Antwerp opened a new exchange building designed exclusively for trading of commodities and bills of exchange.[11] Tawney (1925, pp.62–5) described the international money market of the 16th century as follows:

> In its economic organization the machinery of international trade had reached a state of efficiency not noticeably inferior to that of three centuries later. Before the most highly-organized economic systems of the age were ruined by the struggle between Spain and the Netherlands, and by the French wars of religion, there were perhaps ten to twelve commercial centres whose money markets were the financial power-houses of European trade, and whose opinion and policy were decisive in determining financial conditions. In the Flemish, French and Italian cities where it reached its zenith, and of which England was a pupil, the essence of financial organization of the sixteenth century was internationalism, freedom for every capitalist to undertake every transaction within his means, a unity which had as its symptom the movement of all the principal markets in sympathy with each other, and as its effect the mobilisation of immense resources at the strategic points of international finance. Its centre and symbol was the exchange at Antwerp, with its significant dedication, '*Ad mercatorum cujusque gentis ac linguae*' where . . . every language under heaven could be heard, or the fairs at Lyon which formed, in the words of a Venetian, 'the foundations of the pecuniary transactions of the whole of Italy and of a good part of Spain and of the Netherlands'.

The public good characteristic of such a centralized exchange location was recognized and adapted in other centers. Sir Thomas Gresham personally advanced the funds for the constructing of a similar exchange building in London, the Royal Exchange, opening in 1571. With initial construction starting in 1611 on the new building for the Amsterdam Exchange, by 1613 the transfer of trading to the exchange from different venues around the city was completed.[12]

Fully developed speculative trading in commodities emerged in Antwerp during the second half of the 16th century (Tawney 1925, pp.62–5; Gelderblom and Jonker 2005). The development of the Antwerp commodity market provided sufficient liquidity to support the development of trading in 'to arrive' contracts associated with the rapid expansion of seaborne trade during the period.

Speculative transactions in 'to arrive' grain that was still at sea were particularly active, with trade in whale oil, herring and salt also important (e.g., Emery 1896; Barbour 1950; Gelderblom and Jonker 2005). Unger (1980) provided detailed information on the herring industry during this period. The Dutch herring trade to the Baltic was intimately connected to the grain trade to southern Europe. Thanks to superior technology, the Dutch herring fleets dominated this trade until the second half of the 17th century. The evolution of the herring fishery depended on increased capital requirements; as a consequence, the role of brokers also evolved: "By the mid-fifteenth century the brokers were becoming owners and operators of ships as well. They were merchants with an interest in more assured supplies of preserved fish . . . even individuals with no direct connection with fishing can and did invest in the boats and their supplies" (p.258).

That 'to arrive' contracts came to be actively traded by speculators also directly involved in trading the underlying physical commodity is not surprising. Because transport by sea was a risky business and information about cargoes to arrive at a later date could be sketchy, the quality and quantity of physical commodity available for delivery could not be known prior to arrival of the fleet; a forward sale of such cargoes would be inherently speculative. The concentration of speculative liquidity on the Antwerp Exchange centered on the important merchants and large merchant houses that controlled either financial activities or the goods trade (van der Wee 1977). The milieu for such trading was closely tied to medieval traditions of gambling and insurance where wagering on ships' safe return, a rudimentary form of early insurance (Lewin 2003), was often connected with the conclusion of commercial transactions. A key step in the evolution of exchange-traded contracts came when trading in 'to arrive' contracts involved standardized transactions in fictitious goods for a future delivery that was settled by the payment of 'differences'.[13] Purchasers of such contracts would speculate on the rise in prices before the due date. If such a rise occurred, the contract could then be sold, and the speculator pocketed or, if prices fell, paid the difference in price. This 'difference dealing' was also conducted by goods vendors, selling for future delivery betting that prices would fall.

The development of difference dealing was accompanied by the emergence of 'premium contracts' where: "The buyer made a contract for future delivery at a fixed price, but with the condition that he could reconsider after two or three months: he could then withdraw from the contract provided that he paid a premium to the vendor (*stellegelt*)" (van der Wee 1977). Little is known about the precise evolution of the contracts used for speculative trading, but the premium contract appears well suited to difference dealing by speculators. The 'premium' form of contract for forward sale became a staple of the European securities trade into the 20th century—for example, the contract for the German *prämiengeschäfte* (Hafner and Zimmermann 2009). Such contracts differ from the options traded in modern markets, which have inherited characteristics associated with historical features of US option trading. Following Emery (1896, p.53), the *prämiengeschäfte* "may be considered as an ordinary contract for future delivery with special stipulation that, in consideration of a cash payment, one of the parties has the right to withdraw from the contract within a specified time".[14] As such, this option is a feature of a forward contract, with a fee to be paid at delivery if the option is exercised. For example, on the 19th century Paris and Berlin exchanges the premium payment at maturity was fixed by convention and the 'price' would be determined by the setting the exercise price relative to the initial share price.

Characteristics of trading in commodities and bills of exchange in Antwerp formed the basis for later trading at other venues. Some elements of that trade are still of contemporary relevance. While access to the Antwerp exchange was unrestricted, those unconnected to the bulk commodity trade and seeking to speculate required a broker to establish a position. Brokers could also be dealers in the commodity. The exchange was a largely self-regulatory entity, with broker-dealers clearing speculative difference trades with other broker-dealers. Rules of conduct for trading were largely governed by merchant convention. Penalties for violations involved loss of reputation and an ensuing inability to conduct business. The state provided official recognition to certain 'sworn brokers' and established a civil court system for settling disputes. Physical infrastructure and a sympathetic legal and taxation environment promoted the development of trade. Difference dealing was facilitated by the use of premium contracts. Following traditions developed in the bill of exchange market, the clearing and settling of positions in commodity difference dealing was done by brokers coordinating with other brokers. The 'hand-to-hand' settlement practices in Antwerp involved primarily cash settlement of contracts, eliminating the possibility of contract offset associated with 'settlement by account'.

B   INITIAL TRADE IN JOINT-STOCK SHARES

From Antwerp to Amsterdam

Whatever the origin of the joint-stock company, the emergence of this method of organizing equity capital was slow and progressive. The changes represented by the first joint-stock company were not dramatic compared to other types of business arrangements, such as the regulated companies. In turn, exchange trading in joint-stocks was well established on the Amsterdam exchange before the first important descriptive analysis of the trading in shares of the Dutch India companies became available with Joseph de la Vega's *Confusion de Confusiones* (1688). Prior to this, writings on bourse trading of joint stocks, largely in Dutch, were concerned with controlling the undesirable implications arising from speculative trading activities (Barbour 1950, p.76; De Marchi and Harrison 1994; Gelderblom and Jonker 2004; Gelderblom et al. 2011; Gelderblom et al. 2013). The collapse of Antwerp in 1585 and the resulting diaspora of important merchants contributed substantially to the rise of Amsterdam as the most important commercial center in northern Europe (Gelderblom and Jonker 2004, p.664): "Between 1585 and 1620 the Amsterdam merchant community grew from less than 500 people to about 1500. The immigration of Antwerp merchants alone increased the city's capital stock by an estimated 50 percent."

The commercial decline of Antwerp and the subsequent rise of Amsterdam contributed to the construction of an important exchange in Amsterdam. This development brought Amsterdam in line with other important commercial centres such as London, where the Royal Exchange was established in 1571. While Amsterdam had developed as an important commercial center prior to 1585 (van Dillen 1927; Gelderblom and Jonker 2005), the establishment of a permanent building for the Amsterdam exchange in 1611 marks a symbolic beginning of Dutch commercial supremacy. Given this background, it is not surprising that commercial techniques employed on the Antwerp exchange were also adopted in Amsterdam.

During the 17th and 18th centuries, speculative trading of forward and option contracts on the Amsterdam exchange developed many essential features of such trading in modern derivative security markets. By the middle of the 17th century, speculative exchange trading in Amsterdam for shares in the Dutch East India Company (*VOC*) and, to a lesser extent, the Dutch West India Company,

Figure 6.1 Emanuel de Witte (1653), Courtyard of the Exchange in Amsterdam, *Museum Boijmans Van Beuningen*, Rotterdam

had progressed to where contracts with regular expiration dates were traded (Wilson 1941; Gelderblom and Jonker 2005), and a clearing method with contract offset and settlement by account was fully developed.[15] By the 18th century, the trade involved both Dutch joint stock-shares and "British funds". This trading on the Amsterdam exchange is the first historical instance of speculative exchange trading in financial derivative securities. "With the appearance of marketable British securities, and the application to them of a speculative technique that was already well understood, the Amsterdam [exchange] became the scene of international finance at its most abstract and most exciting—gambling in foreign securities" (Wilson 1941, p.79).

Despite isolated instances of previous joint-stock trading in other centres, the first developed market arose with trade in *VOC* shares in Amsterdam starting from the founding of the company by the States General in 1602.[16] At this time, the Amsterdam bourse was held in the open air near the New Bridge and in the church square near the *Oude Kerk*. It was not until 1613 that trading completely moved to a building dedicated for the Amsterdam exchange. Trading in shares was only a small portion of the general activity on the Amsterdam exchange, which was predominately in bills and commodities. Creation of the company led to a call for initial subscriptions of capital. Prospects for the company were generally perceived to be favorable among the moneyed individuals willing to invest in such a venture, and the closing of the *VOC* subscription lists found numerous individuals still desiring shares. These individuals turned to the Amsterdam bourse to purchase shares and, when they could not do so at par, a 14%–16% premium emerged within a number of days (Ehrenberg 1928, p.358).[17] With such immediate returns, the potential for gain became apparent to bourse traders, and the speculative trade in shares began in earnest, with the selling of shares for deferred delivery not owned at the time of the sale. This initial trade was conducted in bourse fashion, using OTC-style forward contracting.

By the beginning of the 17th century, it was apparent that bourse trading in Amsterdam was becoming the successor to the Antwerp exchange, which had fallen on hard times due to a combination of political, geographic and economic factors. In conjunction with the shift in trading activity, many of the traders also eventually relocated from Antwerp to Amsterdam and brought with them the trading techniques that had developed on the Antwerp exchange. Among these techniques was speculative trading for future delivery. This technique, almost immediately, was applied to trading in *VOC* shares. At least since Ehrenberg (1928, pp.358–9), the sophisticated methods used for trading in *VOC* shares have been recognized:

> From the beginning, the speculation in shares . . . as a means of gain depending on taking advantage of future price changes, made it appear extremely desirable to postpone the fulfilment of the bargains. In the case of bears, who had sold shares which they did not possess, this was an absolute necessity.
>
> Speculative future dealings made possible a twofold simplification of the technique of dealing. First, speculative dealings could be realized before the

date of delivery. Secondly, settling days made it possible to use the same procedure that had done so much in the methods of payment, namely, set off. Both together resulted in an incalculable increase in turnover, since now only a little ready money and stock were required for very large dealings.

Significantly, "it was speculation which made the first modern stock exchange". Speculators provided the liquidity essential for continuous trading and 'accurate' pricing. In turn, traders seeking to acquire or dispose of stock positions provided the 'honest' liquidity needed to clear the market. De la Vega (1688, p.164) suggested that the relative composition of the speculative trading population changed over time, reflecting the evolution from bourse to exchange trading: whereas "formerly twenty speculators ruled the exchange . . . Today there are as many speculators as merchants".

Kellenbenz (1957, pp.139–42) provided a useful summary of de la Vega's discussion of the various types of transactions in the Amsterdam market:

a   There were sales of real stock against immediate payment of cash.

b   There were comparable sales where the money to cover payments was borrowed from individuals, up to four-fifths of its value.

c   There were transactions in which future settlement dates were specified—that is, beyond the regular monthly settlement dates. These future contracts were seemingly used for both speculative and hedging purposes, both by speculators and by the lenders on securities. De la Vega implies that the latter parties always hedged by means of such contracts. Hypothecation, which was mentioned as early as 1610 (in the edict of that year), was permitted to the seller presumably during the period of the forward contract. Arrangements also were possible, and were fairly frequently resorted to whereby the date of the termination of a future contract could be postponed, apparently by mutual consent of the parties. This action was called 'prolongation'. A large proportion of the foregoing future sales were really sales '*in blanco*'—or short sales, as we would label them—even though such transactions were prohibited by laws of the state and of the city.

d   There were options contracts. These were at least of the 'call' and 'put' varieties, which have persisted ever since . . . Option contracts were utilized sometimes for hedging purposes by *bona fide* investors, but more commonly for mere speculation . . .

e   In addition there were purchases and sales of 'ducaton' shares. (Such transactions were of recent origin in 1688, and actually had been abandoned in the slump that had occurred just as de la Vega was writing his book.) What this 'ducaton' trading amounted to is a bit uncertain on the strength of what de la Vega actually says. Scholars who have worked on this period assert that the ducaton shares were fictitious . . .

Trading for forward delivery was essential to the 17th-century trade in shares on the Amsterdam exchange (Barbour 1950).[18] Such trading was of practical necessity because the delivery and settlement process for traded shares was much different than the modern process. Though shares could be transferred, the process required the seller to be present at the *VOC* offices to record the transfer in the 'book of shareholders' and to pay a transfer fee. The practice of same-day cash settlement, delivery and transfer was not usually possible—even for trades arranged at the transfer office.[19] Agreements to sell shares typically included a future settlement and transfer date that could be months in the future, though delivery dates longer than one month in the future were discouraged by statute starting in 1610.

KELLENBENZ (1957) ON DUCATON TRADING

The actual trading mechanics for ducaton shares are somewhat obscure. Kellenbenz (p.142) provided perhaps the best discussion of this activity:

At all events the best authorities assure us that in such dealings the 'stock' had a nominal value of a tenth of that of real East India shares. No delivery of securities was expected, of course, and the point of the whole business was the calculation of profit or loss at a monthly settlement date . . . de la Vega describes how, for settlement purposes, the value of fictitious stock was determined on the day appointed . . . Apparently an official of the exchange put a legal termination to the transactions to be included within the given period by raising a stick as a signal. Some folk wanted the raising of the stick delayed others to have it speeded up; and seemingly the speculators gave loud vent to their respective desires.

Isaac le Maire and the First Market Manipulation in Stocks

Recent treatments of Isaac le Maire have attempted to resurrect him as an aggrieved shareholder fighting the 'good fight' against the *VOC* directors' heavy-handed governance. For example, Gelderblom et al. (2012, pp.12–3) claimed that "Isaac Lemaire, a former *VOC* director who had left the board in 1605 after policy dispute, angrily petitioned the Grand Pensionary Johan van Oldenbarnevelt" about a plan being advanced to the States General in 1609 to ignore "the statutory liquidation" of the *VOC* in 1612. Such a plan "would be illegal, improper and unfair to shareholders, Lemaire argued", also warning that "without dividend, full accounts and liquidation, no investor would subscribe to a successor company". While recognizing that le Maire had "earned his reputation as a rancorous renegade", the connection between previous events in his life and the petition to Oldenbarnevelt is undeveloped. The implication that *VOC* directors subsequently "responded by posting dividends" in response ignores the more likely event that this would have happened whether le Maire acted as a shareholder activist or not.

Le Maire is appropriately remembered in modern times for organizing the first 'bear raid' on joint-stock shares. Market manipulation was an important feature of the early bourse and exchange trading in company shares. General public sentiment about initial joint-stock trading was concerned with various schemes that were aimed at rigging the market. This concern generated much of the early analysis of joint-stock trading (e.g., De Marchi and Harrison 1994; van Dillen 1930). Instead of developing analytical methods for determining the appropriate price of shares, much of the early discussion of joint-stock trading centred on describing the negative features of the speculative trade that was taking place. Of course, attempts to manipulate markets did not originate with early share trading in Amsterdam. For example, Aristotle in *Politics* referred to a Sicilian who cornered the cash market for iron by buying up all available supplies. Anecdotal evidence for similar early examples of market manipulations can be identified in the writings of Cicero and others.

The techniques of share trading on the Amsterdam exchange were inherited from techniques used on the Antwerp exchange for commodities and bills of exchange. Market manipulations were not uncommon in Antwerp. Perhaps the most infamous case happened in 1540 when Gaspare Ducci "formed a ring which succeeded in creating panic on the Antwerp [exchange] and in cornering the factor of the King of Portugal. Ducci apparently had piled up a huge store of money by selling bills of exchange on his accomplices abroad" (de Roover 1949, pp.159–60). When the king of Portugal, through his factor, entered the market to pay off maturing debts, Ducci was the only lender with sufficient funds to lend. Such manipulations in the 16th- and 17th-century bill markets were grist for the views of Sir Thomas Gresham, Gerard Malynes and others who were strong proponents of the view that a banker monopoly rigged the exchange market.

Techniques required to corner or otherwise manipulate a security or commodity market were almost certainly common knowledge to the early share traders in Amsterdam. One such trader was Isaac le Maire, who was able to obtain Fl.60,000 of Dutch East India shares in the initial subscription of 1602. Recognizing that "calculating the market value of VOC shares before the 1620s is a hazardous undertaking, for we only have scattered references from a variety of sources" (Gelderblom and Jonker 2004, pp.661–2), evidence indicates that, following an initial increase of 15%, the price of VOC shares continued to appreciate steadily and, by 1607, had possibly reached as high a value as 300, triple the initial par subscription price of 100.[20] By November 1608, the price had fallen to less than 140, and it stayed in a range of 130 to 180 for the next two years. The significant decrease in prices precipitated a notarial protest against the management of the company for improper use of shareholder capital. Around this time, le Maire joined together with eight others to form a private association to deal in East India Company shares "for their common profit" (van Dillen 1935, p.25).

The most noteworthy of the market manipulations engaged in by le Maire and associates constituted a 'bear raid' designed to depress the value of company shares. Precisely how the manipulation was executed is of considerable importance. The group combined short sales for forward delivery, presumably settled using 'differences', with 'cash' sales of company shares. Many of the actual cash sales of company shares were long-dated, with delivery dates well beyond the conventional one-month-or-less delivery date. In examining records of transfer sales, Gelderblom and Jonker (2004, p.657) concluded that the "sheer volume of share transfers belies" the significance of the le Maire syndicate: "Indeed the bear syndicate appears to have been a sideshow, for during 1608–9 its volume of transfers amounted to less than 20 percent of all transfers registered by the Amsterdam Chamber, and the shares dropped to 11 percent during 1610". This conclusion is based on the assumption that the manipulation relied on cash sales, which would be recorded, and not forward contracts that were done through 'settling up' without leaving any trace for historians.

Despite receiving attention from multiple sources, the precise activities of the bear raiders have not been fully detailed. It is more or less certain that a combination of forward and cash trading in shares was supplemented by using personal influence to spread unfavourable rumours about the company's prospects. This presumption is supported by evidence that le Maire was at this time engaged in attempts to found a rival French East India Company. Such an action by le Maire gave credence to the belief that such rumours had at least superficial validity. Profits on the transaction could be gained from settling up of the forward short sales, without delivery. It is not clear what the implications for the transfer process would be if less-than-a-month-to-delivery repurchases of the company shares, made at lower prices than the initial sales, were made to offset long-dated sales of shares. As such, evidence from share transfer records is insufficient to support the conclusions of Gelderblom and Jonker (2004).

Whatever the trading mechanics, the activities of le Maire's group were apparently successful in holding down the price of VOC shares. The potential impact of the bear ring on share prices attracted the attention of the directors and other politically connected investors. The result was a period of political debate that included some of the first writings on stock market structure and performance. The debate ended in February 1610 with the passing of the first substantive legislation designed to limit stock market manipulation. Selling of shares *in blanco*, also known as the '*windhandel*' or 'wind trade', was prohibited. More precisely, short selling of securities, defined to mean the sale of securities not owned by the seller, was banned. This ban covered both cash sales and forward sales. In addition, it was required that shares which were sold had to be transferred no later than one month after the transaction. Private sanctions included le Maire's expulsion as a VOC shareholder.

Unlike modern securities laws, many 17th- and 18th-century prohibitions imposed on security trading activities did not have criminal sanctions. Rather, edicts such as the 1610 prohibition on short selling removed the protection of the courts for the purpose of enforcing contracts. The inability of the edict to control the 'wind trade' speculation in shares was evident with the establishment of the Dutch West India Company in 1621, when shares were sold on a 'when-issued' basis, prior to the initial subscription. This prompted the issuance of another edict reinforcing the ban on selling shares not owned by the seller. Any trader seeking to repudiate a short sale could find refuge in the courts. Similar edicts in 1630 and 1636, during the time Frederick Henry held the office of stadholder, led to the use of the term 'appeal to Frederick' to refer to a trader invoking the protection of the prohibition on short sales to avert payment on a losing position.

Perceptions of speculative abuse associated with the delivery process appeared almost from the start of bourse trade in VOC shares (van Dillen et al. 2007; Gelderblom et al. 2010). "It is not clear that the [le Maire] ring did more than help to hold down the already slumping prices, but the company lodged a protest with the States of Holland and West Friesland in the summer of 1609 to have a ban placed on the sale of shares '*in blanco*' " (De Marchi and Harrison 1994, p.51). The Dutch edict of 1610 banning short sales '*in blanco*', where, at the time of the short sale, the seller does not actually possess the shares being sold, was not permanent, and the "occasion of renewal brought out anew sentiment for and against *VOC*" (De Marchi and Harrison 1994, p.51). Despite opposition, the ban on 'selling in the wind', or *windhandel* trade, was repeated in 1624, 1630, 1636 and 1677. It is important to recognize that the *de facto* impact of the ban on *in blanco* short selling was to make such contracts unenforceable in the courts. There was no direct criminal penalty for entering into such contracts, which provided the basis for difference dealing among the close-knit community of brokers and dealers who dominated the stock and commodity trade on the Amsterdam exchange.

Though the ban on *in blanco* short selling technically applied to both commodities and shares, the character of speculative trading in commodities was less affected due to the practical need for exchange speculators to have a connection to the underlying goods trade. No such constraint was associated with shares. Without the discipline of exchange trading, the potential for abuse of non-transferable forward contracts with option features in the loosely organized Amsterdam share market was considerable. In turn, the ban did not eliminate speculative trading. Rather, the characteristics of trading were altered. Though the Amsterdam exchange had unrestricted access, the exchange also facilitated concentration of commercial activity. Exchange trading was primarily conducted by sworn and free brokers in combination with a group of dominant merchants. This provided a foundation for the introduction of trading conventions that constitute an early form of exchange self-regulation. The *rescontre* settlement emerged from these early methods of exchange self-regulation. Self-regulation of trading in *VOC* shares on the Amsterdam exchange was further facilitated by the bulk of trading activity being conducted by Jewish traders of Iberian descent.

Speculation and the Amsterdam Settlement Process

Modern knowledge about stock-trading activity on the Amsterdam exchange at the end of the 17th century derives primarily from *Confusion de Confusiones* (1688; Fridson 1996) (Cardoso 2006). Though this remarkable book's central concerns are much broader, de la Vega did make detailed references to speculative exchange-trading practices on the Amsterdam exchange. For example, there is a general description (Fridson 1996, p.155) of the potential gains to options trading: "Give 'opsies' or premiums, and there will be only limited risk to you, while the gain may surpass all your imaginings and hopes." This statement is followed by a somewhat exaggerated claim about the potential gains: "Even if you do not gain through 'opsies' the first time . . . continue to give the premiums for a later date, and it will rarely happen that you lose all your money before a propitious incident occurs that maintains the price for several years." Presumably, de la Vega had call options trading in mind, the possibility of trading put options appears later (p.156).

The reference to extending contracts is further elaborated in de la Vega's discussion of the *rescontre* system (p.181), a major technical evolution of the 'settlement by account' method of clearing trades that emerged between 1650 and 1688, when the Dutch first introduced quarterly settlements of share transactions on the Amsterdam exchange. Prior to this time, settlement procedures had been less formal. Wilson (1941, p.83) provided the following description of the settlement process:

> The technique of speculation in the British Funds at Amsterdam . . . was a kind of gamble carried on every three months: no payments were made except on *rescontre* (settlement or carry-over), i.e., the period for which funds were bought or sold and for which options were given or taken. *Rescontredag* (contango day) occurred four times a year, and on these occasions representatives of the speculators gathered round a table to regulate or liquidate their transactions, and to make reciprocal payments for fluctuations or surpluses. Normally these fluctuations were settled without the actual value of the funds in question being paid—only real investors paid cash for their purchases. Speculative buyers paid to sellers the percentage by which the funds had fallen since the last contango day, or alternatively received from them the percentage by which funds had risen in the same interval. After surpluses had been paid, new continuations were undertaken for the following settlement. In such a *prolongatie* (continuation) the buyer granted the seller a certain percentage (a contango rate) to prolong his purchase to the next *rescontre*: in this way he stood the chance of benefiting by a rise in quotations in the interval, without tying up his capital: he was only bound to pay any possible marginal fall.

A key feature of the *rescontre* was the concentration of liquidity, which, for example, permitted prolongations to be done more readily (van Dillen 1927; Dickson 1967, p.491). The term '*rescontre*' was derived from the practice of Dutch merchants to "indicate that a bill had been paid by charging it to a current account—'*solvit per rescontre*' as distinct from '*per banco*', '*per wissel*' and so on" (Dickson 1967, p.491; Mortimer, *Everyman*, 5th ed., p.28n).

In addition to the references to extending option expiration dates, with regular marking-to-market, de la Vega (1688, p.183) took up the uncertain legal interpretation of option contracts at a later point and explicitly recognized that the Dutch restriction on *in blanco* short sales could impact put and call options differently:

> As to whether the regulation [banning short sales] is applicable to *option contracts*, the opinions of experts diverge widely. I have not found any decision that might serve as a precedent, though there are many cases at law from which one [should be able to] draw a correct picture. All legal experts hold that the regulation is applicable to both the seller and buyer [of the contract]. In practice, however, the judges have often decided differently, always freeing the buyer from the liability while holding the seller [to the contract] . . . If . . . the opinion is correct that it applies only to the seller, the regulation will be of no use to me [as a person wanting to seek shelter]

when I receive call premiums, for in this case I am in fact a seller; but it will help me if I have received a put premium, as I am then the buyer of stocks. With regard to the put premium . . . law and legal opinion, the regulation and the reasons for the decisions are contradictory. The theory remains uncertain, and one cannot tell which way the adjudication tends.

The bulk of option market participants appear to have been speculators, attracted primarily by the urge to gamble, usually "men of moderate wealth indulging in a little speculation" (Wilson 1941, p.105). In contrast, drawing from de Pinto (1762), Wilson (1941, p.84) observed that for trading conducted on the Amsterdam exchange during the 18th century: "Options were the province of the out-and-out gamblers."[21]

Initial Trade in English Joint-Stock Shares

When did trading in English joint-stocks emerge? There is evidence of trading in shares of the earliest English joint-stock companies "practically from their beginning' (Morgan and Thomas 1962, p.14). However, the volume of trade was not significant. Sales were typically negotiated privately, though the East India Company would sometimes auction shares at the same events at which imported goods were being sold. Various factors contributed to restrict the sale of shares of early English joint-stock companies. There was a lack of permanence in the capital stock of many companies, with any profits distributed at the end of a venture—sometimes in goods—and numerous setbacks and calls for additional capital. Similar to the regulated companies, there were restrictions on membership embedded in the charter of incorporation, which restricted transferability. Finally, there was the often sizeable value of individual shares, permitting only a select few the possibility of entry into the book of shareholders.

Figure 6.2   London, Royal Exchange (1751); Etching by Robert Havell (1760–1832)

TYPES OF DEALS IN EARLY ENGLISH STOCK TRADING

A deal for 'ready money' or 'money': A transaction for immediate delivery, to be settled within no less than two days. Also called a deal for **cash**.

A deal for 'time': A transaction for future settlement, effectively a forward contract in the security. Where a *rescontre* settlement system was in place, the transaction would typically have the next *rescontre* as the settlement date.

Heavy horse and light horse: Subscriptions to company shares and government debt issues could be paid by instalment. While share subscription practices varied, the first deposit on government debt was generally 15% (Mortimer 1761, p.137), with further payments of 10% or 15% being required each month until the balance was paid. The full amount of the subscription could be paid in advance, with credit being given for the associated interest. During the period in which subscriptions were being paid, secondary market trading had to account for the unpaid balances on a specific security. Heavy horse referred to a security which was fully paid, while light horse had a balance remaining to be paid. Stockjobbers preferred to deal in the light horse, which required a smaller invested capital for the same notional principal: "they have an opportunity for sporting with, and gaining profit on, a nominal thousand, for the same money, that it would cost to buy a hundred, heavy" (Mortimer 1761, p.138).

For much of the 17th century, the Amsterdam stock market was confined to trading primarily in *VOC* stock and, to a lesser extent, in the stock of the Dutch West India Company. Despite evidence of an active secondary market in Dutch *renten*, trading in Dutch government debt did not start until much later (Barbour 1950, p.84):[22]

> Although the investment value of public funds was recognized, they seem not to have been subject to market trading before the end of the third quarter of the [17th] century . . . the obligations of Holland were maintained at par, which discouraged speculation, and if there were fluctuations in the prices of other public securities, the fact that they were widely held in small lots made them less responsive to market manipulation than actions of the India companies, nor were they liable to sharp variations in price such as occurred in commodity values. The sudden downward plunge of these funds, those of Holland included, at the time of the French invasion (1672), acted as an incentive to speculative trading, and thereafter prices were frequently quoted. In 1673 the States General engaged to pay subsidies to the emperor in bonds at current prices on the [exchange] of Amsterdam. Trading in them soon quickened, and with time spread to other countries.

Circa 1688, the time of the Glorious Revolution in England, there was active securities trading on the Amsterdam exchange in Dutch government debt and the shares of the two Dutch India companies. Towards the end of the century, trading in English funds also assumed importance in Amsterdam trading.

SOME EARLY ENGLISH STOCK MARKET TERMS

Lame duck: A defaulter on a loan or securities contract, such as a deal for time. Typically the loan involved the finance of a securities purchase. According to Mortimer, a lame duck was a 'name given in 'Change Alley to those who refuse to fulfil their contracts (see Figure 6.3). There are some of these at almost every rescounters. The punishment for non-payment is banishment from (Jonathan's), but they can still act as Brokers at the offices'.

Stocks and shares: As reflected in Mortimer (1761), the term could apply to securities listed as stocks, which appeared with price quotes in the public newspapers and on brokers' lists. This general category included government funds, joint-stock of public companies, and various debt securities issued by the public companies. Usage of the term evolved during the 18th century. Houghton (1694) still used the European term '*Actions*', a term which for Houghton lumped joint-stocks and lottery tickets together with a range of commodities such as copper, coal, lead and saltpetre. Following Mortimer, 'shares' could refer to either 'stocks of the public companies of England' or to shares in government debt issues, such as 'shares in annuities'. This interpretation of 'shares' differs from Baskin (1988, p.207, n.29).

Chronological neatness suggests dating the commencement of stock trading in London with the ascendency of William III of Orange in 1688.[23] This date is also intuitively appealing as William III was accompanied by an influx of Dutch persons and practices. However, prior to 1688 London was already trading government securities, including Exchequer bills and navy bills. In addition, there was some limited trading in the shares and debt of joint-stock companies, in particular the East India Company, the Royal African Company and the Hudson's Bay Company (Cope 1978, p.2). Still, despite the development of highly sophisticated joint-stock trading in Amsterdam by the mid-17th century, dealing in joint-stock shares in London was 'haphazard and unorganized' before 1680, with a 'highly developed market', complete with trading in options and time bargains, in evidence only by the early to mid-1690s (Houghton 1694; Morgan and Thomas 1962, p.21).

Starting around 1690, English share trading developed rapidly. One reason for this was the supply of joint-stock issues. Just prior to 1690, new joint-stock companies had been created in areas such as fire insurance, paper making and street lighting. Combined with the established joint-stock companies such as the East India Company and the Hudson's Bay Company, circa 1688 there were about "15 joint stock companies . . . enjoying an active life" (Morgan and Thomas 1962, p.22). In addition, the political reforms associated with the Glorious Revolution permitted the commencement of the financial revolution in English government debt issues. From 1688 to 1695 there was an explosion in new joint-stock company issues, in both shares and bonds, and in the supply of government debt. Included in these promotions was the initial subscription for the Bank of England in 1694.

Figure 6.3   "Waddling Out", a well known 18th century cartoon

Source: Adapted from Morgan and Thomas (1962).
Note: Observe the lame duck in the foreground.

Scott (1910) estimated by 1695 that there were no less than 140 British joint-stock companies. Clapham (1958) made reference to "more than one hundred fifty companies, two-thirds English and one-third Scottish, [that] started lives most of which were brief and unfortunate" during the stock-promoting boom of 1692–1695. Of all these issues, the Bank of England was the giant. The deal leading to its creation had elements of the fantastic. The original plan has been attributed to the Scottish projector William Paterson, though "whether he was strictly the originator, or merely the mouthpiece of a City group, we cannot be quite sure". In any event, the government was anxious to obtain large amounts of funds to sustain the 1690–1697 war of the Grand Alliance against France and, in exchange for £1.2 million, Parliament granted a charter to a joint-stock bank with an effective monopoly on the note issue.

The creation of some type of public bank in England by the end of the 17th century was expected. In the preceding century, various jurisdictions had evolved different forms of public banks. The Bank of Amsterdam, founded in 1609, played a key role in the settlement and transfer of funds. The Bank of Hamburg, an imitation of the Bank of Amsterdam, was founded in 1619, with the Bank of Sweden following in 1656. "On the coasts of the Mediterranean, the North Sea, the Baltic, English merchants of the seventeenth century came into touch with public banks: the influence of these merchants on government was on the increase and so were the public banks" (Clapham 1958, p.3). Yet, the Bank of England was to be considerably more than a public bank of the 17th century. It became the model 'public bank' of the 18th century.

The Bank of England was novel in that it combined the notions of joint-stock ownership and bank of issue. As the right to provide the circulating medium had historically been the preserve of the Crown, it took a particular set of circumstances, combined with the payment of a considerable amount of cash, to consummate the deal. The original act that authorized creation of the bank provided for a maximum authorized borrowing of £1.5 million, with payment of £1.2 million by 1 January 1695. In order for corporate privileges to be conferred, at least half of the subscription amount of £1.2 million had to be paid by 1 August 1694. This condition proved to be overly pessimistic. Within 12 days of the June 1694 subscription announcement date, the full amount had been subscribed (with 25% of the price paid up front).

From the government's perspective, the deal between the Bank of England and the government involved a fully funded loan from the bank's subscribers. Derived from taxes on ship tonnage and duties on liquor, the government undertook the obligation to pay 8% on the bulk of the £1.2 million. These regular debt payments contributed substantially to the success of the bank subscriptions, compared to alternatives that were available in the security market (Clapham 1958, pp.19–21):

> Water companies, most of them quite sound; treasure seeking companies, highly speculative; paper, linen, lead, copper, plate glass, bottle glass and mining companies; The Society for improving Native Manufacture so as to keep out the Wet, and the Company for the Sucking-Worm Engines of John Loftingh, merchant, at Bow Church Yard, Cheapside—a sucking-worm engine was a fire hose—had all been projected and supported less or more. Among these, the Bank with its parliamentary backing, its high sounding name, and its guaranteed income from the taxes was a very attractive proposition.

However, though the potential stability of Bank of England shares was attractive to some, for the prime movers in the deal the main objective were the gains to be obtained from the banking business.

Prior to 1696, there were two venues for London stock trading: the Royal Exchange and Exchange Alley. In the Royal Exchange, dealers in stocks and

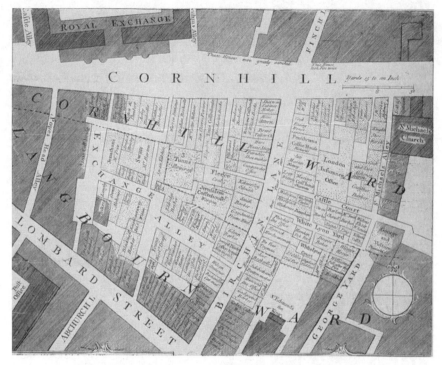

Figure 6.4   Thos. Jeffrey, 1748, A plan of all the houses, destroyed & damaged by the great fire which begun in Exchange Alley Cornhill, on Friday March 25, 1748

shares "had a 'walk' near the centre of the building between the salters, the Italian merchants and the Canary merchants" (Morgan and Thomas 1962). However, due at least partly to abuses arising from the 1696 price collapse of various joint-stock promotions, stock traders left the Royal Exchange, conducting business after that date bourse-style in the environs of Exchange Alley. "There is a certain amount of mystery about [the stock dealers] withdrawal [from the Royal Exchange]. Scott refers to their being turned out, whereas Duguid insists that they were so harassed by their fellow traders, and so short of space that they went voluntarily and in spite of the efforts of the City to prevent them" (p.27). Until 1773, when a group of brokers acquired a building in Threadneedle Street that was, for the first time, called the Stock Exchange, the history of London stock trading was intimately connected to Exchange Alley.

Geographically, Exchange Alley is located across Cornhill Street from the Royal Exchange. Starting at Cornhill, the alley runs to Lombard Street (see Figure 6.4). The alley contained various coffeeshops that were the focus of stock trading. Circa 1696, the chief coffeehouses for stock trading were Jonathan's and Garraway's, though Sam's Coffee House in the Alley and Powell's and the Rainbow in Cornhill were also of some importance (Copes 1978):

> Jonathan's was founded about 1680 by Jonathan Miles, and was from the start connected with financial business. The Garraways were a City family

of the period, who were landlords of the Sun Fire Office in its early days. The coffee-house was started by Thomas Garraway in the early 1670s. The trend to financial specialization, using coffee-houses as a place of business, is typical of the period: other examples are Edward Lloyd's Coffee House, a centre for marine insurance, and Tom's and Causey's Coffee Houses, used in their early days by the Hand in Hand Fire Office and the Sun Fire Office. Jonathan's as a centre for dealers gradually superseded Garraway's (which was concentrating on auction sales by the 1750s), and developed lineally into the Stock Exchange of 1772.

While there was apparently considerable, and almost certainly disreputable, 'curb trading' in Exchange Alley, various city orders, such as those of 1700 and 1703, were aimed at eliminating this type of trading.

C BROKERS, STOCKJOBBERS AND COFFEEHOUSES

London Stock Trading circa 1694

A LIST OF ENGLISH ACTS RELATIVE TO BROKERS, FROM FRANCIS (1850)

13 Edward I. . . . . Statute 5. . . . . . Anno 1284
1 James I. . . . . Statute 21. 1604
8 and 9 William III. . . . Statute 32. . . . . 1697, expired 1707
6 Anne. . . . . Statute 16. 1707
10 Anne. . . . . Statute 19. 1711
6 George I. . . . . Statute 18. 1720
3 George II. . . . . Statute 31. . . . . 1730, for Bristol
7 George II. . . . . Statute 8. 1739
Note: First column is the year of reign of that monarch.

Following the Glorious Revolution, the significant increase in the supply of issues to be traded was accompanied by the emergence of a trading infrastructure composed of brokers and stockjobbers, centred about the Royal Exchange and Exchange Alley. John Houghton (22 June 1694) described the process involved in stock trading at that time as follows:

> The manner of managing the Trade is this; The Monied Man goes among the *Brokers* (which are chiefly upon the *Exchange*, and at *Jonathan's* Coffee House, sometimes at *Garaway's* and at some other Coffee Houses) and asks how *Stocks* go? and upon Information, bids the Broker buy or sell so many Shares of such and such Stocks if he can, at such and such Prizes: Then he tries what he can do among those that have Stock, or power to sell them; and if he can, makes a Bargain.

Houghton followed this brief discussion with a considerable discussion of 'refusals' and 'puts', giving the distinct impression that options trading was a regular component of early London stock trading.

Brokers and dealers have been an essential feature of markets since ancient times. Brokers were used to do business in a wide range of commodities, from cloth and wool to copper and saltpetre.[24] Various jurisdictions imposed laws governing individuals' ability to engage in brokerage and when brokers were required in a business transaction. For example, a 1697 English law restricted to 100 the number of brokers permitted to transact business in joint-stocks. Another example is from medieval Bruges, where alien merchants were required to use local brokers even where a broker was not necessary.[25] Heuristically, brokers do business by connecting buyers and sellers, charging a commission for this service. A broker does not take a position in the security being traded.

In contrast, dealers buy and sell for their own account. Dealer activity can take various forms. In modern financial markets, a dealer typically makes markets in securities, quoting prices for both buying and selling, adjusting bid and offer prices in response to perceived changes in demand, often as reflected in the level of dealer inventory. Such traders were apparently not present in the early English stock market (Cope 1978, p.5):

> It has been suggested that in the first half of the [18th] century there were bankers, stockbrokers, merchants and speculators, even clerks in the transfer offices, who had adopted the role of a professional dealer, 'a stabilizer in the market, normally ready to buy and sell, and professionally interested in adjusting supply and demand' (Dickson 1967, p.496). A dealer in this sense was not mentioned by Mortimer or by any other contemporary writer. Isaac de Pinto described such intermediaries in Amsterdam, but said nothing about them in London.

The first published account of such modern-day 'jobbing' appeared in 1796.[26]

The relationship between dealing and brokerage is an important feature of market microstructure (pp.7–8):

> There are various ways of organizing a security market. One is that found in the London Stock Exchange of today, which has two classes of members: brokers, who act as agents on behalf of clients, and dealers or jobbers, who act as principals. Another way is to have only brokers, who are purely agents, and who have to find other brokers with whom they can match their orders. The third way is to have brokers in name who are in fact dealers who buy from and sell to their clients. Most stock exchanges combine the second and third of these methods, and this was the practice in the securities markets in London in the eighteenth century. In the last quarter of the century there were signs of a transition to the first system, with the emergence of jobbers who 'made the market' and who had no dealings with the public.

The early 18th-century English share market definitely blurred the distinction between dealers and brokers. For example, it was typical for market participants to act as brokers in a transaction for, say, share X while still conducting transactions for their own account in share X, such as where the brokers charge brokerage for, say, a sale while purchasing the share for their own account. The potential for abuse was considerable, especially when trading for forward delivery and trading in options was common.

Venomous Attacks on Stockjobbing

The considerable discussion and analysis aimed at early English stockjobbing activities was particularly venomous. Consider, for example, the full title of a Daniel Defoe work on the subject: *The Anatomy of Exchange Alley or, A System of Stock-Jobbing: Proving that Scandalous Trade, as it is now carried on, to be Knavish in its private practice, and Treason in its Public* (1719). Stockjobbing, it seems, was much more than simple dealing in shares and government funds. Defoe's view on stockjobbers is quite clear:

> if you talk to them of their occupation, there is not a man will own it is a complete system of knavery; that it is a trade founded in fraud, born of deceit, and nourished by trick, cheat, wheedle, forgeries, falsehoods, and all sorts of delusions; coining false news, this way good, this way bad; whispering imaginary terrors, frights, hopes, expectations, and then preying upon the weakness of those whose imaginations they have wrought upon, whom they have either elevated or depressed.

Though Defoe was among the best at thrashing the stockjobber, Thomas Mortimer provides a much more insightful description of stockjobbing activities.

Stockjobbing was not so much an occupation as an activity. Defoe recognized that the activity attracted a range of participants, not just "the Alley throngs [of] Jews, jobbers, and brokers; their names . . . needless, their characters dirty as their employment" (Defoe 1719):

> to see statesmen turn dealers, and men of honour stoop to the chicanery of jobbing; to see men at the offices in the morning, at the P————house about noon, at the cabinet at night, and at Exchange Alley in the proper intervals, what new phenomena are these? What fatal things may these shining planets . . . foretell to the state and to the public; for when statesmen turn jobbers, the state may be jobbed.

Despite some insights, Defoe's brief tract is more a polemic than a reasoned discussion of stockjobbing. Appearing on the eve of the South Sea bubble, the tract was somewhat prophetic.

Compared to Defoe, Mortimer was much more analytical in his discussion of stockjobbing. For example, Mortimer (1761, pp.33–4) gave a precise description of the 'sorts' of individuals involved in stockjobbing:

STOCK-JOBBERS may be divided into three different sorts.

The first are foreigners, who have property in our funds, with which they are continually JOBBING.

The second are our own gentry, merchants, and tradesmen, who likewise have property in the funds, with which they job, or, in other words, are continually changing the situation of their property, according to the periodical variations of the funds, as produced by the divers incidents that are supposed either to lessen, or increase the value of these funds, and occasion rises or falls of the current price of them.

The third and by far the greatest number, are STOCK-BROKERS, with very little, and often no property at all in the funds, who job in them on credit, and transact more business in the several government securities in one hour, without having a shilling of property in any one of them, than the real proprietors of thousands transact in several years.

Mortimer explicitly identified the blurring of the dealer and broker functions. This was reflected in the common language of the time, which "used broker and jobber as interchangeable terms" (Dickson 1967, p.494).[27] However, Mortimer was quite clear that stockjobbers included others than brokers.

What was stockjobbing? Mortimer (1761, p.27) had a useful description:

Now, the Dutch and other foreigners have so large an interest in our public funds, has given rise to the buying and selling of them for time, by which is to be understood, the making of contracts for buying and selling against any certain period of time; so that the transfer at the public offices is not made at the time of making the contract; but at the time stipulated in the contract for transferring it; and this has produced modern STOCK-JOBBING, as I shall presently shew.

Nothing could be more just or equitable than the original design of these contracts, nor nothing more infamous than the abuse that has, and still is made of it.

Unlike the modern-day market, stockjobbing in the 18th century was associated with forward trading of securities, at least according to Mortimer (p.32):[28]

the mischief of it is, that under this sanction of selling and buying the funds for time for foreigners —— Brokers and others, buy and sell for themselves, without having any interest in the funds they sell, or any cash to pay for what they buy, nay even without any design to transfer, or accept, the funds they sell or buy for time. The business thus transacted, has been declared illegal by several acts of parliament, and this is the principal branch of STOCK-JOBBING.

Mortimer made no reference to the use of options in stockjobbing activities, giving some support to the position that Barnard's Act of 1734 was effective in deterring this activity.

Almost from the beginning of English stock trading, attempts were made to severely restrict stockjobbing. The first important piece of legislation was the 1697 Act 'To Restrain the number and ill Practice of Brokers and Stock-jobbers'. This act did not actually have much application to stockjobbing, as conceived by Mortimer. Rather, stockjobbing was conceived as 'pretended' brokerage. From the preamble to the Act (Morgan and Thomas 1962, p.23):

> whereas divers Brokers and Stock-Jobbers, or pretended Brokers, have lately set up and on most unjust Practices and Designs, in Selling and Discounting of Talleys, Bank Stock, Bank Bills, Shares and Interests in Joint Stocks, and other Matters and Things, and have, and do, unlawfully Combined and Confederated themselves together, to Raise or fall from time to time the Value of such Talleys, Bank Stock, and Bank Bills, as may be most Convenient for their own private Interest and Advantage: which is a very great abuse of the said Ancient Trade and Imployment, and is extremely prejudicial to the Public Credit of this Kingdom and to the Trade and Commerce thereof, and if not timely prevented, may Ruin the Credit of the Nation, and endanger the Government itself.

Stockjobbers were seen as interlopers in the legitimate trade of brokerage. As a consequence, the act specifically restricted the trade of brokerage to those brokers licensed by the City of London. The act then limited the number of licensed brokers to 100.

Though it had some impact, the Act of 1697 was insufficient to stem the stockjobbing abuses, as reflected in the need for subsequent English legislation. Unlicensed brokers continued to operate throughout the 18th century, and licensed brokers were often involved in dealing activities (e.g., Dickson 1967, pp.493–7). Though there were definitely political considerations in its passage, the Bubble Act of 1720 was designed to eliminate the rampant stockjobbing in the initial public offerings of the numerous bubble promotions (Harris 1994). The significant role that options still played in stockjobbing activities, both during and after the South Sea bubble, is reflected in the specific inclusion of restrictions on options trading in Barnard's Act of 1734, which also attempted to restrict time bargains. Various other attempts to get anti-speculation and anti-stockjobbing bills passed were unsuccessful.

Interest in restrictive legislation was often sparked by the decline of stock values during periods of military hostility or severe commercial difficulties. With war breaking out between England and France in 1744 (Cope 1978, pp.9–10):

> In 1746, a bill was introduced which indicated the ways in which its sponsors (who included Sir John Barnard) thought bear speculators had been operating. The bill would make it an offense to 'conspire' to lower prices and to sell for time at a price below the price for money. Lenders were not to sell the collateral security they held, unless it had

depreciated or the loan was in default; those holding stock for nominees were not to sell for their own personal account with a view to repurchasing, and stocks were not to be sold conditional on the happening of a future event.

Further attempts at legislation were made in 1756, 1762 and 1773. What is apparent from all this is that stockjobbing was rather loosely defined and could include a range of trading activities, some speculative, some manipulative. Despite Mortimer's rather restrictive definition, the colloquial meaning of 'stockjobbing' could include both cash and forward trading. However, as reflected by the introduction of the quarterly 'rescounter' system to London sometime during the 1740s (Dickson 1967, p.507), the jobber speculation may well have been centred, in practice, on forward trading when Mortimer was writing.[29]

The English Coffeehouses[30]

Coffeehouse trading was a novel feature of English securities markets in the late 17th century and for most of the 18th century, e.g. Ellis (2006). Though none of these original English establishments survives, at least three modern English financial institutions can be traced back to the coffeehouses located near the Royal Exchange: the London Stock Exchange, which evolved from Jonathan's; the insurance syndicate Lloyd's of London, which originated at Lloyd's coffeehouse; and the Shipping Exchange, which can be traced to the Baltic coffeehouse (Gibb 1957, p.4). Though the Royal Exchange was also an important venue for commodity trading, certain features made the coffeehouse environment better suited to trading in shares and government funds during the late 17th and early 18th centuries. Various sources identify the importance of English coffeehouses to the development of the 'public sphere' and the emergence of "the inordinate appetite of the English public for news" (Cowan 2004, p.349).

The introduction of coffee into the English milieu is often credited to Archbishop Laud, who helped Christian refugees escape the Islamic empire in the Middle East (Gibb 1957, p.1). A few years before 1650, the archbishop brought one of these refugees, a Cretan scholar named Canopis, to Balliol College, Oxford. Soon after arriving at Oxford, Canopis introduced his colleagues to coffee, "a drink of soote colour dryed in a furnace and that they drink as hot as can be endured". The coffee-drinking habit spread quickly among the scholars and students of Oxford and Cambridge and, in 1650, a coffeehouse appeared in an apothecary's house 'against All Soules College'. By 1677, the habit had become so popular that a Cambridge don was quoted as saying: "Why doth solid and serious learning decline and few or none now follow it in the University? Answer: because of coffeehouses where they spend all their time" (Gibb 1957, p.2). However, while there was growth in coffee culture throughout England during the second half of the 17th century, the bulk of the growth was in London.

THE MIDEAST ORIGINS OF THE EUROPEAN COFFEEHOUSE

The origins of coffee drinking are obscure, though it is reasonably certain that the practice of consuming the fruit of the coffee plant originated in Ethiopia, possibly in the Kaffa region, where coffee is a native plant. Though Ethiopia was likely the original source, the practice of coffee drinking can "almost invariably" be traced to Yemen, where "most stories connect it to a man or men of one of the mystical Sufi religious orders" (Hattox 1985, p.14). Though coffee drinking by Sufis in Yemen may have originated earlier, the "available evidence" dates the practice from the mid-15th century. "By the first decade of the sixteenth century . . . coffee had spread from Yemen to the Hijaz and Cairo . . . it was another decade or so before it reached Syria, probably by the pilgrimage caravan, and from there it was carried to Istanbul around the middle of the 1500s" (p.28).

Though the "social use of coffee may be traceable to Sufi practice . . . the roots of its social importance must be sought elsewhere", more precisely in the coffeehouse. "From all indications the coffeehouse, like coffee, must be considered of Arab origin" (p.76). By the beginning of the 16th century, rudiments of coffeehouse society had appeared in Mecca, where an official judicial report of 1511 attempted to outlaw coffee drinking. This was the first of numerous attempts over the next two centuries to ban coffee drinking in various locales in the Mideast and Europe. The object of the bans was not usually coffee drinking, *per se*, but rather the social activities which were taking place at the coffeehouses. Recognizing that the severe restrictions Islam placed on alcohol effectively prevented the tavern from being a gathering place, the social attractions of the coffeehouse in the Muslim world were considerable. As such, attempts to ban coffeehouses were almost invariably unsuccessful.

By the end of the 16th century, the coffeehouse craze was evident throughout the Middle East. Cities such as Istanbul, Damascus and Cairo featured a wide range of establishments: from the 'take-out shop' catering to local merchants, to the small local shops with a few benches, to the grand-style coffeehouses catering to important clientele. By 1575, it was estimated that Istanbul had over 600 coffeehouses. The coffeehouse became a microcosm of Islamic society. To attract customers, certain coffeehouses would provide storytellers, puppet shows or musicians. Other establishments used the coffeehouse venue as a front for gambling, prostitution and drug use. This connection between certain coffeehouses and unseemly social practices gave support to the ongoing efforts, primarily from religious fundamentalists, to ban either coffeehouses or coffee drinking.

In 1652, not long after Canopis introduced coffee to the English scholarly community, the first London coffeehouse was opened by an Italian merchant, Pasqua Rosee, originally from Ragusa in Sicily. The subsequent proliferation of coffeehouses was dramatic. By 1679, there were at least 100, and by 1702 there were over 500 (Wright and Fayle 1928, p.9). What explains the remarkable popularity of the coffeehouse? Compared to taverns, the coffeehouse was quieter and the refreshments offered were much better suited to conducting business and leisurely daytime activities. For the usual price of a penny, a customer would be entitled to a drink of coffee and a seat to linger with friends or read the newspapers. In winter, there would invariably be a fire to warm the customers from the damp and dreary London weather. Such an environment was excellent for obtaining news and information of interest. In addition to the added expense, taverns were not well suited to conducting business or civil conversation.[31]

Almost from the beginning, coffeehouses became specialized to certain clientele. Given the need to generate business, the type of coffeehouse clientele was primarily determined by proximity to important locations. For example, the Royal Coffee House and Charing Cross coffeehouse were near to Whitehall and catered to 'beaux and courtiers'. Important coffeehouses for transacting business, such as Garraway's, Jonathan's and Lloyd's, arose near the Royal Exchange. In addition to endeavouring to offer an ambience agreeable to the specialized clientele, coffeehouses provided a range of other attractions. In particular, after 1682 "the London coffeehouses also formed part of a delivery and collection system for the Penny Post" (Dale 2004, p.12). Certain coffeehouses also provided a private courier service for overseas mail using a network of ship masters. "For many years these private arrangements were evidently more efficient than those of the Post Office" (p.12).

Coffeehouse proprietors made special efforts to provide information of importance. As such, the coffeehouses played an essential role in the early development of English newspapers. Newspapers available at coffeehouses could be used to advertise promotions, subscriptions and equity capital calls, allowing for rapid communication with shareholders. Like the *Tatler* and the *Spectator* in the literary and social sphere and the *London Gazette* and the *London Journal* in the political sphere, newspapers specializing in commercial events such as the *Daily Courant* and the *Weekly Journal* could be found in the coffeehouses near the Royal Exchange. By the early 1700s, there were at least 18 newspapers, publishing about 44,000 copies per week (p.15). The cost of providing many newspapers was a source of constant aggravation between the coffeehouse proprietors and those producing papers during the period. In addition to providing a relevant selection of newspapers and an ambience suitable for the clientele, the coffeehouse was a place where letters of general interest could be obtained and posted. 'Accommodation addresses' were provided, not unlike a modern General Post Office. These addresses could be used as the equivalent of newspaper box numbers. This service was especially important to coffeehouses, such as Lloyd's, that catered to the maritime trades.

In the regular course of many businesses, including those involving share-trading transactions, coffeehouses served as makeshift offices. An interesting example of this use is evidenced by the following advertisement appearing in Houghton's *A Collection*: "John Castaing, at *Jonathan's* Coffee-heuse, or *Exchange*, buys and sells all Blank and Benefit Tickets; and other Stocks and Shares". Initial copies of the famous Castaing's *Course of the Exchange* ended with: '*By* John Castaing, *Broker, at his Office at* Jonathans *Coffee-house*'.[32] Abraham de Moivre conducted his business of calculating odds for gamblers and reckoning values for underwriters and annuity brokers in Slaughter's Coffee House in Saint Martin's Lane. Specialized coffeehouses, such as Jonathan's, became important centres of business and were able to charge admission. Ultimately, however, specialized coffeehouses were not able to keep pace with the growth in business, and they slowly diminished in importance as the 18th century progressed.

Jonathan's is a case in point. By 1762, the stock-trading business centred at Jonathan's was sufficiently developed that 150 of the more reputable brokers formed a club and entered into an agreement with the proprietor of Jonathan's for the exclusive use of the establishment in return for a rent of £1,200 a year, which they raised by a subscription of £8 per head. This action, aimed at excluding specific individuals from the coffeehouse, was problematic as coffeehouses were businesses serving the public. Shortly after Jonathan's attempted to enforce exclusivity (Morgan and Thomas 1962, p.68):

> A broker who had been ejected from the coffee-house brought an action against the proprietor. The case was tried before Lord Mansfield and a special jury, who found that Jonathan's had been a place of resort for dealers in stocks and shares since time immemorial, and upheld the plaintiff's right of access.

Shortly thereafter, in 1773, the brokers club purchased a building in Threadneedle Street and called the building the 'Stock Exchange'. Oddly enough, they did not try at first to limit membership, but allowed the use of its facilities to anyone on payment of 6d a day. This gradual progress from public coffeehouse to restricted private quarters was roughly paralleled in the maritime insurance trade, where Lloyd's coffeehouse served a similar role to Jonathan's.

The coffeehouse phenomenon was not restricted to England. Coffee first appeared in Venice in 1615 and Paris in 1643. There was a coffeehouse craze in Paris, similar to that in London, with around 250 coffeehouses appearing in Paris by the end of the 17th century. Coffeehouses were also popular in Amsterdam, as indicated by de la Vega (1688, p.199):

> Our speculators frequent certain places which are called *coffy-huysen* or coffee-houses because a certain beverage is served there called *coffy* by the Dutch and *caffe* by the Levantines. The well-heated rooms offer in winter a comfortable place to stay, and there is no lack of manifold entertainment. You will find books and board games, and you will meet there with visitors with whom you can discuss affairs. One person takes chocolate, the others coffee, milk, and tea; and nearly everybody smokes while conversing. None of this occasions very great expense; and while one learns the news, he negotiates and closes transactions.

While there are numerous studies on the role of the English coffeehouse in trading shares and government funds, evidence for similar activity in Amsterdam, Paris and other locales is scant. To what extent coffeehouses in Europe performed a social and political function, similar to that performed in England associated with the struggle for press freedom, is unclear. Inns, taverns and the like played a key role in commercial activity long before the arrival of coffee; the use of bourse (*beurs*) to describe a trading venue originates with the name of a tavern owner. However, the presence of important exchanges in the major continental European cities likely meant that these were the key venues for trading

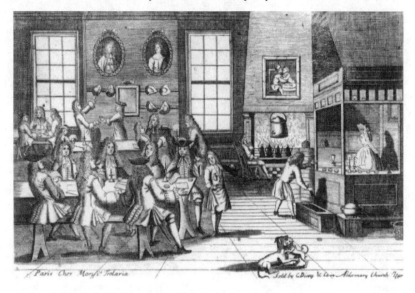

Figure 6.5 Coffeehouse interior, from Douce Prints W.1.2(203), the Bodleian Library, University of Oxford.

Source: Klein (1996, p.32)

shares, unlike in England, where share traders had relocated to more conducive environs outside the Royal Exchange by the end of the 1690s.

Coffeehouses, the Public Sphere and the Press

The rise of the coffeehouse in England had many facets. The connection between coffeehouse culture and financial 'news' was essential to certain coffeehouses becoming the primary venue for trading in government funds, company shares and debt from the late 17th century until the latter part of the 18th century. The development of coffeehouse culture was part of a social progression that has been referred to as emergence of 'the public sphere' (Habermas 1989; Pincus 1995; Cowan 2004a,b). The public sphere was a 'novel form of bourgeois public life developed in the century before the French Revolution'. For Habermas, "the [English] coffeehouse is portrayed as a social space dedicated to high-minded discourse on a wide range of affairs; it is also assumed to be open to any man who wanted to participate in the discussions conducted therein, regardless of social rank" (Cowan 2004a, p.345). For Habermas (1989, p.57): "a public sphere that functioned in the political realm arose first in Great Britain at the turn of the eighteenth century." While "few historians have taken Habermas's rosy view of the Augustan coffeehouse at face value, the central and innovative role of the coffeehouse in the political culture of the period has been often endorsed" (Cowan 2004b, p.24).

This fundamental connection between the political and commercial elements is typically obscured in modern examinations of English coffeehouse culture.

Those concerned with share trading, and the associated development of the financial press and networks of information, typically start the coffeehouse narrative from just prior to the Glorious Revolution of 1688 (e.g., Neal 1988; Dale 2004, ch.1). "After 1695, the newspaper industry began to flourish and the coffee houses responded by providing an ever wider range of publications for their clientele. The coffeehouse then became not just a place of discourse but a library where journals could be studied by a news-hungry public" (Dale 2004, p.10). In a share-trading context, the English coffeehouses in Exchange Alley opposite the Royal Exchange were the preferred venues. Absence of reliable accounting information meant the valuation of shares, government funds and debts depended heavily on the 'news', and those coffeehouses were the locations where newspapers and oral information networks could be accessed for intelligence about general economic developments, legislative actions, firm prospects and the like.

In contrast, those concerned with the political and social aspects start the narrative much earlier in order to examine events arising during the Restoration, when the monarchy and related interests tried to constrain the growth of political discourse associated with coffeehouses (e.g., Pincus 1995; Cowan 2005, 2004a). The struggle for freedom of the press in England, against licensing and other restrictions on 'news' and political discourse, took a significant turn when the Licensing of the Press Act (1662) was allowed to lapse in 1695. The lapsing of this act, which required any printed publication to obtain a government licence, permitted the emergence of a substantial newspaper industry. Common-law libel suits—a blunt tool at best, but one the government could and did use against opponents—became the method for controlling published 'news'. In the absence of print media, the coffeehouse became an important focal point for 'news', in all its forms. Prior to 1695, coffeehouses "were perhaps the main source of news".

O'Neill (2013, p.216) documented "an older world of news, dependent upon oral and manuscript circulation and a relatively limited and slow dispersal of information" that prevailed both before and after the emergence of the newspaper industry. In the absence of print media, letters, manuscripts and visits with members of a coffeehouse or tavern were essential sources of information. The prevalence of newsmongers meant that more traditional letter writing and personal contacts still had 'news' value after the emergence of newspapers (p.220):

> As the distrust of newsmongers reveals, the value of news resided not merely in its credibility but in its freshness. Old news was no news, as "Thomas Quid-nunc" wrote in a letter to *The Spectator*: "A Piece of News loses its Flavour when it hath been an Hour in the Air." Letter writers, who often knew that their information would soon be stale, recognized this. One correspondent lamented that he "had writ my Thursdays letter before I heard of the debate that happen'd in the House of Lords that day and therefore probably tel you old news in mentioning it." They perceived, however, that the private letter was not known for conveying fresh news but rather for allowing for the exchange and evaluation of news. The

bastions of fresh news were newspapers, whose survival depended on sales, and oral networks, which could transmit news rapidly. Because newspaper editors relied on fresh news rather than true news, however, their credibility became suspect. As Samuel Butler said in his portrait of a newsmonger: "True or false is all one to him; for novelty being the grace of both, a truth goes stale as soon as a lie." On the whole, British news readers trusted stale epistolary news more than fresh printed news. John Perceval assured his correspondent, "I don't write you this from the Publick prints, but private letters which may be depended on."

Dale (2004, p.7) estimated there were over 2,000 coffeehouses in London by 1700. This represents considerable growth from an estimate of "over eighty coffeehouses" in 1663 (Pincus 1992, p.812). As reflected in the specialization of coffeehouses to particular clientele, this growth encompassed different facets of English society (Dale 2004, p.8):

> There were houses for literary "wits" (notably Wills in Covent Garden), learned scholars and scientists (the Grecian in Devereux Court), politicians (Whigs at the St James, Tories at the Cocoa-Tree, near Pall Mall), lawyers (Nandos in Fleet Street) and clergy (Child's in St Paul's). Similarly, for the commercial classes there were specialist coffee houses catering for, inter alia, marine underwriters (Lloyds in Lombard Street), life insurance (Tom's in Exchange Alley), regional trading interests (The Jamaica, Jerusalem and Pennsilvania in Exchange Alley) and . . . stock-jobbers (Garraway's and Jonathan's in Exchange Alley).

Given the large number of coffeehouses in London, the listing of specific venues is only indicative. It is significant that the character of 'news' and discourse differed by venue. In the post-1695 context of coffeehouse share trading, the political character of the English coffeehouse was less significant than the negative public perception of the stockjobbing activities that were associated with the trading venues.

NOTES

1 Some of the earliest examples of written language, the Sumerian cuneiform tablets, contain such notarial protests. See, for example, http://www.sfu. ca/~poitras/Brit_Mus.ZIP, which provides a picture of a Sumerian tablet circa 1750 BC from the British Museum collection: "A letter complaining about the delivery of the wrong grade of copper after a Gulf voyage".

2 In the following quotes, the old English spelling used by Malynes in the original text has been modernized (e.g., "booke" to 'book', "necessarie" to 'necessary'). No alterations have been made to grammar.

3 "In 16th century England, the bulk of the export trade was in the hands of the Merchant Adventurers, but the import trade was largely controlled by the merchant strangers, especially Italians, Spaniards and Flemings" (de Roover 1949, p.110). The Merchant Adventurers were an important English regulated

company, a guild association of merchants with a royal charter providing a grant of monopoly for the export of cloth from England. Regulated companies differed from joint-stock companies in that each merchant member provided capital and conducted business on an individual basis. Admission to regulated companies such as the Merchant Adventurers could be obtained by patrimony or apprenticeship or, in some instances, by paying an admission fee. It was also possible to obtain admission by 'free gift'.

4 Max Weber (1924, 2000, p.339) provided an example of such a definition: "A stock or commodity exchange is a *market* in which the purchase and sale of large quantities of goods and money, of stocks and commercial bills of exchange, take place between professional businessmen". Weber (1894, 2000) aimed to defend the exchange process from the view that "one is dealing with an wholly dispensable organization—one that must be judged by its very nature to be a sort of 'conspirators club' aimed at lying and deception at the expense of honest laboring people."

5 The term 'bill of exchange' is being used loosely. The subtle differences in the features of the bill of exchange contract (e.g., transferability) that evolved over time are being ignored. Munro (1998) and de Roover (1949) discussed these differences in some detail. Until the latter part of the 16th century, the bill of exchange was the dominant means of settlement in southern Europe, while the bill obligatory (letter obligatory, writings obligatory) was prevalent in the north: "The bill of exchange was definitely not unknown in the north; on the contrary. But before 1550 the bill of exchange was certainly not yet the characteristic, dominant instrument of foreign trade. Within the Hanseatic League the bill of exchange remained marginal. From the second third of the sixteenth century . . . use of the bill of exchange quickly became general in the north . . . The letter (or bill) obligatory, based on extension of payment, had from the late Middle Ages been the characteristic, dominant security in the foreign trade of the north. It continued to hold this position in the fifteenth and sixteenth centuries" (van der Wee 1977, pp.324–5).

6 De Roover (1954, p.205) traced the progression of the banking practices from the fairs to fixed metropolitan locations: "By 1325 . . . the role of the fairs of Champagne was played out, both as trading and financial centres. In the fourteenth and fifteenth centuries, the banking places of Europe were: Bologna, Florence, Genoa, Lucca, Milan, Naples, Palermo, Pisa, Siena, Venice and the court of Rome in Italy; Avignon, Montpelier, and Paris in France; Barcelona, Valencia, and Palma de Mallorca in Spain; Bruges in Flanders; and London in England . . . Paris declined shortly after 1400 . . . and its place was taken by the fairs of Geneva and, after 1465, by those of Lyons. There were no banking places east of the Rhine, although the fairs of Frankfort-on-the-Main began to emerge as a clearing centre toward the end of the fifteenth century."

7 Relevant English legislation on enforceability of interest payments is detailed in de Roover (1949, p.110, n.31). Henry VIII made the first substantive effort in 1545.

8 A similar description can be found in van der Wee (1977, pp.318–9).

9 The contrast in settlement practices between different trading venues is a historical theme that continues to the present. Lyons was an important Renaissance financial centre for trading in bills of exchange, while Antwerp was an important commercial centre. From the settlement practices employed at Lyons, the Continental and British practice of 'settlement by account' developed. In contrast, commercial trading in Antwerp was primarily based on cash settlement and short-dated forward contracts. It was this general 'cash' approach to settlement that emerged in the US stock market.

10   Buckley (1924, p.590) made the following observation about the treatment of
     the English merchants of the Staple in Bruges: "It was, apparently, an important
     concession which the city Bruges made to the English merchants of the Staple
     in 1559, when it was agreed that the latter should be free of brokers when
     buying. It was asserted in 1562 that in most foreign countries no 'stranger'
     bought or sold except through a sworn broker, and the English Statute Book
     contains a number of regulations of similar import. Such arrangements were
     general, being due to the universal prejudice against foreigners". Buckley also
     made another observation which is indicative of the pervasiveness of brokers
     at Gresham's time: "Dealings in Bills of exchange without the intervention of
     a broker were exceptional" (p.591).

11   This statement disguises a number of characteristics of exchange trading in Ant-
     werp. Following the practice in Bruges, which preceded Antwerp as the centre
     of economic activity in northern Europe, bourse trading consisted primarily of
     dealings in money and bills of exchange located in a building around a specific
     square. Trade in commodities was conducted "either in the large 'Halles' or in
     the houses and warehouses where the goods were stored" (Ehrenberg 1928,
     p.237). In 1531, Antwerp's city council opened a building dedicated to com-
     mercial trading. While intended to accommodate trading in both bills and com-
     modities, the Antwerp exchange emerged as the venue for trading in bills, while
     trading in commodities was conducted on the 'English bourse'. Whereas in Bru-
     ges and other medieval trading venues, traditional bourse trading was organized
     along national lines, in Antwerp trade was segmented by the type of transaction.
     An impediment to trading in Antwerp was the rudimentary settlement prac-
     tices. In contrast to the clearing-house methods that sustained the importance
     of Lyons as a financial centre, settlement in Antwerp was 'hand-to-hand'.

12   Kellenbenz (1957, p.134) gave more precise information on the evolution
     of the Amsterdam exchange: "The institution began as an open-air market
     in Warmoestreet, later moved for a while to New Bridge, which crosses the
     Damrak, then flourished in the 'church square' near the Oude Kerk until
     the Amsterdam merchants built their own exchange building in 1611". The
     Amsterdam exchange was fully open for business in 1613.

13   The identification of this early trade as 'futures' contracting is found in Gelder-
     blom and Jonker (2005). This approach is at variance with the conventional
     view that futures trading began in Chicago in the 19th century or the less
     conventional view that such trading began in the 17th-century Japanese rice
     market (Schaede 1989).

14   Emery (1896, pp.51–3) provided a number of references to late 19th-century
     German and French sources on options trading. Emery also discussed the con-
     nection between German and English terminology (1896, p.91).

15   'The Dutch East India Company' is the English translation of the *Verenigde
     Oostindische Compagnie*.

16   In addition to Amsterdam, van Dillen et al. (2006) made reference to trading
     in shares occurring in Hamburg, Frankfurt, Middleburg, Cologne, Rouen and
     other locations. However, there is no evidence that this bourse trading was
     anything other than small, occasional and generally unorganized (Barbour
     1950, p.76).

17   As shares were issued by specific chambers, trading was confined almost
     exclusively to those issued by the Amsterdam chamber. Even later, when trad-
     ing in shares of other chambers emerged, shares of the Amsterdam chamber
     still demanded a substantial premium (e.g., Barbour 1950, p.77).

18   The primary documentation associated with the Dutch Edict of 1610, which
     removed legal protection for '*windhandel*' contracts, contains an important

memoir, probably written by Isaac le Maire, which outlines arguments in favour of retaining short sales (van Dillen 1930; De Marchi and Harrison 1994; Gelderblom et al. 2011). A number of arguments draw on the similarity of the trade in shares to the trade in goods: "the authors proceed from free trade in goods (perfectly conventional from a common weal point of view), move on to the freedom to make forward purchases of commodities (accepted practice for at least several decades), and end with the freedom to trade in shares. This bundling, as well as the progression itself, may have been intended to persuade the reader that (all) share trading practices should unquestionably be regarded as no different in principle from trade in goods" (De Marchi and Harrison 1994, p.55).

19 Though the actual recording of the transfer could be effected within the day, there were often delays associated with settlement if cash was not paid directly—for example, the sale could be made by installments and the transaction would require a contract to be drawn up. Problems could also arise in verifying the identity of the person transferring the shares and where bills of exchange were required for payment—for example, if the seller was an off-shore investor.

20 Barbour (1950) differs from De Marchi and Harrison (1994) in the description of the early price history of the *VOC*. The latter source has been taken as accurate in the following discussion. Following Barbour (1950), the impact of the bear ring on *VOC* prices was substantially greater.

21 Wilson (1941, pp.84–5) described the options trade: "A *prime à délivrer* (a call) was the option which *A* gave to *B*, obliging him to deliver on the following *rescontre* certain English securities—say £1000 East India shares—at an agreed price. If the speculation of the giver of the option was unsuccessful, he merely lost his option: if, on the other hand, the funds rose, he had the benefit of the rise. The *prime à recevoir* (a put) was the option given by *A* to *B* by which *B* was pledged to take from *A* on *rescontre* £1000 East India shares, say, at an agreed price. *B* became, in fact, a kind of insurance for *A*, obliged to make good to him the margin by which the funds might diminish in the interval".

22 Tracy (1985, p.90) drew this conclusion from an examination of the government transfer books where "sales in the secondary market are indicated . . . by notations that so-and-so is the beneficiary *bij transport van* (by transfer from) from the original buyer or a previous owner". However, records of secondary market prices are rare. Tracy (1985) quoted a 1530 trade at 86.25% of par value.

23 For example, Dickson (1967) identified the Revolution of 1688 as a defining event for London stock trading.

24 In the Advertisements section of *A Collection for the Improvement,* Houghton would provide various lists, such as those for Counsellors and Attorneys on 20 July 1694. In a 6 July 1694 listing which also included Coaches and Carriers, Houghton provided a list of Brokers, in this case for Corn (2), Dyers Wares (3), Exchange (6), Grocery (7), Hemp (1), and Silk (10), with the number in brackets representing the number of names listed as brokers.

25 Buckley (1924, p.590) made the following observation about the treatment of the English merchants of the Staple in Bruges: "It was, apparently, an important concession which the city Bruges made to the English merchants of the Staple in 1559, when it was agreed that the latter should be free of brokers when buying. It was asserted in 1562 that in most foreign countries no 'stranger' bought or sold except through a sworn broker, and the English Statute Book contains a number of regulations of similar import. Such arrangements were

general, being due to the universal prejudice against foreigners". Buckley also made another observation which is indicative of the pervasiveness of brokers at Gresham's time: "Dealings in Bills of exchange without the intervention of a broker were exceptional" (p.591).

26   This account follows Cope (1978). However, consider the following quote from Houghton in 1694: "Sometimes the Dealers in *Stock* sell to one, and buy of another different Shares of the same *Stock* for different prices, and so make Advantages".

27   Dickson (1967, pp.493–7) provided a detailed analysis of the evidence on dealer activities as reflected in the transfer records.

28   In contrast, Defoe (1719) made no reference to forward trading, using examples which usually relate to cash transactions, such as using false rumours to influence the stock price, the idea being to buy low on negative rumours and sell high on positive rumours (pp.39–40). However, it is not clear that Defoe had the best grasp of the financial transactions which were being done. One quote of interest is "the bear-skin men must commute, and pay differences money" (p.148), indicating that forward trading mechanisms similar to those used in Amsterdam were in place in London circa 1719.

29   Rescounter was the adopted English spelling for the Dutch *rescontre*. Early editions of Mortimer contained the following footnote: "The author is wholly at a loss for the etymology of this word (rescounter); and is obliged to suppose that, like most cant words, it is a corruption, and probably taken from the French *rencontre*, tho' with what propriety he cannot imagine" (Mortimer 1761, p.30). By the fifth edition, in 1762, Mortimer had resolved that the word originated from Dutch merchants' practice of indicating that a bill had been paid by charging it to a current account (Dickson 1967, p.491).

30   There are numerous discussions on the history of English coffeehouses, starting with a 17th-century pamphlet literature which includes titles by 'Anonymous' such as *Coffee Houses Vindicated* (1675). This pamphlet literature largely revolved around the question of whether coffeehouses were nuisances (Wright and Fayle 1928, pp.7–10), though there are also descriptive works such as *The Character of a Coffee-House* (1673) (Straus 1938, p.48) and R. Bradley, *A Short Historical Account of Coffee* (1714). Numerous discussions about coffeehouses appear in more general sources such as Samuel Pepys' *Diary*. The subject has attracted attention, even up to modern times, with E. Robinson's *The Early History of Coffee Houses in England* (1893), W. Dawson's *The London Coffee-Houses and the Beginning of Lloyd's* (1930) and Lillywhite (1963) being three interesting examples.

31   Jamieson (2001) provided a helpful account of the relationship between the popular 'caffeine' drinks of the 17th- and 18th-century coffeehouses—coffee, tea and cacao—associating the prevalence of a particular drink with the products of the different colonial empires. "For each of the caffeine beverages there is a unique history of the European encounter with a non-western drink, including not only the drink itself but social signals as to its proper use" (p.270). From the time of the early American colonial conquests, the Spanish favored the native plants, cacao mixed with an additive such as vanilla. This drink was in high demand in New Spain prior to and after the adoption of chocolate by the European Spanish starting in the late 16th century. The adoption of coffee and tea involved the 'East Asia' trading companies working in regions where these drinks were a staple. Again, these companies profited from the intra-regional trade in these commodities, especially tea, prior to significant adoption of these drinks in Europe. It is not surprising that the central place of tea in the 18th- and 19th-century English social milieu coincided with

the commercial dominance of the British East India Company in trade with and within the primary tea-producing regions.

32 *The Course of the Exchange* is the primary source for 18th-century stock prices and is the historical precursor of the 'Official List' of the modern London Stock Exchange. An excellent treatment of the historical evolution of *The Course of the Exchange* is provided in Neal (1990b).

Part III

The Rise of Limited Liability Corporations

7 Mania, Manipulation and Joint-Stock Valuation

Ye wise Philosophers explain
What Magick makes our Money rise
When dropt into the Southern Main
Or do these Juglers cheat our Eyes

Jonathan Swift (1667–1745)
First stanza of the poem *The Bubble* (1721)

A MANIA, MANIPULATION AND THE FIRST BUBBLES

John Law (1671–1729): The Great Projector

Adam Smith (1776, p.302) characterized John Law's Mississippi scheme as "the most extravagant project of both banking and stock-jobbing that, perhaps, the world ever saw". Compared to the Mississippi scheme, the South Sea manipulation was "a mere fraud" whose "fall was not very prejudicial to the nation" (p.219). Smith also maintained that "This scheme of Law's was imitated all over Europe. It gave occasion to the South Sea Company in England". This statement characterizes much of Smith's contribution to financial events. While Smith was able to identify the general characteristics of this major financial event, Law's Mississippi scheme, the details are brief, rendering Smith's analysis too cursory and sometimes confusing. Upon closer inspection, while there are striking similarities, Law's scheme did have some substantive differences with the South Sea bubble. The claim that the South Sea manipulation was an 'imitation' of the Mississippi scheme is not entirely supportable.

John Law qualifies as one of the truly colourful figures of political economics. His life and contributions have been examined in numerous sources, with Murphy (1997) being a particularly impressive account.[1] Law's main theoretical work, *Money and Trade Considered; with a Proposal for Supplying the Nation with Money* (1705), "presented fundamental insights into the nature and functions of money" (Hutchison 1988, p.135). Schumpeter (1954, p.295) observed that Law "worked out the economics of his project with a brilliance and, yes, profundity, which places him in the front rank of monetary theorists of all time". Despite being a noted monetary theorist, e.g., Murphy (1991), it was Law's limitations as a financial innovator that ultimately led to his fall from grace. As Adam Smith recognized, what made John Law's project particularly destructive was the notion of combining joint-stock distributions with bank note issues. The use of these joint-stock issues to undertake an immense refunding of the government debt led ultimately to the collapse of the French monetary system and financial markets.

John Law was born in Edinburgh in 1671, the eldest son of a successful goldsmith and banker. At the age of 14, he entered his father's counting house and spent three years acquiring knowledge of the Scottish banking business. With the death of his father in 1688, Law left the counting house and, bolstered by revenues from the estates he inherited from his father, moved to London to undertake the "gay life" (Mackay 1852, p.3). For the next six years, Law engaged in an extravagant lifestyle and became heavily involved in gambling. While initially quite successful in his gambling ventures, he eventually became consumed, and his gambling losses led to mortgaging of the family estate. In April 1694, this life came to an abrupt end when Law engaged a Mr. Wilson in a duel and had the misfortune of shooting his antagonist dead.[2]

The reason for this duel apparently stemmed from Law's actions towards a Miss Elizabeth Villiers (later Countess of Orkney). Whether there was a love affair or even a slight flirtation between Law and Miss Villiers is unclear. There is considerable evidence for a protracted relationship between Mr. Wilson and the lady. In any event, Law was arrested immediately following the duel, and Mr. Wilson's relatives pressed for his trial on murder charges. In the subsequent trial, Law was found guilty and sentenced to be hanged, a sentence which was commuted to a fine when the charge was reduced to manslaughter. This disposition did not satisfy Mr. Wilson's family. An appeal was launched, and while in detention in the King's Bench, Law escaped and fled to the Continent. In subsequent years, Law did make attempts to obtain a pardon. The pardon was eventually obtained in 1719.

"Little is known of Law's life between his escape from prison in 1695 and his involvement in the land bank debate in England and Scotland in 1704–5. Archival material that has been trawled yields a meagre catch of occasional sightings and passing references to him" (Murphy 1997, p.35). Based on the little primary evidence available, it appears that, following his escape from England, Law engaged in travel, primarily in France, Italy and Holland. During these travels, Law became absorbed in the general study of finance and trade. While in Amsterdam, he "speculated to some extent in the funds" (Mackay 1852, p.4), gaining familiarity with both the Dutch securities market and the operations of the Bank of Amsterdam. With this accumulated study and practical experience, Law began to formulate projects on various topics. During his travels and study, Law became impressed with the benefits that paper currency had introduced in England and Holland. By contrast, countries such as France and Scotland, where resistance to paper currency was significant, were economically depressed.

Mackay (1852, p.5) and others claimed that during his travels Law supported himself by gaming. "At every gambling-house of note in the capitals of Europe he was known and appreciated as one better skilled in the intricacies of chance than any other man of the day". There is much more to this part of Law's story than might appear, as it provides important clues as to how a Scotsman, fugitive from English justice, making an abundant living solely from gambling, could persuade the despotic French government to undertake revolutionary financial gimmicks: "Though Law made a fortune out of gambling it is inaccurate to describe him as a gambler in the traditional sense of the term. His gambling activities involved his use of his mathematical skills to calculate rapidly the most advantageous gambling odds allied to his adoption of the key position at the gaming tables, that of banker" (Murphy 1997, p.37).

John Law was so much more than a simple gambler, combining his innate ability at calculation with intensive study of games of chance. In a era when the basic calculations of modern probability were just being developed, John Law was hard at work calculating the odds for various games of chance. It is hardly surprising that Law discovered how the banker in certain games was similar to a modern bookmaker. The two games that Law is known to have specialized in, *faro* and *basset*, were both games in which "the odds were stacked in favour of the banker" (p.38). Gambling in Law's day was a much more socially ingrained activity, featuring a willingness to engage in novel games of chance, such as betting on lives. Law was known to devise games that would stack the odds in his favour, such as one described in a letter from the Abbe Conti to Madame Caylus: "[Law] offered 10,000 sequins to any who could throw six six times in a row, but each time that they fail to do so they give him a sequin". The odds of throwing six sixes in a row are 46,656 to 1.

Precisely when John Law made the transition from 'gambler' to projector is unclear, though Murphy estimated that "Law started writing on money and banking issues sometime between 1701 and 1704" (p.43). This posture as a projector was appealing in an era populated by the likes of William Paterson, Hugh Chamberlain, and Nicholas Barbon. Although Law was a wanted man in England, until the Union with England in 1706 this peril did not extend to Scotland. Around 1700 or shortly thereafter, Law returned to Scotland and attempted to get some of his projects implemented. Though an initial attempt at establishing a council of trade attracted little attention or support, Law was successful in gaining considerable attention with a proposal for a land bank.[3]

Law departed Scotland in 1705 for the Continent, where he continued his efforts to be a financial projector. In 1712, Law surfaced in Turin, where he was advisor to Victor Amadeus, the Duke of Savoy, on establishing a bank, along the lines of the Bank of England. As in Scotland, Law's plan was also not implemented in Turin. Shortly after this, Law's projecting efforts in France began to bear fruit. In 1714, Law was in the process of establishing permanent residence in France, and "during the summer of 1715 Law appeared finally to have persuaded Louis XIV and Nicolas Desmarets to accept his plan for a bank" (p.124). Unfortunately for Law, on 12 August 1715, the king became ill, and on 1 September the 76-year-old monarch died, leaving his five-year-old great-grandson to carry on the legitimate Bourbon dynasty. Louis XIV's nephew, Phillipe, the Duke of Orleans, was selected as regent. It was under Phillipe that Law's fantastic plans came to fruition (p.130):

> The key to analysing Law's rise and fall lies partially in understanding the operations of the financial system and the political power structure behind this financial system. Law came to power because of the near collapse of the financial system under Louis XIV. The bankruptcy of the financial system encouraged the search for a financial innovation that might remedy 'les finances' and encourage the growth of the real economy. Law, with his fertile and imaginative mind, his ability to master statistical detail, along with his desire to think of solutions outside those normally presented to the administration, represented the type of person that not just the Regent, but even prior to him Louis XIV and Desmarets, wanted to consult over the financial situation.

With this, the ground was set for the execution of what is, possibly, the most amazing sequence of financial events in recorded history.

The Mississippi Scheme

Almost from the beginning of trading in joint-stocks, periods of seemingly irrational pricing have been observed. Providing theoretical explanations for such behaviour has occupied a considerable amount of energy in numerous academic, political and social venues. Yet, closer examination of specific historical events reveals an array of determining factors, with each event featuring its own particular profile. This observation is well illustrated in the two most significant episodes of seemingly irrational pricing in the 18th century: the so-called 'Mississippi scheme' in France and the related South Sea bubble in England. Both these events came to a head in 1720, the collapse of the Mississippi scheme preceding that of the South Sea bubble. Despite the proximity of these two events and similarities in certain details, the Mississippi scheme seems to have been the result of well-meaning but misguided policy, while the South Sea bubble had the distinct smell of fraud and manipulation.

The Mississippi scheme, the brainchild of John Law, began in 1716, when Law gained approval from the Duke of Orleans to establish the *Banque Generale* in Paris. Law's bank was given authority to issue notes and to participate in the management of royal revenues. Continuing a practice of state revenue farming going back to ancient times, the French state would lease the right to collect specific state revenues in return for a fixed payment. This ensured the state would have sufficient revenue to meet political and military obligations without the expense of maintaining a bureaucracy to collect the taxes and other revenues. Initially, the note issue was restricted in size and, as a protection against debasement of the coinage, was made payable on demand in the coin in use at the time of issue. While France had some experience with paper currency, in the form of the *billets d'etat* issued by Louis XIV, this project was the first significant case of a private French bank issuing paper currency.

Somewhat to Phillipe's surprise, Law's bank met with resounding success, and branches were soon established in Lyons, Tours, Rochelle and Orleans. There was also a noticeable positive impact on credit conditions and payment of state taxes. Around this time, France's finances and general economy were in serious disorder, having suffered greatly from the excesses of the recently deceased Louis XIV. The regent seized on the opportunity, and, in December 1718, Law's bank was converted from a private to a public institution, the *Banque Royale*. This bank was conceived to be a note-issuing central bank, with provincial branches, to which was added a range of monopoly powers over activities such as the sale of tobacco and the refining of gold and silver. This merger of state tax-farming and bank note issue in the same firm is, at first glance, an ingenious public policy initiative.

One of the first acts of the *Banque Royale* was to print unbacked notes in the amount of one thousand million *livres*. This step was a harbinger of the financial mayhem that was to follow. Law's private bank had been careful to restrict note issues to an amount that could be managed with the specie reserves that were within the control of his bank. Whether Law concurred with this unbacked note issue is unknown, though his attentions were at least partly diverted by the granting in September 1717 of letters patent to a company with exclusive trading privileges on the western bank of the Mississippi River, in the province of Louisiana. This company was formally known as the *Compagnie d'Occident* or, in English slang, the Mississippi Company. The increasing value of the shares in this venture proved to be another success for Law, and in May 1719 the Mississippi Company evolved into the *Compagnie des Indes*, which was granted further exclusive trading privileges in the East Indies, China and the South Seas.

The creation of the new *Compagnie des Indes* was accompanied by an offering of 50,000 new shares. Accounting for the method of payment, Law promised an annual dividend on the shares exceeding 100%, triggering an almost staggering interest in the new issue. What followed was a sequence of arrangements: first, to lease the bulk of the indirect taxes, the General Farms, in August 1719; and, starting in October 1719, to use the proceeds of further issues of *Compagnie des Indes* shares to pay off virtually all the French government's debt. Throughout this period there was frenzied, almost unbelievable, trading in shares of the company. Propelled by the unbacked note issues of the central bank, the scheme started to slowly unravel during 1720, collapsing completely during September. On 29 September, the government announced *Banque Royale* notes would not be accepted for state revenue payments. In December, John Law fled to Brussels, fearing for his life.

The South Sea Bubble

Since the collapse of the bubble in 1720, the story of the South Sea bubble has been told and retold, sometimes profoundly.[4] Dale (2004) and Kleer (2012) are useful recent efforts. Included in these stories are revisionists making claims similar to Harrison (2001, p.270):

> Contrary to popular perceptions, investors in the early eighteenth century, and even during the height of the bubble, used modern valuation techniques

DICKSON (1967) ON ENGLAND IN 1720

The economic and social conditions in 1720 England stand in stark contrast to those prevailing in France. Dickson (1967, p.90) highlighted many key differences:

> By 1720 the new English state initiated so precariously in 1688 could congratulate itself on immense achievements. In the long wars of 1689–1713 it had led and partly paid for the successful resistance to Louis XIV's last and most costly attempt to expand French power in Europe. It had carried through the Union with Scotland. It had broken the legitimate succession to the English throne, excluded the Stuarts from it, and forced the Bourbons to recognize this exclusion. The pro-Stuart uprisings of 1715 and 1719 had been brushed aside. Civil and religious liberty had been effectively established, and all this had encouraged considerable investment and innovation in domestic finance and foreign trade. If England on the eve of the 'never-to-be-forgot or forgiven South Sea Scheme' was bolder and more confident than ever before, it was because of her successes, and not from mere bravura.

based on fundamentals and that were strikingly similar to those of today. The existence and use of such valuation methods cannot establish that the bubble was rational, only that the economic principles underlying market analysis and valuation were well understood by investors almost three hundred years ago.

The actual story begins with the first of the three great English joint-stock companies, the Bank of England. This flotation was particularly successful, both as a business venture and, more importantly, for validating the effectiveness of using company charters as a vehicle for funding government debt. The basic scheme was quite ingenious: The government had the ability to grant monopoly privileges for certain activities, such as the right to conduct trade to a particular region or the right to issue the 'coin of the realm'. The share market could be used as a mechanism to capitalize the value of these rights, which, in turn, could be sold in exchange for funding government debts, either new or outstanding as the case may have been.

The basic difficulty with this scheme is that the pool of such rights is small, with an even smaller number of truly valuable rights. The success generated by the Bank of England issue spurred calls for more such deals. However, the right to issue notes proved to be far and away the most lucrative monopoly that the British government could issue. The demand for new charters was such that (Morgan and Thomas 1962, p.29):

> In 1698, the subscribers to a government loan were incorporated as, 'The General Society entitled to the advantages given by an Act of Parliament for

ENGLISH WAR EXPENDITURE AND PUBLIC BORROWING 1688–1763

Year	Total Expenditure	Total Income	Balance raised by loans	Col. (4) as % of (2)
	£	£	£	
1688–97	49,320,145	32,766,754	16,553,391	33.6
1702–13	93,644,560	64,239,477	29,405,083	31.4
1739–48	96,628,159	65,903,964	29,724,195	31.1
1756–63	160,573,366	100,555,123	60,018,243	37.4

Source: Dickson (1967, p.10)

ENGLISH GOVERNMENT LONG-TERM DEBTS, AT MICHAELMAS 1719 (EXCLUDING LIFE ANNUITIES)

	£	£
I) Owed to companies		
(a) Bank of England	3,375,028	
(b) East India Company	3,200,000	
(c) South Sea Company	11,746,844	
Total		18,321,872
(2) Redeemable Government Stock		16,546,202
(3) Annuities for terms of years		
(a) Long annuities, £666,566 valued at 20 years' purchase	13,331,322	
(b) Short annuities, £121,669 valued at 14 years' purchase	1,703,366	
Total		15,034,688
Total Long-term Debts		49,902,762

Source: Dickson (1967, p.93)

advancing a sum not exceeding two million for the service to the Crown of England'. The 'advantages' were that the subscribers were entitled to share in the trade to India, each in proportion to his subscription, and that such of them as chose might form a joint stock for carrying on their trade.

The right to trade with India was an important concession that had already been conveyed on the East India Company. Yet, the government had a limited number of viable concessions that could be exploited.

The creation of the New East India Company came at the expense of the 'old' East India Company, creating an arrangement that was to prove unworkable. In 1702, the two East India companies were merged, and once again Parliament made the traders pay for their privileges. The deal was for the company to assume the government debt held by the 1698 East India company, £2 million at 8%, together with an additional £1.2 million, at no interest, producing a total loan to the government of £3.2 million paying 5%. Such capitalized transactions were an immediate relief to a government spending, on average, 30% more than could be supported by revenue sources. By 1710, the pressures of financing a protracted war had become considerable. After tapping the two existing joint-stock companies for additional funds, once again the government resorted to the granting of charters in exchange for paid-in share capital.

The 'Company of merchants of Great Britain, trading to the South Seas and other parts of America and for the Encouragement of the fishing', better known as the South Sea Company, was given royal assent on 11 June 1711. During times of war, the government typically paid for the war effort using short-term debt such as Navy tallies and Army and Transport debentures. Circa 1711, the amount of this short-term unfunded debt was over £9 million. It was this debt that the South Sea Company agreed to assume. Compared to the operations associated with the Bank and East India Companies, this deal was immense. For over two years the South Sea Company took subscriptions, ultimately raising £9,177,968, for which the government was to pay annually £550,678 in interest and £8,000 in management fees.

The early history of the South Sea Company was not good, due in part to funding the debt with tax sources that did not apply until 1715–1716—that is, interest to be paid to the company on the debt from general revenue of the Treasurer of the Navy. During the almost predictable period of suspended interest payments, shareholders were obliged to accept bonds in lieu of interest, further increasing their stake in the company. However, by 1717 the various encumbrances on South Sea stock had been eliminated, and Parliament further enhanced the attractiveness of South Sea stock by an enactment requiring that any deficiencies in interest payments from funded sources would be met with payments from the general sinking fund. By 1717, there were also renewed prospects for the most important segment of the monopoly business granted to the South Sea Company: trading with Spanish America.

John Blunt is an oddity in the South Sea affair. He has, ultimately, been singled out as the kingpin of the manipulations that produced the South Sea bubble, yet his initial involvement was by request of the government. It was Robert Harley, the newly appointed Chancellor of the Exchequer, who, in August 1710, sought out John Blunt, George Caswall and Sir Ambrose Crowley for their advice on dealing with the pressures of government finance. That both Blunt and Caswall were affiliated with the Sword Blade Bank, the former as secretary and the latter as partner, was eventually to prove a fatal error. "Directors and officials of the Sword Blade held five seats on the Original Court of Directors of the South Sea Company and the provision of credit by the bank played an essential part in Blunt's manipulations" (Morgan and Thomas 1962, p.31).

Another key element in the South Sea bubble mix was the presence of a complicitous minister: John Aislabie, Chancellor of the Exchequer. Aislabie was a man with a mixed character. His contemporary Arthur Onslow described him as "a man of good understanding . . . and very capable of business; but dark, and of a cunning that rendered him suspected and low in all men's opinion . . . He was much set upon increasing his fortune and did that" (Dickson 1967, p.95). In the summer and autumn of 1719, the apparent success of John Law's scheme in France generated plans for similar 'projects' in Britain. One such project was proposed by John Blunt: to incorporate all of the national debt, including that embodied into the Bank of England and the East India Company. The result would be a company very much like the company constructed by Law, with powers of note issue combined with profitable trading monopolies to support the interest income from government.

Whatever John Blunt's precise proposals were, the deal that was ultimately consummated left the two other joint-stock companies in place, with the South Sea Company to undertake a conversion of the remainder of the relevant government debt, some £31 million. This was a considerable undertaking for a company whose primary earning asset was government debt. Cantillon (1755, p.323) captured the essence of the scheme from this point: "a Bank with the complicity of a Minister is able to raise and support of the price of public stock and to lower the rate of interest in the State . . . and thus pay off the State debt. But these refinements which open the door to making large fortunes are rarely carried out for the sole advantage of the State, and those who take part in them are generally corrupted." In the case of the South Sea bubble, the bank involved was the Sword Blade Bank and the minister was John Aislabie.

After a bidding process involving the bank and the South Sea Company, the deal eventually reached was for the South Sea Company to be permitted to undertake the conversion of government debt into South Sea stock, with the South Sea Company agreeing to a reduction in the government debt payments to 4% in four years and an additional cash payment from the company to the government that would range from £4 million to £7.5 million. For this deal to make financial sense, the company would have to convince current holders of the government debt to take less than equal par value in South Sea stock. If only the interest payments are compared, the promised income from South Sea stock would be considerably less than many debt holders were receiving. For the conversion process to be profitable, it was necessary to create the illusion that South Sea stock was more valuable than its potential earnings would justify.

The result of the machinations by Blunt and his confederates is surpassed only by the magnitude of the collapse of the Mississippi scheme (Morgan and Thomas 1962, p.32):

> Even before the bill became law, South Sea stock had risen above par, and Blunt and his friends now used every means in their power to enhance the rise. Their technique included carefully staged offers of stock for cash at a little above the current price; the use of this cash together with the Exchequer bills which the Company had undertaken to 'circulate' and its credit at the Sword Blade to support the market; the making of loans against the Company's own stock, so enabling holders to buy still more; the promise of lavish dividends; securing the interest of prominent people by thinly veiled bribes; and extracting the utmost propaganda value out of current events from the peace negotiations with Spain to a carefully contrived reconciliation between the King and the Prince of Wales.

On 14 April 1720, one week after the passage of the act validating the conversion, the company announced its first 'money subscription', at a price of £300 for £100 par value in South Seas stock. Debt holders were required to register for conversion by 28 April, with terms of the conversion to be announced on May 19. To sustain the rate of conversion indicated by the first money subscription, the company boosted the half-yearly dividend to 10%, where 3% was expected based on company dividends prior to the conversion. Two additional, even fundamental, inducements were: (1) the requirement of only a 20% (£60) down payment on the subscription; and (2) in conjunction with the Sword Blade Bank, loans against stock. In effect, share speculators could borrow the subscription payment.

Following the debt-financed success of the first issue, the scheme proceeded with an additional £400 'money subscription' at the end of April, with the king and the Prince of Wales being the first subscribers. And so it goes, on 19 May the conversion rate for government debt holders was announced as £800/£100, and this was followed by yet another money subscription, on 17 June, at £1,000. These prices were sustained by the announcement of a 30% dividend for the year and a guarantee of a 50% dividend for the following 10 years. The most remarkable feature of the South Sea bubble is the extent to which the fraud succeeded. In particular, the £1,000 money subscription was a triumphant success, with subscription lists including half of the House of Lords and more than half of the House of Commons. Even the sole voice of reason who spoke out against the initial South Seas scheme, Robert Walpole, was tempted into this scheme.

Predictably, the scheme foundered. The Sword Blade Bank could not sustain the large loans that the South Sea Company was incurring to support the high price of the stock. In addition, the driving force behind the scheme was the rise in prices. In the early stages of the scheme, money could be borrowed for the initial subscription payment and the resulting subscription receipt sold 'light horse' in the market. In order to prevent an oversupply of subscription receipts, effectively in-the-money subscription warrants, the company would enter the market and purchase both light and heavy horse securities, using credit extended by the Sword Blade Bank. In a rising market, the profit potential of this plan was immense. If the credit underlying prices collapsed, prices would peak and the ensuing price collapse would be more intense than the rise. From 8 to 30 September 1720, South Sea stock fell from 670 to below 200.

When the dust had settled, Aislabie and the directors of the company had been required to forfeit a large part of their estates, and arrangements had been made to do 'rough justice' to other participants (p.32):

> The main points of the ultimate financial settlement were:
>   The £7 million liability of the company to the state was cancelled.
>   Borrowers against stock were to repay only 10% of their loan, but to have the stock which they had deposited against it cancelled.
>   Outstanding calls on money subscriptions were cancelled and stock allotted to all subscribers on the basis of £100 stock for each £300 cash already paid.
>   The parties to the August conversion received additional stock to bring their terms to the same as those of the May conversion.
>   The remaining stock, after discharging all these obligations was divided proportionally among all holders, old and new . . .
>   The net result was . . . to leave the cost of servicing the National Debt much as it would have been if the South Sea scheme had never been thought of.

Even though the scheme did not have substantial fallout for the direct participants, there was one event produced by the South Sea bubble that would have lasting consequences.

The South Sea scheme involving the government debt conversion did not take place in a vacuum. The fantastic promotion of John Law was in the process of unwinding just as the South Sea scheme was beginning, though the full extent of the financial market collapse in France could only be guessed at. The markets in England and France were awash with speculative capital. In England, this produced a competing array of small joint-stock promotions, involving companies either acting without a charter or using a charter that did not provide for the firm's current activities. Scott (1910) identified 120 such issues appearing between September 1719 and August 1720, with a potential market capitalization of £220 million. To stem the flow of speculative capital out of the market for South Sea shares, the South Sea Company was able to get the so-called Bubble Act invoked. It is an oddity of history that the 'Bubble Act' (1720) was aimed not at preventing the South Sea bubble but, rather, at the flurry of speculative share promotions that were competing with the refunding objectives of the government.

The Bubble Act was not a specific act, per se. Rather, the Bubble Act was some clauses attached to a bill enabling the charter for two insurance companies, the Royal Exchange Assurance and London Assurance Companies; yet another instance of the government exchanging exclusive rights in exchange for the paid-in capital of the venture. These clauses prohibited promoters from "presuming to act as if they were corporate bodies and pretending to make their shares or stocks transferable or assignable without any legal authority". The prohibition was extended to companies operating "under the authority of charters that were obsolete or had been given for some other purpose". The effect of this act was to severely restrict joint-stock issues, leaving the two insurance companies, together with the Bank, the East India Company and what remained of the South Sea Company as the main components of the English share market until the emergence of canal ventures toward the end of the century.

The Collapse of the Paris Bourse

The issuing of *"les primes"* by the *Compagnie des Indes* at the height of the Mississippi scheme speculation is, perhaps, the most remarkable event in the history of equity share speculation. The extent of the Mississippi scheme went far beyond the considerable losses of investors. For two generations and longer, the French were wary of financial securities such as bank notes, letters of credit and company shares. There were government efforts to organize a formal stock market, with a 1724 order authorizing the creation of a stock exchange in Paris. Restrictions on the number of brokers (*agents de change*) implicitly encouraged the trading of securities in informal markets organized outside the exchange. Though scepticism of joint-stock financing was widespread, this arrangement suited the French government. From the collapse of the Mississippi scheme until the closing of the Paris bourse in 1793, the government managed to use the facilities of the Paris bourse to bring a considerable amount of debt to market (see Table 7.1). From 1777 to 1788 "Necker and his successors obtained more than 776 million livres in return for life annuities of 8 to 10 per cent constituted on from one to four 'heads' without regard to life expectancy" (Taylor 1962, p.963).

   During the 18th century, French government loans were of two types: long-term fixed rate annuities (*rentes à terme*) and life annuities (*rentes viageres*). The life annuity issues that became an increasingly important element of French government finance as the 18th century progressed were the essential element in the emergence of exchange-traded funds based on pools of such securities. Though life annuities could be traded, such trade was complicated by lack of market information about the life on which the annuity was written. Early attempts at creating a more tradeable security used the life of a well-known individual, such as Louis XV or Frederick the Great (p.962). The practice of issuing *rentes viageres* without reference to age was not common prior to the dismissal of Turgot in 1776, while the 'uniform rate' for a life annuity after this time was "10 per cent on one 'head', 9 or 8½ on two, 8 on three or four" (p.961). Using actuarially sound pricing methods, the uniform rate prices for the single life annuity were fairly priced for an adult about age 50 (Velde and Weir 1992). For various reasons, interest rates on the life annuities, guaranteed by the monarchy, were high enough to be "scandalous" (Taylor 1962, p.965). This perceived mispricing led quite quickly to the seminal creation

E. CLAVIÈRE

Né à Genève,

le ... janvier 1735.

mort en 1793.

Ministre des Finances sous Louis XVI. en 1792.

Figure 7.1   Étienne Clavière (1735–1793), French banker, speculator and Girondist

Table 7.1   Direct Loans of the French Government, 1747–1771

Date of Edict	Finance Minister	Loan Term	Net Sum Raised	Loan Yield	Bond Yield
November 1740	Orry	Life	6.0	5.88	
October 1741		life	8.0	5.82	
June 1742		15 years	12.0	5.00	
December 1743		life	8.4	?	
November 1744		life	4.7	8.18	
July 1747	Machault	life	11.8	7.95	6.03
October 1747		12 years	30.0	6.71	6.22
September 1748		12 years	20.0	6.71	5.70
May 1749		12 years	36.0	5.00	5.18

(Continued)

Table 7.1   (Continued)

Date of Edict	Finance Minister	Loan Term	Net Sum Raised	Loan Yield	Bond Yield
May 1751		22 years	<30.0	?	4.88
May 1751		life	21.8	6.04	4.88
October 1752		9 years	22.5	6.17	4.55
November 1754	Séchelles	life	56.7	5.10	4.36
November 1755		12 years	30.0	5.86	5.86
July 1756	Moras	10 years	36.0	5.00	4.95
March 1757		12 years	36.0	6.20	5.02
June 1757		11 years	40.0	7.35	5.08
November 1757	Boullongne	life	60.0	6.4–9.0	5.15
April 1758		30 years	40.0	6.65	5.19
November 1758		life	39.0	7.0–9.0	5.20
April 1759	Silhouette	'shares'	72.0	6.50	5.23
December 1759	Bertin	tontines	46.9	9.53	6.85
May 1760		10 years	20.0	9.66	6.87
May 1760		32 years	< 60.0	?	6.87
July 1761		32 years	< 30.0	?	6.58
November 1761		life	43.5	6.4–9.0	7.30
January 1766	Laverdy	life	60.3	5.2–8.0	6.15
December 1768	Maynon d'Invau	life	44.6	5.2–8.0	6.34
June 1771	Terray	life	62.4	8.8–11.0	10.32

Source: Adapted from Velde and Weir (1992)

Notes: The Loan Yield is the expected internal rate of return on the loan at the government's offer price. Yields on life annuities are based on Deparcieux's life table. When the age of distribution of annuitants is unknown, the rates apply to lives at age 52 and age 7 at nomination, respectively. Bond Yield is the market yield on the October Loan at the date of the edict. Sums raised (in millions *livres*) exclude the value of old debt accepted as payment. Missing values represent incalculable yields.

of exchange-traded funds based on pools of these annuities. Trading in these funds played a central role in the *agioteur*-driven frenzies and manipulations that characterized the Paris bourse from the mid-1780s to the eve of the French Revolution.

This investment scheme, colloquially referred to as '*trente demoiselles de Geneve*', initially involved Genevan banks creating 'investment trusts' or 'syndicates' that were formed by pooling life annuities issued by the French government. Even though there was an expected gain to purchasing life annuities written on young nominees, there was still the risk of unforeseen events. Extending Taylor (1962, pp.992–6), Velde and Weir (1992) observed that the Genevan banks:

developed lists of young girls from Genevan families to name as the contingent lives. The families were selected for their record of health and longevity. The girls were mostly between the ages of five and ten, and were selected only after surviving smallpox . . . The Genevan banks purchased large amounts on each life to reduce transactions costs, but pooled together annuities on enough different lives to reduce the risk. The most common number of lives in a pool was 30, hence the name of the scheme.

The banks then "resold small fractions of their pools of annuities to individual investors". Sometimes the cash flows from the life annuities were passed-through directly to investors; in other cases the cash flows were repackaged in other forms, such as tontines. Included among the investors were prominent speculators, including the banker Étienne Clavière (1735–1793), the best known of all the French speculators operating on the eve of the Revolution.[5] As Clavière observed in 1782, "The Genevans are the first who have seen in the annuity loan a means of increase of fortune as advantageous to cultivate as most of the other objects of which industry is practiced."

All this reflects a relatively modern state of financial sophistication. In addition to capturing the gains from risk pooling, claims against the pools were "an easily negotiated asset . . . because the bank's dispassionate selection of lives eliminated problems of asymmetric information and moral hazard" associated with life annuities written on single lives (Velde and Weir 1992, p.32). This process was facilitated by the substitution of "the paper of the investment trust for the paper of the annuities themselves". In addition to capturing the French government's perceived 'scandalous' mispricing of life annuities written on young, healthy lives, the pools were able to capture the risk premium available from portfolio diversification. The result was that the claims against the pools could be sold at yields well below those directly paid on individual life annuities issued by the French government. At what point the bankruptcy of the French monarchy could have been anticipated is difficult to determine. In any event, Taylor (1962, pp.964–6) provided an insightful examination of the "rationalization of the risks taken" by the *agioteurs* as the bankruptcy approached.

Over time, the investment technology developed by the Genevan banks spread to other countries, most notably the Dutch Republic.[6] The Dutch schemes, often organized by important brokers instead of banks, introduced an additional wrinkle. This involved using the surplus of interest received from the French government over interest paid to claim holders to buy back shares in the pool. In some cases, the allocation of surplus was not complete, with the residual cash flow going to the brokers who originated the scheme (Alter and Riley 1986, p.28). In any event, the 'share buyback' feature would act to reduce the number of claims on the fund, thereby increasing potential future returns of pool claimholders. In summary, the pooling scheme involved many modern notions, including: the gains to diversification; investment trust/mutual fund origination; security pass-through; and share buybacks. This combination of features provides strong support for the selection of the '*trente demoiselles de Geneve*' as the most appropriate historical starting point for the study of exchange traded funds.

The creation of tradeable equity claims against a pool of securities reflects the remarkable level of sophistication that financial markets at that time had achieved about the notions that Markowitz and others were to explore almost two centuries later under the guise of 'modern portfolio theory'. In particular, the investment scheme that first appeared in 1771 reflected intimate understanding of the gains accruing to portfolio diversification (Taylor 1962; Alter and Riley 1986; Velde and Weir 1992). However, by the 1785 peak of an *agioteur*-driven speculative frenzy on the Paris bourse (Taylor 1962, pp.965–6), the bankruptcy of the state was all too apparent; the suspension of payments in 1788 and 1789 was a case of 'not if but when'. Oddly enough, it was *agioteurs* who were willing to engage in large operations supporting the French government annuity loans as the end neared. For the *agioteurs*, "political action was an important technique of speculative success" and the use of "intrigue, propaganda and manipulation" had proved sufficient in the past. As Clavière observed in 1786: "My fortune, it must be said, is bound to that of the Kingdom. I cannot conceive of the risk of bankruptcy in a country so favored by nature".

In the history of equity capitalists, Étienne Clavière is remembered as the bear speculator able to commission the great French revolutionary, orator and politician M. le comte de Mirabeau (1749–1791) to produce anti-agiotage polemics and tracts designed to support an uncovered bear squeeze of longs with forward contracts (*vente à terme*) in several joint-stock companies starting around 1785.[7] A number of such operations were launched against the Paris Water Company. This trade was sustained by the reappearance of joint-stock share issues starting around 1777 with the Paris Water Company and in 1778 with the Discount Bank. The bear squeeze involved spreading negative sentiment, depressing the cash price in order to permit the bear syndicate to purchase shares for values well below the delivery price on the short *vente à terme* position. The closing of the Paris bourse and the abolition of French joint-stock companies were two consequences of the turmoil of 1793. These events mark a symbolic end to the rudimentary financial transactions of the 18th century, just as the official recognition of the new-style Paris exchange in 1801 marks the beginning of more sophisticated and accepted equity security trading practices.

G. Taylor (1962, p.951) described activities on the Paris bourse approaching the eve of the French Revolution as follows:

> Directly and indirectly banks and big commercial houses were involved. In a crash many of them would be ruined, and their bankruptcies would shatter the Paris money market and extend themselves as though by chain reaction to all the provincial centers, paralyzing business and unleashing social and political reactions. The minister Calonne, who directed royal finance during 1783–1787, understood the danger and feared it, not only for its political implications but also because any serious contraction of private capital would narrow the market for the annual loans on which his budgets depended. He therefore entered the market with treasury funds and tried to shore up prices by buying falling issues. At heavy cost he liquidated private speculative contracts which, by their volume, threatened to bring on a general collapse. Scandals broke out. They were publicized. Nobles, clergymen,

even ministers figured in them. Rightly or wrongly the belief spread that the government was permitting irresponsible men to endanger public prosperity, and the ill-fated ministerial interventions in the Bourse undermined confidence in the government, sapped its prestige, and, like the failures in finance and foreign policy, helped create a demand for a representative regime.

Substitution of New York for Paris and Paulson for Calonne makes for an eerie connection with events of 2008–2009.

B EARLY CONTRIBUTIONS ON JOINT-STOCK SHARE VALUATION

Problems of Valuing Joint-Stock Shares

Unlike the well-developed mathematical theories for pricing life-contingent claims (Poitras 2000, 2005), publicly available 17th- and 18th-century analyses of trade and pricing for joint-stocks shares is quite sparse. Many contributions were little more than descriptive accounts, such as John Houghton's 1694 contributions to his weekly journal *A Collection for the Improvement of Husbandry and Trade* (1692–1703). There were the statistical contributions, most notably John Castaing's *The Course of the Exchange*, a regular publication that started sometime before 1699 and recorded market information such as foreign exchange rates and the prices for selected securities. Castaing's publication is recognized as the starting point for what is the *Official List* of the modern London stock exchange. Houghton's *A Collection* also contained stock price and exchange rate quotations, as did specialist newspapers that were readily available at selected coffeehouses.[8]

Another class of contributions to the analysis of joint-stocks was concerned with moralizing about the nefarious activities of stock market players: "this medley of Barbers, Bakers, Butchers, Shoe makers, Plaisterers, and Taylors, whom the mammon of unrighteousness has transformed into Stock-Brokers" (Mortimer 1761, p.xiii). This group includes Daniel Defoe's *The Villany of Stock-Jobbers detected* (1701) and *The Anatomy of Exchange Alley* (1719), as well as various Dutch publications of the 17th century examining *windhandel* trading, a number of which are reproduced in van Dillen (1930). Typically, periods of market turbulence were followed by "the usual crop of pamphlets" (Morgan and Thomas 1962, p.22). However, the pamphlet literature is invariably concerned with causes, consequences and remedies of turbulence, and it generally has little to offer in the way of reasoned fundamental analysis of share pricing. Fortunately, recent careful study of the primary literature by Murphy (2009a, esp. ch.4–5), Harrison (2001) and others have uncovered a wealth of detail on the information networks of those involved in share trading before the Bubble Act, observing: "while printed information might have been abundant, its utility for the active investor was questionable" (Harrison 2001, p.114).

The relative lack of public sources detailing the use of fundamental analysis to determine share prices has to be connected to the sources of information available and the social and political context surrounding joint-stock shares. Some very basic, general principles of share valuation were apparently well known. For example, de la Vega (1688) identified three key factors driving the price of *VOC* shares: "the conditions in India, European politics, and opinion on the stock exchange itself". No reference is made to accounting statements. Instead, private information networks played an essential role in obtaining important information relevant to share pricing. Murphy (2009a, p.115) documented the situation in early 18th-century England:

> London was the seat of political power and the connections between Westminister and Whitehall and the City were strong. Wealthy London merchants remained the key source of government funds and the Treasury was, at this time, reliant upon the innovation of private individuals in its search from funding solutions. The main moneyed companies, such as the East India Company and the Bank of England, were as much political entities as economic ones. They were dependent on government for the protection of their monopolies, and companies used lobbyists in an attempt to promote their business in Parliament and at Court.

The essential role of the coffeehouses as central clearinghouses for information and, on occasion, misinformation (Dale 2004, ch.1) has received considerable attention.

Even though joint-stock companies played an important role in both commercial activities and state finance, there were other reasons for holding shares than financial gain (Murphy 2009a, p.7):[9]

> For many investors, the dominant view of shareholding during the late seventeeth century was one in which shareholder and company had reciprocal rights and responsibilities. Loyalty was demanded on both sides. Thus, the ability to pursue the rational course, that of switching into a more profitable area of investment, was constrained not only by lack of information but also a sense of loyalty and by the perceived advantages that joint-stock ownership afforded—voting rights, status and, to some extent, political and economic power. The stability that this gave to the larger joint-stock companies of the period formed the foundation for the long-term survival of financial markets.

Detailed analysis of the broader implications of joint-stock organization in the scholarly efforts of the period failed to produce connections to share pricing and valuation. For example, Adam Smith (1776, p.699) recognized that joint-stock companies possessed two essential features not embodied in the typical partnership: transferability and limited liability. These features permitted joint-stock companies to raise initial capital substantially greater than could be raised with a partnership. Yet, despite a detailed historical examination of the performance of various English joint-stock companies, all that Adam Smith was able to conclude about joint-stock share pricing was: "The value of a share in a joint stock is always the price it will bring in the market; and this may be either greater or less, in any proportion, than the sum which its owner stands credited for in the stock of the company".

The Relevance of Accounting Valuations

The quote from Adam Smith implicitly recognizes the role of accounting in the valuation of joint-stock shares. The notion of 'a sum credited in the stock of the company' implies a numerical calculation of firm capital, presumably using double-entry bookkeeping. The risk and long investment time horizon involved in the seaborne trade to Asia during the 17th century required a transition from 'joint-stock' capital that would be liquidated after one or two voyages to a more permanent 'joint-stock' capital. Instead of there being a settling of accounts and return of equity capital and profit, if any, at the end of a voyage, funds were tied up for periods much longer than required for a single voyage. The construction of settlements and trading posts, ships seconded for defense and lost in trade and warfare, the risks of outbound and inbound voyages, and the loss of trade and goods to factors (employees working for the company in the foreign jurisdiction) put considerable pressure on the rudimentary accounting methods of the 17th century. These problems were compounded by the large number of investors required to raise the capital needed to sustain the trade to Asia and other far-flung regions.

The need for accurate accounting was a central issue for the joint-stock companies of the 17th century. Differences in context resulted in different approaches in Dutch and English companies. The charter of the VOC explicitly recognized the need for a settling of accounts after 10 years, though the initial grant of monopoly was for 21 years. Gelderblom et al. (2011, p.50) and Robertson and Funnell (2012, p.354) documented the failure of the directors (*bewinthebbers*) to provide accurate accounting to shareholders, in effect viewing the States General as the controlling group, not shareholders. The failure of directors to disclose the accounts was central to le Maire's 1609 "diatribe" against VOC governance. When the initial 10-year period had expired, there was no return of capital; though a dividend was paid, the required accounting information was not provided. Equity capital from the initial 10-year venture was rolled into the next venture, resulting in a *de facto* permanent capital stock. Again in 1623, when the States General renewed the initial charter of the VOC, shareholders protested the *bewinthebbers'* failure to disclose the accounts.

As Robertson and Funnell (2012, p.353) demonstrated, the *bewinthebbers'* failure to release accounting information was not due to the absence of such information. Both the Amsterdam and Zeeland chambers employed sophisticated, if different, bookkeeping methods. Being closer in proximity to Antwerp, where use of double-entry was well established, Zeeland adopted that practice:

> Not only did Zeeland's bookkeeping practice between 1602 and 1607 meet the best standards of the time . . . its fully integrated bookkeeping system

incorporated the data necessary to calculate periodic net profit and maintained the integrity of its capital sum which was used to equalise its Balance Accounts. Indeed, prior to 1608 Zeeland's bookkeeping practices compared favourably with modern double-entry bookkeeping practice and complied with the principles of capitalist double-entry bookkeeping.

In contrast, "Amsterdam's bookkeeping, on the other hand, remained grounded in a form of Hanseatic venture accounting in which a capital account was not a necessary element and profit or loss only determined on the liquidation of an enterprise". One argument advanced by the directors for withholding accounting information was "resistance to a general accounting as a consequence of the war with Spain which, they claimed, created a special set of circumstances that made it contrary to the national interest to disclose details about a major asset, such as the *VOC*, which was involved in the conflict". This illustrates a fundamental connection between the mercantilism of Dutch national policy and the mercantile activities of the *VOC* as an instrument of state power. However, the tenuous character of this permanent equity capital resulted in a reliance on circulating capital, raised from inventory sales and returning capital, supplemented by short-term loans, to sustain operations.

The (English) East India Company employed accounting methods that were similar to those used in Amsterdam. Scott (1912, pp.123–5) provided the accounts for the initial 12 voyages before 1613, the three Persian voyages of 1628–1630 and five joint-stocks from 1613 to 1650. Accounting results are provided for a capital account and a 'divisions' account related to profit and loss. Prior to the grant of a charter by Cromwell in 1657 for an East India Company with a permanent equity capital stock, the traditional 'settling up' process for equity capital at the end of a voyage or sequence of voyages was used: "From 1600 to 1657, the Company operated with terminable stocks, issued for a single or a series of voyages. At various points in the life of a particular stock or venture, available proceeds were divided pro rata and distributed to the adventurers (shareholders)" (Baladouni 1986, p.19). Some early voyages rolled the paid-in capital to a subsequent voyage; some did not. With the appearance of joint-stock circa 1613, quotes were provided for 'prices of adventures', indicating some limited trading of shares at company venues. Scott (1912, pp.88–227) still provides the most authoritative examination of the early history of the East India Company.

The failure of the *VOC*'s directors to provide any information about company accounts was an ongoing source of conflict with shareholders. The situation was different in England. The appearance of 'joint-stock' issues generated a need for more detailed accounting, which was addressed as follows (Baladouni 1986, p.20): "Article 306 of the East India Company's bylaws, published in 1621, states that 'They [Accountants General] shall yearely deliver up unto the Court [of Committees] at the Fine of June, a perfect Ballance of all Accompts in their charge'". This ideal situation was difficult to meet in practice due to a variety of problems, such as the number of independent voyages and the need to determine the value of goods and ships in transit. Unlike the *VOC*, which ignored demands from shareholders, for the East India Company:

Delays in presenting the yearly balance of accounts to the shareholders gave rise to suspicions concerning the reliability of accounting figures in general. Many of the shareholders maintained that management were their delegates and should, therefore, keep them abreast of the Company's state of affairs. They also demanded that all matters of importance be referred to them for decision. It was not uncommon for shareholders to take the liberty "to come into the Accountants and Auditors' offices to peruse the Company's letters and accounts".

However, again the ideal appears to conflict with the practice (Murphy 2009a, pp.126–7):

> The quality of information produced by the joint-stock companies was . . . questionable. There was a culture of secrecy within some companies. The East India Company was notable in this regard. At times when the Company was experiencing difficulties or was in the process of complex negotiations, it insisted that its directors keep details of their meetings secret . . . The Hudson's Bay Company concealed evidence of private sales of furs and swore its Committee and General Court to secrecy over the matter. Willan's study of the Russia Company also found evidence of concealment of relevant facts . . . Even when companies did publish pertinent information it was not necessarily to be relied upon.

Baladouni (1986, p.28) made a similar observation about the East India Company during the 17th century:

> With regard to the reliability of the Company's statements, one cannot but conclude that there existed sufficient evidence to question the validity of information presented in the financial statements. The continual delays in reporting; management's refusal of an independent audit; and management's decision to conceal the Company's indebtedness from the shareholders are surely reasons enough to shed serious doubts as to the reliability of the financial statements produced during this period.

For example, Murphy (2009a, p.127) observed "in 1696 when the East India Company presented a valuation of its net assets to the House of Lords, its calculations were challenged on almost every point. The Company's valuation of £1,224,502 was adjusted by the Lords to a mere £217,721." Problems of accurate accounting contributed to demands, primarily from small investors, for 'joint-stock' companies to convert to regulated companies.

J. de la Vega and the *Confusion de Confusions*

Against the blank backdrop of late 17th- and 18th-century tomes on share trading stand two interesting anomalies: Joseph de la Vega's *Confusion de Confusiones* (1688) and Thomas Mortimer's *Everyman his own Broker* (1761).[10]

Confusion de Confusiones was written as four dialogues between a shareholder, a philosopher and a merchant. Each dialogue describes different features of the activities of the Amsterdam exchange in the later 17th century. In *Confusion*, de la Vega (1688, p.156) demonstrated a modern understanding of the use of fundamental information to value stocks:

> The price of shares [in the Dutch East India Company] is now 580 . . . it seems to me that they will climb to a much higher price because of extensive cargoes that are expected from India, because of the good business of the Company, of the reputation of its goods, of the prospective dividends and of the peace in Europe.

Recognizing the uncertainties in seaborne trade and the difficulty in obtaining information about incoming cargoes, de la Vega went on to describe how some traders could profitably trade on information about incoming cargoes from the East. He correctly recognized that the usefulness of such information would depend on European conditions and the safe arrival and unloading of cargo.

The modern theory of discounted cash flow valuation models the problem as determining the discounted value of expected future cash flows. De la Vega explicitly recognized this reliance of the valuation problem on expectations and gave this story an additional twist (p.165):

> The expectation of an event creates a much deeper impression upon the exchange than the event itself. When large dividends or rich imports are expected, shares will rise in price; but if the expectation becomes a reality, the shares often fall; for the joy over the favourable development and the jubilation over a lucky chance have abated in the meantime.

PARTICIPANTS IN THE AMSTERDAM MARKET

Kellenbenz (1957, p.139) gave the following summary of de la Vega on the individuals populating the Amsterdam stock market:

> The elements in the market at Amsterdam were as follows: wealthy investors; occasional speculators, mostly merchants of the city; persistent speculators, either in real stock or a lower-denomination substitute; the Bank of Amsterdam; persons who loaned money with stock as security (who may also individually have been 'wealthy investors'); brokers of various types; 'rescounters' for the settlement of 'differences' relative to transactions in real shares, and at least one comparable individual who had, until shortly before 1688, adjusted 'differences' relative to transactions in the substitute (ducaton) stock.

Recognizing that there were "natural reasons for this phenomenon", de la Vega attributed this share pricing behaviour to a struggle between bulls and bears over market sentiment: "the leaves tremble in the softest breeze, and the smallest shadow causes fear".[11]

In the second dialogue, de la Vega (1688, pp.158–9) provided four useful rules to guide investment activities in shares: 'The first principle: . . . Never give anyone the advise to buy or sell shares . . . The second principle: Take every gain without showing remorse about missed profits . . . The third principle: Profits on the exchange are the treasure of goblins . . . The fourth principle: Whoever wishes to win in this game must have patience and money'. Variations of the second and third of these principles could easily pass as commonsense advice given to modern traders. The fourth principle is evidence that de la Vega, an astute 17th-century observer of share trading, adhered to what is known in modern markets as 'long-run investment strategies'. Combining this fourth principle with de la Vega's recognition of the importance of fundamental information anticipates the approach to security investment pioneered by Ben Graham more than 250 years later.

Even though de la Vega identified how the price of joint-stocks could be determined by fundamental information, much of his dialogue is taken up in a description of how prices will deviate from the fundamental values based on the expectations of bulls and bears. In particular, the last of the four dialogues is concerned with detailing methods of market manipulation: "the acme of Exchange operations, the craftiest and most complicated machinations which exist in the maze of the Exchange and which require the greatest possible cunning" (p.191).[12] The manipulation of securities markets in the 17th and 18th centuries was facilitated by the social practice of using securities for purposes of gambling. This practice was in keeping with the widespread public acceptance of gambling—reflected, for example, in the use of lotteries to increase the attractiveness of government debt operations (Cohen 1953; Daston 1988, Sec. 3.4.1).

However, gamblers were not the only participants in the stock markets (de la Vega 1688, p.150):

> it should be observed that three classes of men are to be distinguished on the stock exchange. The princes of business belong to the first class, the merchants to the second, and . . . gamblers and speculators to the third class.

Of the investment motives of the 'princes of business', de la Vega observed (p.151): "their interests lies not in the sale of the stock but in the revenues secured through the dividends, the higher value of shares forms only an imaginary enjoyment for them". Even though share trading in Amsterdam, circa 1688, was largely conducted in one stock, the *VOC*, this recognition of dividends as a key element in stock investment is another insight. The use of attractive dividend payout as a criterion for stock investment is one of the modern strategies for successful investment suggested by Graham et al. (1962).

That *Confusion de Confusiones* is a rare gem in the history of equity capital is an understatement. The book itself is an oddity, initially written in Spanish, published in Amsterdam by a Jewish writer of Portuguese descent. Joseph de la Vega was the second son in a family of four sons and six daughters. His parents were Isaac Penso and Esther de la Vega. Though his formal name was Joseph Penso de la Vega Passarinho, according to custom he typically used the shortened name derived from his mother. Isaac Penso was born in Spain, though the family's ancestral roots appear to have been in Portugal. The Inquisition forced many Jews in 17th-century Spain to emigrate, and his parents moved first to Antwerp, then Hamburg and finally Amsterdam. Joseph was likely born sometime around 1650, soon after the family had relocated to northern Europe.

Isaac Penso achieved success as a banker in Amsterdam and became a prominent member of the community. Though in Amsterdam the activities of Jews were relatively unrestricted in comparison to almost all other cities, there were still considerable barriers to Jewish participation in various trades. However, Jews were permitted to engage in activities such as wholesale trading in goods, shipping and banking functions such as moneylending and money changing. Some Jews were also permitted to engage in brokering. Not surprisingly, Jews were central players in the business of trading stocks. Anecdotal evidence indicates that as much as 85% of Amsterdam stock trading circa 1700 was in the hands of Jews, many of whom were of Iberian descent.[13] Based on this, de la Vega was in an excellent situation to gather the type of information needed to write a detailed account of stock trading on the 17th-century Amsterdam exchange.

There is considerable evidence that valuation methods for joint stocks making use of fundamental information were in general use by brokers to support their activities relative to de la Vega's first and second types of participants. For example, Wilson (1941, p.124) quoted a 19 April 1720 correspondence between London attorney and stockbroker Peter Crellius and Dutch investor David Leeuw: "Shares seem to be notably higher, but it looks to me as if the best-informed people are against the rise and great projects of the South Seas Company, believing the Bank and East India Company to be, in general, more secure and reliable." Unfortunately, as is usual in such a situation, the methods used by 'informed people' to arrive at such conclusions were not recorded. The information networks of the coffeehouses and 'brokers offices near the transfer offices' have left little for historians to examine.

Houghton on London Share and Share Option Trading

Houghton's 1694 contributions to his circular *A Collection for the Improvement of Husbandry and Trade* can be fairly recognized as containing possibly the first coherent and balanced description of early share trading in London (e.g., Neal 1990a, p.17), though the description provided by Houghton is so brief that Copes (1978, p.4) credited Mortimer (1761) with being the "first detailed description of the market". Though Houghton (1694) did provide some description of stock trading, the most significant contribution was on the specific subject of share option trading. For seven weeks, from 8 June until 20

July 1694, Houghton dedicated the first page of his circular to discussing stock trading. About 2-1/2 of the seven weeks are dedicated to trading in 'puts and refusals'. On 22 June 1694, Houghton provided the following insightful discussion of the profit to be obtained from call option (refusal) trading:

> The manner of managing the Trade is this: The Monied Man goes among the *Brokers*, (which are chiefly upon the *Exchange*, and at *Jonathan's* Coffee House, sometimes at *Garaway's* and at some other Coffee Houses) and asks how *Stocks* go? . . . Another time he asks what they will have for Refuse of so many Shares: That is, How many Guinea's a Share he shall give for liberty to Accept or Refuse such Shares, at such a price, at any time within Six Months, or other time they shall agree for.
>
> For Instance; When *India* Shares are at Seventy Five, some will given Three Guinea's a Share, Action, or Hundred Pound, down for Refuse at Seventy Five, any time within Three Months, by which means the Accepter of the Guinea's, if they be not called for in that time, has his Share in his own Hand for his Security; and the Three Guinea's, which is after the rate of Twelve Guinea's profit in a year for Seventy Five Pound, which he could have sold at the Bargain making if he had pleased; and in consideration of this profit, he cannot without Hazard part with them the mean time, tho' they shall fall lower, unless he will run the hazard of buying again at any rate if they should be demanded; by which many have been caught, and paid dear for, as you shall see afterwards: So that if Three months they stand at stay, he gets the Three Guinea's, if they fall so much, he is as he was losing his Interest, and whatever they fall lower is loss to him.
>
> But if they happen to rise in that time Three Guinea's, and the charge of Brokage, Contract and Expence, then he that paid the Three Guinea's demands the Share, pays the Seventy Five Pounds, and saves himself. If it rises but one or two Guinea's, he secures so much, but whatever it rises to beyond what it cost him is Gain. So that in short, for a small hazard, he can have his chance for a very great Gain, and he will certainly know the utmost his loss can be; and if by their rise he is encouraged to demand, he does not matter the farther advantage the Acceptor has, by having his Money sooner than Three Months to go to Market with again; so in plain *English*, one gives Three Guinea's for all the profits if they should rise, the other for Three Guinea's runs the hazard of all the losses if they should fall.

This insightful description is quite remarkable in that, unlike de la Vega or de Pinto, Houghton was not an active participant in the market; Houghton was "not much concern'd in Stocks, and therefore [had] little occasion to Apologize for Trading therein".

An important, but overlooked, feature of Houghton's discussion appears in the contributions of 29 June and 6 July, in which samples of put and call option contracts are given in detail. That standard contracts were available indicates that the market was well developed and that brokers, in conjunction with notaries, were the likely vehicles for executing trades. Examination of the specific clauses in these contracts provides useful information about option-trading practices.[14] In the 29 June 1694 circular, Houghton provided a sample contract for a "refusal" or call option, how "for Security to the giver out of Guinea's, the Acceptor gives him a contract in these or like words". Upon signing of the contract and payment of the three guineas, the Acceptor then provides the purchaser with a receipt for payment. Poitras (2000, pp.351–2) provided the text of a sample option contract to purchase shares used in late 17th-century English trading. Murphy (2009a, p.26) included a picture of an actual contract and discussed English share-option trading during this period in detail.

The first useful piece of information in Houghton's sample contract is the price, 3 guineas for a three-month call option, with exercise price of 75.[15] Though Houghton did give weekly quotes for East India stocks, such prices are not available for 19 June. Houghton quoted prices for 15 and 22 June at £73, so £75 could represent an option which is at-the-money.[16] This is consistent with the option practices observed by Cope (1978, p.8) in which the "price at which the option was exercisable was the same as, or very close to, the price of the stock for ready money when the option was arranged". How the option price was determined, and the interest rate associated with the put-call parity arbitrage, were not examined by Houghton. The statement about profit at a "rate" of 12 guineas per year indicates that these issues were not well understood.

The next point of interest concerns the description of the parties. The writer of the option was described as 'A.B., my Heirs, Executors and Administrators', while the purchaser was "C.D. his Executors, Administrators or Assigns". This wording bound the writer to the contract, whether in death or bankruptcy, while permitting C.D. to 'assign' the contract to another party. The well-developed case law on negotiable instruments (e.g., Munro 1998) is found to apply to the option contract, with the result that the option purchaser could resell the contract prior to the expiration date. While this feature substantially enhances potential market liquidity, the mechanism for assigning a contract, particularly where there has been a significant change in the price and there had been dividends or other advantages paid in the interim, is unclear.

Modern exchange-traded options contracts, such as those traded on the Chicago Board Options Exchange, are American-style—that is, the option can be exercised at any time up to and including the expiration date—and are not dividend-payout protected.[17] Houghton's sample contract provides information about related features at his time. The sample contract contains the agreement to transfer the share together with "all Dividends, Profits, and Advantages whatsoever, that shall after the Date hereof be voted, ordered, made, arise or happen thereon". Taking the "Date hereof" to be the date the option contract was signed, this feature provided what in modern terms is known as 'dividend payout protection'. This feature was combined with the feature that, upon proper notification, the writer agreed to sell one share of stock "at any time on or before the Nineteenth day of September". The Houghton option contract was American-style with dividend-payout protection.

Perhaps the most important theoretical result in the modern study of options is the Black-Scholes option pricing formula. As originally presented (Black and Scholes 1973), this formula provides a closed-form solution for the price of a European call option on a non-dividend-paying stock. Hence, even though most traded options are American, the European feature plays an important role. As conventionally presented, a European option can only be exercised on the expiration date. In general, the price of an American option is equal to the price of a European option, plus a non-negative early exercise premium. An American **call** option on a non-dividend-paying security is a special case where the early exercise premium is zero because, in the absence of transactions costs, the option will never be exercised early. Significantly, inclusion of a dividend payout protection provision in the option contract converts the option valuation problem for a dividend-paying security to the non-dividend-paying case.

What has all this to do with Houghton? The origins of the European and American features in options contracts are obscure, though early sources such as Bachelier (1900) indicate that the European feature predates the American. What Houghton provided is evidence that 17th-century option contracts were transferable, dividend payout protected, American options with settlement which required physical delivery of the shares. Yet, in the absence of transactions costs, an American option with dividend payout protection will not rationally be exercised early; it will always be more profitable to sell the option.[18] This effectively equates the American option to a European option. The upshot is that the modern interpretation of the European feature may be a fiction. Instead of restricting exercise to the expiration date, the 'European' option contract was structured with transferability and dividend payout protection provisions that made early exercise unprofitable.

Other less significant features of Houghton's option contract are also of some modern interest. In particular, modern exchange-traded option contracts permit cash settlement, in lieu of the exchange of stock for money. The Houghton contract only allowed for the actual purchase of stock. The possibility of a *rescontre* method of settlement was not admitted, though de la Vega's option contracts would seem designed for *rescontre* trading. There is also a provision in Houghton's contract for Advance money, which may have been akin to a margin account, to ensure that the option purchaser actually had sufficient funds to complete the transaction. However, why this would be required in an options transaction is unclear. Finally, as evidenced by the issue of a receipt, the option contract did require that the 3-guinea premium be paid up front. The possibility of delaying the premium payment until the expiration date was not admitted.

Table 7.2 In the Guildhall Library from and Anonymous Contributor. An Estimate of the Intrinsick Value of South-Sea Stock. *The* CAPITAL *of the* SOUTH-SEA Company, *at Midsummer, 1720, is Computed as followeth*, viz.

By the Two Thirds of the Absolute Terms, supposed to be Subscribed	*l.* 3,430,000	
By the Two Subscriptions, at 300 *l.* and at 400 *l.* Per Cent.	3,650,000	
	l. 7,080,000	
The Old Capital supposed to be	11,200,000	
		l. 18,280,000

(*Continued*)

Table 7.2   (Continued)

10 *l. per Cent.* for *Midsummer* Dividend		1,828,000
The Total Capital will then be		20,108,000

Debts due from the Company.

To their Bonds to the Proprietors of the Absolute Terms taken in,	*l.* 2,720,000	
To Purchase the remaining One Third Part of the Long and Short Terms, at 32 and 17 Years Purchase,	7,780,000	

	l. 10,500,000	
To Purchase the Redeemables,	16,500,000	
	27,000,000	
To be Paid the Publick,	7,600,000	
		l. 34,600,000

In Cash, or due to the Company towards the Discharge of this Debt,

By the Produce of the First Subscription of 2,250,000 *l.* at 300 *l. per Cent.*	*l.* 6,750,000	
By the Produce of the Second Subscription of 1,400,000 *l.* at 400 *l. per Cent.*	5,600,000	
		12,350,000
Remaining Debt will be		22,250,000

But suppose the Capital at *Midsummer*, 1720, to be
  20Millions; the Debt due to the Company from
  the Publick to be 42 Millions; and the Debt due
  from them to particular Persons 22 Millions;
Then the Value of 100 *l.* Stock at *Midsummer*
  1720, will be 100*l.* viz.

	l.	*s.*	*d.*	*l.*	*s.*	*d.*
The Proprietors of 20 Millions being Intitled to 42 Millions, each 100 *l.* in the Capital of 20 Millions is Worth	210	00	00			
But the Debt of 22 Millions on the Said Capital, is a Debt on each 100 *l.* Stock of	110	00	00			
The remaining Value is				100	00	00

A few Millions more or less in a Matter of this Magnitude, according to the present high Price of *South-Sea* Stock, seems to be very Inconsiderable; I will therefore suppose, That the Company, by encreasing their Capital only to 21 Millions, will be entirely out of Debt, and will be then Intitled to the 42 Millions due from the Publick. Is it not apparent, that this Capital of 21 Millions (exclusive of the Profits by Trade)

Table 7.2 (Continued)

is Worth only 42 Millions; and that every Share therein can be but of a proportionable Value; and so 100 *l*. Stock, Worth only 200*l*. exclusive of the Profits by Trade.

If, after the *Midsummer*-Moon is over, the present reigning Madness should happen to cease, and no new Purchasers should be found; but the present Proprietors of the *South Sea* Stock left to please themselves, with the imaginary Value thereof, until the Debt due to them from the Publick should be repaid; Could it possibly be of any more intrinsick Worth than I have before supposed; and if not to them, Can it become more Valuable to any others, to whom they shall Transfer the same?

I will readily agree, That if new Purchasers come in at high Prices, the Condition of the present Proprietors will be thereby mended; but whatever they Gain the others Lose. For whether the Stock be 21 Millions, Intitled to a Dividend of 21 Millions more; or be 50 Millions, Intitled to a Dividend of 12 Millions more; or be compleated to 42 Millions, without any further Dividend in Stock; it is evident, that the whole Capital can be intrinsically Worth only 42 Millions, and no more, exclusive of the Profits on Trade.

It is also evident, That whether the Company divide the remaining 21 Millions amongst their present Proprietors in Four, Fourteen, or any other Number of Years, it can be only of an equal Value to an immediate Dividend at once of the said remaining 21 Millions; and in that Case, 200 *l*. in such encreased Capital Stock would be Worth no more than 100 *l*. in the present Capital. Because such encreased Capital would be Intitled to no further Dividend in Stock; but the present Capital is Intitled to a Dividend of 21 Millions; *viz*. of *Cent. per Cent*. And there cannot, surely, be a greater Delusion; and yet it seems to prevail, that after several Dividends made in Stock, that the remaining Stock will still continue as Valuable as that which was before disposed of; or that 100 *l*. Stock in such encreased Capital is Worth as much as 100 *l*. in a lesser Capital; as if 100 *l*. Stock in the Capital of 21 Millions, Intitled to a Dividend of 21 Millions more, were not of a much greater Value than 100 *l*. Stock in a Capital of 30 Millions, Intitled only to a Dividend of 12 Millions; or in a Capital of 42 Millions, Intitled to no further Dividend in Stock.

☞It is not pretended, that the aforegoing *Calculations* are Exact; or that there are no Mistakes in the Inferences made therefrom; But People must be left to compute and reason as they are able, until the *Directors* of the *South-Sea* Company shall think fit to publish an exact State of this Matter; and thereby shew, the real and intrinsick Value of their Stock.

And if they can make it appear to be really Worth the Prices at which they have hitherto Sold, or shall here-after Sell the same, they will bless the Nation with a most agreeable Discovery of an immense hidden Treasure, which they only were able to bring to Light.

A number of famous English writers of the late 17th and early 18th centuries made passing contributions to the history of equity capital. Samuel Pepys (1633–1703) mused in his *Diary* about the coffeehouse in Exchange Alley, and Daniel Defoe (1660–1731), author of *Robinson Crusoe* (1719), contributed tracts such as *The Villany of Stock-Jobbers detected* (1701), *The Freeholders Plea Against Stock-Jobbing Elections of Parliament Men* (1701) and *Anatomy of Exchange Alley* (1719). Defoe was, in many ways, one of the most remarkable

Englishmen of the late 17th and early 18th centuries. His social and political writing was not confined to contributions that are descriptive or polemical, with little analytical content. Defoe was a prolific writer in a time when 'newspapers' were only rudimentary operations, and 'journalism' was associated with the pamphlet literature. Raised and educated as a dissenter, at a time when opposition to the High Church was a dangerous religious choice, Defoe is credited with using almost 200 pseudonyms, making it difficult to determine all his contributions. His substantive writings begin with *An Essay upon Projects* (1697). By this time, Defoe had become an experienced, if disreputable, merchant and was able to afford the leisure time needed to undertake the considerable number and variety of writings that were subsequently produced. Backscheider (1989) detailed the role that Defoe played in the creation of the South Sea Company. His most significant literary efforts were produced between 1719 and 1724, when *Roxanna: The Fortunate Mistress* appeared.

Another of the giants of 18th-century English literature, best known for the biting satire of *Gulliver's Travels* (1726), was Jonathan Swift (1667–1745). Far less remarkable and decidedly more closely aligned to the aristocracy and political establishment than the dissenter Defoe, Swift made a passing effort at capturing one of the important financial events of his time, the South Sea bubble. This effort, a poem, was sent by Swift to a friend, Charles Ford, with instructions to have the poem published. The covering letter attached to the original manuscript is dated 15 December 1720. The original manuscript bore no title, though the title 'The Bubble' was inserted, presumably by Ford, when the poem was first published in January 1721 (Williams 1958, pp.248–50). Poitras (2000, pp.407–15) contains both the text of the poem and a detailed discussion of numerous points in the text that survive to the present. Bartlett (1992) credits Swift with being the 'father' of supply-side economics.

Thomas Mortimer and *Everyman his Own Broker*

The middle of the 18th century produced one contribution that was roughly comparable to de la Vega's *Confusion*: Thomas Mortimer's *Everyman his Own Broker* (1761). A related effort, Isaac de Pinto's *Traite de la Circulation et Credit* (1771), contains some descriptive material on 'stock' trading but is largely concerned with issues of debt management. Cope (1978) described *Everyman his Own Broker* as the first detailed account of the English stock market. The book proved extremely successful, reaching four editions within the first year of publication and achieving a 14th edition in 1807. As for Mortimer himself (Cope 1978, p.4):

> Mortimer is an interesting character. Born in 1730 he published his first work at the age of 20, and became a prolific writer on political, economic and business subjects. In 1756, according to his own account, he speculated in the newly issued scrip of the loan of that year, dealing on his own at Jonathan's instead of employing a broker, in order to save the cost of the brokerage. The result was disastrous, and he lost what he described as a 'genteel fortune' . . . Somewhat embittered by his experience, his works

show him hostile to jobbers and other speculators. It has been said that he was a broker, but of this there is no record.

As for every man actually being his own broker, Mortimer counselled against going to Jonathan's, where trading was broker-with-broker, and there was resentment toward those trading for their own account in order to avoid the brokerage. Rather, it was better to go to the transfer offices located at or near the Bank of England, where deals for money were often conducted.

Writing well after the Bubble Act, Mortimer was concerned with a securities market that was dominated by "government funds", mostly 'consols', Bank annuities, "long annuities" and lottery tickets, and the 'capitals or stocks' of the Bank of England, the South Sea Company and the India Company. Recognizing that the "printed lists published by a broker, which printed lists are to be had daily, at or about one o'clock in the afternoon, at any of the broker's offices near the Exchange" lumped "funds of particular societies, and those of the government" under the heading of "stocks", Mortimer took considerable effort to distinguish 'stock' from 'government funds' (p.5–6):

> The word STOCK, in its proper signification, means, that capital in merchandise, or money, which a certain number of proprietors have agreed to be the foundation for carrying on an united commerce, to the equal interest and advantage of each party concerned, in proportion to the sum or share contributed by each ... From this definition of the word it follows, that the application of it to the list of government securities ... is highly improper, as they are absolutely public DEBTS, and not STOCKS.

Public debt, authorized by acts of Parliament, was supported by National Credit, "not the least shadow of STOCK or CAPITAL; but which amply supplies the place of it" (Mortimer 1761, p.7). As long as the government "can find

Witzel and Poitras (2004) provided some helpful biographical detail on Mortimer:

MORTIMER, THOMAS (1730–1810)

Mortimer was born in London on 9 December 1730, and he died there on 31 March 1810. His father was a lawyer and secretary to the Master of the Rolls. He was educated at Harrow and then, following his father's death in 1741, at a private school in the north of England. Having inherited an ample income, he devoted himself to study and scholarship, especially of languages and modern history. He also dabbled in the stock exchange, losing by his own account a great deal of money in 1756 when an investment went sour, and thereafter he was faced with the need to earn a living. In 1762, at the recommendation of the Earl of Sandwich (then secretary of state), Mortimer was appointed British vice-consul in the Austrian Netherlands and took up residence at Ostend. He held this post until 1768, when he was suddenly dismissed following a political intrigue; the exact details of this are unclear, but Mortimer's supporters spread a rumour that he had been too ardent in his anti-Jacobite sentiments.

Settling once again in London, Mortimer became a writer by profession and produced a large number of histories and works on economics and finance. His major works were *The British Plutarch* (1761), a six-volume compendium of biographies of notable Englishmen from the 16th to the 18th century, and the three-volume *A New History of England* (1763). His interest in finance developed out of his own unfortunate experience on the stock exchange, which he described in *Every Man his own Broker: or, a Guide to Exchange-Alley* (1761), a handbook for would-be investors which was frequently revised and reprinted. He was greatly concerned to improve the level of public knowledge, and his *The Elements of Commerce, Politics and Finances* (1772) was intended, as the flyleaf says, "as a supplement to the education of British youth, after they quit the public universities or private academies". In this respect Mortimer can be seen as part of a growing realization that the increasing volume and complexity of commercial and financial activity required people to have at least a basic knowledge of financial and commercial methods. This movement would ultimately lead to the establishment of the East India Company's training college at Hayleybury in 1805.

ways and means of paying the annual interest on this debt, in the same punctual manner that it is paid at present, so long will NATIONAL CREDIT, supply the place of STOCK to the government".

Everyman is much more than a how-to book about trading 'stock' in public companies and government funds, though numerous how-to insights are provided. For example, Mortimer (1761) observed: "Always suspect the man who wants to engage you to be continually changing the situation of your money, to be influenced by some private motive, unless you are a JOBBER yourself". As for the specific topic of joint-stock valuation, Mortimer stated (p.9):

> Every original share of a trading company's STOCK must greatly increase in value, in proportion to the advantages arising from the commerce they are engaged in; and such is the nature of trade in general, that it either considerably increases, or falls into decline; and nothing can be a greater proof of a company's trade being in a flourishing condition, than when their credit is remarkably good, and the original shares in their stock will sell at a considerable premium. This, for instance, has always been, and still is the case of EAST INDIA STOCK in particular, not to instance any other. The

present price of a share of £100 in the company's stock is £134. The reason of this advance on what cost the original proprietor only £100 is, that the company, by the profits they have made in trade, are enabled to pay £6 *per annum* interest or dividend for £100 share. But then it is uncertain how long they may continue to make so large an annual dividend, especially in time of war; for several circumstances may occur (though it is not likely they should) that may molest their trade in their settlements, and diminish their profits.

It follows that Mortimer subscribed to the view that share price was driven by the sustainable level of dividend payout, which, in turn, was affected by the various factors driving firm profitability. The dividend level was implicitly being compared to the prevailing level of interest rates on government funds. Dividends, firm profitability and interest rates drove share valuation. This view was an early precursor of what, in modern times, is referred to as fundamental analysis.[19]

Mortimer took considerable care in detailing differences between factors that influenced government funds and the "stock of any trading company" when trading at a premium and a discount to par value. In the particular case of a discount, "a rupture with a foreign power, which is almost the only thing in time of peace, that ought to affect the price of government securities, is presently known". In contrast (pp.14–5):

> A time of peace is no security for the premium given on the STOCK of any trading company, because many events may happen as easy to conjecture as to mention, by which they may sustain great losses, and which may occasion the premium on shares to totally subside. Again, the transactions of no society whatever are so open, nor so soon known, when they concern the public, as the transactions of the British government. A number of fatal accidents may be concealed for a long time in private societies.

While rumours of war may produce a "small loss" of 4% or 5% on government funds, "whenever a long, concealed misfortune, that has happened to any trading society comes to be divulged, or that society takes any unexpected measures, the fall of the shares in the STOCK of such a society, may be 20 or 30 *per cent* in one day". To support this claim, Mortimer used an example of a dividend cut by the (British) East India company in 1755.

In the case of government funds and "stock of trading companies" selling at a discount to par value, Mortimer observed "very great" differences (1761, pp.15–6):

> should it ever happen, that the shares in the CAPITAL or STOCK of any society, sell considerably under par, it may reasonably be concluded, that the finances of the society are in bad condition, and their trade on the decline; but the government annuities selling at a great discount is only a proof of

the increase in the value of money which will always be in proportion to the demands of the state for it.

In assessing the relative attractiveness of available securities, Mortimer concluded (1761, pp.19–20): "the government securities of England are absolutely preferable to all others whatever. That shares in the STOCKS of the public companies of England are nearly equal to the government securities; and far preferable to the securities given by private societies, or particular persons".

C   THE BEGINNINGS OF DISCOUNTED CASH FLOW VALUATION

Value of Shares and Simple Interest in Partnerships

An important topic in the early history of interest concepts is the process underlying the transition from simple to compound interest calculations. In many early commercial situations, there was no need for compounding, as transactions were often not more than a year in duration. In seaborne trade, capital and profits would be distributed at the end of a return voyage. Where compounding of profit on profit was applicable, there is historical evidence indicating that compound interest was used in business transactions going back to ancient times. However, especially during the Dark and Middle Ages, there was considerable social resistance to compound interest, as reflected in various legal and ecclesiastic prohibitions. Such restrictions still survive in modern Islamic finance, where *riba* is considered illicit. At the beginning of the 16th century, methods for calculating interest taught by reckoning masters typically involved simple interest and the rule of three. Where compound interest was used in Christian business, the practice was not advertised, though there is evidence that groups not subject to canon law, such as Jewish moneylenders, did use compound interest.

One question raised by the historical transition of market practice from simple to compound interest concerns the impact of social restrictions, such as the scholastic usury doctrine, on the recorded methods for calculating interest. To what extent were social restrictions responsible for the use of simple interest, as reflected in the commercial arithmetics up to the end of the 16th century? Was the proposed use of simple arithmetic a ruse, with compound interest being the conventional but unstated commercial practice? Or, were reckoning masters, bound by training using operations such as the rule of three, unable to handle the more advanced calculations required to determine compound interest? A related question concerns the mathematical prerequisites needed to do compound interest calculations. Did reckoning masters have the advanced mathematical training to undertake such alternative calculations?

Resolving questions surrounding the transition from simple to compound interest calculations is not easy. There is no specific landmark text that serves as a benchmark for the change in methods. If such calculations were done, the social conditions of the time dictated the need for secrecy or involved casuistry. The potential civil and ecclesiastical penalties associated with violating Church doctrine on usury meant that merchants disguised interest payments in various types of seemingly non-usurious contracts, such as bills of exchange. However, it is possible to make some indirect inferences based on information about the state of mathematical knowledge. If the typical reckoning master was not equipped to understand compound interest calculations, then it is unlikely that compound interest would be a method that was widely used to determine a 'fair and just' return on a fixed-income investment or partnership.

Interest rate methods of calculating the value of equity capital shares are examined in the *Treviso* in three problems involving the returns from partnership (Swetz 1987, pp.138–9). No other attention is given to any situations involving such payments. The first of these problems is an elementary application of the rule of three:

> Three merchants have invested their money in a partnership . . . Piero put in 112 ducats, Polo 200 ducats and Zuanne 142 ducats. At the end of a certain period they found that they had gained 563 ducats. Required is to know how much falls to each man so that no one shall be cheated.

The solution to the problem is uninteresting from a mathematical viewpoint.[20] However, the problem is of interest in illustrating the general framework for practical partnership problems. In addition, the author was careful to implicitly observe that if all partners have funds invested for the same length of time, the solution to the problem is independent of the endpoint of the partnership.

The second of the *Treviso* problems is more complicated in that the partners are permitted to be involved in the partnership for different time periods (p.143):

> Two merchants, Sebastino and Jacomo, have invested their money for gain in a partnership. Sebastino put in 350 ducats on the first day of January, 1472, and Jacomo 500 ducats, 14 grossi on the first day of July, 1472; and on the first day of January, 1474 they found that they had gained 622 ducats. Required is the share of each (man so that no one shall be cheated).

The proposed solution to this problem follows as an extension of applying the rule of three given in the first problem. As such, this is also a simple interest method of solution. Observing that the stated solution does not admit the possibility of compound interest provides considerable insight into the methods of calculation used in mercantile practice during this period.

Considering the proposed solution in more detail requires knowing that 1 ducat = 24 grossi and 1 grossi = 32 pizoli. The solution to the problem proceeds by applying the rule of three, which, in this case, involves expressing the two contributions in grossi—8,400 grossi for Sebastino and 12,014 grossi for Jacomo—with the addendum that 'since Sebastino has had his share in 6 months longer than Jacomo, we must multiply each share by the length of its time'. Multiplying by 24 months gives Sebastino's share as 201,600 and by 18 months gives Jacomo's share as 216,252. Taking the sum of these two shares (417,852) for a divisor and applying the 'rule of three' gives the solution of 300 ducats, 2 grossi, 8 pizoli and a remainder for Sebastino and 321 ducats, 21 grossi, 13 pizoli and a remainder for Jacomo.

The *Treviso* solution to the partnership problem does not involve the use of compound interest. Using semi-annual compounding, the inclusion of compound interest would involve solving:

$$850\frac{14}{24}+622=350\left(1+\frac{r}{2}\right)^4 + 500\frac{14}{24}\left(1+\frac{r}{2}\right)^3$$

The solution of $r = 34.694\%$ requires the evaluation of a quartic equation. The associated shares would be 308.4 ducats (308 ducats, 9 grossi, 19 pizoli and remainder) for Sebastino and 313.6 ducats (313 ducats, 14 grossi, 12 pizoli and remainder) for Jacomo, a decidedly different result than the 'just' result proposed in the *Treviso*.[21]

While this failure to allow for compound interest was conventional in the early commercial arithmetics, there is evidence that accepted practice was not due to a general ignorance of the concept. For example, manuscripts from 14th- and early 15th-century Tuscany contained variations of the following problem: 'A man loaned 100 lire to another, and after 3 years he gives him 150 lire for the principal and interest at annual compound interest. I ask you, at what rate was the lira loaned per month?' (Franci and Rigatelli 1988). In other manuscripts, four-year compound interest problems were proposed. The solutions proposed to these problems represent important contributions to the early development of algebra in Europe. Also of interest is Pegolotti (1936), which provides a 14th-century Italian manuscript containing tables for the compound interest calculation $(1+r)^n$.

At least two possible factors can be identified for the failure to incorporate compound interest in valuing partnership returns, as reflected in 15th-century and early 16th-century commercial arithmetics. A first possible factor is simplicity of calculation. Even though the compound interest solution had been identified, the tables required for such calculations were not widely available; neither was the mathematical knowledge required for the merchant community to understand compound interest. While a reckoning master could be consulted on the 'just' solution to complicated problems, those involved in the day-to-day implementation of commercial arithmetic were primarily clerks and merchants. The *Treviso* algorithm, while inexact, only required applying the rule of three, a result that was at the heart of early commercial arithmetic.

Simplicity of calculation and general lack of mathematical knowledge imply that compound interest concepts were not typically incorporated into the business decisions of the time. Another possible factor supporting the *Treviso* solution were the usury restrictions imposed by canon law. While partnerships could be used to disguise the payment of simple interest, the explicit recognition of a 'profit on profit' payment could bring the sanctions of canon law upon those requiring the receipt of such a payment. For flagrant violation, these sanctions could include excommunication and even banishment. If such payments were made, and there is some anecdotal evidence that payment of compound interest was a regular business practice at the time of the *Treviso*, such payments were made in silence.

Strong evidence that the use of compound interest was common in the commercial practice of the 15th century, at least in the important financial centres such as Lyons, can be found in Chuquet's (1484) *Triparty*. On the subject of compound interest, *Triparty* makes explicit reference to the incongruity between the theoretically correct mathematical calculation and recommended commercial practice for calculating shares in partnerships reflected in the basic commercial arithmetics. The manuscripts contained in *Triparty* are actually three main sections concerned with algebraic theory, and three other parts containing problems, a geometry and a commercial arithmetic. The latter is generally similar in content to the *Treviso*, reflecting the similarity in the study of commercial arithmetic throughout Europe. However, unlike the *Treviso*, the handling of compound interest is recognized directly (pp.306–7):

> Three merchants formed a company, one of whom put in 10 ecus which remained there for the space of three years. The second put in 6 ecus which remained there for 7 years, and the third put in 8 ecus which remained there for four years. At the end of a period, 20 livres of profit was found. One asks how much comes to each, considering the money and the time that each has used it.

The answer proceeds with the usual application of the rule of three as in the *Treviso*. After presenting this method and the solution, Chuquet stated:

> And the calculation is done, according to the style and opinion of some. And in order for such reckoning to be of value, it is necessary to presuppose that the principal or the capital alone has made a profit, and not the profit (itself). And inasmuch as it is not thus, for the profit and the profit on the profit made in merchandise can earn profit and profit on profit in proportion to the principal, from day to day, from month to month and from year to year, whereby a larger profit may ensue. Thus such calculations are null, and I believe that among merchants no such companies are formed.

Though the compound interest solution was not provided, Chuquet definitely held that calculation of compound interest was the regular practice in calculating the returns from partnerships of unequal duration.

The upshot of this discussion is that it is difficult to tell from an examination of the text of the basic commercial arithmetics, such as the *Treviso*, whether the use of compound interest in determining shares in partnerships was a widespread commercial practice. It is possible to rationalize the *Triparty* manuscript evidence indicating common usage of compound interest by arguing that social and commercial convention did not permit acknowledging that compound interest calculations were used. In turn, the usury restriction was sufficiently binding that it would have been unwise to incorporate payment of compound interest, profit on profit, into the curriculum used to educate merchant apprentices. In addition, the mathematical concepts involved would have required a level of instruction substantively more advanced than that required for motivating fundamental concepts such as the 'rule of three'. On balance, it seems possible that the practice of using compound interest to calculate partnership shares for investment periods of unequal duration was conventional and that the practice was not revealed in written sources in order to avoid the usury sanctions.

Compound Interest

Problems involving compound interest were well known by the end of the 15th century. Mathematical tracts often used compound interest problems to motivate the solution of algebraic equations. For example, Franci and Rigatelli (1988, p.20) quoted a 1395 Italian manuscript that poses the following problem:

> A man loaned 100 lire to another and after three years he gives him 150 for the principal and interest at annual compound interest. I ask you at what rate was the lira loaned per month?

The stated equation used to solve for this problem is the cubic equation ($x^3 + 60x^2 + 1200x = 4000$). The 1395 manuscript recognizes that the rule provided for solving the problem is not a general algebraic solution to cubic equations but is applicable to the general interest rate calculation problems being posed.[22]

The level of algebraic sophistication in 14th-century Italian mathematics extends beyond the solution of specific cubic equations. Quartic equations and, in a very few cases, higher-order algebraic equations were also presented and solved. For example, the same 1395 Italian manuscript poses a compound interest problem requiring the solution of a quartic equation:

> A man loaned 100 lire to another and after four years he gives him for the principal and interest 160 lire at annual compound interest. I ask you are what rate the lira was loaned per month?

The associated quartic equation ($x^4 + 80x^3 + 2400x^2 + 32000x = 96000$) is again stated and solved, with the recognition that the solution procedure to these types of compound interest problems is not algebraically general. This type of quartic problem reflects the ability of Italian mathematics of the time to solve algebraically for the interest rate in practical compound interest problems.

The use of compound interest problems to motivate algebraic solutions became increasingly common in mathematical manuscripts of the 15th and 16th centuries. However, as in the stated solution in the 1395 manuscript, compound interest problems were often used to illustrate the methods of algebra, not to facilitate commercial applications, where the price-given-interest-rate calculation would typically involve substantially less mathematical skill. Widespread practical use of this type of compound interest calculation did require the availability of compound interest tables. The presence of such tables in printed commercial arithmetics or 'ready reckoners' is an excellent reflection of the extent of commercial use of compound interest valuations. Such tables did not begin to appear in print until about the mid-16th century, with detailed tables appearing only in the late 16th century.

As for the content of commercial arithmetic texts, until the later part of the 16th century compound interest problems were typically treated as mathematical, as opposed to commercial, problems. Basic commercial arithmetics, such as the *Treviso*, do not mention the subject. The treatment of compound interest was restricted to the more sophisticated mathematical texts, in which a commercial arithmetic was included as one part of a text also dealing with the theoretical aspects of mathematics. Many of the mathematical texts that contain a section dealing with commercial arithmetic, such as *Triparty*, either do include compound interest problems or include compound interest problems in a section other than that devoted to commercial arithmetic. Other texts, including Pacioli's *Summa*, provide a description of compound interest within the commercial arithmetic, without much elaboration.

Yet, it is fair to say that, at the time of the *Treviso*, the calculation of compound interest was recognized and understood. There were certainly reckoning masters with the skill required to do the required commercial calculations, if such calculations were needed, though compound interest rate problems were still mostly of interest only to mathematicians. By the later part of the 16th century, compound interest calculations were much more widespread, as evidenced by the availability of tables needed to do compound interest calculations. From this time to the middle of the 17th century, progress in mathematics and commercial practice was substantial. Compound interest problems were no longer of much interest to mathematicians, and commercial arithmetic gradually became the preserve of accountants and other specialized merchants.

Compound interest was still of mathematical interest in the 15th and early 16th centuries. Yet, the basic commercial arithmetics did not treat this subject. Given that these texts were designed for instruction in reckoning schools, this is not surprising. Merchant apprentices, struggling to understand the rule of three, could not be expected to have the mathematical skills to handle a concept that involved raising values to powers. Yet, many reckoning masters would have such conceptual ability. The implications of compound interest would be obvious to merchants, even if social restrictions prevented overt discussion. All this raises questions about the extent of compound interest calculations being used in practice,[23] with an important clue being found in Chuquet's *Triparty*.

Seemingly, Chuquet's observation appears to call into question the validity of attributing the absence of compound interest problems in the early commercial arithmetics to the complexity of the solutions. Yet, the problem of determining a precise interest rate is more a mathematical problem than a practical one. The mathematical motivation for compound interest problems is associated with solving for the rate of interest, given the starting and ending values of the investment. However, conventional practice was to state a rate of interest, and from this the ending or starting value for an investment could be readily calculated. Customary fixed interest rates were quoted regularly, one instance being the triple contract, which was often referred to as a five-percent contract (Homer and Sylla 1991, p.75). Interest-bearing securities, such as annuities, mortgages, the *census* and the Venetian *prestiti*, typically offered annual coupon payments, reducing the need to deal with compounding.

Where solutions to compound interest problems were required, reckoning masters such as Chuquet had the ability to make such calculations. For example, Chuquet posed the following problem:

> A merchant has lent to another a sum of money at the interest of 10%, and the interest earned like the principal at the end of every year. It happened that at the end of three years, the debtor is found to owe, as much in interest as in principal, the sum of 100 livres . . . determine how much had been lent to him in the first year.

Chuquet's algebraic solution to this problem provides an answer that correctly incorporates the use of compound interest. Chuquet posed at least seven compound interest problems. Yet, none of these problems appears in the commercial arithmetic. Rather, these problems appear in a general section dealing with mathematical problems. Significantly, Chuquet continued the received practice of treating compound interest as being of mathematical, as opposed to commercial, importance.

More precisely, *Triparty* has three main parts, dealing with arithmetic, calculation of roots and algebra. In addition to the main body of *Triparty*, three supplementary sections are provided: a section with applied problems, a geometry and the commercial arithmetic (Flegg et al. 1985, p.197):

> Collections of mathematical problems, ranging from straight-forward calculations in fancy dress to purely logical brainteasers, have a long history, and played a prominent role in the transmission of mathematical culture throughout the Middle Ages . . . In Chuquet's manuscript, the prime purpose of the Problems is . . . to illustrate the applications of his *Triparty*, and in particular of the rule of first terms.

Though it is acknowledged that compound interest was common in commercial practice, and Chuquet had the ability to make the requisite calculations, the concept was still not included in the commercial arithmetic. This situation changed during the 16th century.

In a detailed examination of 14 French commercial arithmetics written during the 16th century, Davis (1960, pp.22–4) found 10 of the 14 dealing with problems of simple and compound interest, with 2 of the 10 dealing with simple interest only. One of the 10 arithmetics is *Larismethique* (1520, Lyons) by Etienne de la Roche, a probable student of Chuquet who also plagiarized liberally from *Triparty*. La Roche's arithmetic makes a clear distinction between simple and compound interest:

> To merit [interest] is to make one's money earn or work in merchandise or otherwise at so much per livre or per cent at the finish of a year or of a month or of some other period. Simple merit [interest] occurs when

the principal alone earns at the finish of the period. Merit at the finish of term ... [compound interest] occurs when the principal earns at the end of the term, and then the gain and principal both earn ...

The following compound interest problem is then posed:

A man lends another 100 livres for the space of two years and six months, to merit at the finish of term at the rate of twenty per cent. The question is what does it all amount to at the end of the term?

The solution La Roche offers does not go beyond methods provided by Chuquet.

In keeping with the still prevalent social restrictions on usury, 4 of the 10 commercial arithmetics examining simple and compound interest contained criticism of the payment of interest but still discussed the subject because of the prevalence of the practice. One of these arithmetics was the amended 1561 French translation of the commercial arithmetic by important Dutch mathematician Gemma Frisius (1508–1555). Written originally in Latin around 1536, the Gemma arithmetic went into at least 59 editions in the 16th century and more in the 17th century (D. Smith 1958, v.1, p.341). The amended French text states:

Howsoever much this name of usury myst be execrable among Christians, nevertheless because necessity constrains many to this usage, I will speak a little of its computation.

Passing reference is made to compound interest as 'Judaic'.

The connection between compound interest and Jewish business practice was made in at least two other arithmetics. Jacques Chauvet in *Les Institutions de l'Arithmetique* (1578, Paris) described compound interest as 'abominable' and said the practice was used only by Jews. However, this text is somewhat elementary. The more detailed work of Milles Denorry, *L'Arithmetique de Milles Denorry* (1574, Paris), referred to compound interest as 'Judaic usury' and observed that the practice was 'vituperable for Christians, thus punishable, and permitted only to Jews'. However, Denorry went on to observe that compound interest had become 'so common that even the greatest were mixed up in it'. Denorry gave a full treatment to the calculation of compound interest (Davis 1960, p.24).

Of the four arithmetics examined by Davis that do not treat interest problems, two are the earliest considered, 1512 and 1515 respectively, and were printed in Paris, not Lyons. The other two date from the mid-century and were, again, printed in Paris. One of the authors, Pierre Forcadel, offered another commercial arithmetic that did treat compound interest problems. Of the two works treating only simple interest, one is from Poitiers in 1552 and the other is a 1578 French translation of Nicolas Tartaglia. As Tartaglia treated compound interest in other works, if Davis was correct the omission is one of text selection rather than lack of recognition by the primary author. Perhaps the most interesting commercial arithmetic examined by Davis (1960) is the 1515 arithmetic.

This arithmetic, by a French monk and a Spanish monk, deals with problems involving loans with late repayment and loans without interest. It also contains an uncritical explanation of both simple and compound interest.

The Forgotten Work of Richard Witt

By the beginning of the 17th century, commercial arithmetics (as well as academic arithmetics containing chapters on commercial arithmetic) dealing in considerable detail with the subject of compound interest were widely available in Europe's financial centres. A number of sources contained detailed 'breviats' (tables) needed to simplify compound interest calculations for practitioners. Further developments in the area of solving interest valuation problems involved broadening and deepening the subject matter, as well as disseminating advanced knowledge to lesser financial centres. The 17th century witnessed the emergence of technically advanced texts dedicated solely to commercial interest rate calculations, written in the vernacular by commercial algorists.

One important text that reflects the broadening and deepening of interest rate analysis was written by English commercial algorist Richard Witt: *Arithmeticall Questions, touching the Buying and Exchange of Annuities* ... (1613, London) (Lewin 1970). The history of this book is something of an enigma. By standards of early 17th-century commercial arithmetic, the contents of the book are sophisticated. The book was considered of enough significance to warrant a second edition in 1634. This second edition was produced by Thomas Fisher, who made some additions to the original text. However, Fisher observed in his introduction that "the Book is almost forgot and out of use". One element of the enigma surrounding this book is why it failed to have much staying power or later notoriety.

One possible reason for the lapse into obscurity is that the book became a victim of what Thomas Fisher described in his introduction as the "change of times and customs". It is also possible that the book was too much for most practitioners, who could get what was required from more accessible sources, such as the tables of Thomas Clay or, somewhat later, from the ready reckoner of William Leybourn. In turn, little is known of Richard Witt other than his description on the title page as a 'practitioner in the Arte of Numbers'. He was almost certainly alive in 1613 when the first edition was printed and, according to Thomas Fisher's introduction to the second edition, had died by 1634. Witt, apparently, lacked any desire for self-promotion, a trait that probably extended to promotion of *Arithmeticall Questions*.[24]

Witt's book has two significant features: (1) a sequence of detailed interest tables that Witt refers to as 'breviats' and (2) 124 problems that are solved using the tables.[25] The detail and sophistication exhibited in the interest tables is impressive. *Arithmeticall Questions* starts with a discussion of the relationship between the various tables for future and present value, both for single cash flows and for annuities. A future value table listing the factors for $(1 + r)^T$ for $r = 10\%$ and $T \in \{1, 2, \ldots, 30\}$ is provided. Following this table is a demonstration of how to use to the values in the table to construct the associated factors for present value of single cash flows, present value of an annuity and future value of an annuity. The 10% rate of interest is important because this was the prevalent rate in England at that time for financial transactions other than those involving land. After demonstrating the calculations, Witt provided complete present value, present value of annuity, and future value of annuity tables for $r = 10\%$ and $T \epsilon \{1,2, \ldots ,30\}$.

The $r = 10\%$ case was important because of the practical importance of calculations involving this rate. Having demonstrated how to calculate various factors from the future value tables, Witt also provided future value tables for a range of less practically important interest rates, $r \epsilon \{9\%, 8\%, 7\%, 6\%, 5\%\}$ for $T \epsilon \{1,2, \ldots ,30\}$. Lewin (1970, p.124) observed: "The other functions [for present value, present value of annuity and future value of annuity] are not quoted, however, a lack of which was evidently felt by at least one reader, because the British Museum has a copy of the book in which there has been inserted contemporary manuscript tables that give the missing functions at length". As the calculations involved in land valuation conventionally were done using 16 years' purchase, Witt provided a complete set of present and future value tables for 6¼%.

Witt did more than provide tables that were more detailed than Stevin's. In particular, Witt went beyond Stevin in considering less than annual compounding frequencies. He gave future value tables for $(1 + r)^{T/2}$ and $(1 + r)^{T/4}$ for odd values of T, for the practical interest rates of $r = 10\%$ and $r = 6¼\%$. He also gave other tables relevant for less than annual compounding frequencies. The content of certain problems is another feature of *Arithmeticall Questions* that goes beyond Stevin. There is a concern with interest calculations associated with ground leases that had considerable relevance for the use of discounted cash flow to value equity capital shares. For example (Question 99):

A man hath a Lease of certaine grounds for 8 years yet to come: for which he payeth £130 per Ann. Rent, viz. £65 per halfe yeare: which grounds are worth £300 per Ann. viz. £150 per halfe yeare. If this man shall surrender-in his Lease; what ready mony shall he pay with it to his Land-lord for a new Lease of 21 years, not altering the Rent of £130 per Ann. reckoning such int. as men have when they buy Land for 20 years' purchase, and receive the Rent halfe yearly?

The solution requires recognizing that 20 years' purchase translates to 5% interest, which is 2½% 'halfe yearly', an interest rate for which Witt provided a table. The answer of £1,085 1s 6d now follows, because the landlord will have to forego an annuity of £85 per half year for 13 years.

Two other problems provide useful examples of the level of sophistication in Witt's problems. Question 70 poses the following valuation problem:

One oweth £900 to be paid all at the end of 2 yeares: he agreeth with his Creditor to pay it in 5 yeares, viz. every yeare a like summe. They demaund what each of these 5 payments shall be, reckoning 10 per Cent. per Ann. int. and int. upon int.

The solution requires the future value of £900 to be discounted to the present value and, then, the annuity payment to be determined by solving a present value of annuity problem. In this fashion, Witt determined the correct annuity payment of £196 4s 3d.

From a careful consideration of the tables and problems, Lewin (1970, p.128) concluded:

> it is clear that by 1613, the techniques of compound interest were no longer still in their infancy. It was accepted that compound interest should be allowed in ordinary business and legal transactions, and the methods of carrying out the arithmetic were clearly understood. The differences between simple and compound interest were fully appreciated, as well as the difference between, for example, a rate of 10% per annum and a rate of 2½% per quarter.

One additional interesting feature of *Arithmeticall Questions* is the absence of any problems that involve solving for a yield; not even for integer value interest rate problems, let alone the more complicated variants that involve interpolating between factors listed in appropriate tables. The solution of such problems does have a long history within the more mathematical stream of commercial arithmetic. However, Lewin (1970, p.130) was probably correct in stating: "it may be that there was little call for this in practice".

The Beginnings of Discounted Cash Flow Models

Discounted cash flow valuation for equity capital shares involves the application of interest concepts used to value fixed-income securities. More precisely, the objective is to estimate an 'intrinsic value' of an equity capital share by estimating the present value of the future stream of expected annual profits. In modern times, this process is used in the 'dividend discount model', in which expected future dividend payments are discounted at the rate of interest. In the 18th century, using valuation methods developed for fixed-income securities, the discounting process was summarized by valuing the annual profits at a certain number of "years' purchase", similar to the practice used to value fixed-income securities, the value of leases and so on. Harrison (2001, pp.272–3) observed that Archibald Hutcheson (1720), for instance, used a value of 15 years' purchase in his computations for the South Sea Company. As an example, if earnings were 3 percent per year, then the corresponding value of these earnings was 45 (3 times 15).

The valuation provided by Hutcheson implicitly used discounting methods. As Poitras (2000, ch.5) and Lewin (1970) demonstrated, since the late 16th and early 17th centuries, published tables were available for calculating interest payments and present values. Richard Hayes (1726), in *The money'd man's guide: or. the purchaser's pocket-companion,* provided a "showing, at sight, what interest is made by money laid out in the companies stocks, or any other public funds; and also the present value of any yearly income." The interest tables in Hayes (1726, p.92) use present value discounting to calculate the present value of a seven-year annuity if the interest rate were 4% "look in the Table at 4 *l.* per. cent, for the seven years, and even against it you will find 6 *1. 0 s. 3/4 d.* six years purchase . . . and that is the present value of the said Annuity" (p.92). In the fashion of the times, the seven-year annuity was determined to be worth "six years purchase." Such calculations were not novel and can be found in English tracts going back to Richard Witt in the early 17th century.

Hayes (1726) also provided the result for differing interest rates and differing numbers of years. Another example from Hayes shows the direct relation between the years' purchase and the interest rate. Assuming an income for 100 years using an example from an estate, calculations reveal that a 4% interest rate translates into a multiple of £24 11s. 1d., while a 5 percent rate is £19 16 s. 11d., and a 6 percent rate is £16 9s. 0d. The accuracy of these calculations is illustrated by comparison with the results calculated using 1/r as a proxy, which gives 25, 20, and 16.67 as solutions. In such elementary calculations, determining the discounted present value involves a simple multiplication of the number of years' purchase by the yearly income. Though the income stream is for 100 years, the discounted value of the cash flow is only worth as 25 years' purchase on the valuation date. Hayes (1726) is one of several sources with similar tables. For example, Harrison (2001) identified a ready reckoner by G. Clerke in 1725 as an example that provided an easy guide to discounting, forming present values and calculating interest.

As such, 18th-century efforts at discounted cash flow valuation did not advance much beyond the methods of fixed-income valuation that had been available since the previous century. The difficult problem of determining the cash flows was not attempted. The historical transition from traditional fixed-income valuation to discounted cash flow valuation where variation in the cash flows was permitted has been traced to disparate contributions by actuaries, real estate appraisers and engineers starting about the mid-19th century. These more advanced valuation methodologies permitted the future cash flows associated with an equity security to vary over time. In particular, a British mining engineer, William Armstrong, used discounted cash flow methods to value mining company issues and mining leases (Pitts 2001). Similarly, a German forester, Martin Faustmann, is often credited with presenting the first discounted cash flow formula in 1849 (Scorgie and Kennedy 1996; Vitala 2006; Esa-Jussi 2006, 2013), though this primacy has been questioned. There is also evidence that, around this time, actuaries also became interested in valuation for variable annuities.

NOTES

1 Murphy (1997, ch.2) provided detailed information about two precursors in the study of John Law and his system: Paul Harsin and Earl Hamilton. In 1934, Harsin produced the first significant collection of John Law's writings, in which Murphy uncovered some relevant errors and omissions. Earl Hamilton spent almost 50 years accumulating archival material on John Law and his system, though all this effort produced only a few journal articles. The

main body of the somewhat disorganized Hamilton archives are now housed at Duke University and are currently undergoing efforts at classification and compilation which will take 'many years' to complete. Hamilton's collection of books and pamphlets was donated to the University of Chicago Library. Why did Hamilton have so little output from a lifetime of archival work? Murphy (1997, p.12) speculated that Hamilton was "swallowed up in the vortex of minutiae concerning the system . . . Hamilton wanted to write a complete history of the System. Such an objective was unattainable".

2 Melville (1921, p.32) indicated that 'Mr. Wilson' was Edward Wilson, better known as 'Beau' Wilson, "a scion of an old Leicestershire family, a noted dandy, who lived in luxury, apparently on nothing a year. Much curiosity was evinced, and many speculations were rife, as to the source from which he derived his income". Minton (1975) and Murphy (1997) both explored the connection between Beau Wilson and Elizabeth Villiers, a mistress of William III, as a possible basis for the duel. These sources provide considerable detail about events related to the duel, including the trial and Law's escape.

3 Law was, by no means, an originator of the land bank proposal. "The first serious proponent of a land bank in England was William Potter, who in 1656 served as registrar of debentures on the Act for the sale of the late King's lands" (Murphy 1997, p.46). Potter's writings on land banks appeared in 1650.

4 Dickson (1967, p.90) referenced most of the sources available up to 1967. Temin and Voth (2004) and Neal (1990b) included some more recent references. Dickson (1967, chs. 7–8) is also an essential source for examining in detail the period of financial reform and reconstruction following the bubble. Of the available references on the South Sea bubble, Anderson (1764) is seminal. As a clerk working for the South Sea Company during the bubble period, Anderson had firsthand knowledge of events and practical details. Many of the insights found in later works can be traced to Anderson. Scott (1910, 1912) provided, perhaps, the most in-depth account, though there are a number of points at which the discussion is incorrect. Carlos and Neal (2006) discussed the micro-foundations of the London market for equity capital at the time of the South Sea bubble.

5 Taylor (1962, p.952), who discussed Clavière's activities in detail, observed: "We must remember that he was not the only speculator and in respect to the volume of his affairs not even in the first rank". Clavière receives considerable modern interest because the quality of the primary sources—correspondence and accounts—associated with his activities. He also attracts modern interest due to his connection to Mirabeau. For a variety of reasons, not the least of which is an active desire to prevent public disclosure of trading activities, primary sources for the most important *agioteurs* or speculators have not survived. The most important secondary source on Clavière's correspondence with other speculators is still Bouchary (1938).

6 Precisely when schemes to capture the benefits of diversification appeared is unclear. Such schemes likely appeared gradually as the supply of different types of securities became widely available for trade. For example, Goetzmann et al. (2005, p.2) reported on a 1774 scheme (*Negotiatie onder de Zinspreuk Eendragt Maakt Magt*) in which the manager of the fund was directed to hold, as closely as possible, "an equal-weight portfolio of bonds from the Bank of Vienna, Russian government bonds, government loans from Mecklenburg and Saxony, Spanish canal loans, English colonial securities, South American plantation loans and securities from various Danish American ventures, all of which were traded in the Amsterdam market at the time".

7   Étienne Clavière (1735–93) was another of the remarkable figures that populated 18th century equity security markets. Originally from Geneva, Claviere
was involved with the democratic leaders of the Geneva Republic and, as a
result of the collapse of the popular revolution, was forced to take refuge in
Britain in 1782 together with other Swiss expatriates. Many of these expatriates later moved to Paris, where some were engaged in 'banking' before the
revolution. Claviere, in particular, became acquainted with Mirabeau, Brissot,
and other popular leaders. Mirabeau, who had a high opinion of Claviere's
talents, used his assistance in composing speeches and essays on financial matters. Another important expatriate Swiss, Etienne Dumont, claimed the Swiss
banker was the author of almost all of Mirabeau's works on finance. Claviere was chosen deputy to the National Assembly in 1791, and was Girondist
minister of finance from March till June, 1792. He was arrested with other
influential Girondists in June, 1793, on account of Girondist opposition to the
extreme measures of Robespierre and other revolutionary leaders. In December 1793, Claviere committed suicide to escape the guillotine. His wife poi-
soned herself two days afterward.

8   McCusker (1979, pp.29–31) provided a useful discussion of sources for prices
of various commodities, including stocks. These sources, known as 'price currents' in London and 'price courants' in Amsterdam, were what passed for
the commercial and financial newspapers of the time. The first printed price
lists date from the 1580s in Antwerp, Hamburg and Amsterdam, with the first
London price currents appearing around the 1660s.

9   This statement is not meant to imply that the holders of joint-stocks were
numerous. On the contrary, relatively few individuals were involved. For
example, in 1691 the combined stock of the East India and Africa Companies
was divided into 680 holdings (some held by the same person). For both English and Dutch joint-stock issues, most of the holders of joint-stock lived in
London or Amsterdam (Parker 1974, p.559).

10   Though written for a somewhat different purpose, Isaac de Pinto's *Traite de la
Circulation et Credit* (1771) also deserves some recognition.

11   De Marchi and Harrison (1994, p.62) seem to have claimed that de la Vega
proposed a model in which stock prices were a random process, quoting de la
Vega as saying: "shares are enveloped in a veil of almost religious mystery such
that the more one reasons the less one grasps, and the more cunning one tries
to be the more mistakes one makes". The solution, according to de la Vega, is
to trade randomly. Despite this, it would be quite a stretch to claim de la Vega
was a precursor of the random walk model of stock prices.

12   De la Vega recognized that the motives of gamblers and speculators were often
somewhat nefarious and that the presence of manipulation makes accurate
pricing a difficult exercise: "shares are enveloped in a veil of almost religious
mystery such that the more one reasons the less one grasps, and the more cunning one tries to be the more mistakes one makes" (De Marchi and Harrison
1994, p.62).

13   This evidence, quoted in Kellenbenz (1957, p.128) does not imply that Jews
owned 85% of the stock. Rather, Jews, as the brokers, market makers and
gamblers, did 85% of the trading.

14   From de la Vega's sketchy description of Amsterdam options contracts, it
is possible that Houghton's English contract was similar to those traded in
Amsterdam: "For the *options business* there exists another sort of *contract
form*, from which it is evident when and where the premium was paid and
of what kind are the signatories' obligations. The *forms of hypothecating* are
different also. Stamped paper is used for them, upon which the regulations

concerning *dividends* and other details are set down, so that there can be no doubt and disagreement regarding the arrangements" (De la Vega 1688, p.182).

15 The use of guineas to facilitate the premium payment reflects the status of that coin in transacting cash business. The guinea was a gold coin first minted in 1663 under warrant "to the officers of the Mint requiring them to stamp all gold and silver which might be brought to them by the African Company to be coined, with a little elephant, the mark of the Company. This was the fourth company which had been formed to trade with Africa . . . At a time when so many different coins were circulating, the gold pieces with the little elephant were soon distinguished, from the place of origin of the metal as 'guinea pieces' " (Feaveryear 1931, pp.89–90). Due to fluctuations in the gold/silver ratio and among different coins, the price of the guinea in terms of the silver-based pound sterling was variable. Houghton provided regular quotes for guineas. In particular, on 15 June 1694 Houghton quoted guineas at 22 *l.*, and on 22 June 1694 the quote was 23 *l.* In 1696, the government began a process of attempting to fix the value of the guinea in terms of the silver sterling measure. In 1696 a value of 22 shillings was set, which was later lowered to 21*s.* 6*p.* in 1699 and 21*s.* in 1717.

16 An at-the-money option has the exercise price approximately the same as the current stock price. This is in contrast to out-of-the-money (in-the-money) options which have exercise price greater than (less than) the stock price for calls and less than (greater than) the stock price for puts.

17 An American option can be contrasted with a European option, which can only be exercised on the expiration date, and a Bermuda option, which can only be exercised at prespecifed, discrete times prior to expiration.

18 Early exercise for a dividend payout protected put option can occur if the security price is sufficiently close to zero that there is insufficient potential for further increase in the put value due to further reduction in the stock price. In this case, the put can be exercised and the profit invested at interest. In Houghton's time, the securities on which options were traded had prices that were sufficiently above zero that the early exercise event had such a low probability that the early exercise premium for the put could also be set to zero.

19 Modern security analysis has a much more refined treatment of firm profitability, based on the much more elaborate accounting information now available. Graham and Dodd's dictum that security analysis involves the use of financial statements would have been lost on Mortimer because, at his time, accounting information was quite rudimentary and was often proprietary.

20 The stated solution is as follows: for Piero, 138 ducats, 21 grossi, 11 pizoli and remainder; for Polo, 248 ducats, 0 grossi, 13 pizoli and remainder; and, for Zuanne, 176 ducats, 2 grossi, 7 pizoli and remainder. The *Treviso* proceeds to check the solution, so that 'no one has been cheated', by adding together the shares to verify that the total is 563 grossi.

21 The third problem is a more complicated variation of the second: "Three men, Tomasso, Domenego, and Nicolo, entered into partnership. Tomasso put in 760 ducats on the first day of January, 1472, and on the first day of April took out 200 ducats. Domenego put in 616 ducats on the first day of February, 1472, and on the first day of June took out 96 ducats. Nicolo put in 892 ducats on the first day of February, 1472, and on the first day of March took out 252 ducats. And on the first day of January, 1475, they found that they had gained 3168 ducats, 13 grossi and 1/2. Required is the share of each, so that one shall be cheated." The solution procedure is an

extension of the rule of three procedure used to solve problem 2. However, due to crediting Nicolo with three months full investment instead of only one month, "the solution stated does not satisfy the given conditions of the problem" (Swetz 1987, p.147). Ignoring the remainders, the solution is given for Tomasso as 1052 ducats 11 grossi and 8 pizoli, for Domenego as 942 ducats 3 grossi and 21 pizoli, and for Nicolo as 1173 ducats 22 grossi and 17 pizoli.

22   To see how this cubic equation solves the problem posed requires some further discussion. Franci and Rigatelli observed: "The most general formulation of the problem is the following: Calculate at what rate the *lira* was loaned per month knowing the capital is *A lire*, and after three years *B lire* are given back. Further interest must be added to the capital at the end of each year.
Let *x denari* be the rate of one *lira* per month. If we remember that one *lira* is equal to 240 *denari*, we obtain the equation: $x^3 + 60 \ x^2 + 1200 \ x = 8000$ $((B/A) -1)$.' This approach can be compared with the expansion of the modern form of the pricing problem originally posed:

$$100 = \frac{150}{(1 + \frac{i}{12})^3} \rightarrow \frac{150}{100} - 1 = 3\frac{i}{12} + 3\frac{i}{12}^2 + 3\frac{i}{12}^3$$

In the coinage of the time, a *denari* was the same as a grossi, this equivalence originating from the more formal *denari de grossi*. The coinage used further required 20 soldi = 1 lira and 12 grossi = 1 soldo. From this, the relation of 1 *lira* with 240 *denari* is explained. The cubic equation stated for arriving the appropriate solution now follows by solving the modern cubic in terms of *denari*, which requires grossing up by 240. But, in order to obtain a monthly rate which requires division of the annualized interest rate by 12, the equation is only multiplied through by $(20)^3 = 8000$.

23   There are various practical instances where such calculations would be required. For example, a merchant may want to compare the promised return on a one-year investment with the return which would be earned on a six-month investment followed by a reinvestment of principal plus interest in another six-month investment.

24   It is possible to guess about Witt's background. The surname 'Witt' is not a common English name, this surname being more common in the Low Countries. Witt's presence in England at the beginning of the 17th century is consistent with the hypothesis that he was part of the mass emigration from Antwerp and environs associated with the various conflicts which affected that area at the end of the 16th century. This wave of skilled emigration affected many individuals involved in the early history of financial economics. For example, the family of Joseph de la Vega emigrated from Antwerp to Germany and, later, settled in Amsterdam. Gerard de Malynes was also, most likely, part of this emigration. The sophistication of Witt's analysis would have required advanced training. Such training would have been difficult to obtain in England. Such training would have been available in Antwerp during its heyday. If Witt had obtained such training in England and then proceeded to develop an active practice as 'a practitioner of numbers', it is likely that some paper trail would have been left. No such trail has yet been unearthed.

25   The breviats attracted the attention of De Morgan (1846, p.575) as an early contribution to the use of decimal fractions which predates Napier by four years.

8   Joint-Stock, Limited Liability and Incorporation

> The only trades which it seems possible for a joint stock company to carry on successfully, without an exclusive privilege, are those, of which all the operations are capable of being reduced to what is called routine, or to such uniformity of method as admits of little or no variation. Of this kind is, first, the banking trade; secondly, the trade of insurance from fire, and from sea risk and capture in time of war; thirdly, the trade of making and maintaining a navigable cut or canal; and, fourthly, the similar trade of bringing water for the supply of a great city.
>
> Adam Smith, *Wealth of Nations* (1776)

A   ENGLISH CLASSICAL ECONOMISTS ON JOINT-STOCKS AND LIMITED LIABILITY

Pre-Classical Views on Equity Capital Organization

'Joint-stock', regulated companies, limited partnerships, business trusts and general partnerships are all ways of organizing equity capital. It is not surprising that the emergence of the joint-stock company was accompanied by scattered analyses arguing the wisdom of using this approach, if only because the granting of a company charter to form a joint-stock company often conferred some special monopoly right. Such scattered analyses can be found at least as early as the 16th century. For example, Hecksher (1955, v.1, p.396) referred to an early English memorandum dated about 1582 that "described very aptly the pros and cons of the regulated and joint stock company". Similar Dutch documents appeared during the debate over the creation of the *VOC*.[1] Adam Smith was involved in the debate over the relative usefulness of the joint-stock form of organization; this topic occupied a section of *Wealth of Nations*. Other significant contributions by classical economists were made by Senior, Tooke, J.S. Mill, McCulloch and Marx.

One of the more heated debates about the relative merits of joint-stock and regulated companies happened in 1681, with Sir John Buckworth and Dudley North submitting for the regulated company and Sir Josiah Child (1630–1699) replying for the joint-stock company. The underlying dispute involved the Turkey Company, a regulated company with a monopoly on trade with the Levant, and the East India Company, a joint-stock company with monopoly privileges in 'East India'. The period leading up to 1681 was particularly harsh on the Turkey Company, which had been watching its own monopoly decay as a result of the East India Company's successes in adjacent and sometimes overlapping areas. The Turkey Company "became especially vexed when piracy in the Mediterranean and tyranny in Turkey reached a peak, so that trade became more risky and costly than usual" (Letwin 1964, p.32).

The end result was that the conflicting claims of the monopolies led to a Privy Council review of the problem; hence the submission from the regulated company and the joint-stock company arguing the merits of their particular form of business organization (Letwin 1964, p.33):

> The Turkey Company submitted a paper, prepared by Sir John Buckworth and Dudley North, pleading that they be preferred to their rival [the East India Company]. They allege in the first place that their business was more beneficial to the nation, because they exported about £500,000 worth of woollen goods and other English products and imported a great deal of raw silk and cotton that was subsequently worked up in England, all of which, exports and imports alike, gave employment to English labourers. The East India Company, on the other hand, injured the nation by exporting vast quantities of gold and silver, depriving English workmen of labour by importing finished calicoes and silk cloth, and sold at low prices the 'deceitful sort' of raw silk that they brought from India, to the 'infallible destruction of the Turkey trade'. Secondly, they said, the East India Company was much too exclusive. Their own, a regulated company, was open to any qualified merchant on payment of a small fee, whereas the East India Company, being organized on joint stock, could be entered only by buying some of a very small number of shares, whose ownership was, in fact, 'confined to the narrow compass of some few persons'. And the third great complaint was that the joint stock was too small to carry on the trade.

Among other requests, the Turkey Company wanted the king to "reconfirm exclusive right to trade in the Red Sea and all dominions of the Grand Signor and to have free access to those areas by the most convenient passages" (Letwin 1964, p.34).

That Child would be involved in detailing the position of the East India Company was understandable. From 1674 on, Child was probably the East India Company's largest shareholder and, in all years but one, was elected as director. In 1681, Child was elected Governor of the Company "and from then on his policy and the Company's policy were one, so that he became a symbol as well as manager of the Company's rapidly increasing power" (Letwin 1964, p.28). The East India Company's position was (pp.34–5):

> As to the first allegation . . . the Privy Council could undoubtedly discover the truth by checking the customs house records, they themselves were

certain they exported more and better cloth than the Turkey Company, amounting recently to about 19,000 pieces a year, and that the Turkey Company was no less culpable than they themselves in exporting gold and silver. As to the organization of their trade, the experience with all European countries showed that trade with the East Indies was best carried on by joint stock companies. To this, Child's favourite argument on the subject, they added that their Company was by no means so exclusive as the others alleged. If anything, it was more open than the Turkey Company, for while the latter admitted only qualified merchants, such as had served apprenticeships, theirs was open to any Englishmen at all that chose to buy its stock. Furthermore, they denied that its stock was so closely held as alleged; there were, they said, 600 shareholders, and contrary to the assertion that a single shareholder had over 80 votes—that is he owned over £40,000 of shares—no one owned as many as 60, although it would not matter if he did, because the Company's work benefited not only its owners and its employees, but many others.

And so it goes, up to the time of Adam Smith and beyond. Even in Smith's time there was still disagreement over the most appropriate type of business organization for a particular activity, especially those activities operating under royal grant of monopoly privileges. By the middle of the 19th century, the English debate had been settled in favour of the limited liability corporation.

In addition to providing a reasonably coherent statement of the late 17th-century arguments, the 1681 debate is interesting because Sir Josiah Child was a contributor. Child is another of the truly remarkable individuals populating the history of equity capital. Child has some modern status as a noteworthy pre-Smithian economist.[2] "Child came to be the most widely read of seventeenth-century English economic writers" (Letwin 1964, p.45), his writings on the legal maximum interest rates being of particular importance. Yet, in his day, Child was recognized as one of the great English financiers; according to Defoe: "that Original of Stock-Jobbing, Sir Josiah Child". His status as governor of the East India Company was matched by his stock-trading acumen.

In *The Villany of Stock-Jobbers Detected*, one of Child's contemporaries, Daniel Defoe (1701), illustrated the deep-seated cynicism that could be attached to the grand stockjobber of his time:[3]

It would be endless to give an Account of the Subtilties of that Capital [Cheat], when he had a Design to Bite the whole Exchange. As he was the leading Hand to the Market, so he kept it in his Power to set the Price to all the Dealers. Every man's Eye when he came to the Market was upon the Brokers who acted for Sir Josiah: Does Sir Josiah Sell or Buy? If Sir Josiah had a Mind to buy, the first thing he did was to Commission his Brokers to look sour, shake their Heads, suggest bad News from India and at the Bottom, it follow'd, I have Commission from Sir Josiah to sell out whatever I can, perhaps they would actually sell Ten, perhaps, Twenty Thousand Pound; immediately the Exchange (for they were not then come to the Alley) was full of Sellers; no Body could buy a Shilling, 'till perhaps the Stock would fall Six, Seven, Eight, Ten per Cent, sometimes more. Then the Cunning Jobber had another Sett of Men employed on purpose to buy but with Privacy and Caution, all the Stock they could lay their Hands on 'till by selling Ten Thousand Pound at Four or Five per Cent Cost he would buy a Hundred Thousand Pound Stock at Ten or Twelve per Cent under the Price.

Child was one of several 17th-century English writers who promoted Dutch society as a model for England. Evidently, Child also came to master the Dutch financial market techniques, described so accurately by de la Vega.

Figure 8.1 Adam Smith (1723–1790), Scottish philosopher by unknown artist, Scottish National Gallery, Edinburgh

Adam Smith and Joint-Stock Companies

The analysis provided by Adam Smith in *Wealth of Nations* (Bk.V, Ch.1, Pt.III, Art. 1) comparing joint-stock companies with available alternatives is a benchmark, a reasonable reflection of the progress that the debate on joint stocks and other forms of equity capital organization had reached by the second half of the 18th century.[4] Smith's views were, by no means, received opinion. Continuing the tradition of Sir Josiah Child, various influential authors also writing at the time, such as Mortimer, were decidedly in favour of joint-stock ventures (Mortimer 1774, p.143):

> Our East India, and Bank companies, have brought the commerce and mercantile credit of Great Britain to such a degree of perfection, as no age or country can equal; and to suppose that this national success could have been accomplished by private merchants, or even by companies not trading on a joint stock, is an absurdity that does not deserve serious consideration.

On the other hand, periodic English debates in the House of Commons, such as those in 1767 and 1768, would elicit eloquent speeches against the chartered companies. These speeches invariably retraced the arguments made in the 1681 debates.

As far as joint-stocks are concerned, in *Wealth of Nations* Smith was concerned more with how the structure of company ownership impacted company performance than with how the traded market value of the company was determined. On the issue of pricing joint-stocks, Smith (1776, p.254, Blaug edition) was somewhat vacuous, only identifying the difficulties inherent in the valuation of shares in joint-stock companies: "The value of a share in a joint stock is always the price which it will bring in the market; and this may be either greater or less, in any proportion, than the sum which its owner stands credited for in the stock of the company".[5] Smith took much more care with the issue of equity capital organization. Smith went on to provide a significant analysis of joint-stock companies as sources of corporate finance. Some care is required to recognize whether Smith was discussing joint-stock companies with or without "exclusive privilege".

Smith (1776) began his discussion by contrasting the joint-stock company with a partnership, recognizing the features of transferability and limited liability. Transferability brings with it the risk that, at sale, the value received will not equal "his share of the common stock". In this case, 'common stock' refers to retained earnings—which could be composed of goods in inventory, cash-in-hand, improvements to property—plus paid-in capital. This is in contrast to partnerships, in which shares are not usually transferable and 'upon proper warning' a partner may withdraw and receive his appropriate share of the proceeds from the winding up of the partnership. In addition to the market price risk associated with transferability, Smith identified the ability to transfer joint-stock shares to another person "without consent" of the other members of the company.

In keeping with the common-law tradition that descended from the Roman law of partnerships (where share transfer was not possible), Smith (p.254) stated the limitations on transferability of shares in copartnerships:

> In a private copartnery, no partner, without the consent of the company, can transfer his share to another person, or introduce a new member into the company. Each member, however, may, upon proper warning, withdraw from the copartnery, and demand payment from them of his share of the common stock.

He contrasted this with transferability in the joint-stock company:

> In a joint stock company, on the contrary, no member can demand payment of his share from the company, but each member can, without their consent, transfer his share to another person, and thereby introduce a new member.

While capturing well-known general features surrounding transferability, Smith (p.254) took a narrow view on limited liability:

> In a private copartnery, each partner is bound for the debts contracted by the company to the whole extent of his fortune. In a joint stock company, on the contrary, each partner is bound only to the extent of his share.

The possibility of joint-stock companies with unlimited and other forms of liability extending beyond the initial capital subscription went unrecognized. This reflects the historical context within which Smith was writing. In addition, Smith was often concerned with 'joint stock companies' that were "established either by royal charter or by act of parliament". This lack of attention to joint-stock companies without "exclusive privilege" is understandable given that *Wealth of Nations* was written well after the Bubble Act, at a time when 'joint-stock companies' were confined to the chartered companies, and just prior to the canal construction period, when the issue of liability for shareholders re-emerged. As a consequence, Smith often failed to capture essential elements of equity capital organization that impacted later historical developments.

As an illustration, consider the implications of combining separation of ownership and control with limited liability in the joint-stock company. For Smith (p.255), the separation of ownership and control in a joint-stock company, reflected in management by a "court of directors", has the following consequence: "the greater part of . . . proprietors seldom . . . understand any thing of the business of the company", receiving "contentedly such half yearly or yearly dividend, as the directors think proper to make to them". In combination with limited liability:

> This total exemption from trouble and from risk, beyond a limited sum, encourages many people to become adventurers in joint stock companies, who would, upon no account, hazard their fortunes in any private

copartnery. Such companies, therefore, commonly draw to themselves much greater stocks than any private copartnery can boast of.

While recognizing the potential for joint-stock companies to facilitate speculation, Smith failed to fully recognize the impact of limited liability on enhanced share transferability, which became apparent after the collapse of the Glasgow Bank a century later. In turn, instead of developing the theme of speculative excess, Smith preferred to focus on the implications of separating management and control for performance of the joint-stock company.

Adam Smith on Limited Liability

Having recognized essential features of transferability and limited liability, Smith constructed an indictment of the usefulness of the joint-stock form of organization for all but a few economic activities. The crux of his argument depended on the modern notion of **agency costs** (p.233) associated with the separation of ownership and control:[6]

> The directors of [joint stock] companies . . . being the managers rather of other people's money than of their own, it cannot well be expected, that they should watch over it with the same anxious vigilance which the partners in a private copartnery frequently watch over their own . . . Negligence and profusion, therefore, must always prevail, more or less, in the management of the affairs of such a company.

Smith's views on [joint-stock] companies were conditioned by the performance of those companies up to his time (i.e., pre–Industrial Revolution). This included the dealings of the South Sea Company that contributed to the South Sea bubble (pp.235–6):

> The South Sea Company never had any forts or garrisons to maintain . . . But they had an immense capital divided among an immense number of proprietors. It was naturally to be expected, therefore, that folly, negligence, and profusion should prevail in the whole management of their affairs. The knavery and extravagance of their stock-jobbing projects are sufficiently known, and the explication of them would be foreign to the present subject. Their mercantile projects were not much better conducted.

It is unfortunate that Smith did not attempt a detailed discussion of his views on the "stock-jobbing projects' of the South Sea Company." Despite numerous, seemingly exhaustive studies, the causes of the South Sea bubble are still a subject of debate (e.g., Neal 2012; Kleer 2015).

Smith was decidedly negative on the capacity of the joint-stock form of ownership to operate successfully in most branches of trade. In the economically important area of foreign trade, Smith (1776, p.255) observed:

> Joint stock companies for foreign trade have seldom been able to maintain the competition against private adventurers. They have, accordingly, very

seldom succeeded without an exclusive privilege; and frequently have not succeeded with one. Without an exclusive privilege they have commonly mismanaged the trade. With an exclusive privilege they have both mismanaged and confined it.

Similarly, Smith connected joint-stock organization with the wider struggle against trade monopolies associated with mercantilism: "Without a monopoly . . . a joint stock company, it would appear from experience, cannot long carry on any branch of foreign trade" (1776, p.265). However, Smith was willing to admit that a granting a "temporary monopoly" to a joint-stock company could be advisable (p.265):

> When a company of merchants undertake, at their own risk and expense, to establish a new trade with some remote and barbarous nation, it may not be unreasonable to incorporate them into a joint stock company, and to grant them in case of their success, a monopoly of trade for a certain number of years. It is the easiest and most natural way in which the state can recompense them for hazarding a dangerous and expensive experiment, of which the public is afterwards to reap the benefit.

Smith suggested that at the end of the temporary period of monopoly "the forts and garrisons, if it was found necessary to establish any, . . . be taken into the hands of the government, their value paid to the company, and the trade laid open to all the subjects of the state" (p.265).

The recommendation for time limits on 'exclusive privilege' granted by the Crown or legislature was consistent with practices that had been used in the past, though not all charters had time limitations. It is not clear precisely why equity capitalists would be attracted to such temporary monopolies, especially when the 'value paid to the company' for significant improvements was uncertain. Such recommendations seem at odds with Smith's general rejection of monopolies.

After a quite detailed examination of the operating performance for most of the major English joint-stock companies, Smith concluded with the quote that begins this chapter (1776, p.266):

> The only trades which it seems possible for a joint stock company to carry on successfully, without an exclusive privilege, are those, of which all the operations are capable of being reduced to what is called routine, or to such uniformity of method as admits of little or no variation. Of this kind is, first, the banking trade; secondly, the trade of insurance from fire, and from sea risk and capture in time of war; thirdly, the trade of making and maintaining a navigable cut or canal; and, fourthly, the similar trade of bringing water for the supply of a great city.

It is essential to recognize that Smith was referring to joint-stock companies "without an exclusive privilege". In light of the central role that the publicly traded limited liability corporation has in almost all fields of the modern economy, on the issue of joint-stock companies Smith would appear to have been more of an apologist for what was current English legal practice, rather than a visionary. The types of companies identified are those for which "the management of it becomes quite simple and easy", once the initial construction phase is completed, such as with a "navigable canal" or "a great pipe for bringing water to supply a great city".

Adam Smith on Stockjobbing

Being the author of *Wealth of Nations*, Adam Smith is properly considered the father of classical political economy. Yet, beyond the discussion surrounding the joint-stocks, there is relatively little in *Wealth of Nations* of direct relevance to equity capital trading and valuation. To those familiar with the *Lectures*, this is somewhat surprising.

Cannan (1937, p.xxviii) considered the 'Police, Revenue and Arms' portion of the *Lectures* to be an "early draft" of *Wealth of Nations*. Two of three subjects treated in the police, revenue and arms lectures that were "altogether omitted" in *Wealth of Nations* are of interest. These two subjects are stockjobbing and the Mississippi scheme. The discussion of these topics in the *Lectures* is relatively substantial. Section II.13, 'Of the Scheme of Mr. Law', received an eight-page treatment, while Sections III.3 and III.4, 'Of Stocks' and 'Of Stockjobbing', received a total of six pages. By comparison, Section II.8, 'Of Money as the Measure of Value and Medium of Exchange', warranted eight pages. This significant change of course by Smith, away from waters most relevant to equity capital valuation and trading, leaves an unanswered question: Why did Smith choose to omit from *Wealth of Nations* the bulk of the subject matter of these sections of the *Lectures*?

The only writer to consider a potential answer to this question was Cannan (p.xxxviii) who stated: "The description of stock-jobbing was probably left out because it was better suited to the youthful hearers of the lectures than to the maturer readers of the book. The Mississippi scheme was omitted, Smith himself says, because it had been adequately discussed by Du Verney." In other words, Smith recognized that his insights on stockjobbing could offer little over what his readers probably already knew. Compared to what Smith had to offer on other subjects, such as international trade or value and distribution, his views on the inner workings of 18th-century equity capital markets were cursory at best and misguided at worst. As recognized by Cannan, Smith (1776, p.302) acknowledged that his potential contribution was limited by referring discussion and analysis of Law's scheme, "the most extravagant project of both banking and stock-jobbing that, perhaps, the world ever saw", to Mr. Du Verney.

What did Smith have to say in the *Lectures* of relevance to the Mississippi scheme and stockjobbing? Unfortunately, it is difficult to obtain much insight from the *Lectures*. This is partly due to the nature of the *Lectures*. Being recorded by a diligent student and further transcribed by "a person who often did not understand what he was writing" (Cannan 1937, p.xviii), the *Lectures* may not be a particularly reliable source on Smith's views on a range of subjects. This said, consider Smith's (1763, p.251) description of stockjobbing:

> The practice of stock-jobbing, or the buying of stocks by time has, too, on all occasions, a very considerable influence on the rise and fall of stocks.

The method in which this practice is carried on is as follows. A man who has not perhaps £1000 in the world, subscribes for £100,000, which is to be delivered at several fixed times, and in certain portions. He therefore hopes to get these several portions sold out to great advantage by the rising of the stocks before they fall due, but as anything he is worth would go if the stocks should fall, he uses all means to make them rise, he spreads reports at Change Alley that victories are gained, that peace is to be concluded, &c. On the other hand, they who want to purchase a stock, and want that it should fall, propagate such reports as will sink the stocks as low as possible, such as that war will continue, that new subscriptions are thought on, &c. It is owing to this that, in time of war, our newspapers are so filled with invasions and schemes that never were thought of.

The stockjobber is being depicted as a highly leveraged gambler, manipulating the market with rumours aimed at facilitating a quick profit. Whether the stockjobber dealt in shares is unclear; the passage is likely referring to the practice of having government loan issues paid through instalments. Such issues would trade heavy-horse, mostly paid, and light-horse, only fractionally paid, depending on the number of instalments that had been paid since the subscription date.

As stated, Smith's views on stockjobbing are pedestrian compared with those of Thomas Mortimer, an actual securities market "merchant". A similar comment applies to Smith's understanding of stockjobbing trading strategies (p.250):

As there are a great many stock-holders who are merchants, and who keep their stocks in the hands of the government that they may be ready to sell out on any sudden demand, and take the advantage of a good bargain when it casts up, and as these chances occur most frequently in time of war, they have often occasion to sell out, and thus more stock runs to the market, and the new subscriptions sink below par. But further, in time of war, as was observed before, stock cannot be so advantageously employed, and everybody is tempted to subscribe. Even those whose circumstances are but very inconsiderable, subscribe for great sums in hopes that stocks will rise, and that they may sell out before the time of delivery, to great advantage; but when things do not answer their expectations, and they are forced to sell out one way or another to support their credit, they are often obliged to sell below par. In this manner the new subscriptions may fall. Stock-jobbers that are well acquainted with their business, observe particularly when a number of indigent persons are in the subscriptions, and as they are soon obliged to sell out, and consequently stocks fall, it is their proper time to purchase them.

It is difficult to see precisely what is being proposed here. General situations in which stocks, presumably government funds, could fall are identified. Stockjobber profits arise from an ability to recognize "indigent persons", observe when these individuals are selling stock, and profit by buying these securities at a discount. This 'special situation trading' does not seem to be a credible description of a sustainable, actively functioning stock market. Again, the discussion seems to centre on trading of government loan stock, which reflects the limited state of the equity capital market in England during the period of the Bubble Act, when "jobbing in the stock of any company not legally incorporated" could draw severe sanctions, though no convictions were ever obtained (Shannon 1931, pp.268–70; Amsler et al. 1981, p.776).

Classical Political Economists after Smith

The legal transition to permit general availability of limited liability corporations to organize equity capital took place in England between 1844 and 1856. The importance of certain classical political economists in critical policy debates during the first part of the 19th century, such as the suspension of convertibility during the Napoleonic wars (Thornton and Torrens) or the repeal of the Corn Laws (Tooke and Malthus), implies that the British classical political economists had similar influence on the debates surrounding limited liability and incorporation. This was not the case. Some classical economists, such as David Ricardo and Thomas Malthus, had little to say on the issues or simply replicated the views contained in *Wealth of Nations*. Those classical economists after Smith who did express views on legal developments that ultimately resulted in the general availability of incorporation with limited liability were not in agreement. In addition, while important classical economists, such as Nassau Senior and Thomas Tooke, took part in the early deliberations leading to passage of key enabling legislation, other important contributors such as John Stuart Mill (1806–1873) and John Ramsey McCulloch (1789–1864) were reacting to changes that had taken place.

Amsler et al. (1981, p.781) observed: "An examination of the writings of British economists for the half century following Smith discloses no serious attention to questions of either joint-stock management or limited liability arrangements. Any passing comments concerning these issues were entirely Smithian." The first significant contributions are attributed to submissions for the "Report on the Law of Partnership" (1837) prepared by H. Bellenden Ker. The report preceded passage of the Chartered Companies Act (1837). As demonstrated by Fetter (1975) and Hunt (1936), the claim of 'no serious attention' is not entirely correct. The claim is possibly due to an implicit bias by contemporary historians of economic thought to identifying 'British economists' with important 'classical political economists' who had membership in the Political Economy Club, founded by James Mill in 1821 (e.g., Henderson 1986). Among the founding club members are Ricardo, Tooke, Malthus and Col. Robert Torrens. Senior joined shortly after; McCulloch joined in 1829; and John Stuart Mill joined in 1836. Focusing on the period between Ricardo and J. S. Mill, Fetter (1975) demonstrated only a weak connection between these important club members and the holding of a seat in Parliament. Other than Robert Torrens, elected three times in separate boroughs, only J.S. Mill and Ricardo were able to secure a seat for one term.

Classical political economists recognized as important in modern times were relatively late to the public debate over incorporation and limited liability for joint-stock companies, though the Political Economy Club did debate the issue of limited liability on six occasions between 1825 and 1856 (Henderson 1986, p.112). The views expounded were not substantively different than positions that emerged in the period before the Ker report. While Amsler et al. only started the time line with contributions in the Ker report by Tooke—a founding member and prime mover in the creation of the club—and Senior—a club member from 1823 to 1849 and 1853 to 1864—it was earlier decisions by the courts and those involved at senior levels of government that were responsible for developing positions to deal with the emergence of the unincorporated joint-stock company in the first quarter of the 19th century. For example, William Huskisson (1770–1830) was an important early 19th-century British 'economist'—not a member of the club – who actively participated in the debates leading to the repeal of the Bubble Act (e.g., Fetter 1975). At the time the club was founded, Huskisson was in cabinet and, until his untimely death in 1830, he was likely occupied with more essential political duties than the social events at the club.

Given this, classical political economists—those identified with the Political Economy Club—did participate in the various debates on joint-stock corporations and limited liability that took place following the Ker report. These debates were different in character from earlier debates surrounding the increase of unincorporated joint-stock companies and the subsequent Bubble Act repeal. As Hunt (1935, p.1, 2–3) recognized, the earlier debates had a decidedly different social context: "freedom of incorporation was achieved only after a protracted and bitter struggle against deeply rooted prejudice, wide-spread misconception, and even fear". More precisely:

> the history of the business corporation or joint-stock company in England during the one hundred and fifty years following the statute of 1719 is the story of an economic necessity forcing its way slowly and painfully to legal recognition in the face of strong commercial prejudice in favor of "individual" enterprise and in spite of determined attempts of both the legislature and the courts to deny it.

By 1800, over 100 private members' bills had passed Parliament—mostly related to the construction and operation of canals—granting corporate status to joint-stock companies. The resulting erosion in social attitudes and political opposition led to the 1824–1826 boom in the promotion of unincorporated joint-stock companies that precipitated the repeal of the Bubble Act.

As such, the point at which classical political economists associated with the Political Economy Club entered the debate over incorporation and limited liability was relatively late. The Ker report was "appointed to consider the Law of Partnership, and the Expediency of facilitating the Limitation of Liability with a view to encourage useful Enterprise and the additional Employment of Labour" (Report, p.iii). In other words, the initial contributions by Tooke and Senior were considering the possibility of introducing into English law the limited liability partnership, along the lines of the *en commandite* partnerships available in France, for small 'family' partnerships. Adopting the conventional view that limited liability was a special privilege outside the common law of partnership, Tooke argued against adoption because justice would dictate that such privileges also be extended to large partnerships. In addition, widespread availability of limited liability would divert capital away from areas where the granting of limited liability had been identified with a public purpose. Senior argued in favour of adoption, maintaining that (in opposition to the Smithian view that limited liability would discourage proper oversight of the business) the gains from the increased supply of equity capital would more than compensate for any deterioration in oversight.

In addition to important Political Economy Club members expressing divergent views on incorporation and limited liability, there is little evidence that members of the club had substantive influence on policy implementation. In particular, though McCulloch was even more strident than Smith in "consistent advocacy of the anti-corporate, full liability position" (Amsler et al. 1981, p.788), such views were incidental to the larger body of work produced by McCulloch. While the fifth and final edition of McCulloch's *Principles of Political Economy* in 1864 did contain some discussion of incorporation and limited liability, the Smithian narrative derived from the "narrow, lazy and oppressive" character of monopoly still remained. The second edition of McCulloch's *Principles* in 1843, appearing at a critical junction of public debate on incorporation of joint-stock companies, gave the relevant issues only little attention, in the section on 'Interference of Government'. In contrast, this section devotes substantial attention to the implications of the bankruptcy laws that imposed severe penalties on personal bankruptcies but exempted commercial bankruptcy of traders and merchants.

McCulloch maintained a position on incorporation and limited liability that can be found in scattered in works stretching from 1825 to 1864, a position that was not reflected in legislative developments. In contrast, the position of J.S. Mill's *Principles of Political Economy* in 1848 was more in keeping with the direction of legislative developments. The usefulness of incorporation to attract (equity) capital where the funds required exceeded "the means of the richest individual or private partnership" was recognized. The Smithian view on agency costs was retained, though tempered with the possibility of offset through incentive contracting with managers and requiring frequent distribution of financial reports. In addition, the larger firms facilitated by incorporation would allow firms in certain sectors to reap the gains of increasing the scale of production. The resulting increase in profitability would further allow the hiring of "managers of superior intelligence". Mill maintained that the final arbiter of whether to use a joint-stock corporation or private partnership would be the marketplace.

The modern perception of classical political economists proposes a time line that commences with Adam Smith and continues with those dedicated to perpetuating and developing 'economic' ideas initially set down in *Wealth of Nations*. The political aspects have been largely overlooked and, more or less, forgotten. The lack of impact by members of the Political Economy Club on the legislative agenda for incorporation and limited liability is partly due to timing—the club was somewhat late to the debates and lacked individuals with significant political power—and partly due to the political position of important club members. J.S. Mill, Senior and other lesser club members were actively engaged as social reformers seeking improvement for the working classes. The struggles of the poor and working classes against the political monopoly of the aristocracy and propertied classes in England have a long history. Despite a lack of political success, the influence of Chartism on the social fabric from 1838 to 1858 was profound. As social reformers, J.S. Mill and Senior were the 'wrong stripe' to influence legislation impacting the propertied classes. It was to the Select Committee on Investments of the Middle and Working Classes (1850), chaired by the poverty reform campaigner Robert Slaney, that J.S. Mill gave parliamentary evidence on limited liability, not the influential Mercantile Laws Commission (1854).

B   ENGLISH LIMITED LIABILITY CORPORATIONS

Three Elements of Change to English Law

The progress of English law on limited liability corporations has been referenced somewhat haphazardly to this point. Key events have been identified, such as the passage of the Bubble Act in 1719–1720, the Act of Repeal (of the Bubble Act) in 1825, the Chartered Companies Act (1837), the Joint-Stock Companies Act in 1844, the Report of the Mercantile Laws Commission in 1854, the Limited Liability Act of 1855 and the Companies Act of 1856 (and 1862). The acts of 1844 and 1855–1856 may seem to have been watershed legislation that changed the landscape of equity capital organization. However, a detailed examination of the time line reveals that the acts of 1844 and 1855–1856 were the result of a half-century of attempts, legislative and otherwise, seeking to deal with the increasing demands for equity capital in the commercial ventures that were propelled by the Industrial Revolution. These legislative changes required a change in social perception of (joint-stock) 'companies' from "a reference to the people of which they were thought to be composed" to separate entities representing "an object cleansed of people" (Ireland 1996, p.46).

The commercial implications of the changes to English law had three distinct elements: (1) the introduction of 'incorporation by registration' of joint-stock companies in 1844; (2) the subsequent granting of limited liability to such incorporated joint-stock companies in 1855/1866; and (3) the gradual evolution of the tradeable 'autonomous share' that fuelled the 'socialization of equity capital' and the growth of exchange trading of shares in the second half of the 19th century. Though systemically connected, resulting in the emergence of the modern limited liability corporation by the end of the 19th century, factors contributing to the three elements differed. Incorporation was closely associated with the need to provide managerial and legal structure for commercial ventures that required combining equity capital from many individuals. In many cases, such 'companies' had a degree of separation between 'partners' and those responsible for the management of the venture. However, separation of active and passive investors can also be found in much earlier equity capital arrangements, such as the *commenda*.

Though often connected, properties associated with corporate status are distinct from the limited liability property. Even after the legislative changes of 1844 and 1855/1856, some companies still chose to be incorporated with unlimited liability. Circa 1874, unlimited liability banks dominated the British banking business. Using primary data, Acheson and Turner (2008, p.237) estimated that about 80% of bank deposits in England and over 63% of Scottish deposits were in a group of 69 English, 8 Scottish and 7 Irish unlimited liability banks. As the failure of the City of Glasgow Bank in 1878 demonstrated, an insolvent unlimited liability corporation was required to make calls on shareholders for additional paid-in capital to cover the deficit of liabilities exceeding assets. The unlimited liability of many British banks at this time was partly due to the charters granted to the five 'public' banks, such as the Bank of England (established in 1694) and the Bank of Scotland (established in 1695), which prevented the establishment of competing joint-stock banks until enabling legislation in the mid-1820s. "The joint-stock banking legislation, following the common-law tradition, required these banks to have joint and several unlimited liability" (Acheson and Turner 2008). Most of these unlimited liability banks did not convert to limited liability after 1856. Shareholders generally perceived that conversion would reduce profit, because depositors and note-holders viewed unlimited liability as providing better security and would deter risk-taking by bank managers.

At the time of its failure, the Glasgow Bank had the third-largest branch network in Britain, with liabilities about triple the paid-in capital plus reserves. The manager and one director were charged with fraud and sentenced to 18 months in prison for falsifying balance sheets, with three other directors jailed for eight months for fraudulently publishing balance sheets known to be false. Checkland (1975, p.471) reported that, although the deficit was covered by shareholders, only 254 of 1,819 shareholders were solvent after the two calls for additional capital needed to cover the deficit. The collapse had an indelible impact on wealthy shareholders in various sectors, not just banking, and it led to the passage of the 1879 Companies Act to deal with the *en masse* conversion from unlimited to limited liability corporations that was permitted under previous legislation. By 1884, only nine small unlimited liability banks remained in England. No relief was provided for the small shareholders who had been stripped of meager assets, though the favorable treatment of 'commercial losses' in English bankruptcy did prevent the sanctions associated with bankruptcy on personal loans.

The experience of Glasgow Bank reveals, as Loftus (2002, p.94) recognized: "The full significance of limited liability reform cannot be understood if its financial and legal implications are abstracted from the political environment in which debates took place." Through much of the 19th century, the 'old corruption' of the wealthy and the propertied classes that controlled the legislative agenda denied universal manhood suffrage to the working classes, despite the efforts of the Chartists, Christian socialists and other reformers. The evidence presented to the Mercantile Law Commission (1854) led the commissioners to conclude there was "great contrariety of opinion" on the matter of limited liability reform. Combined with the long-standing negative position of Adam Smith regarding the contribution of chartered joint-stock companies, there was a fear expressed to the commission of 'fraud and speculation' and of changing the status quo when there was "abundant evidence of satisfactory progress and national prosperity".

In contrast to those seeking to maintain the status quo, many social reformers were strongly in favour of limited liability (Loftus 2002, p.108):

> whatever their success or failure, the Chartist campaigns and the ten hours movement articulated a critique of political economy based on the structural inequalities of contracting parties in the market. Notions of shared interests through investments had the potential to obscure class differences while promoting the expansion of capital and investment as beneficial to the community.

For social reformers, limited liability typically was seen as "democratization", a step toward a world where class differences were not so biting. Yet, as noted previously, contributions of social reformers such as J.S. Mill to the debate over incorporation and limited liability were typically made to the committees concerned with 'social reform', such as the Parliamentary Select Committee on the Savings of the Middle and Working Classes chaired by the champion of the working poor Robert A. Slaney (1792–1862), and not the Mercantile Laws Commission.

Similar to both incorporation and limited liability, the development of the autonomous share also required a change in the social fabric of Victorian England. In particular, moral attitudes towards speculation and gambling had to change (e.g., Itzkowitz 2002; Acheson et al. 2012). The phenomenal growth in both the number and capitalization of tradeable shares issued by incorporated limited liability companies created equity capital trading venues, such as the London, Paris and New York stock exchanges, with large pools of speculative liquidity to sustain active trading and, presumably, more accurate pricing. The 'democratization' associated with the introduction of limited liability is reflected in the British middle classes purchasing equity capital shares instead of government debt. A 'nation of shareholders' was formed. "By the end of the century, roughly two-fifths of the national wealth was invested in company shares, and large numbers of upper- and middle-class people lived off dividends and interest rates from shares and other securities" (Itzkowitz 2002, p.121).

From Canals to Utilities and Insurance

The transition in markets for equity capital shares during the 19th century was dramatic. In addition to outlawing the formation of companies without a royal charter or act of Parliament, the Bubble Act (1720) also made transactions in the shares of such 'illegal' companies null and void. This effectively stopped the trade in shares of joint-stock companies formed without a royal charter or act of Parliament. This more or less confined the lion's share of equity capital share trading to the moneyed companies, effectively the Bank of England, the British East India and South Sea Companies and the two insurance companies. Against this backdrop, the growth in the public debt—from £5 million in 1698 to £71 million in 1749 to £497 million by 1800—created a market for investment of private funds dominated by trading in gilt-edged securities (Thomas

1973, p.4). Though many acts of Parliament authorized joint-stock issues to fund canal companies in the last quarter of the 18th century, for various reasons these shares did not contribute significantly to the share trading that was centered in London.

An important event occurred on 3 March 1801, when the 'London Stock Exchange' "formally came into existence that not only provided a market for securities but also incorporated regulations on how business was to be conducted" (Michie 1999, p.35). There was much more to this move than a simple transition of trading locations. "By this act the trading of securities in London had moved, decisively, from an open to a closed market as the only way of ensuring that all those who participated both obeyed the rules and paid for the necessary administration. With 363 members by February 1802 the move did appear to be a successful one" (p.35). When the stock exchange moved to a new building in 1802, "the main business of the market centered around gilt edged. Such industrial shares as existed, for example, canals, waterworks and docks were not even listed in the daily list until 1811" (Thomas 1973, p.4–5). It was not until the substantial issues of railway shares starting in the 1830s that there was significant trading in English shares beyond the moneyed companies.

In the last quarter of the 18th century, there was rapid growth in the size and scope of commercial ventures in manufacturing, insurance, transportation, lighting, water works, mining and brewing. Such ventures required equity capital that was initially largely funded using partnerships. This period of growth in demand for 'joint-stock' equity capital commenced with the building of canals. While partnerships and proprietorships were the common method of organizing many ventures, the commercial and industrial expansion of the period fuelled the need, in certain instances, to combine equity capital from many investors to build canal infrastructure, docks and waterworks. Following the Bubble Act, the earliest type of ventures to seek parliamentary approval to form joint-stock companies with tradeable shares were those involved in the construction of canals. Oddly enough, the financial and economic success of an eleven-mile canal from Worsley to Manchester, financed primarily by the Duke of Bridgewater and not by joint-stock capital, fuelled the creation of joint-stock companies for large canal projects.

Arnold and McCartney (2008, p.1188) provided details of early canal construction in England:[7]

> The canal age proper began in 1755 when Liverpool Corporation obtained an Act to improve Sankey Brook, a tributary of the Mersey, make it navigable, and so enable coal from the St Helens area to be carried by water to Liverpool. This prompted the promotion of the Bridgewater canal, from Manchester to the Duke of Bridgewater's collieries at Worsley, seven miles away. Although essentially a private venture, the project involved building an aqueduct to carry the canal over the valley of the Irwell at Barton and an enabling Act of Parliament. The canal opened in July 1761 and immediately halved the cost of coal in Manchester.

As equity capital ventures, canals had a number of distinctive features. In particular, the benefits of a canal accrued locally and mostly to those involved in the production, distribution, sale and consumption of the commodities being transported. As a consequence, suppliers of equity capital were predominately local. It is not surprising that the Duke of Bridgewater was also the owner of the collieries that benefited from construction of the canal. Larger ventures required more share capital; hence the need for a charter. Thomas (1973, p.5–6) described the typical method of raising funds for canal construction during this period as follows:

> Successful promotion of a canal company frequently involved a considerable amount of local support. A promoter without adequate capital enlisted the interest of prominent local citizens, and with their backing set up an investigation fund. Subscriptions to such a fund sometimes only meant that it entitled the contributor to some shares, while in other cases the subscription constituted part of the deposit. Following a favourable decision an act of incorporation was obtained which set out the share capital and its division into a specified number of shares. The deposit on shares was fixed and subscription books were then opened. Frequently subscriptions were collected in the main centres along the route of the proposed canals. In most cases the lists were filled quickly, particularly during the speculative mania of 1792.

The sale of shares by subscription did not initially create difficulties associated with share speculation, though this likely was a contributing factor in the 1791–1792 speculative boom and bust in canal shares.

Canal companies required a permanent equity capital stock and were chartered, permitting the legal transferability of shares. While this would seem to be sufficient to permit active trading in canal shares, similar to the moneyed companies, this was not the case. 'In many instances, provisions in the statutes of the charter prohibited an individual from holding more than a certain number of shares'. The combination of small holdings and a desire for local control meant that 'the disposal of canal shares through the London market' generated only sporadic trade. Though records of canal shares during the 18th century are "very thin", Arnold and McCartney (2011, p.215) provided some evidence:

> Evidence on the scale of canal operations and on their economic success or failure is thus very thin and largely confined to data on construction costs and on the dividends that were paid by some canal companies. Construction costs could be quite variable, ranging from £3,213 per mile on the Trent and Mersey Canal and £3,374 on the Oxford Canal to £16,666 on the Kennett and Avon Canal, but dividends were often very high; the 10 most successful canals in 1825, for example, paid an average dividend of 27.6 per cent and the Sankey Brook Navigation in south Lancashire paid 33.3 per cent dividends for 80 years from its opening in 1757.

The combination of profitable early canal ventures and the use of subscription sales led (in 1791 to 1793) to the introduction of "schemes of all kinds" in which promoters "were anxious to cause the prices of the shares of their projected canals even before the work of construction had begun, to rise to an unduly high figure; and they would unload their stocks upon unsuspecting purchasers so as to net a great profit" (Jackman 1916, pp.394–5). However, as Thomas (1973, p.6) observed, such observations need to be tempered: "There is very little evidence of the extent of the canal share market during the years 1791–93. It is generally agreed that speculation in shares was excessive and that as a result many fraudulent promotions appeared on the market".

Absent sufficient quantitative evidence, qualitative evidence indicates that canal share speculation in 1791 and 1792 appeared in traditional share-trading venues in London—the coffeehouses and the old Stock Exchange—as well as the provinces, where auctions of canal shares impelled the establishment of the provincial stock exchanges. However, this early trade in canal shares "did not provide a sufficient volume of share turnover to sustain provincial stockbroking activity. With the ending of the 1792 mania canal share dealing centered on London and up until 1831 there was a considerable volume of trading, but afterwards stock market interest switched to the growing railway market" (Thomas 1973, p.7). Yet, before the emergence of railway share trading, the English share market experienced several periods of company promotion involving the sale of shares in various companies, including gas works, insurance, brewing, distilling and water works. A number of such ventures resorted to the use of 'trust deeds' as a legal maneuver to attain limited liability for shareholders without gaining a parliamentary charter.

The Repeal of the Bubble Act (1825)

The repeal of the Bubble Act (1825) marks an important change of direction in the organization of equity capital in England. The Industrial Revolution in Britain led to increasing demands for equity capital in a wide range of industries where "individual capital could not be supposed to be adequate for the completion of the object for which the Company was formed" (English 1827, p.31). The experience of the canal companies in obtaining parliamentary charters led other types of companies to seek this route to avoid the sanctions of the Bubble Act. Certain types of companies were more likely to obtain approval than others. English (1827) provided evidence of 624 companies with a capitalization of £372 million that had issued prospectuses just prior to the Bubble Act repeal, with 127 of these companies in operation in 1827. Nominal subscribed capital of the 127 surviving companies was just more than £102 million, of which £15 million was paid on 764,534 shares, leaving about £87 million of unpaid capital associated with outstanding shares, mostly from insurance and banking companies, where ability to make calls on capital provided security to policy holders and depositors.

Inability or excessively long delays to obtain a parliamentary charter led companies in certain sectors to seek other methods to combine sufficient equity capital. As Hunt (1935, p.3) observed, this led to ongoing attempts to circumvent the Bubble Act:

> Several eruptions of company promotion and speculation in defiance of the law, and the opening-up of new industries with which it was impossible for the individual capitalist to cope, were forces which operated finally to break

Table 8.1 Number and nominal capitalization of English companies issuing prospectuses just prior to the Repeal of the Bubble Act (1825)

74	Mining companies	£ 38,370,000
29	Gas	12,077,000
20	Insurance	35,820,000
29	Investment	52,600,000
54	Canal and railroad	44,051,000
67	Steam (navigation)	8,555,500
11	Trading	10,450,000
26	Building	13,781,000
24	Provision	8,360,000
292	Miscellaneous	*148,108,600*
624		£372,173,100

Source: Hunt (1935, p.25)

Table 8.2 Number, paid-in capitalization and market value of selected companies operating in 1827

Companies		Capitalization	Amount Paid	Value
44	Mining	£ 27,766,000	£ 5,455,100	£2,927,350
20	Gas	9,061,000	2,162,000	1,504,625
14	Insurance	28,120,000	2,247,000	1,606,000
49	Miscellaneous	38,824,600	5,321,850	3,265,975
127		£102,781,600	£15,185,950	£9,303,950

Source: Hunt (1935, p.25)

down opposition and to cause Parliament, retracing its steps, gradually to erect the legal framework of the new form of business organization.

This change of legal framework in England, which was not completed until past the middle of the 19th century, involved a change in social conscience to effect the change in legislation. As Taylor (2006) detailed, there was "a persistent and pervasive fear of and hostility to joint-stock enterprise which was by no means the preserve of a reactionary or self-interested few". Arguments against conferring corporate charters were varied and strongly held. For example (p.13):

> In 1800, when Parliament debated the incorporation of the London Company for the Manufacture of Flour, Meal and Bread Tierney vigorously opposed the measure on the ground that "those incorporated could lose only their share of £25 each while their competitors might lose all," speculation would arise, the shares would find their way into a few hands, and thus enable the company to set a monopoly price upon their commodity.

Not only was legal and mercantile opinion hostile to legislative limitation of liability on competitive grounds, there was serious social concern with determining responsibility of shareholders in an unincorporated joint-stock company in the event of financial embarrassment by the company.

The movement of bills for corporate charter through the legislative process was slow, sporadic and unpredictable. In this, there was a strong element of 'old corruption' which stemmed from "the main cause of social oppression" identified by British radicals: "the political monopoly of the propertied elite" (Harling 1995, p.127). The legislative changes surrounding equity capital organization that took place in England in the first half of the 19th century were inspired by radical elements in British society. A continuing tradition of social resistance stretching back to the Levelers propelled radical groups such as the Luddites and the Chartists to exert tremendous pressure on the ruling classes for social and political change. In this struggle, the radicals had common ground with smaller merchants and investors seeking to combine equity capital to support commercial ventures that required more capital than a small grouping could provide. As Philopatris proclaimed in 1807: "Are we now, in this age of civil liberty, to be deprived of commercial freedom? Are the people of small capitals to be restrained from making them productive by uniting to trade as a body?" In addition to denying legislative access to corporate charters for those not connected to the propertied elite, old corruption prevented encroachment on traditional monopolies, such as those granted to the two chartered insurance companies.

Against this backdrop, there was a brief boom in company promotions in 1807 and 1808 involving about 40 companies. Hunt (1935, p.4) listed the types of companies involved:

> 5 insurance companies, 7 brewing companies, 4 distillery companies, 5 companies to import and sell wine, 2 companies to manufacture and sell vinegar, 3 commission agencies, 3 coal companies, 1 medicine and drug company, 1 land company, 1 company to finance canal construction, 2 banking companies, 1 lighting and heating company, 2 copper companies, 1 paper manufacturing company, and 1 woolen company.

Not all of these companies were viable concerns, some being no more than promotions, while a small few were at different stages of the legislative approval process. Some were organized by obtaining limited liability using 'trust deeds' to circumvent provisions of the Bubble Act. In November 1807, old corruption acted against these companies, with the attorney general seeking "a criminal information against two of those recently formed as schemes which violated the 'provisions and plain policy' of the Act of 1719." The response to the legal argument in defence of the companies that no prosecutions had taken place under the Bubble Act since its passage was: "The only probable reason why this branch of the Statute had not been acted upon for so long was because it had corrected an evil it was intended to suppress, till now of late when it had shown itself again, it was necessary to put this wholesome law into force" (p.7).

Such action by the attorney general had the desired impact (Hunt 1935, p.7): "Alarm spread among investors and company promoters. New ventures folded up." This impact was reinforced by the decision in the Court of King's Bench:

> in view of the lapse of eighty-seven years since any authenticated proceeding on the Act, and of the fact that other means of prosecution were open to the attorney-general. Lord Ellenborough, the presiding justice, pointed out, nevertheless, that no person could in the future pretend that the statute was obsolete. Furthermore, he condemned the feature of alleged limited liability as "mischievous delusion calculated to ensnare the unwary public." The subscribers themselves might stipulate with one another for such contracted responsibility, but to the rest of the world each partner was fully liable. Finally, he urged, "as a matter of prudence to the parties concerned, that they should for-bear to carry into execution this mischievous project, or any other speculative project founded on joint-stock or transferable shares."

Despite the considerable passage of time without enforcement of the provisions of the Bubble Act, the court denied that the act was obsolete and strongly reaffirmed its relevance. At this crucial juncture, the progression toward greater permissibility in the granting of corporate status, limited liability and share transferability was overtaken by political and military events associated with the Napoleonic wars. In addition to transforming the political and military landscape of Europe and its colonies, British participation in the Napoleonic wars contributed to old corruption reaching a peak, providing sinecures, reversions, emoluments, government contracts, pensions and the like to the benefit of the propertied elite at the expense of the rest of British society. Such actions provided ample ammunition for William Cobbett (1763–1835), John Cartwright (1740–1824) and others to call for radical parliamentary reform.

As Neal (1998) observed, the repeal of the Bubble Act (1825) was part of a set of reforms in Britain that followed the end of the Napoleonic wars and the resumption of the gold standard. "The government's piecemeal reforms, introduced during the crisis of 1825 and its immediate aftermath, provided smoother patterns of tax collections and interest disbursements, established Bank of England branches throughout England, stimulated country bank competition with joint-stock companies outside of London, and eliminated the Bubble Act of 1720. Even the bankruptcy laws began to be rewritten in 1831" (p.54). Prior to the repeal, trading on the 'stock exchange' was dominated by activity in the stock of British government debt, which had ballooned during the Napoleonic wars. However, the end of war expenditures reduced the supply of new British government debt. This change was accompanied by an unexpected increase in the amount of foreign issues, both government debt and company shares, and an upsurge in domestic share issues seeking legislative approval.

The collapse of Spanish power in the Americas following Napoleon's defeat impelled the floatation on the London stock exchange of foreign debt and share issues from Latin American countries. This revived the sentiments that had led

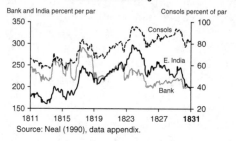

Price Levels of "The Funds"
London Stock Exchange

Source: Neal (1990), data appendix.

London Stock Price Index
1822=100

Source: Compiled from quotes for 50 companies
in the *Course of the Exchange*.

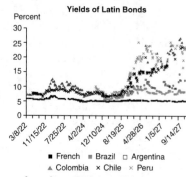

Yields of Latin Bonds

■ French   ■ Brazil   □ Argentina
▲ Colombia   × Chile   × Peru
Source: *Course of the Exchange*, Friday quotes.

Figure 8.2   Selected Data for the London Securities Market, 1811–1831
Source: Neal (1998)

to the boom in joint-stock promotions in 1807 and 1808. Neal (p.64) described
the situation as follows:

> As the London stock market had proved attractive for the new issues of
> debt by the restored European governments and the revolutionary Latin
> American governments, by 1824 a much wider variety of newly formed
> joint-stock corporations offered their shares to London investors. In the
> words of a contemporary observer, "bubble schemes came out in shoals
> like herring from the Polar Seas." The success of three companies floated
> to exploit the mineral resources of Mexico—the *Real del Monte* Associa-
> tion, the United Mexican Company, and the Anglo-American Company
> led to flotations of domestic projects in early 1824. In February 1824,
> the Barings and Rothschilds cooperated to found the Alliance British
> and Foreign Life & Fire Insurance Company. It enjoyed an immediate,
> enormous success. In March there were 30 bills before Parliament to
> establish some kind of joint-stock enterprise, whether a private undertak-
> ing for issuing insurance or opening a mine, or a public utility such as
> gas or waterworks, or a canal, dock, or bridge. In April there were 250
> such bills.

In the face of the avalanche of issues, many with legitimate public purpose funded by credible merchants, the provisions of the Bubble Act prohibiting the formation of joint-stock companies with tradeable shares were repealed. However, this repeal did not grant the right to incorporation with limited liability, creating a difficult legal situation. "Under common law, limited liability was an inseparable incident of incorporation. Henceforth the crown was empowered to prescribe to any extent the degree of shareholders' responsibility. Even so, the grant of charters continued to be very jealously guarded" (Hunt 1935, pp.22–23).

The Boom and Bust in Railway Shares

Into the murky legal environment for joint-stock companies that followed the repeal of the Bubble Act came the steam railway and the need for substantial amounts of equity capital to, ultimately, build a national railway network (Pollins 1954). It is coincidence that the first public railway line to make use of steam railway technology opened in 1825, the same year as the repeal of the Bubble Act. The Stockton and Darlington Railway was authorized by an act of Parliament in 1820 as a public line with an eye to employing steam engine technology that George Stephenson (1781–1848) and others had been developing on private lines for hauling coal. In addition to engine design, steam engine technology required advances in metallurgy to improve the quality of the rails. The opening of the Stockton and Darlington line gave impetus to a number of the joint-stock promotions that surfaced in 1824 and 1825, both for railways and for mines, aiming to benefit from the reduced transportation costs the railways were expected to bring (Reed 1975, p.4):

> By 1825 schemes for trunk lines from London to Manchester, London to Liverpool via Birmingham, London to Bristol and South Wales, and Bristol to Yorkshire were being canvassed in the joint-stock boom of that year, which was chiefly notorious for the many unsuccessful mining ventures which were undertaken. Most of these railway schemes were clearly premature, for there was neither the engineering nor the managerial skill to undertake such projects, and few of them survived the crisis of December 1825.

Similar to canals, railways required the ability to obtain right of way, which made it necessary to obtain a legislative charter; as a consequence, "the essential requirements for railway Bills were taken over from canal legislation" (p.76).

Though unincorporated joint-stock organization was available following the repeal of the Bubble Act, for various reasons public railways required the company to petition Parliament for an act of authorization. The legislative process was subject to standing orders in the House of Commons and the House of Lords. Minor alterations in these standing orders were made following the initial 1834–1837 'mania' in railway shares, the most significant change being an increase from 5% to 10% in the deposit required to introduce a railway bill. Reed (p.80) summarized the key role played by equity capital in this process:

> formal parliamentary requirements and the necessity to survey a line and prepare a case for parliamentary examination meant that a company had to have some sort of corporate existence and to raise substantial amounts of money well in advance of obtaining an Act of Incorporation. The formation of a company and the issue of securities were consequently necessary at an early stage in the promotion of a new railway.

In addition to the deposit, a key feature of the 'formal parliamentary requirements' involved the presentation of a subscription contract and list of applicants: "it was in a company's interest to ensure as far as possible that its shares went to substantial applicants, who could be relied on to pay up instalments . . . It was realized at any early stage that it was sound parliamentary tactics to have a subscription contract which reflected local support" (p.84).

Table 8.3   Railway Shares Issues and Other Public companies known on the London market, c. 1843

Bank of England	£10,914,750	
Bank of Ireland	£ 2,630,769	
Joint-stock banks, England and Wales		
	£15,000,000 (about)	
London joint-stock banks	£ 6,433,500	
Irish " " "	£ 1,850,850	
Scotch " " "	£ 9,619,825	
Subtotal	£46,449,694	
East India Company		£ 6,000,000
South Sea Company		£ 3,662,734
Turnpike trusts		£ 8,774,927
70 Railways		£57,447,903
24 Foreign Mining Companies		£ 6,464,833
81 British Mining Companies		£ 4,500,000
102 Assurance Companies		£26,000,000
59 Canals—main lines	£14,362,445	
branches and feeders	£ 3,500,000 (about)	
Subtotal	£17,862,445	
8 Dock Companies		£12,077,237
27 Gas Light Companies		£ 4,326,870
11 Water Companies		£ 2,536,122
5 Bridge Companies		£ 2,123,874

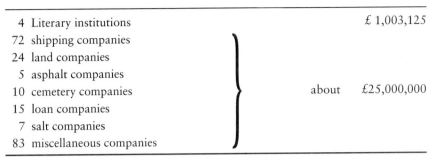

4	Literary institutions	£ 1,003,125
72	shipping companies	
24	land companies	
5	asphalt companies	
10	cemetery companies	about £25,000,000
15	loan companies	
7	salt companies	
83	miscellaneous companies	

Source: Reed (1975, p.2)

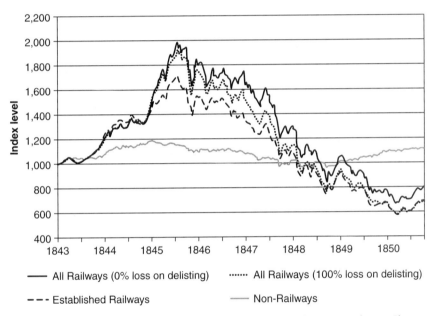

Figure 8.3 London Market Indices for Railway and Non-Railway Shares, 1843–1851

Source: Campbell (2013)
Notes: Railway share indices calculated from weekly share price tables in the *Railway Times* (1843–1850). Non-Railway share index calculated from weekly share price tables in *Course of the Exchange* (1843–1850). The All-Railway index includes all railway securities. The Established Railway index includes only those railways which were constructed before 1843. The Non-Railway index includes the 22 largest non-railways by market capitalisation.

The repeal of the Bubble Act alleviated the demands of certain types of companies to combine equity capital from many investors. However, as Taylor (2006, p.134) observed: "Despite legislation in 1825, 1834 and 1837, companies were in a similar legal position in 1840 as they were in 1800, due largely to the common law interpretation of unincorporated companies, and to the government's desire to maintain its discretion over granting privileges of incorporation." Requiring a charter from Parliament, railway projects were captive to the machinations of old corruption. "There was enormous potential for corruption in the procedure by means of which acts of incorporation were sought. Promoters of joint-stock schemes were quite willing to bribe MPs with shares or directorships in order to secure a favourable hearing for their companies." Following practices used in the raising of equity capital for canal construction, this parliamentary delay provided promoters with a window to raise deposits for subscriptions based on an estimated nominal capital contained in the application for a private members bill. Recognizing that only a small amount of initial capital was required to participate in a promotional venture, the ground was laid for the excess speculation and fraudulent promotions in 1834–1837 and 1843–1847.

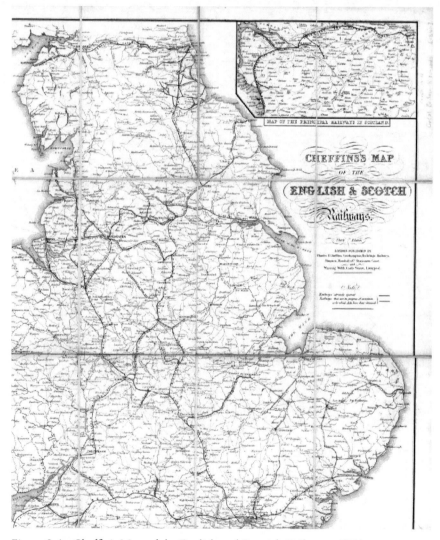

Figure 8.4   Cheffin's Map of the English and Scottish Railways, 1844

Excessive speculation in railway shares was an outcome of the process for obtaining approval for incorporation from Parliament combined with a supply of leveraged equity capital claims in the form of 'scrips' and the like. This provided ample fodder for rampant speculative trading (Alborn 1998, p.189):

> To win Parliamentary approval, [railways] needed to present a subscription list of people who had pledged to buy shares, and various standing orders required [subscribers] to sign contracts for between half and five-sixth's of [railway] capital as a precondition for approval by both Houses. Such requirements created a huge national market in salable securities, whether in the form of "scrip" certificates, letters of allotment, or bankers' receipts, which might thrive for the months or even years it might take for a private bill to pass.

To obtain parliamentary approval, a 5% deposit of nominal capital was required from subscribers, an amount that was raised to 10% following the 1834–1837 wave of promotions. The deposit was raised and paid following a process in which applicants initially applied for shares from the company and a letter of allotment was issued indicating the number of shares that would be issued. When the deposit was paid, either a scrip certificate or a bankers' receipt, exchangeable for scrip, was issued. "The scrip certificate gave the holder a title to the appropriate number of shares when the company was incorporated, and was an acknowledgement that the holder had signed the deeds binding him to pay instalments as demanded" (Reed 1975, p.83).

To appreciate the character of speculative trading during the railway manias, it is essential to recognize that there could be a significant amount of time between the initial promotion and the issuing of the letters of allotment and the signing of the subscription contract required to obtain an issue of scrip. "Though a company might try to ensure that only those to whom an original allotment had been made were permitted to sign the subscription contract, in practice this was difficult to enforce" (p.89). In theory, a scrip certificate was "the acknowledgement that the holder had signed the subscription contract". However, scrip certificates were issued in bearer form, effectively eliminating the need for the signatory to the subscription contract being the individual to ultimately purchase shares in the event that the project received approval. The use of 'nominees' as signatories further clouded the liability issue. A bankers' receipt was evidence that a deposit had been paid against an allotment of shares but the scrip certificate had not yet been issued. This would be an excellent trading vehicle for a speculator willing to "simply throw away the scrip if the company failed". If the venture successfully obtained an act, the price of scrip could jump to more than double the par value.

Seeking a foundation for the 'swindle' hypothesis, Bryer (1991, p.463) claimed that once parliamentary approval had been obtained, "initial subscribers were liable for calls even if they had sold their shares, if the ultimate purchaser was unable to meet them". This uncalled liability deterred wealthy London investors from investing in early railway ventures, leaving merchants and country gentlemen from Lancashire, Manchester and, especially, Liverpool as essential sources of railway share capital. While the claim of liability for calls was theoretically correct, the rudimentary development of the English railway system during the 1830s suggests that the earlier 1834–1837 speculation was associated with bets on the successful granting of parliamentary approval. During the decade, the railway mileage opened rose from less than 100 miles to almost 1,000 miles. Little was known about the eventual return on equity capital invested. The number of petitions, acts and capital authorized from 1834 to 1837 represented a dramatic increase in the supply of equity capital claims—a large portion of this supply was not associated with shares, only with claims to pay a first call on shares in the event the project was approved. Further supply was associated with partially paid shares.

As a consequence, trading of 'scrip' or partially paid shares was speculative compared to fully paid shares. The trading of 'scrip' also had other liability considerations (Alborn 1998, p.189):

> [S]crip was not limited in liability the way shares in incorporated railways were, which tended to keep permanent investors out of the market. Hence, during the long period between projection and incorporation, railway investors were traders, pure and simple: they either held their scrip in anticipation of future stable returns, or they sold at a profit (if they were lucky) when the market price changes. Until incorporation, they had no explicitly political role to play within the company; although scripholders did form loose associations to protect their legal rights.

Given that undercapitalized speculative traders were attracted to 'scrip' and partially paid shares, the 1834–1837 and 1843–1847 events differed substantively in the stage that railway development had reached and the types of ventures being promoted. Though the Stockton and Darlington Railway has claims to being the first steam railway, it was the opening of the Liverpool and Manchester line in 1830 that represented the first major step in the evolution of the British rail system. It was the Liverpool and Manchester line, together with the London and Birmingham line, which overcame cost overruns to make "unexpectedly large profits" which underpinned the increase in the railway share price index from 60.2 in June 1835 to 129.4 in May 1836 (Bryer 1991, p.444, 447).

A CONTEMPORARY DESCRIPTION OF THE ENGLISH RAILWAY PANIC OF 1845

Begbie (1848, pp.72–3) described the mania of 1845 as follows:

What is called "The Railway mania" has given notoriety to the year 1845. The funds had been high for some time before. The interest was low. Money was plenty. The desire to speculate was awakened. It chiefly directed itself to schemes for the extension of internal communication by means of railways at home and abroad. Speculation spread with inconceivable rapidity and force. All classes were smitten with the phrenzy, but more particularly persons in the middle rank of life, with comparatively small amount of capital, for which they were naturally anxious to obtain a higher rate of interest than is allowed on investments in the Funds. Seduced by the names of parties of known standing, wealth, and ability, advertised as the Directors of these projects, the smaller capitalists, who hold among them the bulk of the available property of the country, eagerly took shares, and paid the required deposit. This class of persons, there is every reason to believe, generally entered into these speculations, at first, with the *bona fide* intention of investing their means in what promised to yield them good returns. They saw that established Railway Companies were paying dividends to shareholders, averaging double the rate of interest accruing from money in the Funds. They embarked their money in the railway speculations, expecting like results; and not calculating on the difference in circumstances and of time. The bulk of the speculators early in 1845, appear to have been thus actuated. But there were very many persons who had gone into these speculations, simply with the intention of making money by buying and selling Scrip. The extent to which they carried such transactions, at once discreditable and dishonest, led to the usual conclusion—a Panic, which has been succeeded by the great commercial crisis of 1847–8. There exist no means of ascertaining and distinguishing the classes who, in 1825 and 1835, found money for the deposits then required and paid on account of the schemes of those respective periods. But we do possess a guide, in this respect, for the year 1845, and its Railway speculations . . . On careful examination . . . it is discovered, that more than two-thirds of the amount so paid were disbursed, not by millionaires, but by persons in the middle ranks of life—with incomes averaging from 150*l*. to 2000*l*. a year. That is to say, these monies have been paid by professional men, naval and military men, small manufacturers, shopkeepers, clerks, tradesmen, engineers, schoolmasters, clergymen, annuitants, pensioners, placement, or by their widows, daughters, or sisters. *These,* and not the great commercial men, risked money in such speculations.

From less than 100 miles of opened track in 1830, the British railway system had over 2,000 miles of opened track by 1843. This meant that, in addition to scrip and partially paid shares, the mania of 1843–1847 also had a substantial amount of fully paid shares, providing for a substantively different character to the railway mania of those years.

Swindle or Rational Pricing?

Following Bryer (1991), the so-called railway manias, especially the events of 1843–1847, have received considerable recent scholarly attention (e.g., Campbell 2012, 2013; Campbell and Turner 2012; McCartney and Arnold 2003; Odlyzko 2011). As with the variety of scholarly opinion expressed on other 'manias', academic impressions of the 1843–1847 mania vary from 'swindle' (Bryer) to 'rational pricing' (Campbell and Turner). Unfortunately, the search for historical comparability across manias is hindered by differences in context. For example, unlike the South Sea bubble, the object of speculation did not involve a grant of monopoly for seaborne trade to the 'South Seas'. There was also no exchange of initial equity capital raised for government debt. Capital raised was used toward the construction of a railway line, which may provide local and regional economic externalities beyond the gains to capital invested in the railway project proper. Given this, an important backdrop to the 1843–1847 mania is the claim in Marx (*Capital* III) that: "The period of prosperity in England from 1844 to 1847 was . . . connected with the first great railway swindle". Bryer (1991, p.441) observed: "Marx's view appears to be a classical illustration of Braudel's conception of capitalism as 'an active social hierarchy . . . constructed on top of exchange . . . which they manipulate to their advantage'."

As noted, the method of obtaining equity financing for railways involved three stages: (1) the initial promotion period required to obtain funds needed to seek parliamentary approval; (2) the subscription period where an initial deposit on the equity capital contribution is raised, determined as some fraction of the nominal share capital set out in the petition for the act of incorporation; and (3) the period of railway build out where subsequent calls are made on shareholders toward raising the full amount of nominal capital. As a consequence, three different types of railway 'securities' were available between the repeal of the Bubble Act in 1825 and the railway mania of 1843–1847: (1) securities associated with railway promotions, prior to a parliamentary act; (2) shares for railways with corporate charter under construction and subject to additional calls on capital; and (3) established railways with 'fully paid' shares.[8] While the 1834–1837 speculative mania was primarily associated with numerous promotions inspired by the increasing prospects of railways under construction, the 1843–1847 mania witnessed substantially greater knowledge about the engineering difficulties and construction costs together with a larger supply of fully paid shares and a record of the dividends that had been paid by established lines; "the vast majority of the schemes brought forward in 1844 and 1845 were from existing large companies who appealed to their initial shareholders for more funds" (p.462).

Alborn (1998, pp.189–91) demonstrated the complexities of the historical context involved in the railway manias. In particular, there was an undercurrent of the changing character of financial speculation following the Napoleonic wars. The diminishing flow of new government debt issues found English stockjobbers increasingly doing business in shares:

> By the 1820s, company shareholders were starting to take the place of fundholders . . . By then the state had frozen the debt at around £800 million and fundholding had taken on its modern meaning of "security" as opposed to speculation. There was . . . a direct connection between the disappearance of the creditor-speculator and the rise of the shareholder-speculator, in that the company craze in the first half of the 1820s was due in part to the leveling off of the debt and the consequent dispersion of new investors into different stocks.

As Mortimer and others had recognized, while government debt was relatively homogeneous and fluctuation in prices depended on interest rates and political events, the situation was much different in shares. The trading of debt 'light horse', a preferred instrument for stockjobber speculation, diminished with the absence of new issues. The degree of heterogeneity in shares, combined with the ability to trade shares or equity claims that were not fully paid or simply promotional, provided attractive alternatives to speculative trading of government securities. In addition, "speculation in early-Victorian railways was also qualitatively different, both in volume and political meaning, than trading in other shares at the time. Much of this difference resulted from the railways unique political circumstances" (Alborn 1998). While canals had primarily local economic impact, the geographical reach of the railway was substantially greater: there was "a unique trend among investors to conceive of railways as national and not merely regional undertakings" (p.175).

Bryer (1991, p.443) referred to the Marx-inspired swindle hypothesis associated with the 1843–1847 mania as "a deliberate design by an 'active hierarchy' to: (a) fuel the 'mania' thereby enticing investment in railway shares by unsuspecting middle-class and provincial entrepreneurs; and (b) subsequently squeeze out these investors and deflect critical interest in the new owners, the wealthy London capitalists". As Reed (1975, ch. 4–7) detailed, the bulk of equity capital for the initial period of railway finance originated from "provincial merchants and entrepreneurs (particularly those from Manchester and Liverpool) and the 'middle classes', and not from the very wealthy 'London capitalists' who studiously avoided investing in railways during the initial construction phase" (Bryer 1991, p.441). The 'Commercial Crisis' of 1847 coincided with substantial calls for equity capital from the numerous railway ventures that had been encouraged by the run-up in the price of railway shares starting in 1843. The restriction of credit created by the crisis prevented many shareholders from meeting the calls: "Being unable to meet the calls, many initial investors were forced to sell their shares at heavy losses. The evidence available suggests that the purchasers were the London wealthy" (p.441).

Whether the swindle hypothesis is correct or not, Bryer (p.447) made a fundamental observation about the relevance of accounting practice to the valuation of railway shares. Part of the process of parliamentary approval involved the creation of statutes of incorporation that "invariably included . . . the limitation to only declare 'Dividends out of the clear profits of the said Undertaking', so that 'the Capital of the said Company shall [not] . . . in any degree be reduced or impaired'". Such statements imply that some double-entry based accounting method was used to determine 'profit' and whether 'capital was reduced or impaired'. As Campbell and Turner (2011) detailed, as late as the 1880s, shareholders relied primarily on dividends and the quality of "incentivized boards . . . as an effective market substitute for legal protection" (p.594). Company directors for established lines were more than aware that dividend policy was fundamental to the valuation of shares. Given the weak state of shareholder legal protection in the 1840s, it is not surprising that many established railways found ways to manipulate dividend policy to give the appearance of greater profitability than actual operations warranted.

Dividend policy manipulation by incorporated railway companies was relatively insignificant during the 1834–1837 mania, as only a handful of lines were established enough to pay a predictable dividend. The situation in 1843 was much different. The necessity of manipulating dividends was exacerbated by the commercial crisis of 1847. When confronted with the inability of calls to raise sufficient capital from shareholders, numerous company directors elected to pay dividends from capital. In modern times, such actions would be characterized as a form of Ponzi scheme. However, prior to 1844, substantive legal protection for shareholders was more or less the common-law prohibition on fraud. In the case of unincorporated joint-stock companies, including those railway companies trading securities prior to the receipt of an act of incorporation, "recovery of property from the directors of fraudulent or bankrupt companies in the courts was difficult, for they could exploit the common law illegality of their companies in order to escape punishment: shareholders could not recover from directors if the concerns in question were ruled illegal" (Taylor 2006, p.138). Failure to allow for depreciation provided an accounting basis for reporting an inaccurate 'profit' number from which dividends could be paid.

Though railways were an important component of the share market in the 1840s, numerous other types of companies also sought share capital. Many of these companies were caught in the legal limbo of unincorporated joint-stock companies. The Joint-Stock Companies Act (1844) was well timed, having been the result of legislative action surrounding "a series of insurance frauds which emerged in the late 1830s and early 1840s" (p.137). This Act was introduced to address (p.137):

the various 'modes of deception' adopted by companies, which suggested the danger companies posed to the public as investors in and customers of these concerns. These included the use of fictitious names; the use of

Table 8.4   Private bills presented 1840–1844: Selected private bills presented before Parliament, 1840–1844, and percentage successful

Sector of economy	Bills presented	Acts passed	Percentage successful
Canals/navigations/ferries	35	28	80
Railways	188	137	73
Markets/bridges/cemeteries	49	34	69
Gas/waterworks	63	41	65
'Other' companies	77	49	64
Harbours/piers/docks/fisheriesiers/ docks/fisheries	115	64	56
Total	527	353	67

Source: Companion to the Almanac; or Year-Book of General Information, *1841–1845.*

respectable names without permission; the issue of misleading prospectuses in the newspapers; the prevention of shareholders' meetings; the falsification of share transfer books; the creation of fictitious votes to outvote the real shareholders; the creation of false accounts to deceive shareholders; the declaration of dividends out of capital; and the employment of respectable agents to cloak the want of respectability of the company.

Under the legislative leadership of William Gladstone (1809–1898), it was determined that "such frauds were facilitated by the unincorporated status of the companies involved." The Joint-Stock Companies Act made it easier and less risky to form early-stage companies. While the absence of limited liability dampened the benefits of the act considerably, the strong provisions about 'keeping of books, Auditing of Accounts, publication of Reports, &c' (Wordsworth 1845, p.40) provided important impetus to the development of the accounting profession in England.

Few scholarly sources explore the connection between the Irish potato famine, which hit with a vengeance in 1845, and the collapse of the market for railway shares. By the 19th century, the colonization of Ireland by the English resulted in an agrarian landlord-tenant system of landed estates operated by agents of absentee landlords. The indigenous Irish tenant population was located primarily on marginal farmland, reserving the best agricultural land for grazing animals with products marketed primarily to the English consumer. These estates provided a significant income for the well-to-do and wealthy in England, providing a source of funds for investment in railway shares. Propelled by bumper harvests in the early 1840s, the demand for bulk transport of goods by railway provided established railways with sufficient profit to declare dividends that looked attractive relative to 'the government funds'. Not only did the Irish potato famine expose the cruelty of the English colonization of Ireland, the collapse of the Irish potato crop deprived English landlords of income from grazing animals, as potatoes were also essential fodder. Combined with a poor English harvest, the precipitous drop in profitability of bulk goods transport undermined railway companies' ability to pay dividends, leading to the subterfuge of paying dividends out of capital in order to attract equity capital to satisfy calls.

Interpretation of the 1843–1847 railway mania requires some distinctions to be recognized. In particular, there is the issue of dating. The collapse of railway share prices lasted at least until 1849, arguing for a longer dating. As a consequence, some sources use a longer period—for example, Campbell (2013) used 1843–1850. Other sources identify the mania with a single year, 1845, when prices for railway shares reached a peak (e.g., Bryer 1991). In contrast, Reed (1975), an authoritative source, refers to "the spectacular railway booms of the 1830s and 1840s" without picking specific dates. Any dating of the English railway manias raises questions about the evidence concerning excessive speculation. As Reed (p.97) observed: "Much of the speculative activity which complicates the picture of railway promotion during this period took place in securities which were transferred without record, and it is necessary to rely on secondary evidence to judge the extent of such speculation". Evidence from comparing subscription lists, share lists and the like provided by Reed (1975) and Campbell and Turner (2012) is helpful only for identifying "the degree to which subscribers retained their interest at a later stage" as well as the occupation and location of the shareholder. No substantial evidence about the trade in the most speculative equity capital claims has survived.

Against this backdrop, a number of estimates of railway share performance are available. For example, Arnold and McCartney (2011, p.215) provided estimates for the average dividend record:

> on 15 of the leading (and more profitable) railway companies at only 5 per cent in the period 1840–55, and even the most successful companies hardly

Table 8.5 Average annual capital appreciation and dividend yield by sector, 1825–1870

	Dividend yield (%)	Capital appreciation (%)	Total return (%)
Overall market			
Weighted by market cap.	4.77	4.51	9.28
Unweighted	5.02	5.14	10.16
Banks			
Weighted by market cap.	5.26	5.49	10.75
Unweighted	5.05	8.07	13.12
Bridges (1825–61)			
Weighted by market cap.	4.43	0.03	4.46
Unweighted	2.40	−0.16	2.24
British mines			
Weighted by market cap.	4.09	6.62	10.71
Unweighted	3.92	2.31	6.22
Canals			
Weighted by market cap.	5.21	−0.62	4.59
Unweighted	5.46	−1.07	4.39
Colonial and foreign mines			
Weighted by market cap.	5.49	17.91	23.40
Unweighted	4.83	13.46	18.29
Docks			
Weighted by market cap.	4.89	0.53	5.42
Unweighted	4.94	3.67	8.62
Gas, light, and coke			
Weighted by market cap.	5.95	4.31	10.26
Unweighted	5.84	3.48	9.32

	Dividend yield (%)	Capital appreciation (%)	Total return (%)
Insurance			
Weighted by market cap.	3.90	3.30	7.20
Unweighted	4.20	2.96	7.16
Miscellaneous			
Weighted by market cap.	5.04	7.46	12.50
Unweighted	4.70	3.52	8.22
Railways			
Weighted by market cap.	3.69	10.19	13.88
Unweighted	4.19	10.56	14.75
Roads (1825–35)			
Weighted by market cap.	4.23	–3.77	0.46
Unweighted	4.68	–2.65	2.03
Telegraph (1852–70)			
Weighted by market cap.	7.55	13.85	21.40
Unweighted	7.21	10.80	18.01
Waterworks			
Weighted by market cap.	4.34	2.39	6.73
Unweighted	4.46	2.39	6.85

Source: Hickson et al. (2011, p.1229)

ever paid more than 10 per cent. Returns to equity capital were somewhat higher, but only by 0.5 per cent or so, and the average of a somewhat broader sample of companies across the period 1830–55 was only 4.2 per cent, comparable to the yield on government consols, which ranged from 3.0 to 5.9 per cent in the century to 1855.

These results can be compared to "the 10 most successful canals in 1825 [which] paid an average dividend of 27.6 per cent and the Sankey Brook Navigation in south Lancashire paid 33.3 per cent dividends for 80 years from its opening in 1757". However, following the emergence of competition from the railway for bulk transport, canal share performance deteriorated. Using dividends paid as a measure of share performance is not indicative of overall return. For the 1825–1870 time period, Hickson et al. (2011) found that telegraph companies, foreign and colonial mines and railways experienced the highest relative rates of return. While dividends paid were similar to and competitive with government funds, the bulk of the difference in returns was due to the capital gain or loss. Hickson et al. also reported that relatively high rates of return in banking and insurance appear to be in some measure explained by the presence of extended liability and uncalled capital.

C   AMERICAN COMPANIES AND THE FRENCH *SOCIÉTÉ EN COMMANDITE*

The Rise of American Corporations

Being British colonies prior to 1776, it is not surprising that the founding states of the American republic inherited equity capital organization and valuation methods with distinct similarities to those employed in England. However, from the starting point provided by the Declaration of Independence, the development of incorporation and limited liability in America deviated substantively from the English path. This departure was strongly influenced by a number of American characteristics. In particular, the American republic was a collection of states, each with inalienable rights under the Constitution. While Congress did have the right to grant a federal charter, "its practical force would have been *nil* in a state which refused to recognize it, and effective excuses for such refusal would have been easy to find" (Davis 1917, p.12). Resistance to granting incorporation powers to the federal government meant state legislatures had the primary authority to charter corporations. As a consequence, from the founding of the republic until somewhat after the passage of the New Jersey general incorporation law in 1875, the states used a myriad of legal approaches to granting of corporate status and limited liability.

At the time of the American Revolution, the few "pioneer business corporations" had significance that "even for their time, was but slight and local . . . predecessors rather than prototypes of the present-day business corporation. Only the local public service corporation is well represented" (p.5). Revolutionary America was not yet in need of large combinations of capital to fund canal and railway infrastructure, banks, highways and other such ventures. "Small-scale enterprise was still the order of the day." In addition, the operation of the Bubble Act had been extended to America in 1741, restricting the formation of joint-stock companies without legislative charter. After the revolution, "the situation was materially altered". Assertion of the natural equality of rights and privileges conflicted with the "English tradition that corporate powers were to be granted in rare instances" (p.7). Though constitutions in most states soon recognized the right to general incorporation for ecclesiastical, educational and literary organizations, corporations formed for commercial ventures still required a special legislative corporate charter.[9]

Consistent with the American struggle for religious and political freedoms, granting of corporate status to non-commercial entities varied across states and time. However, the overall result was considerably more acts in America than England: "Prior to 1801 over three hundred charters were granted for business corporations, ninety percent of them after 1789" (p.8). Some states, such as Massachusetts, used the privilege of granting corporate status liberally (Handlin and Handlin 1945, p.4–5):

> by contrast to English and Continental experience, the less advanced economy of the United States produced almost 350 business corporations between 1783 and 1809. By 1799, if not earlier, Massachusetts even had

Table 8.6 Summary of 18th-Century Charters to Business Corporations in the US, Grouped by Period, Sources of Charter, and General Type

Sources of charters	Colonial	1781–1785	1786–1790	1791–1795	1796–1800	Total charters	Per cent
US..............	....	1	....	1	....*	2	0.6
New England.........	6	4	4	69	117*	200*	59.7
Middle states.......	1	2	4	22	38	67	20.0
Southern states......	....	4	14	22	25	65	19.4
Western states.......	....	....	....	....	1	1	0.3
Total charters........	7	11	22	114	181*	335	100
Per cent............	2.1	3.3	6.6	34.0	54.0	100.0	....

General type.........	Colonial	1778–85	1786–90	1791–95	1796–1800	Total charters	Per cent
Financial............	1	5	5	29	27	67	20.0
Highway............	....	5	14	78	122	219	65.4
Local public service....	5	....	....	4	27*	36*	10.7
Business (proper).....	1	1	3	3	5	13	3.9
Total charters........	7	11	22	114	181*	335	100.0

Sources of charters	Financial	Highway	Local public service	Business (proper)	Total charters	Ancillary, additional, or joint charters	Total corporations
US..............	2	....	....	....	2	....	2
New England.........	33	130	30*	8	200*	8	192
Middle states.......	16	42	4	5	67	7	60
Southern states......	16	47	2	....	65	3	62
Western states.......	....	1	....	....	1	....	1

(Continued)

Table 8.6 (Continued)

Total charters	67	219	36*	13	335	18	317
Ancillary, additional, or joint charters...	5	13	....	....	18	....	....
Total corporations....	62	206	36*	13	317	....	....

Source: Davis (1917, p.24)

* Charters to water supply companies issued under the Massachusetts general incorporation act of Feb. 21, 1799 (CLaws, ed. 1801, II, 843–847), cannot be found and are not included.

Table 8.7 18th-Century Charters to Business Corporations, Classified by States and Purposes

Sources of charters	FINANCIAL		HIGHWAY			LOCAL PUBLIC SERVICE		BUSINESS (PROPER)		TOTALS
	Banking	Insurance	Inland navigation	Toll-bridge	Turnpike	Water supply	Dock	Manufacturing	Miscellaneous	
United States............	2	...	...	...	...	...	...	...	...	2
Maine....................	1	1	7	12	...	1	1	...	...	23
New Hampshire..........	1	1	5	19	4	1	1	...	...	32
Vermont.................	...	...	5	5	9	1	...	...	...	20
Massachusetts...........	7	5	5	14	9	15	1	4	...	60
Rhode Island............	4	6	1	3	3	3	...	...	...	20
Connecticut.............	5	2	2	3	23	5	1	1	3	45

New York	4	3	3	1	13	2	...	2	...	28
New Jersey	...	...	4	5	...	2	...	1	1	13
Pennsylvania	3	4	5	5	5	...	...	...	1	23
Delaware	2	...	1	...	...	...	...	...	...	3
Maryland	3	6	4	4	3	1	...	...	...	21
Virginia	2	3	14	...	3	...	...	...	...	22
North Carolina	...	...	11	...	...	...	...	...	...	11
South Carolina	...	2	6	1	...	1	...	...	...	10
Georgia	...	...	1	...	...	...	...	...	...	1
Kentucky	...	...	...	1	...	...	...	...	...	1
Total charters	34	33	74	73	72	32	4	8	5	335
Ancillary, additional, or joint charters	5	...	8	4	...	...	...	...	...	18
Total corporations	29	33	66	69	72	32	4	8	5	317

Source: Davis (1917, pp. 27)

1 One bridge and canal company occasions an additional subtraction.

a general incorporation law. Nor is it enough to point to the relative ease of incorporation in America without answering why it was less difficult to secure charters in the New World. If the weight of common-law inertia was not quite so heavy on one side of the ocean as on the other, and if independence freed colonial merchants from some imperial restraints, it nevertheless would be rash to claim that after 1776 enterprisers in the United States had more influence in government than did their European counterparts.

Significantly, the so-called 1799 Massachusetts general incorporation act was only for ventures organized "for the purpose of conveying fresh water, by subterraneous and other pipes, into any town of place within this Commonwealth" of Massachusetts. Once the project was complete, a settling of accounts was required and the project was leased back to the locality, "it is doubtful if the companies were, strictly speaking, organized for profit" (Davis 1917, p.19). The first steps toward general incorporation, where corporate status was granted without recourse to special charter, were not until the New York Act (1811); albeit, this act appeared in a dual system where corporate status was also conferred by special charter.

Closer inspection of the early American penchant for incorporation poses a number of quandaries. For example, Handlin and Handlin (1945, pp.6–7) observed for the period to 1800:

> The areas of most intense economic development were not the areas where the most corporations appeared. Fully 60 per cent of all charters were in New England while only 15 per cent were in New York and Pennsylvania; New Hampshire alone granted more than either of the two central states. Was the need for this device for accumulating and managing capital more urgent in New Hampshire than in Pennsylvania?

In addition to anomalous practices across states, there were also unusual patterns of incorporation across sectors. "In some of the most important phases of post-Revolutionary economy, in shipping and in trade, in land speculation and in the fisheries, joint-stock companies were prominent; there was only one small, short-lived corporation" (Handlin and Handlin 1945). This differed from the continental European experience, where overseas trade was typically a sector attractive to incorporated companies. In addition, there was no consistent approach used by the various projectors who were prominent in the early years of the Republic: "Duer incorporated his ventures in manufacturing but not in land; John Brown in canals but not in manufacturing; and Mackay, Craigie, Swan, Gorham, and Higginson similarly divided their interests. Yet if the corporate form was so adaptable and so advantageous in the management of capital, it should have been equally irresistible for all types of large-scale enterprise" (Handlin and Handlin 1945).

The timeline and diversity of state actions surrounding incorporation and limited liability, combined with the legal protections provided by the Constitution, provide a helpful backdrop to identify factors that influenced the adoption of specific forms of equity capital organization. Butler (1985, p.138) identified three important stages dating from the Revolution to the passage of the New Jersey general incorporation law of 1875:

> The individual states of the United States did not change their method of incorporation from special charters to general incorporation laws either suddenly or at the same time. These important changes, which took place throughout the nineteenth century, developed in three overlapping stages: first, the era of special charters; second, the dual system under which some companies incorporated under restrictive general incorporation laws while others continued to incorporate through special legislative acts; and third, interstate incorporation competition, which led to the adoption of liberal general incorporation laws.

Special charters were derived from the traditional English method of passing individual corporate charters through the state legislative process. Though there were some targeted instances of 'general' incorporation status granted by selected states previously, the dual system developed after passage of the first general incorporation act of wide coverage in the US—the New York Act of 1811.

The New York Act of 1811

The beginning of the end for the special charter in the US began with the passage of "An Act Relative to Incorporations for Manufacturing Purposes" (the New York Act of 1811) by the New York legislature, e.g. Haar (1941). This act "has long been recognized as a landmark in the history of the law of American business corporations and of public policy with respect to their use" (Howard 1938, p.499). The rules for incorporation under this statute stipulated that five or more persons, in compliance with rules of procedure set out in the statute, could form a corporate body to undertake designated industrial manufacturing ventures. Such corporations were permitted to endure for 20 years from the filing date. The passage of this act marks the beginning of the dual system of incorporation, in which restricted access to general incorporation was given to companies in targeted industries while all other companies still had to secure corporate status through special legislative acts. Significantly, special charters could confer rights not available under general incorporation. In contrast to the common-law practice in England, where legislative granting of corporate status conferred limited liability for shareholders after authorized capital had been fully paid, the New York Act of 1811 continued the practice of denying limited liability.

The Act of 1811 is significant in the history of US corporation law for the granting of general incorporation "permitting automatic self-incorporation if the incorporations followed a certain outlined procedure" (Haar 1941, p.192). The act was initially targeted at the manufacturing industry and was revised significantly in 1828 and 1848. The corporate powers granted under the Act of 1811 did not differ substantively from those conferred to the first manufacturing venture chartered by the New York legislature in 1790: "uninterrupted succession for a stated time; status before the courts with the right to sue and be sued; a common seal alterable at pleasure; the right to buy and sell estate, real or personal; the right to make by-laws and regulations; and, finally, the power to appoint officers and agents" (p.193). Livermore (1935, p.684) correctly recognized that "properly interpreted, this act did not at all usher in the movement of generalized incorporation laws. It was passed simply as a means of encouraging groups with small capital to enter general manufacturing." Prior to 1845, general incorporation laws of "widespread applicability" had been passed in only New York, New Jersey and Connecticut (Butler 1985, p.143).

In contrast to the English experience, American developments in the corporate organization of equity capital varied across states and time. To be sure, there is a close correspondence between the progress and organization of commercial ventures in England and America throughout the first half of the 19th century, the experience of the Baltimore & Ohio Railway being an excellent illustration of the interconnections.[10] However, the American experience was eventually propelled by interstate competition for the employment and tax revenue provided by incorporated companies. As the scope of economic activity in the US increased with the development of canals and the westward expansion of the railways, state economies gradually became integrated into a national economy. The corresponding increased size of commercial ventures, in both physical capital and equity capital, permitted a "flow of corporate privileges, and not just capital, across state lines" (p.143). As a consequence, despite the complexity created by the number of states with separate powers, there are discernible trends in the progress of incorporation across states during the 19th century.

During the initial period of special charters, few corporations were involved in interstate business. Legislatures considering the petition for charter were dealing with companies operating exclusively in that state. Political and social considerations of public versus private interests would be balanced against the 'lobbying, logrolling and bribery' invariably associated with any special interest legislation. Butler (p.139) described the general features of the legislative process surrounding special charters as follows:

> Although interested in using the corporate form to promote industrial independence from England, state governments in the first third of the nineteenth century were conservative in their initial granting of the corporate form to industrial and business organization. The result of these conflicting considerations was an interesting combination of relative generosity in granting special charters and a fairly restrictive policy with respect to their terms. The usual corporate privileges denied by these early charters were perpetual succession and limited liability.

The transition to general incorporation was, to some extent, to alleviate legislative pressure from an increasing number of special charter applications and the deterrent impact of the cost of obtaining a charter on small companies. The 1811 Act limited the capital to $100,000 and the duration of the charter to 20 years.[11] Subsequent legal decisions determined that section 7 of the act, dealing with shareholder liability, continued with a practice of assessing double liability "for all debts of the company at the time of its dissolution" (Howard 1938, p.500).

Limited and Unlimited Liability

Legal and political issues surrounding limited liability in England followed the passage of general registration legislation—the Joint Stock Company Act (1844). The unresolved issues in this act led Robert Slaney, chairman of the Commons Select Committee on the Law of Partnership, to propose a Royal Commission—the Mercantile Laws Commission (1854)—which led to an amendment to the Act of 1844—the Limited Liability Act (1855)—granting limited liability with general registration. Companies could elect to retain unlimited liability, a practice that continued in the banking industry until the collapse of the Glasgow Bank. It is significant that Slaney, "a persistent campaigner for . . . working-class enterprise" (Bryer 1997, p.40) and "a reformer with mild radical views" (Saville 1956, p.419), was on the side arguing for general limited liability. At the time, conventional working-class wisdom saw limited liability as a benefit to the wealthy. As a class, the wealthy saw the move to general registration and limited liability as encroachment on old corruption and the perpetuation of privileged status. In addition, there was the generally held perception that "there was no way of preventing fraud unless, 'the man with the money should be responsible for the character of the business'" (Bryer 1997, p.41).

In the US, the situation was different. In the early years of the republic, "the great majority of projects were launched without charters; they apparently did not regard unlimited liability as a serious business handicap" (Livermore 1935, p.676).[12] Corporations initially appeared in "spheres that were at first thought to involve relatively little risk. They emerged not in land speculation or in trade where failure was likely, but primarily in fields where success seemed almost certain. And the disappointed took for granted the assistance of generous governments which came to their aid with lotteries, grants of land, and increased tolls when profits slackened" (Handlin and Handlin 1945, p.16). The English common-law connection of corporate status and limited liability was less binding in America. The rules governing general corporate registration were initially unclear on the degree of legal liability. The allowable nominal capital and the duration of the charter were restricted. This gave legislatures considerable flexibility in constructing special charters with additional features, such as limited liability for directors and larger approved nominal capital.

Evidence on the number of special corporate charters and general incorporations reveals the complicated character of limited liability. In the New England states from 1863 to 1875, a period for which the best data is available and these states all had general incorporation laws, 4,575 companies were incorporated: 2,390 by special act and 2,185 by general law. About 69% of the total number of incorporations were in the mining and manufacturing sectors. "Thus it appears that the New England states, while showing greater proclivity to use their general incorporation laws than other states . . . maintained a functioning market for special charters" (Butler 1985, p.146). In Wisconsin, where access to general incorporation was constitutionally mandated, between 1848 and 1871 there were 143 corporations formed under the general incorporation law and 1,130 created under special acts. Such evidence illustrates the subtle impact of the different wording and legal interpretation that limited liability provisions could have.

While the judicial interpretation of shareholder liability arising from the initial New York Act of 1811 imposed double liability on shareholders (Howard 1938), the legislative treatment of liability limitation was 'experimental' (Haar 1941, p.206). The designation of the directors as "trustees" implied a legal responsibility beyond that required of shareholders. This 'trustee' language appeared in the Revised Statutes of 1828, which "provided the first true and complete limited liability" to shareholders (Haar 1941, p.196). The distinction between limited liability for shareholders and directors was a primary driver for the use of special charter and general incorporation during the period of dual routes to incorporation (Butler 1985, p.146):

> A major and perhaps the most important difference between the terms of general and special law charters related to the rules affecting the liability of the corporations' directors, who were concerned with their individual exposure to suit. Some of the general incorporation laws in dual-system states contained very strict rules for directors' liability. Almost all special corporate charters, on the other hand, were silent with respect to directors' liability, and the common law did not hold directors personally liable to creditors. Special charters thus enabled directors to avoid personal liability for their mistakes.

In many cases, judicial decisions ultimately were needed to supply answers to the assessment of liability: "none of the changes in law or interpretation had any discernible effect upon the rate of incorporation, a significant indication of the unimportance of limited liability in the minds of incorporators" (Handlin and Handlin 1945, p.17). In an odd twist, even though most states had general registration with limited liability, until 1929 all California corporations had pro rata unlimited liability (Weinstein 2003).

With the passage of the New Jersey general incorporation act of 1875, the era of interstate incorporation competition began in earnest. New Jersey was not the first state to impose an absolute prohibition on special charters for commercial ventures—that distinction falls to Louisiana, which adopted the prohibition in its 1845 constitution. By 1875, approximately half of the 37 states had made special acts of incorporation unconstitutional via the mechanism of constitutional assembly. Several others had a constitutional mandate for general registration while still permitting special charters under exceptional circumstances. Constitutional assemblies could impose absolute prohibitions on special charters, but the implementation of specific rules was left to legislators. Against this legislative backdrop, the growth of interstate commerce began to raise significant legal issues surrounding the legal existence of a 'foreign' corporation, operating outside the state of incorporation. "As late as the 1860s, the status of operating a corporation in a foreign jurisdiction was uncertain" (Butler 1985, p.155).

In 1869, the US Supreme Court made a key decision in *Paul vs. Virginia*. Though seemingly upholding a state's right to regulate commerce within the state, "the effect of the decision was that a state could exclude a foreign corporation from engaging in intrastate commerce . . . but, that a state could not exclude a foreign corporation from doing interstate business" (p.155). Prior to *Paul*, in order to avoid the uncertainties of foreign corporate status, corporations involved in interstate commerce would be obliged to obtain charters in the states in which business was conducted. State legislators would no longer be able to extract rents—such as taxes, license fees and bribes—from each corporation doing business in the state in order to obtain corporate status. New Jersey was the first state to enter this new interstate market for corporate charters by passing "the nation's first modern general incorporation law in 1875" (p.157). There were some legitimate legal reasons for New Jersey obtaining first mover status, including a motivated legislature and the ability to work by legislative constitutional amendment, instead of the more cumbersome constitutional assemblies.

The New Jersey Act of 1875, "when enacted, was the broadest and most enabling general law ever passed. The procedure for incorporating under the law was very simple—clearly the dominant ancestor of modern incorporation procedure" (p.157). A key feature of the act was that corporations could be created without having state residency of the incorporators or having the state being the primary location of the commercial venture. Following the 1875 Act, the granting of special charters was "drastically altered" in those states that still permitted special charters, and especially in New England, where the issue of special charters quickly disappeared. New Jersey became the preferred state for incorporation for the next 40 years. An amendment to the 1875 Act adopted in 1888 that permitted corporations to hold and dispose of the 'shares' (i.e., common stock) of other corporations laid the foundation for the 'trust organization'. The effect of the change was considerable. For example, in 1894 the bulk of the New Jersey state budget "was funded by fees and taxes on firms incorporated in New Jersey but primarily conducting business in New York" (p.162).

Ultimately, the 1888 amendment had unforeseen consequences that resulted in Delaware becoming the favoured state for incorporation. Being the preferred state for incorporation and also permitting trust structures resulted in New Jersey incorporated companies being involved in various anti-competitive commercial practices that, rightly or wrongly, attracted tremendous social resentment resulting in federal legislation such as the Sherman Anti-trust Act and the Clayton Anti-trust Act (1914). Acting within areas of state jurisdiction (p.163),

> Governor Woodrow Wilson of New Jersey engineered passage of the "Seven Sisters Acts"—antitrust measures that severely restricted the permissible corporate activities in New Jersey. Corporations flocked to Delaware, and the phase 'Delaware corporation' passed into the bloodstream of the English language. The "Seven Sisters Acts" were repealed in 1917, but New Jersey had lost its advantage . . . Today Delaware is undeniably the leader in the marketing of corporate privileges.

Delaware's success was not without a keen sense of opportunity by legislators in that state to conform Delaware's incorporation act of 1899 almost verbatim with the New Jersey Act, creating a secure legal environment for corporations to change states. However, legal failings arising from the 'rush to the bottom' in the provision of corporate privileges led the American Bar Association, starting in the 1940s, to draft a 'Model Business Corporation Act' and for others to call for a federal presence to ensure uniform standards of corporate conduct across states.

The French *Société en Commandite Simple*

Though modern equity capital markets are dominated by the limited liability corporation, there is still considerable scope for other legal forms of equity capital organization (e.g., Guinnane et al. 2007). Scattered among the equity claims in modern stock markets are shares in master limited partnerships and units in real estate investment trusts, entities that do not have the same legal structure as limited liability companies. Despite the availability of such alternative legal forms, the limited liability corporation is the organizational form of choice among the largest and most influential modern commercial ventures—measured in economic, financial, political and social terms. The rise of the limited liability corporation in the 19th century had three interrelated facets—incorporation, limited liability and autonomous shares. The limited partnership associated with the French *société en commandite simple* provided limited liability for 'silent partners' but retained partnership liability for those involved in running the commercial venture. Shares of silent partners could be traded, though the extent of this trading varied across time and location. The liability of managing partners would retain the feature of 'hands on' management valued by those opposed to the corporate form of equity capital organization.

The relevance of limited liability to equity capital organization is a subject of debate that survives to modern times. For example, Kessler (2003, p.513) observed:

> As Adolf Berle and Gardiner Means so influentially argued more than a half-century ago, investors seek limited liability in order to minimize investment risk, but precisely because they have minimal risk, they lack incentive to engage in hands-on management of the business. The result, claimed Berle and Means, is a separation of ownership and management.

This begs a fundamental question: Is it limited liability or corporate status that is the root cause of the separation of ownership from control? Halpern et al. (1980) and Halpern (1998) argued convincingly that limited liability makes exchange trading of shares possible. However, this observation does not imply that other, possibly superior, variations of limited liability would also 'make markets possible' (e.g., Easterbrook and Fischel 1985, p.92). Failure to make a distinction between the liability limitations of shareholder, manager and director haunts the Berle and Means claim that limited liability is a root cause for the separation of ownership and control. Interpreting the impact of limited liability is aided by considering the history of equity capital organization in France (and elsewhere in continental Europe); a history with roots in the medieval *commenda* that, again, reveals the influence of political and social norms on the legal organization of equity capital.

The organization of equity capital in France has three significant dates: (1) proclamation of the Royal Ordinance of March 1673 issued by Louis XIV, entitled *Pour le Commerce;* (2) promulgation of the Napoleonic *Code de Commerce* in 1807, which "follows the same general organization and incorporate verbatim much of the Edict of 1873" (Freedeman 1965, p.185); and (3) the granting of free incorporation in 1867. Braudel (1982) recognized that it was not the *societas maris* of maritime Genoa but, rather, the *compagnia* of the inland Italian family firms that provided the basis for the French Ordinance of 1673: "In the end, the large firms of the inland Italian cities were far more important individually than those of the seaports, where firms were numerous but mostly small and short-lived" (p.436). The *compagnia* (*cum panis* = with bread) was typically a family firm composed of father, sons, brothers and other relations where "everything was shared—bread and risks capital and labour". Such a joint liability venture was not well suited to raising capital from outside the family unit. The solution was the *société en commandite.*

The first recorded use of the limited partner arrangement was an *accomandita* from Florence in 1532. While similar to the *societas maris* and likely inspired by this arrangement, the *accomandita* had a permanent capital stock that was not returned at the end of a venture. "The limited partnership firm made its way through Europe, slowly replacing the family firm. It only really prospered to the extent that, by resolving new problems, it corresponded to the growing diversity of trade and to the increasingly frequent practice of long-distance partnership. It was also favoured by partners who wished their holding to be discreet" (p.438). During an era of religious and monarchial conflicts when the profits of colonization required capital from diverse quarters, both geographically and socially, the limited partnership was a useful addition to the other form of commercial *société* recognized by the 1673 Ordinance: the *société générale,* the traditional partnership arrangement, referred to as the *société en nom collectif* in the *Code* of 1807. It is significant that the right to form a joint-stock company with corporate privileges, a *société anonyme,* was reserved by the Crown. This right of the government was clarified in the 1807 *Code,* ostensibly to provide a joint-stock form of organization to attract 'large enterprises'.

Braudel provided an insightful description of the situation in France at the time of the Ordinance of 1673 (p.439):

> Since the 1673 ordinance (which made it compulsory for limited partnership agreements to be signed in front of a lawyer by the interested parties) only referred to 'partnerships between merchants and wholesalers', the current interpretation was that anyone 'not engaged in a mercantile profession' was not obliged to be listed among the partners on the agreement registered with the statutory authorities. In this way, noblemen could be protected from loss of rank and royal officials could avoid revealing that they had commercial interests. This undoubtedly explains the success of the

Table 8.8 French Commercial Sociétés Anonymes and Their Initial Nominal Capital by Type of Enterprise, 1819–1867 (thousands of francs)

Type of Enterprise	1819–30		1831–39		1840–48		1849–67		Total 1819–67	
	No.	Cap.	No.	Cap.	No.	Cap.	No.	Cap.	No.	Cap.
Insurance and Banking	17	143,400	30	71,186	47	73,800	94	758,300	188	1,046,686
Mining and Metallurgy	20	39,637	4	3,881	13	unknown	27	unknown	64	43,518 (1819–39)
Canals and Waterways	10	136,350	6	41,965(for 5)	1	1,500	2	unknown	19	179,815 (1819–48)
Railroads	3	21,000	9	205,250	19	1,156,500	30	671,050*	61	2,053,800*
Other Transportation	13	20,610	16	5,962	10	8,300	18	unknown	57	34,872 (1819–48)
Textiles	5	17,580	2	4,300	3	3,190	6	unknown	16	25,070 (1819–48)
Bridges	10	14,932	27	8,002 (for 21)	18	unknown	5	unknown	60	22,934 (1819–39)
Miscellaneous	29	46,326	23	12,063	28	15,907 (for 18)	54	256,053 (for 28)	134	339,329 (for 98)
Total (where known)	107	439,335	117	352,609	139	1,259,197	236	1,694,383	599	3,746,024

Source: Freedeman (1965, p.201)

* The capitalization for the railroad companies Ouest and the Paris, Lyon et la Méditerranée are excluded from these figures for they were formed by a consolidation of previously authorized roads.

commandite system in France, where those who were 'in trade' were still not readily admitted to high society, even during the business explosion of the eighteenth century. Paris was not London or Amsterdam.

The limited partnership did not originate with the Ordinance of 1673, which was primarily designed to address merchants' concerns about the lack of proper legal documentation for commercial dealing. "The institution of the *société en commandite*, clearly recognized and in a measure provided for by the Ordinance of 1673, was not, of course, created by it. For it was already an old, even if, on the legal side, a hitherto imperfectly developed form of collective business operation" (Howard 1932, p.246). The *Code* of 1807 was subject to a much different set of circumstances. The severely negative social memory of the Mississippi scheme collapse was compounded by the speculative boom in joint-stock 'company' shares preceding the Revolutionary end of the *ancien régime*. This resulted in a particularly negative attitude toward joint-stock companies, reflected in the *Code de commerce* of 1807, one of five major codes of the Napoleonic period.

It is not surprising that at the same time that the English were chartering canal companies and unincorporated 'joint stock companies' were seeking parliamentary approval (or not, in the case of fraudulent schemes), similar activity was happening in France. "Those joint-stock companies that existed during the seventeenth and eighteenth centuries in France were either chartered by the crown, or simply existed as unincorporated companies of shareholders" (Freedeman 1965, p.185). It was speculation in shares of the royal chartered companies that constituted the bulk of share trading preceding the collapse of the *ancien régime*. This history restrained the use of joint-stock companies in France in the 19th century until passage of the general incorporation law. While shares in *commandite* partnerships (*commandites par actions*) were traded on the Paris bourse prior to general incorporation: "The years following 1867 witnessed a large increase in the number of *anonymes* formed annually, while *commandites par actions* were little used after 1867" (p.198).

The New York Limited Partnership Act (1822)

The first half of the 19th century was not a gradual evolution toward general incorporation with limited liability. Many people strongly believed in the efficacy of partnerships in ensuring that commercial ventures were run in the most profitable fashion for shareholders. It is not surprising that in both England and America there were calls for the introduction of the limited partnership as a method of organizing equity capital that would provide the benefits of shareholder limited liability while retaining the incentives of partnership liability for management of the venture. Livermore (1935, p.685) described an important event in the American timeline, the passage of the Limited Partnership Act (1822) in New York, as follows:

> New York made an indirect attack upon the business value of corporate charters in 1822 by passing the Limited Partnership Act . . . From the practical legislative point of view, the act was favored by many out of

resentment at the clause in the Constitution of 1821 requiring that all charters must receive assenting votes from two-thirds of both houses. Obviously the opportunity to secure a limitation of future liability in a limited partnership, protecting the large contributors of capital to an enterprise, reduced sharply the incentive to secure a charter. This law of New York was not generally imitated in other states until after 1835.

The influence of the Napoleonic *Code* is reflected in substantial sections of the act being a translation of corresponding sections in the *Code*. By 1886, limited partnerships had been authorized in all but three states and territories.

Hilt and O'Banion (2009) provided a fascinating account of the limited partnership in New York City from 1822 to 1858. This is a period from which we have only scant information and, even though the results are skewed to the types of ventures found in a major financial center, there is valuable insight in the conclusions (p.642):

> Compared with ordinary partnerships, New York's limited partnerships had more capital; operated disproportionately in mercantile sectors, particularly in buying and selling dry goods; and failed at a lower rate, even conditional on the amount of capital they had. These were elite firms, formed by wealthy and successful merchants and given abundant resources to pursue lucrative business opportunities. The investors who provided capital to these firms often knew the general partners from previous connections in the business world, and were only rarely related to them. This was quite different from most ordinary partnerships, where the partners were often from within the same kinship network, and this difference is not simply due to selection. The special partners' own ordinary partnerships were much more likely to be formed on the basis of kinship ties. The limited partnership appears to have facilitated investments in the businesses of talented young merchants who wealthy investors knew through their business dealings. The superior performance of the limited partnerships, even conditional on the amount of capital they held, is an indication that these investments were indeed made with men chosen on the basis of their talent and potential.

Up to 1858, a total of 1,058 limited partnerships were formed in New York City. The use of limited partnerships did not disappear with the movement to general registration with limited liability. By the end of the 19th century, approximately 3,000 limited partnerships had been formed in New York City. It is significant that few of the limited partner ventures described by Hilt and O'Banion would have been substantially advantaged by the ability to trade shares. The relatively intimate character of the ventures would have made active share trading difficult. Most of those ventures desiring this feature could have accessed the New York general registration statutes.

In 1836 and 1837, both New Jersey and Pennsylvania introduced statutes permitting the formation of limited partnerships. There were two primary motivating factors behind this legislative action (Howard 1934, pp.298–9): (1) the desire to stimulate commerce and industry by allowing those with capital to combine with skilled workers lacking capital and, perhaps more importantly, (2) a "second motivating force was a fear of economic domination by business corporations— a fear which produced an inclination to experiment with other forms of joint-stock trading" (pp.298–9). Similar to other state limited liability statutes at this time, the limited liability for special partners came with strings attached. There were detailed registration requirements that had to be followed precisely or limited liability could be revoked. There were restrictions on the payment of dividends from capital, intended to prevent the wealthy partner from exiting the venture prematurely. In New Jersey, the limited partnership statutes underwent revision in a number of years until the passage of the Uniform Limited Partnership Act of 1919, which eliminated the bulk of restriction of limited partnership formation.

Similar to initiatives in America, various attempts were made to introduce limited partnerships in England. However, unlike Americans who desired to experiment with different forms of equity capital organization, the English were propelled along the path of general registration. The limited partnership appeared: in 1818, when an attempt to introduce the *société en commandite* failed in the Commons; in 1825, during the debates in Parliament surrounding Repeal and in the associated pamphlet literature; in 1836 and, to a lesser extent, in the early 1840s, surrounding the lead-up to the Joint-Stock Companies Act (1844). Following this act, "between 1844 and 1849 there was no discussion of *en commandite* in Parliament" and, with some exceptions, "comment outside was meagre" (Saville 1956, p.419). When the debate began again, it originated from an unusual quarter (p.419):

> The initial impetus in the early 1850s to the Parliamentary debates and the public discussion that led to the coming of general limited liability in 1856 came not from the side of the investors, nor from that of the entrepreneurs, nor from those who argued in terms of freedom of contract. The movers were a group of middle-class philanthropists, most of whom accepted the title of Christian Socialist. Their spokesman in Parliament, not formally a Christian Socialist himself, was Robert Aglionby Slaney, a reformer of mild radical views whose philanthropic interest in the working people had long been known.

Even if the advantages of general registration and limited liability were well suited to the desire of the City to trade shares, this was politically incidental when those seeking universal suffrage and other goals of social justice were vocally supporting general liability.

NOTES

1 Consider the title of a 1677 work by Robert Ferguson, '*The East-India Trade a most profitable trade to the Kingdom, and best secured and improved in a company, and a joint stock*'.

2   There is considerable evidence that Child plagiarized much of his work, either consigning the work to be written by someone else, presumably under his direction, or by direct copying. "It is hardly too much to say that the *Brief Observations* is merely a compendium of statements made by a series of authors whom Child followed more or less closely, but never with acknowledgment" (Letwin 1964, p.15).

3   Comparison of this quotation with the associated text from *The Anatomy of Exchange Alley* (p.139) reveals much similarity in the text, but 'Sir Josiah' has been changed to Sir F————, and a reference is made to: "The subject then was chiefly the East India stock". This and other attempts to update the text to 1719 would seem to bring into question the statement of Morgan and Thomas (1962, p.28) that *The Anatomy of Exchange Alley* was probably "by Defoe, published in 1719 but referring to the sixteen-nineties".

4   Smith was not the first to deal with the problems of the joint-stock form of ownership. For example, the problems of inefficient production associated with 'stock-jobbing management' were raised in parliamentary enquiries going back to at least 1696 (Morgan and Thomas, pp.22–3). Smith also referenced a number of earlier works on joint-stock companies, such as Abbe Morellet's *Examen de la Reponse de M. Necker* (1769) and, especially, Adam Anderson's *The Historical and Chronological Deduction of the Origin of Commerce* (1764).

5   Page references are to volume II of the Blaug 1963 edition of *Wealth of Nations* (1776).

6   Smith (1776) was not the originator of the notion of agency costs. Similar comments can be found in early writers, such as Houghton.

7   Arnold and McCartney (2008, p.1188) provided further background on the early evolution of the English canals: "The success of the Bridgewater Canal in turn encouraged the promoters of the Manchester Runcorn Canal to provide a better alternative to the existing Mersey and Irwell Navigation and, when it opened in 1767, the existing levies for carriage were halved. The new canals were not only used for freight; the Manchester Runcorn introduced passenger boats in the 1770s, charged rates that varied according to passenger class and but also offered refreshment facilities. Other more ambitious schemes followed, including the Trent and Mersey and the Leeds and Liverpool Canals, as heavy outlays of capital were seen to bring 'huge savings in manpower and horsepower' and to dramatically lower (by as much as two-thirds in some cases) the cost of transporting freight, particularly coal".

8   This description of the three categories of equity claim is not fully descriptive. For example, many established lines did not have 'fully paid' shares due to the ongoing construction of extension lines which involved further calls on capital following parliamentary approval of the petition for an extension line. Similarly, some established lines were operational and paying dividends even though the nominal capital was not fully paid, allowing the directors to draw on equity capital at a future date. Evidence on trading prices of shares invariably are derived from sources such as the *Railway Times* or the London stock exchange which only capture activity associated with trading for actual shares after an act had been obtained.

9   In some states, such as Pennsylvania, proponents of anti-charter doctrine resisted incorporation for both public and for-profit entities. Characteristic of early American debates around incorporation, anti-charter activists made little distinction between public and for-profit corporations: "opponents characterized business corporations, like incorporated cities, as aristocratic and so anti-republican because they gave privileges to the few at the cost of the many" (Maier 1993, p.66).

10 This fascinating connection between British and American technological development is described at http://cprr.org/Museum/First_US_Railroads_Gamst. html: "In 1826, Baltimore bankers Philip E. Thomas and George Brown sent Evan Thomas to England. Thomas transmitted back to his brother information on railroads. William Brown, a resident of Liverpool, sent to his Baltimore brother details of the proposed construction of the Liverpool & Manchester [L&M]. These data convinced the two bankers that a railroad could be operated between Baltimore and the Ohio River. On 12 February 1827, Baltimore businessmen held the first meeting to consider building a Baltimore & Ohio (B&O) railroad similar to those in Great Britain. On 22 October 1828 the line's engineers (Jonathan Knight, William G. McNeill, and George Washington Whistler) traveled to England to learn about its railroads. On 22 May 1829, the now-educated participant observers returned to Baltimore. And, from 6 through 14 October 1829, the line's George Brown and Ross Winans observed the Rainhill locomotive trials of the L&M and discussed rail technology with concerned persons. In October 1828, the B&O began construction, and it opened 16 miles of line to Ellicott Mills on 22 May 1830. The first vertical-boilered Grasshopper locomotive, uniquely American, entered service in September 1832. British designs of the Stephenson kind of locomotive soon displaced these home-grown engines. The B&O opened to Harpers Ferry on 1 December 1834. In the first years of operation, the line handled considerable freight and passenger traffic in horse-drawn rail cars. For the double-track line, the earliest rails were of wood or granite, topped by iron straps".

11 Howard (1938, p.500) correctly recognized that Livermore (1935) incorrectly gave the allowable amounts in the Act of 1811 as $50,000 and five years.

12 Livermore (1935) observed: "It is easy to understand that in enterprises largely experimental in character and backed by enthusiasts, attention would be centered on other desired features of group organization—concentration of power in a few hands, perpetuity of existence, and free transferability of shares". Such traditional views conflict with more recent interpretations by Halpern et al. (1980) that connect limited liability with the transferability of shares.

9   Stocks, Shares and the Science of Investments

> If an investor divides his capital equally among a number of stocks, every one of which is under a different trade influence, then each of these divisions of his capital will constitute a distinct investment risk, and a true system of arranging investment risks is thereby established.
>
> Henry Lowenfeld, *Investment, an Exact Science* (1909)

A   THE GLOBAL GROWTH OF EQUITY CAPITAL MARKETS

The Capitals of Capital

The growth in equity capital markets in the second half of the 19th century and the first three decades of the 20th century was more than dramatic (e.g., Cassis 2006, 2012; Preda 2005). By the end of the 19th century, there were globally important stock exchanges in the 'capitals of capital': London, New York, Paris and, to a lesser extent, Berlin. These centers were bolstered by networks of provincial exchanges and trade on lesser exchanges in Amsterdam, Zurich, Brussels, Frankfurt and other centers. In the period up to World War I, London held a dominant position as the global financial centre (Cassis 2012, p.17):

> The years between 1870 and 1914 were the classical period of London as the world's financial centre—not only in quantitative terms, but also in qualitative terms. The City was the first modern financial centre where an unrivaled range of services were provided. . . . London was the main centre for the issue of foreign loans, with Britain accounting for some 40 per cent of the stock of foreign investment in 1913. The London Stock Exchange was larger than the Paris Bourse and the New York Stock Exchange combined, and one third of all the world's negotiable instruments were quoted there. The City hosted major commodity markets, such as the London Metal Exchange and the Baltic Exchange; it was the world's leading insurance market, in particular with Lloyd's of London.

The transition from London to New York as the dominant global financial center accompanied the comparative growth of the British and American economies.

"While in the 1850s the industrial output of the US was far below that of England, by 1894, the value of American products almost equaled the value of the combined output of the United Kingdom, France and Germany. By the First World War, America produced more than one-third of the world's industrial goods" (Bricker and Chandar 2000, p.533).

Any precise comparison among the major equity capital markets at the end of the 19th century encounters "a statistical dark age", especially for the US (Hannah 2007, p.415). This complicates comparisons related to determining the time line for the separation of the equity capital ownership claim from operational control of the corporation. Following Berle and Means (1932), this is a topic that still attracts considerable scholarly attention. At issue in this line of research is the validity of the Berle and Means (1932, p.244) conclusion: "We have reached a condition in which the individual interest of the shareholder is definitely subservient to the will of a controlling group of managers even though the capital is made up of the aggregated contributions of perhaps many thousands of individuals". Chandler (1990) and others have argued that the transformation from "persistent personal capitalism" to "substantial divorce of ownership and control" (Hannah 2007, p.421) had occurred in the US by World War I. Hannah (2007), O'Sullivan (2007) and others dated the 'transformation' after World War I. Various recent studies questioned the empirical claim that there was *de facto* separation of ownership from control. Zeitland (1974, p.1107) argued that "the 'separation of ownership and control' may well be one of those rather critical, widely accepted pseudofacts with which all sciences occasionally have found themselves burdened and bedeviled". More recently, Holderness (2008) claimed, based on a 1995 random sample of NYSE and NASDAQ stocks, 'diffuse ownership' in the US was a "myth". Cheffins and Bank (2009) detailed the history of conflicting views surrounding the empirical evidence.

Regarding the comparative state of 'joint-stock corporations' circa 1900, Hannah (2007, p.647) observed: "Britain in 1900 had about 30,000 joint stock companies, probably as many as all the rest of Europe put together: Germany, for example, had only 5,400 *Aktiengesellschaftenn* in an economy with a larger population and roughly the same GDP as Britain's." Recognizing the difficulties of obtaining accurate data for the US at the time, Hannah (p.647) attempted a 'best guess estimate': "the federal censuses that all U.S. *manufacturing* corporations operated 40,743 establishments in 1899 and that there were 5,386 incorporated *mining* businesses in 1902. It is likely that the total number of U.S. incorporated enterprises for 1900, including the agricultural and service sectors, was somewhat in excess of 60,000". Based on these estimates, Hannah estimated that "about half—probably more than half—of the world's corporations in 1900 were in the US and nearly a quarter in the UK. The prodigious spread of incorporation in Britain and America was no doubt partly because these were wealthy and innovative countries." While "a majority in the United States, the United Kingdom, and Belgium were already employed by joint stock companies", Germany circa 1900 was "pre-eminently a land of personal proprietorships and partnerships, where *Handwerk* and small-scale traditional firms still out-distanced its 'modern' corporate enterprises".

Despite substantial disagreement about the degree of separation between the ownership claim of equity capital and operational control of a commercial venture in the US, there are some rather substantial points of agreement. Witzel (2006) described "the sheer growth of the American financial community" between 1880 and 1925, about which there is no disagreement, as follows:

> In 1880, Wall Street was like a village, a cozy little financial community in which relatively few Americans participated. Fewer than 100 companies were listed on the exchange, and total issued share capital might have been $300 million. Dealers, brokers and investors were likely to know each other personally in most cases. By 1925, less than half a century later, that figure of $300 million had grown by several orders of magnitude, to an estimated $70 trillion (US Department of Commerce figures). More than 1,000 companies were now listed on the New York Stock Exchange, and 14 million Americans were listed as shareholders.

O'Sullivan (2007) demonstrated effectively that "a broad-based stock market was a long way from being established" in the US until "the impetus provided by World War I, plus the enthusiasm of the 1920s". The explosion in the number of listed shares and trading volume on the NYSE, the Curb and the regional exchanges in the US between 1915 and 1930 is evident in comparison with the 1900 to 1915 period (see Tables). From an exchange that was dominated by railways stocks in 1895, between 1915 and 1930, the NYSE was transformed "into a trading market dominated by industrial and utilities stocks . . . by 1930, the number of industrial stocks on the NYSE had reached 1033 or 81% of the total" (O'Sullivan 2007, p.503). A similar, though less dramatic, change occurred on the Curb, which transited from trading mining stocks to industrial and oil stocks.

Table 9.1 Sectoral Breakdown of NYSE Stocks

	1885	1890	1895	1900	1905	1910	1915	1920	1925	1930
Total	151	264	263	296	341	331	420	670	774	1,273
Railroads	122	194	160	161	168	146	146	150	131	151
(%)	(81)	(73)	(61)	(54)	(49)	(44)	(35)	(22)	(17)	(12)
Utilities	5	15	26	32	34	34	34	11	38	89
(%)	(3)	(6)	(10)	(11)	(10)	(10)	(8)	(2)	(5)	(7)
Industrials	24	55	76	103	139	151	240	509	605	1,033
(%)	(16)	(21)	(29)	(35)	(41)	(46)	(57)	(76)	(78)	(81)
Coal & mining	11	20	19	18	22	30	36	44	29	25
(%)	(7)	(5)	(7)	(6)	(6)	(9)	(9)	(7)	(4)	(2)
Other	13	35	57	85	117	121	204	465	576	1,107
(%)	(9)	(16)	(22)	(29)	(35)	(37)	(48)	(69)	(74)	(79)

Source: O'Sullivan (2007, p.499)

Table 9.2   Aggregate Measures of the Size of the US Stock Market

Number of Traded Stocks	1900	1915	1930
New York Stock Exchange	296	420	1,273
New York Curb	n.a.	349	1,582
Leading NY Trading Markets	296[a]	820	2,855
(%)	(29)[a]	(52)	(65)
Regional Exchanges[b]	732	820	1,505
(%)	(71)	(48)	(35)
Total Traded Stocks[b]	1,028[a]	1,589	4,359
Less Overlaps in Trading			
NYSE—Regional	97	191	148
(%)	(9)	(12)	(3)
NY Curb—Regional	n.a.	32	361
(%)	n.a.	(2)	(8)
Regional—regional	15	14	13
(%)	(1)	(1)	(0)
Other	0	12	4
(%)	(0)	(1)	(0)
All Overlaps in Trading	112	249	526
(%)	(11)	(16)	(12)
No of Traded Stocks (excl. overlaps)	916	1,340	3,832
No of Traded Stocks (excl. Overlaps)/million population[c]	12.1	13.3	31.1
No of Companies with Traded Stocks (excl. overlaps)	682	970	2,659
No of Traded Stocks (excl. overlaps)/million population[c]	9.0	9.7	21.6

Trading Volume in Stocks (millions of shares)	1900	1915	1930
New York Stock Exchange	138	173	811
(%)	(88)	(67)	(70)
New York Curb	n.a.	63	222
(%)	n.a.	(24)	(19)
Leading NY Trading Markets	138[a]	236	1,033
(%)	(88)	(91)	(90)
Regional Exchanges[b]	18[d]	23[e]	118[e]
(%)	(12)	(9)	(10)
Total Share Trading Volume[f]	156	259	1,151
Total Share Trading Volume[f]/Million population	2.0	2.6	9.4

Source: O'Sullivan (2007, p.523)

[a] Excluding New York Curb.
[b] Totals excluding Los Angeles and San Francisco.
[c] Based on population figures: 76.1 million (1900); 100.5 million (1915); 123.1 million (1930).
[d] Includes Boston, Philadelphia, Chicago.
[e] Includes Boston, Philadelphia, Chicago, Baltimore, Cincinnati, Cleveland, Pittsburgh.
[f] Does not exclude trading in stocks traded on multiple trading markets.

Trusts, Pools and Corporations

In conjunction with the transformation of the American equity capital market from 1880 to 1930, there was a corresponding change in the structure of corporate governance (Witzel 2006):

> At the same time, and related to the growth [in equity capital markets from 1880 to 1930], the capital structure of business had also changed. In 1880, most business concerns were privately owned. By [1930], stockholder capitalism had become the norm, and many of American's largest corporations were publicly quoted and traded companies. With this change had come a raft of new regulations and, especially in the wake of the Standard Oil affair, a new attitude to corporate governance. Indeed, the concept of corporate governance might almost be said to have been invented during this period, and played a major role in the shaping of the new world of corporate finance, in terms of both regulation and financial structures and markets.

The substantive connection between this change in 'attitudes' to corporate governance following World War I and the organization of equity capital in the period between 1880 and 1914 has gone largely unexplored in recent scholarly efforts. More precisely, the emergence of the limited liability corporation with autonomous shares to organize equity capital led, in the US after 1880, to the emergence of trusts, pools and holding companies to create monopolies in various industries. The period from the formation of the Standard Oil Trust in 1882 to the passage of the Clayton Act in 1914 was punctuated by persistent federal and state actions to curb the use of equity capital ownership structure to secure monopoly control of supply in markets for commodities and industrial products. In addition to the Standard Oil Trust, which controlled 90%–95% of the oil refining capacity, trusts soon appeared in the areas of cotton oil (1884), linseed oil (1885), whisky distilling, cordage, lead and sugar refining (1887).

The roots of the 'trust structure' are found in the accumulation of shares during the 1870s owned by John D. Rockefeller and associates but held in the hands of proxies for the benefit of the Standard Oil Company. "In order to centralize more fully the control of these properties, it was decided in 1879 to organize the Standard Oil 'trust'" (Jones 1921, p.19). As a consequence, the Standard Oil Trust involved the creation of a formal 'agreement': "The 'trust' agreement as revised in January 1882, included about forty companies, controlling 90 to 95% of the refining capacity of the country. It provided for nine trustees." Included in the list of trustees were two Rockefellers. "The trustees received from each of the parties to the agreement an assignment of their stock with voting power, and in return therefor gave 'trust certificates' representing the valuation of the properties" (p.19). Four of the trustees held a majority of the trust certificates. Shares deposited with the trustees were held "for the joint account rather than for the individual account of certificate holders; a stockholder in any one company lost by the trust agreement his title to the stock of that particular company, and secured instead a proportionate interest in all the stocks and properties held by the trustees".

Having effective control of the majority of trust certificates, trustees were "able to elect the officers and directors of each of the constituent companies", resulting in managements that acted in concert. The actions of the sugar refining trust are revealing (pp.21–2):

> During the seventies and eighties competition in the sugar refining industry had been quite keen; between 1867 and 1887 some thirty-six refineries had been closed. By 1887 there were left only twenty-six refineries, operated by twenty-three companies. The concerns that survived this period of severe competition were those that resorted to large-scale production, with its resulting economies. In August 1887, seventeen of these companies, owning twenty refiners, and possessing among them approximately 78% of the refining capacity, entered into a trust agreement.

The outcome of the trust was that of 20 refineries controlled by the trust, 12 were closed down and the remaining 8 were consolidated into 4. While such actions of plant 'consolidation' seem commonplace today, the late 19th-century American political and social context was decidedly different (p.23):

> numerous laws forbidding combinations and trusts [were] enacted by the state legislatures from 1889 to 1893, and by the passage by the National Congress in 1890 of the Sherman Anti-trust Act, which prohibited every contract, combination in the form of trust or otherwise, or conspiracy, in restraint of trade or commerce among the several states, or with foreign nations, and every monopoly or attempt to monopolize.

Being a contract, a trust agreement was explicitly voided by these legislative actions. Given the long common-law tradition voiding contracts in restraint of trade, the need for such legislation reflects the legal complications posed by the newly emerging limited liability corporation with autonomous shares.

Laws prohibiting combinations in restraint of trade did not prohibit combinations that were not anti-competitive, such as the US Steel Corporation and the American Tobacco Company, or, following passage of the General Corporation Act of New Jersey in 1899, the creation of non-operating 'holding companies' that held common stock in constituent companies. Nonetheless, companies still pursued other methods to 'restrain trade', such as the use of 'pools' (pp.6–7):

> The term pool . . . is a catch-all for the various agreements and associations whereby a number of concerns, each preserving its own organization and to a large degree its own independence, adopted provisions looking toward the maintenance or raising of the prices of the articles produced by them— the power to fix prices may or may not have been conferred on a governing body—or looking toward depression of the prices of the materials and supplies required by them.

As such, pools were also illegal restraints of trade, but the absence of a formal agreement made 'pool' acts more difficult to discern. Pools could be structured using a gentlemen's agreement or by other secret arrangements. In any event, the widespread use of trusts, pools, holding companies and the like are strong anecdotal evidence for a lack of separation between *de facto* equity capital owners and operational control involving pools, trusts, consolidation and the like.

Reminiscences of the US Stock Operators

Almost from the beginning of equity capital share trading in the US, it is evident from some articles in the financial press that the practice of share valuation was more than rudimentary. This is not that surprising when it is recognized that valuation practices in the US were transplanted from European centers, such as London, Paris and Amsterdam, where there was more than a century of development in equity securities trading. With this in mind, it is not easy to pick a starting point for the relevant American contributions from the trade and financial press. In general, the published contributions chronologically increase in depth and understanding of valuation issues, roughly consistent with the growth of New York as the world's financial capital. As late as the 1820s, Philadelphia had as strong a claim as New York to be the nation's financial capital. In the period before the Civil War, London was still, by far, the world's dominant securities market. Even with the sizeable influx of funding issues associated with the Civil War, around 1866 London still had a market cap of around $10 billion, compared to $3 billion for New York (Gordon 1999, p.123).

Despite the availability of expertise in the industry, before Graham and Dodd's *Security Analysis* (1934) there was no widely cited American source which systematically developed the techniques of the fundamental approach to equity security valuation. Armstrong (1848) was strongly of the opinion that stocks are gambling transactions conducted in a trading environment characterized by corners, bubbles and "fancy stock manoeuvres". Biographical and autobiographical accounts of those involved in the industry, such as Henry Clews' *Fifty Years in Wall Street* (1908) and Edwin Lefèvre's *Reminiscences of a Stock Operator* (1923), present a similar picture. This does not mean that the methods of equity security analysis were inadequate compared with those used today. Rather, the studies were strongly influenced by the institutional and cultural milieu of the times. Insightful accounts of strikingly modern equity valuation methods, such as Hartley Withers' *Stocks and Shares* (1910), required a cultural maturation that permitted shares in limited liability corporations to be seen as a socially acceptable means of financial improvement.

From the beginning of trading in joint-stock shares, a range of trade publications have covered the securities industry in general and share valuation in particular. In the US, the *Commercial and Financial Chronicle* was a key source until it was superseded by the *Wall Street Journal* (first published in 1884).[1] The business section of the major newspapers, such as the *New York Times* in the US and the *London Times* in England, also were important sources of information useful for share valuation. As daily or weekly publications, these sources did not usually offer much beyond a focus on current events until the turn of the century. By the 1920s, it was common for the financial press reporting on equity securities to feature indexes, volume statistics and the like. Though the discussion often involved valuation aspects of specific stock issues, there was no scope to present a reasoned development based on accurate and detailed accounting statements. Much like business reporters today, financial reporters would gather information from those involved in the trade who were knowledgeable about the topic of interest.

In examining the stories and accounts of market participants, it is possible to go back as far as, say, 1792, when 21 individual brokers and three firms signed the Buttonwood Agreement "not to buy or sell from this day for any person whatsoever any kind of Public Stock, at a rate less than one quarter per cent Commission on the specie value, and that we will give preference to each other in our negotiations" (Eames 1894, p.14). This arrangement eventually evolved into the New York Stock and Exchange Board, formed in 1817 (p.18). In 1863, the Regular Board of the New York Stock and Exchange Board changed its name to the New York Stock Exchange (NYSE). The NYSE emerged as the dominant exchange for trading stocks in New York with its merger with the Open Board of Brokers in 1869 (Gordon 1999, pp.95,124–5). The Open Board was a relative newcomer that flourished in the face of the flood of issues arising from the Civil War.

Until the emergence of a dominant exchange, stock trading in New York was scattered across venues. For example, in 1856, shares of 360 railroad companies, 985 banks and 75 insurance companies, in addition to hundreds of corporate, municipal, state and federal bonds and other types of shares, were being traded in New York (p.87). Most of these were not traded on the New York Stock and Exchange Board, the precursor of the NYSE, as the Board did not trade new and untested issues. These issues were curb traded. The primary venue for curb trading was various lamp posts in the Wall Street area, where brokers who were not Board members, as well as some Board members, would meet to trade securities. Even though the volume of curb trading was usually higher than trading on the Board, the market cap of curb issues was lower. In contrast to curb trading, the Board's activities were conducted at daily auctions held in fixed quarters.

The tales of American stock operators predate the Buttonwood Agreement. Notoriety was, and still is, the result of doing something on a grand scale, often in conjunction with a massive bull market speculation, an immense market manipulation or the creation of a colossal conglomerate. An early example is William Duer, who in the early 1790s was at the center of a speculative scheme to inflate the value of bank stocks, particularly the Bank of New York (pp.40–5). The scheme was based on leveraged speculation and trading on insider information. At the height of the speculative frenzy, a number of banks were incorporated that, ultimately, did not open. As such, these stocks represent an early American instance of bull market 'paper hanging'. The collapse of the scheme bankrupted many of the players, including Duer. The scheme prompted Alexander Hamilton to write: "'Tis time there should be a line of separation between honest Men and knaves, between respectable Stockholders and dealers in the funds, and mere unprincipled Gamblers". This seeking of the line of separation is a task that has occupied regulators up to the present day.

The formation of the New York Stock and Exchange Board in 1817 also marked the beginning of the Wall Street career of Jacob Little, the first of a long line of big-time Wall Street speculative operators (pp.59–62, 89–90). Unlike Duer, who only used Wall Street as a trading venue, Little made a career on Wall Street. Though Little was also a broker, gaining membership to the Board in 1825, it was his activities as a speculator that made his reputation. Little's trading strategies were typically short-term, aimed at anticipating market movements. During his career, Little made and lost four fortunes in speculative trading activities. In the end, he was unable to recover from his last insolvency brought on by the market panic of 1857. From that time, until his death a few years later, Little ended his Wall Street career as a trader of penny stocks and odd lots.

Though Little was primarily a short seller, he made his first fortune in a 1834 short squeeze involving the Morris Canal and Banking Company. The objective of a short squeeze in a stock issue is to gain control of the quantity of that stock available for trading (the 'float' or 'floating supply') at a time when a sizeable amount of stock has been sold short by traders who do not have a sufficient amount of stock to deliver. As was the case in the squeeze on Morris Canal and Banking, the capital requirements for gaining control of the stock for delivery usually involves a group or pool of speculators operating in concert. When the time comes for the short to make delivery of the stock, the short has to enter the market to buy—but there is no supply available because the short squeezers have already gained control. The result is a rapid rise in stock prices as short sellers bid up prices to tempt new supply onto the market (either from accounts of long-term investors or from the short squeezers). At Little's time, most short sellers were brokers who had sold stock they did not own to investors, speculators or other brokers. The short position was sometimes the outcome of longer settlement periods than in modern times. In other cases, the objective of both parties was to engage in speculative forward trading, resulting in delivery dates on the short that could be many months in the future.

Prior to the wide-reaching regulatory reforms of 1933 and 1934, stock market self-regulation was an important theme of government policy toward the securities market. Yet, self-regulation suffered from the conflicting interests of the legitimate brokers, who recognized the negative impact associated with widespread unscrupulous trading activities, and the big-time speculators, who saw the market as a conduit for achieving big profits from a range of trading schemes—many of which, such as trading on insider information or in bucket shops or the formation of pools to engage in trading activities aimed at creating price movements favorable to speculation on stock price changes—are illegal in modern markets. The process of reform using self-regulation was slow and problematic. It was not until November 1868, just prior to the merger of the Open Board and the New York Stock and Exchange Board, that registration of securities and 30 days' notice of new issues were required of companies listed on the two Boards.

The imposition of the listing requirement had an immediate impact on the activities of the big-time speculators Daniel Drew, Jay Gould and James Fisk involving the Erie Railway. The 1864–1869 manipulations associated with the securities of the Erie are almost epic, reflecting the state of securities markets of that time. On one side of the struggle was 'Commodore' Cornelius Vanderbilt, a giant in the transportation industry, who wanted to control the Erie in order to be able to control the pricing of railway freight rates into and out of New York City. On the other side was a group including Drew, Gould, Fisk and other big-time speculators who were seeking to control the Erie as a vehicle for making speculative gains through manipulation of the company's security issues. The machinations of the two camps has been captured in some of the early classics of business finance—for example, Adams and Adams' *Chapters of Erie* (1871) and Henry Clews' *Fifty Years on Wall Street* (1908). The struggle between these two groups is the epitome of the problems that prevailed in securities markets of that time (e.g., Medbery 1870, ch.9; Gordon 1999, ch.6).

Vanderbilt was concerned with securities markets only as a vehicle for creating and managing a business empire, primarily involving railways. As part of the ongoing process of expanding this empire, Vanderbilt moved to acquire a controlling position on the Erie board of directors during the late summer and early fall of 1867. Vanderbilt had been involved with the Erie as recently as 1865, when he resigned from the board over concerns about the evident manipulations in the stock that took place during 1864 and 1865. A major player in these manipulations was Daniel Drew, also a board member who, conveniently, served as treasurer. In his position as treasurer, Drew was able to issue securities, and in 1866 he had done so by loaning the company $3.5 million in exchange for 28,000 unissued shares and $3 million in convertible bonds that had the provision that the 30,000 shares obtained from conversion could be reconverted back into convertible bonds. This provided Drew with the ability to expand and then contract about 10% of the outstanding stock—providing effective control of the floating supply.

When Vanderbilt was unsuccessful in using his influence to control the Erie board of directors, starting in January 1868 he moved to gain control of the company by purchasing as much of the outstanding stock as could be obtained. The speculators saw this as an opportunity to issue more convertible bonds, which became a conduit to print stock certificates that were then sold to Vanderbilt. From late February to mid-March, Drew and his group were able to sell 100,000 newly issued shares. The absence of registration and listing requirements prevented the New York Stock and Exchange Board from knowing what was happening. All this was set against a backdrop of corrupt judges issuing injunctions and arrest warrants and legislators being bribed to pass laws favorable to one or the other of these groups. On 19 April Vanderbilt was able to strike a deal with Drew, Gould and Fisk and recoup his potential losses from his stock dealing. Following this, Gould and Fisk continued to manipulate Erie stock issues, until the listing and registration requirements were introduced by the two Boards. Gould attempted to resist the requirements, even trying to establish a new exchange for the purposes of trading Erie stock. In September 1869, Gould capitulated and agreed to the new regulations. At that time, it was revealed that the number of Erie shares outstanding was around 700,000, about double the 351,000 shares outstanding at the time of the Vanderbilt agreement of April 1868.

The Formation of the Trusts

To modern observers, events surrounding the Erie have the appearance of a classical farce. A business titan attempting to control a railway company in order to implement a pricing cartel enters battle with a group of big-time speculators seeking to use the company as a vehicle for generating profits from stock price manipulation. Drew, Gould and Fisk are usually lumped in with Andrew Carnegie, J.D. Rockefeller and Commodore Vanderbilt as the 'Robber Barons' who dominated American industry through their financial dealings from 1870 to 1890 (e.g., Geisst 1997, ch.3), which took place against a backdrop of increasing concentration of economic power in the hands of trusts such as American Telephone and Telegraph, General Electric, Standard Oil and the American Tobacco Company. During the 1890s, there were about 50 trusts operating throughout the US, involving most of the major industries. This number includes some agricultural trusts concentrated primarily in the South. The trusts were formed largely as a way of circumventing laws that, up to around 1900, prevented corporations from holding stock in other corporations.

Prior to the changes in state corporation law that started with New Jersey during the 1890s, the ability of a corporation to act as a holding company was quite limited. Trusts provided a way around these restrictions. In a trust, the companies to be merged or taken over would exchange the common shares in the original corporations for trust certificates that possessed a claim to earnings of the trust as well as voting rights to elect the trustees. Standard Oil, for example, had nine trustees. Trust certificates were traded like common stocks on the stock exchanges. Trusts were a useful legal mechanism for the emerging industrialists' takeover ambitions. Instead of a company diluting the ownership claim by having to issue new shares to raise new capital for a takeover, trusts could pay for the takeover using trust certificates or internal sources of funds.

Due to changes in state corporation laws, trusts had a relatively short life span. The legal status of trusts did not prevent various states from initiating legal actions on other grounds, such as the common-law restrictions on monopoly, aimed at preventing the increasing monopolization of specific industries. In addition, the public perception of economic and social problems posed by the trusts was addressed in 1890 with the passage of the Sherman Anti-Trust Act. Though this act did not result in many successful prosecutions, it did provide a federal definition and jurisdiction for what constituted a monopoly. The trusts gradually reorganized as holding companies, and trust certificates were replaced by common shares. Standard Oil, for example, completed the shift in 1899. Whether it was trading in trust certificates or common shares, the changes in American industrial structure were good for Wall Street. The importance of trading in shares of these industrial companies gradually came to surpass the railroads. The volume and value of trade on the NYSE doubled between 1875 and 1885.

Yet, despite the growth, the securities markets of that era justly deserved their public perception as a speculator's haven. Henry Clews (1908, p.19), a veteran broker and investment advisor, provided an informed view of "How to Make Money on Wall Street":

To the question often put, especially by men outside of Wall Street, "How can I make money in Wall Street?" there is probably no better answer than the one given by old Meyer Rothschild to a person who asked him a similar question. He said, "I buys 'sheep' and sells 'dear'".

Those who follow this method always succeed. There has hardly been a year within my recollection, going back nearly thirty years, when there has not been two or three squalls in "the Street", during the year, when it was possible to purchase stocks below their intrinsic value. The squall usually passes over in a few days, and then the lucky buyers of stocks at panic prices come in for their profits ranging from five to ten per cent on the entire venture.

The question of making money then becomes a mere matter of calculation, depending on the number of squalls that may occur during any particular year.

If the venture is made at the right time—at the lucky moment so to speak—and each successive venture is fortunate, as happens often to those who use their judgment in the best way, it is possible to realize a net gain of fifty per cent. per annum on the aggregate of the year's investments.

Coming from an individual so intimately connected to the dealings of 'the Street', it is difficult to deny the essential role played by speculation in US securities markets of the time. Given the numerous abuses associated with common stocks, the disposition of the small investor to favor bonds over stocks during this period is understandable.

Many of the systemic problems raised by the predominance of speculators in securities markets persisted until the regulatory reforms following the Great Depression. The introduction of legislation such as the Securities Act (1933) involved a radical realignment of the federal government's role in securities markets. The collapse of securities markets from late 1929 to early 1933 was sufficient to end the period of self-regulation that had largely governed securities trading up to that time. Yet, the period of self-regulation was not without contributions. Many of the tools needed to lay the foundation that Graham and Dodd used to launch security analysis had evolved without government intervention. The growth of securities markets witnessed the emergence of professionals who made their living in the market and had a vested interest in making sure the game was played, if not always fairly, at least according to accepted rules. For example, the listing and registration requirements imposed by the newly formed NYSE were a direct assault on Jay Gould's manipulations of Erie Railroad Company securities.

B   THE SCIENCE OF INVESTMENTS

Origins of Equity Indexing

The distinction between "vernacular" and "academic" analysis has been introduced by intellectual historians and sociologists studying the popularization of investments in stocks and shares during the 19th century (e.g., Preda 2006, p.150).[2] Vernacular analysis aimed at 'real time' financial decision making and typically is anecdotal, imprecise and uses simple language. It is "a heterogenous set of practices, know-how techniques and rationalization procedures". In contrast, academic analysis is "a body of homogenous, abstract, formalized explanations" aimed at the community of academics staking claim to the subject area. It is theoretical, precise and involves formal language. Such a distinction continues to the present, with modern finance being the dominant school of academic analysis, while trade publications, market commentary, newsletters and the like, associated with the old finance 'Wall Street approach', dominate the vernacular realm. The origin and development of equity indexing lie at the intersection of the academic and vernacular approaches.

While advice manuals and financial periodicals have a much longer history, the dramatic expansion of joint-stock issue supply in the first half of the 19th century initiated a demand for information about equity securities from the general public. Especially after 1840, this expansion was associated with railway companies, which often required substantially more capital than could be financed locally. This coincided with an increasing international integration of European and American markets for stocks and shares in the second half of the 19th century and until the beginning of World War I. This transformation resulted in widespread use of internationally diversified portfolios, particularly in the UK (Rutterford 2006).[3] In order to attract middle-class investors, the social and moral perception of investment in shares had to be transformed from one of 'evil gambling' to 'social good' based on rational and scientific principles. The result was a vernacular 'science of financial investments' that has, ever since, had a complicated relationship with the development of the academic 'science of financial investments' (e.g., Jovanovic 2006).

Considerable confusion has been created by a failure to identify the connection between vernacular and academic approaches to the equity valuation aspect of the science of financial investment. Similar confusions can found in almost all areas where scientific ideas are needed—for example, medical research, nuclear energy and climate change. A range of questions can be identified. Are vernacular and academic approaches basically the same, differing mainly in level of rigor? Or, are vernacular and academic approaches "incommensurable" (Preda 2006, pp.150–1), with aims and principles that are only marginally similar? Do vernacular approaches produce rationalizations for financial investment decisions that influence academic theories? To what extent do vernacular theories set the framework with which the general public interprets the results of academic contributions? In the context of equity security valuation in general and the use of equity indexes in particular, answering such questions is made more difficult by the mixing of actors from the vernacular and academic realms.

The trade publications *Banker's Magazine* in the UK and the Dow, Jones and Co. *Customer's Afternoon Letter* introduced equity indexes in 1884 (Hautcoeur and Petit-Konczyk 2006). In some ways, it is not surprising that equity indexes first appeared in the vernacular realm. Instead of using the stock index to determine the direction of the stock market, academics were more concerned with the stock index as a predictor of business conditions (e.g., Mitchell 1910, 1916; Copeland 1915; Frickey 1921). The need for reasonable sample sizes, appropriate estimators and careful empirical analysis prevented an earlier examination of the subject. The divergence in usage is reflected in the following academic criticism of the Dow Industrial index by Copeland (1915, pp.532–3):

> The stock market index of the Wall Street Journal has been more commonly used for showing movements of security prices; but amongst the twelve industrials which it formerly included there was one quotation for United States Steel preferred, one for United States Steel common, one for United States Rubber preferred, and one for United States Rubber common. The weight thus given to steel and especially to rubber seems to have been unwarranted.

The computational problems of generating an average value for 24,000 price quotations covering 40 NYSE stocks over a 26-year period was "bewildering" (Mitchell 1916, p.655) for academics but posed little difficulty for the less precise Dow indices generated by the vernacular approach.

For various reasons, prior to World War I most of the literature on equity security analysis was written using the vernacular approach. Contributions from those in the trade and the financial press, such as Henry Clews (1908), Alexander Noyes (Klein 2001), Edwin Lefèvre (1923) and Hartley Withers (1910), were typical, though contributions with a more academic flavor were beginning to appear (e.g., Lowenfeld 1909; Babson 1910 a,b, 1911). Works written by academics, designed primarily to appeal to other academics, appeared in strength following World War I. Included in this grouping are contributions by Irving Fisher, Alfred Marshall, Edgar L. Smith, John Maynard Keynes and John Burr Williams.[4] Even though some members of the academic grouping, such as Irving Fisher and J.M. Keynes, did make some contributions that could easily be included in the second grouping, there is generally a different flavor to the contributions of the vernacular and academic groupings.

Charles Dow and the Dow Indexes

A key historical initiative in the popular science of financial investments involved increasing the availability of accurate information to the individual investor. Similar to the telecommunications and computer-driven technological revolution that has transformed modern equity securities markets, the 19th century witnessed the development of first the telegraph, then the ticker tape and finally the telephone. The securities industry was at the forefront in implementing these new technologies. It was during the 1890s that the NYSE required listed companies to produce annual reports. Though, even with this change, many of the annual reports did not have much substance by modern standards, the rise of the professional investment advisor necessitated that some useful information be made available. Though much of the trade literature was largely concerned with pontificating on the good or evil of speculation, or glorifying the deeds of the big-time speculators, or documenting use of the securities market to propel the rise of a business titan, the 'green shoots' of an emerging 'science of financial investments' were apparent by the turn of the century.

Figure 9.1   Charles Dow (1851–1902), American journalist

The financial press spearheaded a number of important innovations. Of particular importance is the introduction of price indexes to measure the performance of the aggregate stock market. Charles Dow (1851–1902) is often credited as the father of the modern stock market index. Dow is also important for having, together with Edward Jones and Charles Bergstresser, founded Dow Jones & Co., the company that created the *Wall Street Journal*. Charles Dow is a caricature of the changes that were taking place in the US securities markets of the late 19th century. Dow was a lifelong newspaper journalist who started covering financial news in 1879. Dow was able to achieve success in financial reporting by feeding the growing need for information to do security analysis. In 1880, Dow moved to New York, where he started with a stint reporting on mining stocks. In 1882, he joined with Edward Jones, a fellow reporter, to form Dow Jones & Company. With offices behind a soda shop next to the entrance of the NYSE, the company's main activity was to collect and distribute 'flimsies' or 'slips' containing market news of the day. It was in this 'Customers Afternoon Newsletter' that on 3 July 1884 the first version of the index appeared. The

Table 9.3 Components of the Dow Jones Industrial Average 17 July 2009, with additions to 11 September 2015

COMPANY NAME	PRIMARY EXCHANGE	TICKER	ICB SUBSECTOR	WEIGHT PCT	USD CLOSE
3M Co.	New York SE	MMM	Diversified Industrials	5.438202247	62.92
°Alcoa Inc.	New York SE	AA	Aluminum	0.883318928	10.22
American Express Co.	New York SE	AXP	Consumer Finance	2.422644771	28.03
°AT&T Inc.	New York SE	T	Fixed Line Telecommunications	2.072601556	23.98
°Bank of America Corp.	New York SE	BAC	Banks	1.114088159	12.89
Boeing Co.	New York SE	BA	Aerospace	3.574762316	41.36
Caterpillar Inc.	New York SE	CAT	Commercial Vehicles & Trucks	2.937770095	33.99
Chevron Corp.	New York SE	CVX	Integrated Oil & Gas	5.628349179	65.12
Cisco Systems Inc.	NASDAQ NMS	CSCO	Telecommunications Equipment	1.772687986	20.51
Coca-Cola Co.	New York SE	KO	Soft Drinks	4.349178911	50.32
E.I. DuPont & Co.	New York SE	DD	Commodity Chemicals	2.382886776	27.57
Exxon Mobil Corp.	New York SE	XOM	Integrated Oil & Gas Broad	5.922212619	68.52
General Electric Co.	New York SE	GE	Diversified Industrials	1.006914434	11.65
°Hewlett-Packard Co.	New York SE	HPQ	Computer Hardware	3.455488332	39.98
Home Depot Inc.	New York SE	HD	Home Improvement Retailers	2.132238548	24.67
Intel Corp.	NASDAQ NMS	INTC	Semiconductors	1.624027658	18.79
Interntl. Bus. Machines	New York SE	IBM	Computer Services	9.975799481	115.42
Johnson & Johnson	New York SE	JNJ	Pharmaceuticals	5.119273984	59.23
JPMorgan Chase & Co.	New York SE	JPM	Banks	3.188418323	36.89
°Kraft Foods Inc. Cl A	New York SE	KFT	Food Products	2.370786517	27.43
McDonald's Corp.	New York SE	MCD	Restaurants & Bars	4.999135696	57.84

(Continued)

Table 9.3 (Continued)

COMPANY NAME	PRIMARY EXCHANGE	TICKER	ICB SUBSECTOR	WEIGHT PCT	USD CLOSE
Merck & Co. Inc.	New York SE	MRK	Pharmaceuticals	2.392394123	27.68
Microsoft Corp.	NASDAQ NMS	MSFT	Software	2.099394987	24.29
Pfizer Inc.	New York SE	PFE	Pharmaceuticals	1.292999136	14.96
Procter & Gamble Co.	New York SE	PG	Nondurable Household Products	4.833189283	55.92
Travelers Cos. Inc.	New York SE	TRV	Property & Casualty Insurance	3.493517718	40.42
United Technologies Co.	New York SE	UTX	Aerospace	4.649956785	53.8
Verizon Comm. Inc.	New York SE	VZ	Fixed Line Telecommunications	2.557476232	29.59
Wal-Mart Stores Inc.	New York SE	WMT	Broadline Retailers	4.191011236	48.49
Walt Disney Co.	New York SE	DIS	Broadcasting & Entertainment	2.11840968	24.51

* Indicates removal from DJIA since 17 July 2009

Additions as of 11
Sept. 2015:

Apple	AAPL	NASDAQ
Visa	V	NYSE
Nike	NKE	NYSE
United Health	UNH	NYSE
Goldman Sachs	GS	NYSE

Table 9.4 Dow-Jones Industrial Average, Component History, selected years, 1896–2003

1896	1916	1928	1997	2003
American Cotton Oil	American Beet Sugar	Allied Chemical	Allied-Signal	Alcoa
American Sugar	American Can	American Can	Alcoa	Altria (Philip Morris)
American Tobacco	American Car & Foundry	American Smelting	American Express	American Express
Chicago Gas	American Locomotive	American Sugar	American Tel & Tel	American Tel & Tel
Distilling & Cattle Feeding	American Smelting	American Tobacco	Boeing	Boeing
General Electric	American Sugar	Atlantic Refining	Caterpillar	Caterpillar
Laclede Gas	American Tel & Tel	Bethlehem Steel	Chevron	Citigroup
National Lead	Anaconda Copper	Chrysler	Coca-Cola	Coca-Cola
North American	Baldwin Locomotive	General Electric	DuPont	DuPont
Tennessee Coal and Iron	Central Leather	General Motors	Eastman Kodak	Eastman Kodak
US Leather pfd.	General Electric	General Railway Sig.	Exxon	Exxon
US Rubber	Goodrich	Goodrich	General Electric	General Electric
	Republic Iron & Steel	International Harvester	General Motors	General Motors
	Studebaker	International Nickel	Goodyear	3M Co.
	Texas Co.	Mack Trucks	Hewlett-Packard	Hewlett-Packard
	US Rubber	Nash Motors	IBM	Home Depot
	US Steel	North American	International Paper	Honeywell
	Utah Copper	Paramount Publix	JP Morgan	IBM
	Westinghouse	Postum, Inc.	Johnson & Johnson	Intel
		Radio Corp.	McDonald's	International Paper
		Sears. Roebuck	Merck	Johnson & Johnson
		Standard Oil (NJ)	Minn. Mining	JP Morgan Chase

(*Continued*)

Table 9.2 (Continued)

1896	1916	1928	1997	2003
		Texas Corp.	Philip Morris	McDonald's
		Texas Gulf Sulphur	Procter & Gamble	Merck
		Union Carbide	Sears Roebuck	Microsoft
		US Steel	Travelers Group	Procter & Gamble
		Victor Talking Machine	Union Carbide	SBC Communications
		Westinghouse Electric	United Technologies	United Technologies
		Woolworth	Wal-Mart	Wal-Mart

price-weighted average was calculated by summing the prices of the stocks in the index and dividing by the number of stocks.

According to Siegel (1998, p.55), Dow began publishing a daily index of actively traded, high capitalization stock starting in February 1885. The original index contained 10 railways and 2 industrials. This collection was roughly consistent with the importance that railway stocks played in the stock market. Dow expanded the index four years later to cover 18 railways and 2 industrials. The same year, Dow Jones & Co. started the *Wall Street Journal*. At that time, the *Commercial and Financial Chronicle* was the most important financial newspaper. (Judging from the accounts of Richard Wychoff (1930, p.44), the *Chronicle* continued to be the leading source of financial news until after Dow's death.) Recognizing the importance of the emerging industrial sector, in May 1896 Dow changed the index to 12 industrial stocks. The first version of the Dow Jones Industrial Average appeared in the *Wall Street Journal* in October 1896. The index of 20 railway stocks, the precursor of the modern Dow Transportation Index, was renamed the Rail Average. Brown et al. (1998) discuss the evolution of the 'Dow theory' by a subsequent editor of the *Wall Street Journal*, W.P. Hamilton.

The original 12 stocks of the Dow Jones Industrial Average (DJIA) reflect the nature of the stock market at that time (see Table 9.2). All but US Leather survives today in some form, though only General Electric remains in the DJIA. The DJIA was expanded to 20 stocks in 1916 and to 30 stocks in 1928. The use of 30 stocks has continued up to the present day. Only 3 stocks (American Sugar, General Electric and US Rubber) of the original 12 appeared in 1916, with 7 of the 20 from 1916 appearing in 1928. Oddly enough, American Tobacco and North American reappeared in 1928 after being left off the 1916 list. This reflects the ongoing practice, still used today, of updating the average to reflect the changing composition of trading, market capitalization and industrial composition of the leading common stocks.[5]

The Science of Equity Valuation

Following Jovanovic (2006a, b), notions central to modern finance—such as the random walk hypothesis and the associated 'science of the stock market'—can be traced to the latter half of the 19th century, when French writers such as Jules Regnault (1834–1894) and Henri Lefèvre (1827–1885) extended the positivist program of Auguste Comte (1798–1857) to financial markets. Alex Preda (2004, 2006) detailed the social and economic developments that laid the foundation for this early progress towards the modern theory of efficient markets. The needed cognitive and cultural background required transforming financial investing into a science, helping the public to see financial securities as investments rather than gambling. Consistent with the central role of London in the global securities market, similar developments to those in France were emerging in the UK, where the founding of the Foreign and Colonial Government Trust in 1868 "was the first British investment trust, designed to provide investors with the opportunity . . . to allow ordinary investors to earn the higher yields that were available on overseas government bonds, compared with domestic

Consols . . . to reduce the risk of possible loss through default on coupon or final payment by investing in a range of different securities" (Rutterford 2009).

While French contributions to the science of the stock market included a number with an academic bent, British contributions were decidedly in the vernacular realm. By the beginning of the 20th century, the vernacular contributions had progressed to where Lowenfeld (1909, esp. p.25) was able to use analysis of price charts for representative common stocks, preferred stocks and debt in eight different countries to conclude the following "law" for "the foundation of profitable investment":

> *The realizable values of all securities controlled by the Stock Exchanges of any one country are entirely under the influence of the general state of trade of that country.*

This law led to the lesson (p.26):

> *Every investor who places his money exclusively in the investments of any one country is simply speculating on the future trade prosperity of that country.*

Recognizing that the "trade prosperity of each country differs from that of all other countries, so the price movement of stocks in each country differ from those of all other countries" (p.40), Lowenfeld proposed the following international diversification rule:

> *If an investor divides his capital equally among a number of stocks, every one of which is under a different trade influence, then each of these divisions of his capital will constitute a distinct investment risk, and a true system of arranging investment risks is thereby established.*

This 'top-down' equally weighted by country approach to diversification differed from the more 'bottom up' conventional approach of selecting securities on the basis of a portfolio yield target and the associated quality of the securities being purchased.

The title of Lowenfeld's 1909 book, *Investment: An Exact Science,* reflected the remarkable transformation in public attitudes regarding foreign government stocks and, to a much lesser extent, company shares that had taken place in the UK from around 1870 until World War I. *Investment: An Exact Science* was one of a number of contributions appearing in the *Financial Review of Reviews,* first published in 1905 and associated with the Investment Registry. Founded in 1881, the Investment Registry was one of a number of managed funds that used the portfolio management methods of 'average investment trusts' (Scratchley 1875; Hutson 2005). Based on the initial success of the Foreign and Colonial Trust, the key insights behind the average investment trust are outlined in the "Publisher's Note" to Lowenfeld (1909):

The key to investment success lies in a true system of averages with the view to the depreciation in one portion of the securities held being counterbalanced by a simultaneous rise in another portion of them. The proper and systematic selection of stocks is the whole secret of Capital Stability, and in Capital Stability lies the whole science of successful investing.

From the perspective of the history of equity securities, it is the traded claims against the different managed funds that still has significance.

Starting with the Foreign and Colonial, the "stocks" held by the funds were, initially, all bonds. This is consistent with the typical British investor of that period: "Many belonged to the upper and upper-middle classes . . . who lived on the income from their invested capital. Security of capital and regular interest payments were therefore vital" (Hutson 2005, p.441). For example, Rutterford (2009) lists the 18 debt securities of the 1868 Foreign and Colonial trust totaling about £1 million initial market value, spread over 14 countries, with the smallest market value being a £15,000 New South Wales (5%) and seven country positions being about £100,000: Spanish 3%; Italian 5%; Turkish 5% and 6%; Austrian 6% and 5%; Chilean 6% and 7%; Egyptian 7% and 7% Railway Loan; and Peruvian 5%. The combined market value of the US (10/40), Nova Scotia (6%) and Brazilian (5%) positions was about another £100,000, with the remainder being made up of Russian Anglo Dutch company bonds (£80,000), Danubian (£60,000) and Portuguese (£50,000). A number of the securities, such as the Spanish, Portuguese, Italian and Turkish bonds, were selling well below par value, indicating the likelihood of default on coupon payments.

The 'exact science of investments' did make a number of substantive initial contributions to equity security valuation. Prior to this, ordinary shares were typically assessed for valuation on much the same principles as debt securities, comparing the dividend current yield with the bond coupon current yield. Safety of capital and income received were the two chief characteristics. The initial average investment trusts aimed to employ equally weighted, geographically diversified portfolios to improve the safety of capital. As Lowenfeld (1909, p.10) observed: "The safety of Capital is obtained by its *even division* over a number of sound stocks of *identical width of fluctuation*, and every stock held must also be subject to an entirely *different market influence*." Due to the declining coupon rates on British government and corporate bonds between 1870 and 1900, this approach to diversification also coincided with a potential increase in income received due to the higher, sometimes much higher, yields on foreign bonds. For example, the weighted average yield on the Foreign and Colonial Trust of 1868 was just over 8% at a time when British government bonds were yielding around 3.5%.

An essential insight from the science of investments for equity valuation is that value is conceived in a portfolio context. In addition, there is explicit recognition that the values of stocks within a given country are, more or less, all subject to "the influence of the general state of trade of that country". In the context of modern finance, this would correspond to a one-factor model where the expected return on individual stocks depends on a combination of the riskless rate of interest and the expected return on the market. However, unlike modern finance theories of equity value, the problem of identifying an appropriate market index was avoided by exploiting the low correlations between 'stock' markets in different geographical locations. The equity value of a geographically diversified portfolio was distinguished from the value of a domestically diversified portfolio involving "a mixed assortment of British stocks . . . That any counterpoise of this sort is ever to be derived from an all-British Investment List is an absolutely vain hope" (p.23).

British Equity Valuation on the Eve of World War I

While the 1890s are a potential reference point for exploring the precursors, Graham and Dodd (1934, p.14) made specific reference to "the last three decades" of security analysis. This suggests the first decade of the 20th century as a starting point for 'fundamental analysis' of corporate securities. Hartley Withers (1910), a financial journalist from "the City" in London, provided an excellent benchmark for examining the techniques of equity security analysis that predate Graham and Dodd. Withers' objective was "to glean among the best brains of the world of finance" and "to pass on the gleanings to readers", giving ample attention to both English and US securities markets. After an initial chapter on the historical evolution of securities, starting from the 16th century, Withers proceeded with a chapter on the form of securities, dealing with topics such as the definitions of stocks, shares and bonds and the difference between registered and bearer securities. While this material is somewhat pedestrian, the next four chapters are recognizable precursors of Graham and Dodd (1934).

The first chapter of four in Withers (1910) details how the capital structure of companies related to the various classes of securities: the role of the shareholders in choosing the board of directors, the difference between preferred and ordinary shares and stock splits. The presentation was structured around the fictional creation of the "Hygienic Tooth-powder Company" by "Mr. Cleanbite", who lived in Brixton and had a small dental practice in Finsbury Circus. 'Mr. Cleanbite' had developed an effective toothpowder but did not have the capital to produce it on a large scale. As chance would have it, one of his business neighbours in Finsbury Circus, "a certain Mr. Mortimer . . . who carries on the mysterious profession of company, promoter, underwriter, financier, and organizer of syndicates" happened to visit Cleanbite's dental office for treatment. The machinations and complications of the ensuing formation of a public company, complete with issuing of stock, selection of the board of directors, watering of stock and so on, reflects a solid understanding of the initial public offering. Having laid this foundation, Withers presented a chapter with a detailed examination of company prospectuses.

Withers' chapters 5 and 6 can fairly be considered early gems of equity security analysis, in the sense of the Graham and Dodd mantra: "All security analysis involves the use of financial statements". Chapter 5 is a detailed dissection of the balance sheet and income statement of Babcock and Wilcox Ltd., a well-known engineering firm. After going over items on the liabilities side of the balance sheet, Withers observed (p.127):

It is when we come to the assets side of the balance-sheet that its difficulty really begins. On the liabilities side we have been faced with sums about which there is no doubt. Every penny that the company has to account for to its shareholders or pay to its creditors is a definite penny, no more and no less. But when we look into the assets that it holds against these liabilities there is room for infinite variety in the meaning of the figures attached to them.

Withers went on to demonstrate that the simple process of accounting for asset values according to the values paid for purchase is "quite useless as a guide to its actual position at the moment". This lays the basis for chapter 6, which is concerned with the notions of depreciation and profitability. The connection of these concerns with Graham and Dodd (1934) are apparent where Part VI is composed of four chapters concerned with the implications of asset values for balance sheet analysis. In addition, Part V is concerned with analysis of the income account and has a chapter on "the relation of depreciation and similar charges to earnings power".

Accounting standards were considerably less well defined at the time Withers was writing. Rules and practices that are taken for granted today were either non-existent or subject to dispute. Legal decisions associated with bankruptcies, securities frauds and the like often acted as a barrier to implementing sound accounting practices. This led Withers (1910, p.151) to make the following statement about the position of the auditor:

> The position of an auditor of a joint stock company is doubly difficult, from the indefinite and hazy nature of his duties, and from his relation to the shareholders and the Board. As we have seen, his duties are reduced by legal pronouncements to those of a checking-clerk, and the fees that he receives are very inadequate to the real importance of his task; while in practice, if a company gets into difficulties, the auditors are always likely to be blamed for not having pointed out that its published figures, though correct, were not veracious. Though originally, as a rule, appointed to be watch-dogs in the interests of the shareholders, to see that the Board and the officials are publishing true and correct statements. Their duty is to the shareholders, but their direct relations are with the Board and officials. When they take a high view of their duties, and call attention in their reports to matters which ought to be amended, it sometimes happens that their action is very foolishly resented by the shareholders, whose best interests they are trying to serve, and they sometimes get removed from office for having done their duty well.

In light of the more recent events surrounding Enron, WorldCom, Tyco and the collapse of major accounting firm Arthur Andersen, this statement seems almost prophetic.

After three chapters, one on government and municipal securities, one on the stock exchange, and one on stock exchange transactions, Withers concludes with three remarkable chapters that explicitly deal with the implications of the distinction between speculation and investment, a distinction that also plays a key role in Graham and Dodd. Yet, Withers in these chapters goes beyond Graham and Dodd in some ways. The last three chapters of Withers have many elements that later appear in J.M. Keynes (1936, ch12). It is difficult to do justice in a short discussion. Chapter 10 is concerned with the price movements of securities. In this chapter, Withers (1910, p.283) starts by recognizing the role of psychological factors in determining stock prices, saying, "price movements are chiefly a psychological question". After an insightful observation about the impact of dealers on pricing ("it often happens that an unexpectedly favourable traffic return or dividend announcement makes the dealers in a market raise the price of stock because they infer a quick rush of buying that will follow it"), Withers recognizes that share pricing ultimately has to be supported "by the action of the public".

Withers followed this introduction with a discussion that is clearly reminiscent of Keynes:

> One curious result of this dependence of securities on public opinion in the matter of their price movements, is that it is often dangerous to be too clever and far-seeing concerning the influences that may be expected to improve or depress prices. It has happened before now that long-sighted operators have foreseen trade developments or other happenings that could not fail ultimately to have an important effect on prices, have backed their opinion by buying the securities likely to be affected, and have lost money by being too keen of vision. All that they foresaw may have happened, but if its effects did not dawn on the intelligence of a large enough number of buyers, the stocks that ought to be affected would not move . . . It is not enough for a stock to be worth buying. It must be recognized to be worth buying by the multitude before it will go up in price. Further, the fact that a stock may be absurdly over-valued will not for a moment prevent its rising still further if there are folk enough who believe that it is still cheap and are prepared to back their opinions by buying it.

This is not the only connection to Keynes (1936, ch.12). After examining the bull and bear operations of speculators, Withers (1910) observed that the impact of such operations on security prices are "more or less temporary" and "what finally determines the price of a security is what the real investor thinks about it. Bulls and bears produce the waves on the surface, real buying and selling are the flow and ebb of the tide which determine the depth of the water" (pp.293–4). This is followed by the remarkable statement: "The real investor . . . is likely to be guided by convention". Though the connection to the elaborate process of decision making under 'true uncertainty' is unrecognized, Withers did dedicate substantial discussion to the social status of the real investor, "in most cases a member of the upper or middle classes of society", and the social and psychological factors that would influence the conventions that guide their investment decisions—for example, "old-time convention had been very much in favour of investments at home". It is difficult to tell whether Keynes was aware of Withers

(1910), as Keynes did little referencing of the ideas gleaned from others and no reference is given to Withers in Keynes (1936).

The last two chapters of Withers (1910) are devoted to detailed examination of 'the real investor' and 'the speculative investor'. After recognizing that making such a distinction is artificial because "every investor is a speculator, and the difference between the two classes is finally, like most other differences, one of degree", Withers observed that real investors "look most of all to security of income and least to the hope of capital appreciation, while the pure speculator sets no store by income, and looks entirely to the chance of being able to make a big profit by a resale" (p.317). Between these extremes are a range of speculative investors and investing speculators. The motivations of these speculative investors and investing speculators are of interest. In particular, much like the 'value investor' of modern times, the investing speculator can follow the course "of buying good securities which the investing public is at present neglecting, knowing that some day or other it will come back to them, and in the meantime earning a good round yield on his money by buying stocks which are discredited".

Two final points of interest in Withers (1910) were "well known saws on the subject of investment" that are explored: 'the higher the yield, the lower the security' and 'never put all your eggs in one basket'. On the latter saw, Withers made the remarkable (why?) statement: "expert advisers of the public are fertile in schemes for scientific distribution of risks by climate, or by geography, or by industries, etc., etc." Withers found that neither of the old saws was "quite sound". The text ends with an exhortation (pp.344–5): "the preceding pages have been written in vain if they have not shown that stocks and shares and market movements are a weltering chaos of uncertainty and haphazard guesswork, based on figures that often mean nothing—or worse than nothing, because they seem to mean so much—and on gusts of opinion blown hither and thither by causes which have no logical connections with the merits of the stocks affected. Whosoever is wise will ponder these things and try to be a real investor, exposing himself as little as possible to speculative anxieties and pitfalls". Sounds like a strong vote for bonds over stocks, circa 1910.

Roger Babson and the Barometric Indices

It is a quandary that Roger Ward Babson (1875–1967) is remembered today primarily for founding Babson College in Wellesley, Massachusetts instead of other important contributions that transformed equity security markets. In particular, together with his wife Grace, Babson founded Babson's Statistical Organization, the first American investment advisory company aimed at providing advice to individual as well as institutional investors.[6] The founding of the Babson Institute (later Babson College) was part of the pioneering effort that revolutionized the American financial services industry, making Babson a considerable fortune in the process. A graduate of MIT in 1898, Babson acquired a considerable academic reputation over his career. Initial contributions included a number of influential papers in the *Annals of the American Academy of Political and Social Sciences* (Babson 1910 a,b, 1911) and a paper presented at the 1911 meetings of the American Statistical Association. Babson went on to publish over 40 books, including *Business Barometers*, which reached eight editions, to be followed by *Business Barometers for Profits, Security, Income*, which had ten editions. He was a Fellow of the Royal Statistical Society of London.

In the academic realm, Babson was part of the pre-history of the institutional school of economists that commences with the manifesto of institutional economics—Hamilton (1919)—and the establishment of the National Bureau of Economic Research (NBER) in 1920. Institutionalism was, arguably, the dominant school in American economics in the inter-war period. While institutionalism as an intellectual force was not able to recover from the post–World War II 'measurement without theory' criticism leveled by Koopmans (1947) and others, this school of economic thought made contributions to the conduct of economic policy and government practice that survive to the present. Following Rutherford (2001), the institutionalist agenda emerged in the immediate aftermath of World War I and was propelled by a desire to support an enhanced role for government in the economy to achieve much needed social and economic reform. This created a demand for improved economic data and policy analysis, which were the touchstones of institutionalism. Proposing a "modern" and "scientific" empirical approach analogous to that used in the natural sciences, institutionalism aimed to replace the theoretically driven neoclassical approach to economics that dominated economics prior to World War I (e.g., Yonay 1994).

By the time that institutionalists were in vogue, Babson was firmly ensconced in the vernacular realm. In addition to a newspaper column, which commanded 16 million readers, he wrote hundreds of magazine and newspaper articles.

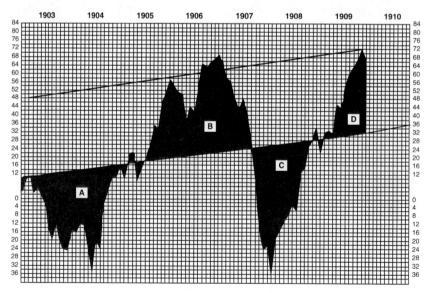

Figure 9.2   Time Series of the Babson Barometer, 1903–1910

Source: Babson (1910, p.122)

Babson's intellectual influence within the vernacular community is evident from *The Stock Market Barometer* (Hamilton 1922), which is the defining work of the classical Dow Theory. On 5 September 1929, Babson gave a speech saying: "Sooner or later a crash is coming, and it may be terrific". Later that day, the stock market declined by about 3%. This became known as the "Babson Break":

> The safest and most successful method of investing is to watch the barometer figures on the twenty-five subjects . . . and then to buy and to sell only when these subjects plainly show which to do, *confining all purchases to the very highest grade securities*. By such a method purchases are made only at the end of a long period of declining prices, after which securities are held from two to four years until the figures on these twenty-five subjects show that prices have about reached the top. Then they are sold, the proceeds reinvested in short-term municipal notes and high-grade bonds maturing in from one to three years, or else deposited in banks. During these years a panic invariably comes when this money will again purchase, at from 20 to 50 per cent less price, the same high-grade securities that were sold a few years previous. (Babson 1910, p.614)

THE FOUNDING OF BABSON COLLEGE (FROM WWW. BABSON.EDU)

Beginning in 1908, Roger Babson offered through Babson's Statistical Organization a correspondence course on how to sell bonds. This endeavor was an instant success, and courses in economics, finance, and distribution soon followed. Babson then saw the need for a private college that specialized in business education. In June 1919, in a special letter to clients of the B.S.O., he announced the establishment of a school of business administration to provide not only practical but also ethical training for young men wishing to become business executives. On September 3, 1919, with an enrollment of 27 students, the Babson Institute (renamed Babson College in 1969) held its first classes in the former home of Roger and Grace Babson on Abbott Road in Wellesley Hills.

From the very beginning, Roger Babson set out to distinguish the Babson Institute from other colleges offering instruction in business. The Institute provided intensive training in the fundamentals of production, finance, and distribution in just one academic year, rather than the standard four. The curriculum was divided into four subject areas: practical economics, financial management, business psychology, and personal efficiency, which covered topics such as ethics, personal hygiene, and interpersonal relationships. The program's pace did not allow time for liberal arts courses, and it was assumed that students would learn these subjects elsewhere.

Believing experience to be the best teacher, Roger Babson favored a curriculum that was a combination of both class work and actual business training. Seasoned businessmen instead of career academicians made up the majority of the faculty. To better prepare students for the realities of the business world, the Institute's curriculum focused more on practical experience and less on lectures. Students worked on group projects and class presentations, observed manufacturing processes during field trips to area factories and businesses, met with managers and executives, and viewed industrial films on Saturday mornings.

The Institute also maintained a simulated business environment as part of the students' everyday life. The students, required to wear professional attire, kept regular business hours (8:30 a.m. to 5:00 p.m., Monday through Friday, and 8:30 a.m. to noon on Saturday) and were monitored by punching in and out on a time clock. They were also assigned an office desk equipped with a telephone, typewriter, adding machine, and Dictaphone. Personal secretaries typed the students' assignments and correspondence in an effort to accurately reflect the business world. Roger Babson prepared his students to enter their chosen careers as executives, not anonymous members of the work force.

C EQUITY CAPITAL, SPECULATION AND DERIVATIVE SECURITIES

The Evolution of Stockjobbing

To the uninitiated, much confusion is created by applying modern security market norms to historical events. As a consequence, valuable historical lessons can be misinterpreted, to the detriment of those seeking insights such as investors attempting to value equity securities or regulators seeking to maintain a level playing field for efficient equity security trading. The use of derivative security contracts in the trading of equity securities is a case in point. Poitras (2002) referred to a "derivative security renaissance" that characterized the last quarter of the 20th century. In combination with a revolution in computing and communications technology, the removal of a plethora of restrictions on derivative security trading and related 'stockjobbing' types of transactions has transformed trading practices in modern equity security markets. Innovations such as 'credit default swaps' and 'double short exposure' exchange-traded funds on equity indexes and commodities raise important questions concerning "unnatural" (Armstrong 1848) fluctuations in market prices associated with the availability of such securities. Centuries of history detailing the abuse of derivative security contracts has been ignored in favour of a 'brave new world' vision for financial security trading.

With this in mind, consider a theme that appears repeatedly in stock market history since the late 17th century: the nefarious practice of 'stockjobbing'. Following Attard (2000, p.7), "the term 'stockjobber' has been used pejoratively since the seventeenth century to describe any person who dealt fraudulently, speculated, or simply traded on his own account". For example, recall the title by Daniel Defoe on the subject discussed in chapter 6: *The Anatomy of Exchange Alley or, A System of Stock-Jobbing: Proving that Scandalous Trade, as it is now carried on, to be Knavish in its private practice, and Treason in its Public* (1719) and the contributions by Thomas Mortimer on this subject. Another example is Adam Smith's (1763, p.251) description of stockjobbing in the *Lectures* discussed in chapter 8. The stockjobber is often being depicted as a gambler using the leverage obtained through time contracts, manipulating the market with rumours aimed at facilitating a quick profit. In chapter 7, Mortimer explicitly identifies the blurring of the dealer and broker functions. This is reflected in the common language during the 18th century that "used broker and jobber as interchangeable terms" (Dickson 1967, p.494).[7] However, Mortimer is quite clear that stockjobbers also include others than just brokers.

What was stockjobbing? Mortimer (1761, p.27) has a useful description:

> Now, the Dutch and other foreigners have so large an interest in our public funds, has given rise to the buying and selling of them for time, by which is to be understood, the making of contracts for buying and selling against any certain period of time; so that the transfer at the public offices is not made at the time of making the contract; but at the time stipulated in the contract for transferring it; and this has produced modern STOCK-JOBBING, as I shall presently shew.
>
> Nothing could be more just or equitable than the original design of these contracts, nor nothing more infamous than the abuse that has, and still is made of it.

In keeping with the modern-day renaissance of derivative securities, stockjobbing in the 18th century was also associated with forward trading of securities. According to Mortimer (p.32):[8]

> the mischief of it is, that under this sanction of selling and buying the funds for time for foreigners—Brokers and others, buy and sell for themselves, without having any interest in the funds they sell, or any cash to pay for what they buy, nay even without any design to transfer, or accept, the funds they sell or buy for time. The business thus transacted, has been declared illegal by several acts of parliament, and this is the principal branch of STOCK-JOBBING.

Mortimer makes no reference to the use of options in stockjobbing activities, giving some support to the position that Barnard's Act of 1734 was effective in deterring this activity.

Almost from the beginning of English stock trading, attempts were made to severely restrict stockjobbing. The first important piece of legislation was the 1697 Act 'To Restrain the number and ill Practice of Brokers and Stockjobbers'. This Act did not actually have much application to stockjobbing, as conceived by Mortimer. Rather, stockjobbing was conceived as 'pretended' brokerage. From the preamble to the Act:

> whereas divers Brokers and Stock-Jobbers, or pretended Brokers, have lately set up and on most unjust Practices and Designs, in Selling and Discounting of Talleys, Bank Stock, Bank Bills, Shares and Interests in Joint Stocks, and other Matters and Things, and have, and do, unlawfully Combined and Confederated themselves together, to Raise or fall from time to time the Value of such Talleys, Bank Stock, and Bank Bills, as may be most Convenient for their own private Interest and Advantage: which is a very great abuse of the said Ancient Trade and Imployment, and is extremely prejudicial to the Public Credit of this Kingdom and to the Trade and Commerce thereof, and if not timely prevented, may Ruin the Credit of the Nation, and enndanger the Government itself.

Stockjobbers were seen as interlopers in the legitimate trade of brokerage. As a consequence, the Act specifically restricted the trade of brokerage to those brokers licensed by the City of London. The Act then limits the number of licensed brokers to one hundred.

Though it had some impact, the Act of 1697 was insufficient to stem the stockjobbing abuses, as reflected in the need for subsequent English legislation. Unlicensed brokers continued to operate throughout the 18th century and licensed brokers were often involved in dealing activities (e.g., Dickson 1967, pp.493–7). Trading practices in both Amsterdam and Paris also involved licensed and unlicensed brokers. Though there were definitely political considerations in its passage, the English Bubble Act of 1720 was designed to eliminate the rampant 'stockjobbing' in the initial public offerings of the numerous joint-stock bubble promotions (Harris 1994). That option contracts still played a significant role in stockjobbing activities, both during and after the South Sea bubble, is reflected in the specific inclusion of restrictions on options trading in Barnard's Act, which also attempted to restrict speculative time bargains. Various other unsuccessful attempts to get anti-speculation and anti-stockjobbing bills passed were launched.

Some general themes of modern interest emerge from a closer inspection of the activities involved in the nefarious practice of stockjobbing. The negative outcomes that were identified arose from a combination of factors, including: (a) the lack of separation between brokerage and dealing functions; (b) the abuse of time contracts and privileges; and (c) the inability to regulate access to market trading by fraudsters and manipulators. Each of these factors continues to plague modern equity security markets, despite ongoing efforts by government regulators and self-regulatory organizations to mitigate undesirable outcomes. It was around the last quarter of the 18th century that the functions of jobbing and dealing began to converge. Regulations on the London Stock Exchange aimed to prevent conflict of interest between jobber and brokerage activities by prohibiting member firms to engage in both capacities date from 1847. Following a restatement of the ban in 1878, the Exchange entrenched the separation of brokerage and jobbing functions in regulations of 1908 and 1912. The separation of function was removed in the Big Bang financial reforms of 1986 (Attard 2000).

Brokers have been an essential feature of markets since ancient times. Brokers were used to do business in a wide range of commodities, from cloth and wool to copper and saltpetre.[9] Various jurisdictions imposed laws governing the ability of individuals to engage in brokerage and when brokers were required in a business transaction. For example, the 1697 English law restricted to 100 the number of brokers permitted to transact business in joint-stocks. Similar restrictions were imposed by the French government in setting up the Paris bourse following the collapse of the Mississippi scheme, though trading by unlicensed brokers on the *Coulisse* in the 19th century did play a fundamental role in bourse development (Walker 2001). Another example is from medieval Bruges, where alien merchants were required to use local brokers even where a broker was not necessary.[10] Heuristically, brokers do business by connecting buyers and sellers, charging a commission for this service. A broker does not take a position in the security being traded. In contrast, dealers buy and sell for their own account. Dealer activity can take various forms, some of which can create conflicts of interest with the brokerage function.

Modern equity markets have blurred the distinction between brokers and dealers. Even the UK abolished the long-established distinction in the Big Bang financial reforms of 1986. This has led to a variety of difficulties. In particular, during the lead-up to the collapse of the technology stock bubble in 2000, inaccurate brokerage house recommendations touted IPOs that the investment banking arm of a number of broker-dealers were bringing to market. In the most high-profile case, the subsequent prosecution of Frank Quattrone, former star investment banker with Credit Suisse First Boston, illustrates the difficulties in penalizing such manipulations.[11] That Quattrone was able to obtain hundreds of millions in 'overdue' compensation payments after his 2004 conviction was overturned reflects the modern difficulties of preventing firms from exploiting the advantages of combining the investor information aspect of full-service brokerage with the dealing function associated with equity IPO distributions. In the US, broker-dealers are subject to oversight by the SEC and by the self-regulatory functions of exchanges. The SEC reacted to this most recent round of difficulties associated with lack of sufficient broker-dealer separation by introducing Reg. AC in April 2003.

What Is a Derivative Security?

The negative feature of stockjobbing most often identified by informed observers of early stock markets was the abuse of time contracts and privileges, referred to as derivative securities contracts in modern markets. This has a number of implications for equity security valuation. In an insightful early examination of security markets, Sir Robert Giffen (1877, pp.85–93) identified four general causes for differences in security prices: "the security and safety of the income yielded by the investment"; "the difference of marketability"; "the effect of extrinsic regulations, such as those of the law courts, which direct the investment and reinvestment of funds"; and "the estimation of the public . . . in favouring some securities more than others by qualities unconnected with the solidity of income or mere marketability". The advantages of derivative security trading relate to the first two causes and the disadvantages with the last. Disentangling these elements has created problems from the first trades in joint-stock shares. Yet, while severe bans and restrictions on various aspects of derivative security trading that were imposed prior to the current renaissance period were reasonably successful in curbing speculative abuses, the bans and restrictions also resulted in losses associated with reduced market liquidity and, possibly, increased price volatility.

Despite its being a widely used term, it is difficult to precisely define a 'derivative security contract'. In particular, all derivative securities involve a traded contingent claim, where some essential feature, typically the price, is derived from some future event. This event is often, though not always, associated with a security or commodity delivery to take place at a future date. However, defining derivative securities as tradeable contingent claims is not precise enough, because financial markets are riddled with contingent claims, not just those associated with derivative security contracts. In addition, contingent claims may be combined with other security features or traded in isolation. In some cases in which the contingent claim involves a notional equity security transaction to take place at a later date, such as with a convertible bond or convertible preferred share, the traded value of the contingent claim and the underlying security is combined. Recognizing that such bundled securities could also be defined as derivative securities, the definition is usually restricted to cases in which the contingent claim contract is unbundled or "free standing" (FASB 1998, 2000).[12] This includes the following types of contracts: forwards and futures; put and call options; subscription rights and warrants; and bundles of these contracts, such as plain vanilla swaps.[13]

Significantly, the historical use of derivative securities in equity security trading developed differently in the US than it did in Europe, due to differing cash market settlement practices. More or less from the beginning of security trading in the US, "each day is a settling day and a clearing day for transactions of the day before . . . This is a marked difference from European practice", where "trading for the account" involves monthly or fortnightly settlement periods, with allowance for continuation of the position until the next settlement date (Emery 1896, p.82). In effect, the UK and continental stock exchanges used settlement methods that directly involved the use of extendible, short-dated time contracts. On settlement day, there was a continuation process for a buyer seeking to delay delivery that involved the immediate sale of the stock being delivered and the simultaneous repurchase for the next settlement date. As this transaction would involve the lending of money, an additional 'contango' payment would typically be required.

Daily or short-dated settlement had dramatic implications for derivative security trading in the US stock market. Instead of trading for time, with regularly scheduled settlement dates and allowance for continuation as in Europe, it was often more expedient to speculate by selling (shorting) borrowed stocks and buying stocks on margin. Armstrong (1848, p.10) made a telling observation: "When such a time operation as is desired cannot be conveniently obtained, it is customary to buy the stock for cash, and then borrow as much money upon it as possible, and deposit the certificate of Stock with the lender as security for repayment of the amount borrowed. The market value less five or ten per cent. can almost always be obtained". As Poitras (2002, p.6) explained, derivative securities are difficult to define because similar payouts can often be obtained by combinations of other securities. For example, a long position in a time contract for purchase of stock with delivery in 30 days and a margin deposit of 5% has similar cash flows to a purchase of stock using a 30-day loan for 95% of the purchase price.

Use of day-to-day 'hypothecation' to finance inventories instead of 'trading for the account', at times, has had severe implications for liquidity in the US short-term credit markets, especially following the Great Depression and, more generally, during the gold standard period. In addition to Keynes, who made important contributions, other economists of the inter-War period were concerned with this issue (e.g., Machlup 1940). As a consequence of a largely cash market for equity securities, the venue for evolution of derivative security trading in the US was in the bulk commodity markets, where, during the 19th century, exchange trading of derivative securities experienced a revolution that can be attributed to the subtle impact American culture had on specific business practices. Writing in 1896, Emery (1896, p.7) captured the main theme: "The American people are regarded by foreigners as the greatest of all speculators". This drive to speculate facilitated American innovations in derivative securities. "It was not until the (19th) century . . . that the system (of dealings for time) became widely developed and not until the great expansion of foreign trade in the last fifty years that it became of great importance".

The start of the modern renaissance in equity derivative security trading can be identified with the commencement of trading on the Chicago Board Options Exchange (CBOE) in 1973. Though equity option trading in the US began as early as 1790 and time bargains even earlier, both played a significant role at one time or another in various market manipulations. As early as the 1890s, option pools were in operation. Two general types of pools were present in the 1920s: trading pools and option pools, with the latter being the most common. While trading pools acquired stock on the open market, option pools would acquire all or most of their securities by obtaining call option contracts to purchase stock at favorable prices. These options were acquired OTC from various sources, such as the corporation, where the options took the form of warrants, as well as large stockholders, directors, officers, large speculators and banks. While there was considerable diversity in the maturity of the options granted and the types of schemes involved, the primary objective of the option pool was to benefit through manipulation of the common stock price. The option pools were symptomatic of the types of abuses that contributed to the 1929 stock market collapse. The regulatory response implemented in the 1930s, culminating in the Securities Act (1933) and the Securities Exchange Act (1934), was to prohibit all activities aimed at manipulating market prices and trading on insider information.

Franklin and Colberg (1958, pp.29–30) illustrated the importance of options trading in the 1929 market collapse as follows:

> Testimony before the Senate Committee on Banking and Currency in 1932 and 1933 disclosed that many of the financial abuses of the 1920s were

related to the use of options. A favorite device of large stockholders was to grant options without cost to a pool which would then attempt to make these profitable by "churning" activities designed to bring the general public in as buyers of the stock. In addition, long-term and even unlimited-period option warrants were issued frequently in connection with new stock issues.

During the wave of securities market reform following the financial market collapse of 1929–1933, considerable attention was given to terminating option trading altogether. One of the most profitable pools was the Sinclair Consolidated Oil option pool of 1929. While Sinclair stock was selling in the $28 to $32 range, a contract was obtained from Sinclair granting the pool an option to buy 1,130,000 shares at $30 per share. The pool then purchased 634,000 shares in the open market to bid up prices. The pool exercised its option and liquidated all its holdings while the stock was selling for around $40. The pool also sold 200,000 shares short as the price fell. The pool's total profit was approximately $12.5 million from the following sources: $10 million profit from optioned shares purchased at $30 per share, $500,000 profit from shares purchased in the market, and $2 million profit from the short sales.

In the process of developing a regulatory response to the market abuses which contributed to the financial market turbulence of 1929–1933, it was accepted that the abuses associated with option pools would become illegal. However, in addition to the use of options in pool operations, there were other, more legitimate reasons for stock option trading. In the end, the brokerage industry was able to avoid the outright ban associated with commodity options. The initial legislation aimed at regulating the securities markets, the Fletcher-Rayburn bill (1934), called for a total ban on stock options. The brokerage industry was able to prevent this result. Instead, the Securities Exchange Act (1934) empowered the newly created Securities and Exchange Commission (SEC) to regulate the market and introduced the Put and Call Brokers and Dealers Association (PCBDA) (1934), which was designed to act as a self-policing agency, working closely with the SEC and other agencies to avoid further government regulation. It was member firms of the PCBDA which formed the basis for the OTC market trading of options which took place in the period leading up to the creation of the CBOE.

To appreciate the major advance that the CBOE represented, consider the state of equity option trading prior to the CBOE. Franklin and Colberg (1958, p.22) described the general state of trading at the end of the 1950s as follows:

> Practically all of the Put and Call business in the US is handled by about twenty-five option brokers and dealers in New York City. The brokers operate through [the PCBDA]. All the contracts in which they deal are guaranteed or indorsed by member firms of the New York Stock Exchange . . . The Put and Call business is largely self-regulated, but a great deal of the aura of secrecy which surrounds this activity seems to stem from the early 1930s when the threat of strict regulation or even legislative extermination haunted the entire options trade.

At this time, the options market was relatively small. Self-regulation, both by the exchanges and by the PCBDA, coupled with the SEC's ability to require reporting of options trading, were sufficient to prevent the abuses of previous years. However, the markets were relatively illiquid and it was difficult to resell positions. Upon closer inspection, though the options being traded through the PCBDA were transferable and, in a sense, protected by a clearing mechanism, some common drawbacks of OTC trading of derivative securities were present. In addition to illiquidity, trading in the market primarily involved large institutional investors writing overpriced options to small investors seeking to gamble in stocks with limited capital. In effect, OTC trading was aimed at capturing rents from control of the information and transactions technology of options trading.

Among other significant regulatory changes introduced by the Securities Act and the Securities Exchange Act, the SEC required all options sellers to post margins. Unscrupulous activities such as granting brokers options for touting a stock were banned together with the use of options to trade on inside information. In addition to the increased government regulation, self-regulation by the PCBDA played an important role. Despite the success in reducing market abuses, the options traded in the OTC market were often illiquid, making it difficult to resell or transfer a given options contract. In 1972 this started to change with the creation of the Options Clearing Corporation, a subsidiary of the CBOE. In following years, the American, Philadelphia, Pacific and Midwest stock exchanges also introduced options trading. Trading on the CBOE commenced in April 1973 with 16 stock options. While initial interest in options trading was small, by 1977 volume had increased substantially, to the point where put options were introduced. The ensuing implications of inter-exchange competition undermining the self-regulatory function of exchanges, a phenomenon which has overtaken equity cash and derivative markets in recent years, was not adequately appreciated at the time. The advantages associated with combining options with cash trading, a tradition on European exchanges stretching back to early 19th-century France (Viaene 2006), is unrecognized.

The common use of options contracts to trade equity securities can be traced to the 17th century. Such contracts made sense in the equity markets of the time, due to the difficulties of locating shares for sale. For a time contract, a deposit would be paid—typically similar in size to the premium on an options contract—and a price established for future delivery. The buyer's right to refuse delivery would produce a higher settlement price than for a time contract. The abuse of time contracts in general and options contracts in particular led to restrictions on usage. While important merchant manuals of the 18th century, such as Jacques Savary's *Dictionnaire Universel de Commerce* (1730) and Malachy Postlethwayt's *Universal Dictionary of Trade and Commerce* (1751), have detailed discussion of the trade in *actions*, there are no entries for privileges, *prime à délivrer* or *prime à recevoir*; premiums; *jeu d'actions*; or puts and refusals. With the exception of Houghton (1694), primary sources on the 17th and 18th century share-options trade are either obscure or were part of numerous legislative attempts to regulate or abolish the trade. It was not until the 19th century that knowledge and understanding of equity options trading moved outside the narrow confines of a small group of specialized traders and gradually acquired a better reputation in Europe (Poitras 2009).

The German option contract (*prämiengeschäfte*) that concerned Bronzin early in the 20th century (Hafner and Zimmerman 2009) differed from the options traded in modern markets, which have inherited characteristics associated with historical features of US option trading. Following Emery (1896, p.53), the *prämiengeschäfte* "may be considered as an ordinary contract for future delivery with special stipulation that, in consideration of a cash payment, one of the parties has the right to withdraw from the contract within a specified time". As such, this option is a feature of a forward contract, with a fee to be paid at delivery if the option is exercised. Circa 1908 on the Paris and Berlin bourses, the premium payment at maturity was fixed by convention and the 'price' would be determined by setting the exercise price relative to the initial stock or commodity price. In Castelli (1877, p.7), the premium to be paid at maturity "fluctuates according to the variations of the Stock to be contracted". In contrast, the modern call option is a tradeable 'privilege' or 'refusal' with fixed terms in which an agreed-upon fee would be paid in advance.

NOTES

1 You can find a discussion of the history of the *Wall Street Journal* in Wendt (1982).

2 In examining opinion on futures market speculation during the late 19th and early 20th centuries, Jacks (2007) referred to "populists" versus "theorists", which corresponds to a distinction between the vernacular and the academic views. Jacks connected 'theorists' with "professionals", which is consistent with the absence of a sizeable community of 'academic' theorists. The vernacular 'populists' were typically anti-speculation. The 'professional' theorists were usually involved in the trade and were opposed to government intervention.

3 For example, Hautcoeur (1997) identified 238 financial periodicals published in Paris during 1881. A somewhat similar list could be assembled for London, with some important sources being *Chadwick's Investment Circular; Beeton's Guide;* and the *Investor's Monthly Manual.* Following Ott (2008), O'Sullivan (2007) and Michie (1986), the retail investor in the US emerged somewhat later than in Europe, with 1885–1890 being identified with "the origins of conservative belief in the ability of laissez-faire financial markets to provide economic security and justice for all" (Ott 2008, p.619). Means (1930) is an early study documenting these changes.

4 Though Edgar Smith was also a financial analyst and investment manager during the 1920s, he is included in the academic group because many of his contributions were aimed at the academic audience (e.g., Smith 1927, 1931). In McCloskey's terminology, Smith was actively involved in conversations with academics.

5 You can download the complete history of changes in the Dow Jones Averages at: www.dowjones.com.

6 The company was later called Business Statistics Organization and then Babson's Reports. In 1986, Babson's Reports was sold to United Business Service

Company, which became Babson-United Investment Advisors, Inc., and the weekly newsletter became United & Babson Investment Report. In 2001, this report ceased publication. Further information can be obtained from www. babson.com.

7   Dickson (1967, pp.493–7) has a detailed analysis of the available evidence on dealer activities as reflected in the transfer records.

8   In contrast, Defoe (1719) made no reference to forward trading, using examples which usually relate to cash transactions, for example, using false rumours to influence the stock price, the idea being to buy low on negative rumours and selling high on positive rumours (pp.139–40). However, it is not clear that Defoe had the best grasp of the financial transactions which were being done. One quote of interest is: 'the bear-skin men must commute, and pay differences money' (p.148), indicating that forward trading mechanisms similar to those used in Amsterdam were in place in London, circa 1719.

9   In the Advertisements section of *A Collection for the Improvement,* Houghton would provide various lists, such as those for Counsellors and Attorneys on 20 July 1694. In a 6 July 1694 listing which also included Coaches and Carriers, Houghton provided a list of Brokers, in this case for Corn (2), Dyers Wares (3), Exchange (6), Grocery (7), Hemp (1), and Silk (10), with the number in brackets representing the number of names listed as brokers.

10   Buckley (1924, p.590) made the following observation about the treatment of the English merchants of the Staple in Bruges: "It was, apparently, an important concession which the city Bruges made to the English merchants of the Staple in 1559, when it was agreed that the latter should be free of brokers when buying. It was asserted in 1562 that in most foreign countries no 'stranger' bought or sold except through a sworn broker, and the English Statute Book contains a number of regulations of similar import. Such arrangements were general, being due to the universal prejudice against foreigners". Buckley also made another observation which is indicative of the pervasiveness of brokers in Gresham's time: "Dealings in Bills of exchange without the intervention of a broker were exceptional" (p.591).

11   This is not to say that CSFB and Quattrone were the central figures in the misuse of analyst ratings to tout questionable stocks. Rather, the 28 April 2003 press release by the SEC, the NASD, the NYSE and New York state attorney general Eliot Spitzer named 10 Wall Street firms in the landmark $1.4 billion settlement for conflicts of interest, with Salomon Smith Barney getting the highest penalty at $400 million and CSFB and Merrill Lynch at $200 million. Morgan Stanley and Goldman Sachs also had fines greater than $100 million. It was the investigation by Eliot Spitzer that commenced in 2001 of the Internet research analysts at Merrill Lynch, led by Henry Blodget, which eventually led to settlements with a much larger number of firms found to be engaging in predatory activities.

12   The modern renaissance in derivative security trading has posed considerable problems for the accounting profession. In order to address the accounting problems raised by the use of derivative securities by firms for risk management and other purposes, the notion of 'free-standing derivatives' was introduced. This reference to free-standing derivatives is precise accounting terminology borrowed from the financial accounting standard FAS 133. Being 'free-standing', derivative security contracts pose fundamental problems for conventional methods of preparing accounts. This point has not been lost on the accounting profession, which for decades has attempted to produce a set of standards that permit an accurate financial presentation of the accounts of the firm which do not permit substantial discretionary variation in the accounts. In a perfect world, two otherwise identical firms, both involved with

using derivative securities, would not be able to present accounts which were substantively different, based on discretionary accounting choices, such as the method used to recognize gains or losses on the offsetting spot position.

13 Though commonly used, there are difficulties with this definition. For example, combinations of bundled contingent claims can produce payoffs that are almost identical to the payoffs for combinations of derivative securities—for example, simultaneous buying and selling of equal cash value in bills of exchange with different maturity dates produces a payoff which is equal to a calendar spread using currency forward contracts.

Part IV

Conceiving Modern Equity Capital

10 Old Finance and Modern Finance

Before World War I the typical common stock was basically speculative, for reasons related chiefly to the company itself. The capitalization structure was often top-heavy, the working capital inadequate, the management deficient in various respects, the published information sketchy and unreliable. The junior issue's dividend history was nonexistent or erratic, its earnings subject to wide fluctuations, and its market action to crass manipulation. Virtually, all these defects have been greatly ameliorated or abolished, as far as today's representative common stocks are concerned.

Graham and Dodd, *Security Analysis* (1934)

A OLD FINANCE AND THE 1929 CRASH

The Landscape of Equity Capital Share Valuation

As Mortimer observed in the 18th century, unlike fixed income debt securities, the cash flows associated with equity capital shares are typically much less predictable, making valuation a more uncertain exercise. In modern times, common stock valuation is complicated by numerous factors involved in the estimation of firm cash flows, which, in turn, involve qualitative variables such as market conditions and other fundamentals of the business. This valuation process is impacted by an agency problem brought on, at least partly, by the separation of ownership and control embodied in the modern limited liability corporation with autonomous, exchange-traded equity capital shares. Given this, joint-stock valuation in the 18th century differed significantly from modern common stock valuation. In the 18th century, accurate accounting information was scarce and fragmentary; and shares were not 'autonomous'. The limited number, quality and type of joint-stock shares traded meant modern portfolio diversification opportunities were unavailable.

Following the Bubble Act of 1720, share trading in England focused largely on the three great joint-stock companies: the Bank, the East India Company and the South Sea Company. These companies, and other important European joint-stock companies such as the *VOC*, typically aimed at regular dividend payout that, by modern standards, was quite high. Efforts were made to sustain the dividend at levels that made such joint-stock shares a comparable alternative to debt securities. In the English chartered companies, paid-in subscription capital was exchanged for government debt, which partially supported the dividend. The remaining support for the dividend depended on the characteristics of the public purpose for which the charter was granted. For example, the public purpose of the East India Company was subject to suspension of payments due to military misadventures undertaken by the company to further British foreign policy objectives. The inherent similarity and substitutability between joint-stock shares and government debt stock was captured in the use of par values in the trading of both debt stock and joint-stock shares.[1]

In any event, it is difficult to compare 18th-century joint-stock share valuations with similar procedures used in modern stock markets. There is considerable disparity in the various modern techniques proposed for common stock valuation. Because market efficiency is assumed, the modern finance approach to valuing common stocks lacks a **theoretical** pricing model that has the practical accuracy of fixed income pricing models, offering in its place a theory of portfolio management of asset classes. The key assumption underlying this approach is that, because markets are efficient, stock prices will be 'best available' representations of available information. Hence, the best approach to investment decisions is to focus on optimal portfolio diversification strategies across 'asset classes'. The acceptance of this approach is reflected in the awarding of the Nobel Prize in Economics to two of the modern 'originators' of this approach, Harry Markowitz and William Sharpe. The connection to specific aspects of the commercial ventures associated with the equity capital is lost in this process.

In contrast, the popular practical approach of 'old finance' stock valuation relies on analysis of fundamental information, especially the data gleaned from the firm's accounting statements and public filings. Benjamin Graham is often identified as the modern father of this approach, with investor Warren Buffett of Berkshire Hathaway as a leading proponent. In addition to representing a significant evolution of accounting valuation, the search for heterogeneous properties of individual firms associated with the fundamental approach is not readily adapted to the systematic data analysis required for the science of modern finance to be useful. The practical importance of the equity capital share valuation problem energizes the historical connection between share valuation and accounting, undermining academics' attempts to claim intellectual supremacy of common-stock valuation using a 'capital asset pricing' framework. The old finance approach is aimed at identifying accurate valuation of individual companies using the legally required information in public filings and other sources.

Irving Fisher's Prediction and Equity Capital Share Valuation

The roots of the 'modern finance' approach to equity capital share valuation can be traced, without much difficulty, back to Irving Fisher. As time has advanced, a tendency has emerged to start the chronology of modern finance with Markowitz (e.g., Markowitz 1999; Rubinstein 2002). Given the substantive institutional changes in securities markets that have taken place since World War II, this tendency is understandable. However, Irving Fisher's seminal contributions spanned so many related areas, from index numbers to the theory of interest to the use of mathematical analysis in valuation problems, that Fisher can reasonably be identified as having laid the foundations for the theoretical superstructure that dominates the landscape of academic finance. Siegel (1998, p.44), for example, referred to Fisher as "the founder of modern capital theory". Yet, Fisher's importance extends beyond his academic contributions. Fisher harks back to an era when leading academics, such as J.M. Keynes, also played important roles outside the academic realm. In addition to writing investment newsletters and giving speeches to business leaders on financial topics, Fisher started a profitable card indexing firm based on an invention that he had patented. Prior to the stock market collapse of 1929, his personal net worth was around $10 million.[2]

Based on this background, it is somewhat unfortunate that, in the annals of equity capital, Irving Fisher is most remembered for comments and prognostications made just prior to the stock market collapse of 1929 and in the following year (e.g., Fisher 1930b). Siegel (1998, pp.43–4) provided a lively description of a most telling incident:

> It was a seasonably cool Monday evening on October 14, 1929 when Irving Fisher arrived at the Builders' Exchange Club at 2 Park Avenue in New York City. Fisher, a professor of economics at Yale University and the most renowned economist of his time, was scheduled to address the monthly meeting of the Purchasing Agents Association . . . Members of the association and the press crowded into the meeting room. Fisher's speech was mainly designed to defend investment trusts, the forerunner of today's mutual funds. But the audience was most eager to hear his views on the stock market.
>
> Investors had been nervous since early September when Roger Babson, businessman and market seer, predicted a "terrific" crash in stock prices. Fisher had dismissed this pessimism, noting that Babson had been bearish for some time. But the public sought to be reassured by the great man who had championed stocks for so long.
>
> The audience was not disappointed. After a few introductory remarks, Fisher uttered a sentence that, much to his regret, became one of the most quoted phrases in stock market history: "Stock prices have reached what looks like a permanently high plateau".
>
> On October 29, two weeks to the day after Fisher's speech, stocks crashed. Fisher's "high plateau" transformed into a bottomless abyss.

Keen to promote the notion of "Stocks for the Long Run", Siegel was an apologist for Irving Fisher. The depth of Fisher's misconceptions were not adequately explored or recognized. For example, the actual quote by Fisher could be more accurately given as: "Stocks have reached what looks like a permanently high plateau . . . I expect to see the stock market a good deal higher than it is today within a few months" (Klein 2001, p.201). Fisher was not the only prominent academic bulling the stock market. For example, just prior to the crash, Charles Amos Dice, a professor at Ohio State University, published *New Levels for the Stock Market,* which provided a range of arguments as to why stock prices had to continue climbing.

Though Fisher was only a leading voice in a chorus of academics cheering the virtues of common stock investment, it is disturbing to see the soundness of his arguments being undercut by the brutal reality of the subsequent collapse in stock prices. Fisher's outstanding academic and public reputation was justly deserved. He was a careful and methodical researcher employing valuation models that are similar to those employed today. For example, Fisher (1930b, p.xxii) explicitly used discounted cash flow valuation to describe common stock prices:

> Since every stock price represents a discounted value of the future dividends and earnings of that stock, there are four reasons that may justify a rise in the price level of stocks: (1) Because the earnings are continually plowed back into the business instead of being declared in dividends, this plowing-back resulting in an accumulation at compound interest, so to speak; (2) Because the expected earnings will increase on account of technical progress within the industry; (3) Because less risk is believed to attach to those earnings than formerly; (4) Because the "basis" by which the discounting is made has been lowered.

Writing at the end of 1929, following the 40+% decline in stock prices of September to mid-November, Fisher (1930a) explored all of these four points in detail and concluded (pp.267–9): "the general plateau of the stock market is still the plateau of 1926–1929, still 55% higher than it was in 1926, and still higher than any previous plateau . . . For the immediate future, at least, the outlook is bright".

Fisher went far beyond a simple recognition that earnings were the key factor driving stock prices (1930b, p.67): "The percentage increase in prices of stocks should be equal to the percentage increase in earnings per share if the ratio of price to earnings were to remain constant". Yet, the data indicated that from 1922 to 1927 industrial stock prices increased 14.1% per year while "total profits" (earnings?) increased only 9%. Fisher attributed this difference to the gains to common stock from the low "rate of return on preferred stock" that permitted a greater share of the earnings growth to be captured by the common stock. In addition, the plowing-back of earnings permitted industrial corporations to purchase new plant and equipment that enhanced earnings capacity. Fisher recognized that the plow-back rate for industrial corporations had increased since 1927 and viewed this as a reinforcing force (p.80): "During the long bull market there was the record of increased real income, while plowed-back earnings gave promise of future values resident in the productive and consuming plant of the nation that were properly reflected in a heightened level of stock prices".

Fisher (p.67) credited Edgar L. Smith with the argument that the plowing-back of earnings was the main factor driving the increase in common stock prices. Fisher (p.66) put the argument this way:

> The increase both in dividend payments and in plowed-back earnings during 1929 over 1928, was not only a primal cause of the new plateau of stock prices, but gave promise of continuing prosperity to business for 1930. This increase should minimize the effects of the panic, which was largely restricted to the stock market.
>
> When earnings are turned back into a business it is in order to increase the rate of profits according to the same method by which interest is compounded on savings. There has always been a plowing-back of earnings, but it has been especially done in the last few years.

Having proposed the importance of plowing-back of earnings, Fisher asked the question: "Are the conclusions . . . with respect to the increased rate of plowed-back earnings, stated with too great optimism?" (p.81). Fisher addressed this question with a reasoned analysis of the behavior of the aggregate price-earnings (P/E) ratio.

Modern fundamental analysts are well versed in the difficulties of interpreting P/E ratios. Earnings can be an elusive number that, in order to interpret adequately, requires careful inspection of additional information from the financial statements and other sources. Unlike modern stock market prognosticators,

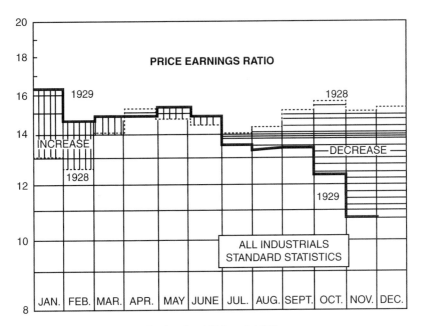

Figure 10.1   Price-Earnings Ratios for 1928 and 1929

Source: Fisher (1930b, p.82)

Fisher was hampered by lack of data on earnings and many other variables that are considered essential today for doing equity security analysis. For example, data on both a price index of industrial stocks and the associated earnings of those companies, calculated by the Standard Statistics Company (later to merge with the publisher of *Poor's Manual* to form Standard and Poor's), are only available from May 1927. Fisher was able to obtain his estimate of the increase in earnings of industrial companies from 1922 to 1927 of 9% from a government report (Committee of Recent Economic Changes). From the bulletin of the National City Bank of New York he was able to obtain evidence that the increase in earnings from 3Q 1928 to 3Q 1929 was 14%. Excluding railways and utilities, the remaining manufacturing and trading companies had a gain of 15%.

Given the state of financial reporting requirements prior to the Securities Act (1933), the crude earnings numbers that Fisher had to work with are somewhat suspect. Fisher (1930b, p.88) observed: "There are also difficulties to be faced in the choice of stocks that publish annual earnings figures, and in those stocks where there is concealment of earnings for tax evasion purposes." Fisher was also somewhat unclear about what P/E multiple to apply to individual stocks (p.88):

> The price-earnings ratios of the old-fashioned type should be perhaps ten times annual earnings, which is the traditional ratio for a fair selling price for stocks during the period prior to 1922. But for the new type of rapidly expanding corporation the price-earnings ratio might be 100 to 1, or even literally to infinity in the initial stages of investment when earnings are not being realized.

With this background, Fisher proceeded to examine aggregate stock price index and earnings data from the Standard Statistics Company (see Figure 10.1). Examining the aggregate data (industrials including railways), Fisher concluded that the 9.8 P/E for November 1925 was justified. It was 40% below the peak of 16.2 in January 1929 and lower than the previous low of 11.2 for May 1927, "the earliest month for which such statistics are available".

In addition to examining the aggregate P/E data, Fisher made a number of astute observations about the behavior of aggregate and individual stock prices in the months surrounding the crash. In particular, he observed that the run-up in prices was selective (p.93): "As the market marched to its peak about half of the groups listed (on the NYSE) receded in price, while half went up". It was the high flyers that came crashing down. Using his own index for aggregate stock prices that took in all NYSE groups, Fisher estimated that stocks fell 38% overall during the crash, with railway stocks falling only 28% but the most speculative stocks falling over 50%. He attributed the downturn in "the best stocks" to the impact of "overextension of loans" to buy stocks. After reviewing the data surrounding the crash, Fisher remained a bull (p.98): "the precipitous fall in the market went too far, in the light of sound reasons justifying the long bull market, namely, justifiable expectation of great and increasing earnings, the fact they were so generously plowed-back, the warranted expectation of safety through diversification of investments and, finally, a consequent lowered basis of discounting the future as apparently reflected in price earnings ratios".

The Common Stock Theory

Like many others of his time, Fisher was deeply impressed with the work of Edgar L. Smith on the long-run performance of common stocks versus bonds. Prior to Smith's *Common Stocks as Long-Term Investments* (1924), Fisher (1912) held to the prevailing view that stocks would outperform bonds in periods of rising prices, while bonds would outperform stocks during periods of falling prices. Smith carefully demonstrated that this view was mistaken. Harold (1934, p.46) summarized what subsequently came to be known as the common stock theory:

> Proponents of the theory do not claim that a given stock is a better investment than a given bond nor that any group of stocks are better than any group of bonds. The theory, as expounded by Smith and Van Strum, is that over long periods diversified portfolios of common stocks in leading corporations yield the investor more income, more safety, more market value per portfolio, and also that such common-stock investments, as a group, keep better pace with the cost of living than do bonds as a group.

Smith took care in recognizing that the stock holdings had to be well-diversified across companies that represented the major industries. In addition, stocks had to be held long enough to permit liquidation at favorable prices. Smith recognized that the length of the holding period to liquidation could be as long as 6 years—extending to 15 years in extreme cases. Fisher (1930b, pp.198–200) explicitly recognized the contribution of Smith (1924) to "a material change during (1923–30) in the estimate of the public as to the risk of investing in common stocks."

Irving Fisher was well off the mark in terms of predicting future stock price movements. Yet, in *The Stock Market Crash—and After* (1930b) and other contributions, Fisher laid the methodological foundation for the approach of modern finance to equity capital valuation. Fisher (1930b, ch.13) was concerned with "Flight from Bonds to Stocks"—developing a theoretical basis for the rationale of why stocks are a better long-term investment than bonds. Fisher first explored the notion that bonds are "far safer" than stocks. Working with Smith's data, Fisher adjusted for the impact of price level changes and estimated the yield on a bond investment for 1866–1885, a period of falling prices, as 11.7% in real terms (6.8% nominal); the same calculation for 1901–1922 was 1.1% real (4% nominal). "This analysis indicates clearly enough that during periods of marked fluctuations in the general price level, bonds have a speculative character . . . bonds are not, as compared with a well-selected and diversified [portfolio of] stocks, what they have been cracked up to be . . . even when prices are falling they are not usually superior to stocks" (p.202).

In a precursor of modern portfolio theory, Fisher identified "five reasons for the now proved fact that stocks are a better investment than bonds" (p.203):

> first, because the stockholder stands to win as well as to lose; second, because modern dividend policy is toward steadiness; third, because a portion of stockholders' earnings is reinvested for him and ultimately yields further dividends; fourth, because the unstable dollar tricks the bondholder, but any effect on the shareholder is largely neutralized; and fifth, because diversification can correct the irregularities of the stockholder's income but not that of the bondholder.

Fisher recognized that Edgar L. Smith, K. van Strum and other writers emphasized the importance of diversification—he did not claim originality on this point. Yet, Fisher was a vocal and active proponent of "investment trusts" run by "expert counsel"—precursors of modern closed-end funds and actively managed mutual funds. For Fisher, diversification had to have another element added: "It is the principle of constant inspection or check-up as to the status of companies issuing stocks, and constant turnover accordingly . . . For the sound investor in common stocks must turn them over constantly, selling those that are losing in value and investing in those that are gaining" (p.207). The skilled investment counsel situated in investment trusts were an essential element to achieving the gains associated with diversification that made stocks a better investment than bonds.

Based on the limited data available, Fisher was able to observe the phenomenon, common to periods of intense speculation in stocks, of substantially increased equity issues at the end of the 1920s. A comparison was made between corporate financing during the first eight months of 1925 ($2.353 billion in long- and short-term corporate bonds, with $804 million in stock issues) with the first eight months of 1929 ($2.360 billion in long and short corporate bonds, with $4.794 billion in stock issues). Fisher also observed that the bond issues in 1929 had relatively more equity-related provisions, such as conversion features. Oddly enough, Fisher interpreted this data as a positive development for stock valuation. Fisher failed to foresee the precipitous fall in stock prices from 1930 to 1932. More importantly from the standpoint of individual investors at that time, he failed to foresee that the general level of US stock prices would not recover to 1929 levels until after World War II.[3] As late as 1939, when the extent of the stock market collapse was all too evident, Fisher still argued: "there is considerable evidence to support the conclusion that stocks in general sold at about three-quarters of their true value as measured by the return to the investor" (Fisher 1939, p.433).

In continuing to support "the common-stock theory" in the aftermath of the collapse of equity values associated with the Great Depression, Fisher was not alone. Bierman (1991, 1998) continued a tradition stretching back to Eiteman and Smith (1953) and Harold (1934, p.59) in which, at the depths of the equity security market downturn, it was concluded: "the common-stock theory stands upon a firm base, shaken by the developments of 1932, but not destroyed." Similar empirical results were presented in Bosland (1937) for the 1890s to the early 1930s. However, Bosland reflected Americans' increasing wariness of the common stock theory: "no criticism of the common stock theory of investment is so impressive as the one which warns that the findings of the past may be of little value for the future. Specifically, the question is whether the factors favorable to increased common-stock earnings in the earlier period are likewise favorable for the period we have now entered, or, if not, whether new factors affecting common stocks have entered the picture" (p.73).

Irving Fisher never wavered in his support of common stock theory, despite considerable empirical evidence suggesting otherwise. It is easy to look back on what Fisher said and conclude that he was just another prognosticator who got it wrong. Yet, Fisher was so much more than another prognosticator. With all the skills and information at his disposal, Fisher failed to provide an able answer to the problems confronting vernacular equity market practitioners. In particular, practitioners have to deal with the "American question" (McCloskey 1985; Poitras 2011, p.84): If you're so smart, why ain't you rich? Though modern finance academics may want to ignore Fisher's foibles, perhaps this is a reflection on the goals associated with academic approach to equity security valuation. Based on as careful an implementation of the scientific approach as he could muster, Fisher was a strong proponent of stocks for the long run—a view that, in his time, proved profoundly incorrect. Perhaps more personally disturbing to Fisher was that his longtime academic rival, J.M. Keynes, was so much closer to the mark both academically and in the world of investment returns.

Graham and Dodd (1934): The 'New Era Theory'

Graham and Dodd's *Security Analysis* (1934) was a product of the severe collapse in the corporate securities markets that started in October 1929 and continued until February 1933. This is evident from page 1: "Any present examination into financial principles or methods must start with recognition of the distinctive character of our recent experiences, and it must face and answer the numerous questions which these experiences inspire". For Graham and Dodd, "recent experiences" stretched back to 1927 (p.1):

> Economic events between 1927 and 1933 involved something more than a repetition of the familiar phenomena of business and stock market cycles. A glance at . . . the Dow-Jones averages of industrial common stocks since 1897 will show how entirely unprecedented was the extent of both the recent advance and the ensuing collapse. They seem to differ from the series of preceding fluctuations as a tidal wave differs from ordinary billows and, as such, would undoubtedly be governed by special causes and produce unparalleled effects.

Words like "unprecedented", "tidal wave", "special causes" and "unparalleled effects" were used to describe this period relative to the usual "repetition of business and stock market cycles" that typically characterized stock market price behavior. In contrast, a number of recent studies (e.g., Santoni 1987; Bierman 1991, 1998) concluded that "overall [the] stock market was not obviously excessively high in September 1929 and the business outlook was favorable. Thus the October crash did not occur because the market was too high" (Bierman 1998, p.17). Such views lend support for the position that Irving Fisher held regarding equity valuations during the crash period.

Were Graham and Dodd incorrect in their observations about security markets events that were, perhaps, too close to be judged accurately? This seems unlikely. If Graham and Dodd were correct, then Bierman and other observers have misinterpreted the significance of 'the crash of 1929' by focusing on the mechanics of common stock valuations surrounding the crash instead of dealing with the role of the crash in contributing to the ongoing collapse of stock market values that continued until February 1933. Based on analyses starting from Fisher (1930b) and continuing to the present, it is evident that theoretically sound rationales for the level that stock prices attained in 1929 can be provided. Yet, consistent with J.M. Keynes' argument in *The General Theory* (e.g., Chapter 11), the crash acted by changing investor perceptions; it was the severity of the blow to perceived return on investment that fuelled the aggregate economic problems that plagued the industrial world in the 1930s. Such events deny theoretical rationality.

Equity security valuation requires more than a mechanical application of predefined rules. The uncertainty inherent in common stock returns can be resolved in different ways, depending on the impact of the historical context on investor psychology. Graham and Dodd (1934, p.6) clearly recognized this point:

> we do not accept the premise that the 1927–1933 experience affords a proper norm by which to judge the future of investment. The swing of the speculative pendulum during this period was of such unprecedented amplitude as to warrant the belief that it will not recur in similar intensity for a long time to come. In other words, we should regard it more as an economic phenomenon akin to the South Sea Bubble and other isolated instances of abnormal gambling frenzy than as an indication of what the typical speculative cycle will be. As a *speculative* experience, the recent cycle differed from previous ones in kind rather than degree; but in its effects upon the *investment fabric* it had unique characteristics, seemingly of a nonrecurrent type.

This is by no means an isolated quote. For example, "One of the striking features of the past five years has been the domination of the financial scene by purely psychological elements" (p.11). The impact of the historically abnormal previous five years of common stock pricing on the analysis and principles advanced by Graham and Dodd is systemic; it affects the whole text.

Graham and Dodd were concerned about the inadequacies of an approach to equity security analysis that appeared in the latter part of the 1920s. Graham and Dodd referred to this approach as "**The New Era Theory**" (p.307):

> During the postwar period, and particularly during the latter stage of the bull market culminating in 1929, the public acquired a completely different

attitude towards the investment merits of common stocks . . . The new theory or principle may be summed up in the sentence: "The value of a common stock depends entirely upon what it will earn in the future."

From this dictum the following corollaries are drawn:

1 That the dividend rate should have slight bearing upon the value.
2 That since no relationship apparently existed between assets and earning power, the asset value was entirely devoid of importance.
3 The past earnings were significant only to the extent that they indicated what changes in earnings were likely to take place in the future.

This complete revolution in the philosophy of common stock investment took place virtually without realization by the stock buying public and with only the most superficial recognition by financial observers.

Graham and Dodd were clear that "the new-era style of investment—as exemplified in the general policy of the investment trusts—was practically indistinguishable from speculation" (p.52). Given the valuations of the NASDAQ-5000 tech stock bubble at the turn of the millennium, these statements have a timeless quality.

By referring to "a completely different attitude towards the investment merits of common stocks", Graham and Dodd's observations about the New Era Theory implicitly made reference to previous approaches to equity security valuation that, presumably, took a more informed view of "investment merits". As such, *Security Analysis* represents a revival of the "advance of security analysis [that] proceeded uninterruptedly until about 1927, covering a long period in which increasing attention was paid on all sides to financial reports and statistical data". The "new era" was a diversion where facts and figures were "manipulated by a sort of pseudo-analysis to support the delusions of the period" (p.14). Reliance on analysis of financial reports permits a rough correspondence between the development of equity security analysis and the emergence of the professional accountants required to prepare the corporate accounts. "The importance and prestige of security analysis have tended to increase over the years, paralleling roughly the steady improvement in corporation reports and other statistical data which supply its raw material" (Graham et al. 1962, p.24). In the pre-1933 world of security market self-regulation, a professional self-regulating accounting profession was needed to ensure that financial reports would be a reliable source of information.

Compared to the English market, professional accounting was relatively slow to develop in the US. A useful reference date is 1882, when the Institute of Accountants and Bookkeepers was formed in New York State. The institute issued certificates upon successful completion of a comprehensive examination. This development was significant because it reflected the growing need for independent accountants to prepare and audit accounts. While, in 1884, there were only 81 independent accountants listed in the city directories of New York, Chicago and Philadelphia, just five years later there were 322 (Gordon 1999, p.173). In 1887, the precursor of the modern-day American Institute of Certified Public

Accountants was established as the American Association of Public Accountants. Recognizing states' important role in regulating the accounting profession, in 1896 New York State established criteria for individuals to be qualified to prepare and audit company accounts. This New York legislation, which was soon adopted by other states, was responsible for introducing the term 'certified public accountant'.

The Bible of Security Analysis

In contrast to Withers (1910), *Security Analysis* is a significant advancement in terms of depth, breadth of analysis and lasting influence. Few modern sources reference Withers (1910), while Graham and Dodd (1934) is viewed with reverence by modern 'value investors', with this first of six editions sometimes being referred to as the 'Bible of Security Analysis'. Given that Withers was an English financial journalist recounting ideas gleaned from discussions with market practitioners in 'the City', this is not surprising. By 1934, Graham was a market practitioner par excellence, with a wealth of personal experience to draw on. In the quarter of a century separating these two texts, there was a substantive increase in the breadth and depth of accounting and other statistical information that are essential ingredients in fundamental analysis. The two texts were also separated by a major security market event, the collapse of security markets from 1929 to 1933. Yet there are enough similarities that *Security Analysis* can be seen as part of a centuries-long progression of ideas about the valuation of equity capital shares. The seminal status often attributed to *Security Analysis* is due more to the impact and influence of that text than to the seminal nature of the ideas presented.

Close examination of the 'fundamental analysis' in Withers (1910) reveals that Graham and Dodd (1934) had themes that can be found in previous contributions to equity capital share valuation. These themes include: (a) the relevance of the distinction between investment and speculation; (b) emphasis on the use of financial statements to form opinions; and (c) the problems raised by the vagaries of market pricing. For example, chapter 4 of *Security Analysis* is dedicated to "distinctions between investment and speculation". On the vagaries of market pricing, Graham and Dodd explicitly recognized that the "intrinsic value" of an equity security may well differ from the market price (p.23):

> the influence of what we call analytical factors over the market price is both *partial* and *indirect*—partial because it frequently competes with purely speculative factors which influence the price in the opposite direction; and indirect, because it acts through the intermediary of people's sentiments and decisions. In other words, the market is not a *weighing machine*, on which the value of each issue is recorded by an exact and impersonal mechanism, in accordance with its specific qualities. Rather we should say that the market is a *voting machine*, whereon countless individuals register choices which are the product of and partly of emotion.

Together with "inadequate or incorrect data" and "uncertainties of the future", the "irrational behavior of the market" is a principal obstacle to the success of the old finance fundamental analyst.

In a fashion, Graham and Dodd dealt with certain epistemological problems arising in the process of generating knowledge about the value of equity capital shares. Such problems were recognized as early as 1921 (Knight 1921). Knowledge in the human sciences does not progress in the same linear fashion as in the natural sciences, where more theoretical and empirical information can usually be obtained about a given phenomenon. In the human sciences, authoritative contributions can be timeless. *Security Analysis* is an excellent example of this point. To be sure, the historical context has changed since the text was written, but many of the insights still have value. Consider the following comment about the objectives of security analysis (Graham and Dodd (1934, p.14):

> Analysis connotes the careful study of facts with the attempt to draw conclusions therefrom based on established principles and sound logic. It is part of the scientific method. But in applying analysis to the field of securities, we encounter the serious obstacle that investment is by nature not an exact science. The same is true of law and medicine: both individual skill (art) and chance are important factors in success or failure. Nevertheless, in these professions analysis is indispensable, so that the same should probably be true in the field of investment and possibly in that of speculation.

It seems that in seeking a definition for 'security analysis', Graham and Dodd grappled with many of the epistemological issues raised by Gadamer (1960) and others.

In surveying the scope of security analysis, Graham and Dodd (1934) identified three functions: descriptive, selective and critical. Of these, it is the selective function that deals with "whether a given issue should be bought, sold, retained, or exchanged for some other"—the other two functions deal with the preparing of company reports or evaluating the terms and conditions of a particular security issue. For purposes of equity valuation, the selective function is of greatest interest. While the descriptive and critical functions are needed in the process of determining an estimated value, this estimated value can be above or below the observed market price. Equity security selection is based on heuristics regarding the difference between the estimated 'intrinsic value' and the market price. This is consistent with methods of equity capital share valuation and selection methods going back to the earliest trade in joint-stock shares. Following a long tradition, Graham and Dodd referred to this estimated value as the 'intrinsic value' of the security.

What Is "Intrinsic Value"?

In *Security Analysis*, the key element in the selective function is the "intrinsic value" of the security. Significantly, the precise definition of intrinsic value evolved through the editions. Initially, the concept was rather vague: "the intrinsic value is an elusive concept. In general terms, it is understood to be that value which is justified by the facts, e.g., the assets, earnings, dividends, definite prospects, as distinct, let us say, from market quotations established by artificial manipulation or distorted by psychological excesses" (Graham and Dodd 1934, p.17). This is remarkably similar to the notion of "intrinsic value" proposed in Armstrong (1848, pp.6–7):

> The market price of Securities is principally determined by their intrinsic value, that is, the state of affairs of the Company which the Stocks represent, the amount of dividend which they pay, the state of interest, &c. We say principally, but not entirely. The prices of all Securities for the investment of Capital, the value and returns being unaltered, are affected more or less by the general condition of the country, as it may be influenced by foreign and domestic affairs, and especially by the state of the money market . . . we can draw a distinction between the *natural* elevations and depressions [of market prices] which are inevitable, and those *unnatural* ones which are the effect of design.

As much of *Security Analysis* is concerned with appropriate methods for determining the intrinsic value of a security, it may seem odd that only a vague definition was proposed. Yet, in adopting a relatively vague definition of intrinsic value, Graham and Dodd were following a long line of inquiry.

The origins of 'intrinsic value' or, in older English, 'intrinsick value', are not clear. Locke (1695) used 'intrinsick value' in the context of "Money":

> SILVER is the Instrument and Measure of Commerce in all the Civilized and Trading parts of the World.
>
> It is the Instrument of Commerce by its intrinsick value.
>
> The intrinsick value of Silver consider'd as Money, is that estimate which common consent has placed on it, whereby it is made Equivalent to all other things, and consequently is the universal Barter or Exchange which Men give and receive for other things they would purchase or part with for a valuable consideration: And thus as the Wise Man tells us, Money answers all things.
>
> Silver is the Measure of Commerce by its quantity, which is the Measure also of its intrinsick value. If one grain of Silver has an intrinsick value in it, two grains of Silver have double that intinsick value, and three grains treble, and so on proportionably. This we have daily Experience of, in common buying and selling. For if one Ounce of Silver will buy, i.e. is of equal value to one Bushel of Wheat, two Ounces of Silver will buy two Bushels of the same Wheat, i.e. has double the value.
>
> Hence it is evident, that an equal quantity of Silver is always of equal value to an equal quantity of Silver.

John Locke (1691) "presents a detailed analysis of the value of land. Locke's main point, which he presents as common knowledge, is that property value depends on the rent that could be earned from it, so that the value of the stream of rental income is the value of the land" (Harrison 2001). An anonymous lengthy English pamphlet from 1691, *The True Cess, by the Exact*

Intrinsick Value of all Real Estates Rightly Stated, was concerned with determining the appropriate 'intrinsic value' of real estate used in the assessment of parish rate taxes. The use of annual 'rack-rent' estimates to assess the amount of taxes to be paid reflects the rudimentary adoption of discounted cash flow concepts to value a physical capital asset, i.e., landed property producing agricultural rents.

Early English sources referencing 'intrinsic value' in the sense of the traded price of a 'share' appeared after similar references in Dutch and French. This raises translation issues. For example, Cantillon used the term in *Essai sur la nature du commerce en general,* which was written in French around 1730 and published posthumously in English in 1755 (Murphy 1986). Though Cantillon used the term in relation to determining a par value between land and labour, the analysis was explicitly concerned with the difference between intrinsic value and market price. The connection between the 'intrinsic value' proposed by Cantillon and the modern notion of 'opportunity cost' identified by Thornton (2007) is intriguing. As a prominent financier during the Mississippi scheme and the South Sea bubble, Cantillon was deeply influenced by the workings of the securities market. As in other aspects of the *Essai* (Poitras 2000, pp.401–2), concepts gleaned from his activities as a financier may have been an inspiration for his contributions to political economy. However, the connection between the 'intrinsic value' of the *Essai* and 'intrinsic value' as the true worth of shares traded in the stock market is underdeveloped.

While Postlethwayt's *Universal Dictionary* (1755) has no reference for intrinsic value, the terminology was in use in the English stock market of the 18th century. In particular, Mortimer (1761, pp.12–3) provided a clear statement of the intrinsic value of a traded security, albeit in the context of "government annuities":

> As the governments are engaged in no trade, a share in their annuities cannot bear any premium, but what will arise from the real value of such share at the time it bears a premium. To illustrate this, let us suppose that I buy at present 100£ share of 3 *per cent Annuities* for 74£ the current price, the reason I buy it so low is, that money is worth at present 4½ *per cent. per annum* and I am to receive only 3 *per cent.* therefore I give a principal sum in proportion only to the interest I am to receive. In a course of time the nation enjoys profound tranquility, by a lasting and honourable peace; my 100£ share in the 3 *per cent. Annuities* which I bought for 74£ becomes worth 104£ or more; from whence does this great profit arise? not from the uncertain advantages of trade, but from a natural and probable event, as publick peace, which has lowered the value of money (the government not being in want of extraordinary supplies) to such a degree, that more than 3 *per cent.* is not to be obtained any where, nor even that, on such good security as my share in the 3 *per cent. Annuities;* therefore I am offered a premium for it, on account of its **intrinsic value.** (emphasis added)

While the anonymous 1720 valuation of the South Sea Company provided 'an estimate of the intrinsick value of South Seas stock' (see Table 7.2), by the middle of the 18th century, 'intrinsic' had replaced 'intrinsick' in the nomenclature of market valuation.

As for the use of intrinsic value for equity capital shares, Harrison (2001) observed most early 18th-century stock-market authors interpreted intrinsic value by the rate of return on an investment. "One 1720 author describes how to 'estimate the Value of a Thing . . . [by] the yearly Profit which it will bring in' . . . This idea appears to have been common, because it expresses the exact method by which land had been valued for many years—on the basis of the yearly rent that could be earned." Significantly, the intrinsic value concept is reflected without the actual terminology employed. Harrison (2001) quoted *Remarks on the celebrated calculations* (1720): "The main principle, on which the whole science of stock-jobbing is built, viz. That the benefit of a dividend (considered as a motive to the buying or keeping of stock) is always to be estimated according to the rate it bears to the price of the stock, because the purchaser is supposed to compare that rate with the profits he might make of money, if otherwise employed". "Similarly the author of *An argument* (1720) chastises stockholders for not recognizing the intrinsic value: 'They are all in Haste to sell out, at more than half below the real Value, and will not wait with Patience and cool thoughts for the profitable Dividends' " (Harrison 2001, p.272).

The use of dividends as a signal of earnings and asset quality was directly related to the absence of accurate accounting provided to shareholders. Previts and Merino (1998, p.121) subtly connected the 'dividend value' approach to determining the 'intrinsic value' and the methods of US accounting that were employed once such information began to be more widely available near the end of the 19th century:

> The practices of quasi-public enterprises, including . . . transportation and utility companies, were profoundly influenced by legal arrangements based upon cash receipts less cash disbursements notions of reporting and profit. As such, many investors sought information that would assist in establishing and corroborating the "dividend value" of a stock. Such a value-based approach equated bond and stock investments in terms of their cash payout via interest and dividend payouts at a time when each of these two forms of corporate securities was being celebrated by unprecedented listings on the New York Stock Exchange.

Significantly, the early regulatory search for a uniform method of reporting accounts involved a cash-based 'operating statistic'. Such an approach became outdated with the introduction of corporate taxes, the adoption of uniform listing requirements by exchanges and the migration into the US of accounting methods similar to those laid out in the British Companies Act (1900).

Graham and Dodd (1934) are often credited with defining security analysis to mean 'the use of fundamental analysis to value securities issued by publicly traded corporations'. This has led to the mantra: "All security analysis involves the use of financial statements" (e.g., Graham et al. 1962, p.105). As such, equity security analysis and valuation are intimately connected to accounting practices. Yet, this interpretation of Graham and Dodd is too narrow. Determination of intrinsic value requires analysis of both quantitative and qualitative factors. Quantitative factors are associated with statistical information from the accounting statements and additional data on capacity utilization, unit prices, costs and the like. Qualitative factors include: (a) the nature of the business; (b) the company's relative position in the industry; (c) physical, geographical and operating characteristics; (d) the character of management; and (e) the long-term outlook for the unit, industry and business in general. How all these elements fit together to form an estimate of intrinsic value is the essential issue confronting fundamental equity security valuation of old finance.

Absent accurate accounting statements, the determination of an equity capital share's 'intrinsic value' is decidedly difficult to estimate. Dividends paid can provide some assistance, but, as Arnold and McCartney (2011, p.214) observed for the 18th-century English canal companies, dividends provide a weak signal:

> Dividends can provide a tangible signal of earnings, but this function depends upon characteristics of financial reporting that were not always present in early financial capitalism. Although eighteenth-century English canal companies offered low-risk securitized capital approved by Parliament and were important to the development of financial capitalism, little is known about the economic state of the canal industry, beyond observed dividend levels . . . estimates [of] rates of return on equity for a set of major English canals . . . shows that their financial reporting under-represented equity inputs so that dividend rates did not reliably signal operating returns or equity-based rates of return.

In addition, during the 19th century, the context of share trading was idiosyncratic. Hickson et al. (2011, p.1218) found for the period between the repeal of the Bubble Act and the failure of the Glasgow Bank, "relatively high rates of return in the banking, insurance, and miscellaneous sectors appear to be in some measure explained by the presence of extended liability and uncalled capital". In addition, some corporations during this period had large share par values, which also impacted the 'intrinsic value' through liquidity concerns.

B   STOCK MARKET REGULATION AND ACCOUNTING EVOLUTION

Financial Reporting circa 1900

Hannah (2007, pp.653–9) detailed the state of accounting in the capitals of capital circa 1900. At this time, in marked contrast to the Continental and Japanese commercial codes, British companies were pioneering external auditing using professional accountants "under the self-regulating auspices of the Institute of Chartered Accountants of England & Wales and of similar self-governing professional associations in Scotland and Ireland." The British accounting associations have their origins in the separation of bookkeeping and accounting from actuarial science around the middle of the 19th century. The days when a reckoning master could handle business calculation and recording needs using the tools of commercial arithmetic were long gone. The change was reflected in the founding of "The Society of Accountants in Edinburgh, the first official accountancy body in the world, receiving its Royal Charter on October 23, 1854". McRae (1965, pp.255–6) provided a useful discussion of the evolving accounting profession in Scotland up to the middle of the 19th century:

> The accounting profession in Scotland is rooted, as it were, in three types of soil.
>
> First we have the legal soil. The growing numbers of bankruptcies and insolvencies in the 19th century encouraged the growth of a clerical profession to assist the legal profession "to consider the whole accompts and to state the points in controversy and to prepare minutes for the Lord Ordinary". Consequently, the legal outlook has had a profound influence on the growth of the accounting profession in Scotland.
>
> The second soil is the more obvious one of bookkeeping. Glasgow and Edinburgh were thriving commercial centres and certain merchants who developed special skills in preparing books of account set up as specialists in this field.
>
> The third soil, the least known, but currently the most interesting, is concerned with mathematics. The official history of the Edinburgh Institute comments that "there was no separate profession of actuary [in Scotland] and it was among the accountants that there could be found such actuarial skill as there then was." Many insurance companies now of international repute were founded by Scottish accountants, and some of the early life tables were calculated by Scottish accountants.

The founding of the Institute of Actuaries in 1848, following collaborative actuarial efforts among life companies starting in 1843, indicates the start of *de facto* specialization separation. While the enhanced role of external auditor for publicly traded companies was still some years in the future, the roots of the modern accounting profession can be traced to the need for accurate records to be used in bankruptcy proceedings as well as the historically traditional tasks of internal audit and bookkeeping.

Following Anderson et al. (2005, p.5):

> accountants in England and Wales made slower institutional progress. In 1870, accounting societies were formed in Liverpool and London, soon followed by Manchester (1871) and Sheffield (1877). The founding of a national body in 1872, the Society of Accountants in England, provided the stimulus for the 1870 London Institute to also open its doors to provincial members. In 1880, members from these five bodies successfully petitioned for a Royal Charter to create the Institute of Chartered Accountants in England and Wales.

At the point of receiving a charter, the English Institute had 587 members. Without the legal right to prevent others from claiming to be 'accountants', the English Institute sought to bring a standard of professionalism to accounting by preventing members from offering an array of services and by requiring a period of apprenticeship to ensure that members of the institute were sufficiently qualified. In conjunction with the growth in demand for external audit services, this approach proved successful, and by 1901 the membership reached 2,831, with about a tenth of members working overseas (Hannah 2007, p.653).

The demand for 'professional' accountants in England was fuelled by the increase in the number of listed companies. As reflected in the *Stock Exchange Official Intelligence*—which included British-registered companies with securities listed on the London Stock Exchange, as well as some foreign-registered listed companies and some provincially listed companies that traded "over-the-counter" in London—the number of listed companies grew from 1,585 in 1885 to 2,581 in 1895, 4,166 in 1901, and 5,337 in 1915. Hannah (p.653) reported that

> In 1901, the president of the English institute reported that 75 percent of these companies were audited solely by his members, a further 4 percent partly by his members, and 8 percent by members of the Irish and Scottish institutes, leaving only 13 percent (many of these French and American companies) audited by individuals, the corporations themselves or non-members. It is evident that this represents a relatively high degree of both professionalization and externalization of corporate auditing.

In contrast to the US, by the end of the 19th century the British company audit had been largely achieved by the voluntary compliance of company boards. The British Companies Act had included a non-compulsory model for articles of incorporation that required an audited balance sheet and profit statement to be presented at the annual general meeting of shareholders.[4]

In addition to regulatory and legislative encouragement by government, the self-regulatory process of the exchanges played a role in the transition to presentation of accounts. While the NYSE did not start compelling the publication of accounts by listed companies until 1895, for several decades the London Stock Exchange Listing Committee had required listed British companies to publish accounts as a condition of new issues, both primary and secondary. However, enforcement was sporadic. Foreign listed companies were only required to follow rules for their domestic markets. Certain domestic companies, such as some breweries and shipping lines that issued debentures and preference shares, were also exempted, presumably for competitive reasons related to company business. However, all but a few, mainly breweries, "of Britain's largest domestic industrial companies by 1900 published both a balance sheet and a profit and loss account and some laggards had fallen into line by 1907" (Hannah p.656). Circa 1900, this British attention to public disclosure of accounting information differed considerably from the American and continental European experience.

Bunting (1986, pp.16–9) estimated that 43 of the largest 100 American industrial companies did not publish a balance sheet in 1900. Continental European industrial companies were typically required by national commercial codes to present accounts to shareholders from an earlier date than in the US and the UK. However, European countries usually did not typically use external audits done by accounting professionals to comply with national regulations. Whether the presence of external audit increased the quality of accounts that were published

Table 10.1 Condensed Statement of the Condition of General Motors Company, 30 September 1909

ASSETS

Cash and Cash Items	$1,365,235.24
Stocks Owned	16,288,048.59
(Valuations Based on Inventories Sept. 30, 1909)	
Other Investments	690,571.96
Other Assets	37,512.07
Total,	$18,381,367.86

LIABILITIES

Companies and Individuals	$11,593.14
Dividend	237,173.79
(Due Oct. 1, 1909)	
Capital Stock	
Common, $4,211,630.00	
Preferred, 6,782.493.89	10,994,123.89
*Surplus	7,138,477.04
Total.	$18,381,367.86

GENERAL INFORMATION

Volume of Business	$34,000,000.00
Number of Motor Cars Produced During Fiscal Year	28,550
Number of Employees	14,250

OFFICERS

President	W. M. Eaton
Vice-President	W. C. Durant
Vice-President	W. J. Mead
Secretary	Curtis R. Hatheway
Treasurer	Curtis R. Hatheway

BOARD OF DIRECTORS

W. M. Eaton	Curtis R. Hatheway
W. C Durant	H. C. Hamilton
W. J. Mead	John T. Smith
	Henry Henderson

Source: Previts and Merino (1998, p.226)

* After charging of $1,040,000.00 for Depreciation, Patents and Questionable Accounts.

under the moral suasion of the London Stock Exchange has been questioned. In particular, Arnold (1997) compared the published shareholder accounts against the internal management accounts of 30 British companies. Arnold concluded corporate disclosures were "not as bad as they might have been" and were sometimes "uninformative and misleading", with the quality of information in published accounts deteriorating over time.

Examining the evidence on the quality of published accounts during this period, Hannah (2007, p.657) uncovered an interesting early instance of auditor shopping: "Part of the problem was that external auditors, though formally appointed by the shareholders in the annual general meeting, in practice were chosen by the directors. They were no doubt—within the capacious limits of their professional standards—somewhat biddable". The underdeveloped character of accounting for large publicly traded companies was still embryonic. A variety of 'legitimate' accounting methods could be employed (p.657):

> Depreciation accounting rules were not well developed and there remained a wide range of allowable treatments: holding companies were not required to consolidate the accounts of subsidiaries; directors could create secret reserves by understating profits in good years, raiding them—without disclosing this—in bad. A very few companies notoriously observed only the letter of the law (it was a requirement to publish a balance sheet every year, but the law did not until 1928 specify that it had to be a new one every year!).

Hannah made a fundamental observation about the relationship between social values and the function of the British equity capital market (p.657):

> Plainly, this was not a world of rigorously prescribed *rules* (such as modern regulators impose in onerous detail), but it was a world of shared *values* or *standards* (that is, broadly understood norms of equitable practice which directors and accountants—and sometimes, *in extremis,* judges—could be expected to apply). We perhaps underestimate the power of Victorian cultural norms of professional, reasonable, and fair behavior in enabling securities markets to work effectively, even with what by modern standards appear as poorly articulated disclosure laws and investor protections. The great majority of companies in fact published more and better information than was legally required and, in the absence of evidence to the contrary, this was treated by contemporary investors as broadly accurate.

This resulted in a general situation in the UK where shareholders would take company accounts with a grain of salt. However, in comparison with other jurisdictions, investors in the London markets at the end of the 19th century had considerably more consistent and reliable accounting information than found elsewhere at the time.

Though there was difficulty with the public availability of accounts for many publicly traded American companies, there were exceptions. In particular, consider the accounts published by US Steel in 1902. There was an "impressive mass of operational and financial detail that was given from 1902 in the published accounts of U.S. Steel (prepared by the British accountants, Price Waterhouse), though that steel giant was then also a somewhat exceptional U.S. industrial, listed on London as well as New York" (p.659). US Steel was one of the first American firms to adopt the English formality of the shareholders electing auditors. In comparison, Standard Oil published no information on assets or profits, other than reporting the capital stock and annual dividend. In this regard, Standard Oil was considered a "blind pool", with financial accounts that were a largely a private matter of the Rockefellers and other directors. Such a pattern of reporting was commonplace in the US, except in areas where specific legislation compelled reporting, as was the case with the Interstate Commerce Act of 1887, which created the Interstate Commerce Commission (ICC), with the authority to regulate railroads to ensure fair freight rates and to eliminate rate discrimination.

The Securities and Exchange Commission

The early history of accounting in the US has received detailed examination in a number of sources, Previts and Merino (1998) being one such account which dates "the birth of modern accounting practice" in the US to 1850–1899. City directories for New York, Chicago and Philadelphia show the number of listings for accountants rising from 19 in 1850 to 81 in 1884 to 322 in 1889. Increasing regulation from the ICC and the corporate merger wave that peaked during the 1890s contributed to the passage (in New York State) of the first act "recognizing and establishing the title of certified public accountant" (p.133). This followed the establishment of the Institute of Accountants of New York in 1882, "the earliest recognized professional accounting organization in the US". Few records have survived for this association, other than an 1884 list of 80 members. Similar associations were organized in other cities, with the Philadelphia Bookkeepers Beneficial Association being organized in 1874 with 35 members and having "nearly three hundred" in 1884.

While the beginnings of accountancy in the US were influenced by transplanted British accountants, the passage of the CPA law in New York "limited the granting of certificates to citizens or those who duly intended to become citizens, which effectively barred many resident British chartered accountants from certification in New York" (p.186). Such exclusionary competition characterized the infighting that plagued the American accounting profession in the first decades of the 20th century as state-by-state legal recognition was provided to accountants. Struggles to form a national association and improve the acceptability of CPA laws in some states took place against a backdrop of "charges of professional exclusion and meaningless CPA certificates". This put pressure on the emerging accounting profession to introduce uniform standards for education and to produce "a systemic approach to accounting problems through which judgment, guided by experience and education, enabled the practitioner to arrive at appropriate solutions in each specific engagement".

The progression of the accountancy profession in the US during the 1920s saw the American Institute of Accountants—with membership that "tended to be concentrated in urbanized states and its leaders were often connected with large, well-established, and prosperous firms"—slowly gain prominence

Table 10.2 Legal Recognition of Accountants

Year Law Passed	Number of States	States
1896	1	New York
1899	1	Pennsylvania
1900	1	Maryland
1901	1	California
1903	2	Washington, Illinois
1904	1	New Jersey
1905	2	Michigan, Florida
1906	1	Rhode Island
1907	3	Utah, Colorado, Connecticut
1907	3	Ohio, Louisiana, Georgia
1909	5	Montana, Nebraska, Minnesota, Massachusetts, Missouri
1910	1	Virginia
1911	2	West Virginia, Wyoming
1912	1	Vermont
1913	8	Oregon, North Carolina, North Dakota, Nevada, Tennessee, Delaware, Maine, Wisconsin
1915	6	South Carolina, Indiana, Arkansas, Kansas, Texas, Iowa
1916	1	Kentucky
1917	4	Idaho, New Hampshire, Oklahoma, South Dakota
1919	2	Alabama, Arizona
1920	1	Missippi
1921	1	New Mexico
1923	1	District of Columbia

Source: Previts and Merino (1998, p.148)

Note: Reproduced from Eric L. Kohler and Paul W. Pettengill, *Principles of Auditing* (Chicago: A. W. Shaw Company, 1927).

over the American Society of Certified Public Accountants—founded in 1921 by a group of practitioners primarily from the Midwest "to prevent the sale of CPA credentials and to protect the CPA title as the designation for professional accountants" (p.243). Following the collapse of securities markets that started in late 1929 and propelled the change in social conscience that permitted passage of the Securities Act (1933) and the Securities Exchange Act (1934), the "bitter rivalry" between these two accounting associations ended with unification under the threat of external intervention from newly established federal regulatory authority. Previts and Merino (p.271) described the change in social conscience as follows: "politicians could no longer argue that Americans would prosper under a business system managed—or unmanaged—as it had been in the 1920s. The ideological debates of the past began to give way to a new agreement on the practicalities of managing a modern economy".

The goals of the legislation to reform the US securities markets in general and the equity capital market in particular aimed to 'curb managerial power, promulgate uniform reporting rules and to provide information useful to equity capital investors'. Such changes required a transformation of the US accounting profession from the position of accountants during the 1920s (p.249):

> Despite the marked increase in share ownership and the emergence of the small investor, politicians voiced little concern about protection of investors. If capitalism had overcome its materialism and if managers, guided by profit, could be relied upon to protect the public interest, as the dominant view held, then investors needed no other safeguards. CPAs would fulfill their obligation to investors by working with corporate managers to ensure that every firm received a fair return on its investment.

It was difficult for the accounting profession to make the transition from being actively involved in the decision-making process of corporations to being independent actors. In the 1920s, CPAs came to be seen as nearly infallible advisers. "The ASCPA actively promoted advisory services" (Previts and Merino 1998, p.251). The passage of the 1913 income tax act led to a situation where 'advocacy, not independence, became an accepted norm for tax practice'.

The cosy relationship between professional accountants and corporate managers led to a complicated situation during the 1930s (p.271):

> The passage of securities legislation should have changed relationships between accountants and management. It did not because the stated objectives of the legislation—to curb managerial power, to promulgate uniform reporting rules, and to provide information that was useful to investors for decision-making—were not implemented. By the end of the decade, management continued to have great flexibility in the selection of accounting principles; acceptance of concepts of consistency and conservatism did not increase the usefulness of financial reports to the "average" small investor. In many respects, securities legislation appeared to be symbolic, its primary purpose was to mollify public concern.

Against this backdrop, accountants were able to withstand "the threat of loss of professional autonomy" and develop rudiments of a more uniform set of financial accounting rules and reporting standards, spearheaded by the Committee on Accounting Procedure (1936–1959) of the American Institute of Accountants. The initiatives of this group evolved into the Accounting Principles Board (1959–1973), a part of the American Institute of Certified Public Accountants, which evolved on 1 July 1973 into the Financial Accounting Standards Board

(FASB), recognized by the SEC as the organization responsible for setting accounting standards for public companies in the US.

While there were a number of precursor legislative actions, such as the Uniform Sale of Securities Act (1930), the origin of the Securities and Exchange Commission (SEC) can be traced to the passage of the Securities Act of 1933:[5]

> The Securities Act of 1933 was the first general federal law to regulate the issuance of securities. The Act required certain issuers of securities to file registration statements with the Federal Trade Commission and to provide a prospectus to investors. The FTC had the power to issue stop orders to prevent the sale of an issuer's securities. The purpose of the Act was to prevent fraudulent securities offerings and to ensure that the public had adequate information regarding the issuer and nature of a security. The Act was one of the major pieces of legislation enacted during Roosevelt's first 100 days in office.
>
> The original draft of the Act did not require that financial statements be audited ('certified'). Later drafts considered the value of independent audits, and the feasibility of requiring that audits be made by accountants on staff of the agency that would administer the Act. The bill as passed confirmed the requirement of certification by independent public accountants.

This legislative action did not happen independent of activities in the securities markets. For example, in 1932, the NYSE began asking all corporations applying to list securities to provide published annual financial statements, audited by independent public accountants. In 1933, the NYSE further required that listing applications include audited financial statements for the most recent fiscal year. At that time, over 90% of listed companies had independent audits, though the quality of many audits was viewed with skepticism due to the close relationship between accounting firms and corporate management.

While the Securities Act of 1933 dealt with rules and regulations for the issuance of securities, the SEC was empowered by the passage of the Securities Exchange Act of 1934. In February 1934, President Roosevelt requested that Congress pass legislation to regulate the stock exchanges. Following this request, Senator Duncan Fletcher and Congressman Sam Rayburn introduced the Securities Exchange Act requiring registration of stock exchanges. The Securities and Exchange Commission was created pursuant to the act, with power to approve stock exchange rules, prohibit manipulative trading practices, regulate corporate proxy practices and increase disclosure requirements. The prominent Wall Street businessman and Democratic supporter, Joseph Kennedy, was appointed the first chairman of the SEC.

> Confronted in the 1930s with a moribund securities market and a demoralized investment community, the SEC's architects worked first to restore and then to modernize a functioning system of capital markets. They pursued this objective by emphasizing the promotion of disclosure more than the punishment of fraud. They administered the strategy wherever possible through third-party institutions rather than through a large corps of federal

employees. These third parties were the organized stock exchanges, the accounting profession, and the National Association of Securities Dealers, Inc. (McCraw 1982, p.348)

In addition to federal jurisdiction, state regulators played a role in 'restoring confidence and modernizing a functioning system of capital markets'.

The 75th anniversary of the birth of the SEC coincided with the financial collapse of 2008–2009: "Over the course of a few weeks, several of the country's largest financial institutions suffered critical or near-critical crises, requiring the injection of unprecedented bailout funds. In a single week in October, 2008, the Dow Jones Industrial Average fell by more than 20%. In a one-year period, the Dow Jones Wilshire 5000, reflecting most U.S. publicly traded stocks, lost $8.4 trillion in value" (Fisch 2009, p.785). This historic event served to reinforce ongoing criticism that the SEC: improperly regulates derivative securities, especially in the OTC market; is lax in its oversight of securities firms; and, based on various investigations by Congress, is possibly biased in favor of large securities firms. In March 2008, the US Treasury Department issued the "Blueprint of Financial Regulation" criticizing the SEC's 'obsolete approach to regulation', advancing a plan for regulatory consolidation that would severely curtail the SEC's position as the cornerstone of capital market regulation. Against this backdrop, the SEC's failure to deal properly with the $50 billion Ponzi scheme at Madoff Investment Securities fuelled the severe criticisms of its performance of core enforcement operations.

The numerous contemporary criticisms of the SEC stand in stark contrast to its promising formative years when the SEC restored public confidence in the financial markets and encouraged regulated and other interested entities to aid in the implementation of public policy (McCraw 1982). These entities included the accounting profession, the organized securities exchanges, and the brokers and dealers operating in the OTC markets. McCraw detailed some positive early impressions of the SEC (p.347):

In 1940 Sam Rayburn called [the SEC] "the strongest Commission in the Government." In the late 1940s the Hoover Commission Report cited the SEC as "an outstanding example of the independent commission at its best." In 1971, a survey of regulatory literature found the SEC's standing superior to that of all comparable agencies. In a major research project of 1977, the Congressional Research Service of the Library of Congress polled over one thousand members of the regulatory bar in Washington, who "rated the SEC commissioners most positively and the FMC and FTC commissioners most negatively." In the same study, "the SEC also received the most favorable ratings on judgment, technical knowledge, impartiality, legal ability, integrity and hard work." Even the Reagan transition team had a good word in December 1980: "In comparison with numerous oversized Washington bureaucracies, the SEC, with its 1981 requested budget of $77.2 million, its 2,105 employees and its deserved reputation for integrity and efficiency, appears to be a model government agency."

This success was, at least partly, due to 'the first four SEC chairmen—Joseph P. Kennedy, James M. Landis, William O. Douglas, and Jerome Frank', "talented regulators who formulated clear plans to implement their strategy". By 2006, this strong, positive public impression had been eroded to the point where Arthur Levitt, chairman of the SEC from 1993 to 2001, observed: "Events have placed the Securities and Exchange Commission (SEC) at a great turning point. For the first time in its history, the agency is being challenged legally and politically. The anger of various constituent groups and their willingness to challenge the Commission's authority is, in my view, a serious threat to its relevance. An erosion of the power and influence of the SEC would be a tragic blow to the interests of markets, investors, and the nation's continuing primacy as the world's foremost capital market" (Levitt 2006, p.1483).

Graham et al. (1962)

Knowledge can be transmitted in a variety of forms. Consistent with tenets of logical positivism, modern finance proceeds by providing the logical development of a desired proposition, starting from initial assumptions and progressing logically until the proposition is established. Where appropriate and possible, the proposition is then subjected to empirical verification. This pedagogical method can be contrasted with, say, the Socratic approach, which develops notions using an interrogatory interplay. Other methods of transmitting knowledge include the parables of the New Testament, the sayings of Confucius and Sun Tzu, and the fables of Aesop. Even Grimm's fairy tales and Mother Goose nursery rhymes convey knowledge in a fashion that is at odds with the 'scientific' approach. Yet, it is difficult to claim that these different pedagogical methods do not have immense value. It is even possible to go in the other direction and claim that, in the human sciences, false scientific precision can shed more heat than light on matters. As Warren Buffett (Cunningham 2002, p.82) observed about the modern finance approach to measuring risk using beta: "In their hunger for a single statistic to measure risk . . . they forget a fundamental principle: It is better to be approximately right than precisely wrong."

Though a landmark text in security analysis, there is much in the fourth and final edition[6] of *Security Analysis* (Graham et al. 1962) that can be found in other sources, such as Ben Graham's *Intelligent Investor* (1949). Large parts of Graham and Dodd (1934) appear verbatim in Graham et al. (1962). Being a classic text from the era of 'old finance', Graham et al. (1962) shares the institutional and descriptive pedagogical approach that characterizes old finance. Though there is a drift towards the approach of modern finance, Graham et al. (1962) is still clearly from a different tradition. The style used involves a heuristic discussion of a particular topic, typically illustrated with a number of practical examples using actual securities. Sometimes, usually where there is potential for confusion in analyzing a particular situation, the discussion is followed by the statement of an investment principle. Graham et al. (1962) is characterized by certain themes that permeate the analysis. These themes connect Graham et al. (1962) with earlier versions of the text going back to the first edition (Graham and Dodd 1934). However, Graham et al. (1962) is more than an expanded discussion of earlier versions. Though the essence of the discussion is largely unchanged, there are some significant points of evolution and, on occasion, disagreement.

An important theme in Graham et al. (1962) is the distinction between speculation and investment. This distinction was inherited directly from Graham and Dodd (1934), in which the lessons of the stock market collapse of 1929–1933 and the "new era theory" of common stock investing were still fresh in the air. Though concern with the 'new era' theory had been reduced to a historical discussion in Graham et al. (1962), the theme of investment versus speculation persisted: "An investment operation is one which upon thorough analysis, promises safety of principal and satisfactory return. Operations not meeting these requirements are speculative" (p.49). This is an exact repetition of Graham and Dodd (1934, p.54). Graham et al. (1962, e.g., pp.51–2) explicitly recognized that old finance security analysis has considerable limitations in *speculative* situations. Security analysis is "an adjunct rather than . . . a guide to speculation. It is only when chance plays a subordinate role that the analyst can properly speak in an authoritative voice and accept responsibility for the results of his judgments". With limitations in the analysis of speculative securities, the range of common stocks and other securities to which the Graham et al. (1962) techniques of security analysis apply is relatively narrow. More precisely, common stocks that have "too many uncertainties about its future to permit the analyst to estimate its earning power with any degree of confidence" are speculative in nature because "a common stock purchase may not be regarded as a proper constituent of a true investment program unless it is possible to show by some rational calculation that it is worth at least as much as the price paid for it".

Another central theme in Graham et al. (1962) can be summarized as "All security analysis involves the analysis of financial statements". This viewpoint is qualified with the proviso: "the weight given to financial material may vary enormously, depending upon the kind of security studied and basic motivation of the prospective purchaser". However, the authors were clear on the relative importance of "quantitative" versus "qualitative" factors in security analysis. Quantitative factors are associated with statistical information from the income statement, balance sheet and additional data on capacity utilization, unit prices, costs, and so on. Qualitative factors include the nature of the business; the relative position of the company in the industry; physical, geographical, and operating characteristics; the character of management; and the long-term outlook for the unit, industry and general business. The Graham et al. (1962) approach to security analysis is fundamentally concerned with how quantitative and qualitative information is combined. On this point there is an apparent divergence of opinion across the editions.

Comparing Graham et al. (1962) with earlier versions, the weight to qualitative factors in security analysis varies considerably. Graham and Dodd (1934, p.430) maintained: "Quantitative data are useful only to the extent that they are supported by a qualitative survey of the enterprise". In contrast, Graham et al. (1962) maintained that quantitative factors are always an essential element of the analysis (p.86):

Broadly speaking, the important quantitative factors lend themselves to much more precise consideration in appraising a specific company than do the qualitative factors. The former are fewer in number, more easily obtainable, and better suited to the forming of definitive conclusions. Furthermore, the financial results themselves epitomize such qualitative elements as the ability of a reasonably long-entrenched management. This point of view does not minimize the importance of qualitative factors in appraising the performance of a company, but it does indicate that a detailed study of them—to be justified—should provide sufficient additional insight to assist significantly in appraising the company.

The issue is further clouded when Graham et al. (1962) provided an additional criterion for investment: "An investment operation is one that can be justified on **both** qualitative and quantitative grounds". This change in emphasis away from qualitative factors towards quantitative factors associated with financial statements was likely due to the substantially better reliability and availability of this source of information due to historical developments such as the 1933 and 1934 securities reforms.

Another important theme in Graham et al. (1962) carried forward from previous editions, but subjected to change, was the concept of "intrinsic value". Whereas Graham and Dodd (1934, e.g., p.17) emphasized the "intrinsic value" of a stock and provided heuristic methods for determining this "elusive concept" based on examination of a range of factors such as the record of dividends and the ability of earnings to sustain the dividend, Graham et al. (1962) identified intrinsic value with discounted cash flow valuation of equity securities. Graham et al. (1962) adopted the discounted cash flow (DCF) model as the theoretical mechanism for determining the intrinsic value (p.435):

The Valuation Process Briefly Described

The standard method of valuation of individual enterprises consists of capitalizing the expected future earnings and/or dividends at an appropriate rate of return. The average earnings will be estimated for a period running ordinarily between five and ten years. In the case of an issue valued as a "growth stock" the projection may be of a terminal year—e.g., four to five years hence—rather than a long term average. The capitalization rate, or multiplier, applied to earnings and dividends, will vary with the quality of the enterprise and will thereby give recognition to the longer-term profit possibilities which cannot be established with precision. Asset values become a significant factor in the appraisal only at the extreme ranges, where either the tangible assets are very low in relation to earnings power value or the net current assets alone exceed the earning power value.

This approach led Graham et al. (1962) to identify the four basic components of common stock value: expected future earnings, expected future dividends, capitalization rates and asset values. J.B. Williams' influence on Graham et al. (1962) is difficult to ignore.

The Graham et al. (1962) approach to security analysis integrates the price estimates obtained from the DCF model with the 'margin of safety' principle and the benefits of diversification: "In our opinion, margin of safety—in the form of an excess of estimated intrinsic value over current market price—is a prerequisite to investing in secondary [and primary] shares" (pp.438–41).[7] Because the margin of safety is not a guarantee that any given stock will produce a loss, the diversification principle is also required: "A group of, say, twenty or more common stocks will usually average out the individual favorable and unfavorable developments. For this reason, the diversification or group approach is an integral part of the valuation concept itself". Graham et al. (1962) later clarified this number to between 20 and 30 stocks drawn from a list of not more than 100 "primary" common stocks (i.e., large, prosperous and highly capitalized companies with a strong record of earnings). Graham et al. (1962) suggested a further restriction on the amount invested in any one industry. The Graham et al. (1962) recommendation that common stock portfolios contain 20 or more high-grade common stocks that would be regularly adjusted is a distinct point of contrast with the recommendations of a growth stock proponent such as Philip Fisher (1958, 1980), who indicated a significantly smaller number of share holdings for individual investors.[8]

Even though both 'margin of safety' and diversification concepts were adopted from previous editions, there was a decided change in tone in Graham et al. (1962). For example, on the diversification principle, Graham and Dodd (1934, p.320) stated: "In our view, the purchase of a single common stock can no more constitute an investment than the issuance of a single policy on a life or a building can properly constitute insurance underwriting." However, Graham et al. (1962, p.55) substantially qualified this view:

> There is a well-known argument *against* diversification based on Andrew Carnegie's maxim: "Put all your eggs in one basket and watch the basket". We believe this counsel has an application to security investment but only within its strictest interpretation. An investor may concentrate heavily on the shares of one corporation provided that he has a *personal connection* with it—as an executive or a member of a controlling group. Many large fortunes have been built up over the years by such concentration. But where the close personal connection with the company is lacking that policy rarely works out well. When the choice is in fact a very good one, there is a tendency to sell out at a comparatively early stage in the long-term advance. Any other kind of choice will, of course, appear to be a mistaken one during periods of declining prices.

Graham et al. (1962) also recommended a form of 'tactical asset allocation' strategy (see Poitras 2005, ch.10) in which the composition of the investment portfolio would fluctuate between "an upper limit of 75 percent to be held in common stocks and a lower limit of 25 percent" (pp.447–9). The proportion held in common stocks at any point in time would be "geared to the analyst-investor's valuation of the DJIA, Standard & Poor's Composite Index, or some other measure of the market". In effect, Graham et al. (1962) were advocates of index-tracking market timing strategies. In addition, Graham et al. (1962) recommended "the sale of holdings that appear definitely overvalued or replacement of less by more attractive stocks" (p.446). This implies a shorter holding period than the long-term buy-and-hold horizon of Philip Fisher.

Graham et al. (1962) were intimately aware of: the dramatic progression in securities markets; in the professional practice of security analysis; and in the theories of modern finance that emerged between 1934 and 1962. As observed above, the acceptance and adoption of valuation techniques for common stocks based on DCF modeling, started by Williams (1937), was explicitly recognized and rationalized. Graham et al. (1962, p.416) acknowledged that the changes that occurred in securities markets, particularly stock markets, during the 1950s required "new points of view and standards of value":

> Our philosophy and its related standards of value were derived primarily from the actual experience of stock investors (and speculators) during many decades prior to the 1950s. They were consistent with stock-market conditions existing at the time our previous editions were published. We think they proved a useful guide to investors from 1934 through 1954. But . . . the latter half of the 1950s brought record high levels in stock prices and with them new points of view and standards of value. It is a difficult task to examine these new levels and standards as they exist at the beginning of the 1960s and to reach some conclusions as to their validity for investment purposes.

Consistent with the proposed use of DCF for common stock valuation, Graham et al. (1962) criticized the observed practice of doing common stock valuations based on a "too abbreviated forecast of probable future earnings—covering generally only the next twelve months . . . value cannot soundly be established on the basis of earnings shown over a short period of time" (p.434).

On the historical evolution of common stocks, Graham et al. (1962, pp.56–7) observed that the improvement in investment potential of common stocks led to "an upgrading in the public standing of common stocks generally", leading to the misperception that many 'speculative' issues were actually of 'investment' quality. This misperception had been complicated by the rapid pace of technological change, which created the 'growth stock' and led to more rapid erosion in the core business of certain 'primary' stocks due to an inability to adapt to the pace of change. This technological growth factor "is not amenable to dependable prediction" and, as a consequence, stocks in the growth category are "fundamentally speculative". In contrast to Philip Fisher, Graham et al. (1962) also maintained that the quality of the company alone is an insufficient indication of value without also considering the common stock price: "Strictly speaking, there can be no such thing as an 'investment issue' in the absolute sense, i.e., implying that it remains an investment regardless of price" (p.50).

Though the fourth edition of *Security Analysis* is generally a more sophisticated and developed treatment of security analysis than the first edition, there are a number of points where Graham et al. (1962) failed to recognize the value contained in the earlier edition and dropped material that still had considerable insight. The discussion of the 'new era' theory is one of these cases. A modern observer of equity markets will be struck by the similarity of the 'new era' theory of common stock valuation and similar valuation methods that appeared during the technology/dot-com bubble that started around 1995 and continued to early 2000. Writing in the early 1960s, when concerns with the stock market collapse of 1929–1933 had largely faded from view, instead of a close examination of the 'new era' theory all Graham et al. (1962, p.57) could muster was a concern about "the shift of investment emphasis from values established by the past record to values to be achieved *solely* by future growth . . . we are skeptical of the ability of all but the most gifted analysts to chart with precision the growth rate of a given company for many years ahead." More significantly, in proposing DCF to estimate 'intrinsic value', Graham et al. (1962) strayed far from the path of Graham and Dodd (1934).

A Variety of Modern DCF Models

The use of discounted cash flow (DCF) methods to value investments and real assets goes back centuries (e.g., Poitras 2000, ch.4; Parker 1968). The application of these techniques to the earliest issues of equity securities involved the use of valuation methods developed for fixed income securities to determine the 'intrinsick' value of the stock. Well into the 20th century, the dividend yield was considered the most important measure of equity security value, especially for investment-grade stocks (e.g., Rutterford 2004). There were various reasons for this preference, including the absence of sufficiently accurate accounting information prior to reforms of the securities markets begun by the passage of the Securities Act (1933) and the Securities Exchange Act (1934) in the US and the Companies Act (1948) in the UK.[9] Dividends paid were the most visible and reliable source of information about firm performance. In addition, in the UK and Europe corporations tended to have high dividend payout ratios and a preference for raising capital for expansion from new share issues (Graham and Dodd 1934, p.331), instead of having a lower dividend payout and reinvesting retained earnings to expand the business.

One shortcoming with using fixed income methods to value common stock is that the dividend is not fixed over time. The historical transition from traditional fixed income valuation to discounted cash flow valuation for capital assets can be traced to contributions by actuaries, real estate appraisers and engineers made in the mid-19th century. These more advanced valuation methodologies permitted the future cash flows associated with a capital asset, such as an equity security, to vary over time. In particular, a British mining engineer, William Armstrong, used discounted cash flow methods to value mining company issues and mining leases (Pitts 2001). Around this time, actuaries also became interested in valuation for variable annuities. The first Institute of Actuaries textbook (Sutton 1882) contained a section on variable annuities. Todhunter (1901) modelled the common stock price using a perpetuity with a constant growth rate, determining the pricing solution with an infinite number of dividend payments. This approach to equity valuation continued to attract attention until the 1960s (e.g., Clendenin and Van Greave 1954; Durand 1957b; Soldofsky 1966).

While not directly concerned with DCF valuation, *Common Stocks as Long-Term Investments* (Smith 1925) marks the beginning of the transition from equity valuation based on dividend yields to equity valuation based on earnings. Providing detailed empirical evidence, Smith (1925, 1927) changed the perception of earnings relative to dividends. Prior to Smith, the convention was to measure the value of common stock relative to bonds: Being the most junior of all corporate securities, with the greatest variability of cash flow, common stock required the highest yield among the securities on offer from a given corporation. Smith demonstrated that the *ex post* returns on equities outperformed bonds due to the compounding effect on future dividends and future share prices of reinvesting 'this increasing surplus in productive operation' (Smith 1925, p.77). This view was well suited to American companies which had benefited from strong economic growth over the 1866–1922 sample that Smith examined. The superior presentation of accounting information by US as compared to UK and European companies—for example, in the reporting of consolidated versus unconsolidated earnings– also facilitated the use of valuations based on earnings as opposed to dividends.

The connection between equity valuation based on earnings and DCF valuation is that once reinvestment of retained earnings is recognized, the dividend is expected to rise over time with the share price. This represents a significant change in the character of corporate finance, which favoured distributing the bulk of earnings in dividend payments, leaving undistributed earnings in reserves designed to maintain the dividend payment in adverse conditions. Faced with favourable growth prospects, American companies tended to have lower dividend payout ratios than firms in the UK and Europe, which were often more mature and did not have the same need for capital to fund growth opportunities as those operating in the tariff-protected US market. With high dividend payout and lower growth prospects, unconsolidated reported earnings were primarily

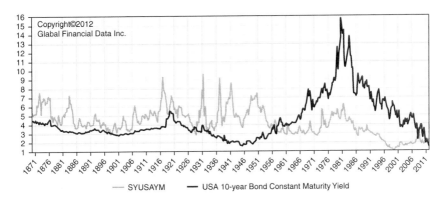

Figure 10.2   S&P 500 Monthly Dividend Yield vs USA 10-year Bond Constant Maturity Yield

used to measure the 'dividend cover'—similar to the use of interest coverage ratios to value corporate bonds. Recognition that the dividend payment will increase over time led to theoretical contributions providing appropriate pricing models. For example, Guild (1931) developed a model of the share price using the sum of a finite period of constant growth in cash flow plus a terminal share value measured using the discounted value of a price/earnings multiple.

While Guild (1931) wrote for the investment trade, similar contributions were appearing in academic publications. Preinreich (1932) presented a model with a capital base that expands as earnings grow over a finite period. Significantly, Preinreich concluded: "only discounted cash flow techniques could value such growth firms correctly" (Rutterford 2004, p.139). Despite the ability to model the price of equity claims using a discounted stream of growing dividends, the widespread recognition and acceptance of these methods by academics and some practitioners to value common stocks began with the theoretical and empirical applications in John Burr Williams' *Theory of Investment Value* (1937). Graham and Dodd (1934) gave no explicit discussion or recognition of discounted cash flow valuation for equities, though in the final edition of *Security Analysis* by Graham et al. (1962), DCF methods are recommended to estimate intrinsic value without actually executing such a calculation.

The basic notion advanced in Williams (1937) was that the present value for an equity security, such as a common stock, can be determined by discounting the future stream of expected cash inflows minus expected cash outflows at the appropriate rate of interest. The notion that "every stock price represents a discounted value of future dividends and earnings of that stock" (Fisher 1930a, p.xxii) was well known. What is significant about Williams (1937) is that the common stock valuation takes centre stage in the discussion. There is detailed discussion of how the distribution of company earnings into dividends and retained earnings impacted the future growth of both earnings and the balance sheet. While only simplistic growth assumptions are used, Williams (1937) devoted pages to actual valuations of companies such as General Motors. Recognizing that "investment value" for Williams corresponded to "intrinsic value" in Graham and Dodd (1934), Williams (1937) provided a promising and well-structured method of determining a numerical 'intrinsic value'.

The theoretical development of the basic discounted dividend model advanced in Williams (1937) reached a climax with Durand (1957b), in which a connection was made between the constant dividend growth version of the discounted dividend model and the St. Petersburg paradox. Though the constant dividend growth variant of the discounted dividend model is often attributed to Gordon (1962), as Durand (1957b, p.351) observed, this version of the model is given in Williams (1937). Durand (1957b) considered a number of theoretical nuances arising from the dividend discount model with growing dividends. Despite this long history, the eponym for the simplified DDM belongs to Myron Gordon (1920–2010). Because Gordon (1962) was concerned with the important practical problem of valuing companies in regulated industries, the formula provided a 'killer application' for the emerging capital asset pricing model to determine the unobservable discount rate for the stock. In recognition of the significance that the model played at that time, the constant dividend growth version of the discounted cash flow model is referred to as the 'Gordon growth model' (e.g., Damodaran 1994, p.99).

Discounted Cash Flow Prior to J.B. Williams

Using discounted cash flow to value a traded equity capital share stretches back at least to the 18th century (e.g., Harrison 2001). Given the well developed state of fixed income valuation at that time, it was natural to apply such techniques to the relatively predictable payouts of shares belonging to 'the English funds'. Despite these beginnings, the practical use of discounted cash flow to value equity capital shares was confounded by the method of keeping commercial accounts, which focused on the capital stock and expenses rather than current and future cash flow. It is apparent from Tuck (1847) that by the middle of the 19th century practical valuation of English railway shares concentrated on authorized capital stock and the land acquisition costs, construction expenses and the like. At that time, the rudimentary state of accounting practice and information combined with the competitive need to acquire equity capital. This created a situation in which dividends paid, when available, were only a weak indicator of the underlying cash flow generated by the firm. In this environment, comparison of current dividend yields for traded shares was the closest that practical valuation came to using discounted cash flow.

In America, Dulman (1989, p.556) reported the situation was not much different:

> During the nineteenth century, no major [US] industrial firm measured its net earnings in relation to total capital investment. Entrepreneurs such as Andrew Carnegie were concerned with controlling costs and improving the efficiency of one economic activity. Most nineteenth century entrepreneurs took their firms' investment as given, and they devoted their attention to managing short-run costs. Railroad and steel firms classified capital investments as operating expenses.

Significant progress on the theory of discounted cash flow valuation started to appear in capital budgeting applications in the last half of the 19th century. Faustmann's seminal formula, which gives the present value of the future cash flow from a forest rotation, appeared in 1849. In the context of determining an appropriate railway location, Wellington (1877, pp.193–7) used discounted cash flow valuation to show "the justifiable present expenditure" for construction of a railway line. Dulman (1989, p.560) claimed: "Wellington was apparently the first to advocate the use of present value analysis to evaluate industrial capital budgeting alternatives". However, the application was not central to the much larger Wellington text, being provided "if only to check the vague visions of his board of directors, as to the probable growth of traffic in the future, and the justifiable present expenditure" (Wellington 1877, p.194). A much larger second edition in 1887 contained a much expanded discussion of applying discounted cash flow valuation in engineering economics.

Edwards and Warman (1981) provided a revealing instance of the perception of discounted cash flow in the later 19th century. The case involves a discounted cash flow valuation of an equity capital share contained in a much larger report on the merger of two companies (p.37):

> In 1889 the Shelton Iron, Steel and Coal Company was incorporated to take over the assets and business activities of two existing companies. To guide the contracting parties in negotiating a price to be paid for the properties belonging to the Shelton Collieries and Ironworks an independent valuation was arranged by Deloitte, Dever, Griffiths & Co., later appointed auditors of the new company.

The two companies being merged were Lord Granville's Shelton Collieries and Ironworks (SCI), a privately held venture, and the Shelton Iron and Steel Company Limited (SISC). The resulting use of discounted cash flow to determine a valuation for SCI can be discounted: "As it turned out, the only use made of Craig's estimate of present value was to demonstrate, to new investors brought in at the time SISC was incorporated, the conservative nature of the basis actually used" (p.48). This indicates that the newly incorporated company was seeking to issue equity capital shares. Though the report was prepared by an accounting firm, the work was contracted to a legal firm, and nothing is known of the professional qualifications of the actual preparer of the discounted cash flow valuation, a William Craig from Cheshire. The ultimate use of traditional balance sheet valuations for the assets reflects the lack of acceptance that valuations based on income had at that time.

Though discounted cash flow methods were widely used to value fixed income securities, the unpredictable character of cash flows from the avalanche of equity capital shares that emerged during the 19th century, combined with the absence of reliable accounting information for cash flow, did not provide enough 'inputs' to estimate a useful discounted cash flow value. As a consequence, it was 19th-century mining engineers, railway engineers, foresters and the like who were able to develop capital budgeting applications associated with valuations of well-defined cash flows that J.B. Williams later adopted. In cases such as mining and forestry, the relatively predictable cash flows were generated by physical assets. These contributions formed the beginnings of capital budgeting analysis, a topic where the theoretical optimum fails to gain traction in the vernacular (p.38):

> Why have . . . inherent errors of principle not deterred companies from using sub-optimal valuation methods in preference to the theoretically pre-eminent DCF techniques? The reasons have not changed since they were first identified by Bonbright in the 1930s. Forecasting future cash flows and selecting a suitable discount rate are subjective exercises difficult to defend in law. Forecasting future cash flows inevitably involves a strong element of crystal-ball gazing and, instead of a series of known returns, estimates used will be, at best, a range of possible outcomes dependent upon the occurrence or nonoccurrence of various future events. Moreover the discount rate which, in theory, should represent the risk-free rate of interest plus a

premium for risk, both unknowns, must, in practice, also be estimated. The effect of these practical difficulties is that DCF techniques have come to be regarded, by many businessmen, as academic ideals with little relevance to the imperfect market in which firms operate.

J.B. Williams (1937) was not the first to propose discounted cash flow as a method of determining the intrinsic value of a particular capital asset (i.e., a common stock price). However, his suggestion that this approach could produce a 'rational' valuation was novel.

Macaulay's *Movement of Interest Rates, Bond Yields and Stock Prices in the United States since 1856* (1938) was a monumental effort involving more than a decade of research. The text is justly remembered for introducing the notion of "Macaulay duration". Macaulay (1938) considered whether discounted cash flow methods, which are at the core of fixed income analysis, can be applied to valuing common stocks. Macaulay (pp.130–2) made the following observation:

> Because the good that the common stock offers to its purchaser is an expectation of future money payments, the relation of its present-money price to its future-money payments is as **unmistakably an interest phenomenon** as is the relation of the present-money price of a bond to its future-money payments. In the fullness of time the stock will have a 'realized' or 'actual' yield just as will the bond. And, though the stock makes no 'promise', as does the bond, and therefore has no 'promised' or 'hypothetical' yield, its price **discounts estimated future payments** as truly as does the price of a bond. (emphasis added)

Despite this recognition of using discounted cash flow methods to value common stocks, Macaulay objected quite strongly to the practicality of using such methods:

> The 'assumption of payment', which must be made before the promised or 'hypothetical' yield of a bond can be calculated . . . may, as we have seen, be a mere mathematical fiction for all except the highest grade of bonds. But, for common stocks it is not only a mathematical fiction but also **an economic absurdity.**

For Macaulay, the difficulty of estimating the cash flows generated by common stock prevented the practical application of discounting methods to value such securities. This scepticism is a useful backdrop to the subsequent use of discounted cash flow techniques to value equity securities.

Dividends, Share Repurchases and Corporate Cash Balances

Against the backdrop of using discounted cash flow to value an equity capital share, a structural change in corporate governance appeared following World War II that undermined the validity of this technique. Under the pretence of aligning the objectives of corporate management with shareholders, a range of contingent equity compensation schemes were introduced that altered the mechanism for returning corporate earnings to shareholders. These schemes provided a legal mechanism for managers to capture a disproportionate share of

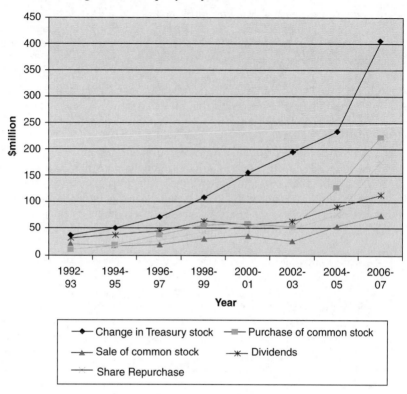

Figure 10.3 Share Repurchases and Dividends: US Industrial Corporations, 1992–2007

Source: Bhargava (2010)

corporate earnings. More precisely, instead of the traditional method of returning earnings to shareholders by paying dividends, the 'excessive' use of contingent equity compensation incentivized managers to use share buybacks and, in some cases, the buildup of large cash and near cash balances to support the price of common stock. The ability of management to set the size and timing of share repurchases to maximize the exercise value of the contingent claim—transferring wealth from shareholders to managers—receives little or no attention in modern academic studies. Available evidence gathering in such studies does not extend much beyond recognition that a dramatic change has occurred.

Recognition of the evolution in the use of different methods to return 'value' to shareholders has led to empirical studies on the properties of 'broad dividends', effectively cash dividends and share repurchases. To this end, numerous studies of 'narrow dividends' document an overall decline in aggregate dividend payout ratios since the 1950s, marked by periods of persistence where the dividend payout ratio is relatively constant. This declining importance of dividends has been paralleled by an increasing importance of share repurchases. For example, using a sample of all industrial firms listed on the Compustat database, Jagannathan et al. (2000) found that from 1985 to 1996 the number of open market repurchase program announcements by US industrial firms increased 650% from 115 to 755, with an announced value increase of 750% from $15.4 billion to $113 billion. Over the same period, dividends increased by a factor of just over two, with aggregate dividends rising from $67.6 billion to $141.7 billion. Grullon and Michaely (2002) reported an increase in the value of share repurchases from $1.5 billion to $194.2 billion over a 1972 and 2000 sample, while dividends only rose from $17.6 billion to $171.7 billion.

The study of share repurchases has progressed considerably as more and more firms have adopted this method of returning cash to shareholders (e.g., Stephens and Weisbach 1998; Jagannathan et al. 2000; Kahle 2002; Lee and Rui 2007). At the time of the seminal work on corporate dividend policy by Lintner (1956), it was acceptable for corporate income to be effectively distributed among dividends, retained earnings, and taxes. Stock repurchases were not a practical part of the mix. But times have changed, and, from the significant number of recent studies, a number of stylized facts have emerged. In particular, share repurchases and dividends are used at different times and by different types of firms. While dividends are typically paid by firms with a higher level of "permanent" operating cash flows, firms using share repurchases tend to have higher "temporary", non-operating cash flows. Both the cash flows and distributions from repurchasing firms tend to be substantially more volatile.

Against this backdrop of increased use of share repurchases, Ferris et al. (2009) examined the number of firms paying dividends in 1994 and 2007 for a sample of 25 countries and examined the global decrease in the percentage of firms that were dividend payers. Combined with the more detailed results in Fama and French (2001) on US dividend payers and Fatemi and Bildik (2012) for an international sample of firms (see Table 10.3), some key developments are apparent. Recognizing that there has been a significant increase in the total number of firms over the period, the percentage of firms paying dividends has fallen over 30% in common-law countries from 74% to 43% between 1994 and 2007, with a more modest reduction of 8% from 70% to 62% for civil-law countries.[10] The aggregate common-law result brings these countries closer in line with the US, which saw dividend payers fall from 36% to 25%. Following a period in the 1970s when the payers exceeded non-payers, since 1980 the number of dividend non-payers in the US has increasingly exceeded the number of payers. The civil-law countries, which include European firms (other than British and Irish) and the important emerging markets of China and Brazil, even saw some increases in the percentage of dividend payers. The percentage of dividend-paying firms in Germany fell from 71% to 46%, while the important sample of Japanese firms fell only from 88% to 86%.

Given the temporal decline in the importance of cash dividend payout relative to share repurchase programs, details on share repurchase activity increasingly assume importance. For example, studies have observed that the increases

Table 10.3 Dividend payers and non-payers, 33 countries and 17,106 listed firms, 1985–2006

Summary Statistics: Annual number of dividend payers and non payers, never payers and former payers, means and medians of payout ratios, numbers and percentages of payers and non payers: 1935–2006 for all countries. Payers pay dividends in year t: non payers do not. The two subgroups of non payers are firms that have never paid and former payers; firms that do not pay in year t but did in a previous year.

	1985	1986	1987	1988	1989	1990	1991	1992	1993	1994	1995	1996	1997	1998	1999	2000	2001	2002	2003	2004	2005	2006
All firms	1434	1623	2059	2433	2697	3052	3556	3855	4105	4823	5519	6459	6997	8047	9128	10837	12407	13388	13895	14928	15714	17106
Mean of dividend payout ratio of payers	38%	38%	37%	33%	34%	35%	37%	38%	38%	36%	35%	35%	34%	35%	34%	33%	35%	37%	36%	34%	34%	34%
Median of dividend payout ratio of payers	34%	34%	33%	30%	30%	31%	32%	34%	34%	31%	30%	30%	29%	30%	29%	28%	30%	32%	31%	29%	29%	29%
Payers	1246	1393	1707	2020	2236	2529	2883	3048	3157	3418	3867	4425	4642	4951	5282	5882	6427	6843	7208	7809	8367	9121
	87%	86%	83%	83%	83%	83%	81%	79%	77%	71%	70%	69%	66%	62%	58%	54%	52%	51%	52%	52%	53%	53%
Non payers	188	230	352	413	461	523	673	807	948	1405	1652	2034	2355	3096	3846	4955	5980	6545	6687	7119	7347	7985
	13%	14%	17%	17%	17%	17%	19%	21%	23%	29%	30%	32%	34%	39%	42%	46%	48%	49%	48%	48%	47%	47%
Never payers	0	169	202	284	343	387	444	571	674	805	1201	1469	1773	2061	2635	3246	4200	5106	5453	5662	5907	6201
	0%	10%	10%	12%	13%	13%	13%	15%	16%	17%	22%	23%	25%	26%	29%	30%	34%	38%	39%	38%	38%	36%
Former payers	0	14	25	21	28	49	76	100	122	142	108	150	203	329	354	392	468	617	514	413	367	485
	0%	1%	1%	1%	2%	2%	3%	3%	3%	3%	2%	3%	4%	4%	4%	4%	4%	5%	4%	3%	2%	3%

Source: Fatemi and Bildak (2012, p.664).

in stock repurchases have been pro-cyclical. Examining the ongoing process of corporations substituting share repurchases for dividends, Grullon and Michaely (2002) provided evidence that firms were not simply cutting dividends and replacing them with repurchases. Rather, large dividend-paying firms were repurchasing stocks rather than increasing dividends, and much of the growth in popularity of share repurchases is due to large dividend-paying firms. Grullon and Michaely reported that although the dividend payout ratio of US companies has been declining since the mid-1980s, the total payout ratio has remained more or less constant, which suggests that corporations have been substituting repurchases for dividends. They also showed the average dividend payout ratio fell from 22.3% in 1974 to 13.8% in 1998, while the average repurchase payout ratio increased from 3.7% to 13.6% during the same period.

The connection of dividend payments with permanent cash flow and share repurchases with temporary, non-operating cash flow fits well with the traditional theory of dividends that originates with Lintner (1956). Based on a survey of corporate managers about the most important factors influencing dividend policy, Lintner found that the most important determinant of a change in the dividend payment is a change in company earnings that results in a dividend that is "out of line" with the firm's target payout ratio. Firms seek to make only partial adjustments in the actual payout ratio toward the target payout ratio and are strongly averse to cutting the regular cash dividend payment. Hence, managers smooth dividends in the short run to prevent fluctuations in the dividend cash flow to shareholders. Lintner's partial adjustment model for dividends can be formalized as: $D(t) = D(t-1) + \lambda \, (D^*(t) - D(t-1))$ where $\lambda \in [0,1]$ is the speed of adjustment coefficient and $D^*(t)$ is the target dividend payment.

The Lintner model of dividend payment behaviour has a number of testable hypotheses. One testable implication is that dividend decreases will be relatively rare and be associated only with historically poor performance. Similarly, following dividend decreases (increases), the bad (good) operating performance of the firm will continue. In more recent studies, this hypothesis has been formulated along the lines that dividend increases will be related to the "permanent" component of cash flow and not to the "temporary" component of cash flows. Another implication of the Lintner model is that, due to the need for higher and more stable cash flows, dividend-paying firms will be larger than non-dividend-paying firms. Strong empirical support for the Lintner model, in one form or another, has continued from the early cross-sectional work as reflected in the recent survey work of Benartzi et al. (1997) and Baker et al. (2001).

The aversion of firms to cutting dividends is understandable given the negative stock market reaction to dividend cuts—for example, Ghosh and Woolridge (1988) and Denis et al. (1994) both reported an average stock price decline of about 6% on the three days surrounding the announcement of a dividend cut. This punitive market response to dividend decreases has been identified as an argument in favour of share repurchase programs where there is no commitment to initiate a new repurchase program when the old program expires. As such, stock repurchases are a sensible way for firms to pay out "temporary" cash flows that have a high likelihood of not being sustainable. The typically favourable investor tax treatment for capital gains over dividend income is another argument in favour of share repurchases. The arguments in favour of share repurchases are so compelling that Black (1976) coined "the dividend puzzle" (e.g., Crockett and Friend 1988; Christie 1990; Frankfurter 1999): Why do firms use dividends to distribute corporate income—and investors prefer this form of distribution—when dividends are subject to double taxation? Perhaps shareholders are more than aware of the rent-seeking objectives of corporate managers and insiders associated with the use of share repurchase programs.

In the US, the dividend puzzle has been largely resolved by the evolution of firm dividend policy. For example, Fama and French (2001) found that the percentage of firms paying cash dividends fell from 66.5% in 1978 to 20.7% in 1998. What has emerged more than three decades after Black introduced the dividend puzzle is that there is considerable heterogeneity in the dividend policy decision. This is particularly true if the scope of discussion includes international firms. Truong and Heaney (2007, p.684, Table 3) demonstrated the importance across firms and countries of corporate ownership composition, particularly the presence of a large shareholder or shareholder group, to the determination of dividend policy. While not as significant an issue with US stocks, in the Truong and Heaney sample of over 8,000 firms from 37 countries, at least 50% of the firms had one shareholder or a shareholder group owning at least 25% of the equity in the firm, with the largest shareholder owning, on average, more than 30% of total voting shares.

The Warren Buffett Synthesis

Often described as the world's greatest investor, Warren Buffett is a symbol of the state of 'old finance' at the beginning of the 21st century. Buffett has developed an approach to equity valuation that synthesizes the traditional Graham et al. (1962) 'analysis of financial statements' approach with the 'focus on the company characteristics' of the growth stock approach (e.g., Lowenstein 1995). Given the well-known relationship between Buffett and Benjamin Graham, the connection to the Philip Fisher growth stock approach is apparent in Buffett's writings, such as the following (Cunningham 2002, pp.100–1):

> Your goal as an investor should simply be to purchase, at a rational price, a part interest in an easily-understandable business whose earnings are virtually certain to be materially higher in five, ten and twenty years from now. Over time, you will find only a few companies that meet these standards—so when you see one that qualifies, you should buy a meaningful amount of stock. You must also resist the temptation to stray from your guidelines. If you aren't willing to own a stock for ten years, don't even think about owning it for ten minutes. Put together a portfolio of companies whose aggregate earnings march upward over the years, and so also will the portfolio's market value.

While there is some overlap in the basic notions advanced by Graham and Philip Fisher, it is on selecting appropriate points of emphasis and divergence that Buffett was able to arrive at a successful synthesis of the value investing and growth stock approaches to equity security valuation. For example, Graham proposed methods of determining whether common stock prices were selling below intrinsic value, emphasizing the use of financial statements. In contrast,

Table 10.4 Berkshire's Performance vs. the S&P 500

| Year | Annual Percentage Change | | |
	in Per-Share Book Value of Berkshire	in Per-Share Market Value of Berkshire	in S&P 500 with Dividends Included
1965	23.8	49.5	10.0
1966	20.3	(3.4)	(11.7)
1967	11.0	13.3	30.9
1968	19.0	77.8	11.0
1969	16.2	19.4	(8.4)
1970	12.0	(4.6)	3.9
1971	16.4	80.5	14.6
1972	21.7	8.1	18.9
1973	4.7	(2.5)	(14.8)
1974	5.5	(48.7)	(26.4)
1975	21.9	2.5	37.2
1976	59.3	129.3	23.6
1977	31.9	46.8	(7.4)
1978	24.0	14.5	6.4
1979	35.7	102.5	18.2
1980	19.3	32.8	32.3
1981	31.4	31.8	(5.0)
1982	40.0	38.4	21.4
1983	32.3	69.0	22.4
1984	13.6	(2.7)	6.1
1985	48.2	93.7	31.6
1986	26.1	14.2	18.6
1987	19.5	4.6	5.1
1988	20.1	59.3	16.6
1989	44.4	84.6	31.7
1990	7.4	(23.1)	(3.1)
1991	39.6	35.6	30.5
1992	20.3	29.8	7.6
1993	14.3	38.9	10.1
1994	13.9	25.0	1.3
1995	43.1	57.4	37.6
1996	31.8	6.2	23.0
1997	34.1	34.9	33.4
1998	48.3	52.2	28.6
1999	0.5	(19.9)	21.0
2000	6.5	26.6	(9.1)
2001	(6.2)	6.5	(11.9)

Table 10.4   (Continued)

Year	Annual Percentage Change		
	in Per-Share Book Value of Berkshire	in Per-Share Market Value of Berkshire	in S&P 500 with Dividends Included
2002.................................	10.0	(3.8)	(22.1)
2003.................................	21.0	15.8	28.7
2004.................................	10.5	4.3	10.9
2005.................................	6.4	0.8	4.9
2006.................................	18.4	24.1	15.8
2007.................................	11.0	28.7	5.5
2008.................................	(9.6)	(31.8)	(37.0)
2009.................................	19.8	2.7	26.5
2010.................................	13.0	21.4	15.1
2011.................................	4.6	(4.7)	2.1
2012.................................	14.4	16.8	16.0
2013.................................	18.2	32.7	32.4
2014.................................	8.3	27.0	13.7
Compounded Annual Gain— 1965–2014......................	19.40%	21.6%	9.9%
Overall Gain- 1964–2014	751,113%	1,826,163%	11,196%

Source: Berkshire Hathaway Annual Report 2014, p.2.
Notes: Data are for calendar years with these exceptions: 1965 and 1966, year ended 9/30; 1967, 15 months ended 12/31. Starting in 1979, accounting rules required insurance companies to value the equity securities they hold at market rather than at the lower of cost or market, which was previously the requirement. In this table, Berkshire's results through 1978 have been restated to conform to the changed rules. In all other respects, the results are calculated using the numbers originally reported. The S&P 500 numbers are **pre-tax** whereas the Berkshire numbers are **after-tax**. If a corporation such as Berkshire were simply to have owned the S&P 500 and accrued the appropriate taxes, its results would have lagged the S&P 500 in years when that index showed a positive return, but would have exceeded the S&P 500 in years when the index showed a negative return. Over the years, the tax costs would have caused the aggregate lag to be substantial.

Table 10.5   List of Berkshire Hathaway Operating Companies

BERKSHIRE HATHAWAY INC. OPERATING COMPANIES
INSURANCE BUSINESSES

Company	Employees	Company	Employees
Applied Underwriters	679	GEICO	32,295
Berkshire Hathaway Homestate Companies	833	General Re	2,317
Berkshire Hathaway Reinsurance Group	626	Guard Insurance Group	346

Table 10.5   (Continued)

Company	Employees	Company	Employees
Berkshire Hathaway Specialty	521	Medical Protective	614
BoatU.S.	457	National Indemnity Primary Group	553
Central States Indemnity	76	United States Liability Insurance Group	744
		Insurance total	**40,061**

NON-INSURANCE BUSINESSES

Company	Employees	Company	Employees
Acme	2,257	Iscar	12,423
Adalet [1]	260	Johns Manville	6,852
Affordable Housing Partners, Inc.	12	Jordan's Furniture	937
AltaLink [2]	816	Justin Brands	1,085
Altaquip [1]	321	Kern River Gas [2]	155
Ben Bridge Jeweler	859	Kirby [1]	494
Benjamin Moore	1,908	Larson-Juhl	1,394
BH Energy [2]	25	Lubrizol	7,865
BHE Renewables [2]	343	Lubrizol Specialty Products, Inc.	151
BHE U.S. Transmission [2]	22	The Marmon Group	19,906
BH Media Group	4,074	McLane Company	21,857
Borsheims	174	Metalogic Inspection Services [2]	82
Brooks Sports	625	MidAmerican Energy [2]	3,575
BNSF	48,000	MiTek Inc.	3,006
The Buffalo News	748	Nebraska Furniture Mart	3,225
Business Wire	497	NetJets	6,355
CalEnergy Philippines [2]	63	Northern Natural Gas [2]	851
Campbell Hausfeld [1]	323	Northern Powergrid Holdings [2]	2,509
Carefree of Colorado [1]	256	NV Energy [2]	2,448
Charter Brokerage	143	Oriental Trading	1,606
Clayton Homes	11,988	PacifiCorp [2]	5,902
Cleveland Wood Products [1]	46	The Pampered Chef	522
CORT	2,388	Precision Steel Warehouse	154
CTB	2,770	Richline Group	2,981

Table 10.5 (Continued)

Company	Employees	Company	Employees
Dairy Queen	476	Russell [4]	1,781
Douglas/Quikut [1]	40	Other Scott Fetzer Companies [1]	187
Fechheimer	417	See's Candies	2,380
FlightSafety	4,168	Shaw Industries	22,074
Forest River	9,788	Stahl[1]	107
France [1]	149	Star Furniture	677
Fruit of the Loom[3]	27,846	TTI, Inc.	4,705
Garan	3,875	United Consumer Financial Services [1]	199
HHBrown Shoe Group	1,140	Vanity Fair Brands [3]	563
Halex [1]	74	Wayne Water Systems [1]	104
Heinz	24,500	Western Enterprises [1]	..235
Helzberg Diamonds	2,305	R.C.Willey Home Furnishings	2,523
HomeServices of America[2]	4,078	World Book[1]	171
Intelligent Energy Solutions [2]	17	WPLG, Inc.	188
		XTRA	393
		Non-insurance total	300,413
		Corporate Office	25
		Total	340,499

Source: Berkshire Hathaway Annual Report 2014, p.125.

[1] A Scott Fetzer Company

[2] A Berkshire Hathaway Energy Company

[3] A Fruit of the Loom, Inc. Company

[4] The Marmon Group consists of approximately 185 manufacturing and service businesses that operate within 13 business sectors.

Fisher was concerned with the characteristics of the business, emphasizing the quality of management and the company's ability to generate sales and profits. Basic Buffett security selection dictums like searching for businesses with excellent management, focusing on a small number of core holdings (because there are only so many outstanding companies) and 'buy a business not a stock' echo Philip Fisher more than Ben Graham, though Graham did make passing reference to these concepts as well.

Buffett started from the old finance, Graham and Dodd view that securities have an intrinsic value and that for a number of reasons, the prices of securities may not trade at intrinsic value, creating trading opportunities. Following Williams (1937), Buffett advocated the use of the discounted cash flow model to estimate the intrinsic value. In order to overcome the difficulties of estimating the future cash flows, Buffett recommended examining only businesses that the analyst is capable of understanding: "You don't have to be an expert on every company or even many. You only have to be able to evaluate companies within your circle of competence. The size of the circle is not very important; knowing its boundaries, however, is vital" (Cunningham 2002, p.100). Once the cash flows have been determined, the margin-of-safety principle is used to decide whether the security is a buying (or selling) opportunity. Because only a few companies will meet the criteria, a Buffett portfolio for a retail investor will have few securities and be relatively inactive in trading.

Examining the evolution of security analysis as reflected in the different editions of *Security Analysis*, it is apparent that the historical evolution of security markets has had a profound impact on the prescriptions for equity security valuation. For example, whereas before World War II it was possible at times to identify significant numbers of companies with common stock prices trading below the net current asset value per share, such companies are relatively uncommon in current US stock markets. Where such situations are available, this is, more likely than not, a situation that is to be avoided because the large balance of net current assets is likely being soldiered to stave off an impending sequence of negative earnings. While the views of Graham et al. (1962) and Fisher may have provided considerable insight into securities markets of earlier times, there is no assurance that markets have not evolved beyond the lessons contained in those texts. This speaks to the importance of the Warren Buffett synthesis. Buffett obtained his track record more recently and, as such, his prescriptions are more relevant to contemporary observers. To this end, Table 10.4 provides evidence on the performance of Berkshire Hathaway versus the S&P 500 and Table 10.5 provides a listing of the companies in which Berkshire Hathaway currently has an ownership position.

Hagstrom (1995, 2000) summarized the 'Buffett approach to investment' into five principles. Though these principles do not do full justice to Buffett's value investing prescriptions (e.g., Cunningham 2002), the basic structure is sound.[11] These principles can be summarized as follows:

1   Don't follow the day-to-day fluctuations in the stock market. The market is a forum for buying and selling, not for precisely setting value. Investors need to be able to ignore significant short-term reductions in the value of a common stock. Follow the market only when the objective is to sell a stock at prices well in excess of intrinsic value.

2   Don't try to predict the direction of the general economy. If the stock market cannot be predicted, then how is it possible to predict the economy?

3   Buy a business, not its stock. A stock purchase can be viewed as though the entire business is being purchased. Four important elements apply to valuing the business: business characteristics, management, financial numbers and value. The business needs to be simple and understandable to the investor, and the business needs a consistent operating history and favorable long-term prospects. The management has to be honest, capable and candid with shareholders. Management with a high fraction of personal wealth invested in a company (e.g. Buffett and Munger at

Berkshire Hathaway) have a greater incentive to manage effectively. Key financial numbers to examine are return on equity, as opposed to earnings per share, profit margin and the ability to add value with retained earnings (return on additions to equity greater than cost of capital).

4 Buffett requires the intrinsic value to be more than the market price by the margin of safety for a security to qualify as an eligible purchase.

5 Manage a portfolio of businesses—act like a business owner rather than a stock trader. The implication is that being widely diversified is inconsistent with being able to manage so many businesses.

In addition to these general principles, Buffett is credited with numerous interesting quotes such as: "It is just not necessary to do extraordinary things to get extraordinary results" and "As far as I am concerned, the stock market . . . is there only as a reference to see if anybody is offering to do anything foolish".

Table 10.6   Berkshire Hathaway's "Acquisition Criteria"

BERKSHIRE HATHAWAY INC.ACQUISITION CRITERIA

---

(1) We are eager to hear from principals or their representatives about businesses that meet all of the following criteria:

(2) Large purchases (at least $75 million of pre-tax earnings unless the business will fit into one of our existing units),

(3) Demonstrated consistent earning power (future projections are of no interest to us, nor are "turnaround" situations),

(4) Businesses earning good returns on equity while employing little or no debt,Management in place (we can't supply it),

(5) Simple businesses (if there's lots of technology, we won't understand it),

(6) An offering price (we don't want to waste our time or that of the seller by talking, even preliminarily, about a transaction when price is unknown).

The larger the company, the greater will be our interest: We would like to make an acquisition in the $5-20 billion range. We are not interested, however, in receiving suggestions about purchases we might make in the general stock market.

We will not engage in unfriendly takeovers. We can promise complete confidentiality and a very fast answer - customarily within five minutes - as to whether we're interested. We prefer to buy for cash, but will consider issuing stock when we receive as much in intrinsic business value as we give. We don't participate in auctions.

Charlie and I frequently get approached about acquisitions that don't come close to meeting our tests: We've found that if you advertise an interest in buying collies, a lot of people will call hoping to sell you their cocker spaniels. A line from a country song expresses our feeling about new ventures, turnarounds, or auction-like sales: "When the phone don't ring, you'll know it's me."

Source: Berkshire Hathaway Annual Report 2014, p.23

Despite all the reverence given to Buffett as the prototypical old finance value investor, it is apparent that individual investors would have difficulty pursuing the types of strategies that have brought considerable success to Berkshire Hathaway. For example, consider the "Acquisition Criteria" in Table 10.6 published in the Berkshire Hathaway annual report. This buy-a-business approach is reiterated in Buffett's various writings. The following statement is contained in the Berkshire Hathaway annual report:

> Our preference would be to reach our goal [of maximizing Berkshire's average annual rate of gain in intrinsic value on a per-share basis] by directly owning a diversified group of businesses that generate cash and consistently earn above-average returns on capital. Our second choice is to own parts of similar businesses, attained primarily through purchases of marketable common stocks by our insurance subsidiaries. The price and availability of businesses and the need for insurance capital determine any given year's capital allocation.

While it would be nice for individual investors to be able to search out companies and take a 100% interest, this is not practical for all but a few investors (see Table 10.6 again). The detailed emphasis on business characteristics, which usually requires on-site visits and access to senior management, also makes it difficult for individual investors.[12] In this regard and in the general approach to detailed fundamental analysis of the business, Buffett has much more in common with Philip Fisher than Graham and Dodd.

Buffett's insights into the use of accounting numbers in business valuation are generally unrecognized. Buffett explicitly recognized the importance and limitations of accounting numbers (Cunningham 2002, p.213):

> Accounting numbers, of course, are the language of business and as such are of enormous help to anyone evaluating the worth of a business and tracking its progress. Charlie and I would be lost without these numbers; they invariably are the starting point for us in evaluating our own businesses and those of others. Managers and owners need to remember, however, that accounting is but an aid to business thinking, never a substitute for it.

Because the most important sources of information for Buffett's views are Berkshire Hathaway's annual reports and letters to shareholders, many of the comments are addressed to accounting aspects of that company. This means giving detailed attention to accounting for taxation, acquisitions and for different levels of ownership in the various companies that comprise the Berkshire Hathaway holding company.[13] However, there are also a number of general observations about accounting that appeal to a wider range of applications.

Buffett recognized the failings of conventional interpretations of accounting numbers and related valuation measures (p.218): "Common yardsticks such as dividend yield, the ratio of price to earnings or to book value, and even growth rates have *nothing* to do with valuation except to the extent they provide clues as to the amount and timing of cash flows into and from the business". A common theme in Buffet's writings is that references to 'growth' and 'value' strategies reflect an ignorance of the valuation process. Growth can destroy value if the cash required to increase assets exceeds the cash generation of those assets in the future. For Buffett (p.218):

> The primary test of managerial economic performance is the achievement of a high earnings rate on equity capital employed (without undue leverage, gimmickry, etc.) and not the achievement of consistent gains in earnings per share. In our view, businesses would be better understood by their shareholder owners, as well as the general public, if managements and financial analysts modified the primary emphasis they place on earnings per share, and upon yearly changes in that figure.

Earnings are too readily manipulated by unscrupulous management or misinterpreted by naive investors. The use of GAAP accounting does not ensure a meaningful earnings number, only that the earnings number is calculated according to 'generally accepted accounting principles': "managers and investors alike must understand that accounting numbers are the beginning, not the end, of business valuation".

Buffett clearly states that the object is to maximize 'economic earnings', not 'accounting earnings'. This point is not original to Buffett. What Buffett brings to the table is the invaluable interpretations of an individual who has accumulated a remarkable record from understanding the difference. One example concerns 'economic goodwill' versus 'accounting goodwill': "You can live a full and rewarding life without ever thinking about Goodwill [*sic*] and its amortization. But students of investment and management should understand the nuances of the subject." On this subject, in 1983 Buffett made a veiled reference to the incorrectness of the Graham and Dodd treatment of goodwill (pp.197–8):

> My own thinking has changed drastically from 35 years ago when I was taught to favor tangible assets and to shun businesses whose value depended largely upon economic Goodwill. This bias caused me to make many important business mistakes of omission, although relatively few of commission.
>
> Keynes identified my problem: "The difficulty lies not in the new ideas but in escaping from the old ones". My escape was long delayed, in part because most of what I had been taught by the same teacher had been (and continues to be) so extraordinarily valuable. Ultimately, business experience, direct and vicarious, produced my present strong preference for businesses that possess a large amount of enduring Goodwill and that utilize a minimum of tangible assets.

Unlike accounting goodwill, which is 'excess of cost over equity in the net assets being acquired', economic goodwill is the capitalized value of the excess over market rates of return on net tangible assets. Both concepts are related to intangible assets, but in different ways.

Economic goodwill provides a connection to the "earnings power value" identified by proponents of 'value investing' (Greenwald et al. 2001, ch.5). To illustrate the concept of economic goodwill, Buffett examined the purchase of See's Candies in 1972, a basically debt-free company that Berkshire Hathaway continues to own up to the present. The purchase price of this company was $25 million and the net tangible assets of the company $8 million.[14] Observing that See's after-tax earnings were approximately $2 million per year, it is apparent that the 25% return on assets represented more than just the market return earned on tangible assets. The excess return above what could be earned on the net tangible assets at prevailing market rates of return, capitalized at an appropriate discount rate, is the economic goodwill. See's had intangible assets associated with reputation, consumer loyalty and quality of product. In contrast, accounting goodwill would depend on a combination of factors (i.e., the premium over accounting book value of the price paid for the firm, adjusted for fair value revaluation of inventories and tangible assets, plus amortization of goodwill and adjustments for deferred taxes). The resulting number may, or may not, capture the implicit value of the intangible assets.

Considerable discussion in value investing analysis is dedicated to the sources of 'earnings power value' associated with "assets plus franchise". Businesses where the return on tangible assets is in excess of market rates of return are strong candidates for increased competition. This competition can arise in various forms—for example, on the price side from competitors already in the market or from the entry of new firms. The end result is irresistible market pressures that force the return on assets to the market rate of return, or possibly below. What factors enable firms to resist these market pressures? Identifying sustainable sources of competitive advantage is the subject of numerous books and theories. A number of such sources of competitive advantage include: (a) licenses, such as television or telecom broadcast rights; (b) production efficiencies due to factors such as patents, specialized human capital or economies of scale; (c) access to cheaper sources of capital, labor or other inputs; and (d) the franchise factor associated with customer loyalty or acquired tastes.[15] It is not surprising that arguably the most important franchise factor business, Coca-Cola, is also a major common stock holding of Berkshire Hathaway.

Another key difference between accounting and economic values identified by Buffett involves the treatment of depreciation. This is directly related to the concept of "owner earnings" (Cunningham 2002, p.211):

> "owner's earnings" . . . represent (a) reported earnings plus (b) depreciation, depletion, amortization, and certain other non-cash charges . . . less (c) the average annual amount of capitalized expenditures for property plant and equipment, etc. that the business requires to fully maintain its long-term competitive position and its unit volume.

Except in special cases, (c) will be difficult to estimate and, as a result, can only be a guess. However, for Buffett: "the owner earnings figure, not the [deceptively precise] GAAP figure [is] the relevant item for valuation purposes—both for investors in buying stock and for managers in buying entire businesses". Buffett cautioned that the use of measures such as EBITDA to determine 'cash flow' will likely lead to "faulty decisions". Economic depreciation is not the same as amortization, and this is another essential feature to be taken into account in arriving at an estimate of intrinsic value.

C   THE RISE OF MODERN FINANCE

Old Finance vs. Modern Finance

Merton (1987, p.150) described "old finance" as "an essentially loose connection of beliefs based on accounting practices, rules of thumb and anecdotes". In contrast, modern finance features "rigorous mathematical theories and carefully documented empirical studies". The battle for the academic high ground in finance between institutionalists—representing the old finance approach—and the neoclassicals—representing modern finance—was particularly vicious, even by academic standards. The opposition, it seems, was completely flattened and forgotten. Any helpful ideas were rolled into the scientific movement express train that was modern finance (e.g., Poitras 2006–7). As it played out, the wide gap between the *ex ante* claims advanced by the modern finance movement and the actual *ex post* performance of the theories in the marketplace brings to mind another observation of Stigler (1965, p.15): "we commonly exaggerate the merits of originality in economics . . . we are unjust in conferring immortality upon the authors of absurd theories while we forget the fine, if not particularly original, work of others".

While recognizing that the benefits of diversification had been identified long before, Markowitz (1999) emphasized the contributions of Markowitz (1952, 1959):

> What was lacking prior to 1952 was an adequate *theory* of investment that covered the effects of diversification where risks are correlated, distinguished between efficient and inefficient portfolios, and analyzed risk-return trade-offs on the portfolio as a whole.

Markowitz (1999) recounted that his motivation to develop a formal optimization model of the risk-return tradeoff for a portfolio of securities was inspired by a rejection of Williams (1937), in which the rule guiding investment decisions was to "maximize the discounted . . . (expected) value of future returns". For Williams, the value of a stock was the discounted expected value of future dividend payments. The resulting investment strategy called for selection of securities with the highest expected return. For Markowitz, the Williams approach to investment decisions ignored benefits of diversification. Though Williams (1937) did deal with the impact of uncertainty, the approach suggested was to assign probabilities to possible future states and evaluate the expected value of the investment. Williams felt that diversification would result in an elimination of security risk premia, a view that does not deal adequately with security covariances.

Markowitz (1999) reviewed many contributions dealing with aspects of diversification, the risk-return tradeoff and the like appearing in the two decades before Markowitz (1952, 1959). The general assessment of prior contributions is that the discussion did not provide much beyond general terms and "did not clearly indicate why it is desirable". As demonstrated by Rubinstein (2006), Dimand (2007) and others, this ignores the contributions of Bruno di Finetti, Irving Fisher and others. To see this, consider the contribution by Fisher (1930b) that receives no mention. In a discussion of "Taking Risk from Speculation", Fisher clearly dealt with the issue of diversification (pp.204–7):

> A little reasoning permits of a startling corollary. It is this: If we can, by sufficient diversification in investments, get a greater certainty and thus run less risks from our speculation, then the more unsafe the investments are, taken individually, the safer they are taken collectively, to say nothing of profitableness, provided that the diversification is sufficiently increased.

This paradox is derived directly from exploiting the old-fashioned fear of common stocks and the consequent refusal to deal in them, except well below their "mathematical value". What follows is a delightful discussion of the fair game model that is used to motivate the notion of the "caution coefficient"—Fisher's term for the cost of risk, a concept developed in Fisher (1906).

Irving Fisher measured the cost of risk as the difference between the expected value ("mathematical value") and the price that will be paid for the gamble: "a sound minded investor will pay less than the mathematical value for a chance to gain money on a risk. That is, he will trim the price by means of a 'caution coefficient'". It is clear that Fisher was advocating the use of mean-variance expected utility functions to model investor choice (1930b, p.205):

> The "caution coefficient" becomes, in practice, greater and greater as the risk grows. If my chance of getting a dollar is a certainty, there would be no reduction on account of the caution factor. If it is like the chance of betting on "heads" or "tails", the caution factor may trim the price of the chance down from fifty cents, in mathematical value, to say, forty cents for the chance to win the dollar. That is a reduction on account of caution to 20 per cent. But if one bets on two heads in succession, the reduction on account of caution would be correspondingly greater, so that instead of paying twenty-five cents, the mathematical value, the investor might insist on a reduction of more than 20 per cent to say, fifteen cents. It is both normal and proper that the higher the risk the cheaper the chance of winning can be obtained, compared to its mathematical value.

What remains is for Fisher to translate this risk-return tradeoff into a portfolio context.

A key result of modern portfolio theory is that the market does not reward the total variability of a security's return, only that part which cannot be eliminated in an efficiently diversified portfolio. Whether Fisher grasped this point is unclear from the key part of the discussion:

> Hence, the more risky the investment would be to a lone individual playing the game, the safer it is, if, by pooling in an investment trust with wide diversification in investment, the individual risk is thereby absorbed. For as the (individual) risk grows it can be constantly absorbed by corresponding

increases in diversification. Thus the individual investor of the trust may gain more on the riskier investments, bought by the trusts at much less than their mathematical value, than if he played the market alone with less risky investments, but bought at much nearer their mathematical value.

Fisher went on to observe that the aggregate risk-reducing benefits associated with increasing use of "investment trusts, investment counsels and other skilled means of diversifying" contributed to the overall rise in stock prices during the 1920s.

Chapter 13 of *The Stock Market Crash—and After* (Fisher 1930b) contains a number of other intellectual gems. For example, Fisher seems to have anticipated what Markowitz was to do over two decades later: "This principle (of higher expected return for the same level of risk through diversification), so far as I know, never has been definitively formulated in the investment market" (p.206). Fisher directly tied the benefits of diversification to the "principle of constant inspection". Portfolios have to be actively monitored—"rebalanced" in modern terminology—in order to achieve the anticipated portfolio expected return. Bond portfolios require less monitoring than stock portfolios. Fisher explicitly identified the value of "scientific appraisals of the stock market" to increasing the value of stocks in general and spoke favorably about the benefits of what has come to be called "fundamental analysis". He recognized the differences between the various entities using the moniker 'investment trusts'—some of which were "avowedly of the most speculative type . . . because they may heavily concentrate their holdings". Finally, he explicitly recognized the diversification benefits of holding foreign securities.

Cowles and Stock Market Forecasting

Alfred Cowles III (1891–1984) is best remembered in modern times for his role in establishing the Cowles Commission (later Foundation) for Economic Research and for the 1871–1939 stock price index that became the basis for the important equity market benchmark S&P index launched in 1957 (Wilson and Jones 2002).[16] Cowles is not typically identified with the academic school of institutionalism, despite having similar philosophical goals (e.g., Yonay 1994). In particular, a primary motivation for Cowles to join forces with Irving Fisher and a group of other influential academic economists to form the Cowles Commission in 1932 was the desire to elevate economics into a more precise science using mathematical and statistical techniques. This is consistent with the general goals of both academic institutionalism and modern finance. Ironically, research developments associated with the Cowles Commission following World War II were central to the demise of the 'measurement without theory' form of institutionalism as an intellectual force in modern economics.

Cowles has gone largely unrecognized in modern times for making other early contributions, particularly to the empirical validity of the efficient market hypothesis for the equity capital market. Cowles produced two seemingly conflicting contributions. Cowles' "Can Stock Market Forecasters Forecast?"

(1933), updated in "Stock Market Forecasting" (Cowles 1944), examines "the attempts of two groups, 20 fire insurance companies and 16 financial services, to foretell which specific securities would prove profitable . . . [and] with the efforts of 25 financial publications to foretell the future course of the stock market". The objective was to "lead to the identification of economic theories or statistical practices whose soundness has been established by successful prediction" (Cowles 1933, p.309). Observing that the sample period predates Graham and Dodd (1934), the results are still quite remarkable (Cowles 1933, pp.323–4):

1   Sixteen financial services, in making some 7500 recommendations of individual common stocks for investment during the period from January 1, 1928, to July 1, 1932, compiled an average record that was worse than that of the average common stock by 1.43 per cent annually. Statistical tests of the best individual records failed to demonstrate that they exhibited skill, and indicated that they more probably were results of chance.

2   Twenty fire insurance companies in making a similar selection of securities during the years 1928 to 1931, inclusive, achieved an average record 1.20 per cent annually worse than that of the general run of stocks. The best of these records, since it is not very much more impressive than the record of the most successful of the sixteen financial services, fails to exhibit definitely the existence of any skill in investment.

3   William Peter Hamilton, editor of the Wall Street Journal, publishing forecasts of the stock market based on the Dow Theory over a period of 26 years, from 1904 to 1929, inclusive, achieved a result better than what would ordinarily be regarded as a normal

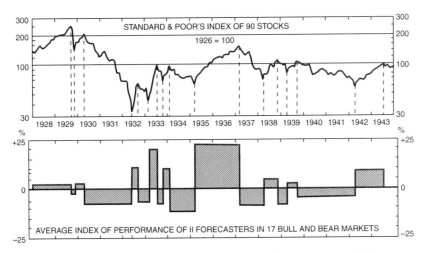

Figure 10.8   Cowles Index of 11 Market Forecasters' Performance, 1928–1943
Source: Cowles (1944, p.211)

investment return, but poorer than the result of a continuous out-right investment in representative common stocks for this period. On 90 occasions he announced changes in the outlook for the market. Forty-five of these predictions were successful and 45 unsuccessful.

4   Twenty-four financial publications engaged in forecasting the stock market during the 42 years from January 1, 1928, to June 1, 1932, failed as a group by 4 per cent per annum to achieve a result as good as the average of all purely random performances. A review of the various statistical tests, applied to the records for this period, of these 24 forecasters, indicates that the most successful records are little, if any, better than what might be expected to result from pure chance. There is some evidence, on the other hand, to indicate that the least successful records are worse than what could reasonably be attributed to chance.

While this is striking, even a casual observer will notice that the forecasting sample period used by Cowles, January 1928 to June 1932, is particularly unusual. For this reason, the update provided in "Stock Market Forecasting" (Cowles 1944) is of interest.

"Stock Market Forecasting" does not replicate "Can Stock Market Forecasters Forecast?". The sample of only 11 forecasters is much smaller. The 4 financial periodicals and 7 financial services firms that are included also appear in Cowles (1933), making for a much longer January 1928 to July 1943 time series, effectively eliminating the questions raised about the 1928–1932 sample used in Cowles (1933). In addition, Cowles was able to obtain forecast data going back to 1903 for the individual forecaster who exhibited the best forecasting performance of the 11 forecasters over the 1928–1943 sample. Though the forecaster is not named, it is likely that the forecaster was Roger Babson. The reported results are as follows (Cowles 1944, p.214):

(1) The records of 11 leading financial periodicals and services since 1927, over periods varying from 10 to 15 years, fail to disclose evidence of ability to predict successfully the future course of the stock market.

(2) Of the 6904 forecasts recorded during the 15 year period, more than four times as many were bullish as bearish, although more than half of the period was occupied by bear markets, and stocks at the end were at only about two-thirds of their level at the beginning.

(3) The record of the forecasting agency with the best results for the 15 years since 1927, when tabulated back to 1903, for the 40 years showed results 3.3 per cent a year better than would have been secured by a continuous investment in the stocks composing the Dow-Jones industrial average. Under present laws the capital-gains tax might wipe out most of this advantage. While prospects for the speculator are, therefore, not particularly alluring, statistical tests disclose positive evidence of structure in stock prices which indicates a likelihood that whatever success may be claimed for the very consistent 40 year record is not entirely accidental.

The results supporting (1) are illustrated in Figure 10.8. The decidedly more sympathetic tone towards the possibility of profitable stock market forecasting compared to "Can Stock Market Forecasters Forecast?" is solidified by the closing statement: "A simple application of the 'inertia' principle, such as buying at turning points in the market after prices for a month averaged higher, and selling after they averaged lower, than for the previous month, would have resulted in substantial gains for the period under consideration".

The tenuous academic connection of Alfred Cowles III with the venerated and academically influential Cowles Commission reflects the sharp division that was beginning to emerge between vernacular old finance and academic modern finance. Cowles' background was decidedly in the vernacular realm: the grandson of Alfred Cowles, Sr., founder of the *Chicago Tribune*, his father, Alfred Cowles, Jr., (1865–1939) also served as a manager and director of the *Chicago Tribune*. For a decade prior to the foundation of the Cowles Commission, Alfred Cowles maintained a private organization for statistical research on problems of investment and finance; partially in support of his activities managing the sizeable financial assets associated with the *Chicago Tribune* fortune. At the time the Cowles Commission was founded, this advisory service was located in Colorado Springs. Despite spending considerable effort monitoring and heeding the advice of leading financial advisory services, Cowles was among those who suffered considerable losses in the equity capital share markets during the downturn of 1929–1932. Deeply troubled by the losses, Cowles set about to establish stock market forecasting on a more scientific basis using mathematical and statistical methods (Christ 1994, pp.30–1). The Cowles Commission was the result of these efforts.

David Durand and Vernacular Finance

Frederick Macaulay, originator of 'Macaulay duration' and author of *The Movement of Interest Rates, Bonds, Yields and Stock Prices in the United States Since 1865* (1938), was of sufficient stature in the vernacular community to warrant selection to form an investment advisory firm, Bernstein-Macaulay, in 1934. At this point, the long-promised effort that was to be *The Movement of Interest Rates, Bonds, Yields and Stock Prices* still was not near completion. In practice, Macaulay had few responsibilities within Bernstein-Macaulay and used the time and resources to finish the project. Peter L. Bernstein reported: "When he finally finished the book, Macaulay told my father he could continue to use his name, but he was tired of coming to an office every day and was going to retire" (Poitras 2007). Given his relatively limited duties in the investment counsel business, Macaulay was able to pursue some research activities. After leaving the National Bureau of Economic Research in 1938, he took up the position of research director with the Twentieth Century Fund for a study commissioned by the NYSE on short selling. The final results of this study, *Short Selling on the New York Stock Exchange* (Macaulay and Durand 1951), is Macaulay's last published research contribution. The results of the study are somewhat anti-climatic, as short selling was not found to significantly impact share prices, though some interesting individual transactions were identified.

The connection between David Durand and Macaulay represents the final step in the demise of institutionalism within academic finance. Like Macaulay, Durand was a Columbia PhD (1941), attracted by the possibility of working with W.C. Mitchell. Earning his B.A. (1934) and M.A. (1938) from Cornell, Durand accomplished the significant academic achievement, prior to receiving his M.A., of publishing an article on marginal productivity theory in the prestigious *Journal of Political Economy* Durand (1937) and another in the influential *Annals of Mathematical Statistics* (Durand and Greeenwood 1937).[17] Though Durand became a member of the National Bureau of Economic Research (NBER) staff after Macaulay's departure, Paul Samuelson recounts that, while at the NBER, Durand "pioneered the empirical study of how long-term bonds usually require a higher yield than short. Everyone understands that today, but he was the first to document it" (Székely and Richards 2004). Given his considerable technical abilities, the NBER connection and the subsequent overlapping work on interest rates, it is not too surprising that Durand and Macaulay would undertake a joint project, such as that on NYSE short selling.

Like so many at the time, Durand's career was interrupted by World War II. He served in the Naval Reserve, stationed in Hawaii and Guam. Following the war, Durand continued his work with the NBER and the Institute of Advanced Study at Princeton University, where he became acquainted with Albert Einstein. Starting as a research associate in 1953, Durand obtained the position of associate professor at MIT in 1955 and professor in 1958, a position he held until his retirement in 1973. Durand played a recognizable role in the pre-history of modern finance. For example, just prior to joining MIT, at an NBER research conference Durand proposed the then-unorthodox position that the financial goal of a firm is to maximize the investment value of the firm rather than to maximize income (Paulo 2003, p.330). In addition, Modigliani and Miller (1958) mentioned Durand as contributing to the formulation of the MM1 theorem. In an interview (Barnett and Solow 2000, p.223), Franco Modigliani observed: "listening to a paper by David Durand suggesting (and then rejecting) the so-called 'entity theory' of valuation, I gradually became convinced of the hypothesis that market value should be independent of the structure of financing . . . This result later became part of the proof of the Modigliani-Miller theorem".

Given the connection to MIT, strong quantitative training and initial insights into the emerging theories of modern finance, Durand was a likely candidate to be at the forefront of this emerging scientific initiative. However, with strong institutionalist roots, Durand was one of the few in a prestigious academic situation to question the rise of modern finance (e.g., Durand 1959, 1968). As a consequence of this decision, Durand is best remembered today for the application of statistical methods to problems in corporate finance. Oddly enough, Durand (1957a, p.362) represents an important early criticism of discounted cash flow (DCF) valuation. More precisely, Durand made a significant connection between the St. Petersburg paradox and the use of DCF to value growth stocks:

> The moral of all this is that conventional discount formulas do not provide completely reliable evaluations. Presumably they provide very satisfactory approximations for high-grade, short-term bonds and notes. But as quality deteriorates or duration lengthens, the approximations become rougher and rougher. With

growth stocks, the uncritical use of conventional discount formulas is particularly likely to be hazardous; for, as we have seen, growth stocks represent the ultimate in investments of long duration. Likewise, they seem to represent the ultimate in difficulty of evaluation. The very fact that the Petersburg Problem has not yielded a unique and generally acceptable solution to more than 200 years of attack by some of the world's great intellects suggests, indeed, that the growth-stock problem offers no great hope of a satisfactory solution.

Székely and Richards (2004) revived the arguments in Durand (1957a) to explain the crash of equity capital valuations for technology stocks during the market crash of 2000.

In the history of equity security valuation, Durand symbolizes the end within academic finance of concern with the vernacular old finance problems of practical valuation and market forecasting. From 1959 to 1968, the resistance was considerable but the opposition was too overwhelming. Durand correctly observed that numerous claims being made by "the new finance", aka modern finance, were inflated. For example, regarding the claim that the emerging modern finance approach was based on mathematical logic and supported by quantitative methods Durand (1968, p.848) observed:

> What comes first to mind [in considering the difference between the new finance and the traditional], namely the use of mathematics and quantitative methods, will not stand a second thought. The quantitative approach is anything but new in finance; in the hands of actuaries, it dates back to the eighteenth century . . . The actuaries have . . . greatly contributed to the development of modern statistics, including hypothesis testing.

Similar to Poitras (2000, esp. ch.6, 2006–7), Durand found a close connection between the early histories of finance and actuarial science. Such a connection was grossly inconsistent with the claims of 'scientific revolution' being made by the founders of the modern finance school. Decades later, on "the fiftieth anniversary of the publication of Harry Markowitz's landmark paper, 'Portfolio Selection' " Rubinstein (2002, p.1042) would claim:

> With the hindsight of many years, we can see that [Markowitz 1952] was the moment of the birth of modern financial economics. Although the baby had a healthy delivery, it had to grow into its teenage years before a hint of its full promise became apparent. What has always impressed me most about Markowitz's 1952 paper is that it seemed to come out of nowhere.

The division of academic modern finance from the vernacular world of old finance was complete. Those wanting to keep faith with the vernacular world, such as Durand, were irrelevant.

From Markowitz to Modigliani and Miller

A number of candidates are available for selection as the intellectual beginning of modern finance. Numerous sources identify Markowitz (1952, 1959) as the starting point (e.g., Brealey 1991; Rubinstein 2002; Markowitz 1999). In contrast, Rubinstein (2003) suggested an earlier beginning, tracing the roots back to Fisher (1906, 1907, 1930a) and Williams (1937). Rubinstein (2006) identified the important role of Di Finetti. Recognizing that the Markowitz approach was not widely recognized until after the contributions by W. Sharpe (Sharpe 1963, 1964), the contributions of Modigliani and Miller (Modigliani and Miller 1958; Miller and Modigliani 1961) (MM1; MM2) are an appropriate starting point. This position is supported by a close reading of the literature at the time. For example, in launching a "hostile review" of MM1 (Bernstein 1992, p.175), Durand (1959) represented a broad consensus of academic opinion at the time that MM1 appeared. Durand (1960) demonstrated that the Markowitz model had not received the close scrutiny that was given to MM1. Initial criticisms of the evolving modern finance approach included individuals who, at first glance, would seem to be disposed to MM1, MM2 and the Markowitz approach (e.g., Durand 1957a).

As Rubinstein (2003) recognized, the attribution of ideas to specific individuals is a difficult task, particularly where the individuals involved are no longer living. As such, the task of identifying the origins of modern finance has been simplified significantly by Bernstein (1992), who provided a wonderful collection of first-hand insights into the individuals involved at the beginnings of modern finance in the 1950s and early 1960s. While it is tempting to push back the time line to individuals writing prior to this period, such as L. Bachelier, J.B. Williams and I. Fisher, there is too much of a temporal gap separating these contributors from the widespread recognition of the "bombshell assertions" (Bernstein 1992, ch.9) that modern finance adherents used to supplant the old finance from the core curriculum of business schools. In this interpretation, the modern finance revolution began with Modigliani and Miller (1958), gathered steam during the 1960s and reached fruition by the middle of the 1970s. Though Markowitz's article "Portfolio Selection" (1952) appeared first, it is Markowitz's book *Portfolio Selection: Efficient Diversification of Investments* (1959) that better fits into the time line suggested here.

The selection of MM1 for the beginning date of the modern finance revolution is not intended to imply that MM1 was the most theoretically significant of the early contributions. Bernstein (1992, p.41) reflected the generally accepted view among modern finance adherents about the relative significance of Markowitz's contribution:

> The most famous insight in the history of modern finance and investment appeared in a short paper titled: "Portfolio Selection". It was published in the March 1952 issue of the *Journal of Finance*, the only journal then in existence for scholars in the field. Its author was an unknown 25-year-old graduate student from the University of Chicago named Harry Markowitz.

Having said this, Bernstein proceeded to recognize a time line that supports the primacy of MM1:

> No one, including Markowitz, was aware that his paper would turn out to be a landmark in the history of ideas. Although his achievements would earn

him a Nobel Prize in economic sciences 38 years later, the paper languished for nearly ten years after publication attracting fewer than twenty citations in the academic literature until after 1960. By that time, Markowitz had written his dissertation on the subject and had converted it into a full-length book.

In contrast to the slow acceptance of the Markowitz theory of portfolio optimization, MM1 gained almost instant notoriety.

Portfolio Selection: Efficient Diversification of Investments (Markowitz 1959), ultimately, became the theoretical foundation for the "modern portfolio theory" that is at the center of the modern finance approach. In contrast, MM1 and MM2 did not make such a wide-reaching contribution. This was, at least partly, due to the nature of the results being presented. MM1 demonstrated that, in perfect capital markets, the capital structure of the firm will be irrelevant to the market value of the firm (i.e., there is no optimal capital structure). Similarly, MM2 demonstrated, again in perfect capital markets, that the dividend policy of the firm was also irrelevant to the market value of the firm. In the case of the firm's capital structure, MM1 proposed that the market value of the firm (= market value of debt + market value of equity) is determined by the assets side of the balance sheet. The liabilities plus equity side of the balance sheet only determines the division of the asset cash flows between security claimholders. It is not possible to change the market value of the cash flows from the assets by reorganizing the division of those cash flows between claimholders.

In addition to the basic demonstration that the value of the firm is determined by the assets side of the balance sheet, the MM1 argument also had to deal with investor preferences for a specific type of capital structure. Given the random behavior of asset cash flows, firms with more debt on the balance sheet will have a higher variability in the payments made to equity claims. While this would seem to indicate that the common stock in firms with higher debt levels is riskier and, as a consequence, will have a different market value than the common stock of an otherwise identical firm with a lower debt level, MM1 demonstrated that by engaging in borrowing or lending activities in conjunction with purchases of the common stock, individual investors are able to create a 'synthetic capital structure' for the firm that is consistent with the desired portfolio cash flow variability associated with holdings of the firm's securities. Because the individual investor is able to synthetically achieve a desired capital structure through portfolio allocation, the market value of the firm's debt and equity claims will not be priced to reflect differences in firm capital structure.

MM2 followed lines similar to MM1. The dividend policy of the firm is irrelevant because individuals are able to create a synthetic dividend that is consistent with the individual's desired dividend payout. From the firm's perspective, dividend payments made to shareholders represent foregone retained earnings. In cases where retained earnings are insufficient to sustain the capital requirements needed to fund the firm's growth, the dividend payments are recouped through new share issues. Where the dividend policy is lower than dictated by the firm's capital requirements, the excess retained earnings will be used to repurchase the firm's common stock. Within this context, if the individual finds the firm's dividend policy is lower than desired, then a fraction of the share holdings can be sold each period to obtain the desired level of 'synthetic dividend' cash flow. Similarly, if the dividend payout is higher than desired, the surplus can be used to purchase shares. While, over time, the number of shares outstanding will differ between otherwise identical firms with different dividend policies, the market value of the equity claims will be the same. As in MM1, this occurs because the value of the firm is determined by the assets side of the balance sheet.[18]

Though MM1 and MM2 did not go on to play a central role in the theoretical development of modern portfolio theory—the core of modern finance— MM1 and MM2 did play a central role in the attack on old finance. Dividend policy and the capital structure of the firm are key concerns in traditional 'value investing'. The theoretical claim that such concerns are irrelevant is potentially devastating. More importantly, the irrelevance results depend on exploiting the analytical properties of perfect capital markets. The rational, maximizing individual operating in a 'frictionless' market environment—a central feature of the intellectual superstructure that characterizes modern finance—represented a metaphor that was to prove irresistible compared to the institutionally and legally driven model of the old finance. However, the topics that concerned MM1 and MM2 were focused largely on the central issues of old finance and did not play a crucial role in the evolution of the core theory of modern finance.

What early contributions did play a key role in the evolution of the core theory of modern finance? The general consensus among modern finance academics (e.g., Rubinstein 2002) is that at the head of the list are the seminal contributions that led to the capital asset pricing model (CAPM) and the market model: Markowitz (1952, 1959) and Sharpe (1963, 1964). In addition, as recognized in Markowitz (1999), Tobin (1958) can also be given some credit for containing the essence of the two fund separation result, albeit within the context of modeling the demand for money in a portfolio optimization framework. Markowitz (1999, p.10) observed: "At a meeting with Tobin in attendance, I once referred to his 1958 article as the first capital asset pricing model". Apparently Tobin did not accept this interpretation. In any event, while making an important contribution to monetary economics, Tobin (1958) did not have a similar impact on finance. It was Sharpe (1963, 1964) who recognized the key revolutionary result: "the expected return on each security is linearly related to its beta and only its beta".

The Scope of Modern Finance

The core theory of modern finance is not limited to the Markowitz mean-variance optimization framework and the Sharpe 'capital asset pricing model' (CAPM). Running roughly in parallel with the development of these concepts was the work on the random character of stock market prices that culminated in Cootner (1965) and Fama (1965). While interesting in itself, this work also laid the foundation for the efficient markets hypothesis (EMH) and the modeling of stock prices (returns) as conditional expectations with information sets characterized as weak form, semi-strong form and strong form.[19] This progression was aided considerably by Fama et al. (1969), who introduced a novel statistical methodology, based on cumulative abnormal residuals, that could be used to empirically test the semi-strong (and strong) form of the EMH. In turn, development of the EMH strengthened the argument for using the CAPM and Markowitz model. More precisely, under the EMH, it was not possible to use available information to earn systematic, risk-adjusted abnormal returns. This substantively undermined the basis for doing 'old finance' security analysis, strengthening the rationale for the elimination of diversifiable risk through portfolio optimization methods.

While circa 1965 modern finance was still in the process of evolving into a coherent package, Fama (1970) illustrated that by the end of the decade modern finance had developed into something resembling a coherent whole. With Fama's *Foundations of Finance* (1976), the revolution against the old finance was largely completed, the corpus of modern finance was solidified and the program of future research was well defined. In addition, by the mid-1970s, the modern finance school's attention was shifting to extending and exploring the seminal contribution of Black and Scholes (1973). Though a connection can be made between the CAPM and the Black-Scholes formula, it is difficult to meld the notion of pricing by arbitrage with that of pricing by expectation. Though there were substantive efforts to exploit the continuous time pricing technology used in Black and Scholes (1973) to the CAPM framework (e.g., Merton 1969, 1973b), a disconnect between these two streams of modern finance survives to the present day.

Modern finance has adopted the rational, maximizing individual as the central abstraction upon which theoretical knowledge about equity security pricing can be obtained. Inductive methods—especially variants of regression analysis—are used to determine whether a particular version of a theoretical model is consistent with observed data. If the null hypothesis is not empirically supported, the model is restructured, typically by altering an assumption, and retested. While sharing this general epistemological approach, there have been several distinct tracks in modern finance: the CAPM and Markowitz mean-variance portfolio optimization model; the EMH; and the contingent claims pricing models that emerged following Black and Scholes (1973). Though there has been some complementarity between each of these tracks, each evolved somewhat differently and, as a consequence, modern finance cannot be viewed as coherent doctrine of interlocking parts. Questioning of one part—such as the EMH being questioned by the 'New Finance'—does not necessarily involve questioning another part—such as contingent claims pricing models.

NOTES

1 The use of par values in trading stock was continued until the 20th century, when stock with either no par value or notional par value was first issued in the US, starting in the 1920s (e.g., Baskin 1988, p.227).

2 The life of Irving Fisher extended well beyond the world of academics (e.g., Klein 2001, pp.86–8). Born in 1867, the son of a Congregationalist minister, Fisher studied mathematics and political economy at Yale University. The claim that Fisher was a self-made business success has to be tempered by the fact that in 1893 Fisher married Margaret Hazard, daughter of Rowland Hazard, a wealthy woollen manufacturer. As a wedding gift, the happy couple was presented with a palatial abode in New Haven. It was not until 1912 that

Fisher developed his card index system that he marketed through his Index Visible Company. In 1926, this company merged with its major competitor to form what was eventually to become the Remington Rand Company. During the 1920s Fisher was able to turn part of the house into a home for his Index Number Institute, staffed by more than a dozen people. The institute prepared a weekly newsletter that was distributed to newspapers around the world. Having suffered tuberculosis in 1898, Fisher was for the rest of his life devoted to pursuing and promoting clean living. This part of his life found him to be a confirmed prohibitionist and one of the founders and organizers of the American Eugenics Society. This society was an active promoter of the cause of "race betterment".

3 This was not the case in the UK, where aggregate stock price levels had recovered to 1929 levels by 1936.

4 Hannah (2007) observed that the process of obtaining voluntary compliance for British firms "had been considerably assisted by Sir Henry Burdett, secretary to the London Stock Exchange from 1881. His annual letters to companies, at home and overseas, including some quoted in the provinces, requesting copies of accounts, were a constant reminder of the desirability of providing timely information to shareholders. Even some unquoted companies (apparently ones contemplating an IPO) were sufficiently impressed by his missives to send typewritten copies of their confidential accounts. The extensive archive of several hundred thousand British and foreign company accounts now held at London's Guildhall Library is a permanent monument to his labors".

5 The web page at http://www.sechistorical.org/museum/timeline/ contains a useful, if brief, history of the SEC.

6 A sixth edition was published in 2008. This edition was only a repeat of a previous edition by another author that wrote an introduction. Graham and Dodd were only directly involved in four editions.

7 GDC did not use the words "primary" and "secondary" in the fashion that is conventional in finance terminology, in which a primary issue is a 'new' issue, such as an IPO for a common stock or a Treasury issue that has just been auctioned, and a 'secondary' issue is a previously issued security, such as the common stocks traded on the NYSE or Treasury bonds traded in the OTC market. For GDC, a 'primary' stock issue was a "first line" or "standard" issue of "large and prominent companies, generally with a good record of earnings and of continued dividends." A 'secondary' issue refers to the more marginal common stock issues that have not obtained 'primary' quality. GDC estimated that about 80% of listed stocks and 90% or more of unlisted stocks belong in the secondary category.

8 The precise specification of the margin of safety is unclear. Recognizing that there is a target level of 20–30 stocks in a portfolio, presumably the margin of safety will change as the level of the market changes. When the market is 'high', there will be a greater proportion of fairly valued and overvalued stocks, and it will be necessary to have a lower margin of safety, say 10%–15%, in order for there to be stocks that will qualify for selection, as there will be 'overvalued' stocks that were purchased previously that now require selling. Similarly when the market is 'low', there will be a proportionately greater number of 'undervalued' stocks to buy and less 'overvalued' stocks in the portfolio to sell. This will require the margin of safety to be raised to, say, 25%–30%, in order for the portfolio rebalancing exercise to avoid being almost all in cash at certain times.

9 The requirement introduced by the NYSE in the 1890s that traded firms provide financial statements was an early impetus to providing investors with accurate financial information, permitting the calculation of crude earnings

numbers. While the securities laws of 1933 and 1934 were revolutionary, prior to this time American investors still received considerably better accounting information than investors in other jurisdictions. The situation in the UK was decidedly murkier. It was not until 1976 that turnover numbers had to be fully disclosed (Toms and Wilson 2003). Until the Companies Act was passed in 1948, balance sheet information was clouded by the absence of a requirement to provide consolidated accounts (Rutterford 2004).

10 Common-law countries include the important equity markets of Australia, Canada, Hong Kong, Malaysia, Singapore, South Africa, the UK and the US. The civil-law countries include the important markets of France, Germany, Italy, Japan, Spain, Sweden and Switzerland.

11 An expanded version of the 13 "owner related business principles" plus one added principle underlying Buffett's approach can be found in the Berkshire Hathaway annual report (2003, pp.68–72).

12 For example, in the 2002 Berkshire Hathaway annual report, Buffett recommended in reference to management: "to be a winner, work with winners". While this is good advice for those like Buffett, who are able to secure a golf game, weekend retreat or cosy dinner with virtually any major figure in American corporate management, it is little comfort to a small individual investor seeking to make a purchase in, say, US Steel.

13 The reference to 'holding company' is intended in a descriptive and not a legal sense. The description of Berkshire Hathaway in the 10-K filing refers to an insurance company that owns a range of non-insurance-related businesses.

14 Any 'economic value' calculation is subject to interpretation. The calculation of net tangible assets is no exception. A common convention is to use (cash + accounts receivable + inventory + property, plant and equipment)—(adjustments to reflect differences between the accounting value of the assets recorded on the balance sheet and the replacement cost of the assets).

15 Various descriptions of the value investing approach in general and the Buffett approach to value investing in particular stress the key role played by the franchise factor as the source of long-run corporate advantage and 'monopolistic' profit. However, while the franchise factor is of central importance in many situations of sustainable competitive advantage, other sources can also produce this result.

16 Christ (1994) and Dimand (2009) discussed the early history of the founding of the Cowles Commission for Research in Economics. The Commission was founded in Colorado Springs in 1932, basically because the investment advisory firm run by Cowles was located in Colorado Springs. The commission was formed primarily at the initiative of Cowles and Irving Fisher, president of the recently formed Econometric Society. The first edition of *Econometrica* in 1933 followed shortly after the Commission was founded. In 1939, the Cowles Commission moved from Colorado Springs to the University of Chicago. Jacob Marschak served as director from 1943 to 1948, when T. Koopmans succeeded to the position. For a combination of reasons, including some opposition to the Cowles Commission within the economics department at the University of Chicago and a desire to attract James Tobin to the directorship, in 1955 the commission moved to Yale University and was renamed the Cowles Foundation. While a graduate student at the University of Chicago in the 1950s, Harry Markowitz was a member of the Cowles Commission.

17 As evidence of quantitative background, Durand and Greenwood (1937) and Gumbel, Greenwood and Durand (1953) are two substantive contributions to mathematical statistics. Biographical information on Durand is available in a number of sources. The 6 March 1996 edition of *Tech Talk*, the official MIT newspaper, has a lengthy memorial by Enders Robinson, a close friend

of Durand. Szekely and Richards (2005) gave good coverage of available sources. See also Durand (1989) and Durand (1992) for more information on how Durand viewed his various contributions.

18 Significantly, implications of the relationship between share price, corporate dividend policy and the use of share repurchase programs to, supposedly, return profits to shareholders goes unrecognized.

19 Though Fama (1970) is often credited with popularizing the weak, semi-strong and strong form terminology, Fama credited the origination of these terms to a colleague at the University of Chicago, Harry Roberts.

11 The Separation of Ownership and Control

> The prime fact concerning us as a nation is the progressive diffusion of ownership on the one hand and the ever-increasing concentration of managerial power on the other.
>
> William Ripley, *Main Street and Wall Street* (1927)

A BERLE AND MEANS REVISITED

The Historical Context

Two texts from the inter-war period have an enduring influence: J.M. Keynes' *General Theory* (1936) and A. Berle and G. Means' *Modern Corporation and Private Property* (1932). The persisting influence of such texts can be found in the diversity of issues being addressed. While some issues still resonate, other aspects have long since been ignored. In the case of Berle and Means, the fundamental issues that still attract attention in corporation law, corporate finance and related subjects are shareholder primacy and the separation of ownership and control. In modern corporate law, *The Modern Corporation and Private Property* is taken to represent 'shareholder primacy', that corporate managers have an overriding responsibility to maximize shareholder value. Shareholder primacy is contrasted with two other viewpoints: those that allow for managerial discretion and those that advocate corporate social responsibility. Millon (1990) detailed the debate between these different positions dealing with "the fundamental nature of corporate activity and the appropriate goals of corporate law" (Bratton and Wachter 2008, p.100).

Bratton (2001, p.739) identified factors that have sustained the continuing influence of Berle and Means in the area of corporation law and corporate governance. This enduring influence is not due to the impact on policy:

> *The Modern Corporation and Private Property*'s endurance is a singular event in the last century of academic corporate law . . . The answer to the question respecting the book's longevity reverses usual expectations concerning elements of scholarly success. We tend to look for real world consequences,

equating success with changes in positive law. But *The Modern Corporation and Private Property*'s academic survival does not result from its influence on New Deal legislation. Indeed, the book's prescription for remedying the problem of separation of ownership and control—a step up in the intensity and scope of fiduciary duties—must be characterized as a policy relic.

Rather, Berle and Means have become a symbol, pointing to something permanent in modern society beyond the contents of the text (p.739):

> Berle and Means survive *despite* their prescription, because they correctly diagnosed a persistent condition. Their book's continued vitality results from its identification and discussion of problems left untreated both then and now. Leading corporate governance discussions still implicate the separation of ownership and control because, as Berle and Means asserted, the separation implied shortfalls of competence and responsibility. Their association with these problems seems permanent and the problems themselves never seem to go away. It follows that we can predict a continuing presence for *The Modern Corporation and Private Property*, both normative and descriptive, in the twenty-first century.

In effect, Berle and Means are synonymous with the separation of ownership and control, a topic that appears in social, political, legal, economic and financial contexts.

Given this, considerable effort has been given to validating or disproving the descriptive element of Berle and Means. The implication is that, if the historical evidence supporting the claims of Berle and Means is inaccurate, then the argument being made is, somehow, faulty. Recognizing and identifying failures in the empirical evidence will, somehow, render a more informed view of the separation of ownership and control. Alternatively, closer reading of the historical evidence could, possibly, reveal that *The Modern Corporation and Private Property* is a "myth" (e.g., Hannah 2007; Holderness 2008; Hilt 2008). Considerable recent effort has been given to debunking those seeking to debunk Berle and Means (e.g., Cheffins and Bank 2009; Cheffins 2008). Others are willing to accept the historical evidence but deny interpretations to the evidence given by Berle and Means—for example, "a purpose that stands Berle and Means story on its head . . . limited liability did not lead to a separation of ownership and management, but rather that a separation of ownership and management led to limited liability" (Kessler 2003, p.513).

Unfortunately, what has survived to modern times from Berle and Means (1932) has been sanitized, largely removed from the social and political concerns that are threaded through the text. To illustrate, consider the concluding paragraph on the reach and importance of the limited liability corporation (p.313):

> The rise of the modern corporation has brought a concentration of economic power which can compete on equal terms with the modern state . . . Where its own interests are concerned, it even attempts to dominate the state. The future may see the economic organism now typified by the corporation, not

only on an equal plane with the state, but possibly even superseding it as the dominant form of social organization.

As Mizruchi (2004, p.581) observed: "Removed from the pressures of stockholders, managers, for Berle and Means, were now viewed as a self-perpetuating oligarchy, unaccountable to the owners whom they were expected to represent". In a broader context: "Berle and Means warned that the ascendance of management control and unchecked corporate power had potentially serious consequences for the democratic character of the United States" (p.579). It is a concern "that economic power was becoming concentrated in the hands of a cluster of corporate managers" that initially together brought the research of Adolf Berle, a law professor, and Gardiner Means, an economics graduate student, (Bratton 2001, p.752).

The Modern Corporation and Private Property "appeared in the early stages of the Great Depression, but it was more a product of the 1920s, or more generally, the period after 1890 that culminated in the stock market crash of 1929" (p.752). The research was well formed before the stock market crash of 1929 and the profound social and political concerns arising from the Great Depression. During the 1920s, there was a pervasive view in law and economics that self-regulation was the appropriate approach to corporate governance.[1] Berle and Means' conclusion was that government control of publicly traded limited liability corporations was required to offset the power that the law and the political system had allowed to become overly concentrated, threatening democratic institutions. This reasoned and seemingly well-researched perspective fit well with the New Deal reforms, such as the Securities Exchange Act (1934), which substantially altered the character of the relationship between 'the corporation' and its 'owners', the common stock holders. For a number of reasons, such concerns are largely absent from recent treatments. Instead, they focus on concerns about 'the data', whether Berle and Means got it right back in the day, and whether similar 'data' apply to more recent time periods.

Building on Means (1930), empirical evidence provided by Berle and Means (1932) involved examining the 200 largest US non-financial corporations in 1929. Berle and Means observed that 44% of these corporations had no individual owner with as much as 20% of the common stock, a threshold that Berle and Means assumed as the approximate minimum needed for effective control. These 88 corporations, which were classified as having sufficiently dispersed ownership to be considered 'management controlled', accounted for 58% percent of the total assets among the top 200. In 11% of the companies, the largest shareholder had a majority of the outstanding shares. Since Berle and Means (1932), considerable effort has been dedicated to determining the validity of the empirical evidence on the separation of ownership and control. As Gilson and Gordon (2013, p.863) observed, the equity capital landscape has changed considerably since Berle and Means (1932). More precisely: "Equity ownership in the United States no longer reflects the dispersed share ownership of the canonical Berle-Means firm. Instead, we observe the reconcentration of ownership in the hands of institutional investment intermediaries".

In addition to debates about the empirical evidence on ownership concentration after Berle and Means, questions have been raised about the validity of Berle and Means' interpretation of the degree of concentration, the separation of ownership and control, in earlier times. For example, Campbell and Turner (2011, p.577) examined the evidence for Berle and Means' (1932, p.56) claim that during the last half of the Victorian era in Britain "the corporation was small enough so that [the shareholder] could maintain direct contact with responsible individuals; and thus either because of his individual influence, or his knowledge of the affairs of the corporation, and community sentiment in general, the law needed to worry little about him". While this observation may have applied to an era of localized US businesses, nearing the end of the century in England the situation was much different: "dividends and well-structured and incentivized boards of directors" played a key role in protecting outside investors. Incentivized management and boards is a theme in the modern agency theory resolution for the problems of separating ownership and control, which proposes the use of executive stock option grants to better align the interests of management and shareholders.

There are other examples of Berle and Means not 'getting it right' regarding the earlier history of US corporations. Examining an 1823 sample of New York corporations, Hilt (2008, p.645) found: "In contrast to Berle and Means's account of the development of the corporation, the results indicate that many firms were dominated by large shareholders, who were represented on the firms' boards, and held sweeping power to utilize firms' resources for their own benefit". Following Bricker and Chandar (2000, p.529), "Berle and Means' omission of the role of investment funds led them to conclude that the separation of ownership from control problem was located between shareholders and company managers". This suggests a drawback in the 'agency theory' approach that is based on corporate managers and diffusely distributed shareholders. Issues surrounding separation of equity capital fund 'ownership' and shareholders in the funds are distinct from the traditional agency model, adding a layer of complexity involving insurance companies, pension funds, hedge funds, mutual funds, index funds and other exchange traded funds. In this approach to alleviating the problems arising from the separation of ownership and control, socially responsible corporate management will seek to maximize shareholder wealth, monitored by managers of equity capital funds with a fiduciary responsibility to ensure the interests of shareholders are looked after. Such is the basic theory of fiduciary capitalism.

Fiduciary Capitalism and Equity Capitalism

'Capitalism' is such an overused word that the concept has become obscured by the variety of meanings that could be attached. At least since Hall and Soskice (2001), many of those currently employing this term have preferred to explore 'varieties of capitalism'. Following Neal and Williamson (2014, p.2), this approach identifies:

> Four elements . . . common in each variant of capitalism, whatever the specific emphasis:
>
> 1   private property rights

2   contracts enforceable by third parties
3   markets with responsive prices; and
4   supportive governments.

Each of these elements must deal specifically with *capital*, a factor of production that is somehow physically embodied, whether in buildings and equipment, or in improvements to land, or in people with special knowledge. Regardless of the form it takes, however, the capital has to be long lived and not ephemeral to have meaningful economic effects.

This approach identifies 'capital' with the left-hand side of the balance sheet (i.e., "long lived" physical, financial and human capital). In contrast to those seeking common factors in varieties of capitalism, Acemoglu and Robinson (2015, p.4) and others did not find:

> the term capitalism to be a useful one for the purposes of comparative economic or political analysis. By focusing on the ownership and accumulation of capital, this term distracts from the characteristics of societies which are more important in determining their economic development and the extent of inequality. For example, both Uzbekistan and modern Switzerland have private ownership of capital, but these societies have little in common in terms of prosperity and inequality because the nature of their economic and political institutions differs so sharply. In fact, Uzbekistan's capitalist economy has more in common with avowedly noncapitalist North Korea than Switzerland.

This again appears to relate the capital in 'capitalism' to the left-hand side of the balance sheet. Despite critiquing capitalism, the ownership claim is associated with physical, not equity, capital, and the accumulation of capital does not identify the increase in book value and market value of equity as earnings are retained over time.

As a consequence of the scattered and disparate interpretations of 'capital', the 'capitalism' associated with the 'equity capital' of the right-hand side of the balance sheet often appears with an adjective: 'financial capitalism', 'money manager capitalism', 'fiduciary capitalism', 'agency capitalism', 'finance-dominated capitalism', 'investment bank capitalism', 'managerial capitalism'. Though the broader concerns of these interpretations of capitalism differ, a common theme is that the bulk of productive capacity in modern society is now owned by limited liability corporations, with equity capital ownership increasingly concentrated in the hands of large financial institutions—pension funds, life insurance companies, investment banks, mutual funds, exchange traded funds, hedge funds. The various adjectives reflect, to varying degrees, the positive or negative interpretation of this state of affairs. Those referring to 'fiduciary capitalism' or 'agency capitalism' see the increasing ownership of equity capital by 'fiduciaries' as a positive development. Such fiduciaries work for 'fiduciary institutions' with legally defined duties, such as prudent investor rules and investment advisor registration.

Hawley and Williams (2000) referred to such 'fiduciary institutions' as "universal investors":

whose investment portfolios are so large and so diverse, and whose time horizons are so long-term, that it no longer makes economic sense for them to focus on the goal traditionally thought to drive individual shareholders—the goal of maximizing the price of the company's shares . . . the universal shareowner—unlike the typical individual investor—has both an interest in and an ability to promote corporate practices that advance not only the narrow interests of the firm's shareholders, but also those of the broader society.

In contrast to the positive view of 'fiduciary capitalism' proposed by Hawley and Williams (2000), Rogers (2014) and others—those referring to 'money manager capitalism', finance-dominated capitalism, 'investment bank capitalism' and the like—took a decidedly negative view. For example, Hein (2012, p.179) provided "a systemic macroeconomic perspective on finance-dominated capitalism and its crisis", arguing from a macroeconomic perspective that the "financialization" inherent in finance-dominated capitalism "has, since the early 1980s, affected long-run economic developments in the developed capitalist economies in particular through the following three channels: redistribution of income at the expense of low labour incomes, dampening of investment in real capital stock, and an increasing potential for wealth-based and debt-financed consumption". On one hand, this concern with increasing redistribution and disparity of wealth is also a key theme in the widely discussed contributions by Piketty (2014); on the other hand, it received no attention from Shiller (2013).

When viewed through the lens of 'equity capital', an alternative vision of 'capitalism' appears. The negative views of 'capitalism' that claim increasing and inexorable wealth inequality and macroeconomic instability find no basis in 'equity capital'. The allocation of domestic production to various groups in society and the associated ability to carry wealth through time is a political and social matter. The Roman Empire and Renaissance Italian city states imposed taxes based on wealth, not income. In contrast, the wealthiest modern societies use personal income taxes and sales taxes to fund government programs. Such taxes fall disproportionately on those groups in society with *de facto* lower income and wealth levels. At the same time, the pressures of globalization mean the use of corporation taxes, wealth taxes and inheritance taxes are being reduced *de facto* in various ways. This has worked well for the so-called "one percent" in terms of capturing a larger and larger share of the increases in real economic output resulting from dramatic technological changes that have been largely financed by equity capital in different forms—for example, venture capital; limited liability partnerships; and, publicly traded common stock. The failing of modern wealthy societies to adequately 'tax' these wealth gains is a failure of the political process, not from the use of 'equity capital' that has facilitated the rapid introduction of new technologies that have driven real output gains.

Unfortunately, the social need to use the tax system for redistributing resources to those in society with lower income and wealth levels is gradually being obscured by the advance of the modern consumer society. There is a real threat to the social fabric from the use of limited liability corporations with global reach increasingly providing the wealthy with a legal vehicle to accumulate physical and financial assets without having to pay for the use of 'the public space' to generate profits. As a consequence, those with positive views of 'capitalism' also find no basis in 'equity capitalism'. By ignoring the fundamental social connection between the concentration of *de facto* equity capital control in a narrow privileged group and the use of that accumulated wealth to exercise political power, the positive views of capitalism fail to account for the perverse implications of a political process that is incapable of action that will more fairly charge the wealthy for benefits received from access to 'the public space'.

What Is an Autonomous Share?

Two essential features of modern equity capital—limited liability and corporate status—have been widely recognized and studied. In comparison, the other essential features—'autonomous' exchange-traded shares—receive scant attention. While the meaning of 'exchange traded' is more than apparent, 'autonomous' is opaque. Following Ireland (1996), the autonomous share is symbolic of 'capitalism without the capitalist'. However, the concept is more scientific than this metaphor. As the number of limited liability corporations with traded shares increased over time and the size of 'permanent' tangible and intangible capital of those corporations also increased, the ownership claim of a given equity capital share diminished to the point of being almost perfectly diffuse. The ability and risk reduction incentive to combine equity capital shares into a diversified portfolio completes the divorce of equity capital share ownership from the control of the commercial entity. In contrast to the raising of local equity capital to finance projects that promote local or regional interests, as in the case of 18th- and 19th-century canal and railway construction, an autonomous share has completely detached the location of corporate physical capital from the source of the equity capital financing.

In modern times, Berle and Means have been associated with shareholder primacy. This objective is complicated when the *de jure* ownership claim of an equity capital share is 'autonomous', completely separated from *de facto* operational control of the commercial venture. Starting in the 1980s, modern finance academics proposed that the agency problem created by this 'separation of ownership and control' could be addressed by providing contingent incentive contracts tied to the share price, which better align the interests of management with shareholders. The ensuing substitution of share repurchase programs for dividend payments has allowed corporate managers to capture excessive compensation at the expense of investors with autonomous shares. The presence of autonomous shares begs the question: If shares are autonomous, entitled to profit only after corporate objectives and management compensation has been determined, then where are the *de facto* 'owners' who do have control? In other words, instead of 'capitalism without the capitalists', the autonomous share allows the *de facto* capitalists controlling corporate assets to access the permanent corporate equity capital stock provided by investors with a diffuse ownership claim.

Gilson and Gordon (2013) recognized the profound evolution of the autonomous share from "the dispersed share ownership of the canonical Berle-Means firm" to the "reconcentration of ownership in the hands of institutional investment intermediaries", giving rise to "the agency costs of agency capitalism". In effect, the agency cost model of Berle and Means locates agency costs between managers and shareholders, while 'agency capitalism' finds a more complicated agency cost relationship between institutional fund managers and diversified investors and between corporate management and institutional fund managers. Driving this relatively recent evolution are two key factors: (1) the transition from defined benefit and public pension plans to the 'privatized provision of retirement savings' through defined contribution pension plans; and (2) the emergence of "investment intermediaries offering low-cost diversified investment vehicles". Gilson and Gordon describe the historical details (p.884):

> The past thirty-five years have seen a sharp increase in U.S. household ownership of equities, but equity mutual funds have been the vehicle. As of 1977, approximately 20% of households owned equities directly. While the percentage of direct owners has remained stable, the rise in mutual fund investment has increased the percentage of households that own equities directly or through mutual funds by 30% to a total of 50%.

This development raises legitimate questions surrounding the institutional and intellectual factors that fuelled this dramatic move to 'agency capitalism'.

Gilson and Gordon identify elements of the institutional changes that have contributed to the rise of agency capitalism (p.884):

> a large fraction of mutual fund owners have come to this form of investment through employer-sponsored defined contribution accounts (in 2011, 32% of all households owned funds only through an employer-sponsored retirement plan), but a significant fraction owned mutual funds even without that connection (31% of mutual fund holders, or 13% of all households, owned funds only outside an employer-sponsored mutual fund plan).

Recognizing that such dramatic institutional changes needed to be rationalized in the intellectual attention space, Gilbert and Gordon raised a fundamental empirical issue. While much of the increasingly widespread use of equity mutual funds in defined contribution pension plans arises from favourable tax treatment, "many investors own mutual funds outside of choice-constrained accounts". This occurs even though "individual mutual fund ownership is commonly less tax-efficient than direct equity investing". In the US, for example: "Mutual funds are 'flow-through' vehicles for tax purposes, and individuals are required to pay tax on net gains realized by the fund even when the fund is selling stock to meet others' redemption requests" (p.885). Gilson and Gordon attributed much of this investment pattern to the "Triumph of Portfolio Theory", an intellectual contribution at the core of modern finance.

Gilson and Gordon provided a helpful overview of: "the application of Markowitz's Nobel Prize-winning theory on the efficiency of mean variance investing, which gives rise to the portfolio theory". The practical lessons to be gleaned from the subsequent development of 'modern portfolio theory' were summarized as follows (p.885):

(i)   diversification improves risk-adjusted returns;
(ii) the broader the portfolio, the greater the diversification; and,
(iii) since secondary markets in seasoned equities are highly efficient, research that adds value is expensive and its fixed cost is best spread across large portfolios.

As detailed in Poitras (2011, ch.1), the 'scientific' basis for such claims fails to recognize the practical and epistemological difficulties of connecting *ex post* 'logical' facts from modern portfolio theory, which are based on deduction and mathematics, with *ex ante* 'empirical' facts, which depend on the ability of the logical theory to accurately predict observed behavior. Modern finance adherents, in general, and modern portfolio theorists, in particular, make the philosophical assumption that 'capital asset' markets are efficient. In contrast, old finance adherents take a different perspective on the ability of equity capital markets to 'efficiently' value shares. Both perspectives argue for diversification, but modern portfolio theory dictates holding widely diversified index funds, while fundamental analysis suggests a much smaller number of carefully selected companies.

On balance, it is not possible to say whether buying equity securities directly or indirectly through diversified mutual funds or exchange-traded funds will have the best *ex ante* performance at a given point in time. The practical upshot is that, as a result of the increase in ownership of autonomous equity capital shares by mutual funds and related intermediaries, it is now that case that these entities (Gilson and Gordon 2013, p.886):

> hold a large percentage of U.S. equities. Over recent years, mutual funds held approximately 25% of the outstanding stock of publicly traded U.S. corporations. Given the concentration in the mutual fund industry, twenty-five mutual fund families hold the voting rights for some 18.75% of outstanding U.S. equities. Thus, by any measure, mutual funds have the power to be a significant force in the governance of large U.S. corporations.

Based on the substantial data on fund activity available in public filings, there is ample evidence that "mutual funds are at least on the surface anything but proactive". As a consequence, the "reconcentration of ownership" in these financial intermediaries has created a strikingly modern type of agency cost, where a significant portion of the ownership claim has eroded, allowing those in *de facto* control to engage in excessive rent-seeking precipitated by the reduced probability of effective oversight.

B   EQUITY SECURITY FUND HODGEPODGE

What Are Managed Funds?

The management of funds has a history that dates back to antiquity. Political, religious and clan organizations have, at various times, been responsible for the management of social resources to provide for the destitute, sick and elderly or to meet the needs of government. For example, the *publicani* of the Roman Empire were involved in the collection of taxes within the territories of the Empire. This required management of funds that accumulated as taxes were paid and involved arrangements made for disbursement of these funds to the regional authorities and the government in Rome.

In contrast, the history of managed funds is much shorter. In the context of equity security valuation, a managed fund requires two basic characteristics: There needs to be a fund manager, and, more importantly, there needs to be a tradeable equity claim associated with the fund. In a sense, royally chartered English joint-stock companies, such as the Bank of England and the East India Company, were managed funds. This follows because the equity capital raised from the joint-stock issue was exchanged for government debt, resulting in a balance sheet that had a sizeable portion of government loan stock on the assets side of the balance sheet.

Due to the legitimate business component of the early English joint-stock companies associated with the grant of monopoly in the royal charter, the managed fund component of the share price was not traded in isolation. Such a broad definition of managed funds supports the view that managed funds have been part of equity security markets from the beginning of trade in *VOC* shares. Joint-stock companies evolved out of partnerships that needed to pool capital to fund ventures. The *VOC* in particular was formed by combining the equity of smaller Dutch trading companies. In effect, joint-stock shares are a claim against a closed-end fund of equity capital used to create and perpetuate a business venture. The managers of the fund are those in charge of running the company. While this stretches the definition of 'fund' considerably, the basic principle is clear: A tradeable share in a managed fund has similar characteristics to other types of tradeable equity securities.

As evidenced in the Mississippi scheme and the South Sea bubble, in many situations it was not the government debt component of the asset value that drove market pricing of the 18th-century joint-stock share. A similar comment applies to the actuarially sound life insurance companies during the last half of the 18th century (e.g., Lewin 2003), even earlier if companies selling other types of insurance—such as the London Assurance and Royal Exchange Assurance, chartered in 1720—are recognized. Such companies managed a fund of financial assets and had a traded equity security. However, again there is a mix of a legitimate business component and the managed fund element. All this leads to an additional restriction: The assets held by the managed fund must be tradeable securities. In effect, a managed fund is a tradeable equity security that holds other tradeable securities. In this amended definition, 'tradeable' is broadly defined to include, say, no load mutual funds. In this case, the broker-dealer sponsoring the fund makes a market by being willing to buy or sell at net asset value.

Recognizing that managed funds involve the creation of tradeable securities, it follows that such funds can capture payoff characteristics not achievable with, say, common stocks individually. The practical realization of this result during the 18th century marked a feasible beginning to what has evolved into the modern managed funds industry. One of the insights of modern finance is that the expected return on a capital asset depends only on the risk of that asset within an efficiently diversified portfolio, after adjustment for the level of the risk-free return. In other words, it is only the undiversifiable or systematic part of risk that matters for determining the expected return, "and this can be defined only in the context of an investment portfolio" (Levi and Sercu 1991, p.26). By reducing transactions costs and the like, intermediaries can benefit investors by creating tradeable funds composed of individual security combinations. The precise method or 'style' used to create a particular fund differs considerably over time, depending in part on the types of securities available. The decidedly uneven evolution of this industry reflects the relative sophistication achieved by national and global securities markets at a given point in historical time.

Structure of Early Managed Funds

The earliest managed funds were closed-end funds, traded on the Paris bourse and other venues starting in the 1760s, invested in debt securities of the French government. The managers were, initially, Genevan bankers, though the investment schemes were soon adopted in other centers, such as Amsterdam, and applied to other securities, such as the debt of different sovereign governments (Taylor 1962). The use of debt issues was a least partly due to the relative lack of joint-stocks available, though gross mispricing by the French government of the life annuities being purchased by the earliest funds also was an important initial impetus. Restrictions various European countries adopted following the bubbles of 1719 and 1720 hampered the ability to issue joint-stock, reducing the supply of such equity securities for inclusion in managed funds. Not until the 20th century did funds composed exclusively of 'ordinary shares' or common stocks become popular. Funds that purchased common stocks for earnings compounding and capital gains purposes instead of the higher dividend yield on common shares than preferred or debenture stock did not appear until the 1920s.

A confusing semantic feature appearing in primary sources for pre-20th-century equity markets is the use of 'stock' for debt issues and 'shares' for common stock. These definitions were conventional in 18th- and 19th-century British security markets at a time when dividend yield comparison was a common method of equity valuation. Following Armstrong (1848, pp.5–6), 'stock' was standard American usage for both "shares of stock" (i.e., common stock) and "government and state stocks . . . upon which a certain rate of interest is allowed". However, when common stock valuations were being specifically discussed, reference was made to "par value of the shares of this Company". By the time Lowenfeld (1909) referred to "the selection of stock for investment", 'stock' was defined loosely to include a range of debt, preferred shares and ordinary shares. While modern 'stock' markets are primarily secondary markets that trade common stock, it was not until the latter part of the 19th century, in conjunction with the introduction of the limited liability corporation, that 'ordinary shares' attracted much attention on the 'stock exchanges', where trading of debt securities was, by far, the most important. At this time, valuation of ordinary shares was driven by factors that were characteristic of debt security selection: safety of capital and stability of income.

From 1868 to 1914, when 'average investment trusts' were popular, ordinary shares were only gradually assuming importance in the UK. From a legal perspective, this is understandable, as it was not until the Companies Acts of 1856 and 1862 that limited liability and readily available company registration encouraged funding using ordinary shares. In any event, other sources of financing were available for companies, and, in addition, there was a plentiful supply of foreign sovereign debt issues to attract the British investor seeking to make up for the progressively falling British government bond yield during this period. For example, the yield on British consols fell from about 3.5% in the early 1860s to below 2.5% around 1900 (Hutson 2005, p.445). In contrast, with consols yields around 3.25%, the Foreign and Colonial Government Trust was able to obtain attractive yields between 5% and 6% on the highest-quality (New South Wales; Nova Scotia) British colony bonds and yields as high 15.5% on the least attractive Turkish bonds. Those coupons might have been suspended from time to time on low-quality sovereign credits, but the full force of the British government could be used to ensure at least some return of principal on such sovereign issues.

The evolution of managed funds proceeded considerably during this period (Burton and Corner 1968; Rutterford 2009). Though a number of previously organized building societies, mutual savings associations and friendly societies had features of managed funds, the Foreign and Colonial Trust was different enough to be considered the first of the British investment trusts. The trust was chaired by Lord Westbury, the Attorney-General who had championed the Fraudulent Trustee Bill (1857) and the Bankruptcy and Insolvency Bill (1861). The legal structure of a trust was preferred to that of a limited liability company, due to the unsavory reputation that companies had attained following the panic of 1866, fuelled by the registration of less than credible limited liability companies following passage of the Companies Act. This panic was another instance of the speculative excess that had characterized the first half of the 18th century, such as the foreign government bond craze of the 1820s and 1830s and the railway bubble and bust of 1845–1847. The Foreign and Colonial was established primarily with the aim of providing investors of lesser means, who depended on receiving a steady investment income, with a 'safe' diversified investment vehicle capable of achieving returns above those being offered on British government securities.

The success of the Foreign and Colonial led to five subsequent issues by 1872 and the creation of eight other investment trusts by 1874 (Burton and Corner

1968, p.17). Circa 1875, the London Stock Exchange listed 18 trusts, growing to 70 listed trusts by the end of the decade, numbers that included different issues by the same investment trust (Rutterford 2009). Some of these early trusts were not well designed, and there were abuses, such as the over-judicious use of founder shares. A legal challenge in 1879 led to virtually all trusts converting to limited liability companies—for example, the Foreign and Colonial converted from trust to investment company status in 1879. This marked the historical beginning of another semantic confusion between the 'investment trust'—which is legally organized as a trust with trustees and contractual similarities to a bond indenture—and the 'investment trust company' or investment company—which is a limited liability company. Among other implications, conversion to company status permitted managed funds: (a) to issue different classes of debt, preferred shares and ordinary shares; and (b) to depart from the fixed investment list and, to some extent, actively trade securities. The relevance of the legal distinction between trusts and companies continues to modern times with the Canadian government's 'Halloween 2006 massacre' of the corporate tax exemption for the unit trust structure, which decimated small investors' retirement savings.

The early investment trusts charged a small front-load fee and an annual management fee to pay for fund expenses, not unlike modern managed funds. There was also considerable variation in the investment style of the early trusts. For example, whereas the Foreign and Colonial selected government bonds outside the UK, the Scottish American Investment Trust selected only US railway bonds. Investment trust features prior to the conversion to company status were dramatically different from modern managed funds (Hutson 2005, pp.448–50). In particular, the funds were fixed. A trust was created by issuing shares or participation certificates, and the funds raised were used to buy specific amounts from a list of securities. Once selected, the portfolio could not be changed except in narrowly defined circumstances. The trust had a fixed life—24 years for the Foreign and Colonial—and promised to pay a fixed dividend. To allow for the creation of a reserve against unforeseen events and to make allowance for future capital to redeem shares, an actuary was employed to determine the correct initial difference between the underlying portfolio yield and the fixed fund dividend payment so that 'in all probability' all certificates could be redeemed within 24 years with a capital surplus still remaining (Rutterford 2009).

The theoretical sophistication of the early investment trusts reflects a careful attention to actuarial detail. These 'average investment trusts' were built on: "The principle of distribution of risk by embodying in a Trust a number of undertakings" (Share Investment Trust prospectus, 1872). Unfortunately, the subsequent history of investment trusts and investment trust companies did not fulfill the early promise. Even before the conversion to corporate status, problems were emerging in the governance structure and with the use of leverage. Unlike modern mutual funds, which are restricted in the use of leverage, there were a number of reasons for early managed funds to use leverage. For example, it was common for initial subscriptions to be partly paid, with the balance to be carried by the company using loans that would be paid down as subscriptions became fully paid. It was a small step to where the fund would be constructed using borrowed money to purchase additional securities that would result in a higher residual payment to founder shares. The abuse of leveraging became particularly acute as the conversion to corporate status permitted funds greater discretion to actively manage the security portfolio and to adjust the composition of equity securities issued by the fund between ordinary, founder and preferred shares.

From Investment Trusts to Mutual Funds

The contributions of Henry Lowenfeld, Sir John Fowke Rolleston and others associated with the Investment Registry that supported the *Financial Review of Reviews* were inspired by the various failings that emerged in UK investment trust companies during the last two decades of the 19th century. Whereas the prudent use of reserve funds had protected the early investment trusts from the bond defaults arising during the 1874–1876 economic downturn, this was not the case for the 55 investment trust companies—up to 100 if hybrids investing in other than tradeable securities are counted—that had been listed on the London stock exchange by 1890. The spread of the Barings crisis that began in 1890 saw dividends being suspended, many trusts folding or merging and trust share values collapsing. By the end of the recession of 1893, only seven trusts had market value greater than issue price (Hutson 2005, p.448). In this process, a number of poorly managed trusts with self-serving management practices were exposed. In the aftermath of this debacle, Lowenfeld and others sought to restore the actuarial foundations that the original investment trusts had established.

Despite the efforts of Lowenfeld and others, investment trusts in the UK did not regain the luster of the late 1880s until the boom years of 1924–1929. By this time, the US had been propelled by World War I into a position of economic importance, reflected in the size and development of equity security markets. "By mid-1928, the US investment trust sector had overtaken that of the UK, with an aggregate capital of $1.2 billion compared with an equivalent $1 billion in capital for British investment trusts" (Rutterford 2009). It was during the 1920s that managed funds, traded primarily in the US equity markets, emerged with investment styles and characteristics closer to actively managed funds traded in modern equity markets. In particular, from the classical closed-end, fixed investment trust model inherited from the UK, the American equity security markets of the late 1920s developed the closed-end fund, active investment management company model. This allowed for actively managed funds that invested exclusively in common stocks, emphasizing capital gains to obtain the compounding power of reinvested earnings and, hopefully, to make speculative gains from a combination of leveraging and experienced management producing sound stock selection and market timing decisions. Such trusts also attracted interest from UK investors from 1924 to 1929.

Though examples of investment trusts in America go back to the 19th century, the few US trusts that appeared prior to 1924 followed the UK closed-end, fixed trust model, with the exception that common stocks of US companies were the primary assets of the trusts. By 1924, only 18 investment trusts had been formed in the US (Chamberlain and Hay 1931, p.104). Following Rutterford (2009), an important factor in the investment trust boom that developed from 1924 to 1929 was "the support given to investment trusts [by] a number of influential authors, most notably Edgar Laurence Smith, Leland Robinson, P.W. Garrett, Irving Fisher and Marshall Williams". The leading figure in the common-stock theory, E. L. Smith, was president of The Investment Managers' Company and had a direct business interest in establishing legitimacy for the practices of the 'new style' investment management companies. In addition to touting stocks for the long run, Smith (1924) recommended the use of professional investment managers able to periodically alter the composition of the fund portfolio.

In addition to being a strong proponent of the 'common stock theory' advanced by Smith, Irving Fisher was a strong proponent of actively managed funds run by investment professionals. "Incessantly vigilant management" was needed to see that 'blue chips did not turn pink' (Rutterford 2009). This recommendation was based on a seemingly obvious point: inflexibility in the holdings of a fixed trust reduced overall returns, as poorly performing securities could not be replaced. This point would have little relevance for the type of UK fixed trust that the Foreign and Colonial had become since 1905. The conversion to corporate status in 1879 resulted in the five individual trusts, each with less than 20 securities, being combined into a single fund holding 90 securities. By 1905, there were 280 securities held by the fund, almost exclusively selected for purposes of geographical diversification, stability of income and safety of principal (Rutterford 2009). Unlike the classical fixed investment trust, the averaging inherent in a particular investment list was not predetermined, and some variation in the portfolio, and the capital structure of the fund, was permitted, because the number of securities held was large.

Not unlike the excesses of the UK investment trust companies in the decade prior to the Barings crisis, tragic excesses appeared in the flexible US investment trusts and investment management companies of the late 1920s. In the explosion of new issues, which saw a more than doubling of managed fund assets from 1928 to 1929, the lack of available common stock for purchase saw trusts and investment companies purchasing the equity securities of other trusts and investment companies. In contrast to the classical fixed UK investment trust that invested in a published list of globally diversified "Class I" fixed income securities—sovereign and high-quality corporate bonds and preferred stock—US investment company managers concentrated on the common stock of a small number of large domestic corporations. The flexible fund feature and corporate structure permitted investment managers to avoid the publication of the specific securities held in the managed fund at any time. Another aggravating factor in the excesses was the use of fixed income securities—primarily associated with preferred shares, though some companies also issued debt—to finance fund capital, while fund assets were almost exclusively in common stock.

The failure of the US investment management companies of the late 1920s was a key event in the history of equity security analysis. More precisely, the speculative investing practices of the actively managed US investment trusts and investment companies inspired Graham and Dodd (1934, p.52) to identify the "new era" theory of investing:

> Certainly, through many years prior to 1928, the typical investor had been interested above all in safety of principal and continuance of an adequate income. However, the doctrine that common stocks were the best long-term investments resulted in a transfer of emphasis from current income to future income and hence inevitably to future enhancement of principal value. In its complete subordination of the income element to the desire for profit, and also in the prime reliance it placed upon favorable developments expected in the future, *the new-era style of investment—as exemplified in the general policy of the investment trusts—was practically indistinguishable from speculation.* In fact this so-called investment could be accurately defined as speculation in the common stocks of strongly situated companies. [emphasis added]

Though Irving Fisher, one of the leading figures in the history of academic finance up to World War II, is infamous in vernacular finance for the brutal call on the stock market in 1929, in the history of equity securities it was touting of the shares in US investment management companies that was more tragic. Oddly enough, J.B. Williams "followed Irving Fisher in valuing an asset as the present discounted value of the expected stream of income from owning it, so that the value of a stock would be the discounted present value of the expected stream of dividends, reduced by some factor to compensate for uncertainty" (Dimand 2009, p.91). It was this discounted cash flow model that Graham, Dodd and Cottle (1962) later used to identify intrinsic value.

Following Rutterford (2009), at the peak of the market in 1929, there were some 675 investment companies in the US and UK, holding over $7 billion in assets. This included 193 investment 'management' companies with $2.7 billion in assets, with both American and British investors participating in these actively managed funds. The benefit of the conservative UK fund structure is evident in the managed fund performance during the market downturn that started in October 1929. From a peak in 1929 to June 1931, the Standard Statistics common stock index of 30 US investment trusts fell more than 75%, while the Institute of Actuaries common stock index for 15 UK investment trusts fell just 17% from the March 1928 peak to March 1931 low (*Economist*, 30 June 1931). Allen (1938, p.237) presented somewhat different numbers with the same general dimensions. Describing the US investment fund industry, Allen (p.233) observed: "From 1930 to 1934, nearly 200 of the 540 management-company units of all types in existence at the end of 1929 had disappeared through merger, voluntary dissolution, or failure". Although some 200 US investment trusts disappeared, there were no similar impacts on UK trusts. At the worst, a number of UK trusts had to pass dividends. The inevitable outcome was a dramatic change in US managed funds during the 1930s.

The Investment Company Act (1940)

Together with the Investment Advisors Act (1940)(IAA), the Investment Company Act (1940) (ICA) was the last major piece of legislation that reformed US securities markets following the collapse of equity security prices from 1929 to 1933. The initial piece of legislation, the Securities Act of 1933, was concerned with the issuing of new securities. The Securities Exchange Act of 1934 dealt with regulations for the trade in securities after issuance, governing the registration of exchanges and the registration of securities listed for trade on the exchanges as well as setting rules for fair conduct. The Securities and Exchange Commission was created by this act to oversee these activities. While these two acts covered much of the ground needed to establish a firm legal foundation for US securities trading, there were still some more focused issues that needed to be legally clarified. These issues were sorted out by the passage of the Trust Indenture Act (1939), which dealt with bond issues, and, finally, to deal with the excesses of the US investment companies, the IAA and ICA. This historic transition roughly marked the beginning of the modern mutual fund industry.

Initially, the US managed fund industry responded to the collapse of the flexible, actively managed closed-end investment company model with a fixed, open-end unit trust model. About 150 such US trusts, with capital of $400 million, were issued in 1929–1931 (Rutterford 2009). These funds had some similarities to classical UK investment trusts, such as: (a) no use of loans to buy securities; (b) a fixed and published investment list; and (c) a passive security selection strategy. While this explicitly prohibited active management, the open-ended feature made some trading necessary. Over time, this created difficulties, as the list of available securities was limited. Trading was made even more difficult by the preference for common stocks of large US companies and rules requiring the sale of shares if the dividend was passed. Not only did rules regarding passed dividends further restrict the initial list, it exacerbated a bear market in shares of these favored companies, brought on by a negative dividend event, as these unit trusts acted in concert with forced sales of shares.

Allen (1938) provided helpful background on the state of the US investment management industry in the period leading up to the passage of the ICA. In particular, there was the relatively poor performance of investment company common stocks: "Over the entire period 1930–36, their composite record did not quite equal that of the stock average and was decidedly inferior to that of bonds or of a bond-stock composite. Their record, moreover, was inferior to that of the older British companies over the same period" (pp.236–7). Recognizing that none of the so-called investment trusts were legally trusts, Allen (p.251) divided the common stock of investment companies into 'leveraged' and 'nonleveraged'. Having identified the poor performance of leveraged investment company stocks since 1929 and characterizing the shares in such investment companies as "among the most speculative stocks in the market", Allen divided the unleveraged investment company stocks into mutual and nonmutual. Of these opportunities, it was the rapid development of mutual companies since 1929, in which "the shareholder is able to resell his holdings at any time at (approximately) liquidating value", that was identified as "highly desirable" (p.253). As early as 1936, the federal government was providing Revenue Act incentives for management companies to convert to the "good" form of mutual fund organization—incentives that eventually evolved into the ICA model of non-leveraged, managed and diversified, open-ended mutual funds that still dominate the managed funds industry.

In contrast to the income-driven, geographically diversified UK invest-ment trust, which invested primarily in fixed income securities and high-quality, dividend-paying common stocks, the early American investment company was concerned with "managed diversification in common stocks", which requires that "the long-run record of investment companies in this country will rest in large part on the validity of the common-stock theory of investment" (pp.234, 248). Similar to Cowles (1944), Allen (1938) explored the strategies used by the cohort of most successful investment companies: "This group included such well-known companies as State Street Investment Corporation, Lehman Corporation, General American Investors, National Bond and Share, Fourth National Investors, U.S. and Foreign Securities, and Tri-Continental Corporation" (p.239). In addition to a group of investment companies with successful security selection strategies involving both debt and equity, "a number of these investment companies built their portfolios around a flexible common-stock policy, involving a sharp shift into (primar-ily) cash and United States government securities in 1930–32 and back into common stocks just preceding or at the beginning of recovery" (Allen 1938, p.247).

A World of Exchange-Traded Funds

The ICA imposed a range of restrictions on the activities and capital structure of US investment companies. Tight control was placed on the use of debt, pro-hibiting its use for open-end funds, including mutual funds. Closed-end funds were permitted to have one issue of preferred and one class of debt, covered by at least 200% and 300% with assets at market value. In addition, the ICA facilitated the development of the open-ended fund, which had become popular in the 1930s. From the passage of the ICA in 1940 until the present, open-ended mutual funds with managed diversified portfolios have proved to be an overwhelming success compared to all other types of managed funds. The Investment Company Institute (www.ici.org) provides a variety of statistics on investment funds. Virtually all of data provided is for the US only, such as the assets of money market funds, though information on global mutual fund assets is also reported. At the end of 2014, the following asset values in Table 11.1 were reported by ICI. Though the managed fund landscape has now recovered, Table 11.2 illustrates the dramatic collapse in asset values for mutual funds, in general, and equity security mutual funds, in particular, which fell from a peak in 2007 at over $12 trillion and did not recover until 2012.

Table 11.1   2014 Facts at a Glance

Total worldwide assets invested in mutual funds and exchange-traded funds	**$33.4 trillion**
US investment company total net assets	**$18.2 trillion**
Mutual funds	$15.9 trillion
Exchange traded funds (ETFs)	$2.0 trillion
Closed-end funds	$289 billion
Unit investment trusts	$101 billion
US investment companies' share of:	
US corporate equity	30%
US municipal securities	26%
Commercial paper	46%
US government securities	11%
US household ownership of mutual funds	
Number of households owning mutual funds	53.2 million
Number of individuals owning mutual funds	90.4 million
Percentage of households owning mutual funds	43.30%
Median mutual fund assets of fund-owning households	$103,000
Median number of mutual funds owned	4
US retirement market	
Total retirement market assets	$24.7 trillion
Percentage of households with tax-advantaged retirement savings	63%
IRA and DC plan assets invested in mutual funds	$7.3 trillion

Source: Investment Company Institute, Factbook 2015

Though calls for the demise of the managed diversified mutual fund may be premature, there are a number of factors other than the global decline in the equity markets to account for the dramatic drop in assets under management at mutual funds between 2007 and 2012. One factor, the impact of higher fees on fund performance, has been recognized at least since Allen (1938, p.242) observed "that expense-tax ratios have been excessively high for investment companies as a group is indicated by the inferior record which these companies have made over the period". At a time when most managed funds were closed-end, Allen also observed that the 'closed-end fund discount' could be explained by poor performance relative to fees charged: "investment company shares continue to sell on the market at prices below liquidating values, evidence that investors feel that operating results after expenses have not been as satisfactory as returns from direct investment in common stocks". Faced with a decline in assets under management during the bear market of 2000 to 2003, "the GAO estimates that the largest

Table 11.2   Investment Company Total Net Assets by Type (*billions of $; year-end 1997–2004*)

	Mutual funds[1]	Closed-end funds[2]	ETFs[3]	UITs	Total[4]
1997	$4,468	$152	$7	$85	$4,711
1998	5,525	156	16	94	5,790
1999	6,846	147	34	92	7,119
2000	6,965	143	66	74	7,247
2001	6,975	141	83	49	7,248
2002	6,383	159	102	36	6,680
2003	7,402	214	151	36	7,803
2004	8,096	253	228	37	8,614
2005	8,891	276	301	41	9,509
2006	10,398	297	423	50	11,168
2007	12,000	312	608	53	12,974
2008	9,603	184	531	29	10,347
2009	11,113	223	777	38	12,151
2010	11,833	238	992	51	13,113
2011	11,632	242	1,048	60	12,982
2012	13,052	264	1,337	72	14,725
2013	15,035	279	1,675	87	17,075
2014	15,852	289	1,974	101	18,217

Sources: Investment Company Institute and Strategic Insight Simfund

[1] Mutual fund data include only mutual funds that report statistical information to the Investment Company Institute, and do not include mutual funds that invest primarily in other mutual funds.
[2] Closed-end fund data include preferred share classes.
[3] ETF data prior to 2001 were provided by Strategic Insight Simfund. ETF data include investment companies not registered under the Investment Company Act of 1940 and exclude ETFs that primarily invest in other ETFs.
[4] Total investment company assets include mutual fund holdings of closed-end funds and ETFs.

Note: Data are for investment companies that report statistical information to the Investment Company Institute. Assets of these companies are 98 percent of investor assets. Components may not add to the total because of rounding.

mutual fund managers in the United States raised their fees by an average of 11% from 1999–2001".

As illustrated in Table 11.2, the equity security component of the US mutual fund industry faces systemic problems when faced with poor performance of equity securities. It is difficult to achieve sufficient upside performance to justify management fees when the overall market is down. In addition to the systemic problem of attracting and retaining funds when returns are poor to negative, mutual funds sustained a serious blow to their image in 2003 as a result of illegal late trading and market timing practices by certain hedge fund and mutual fund companies. Coming shortly after the $1.4 billion settlement reached with the SEC surrounding the fraudulent touting of investment banking clients by the research departments of the firms' brokerage divisions, the mutual fund scandal was more technical in character and conducted on a much smaller scale. However, the perception of wrongdoing was widespread and well published due to the prosecution of the case by the same white-collar-crime-buster responsible for initiating the stock-touting investigation: New York State attorney general Eliot Spitzer.

The initial case uncovered by Spitzer, acting on a phone tip, involved a New Jersey hedge fund, Canary Capital Partners LLC, conducting 'late trades' with a Bank of America–run mutual fund. Soon joined by the SEC, the investigation grew to include 'market timing' violations by some major mutual funds, including Janus, Bank One (One Group) and Strong Capital. As with the initial Canary Capital Partners case, hedge funds were often involved as counterparties. In some instances, a financial intermediary affiliated with the mutual fund would lend the hedge funds the money to purchase the fund shares. For late trades, the fund permitted trading in fund shares after 4:00 p.m. at the closing price for trades done prior to 4:00 p.m. As Spitzer observed in the initial indictment, this was "like allowing betting on a horse race after the horses have crossed the finish line". Less insidious is market timing, in which the fund permits certain individual traders to do more trading than permitted by the fund prospectus. Fees and expenses for mutual funds are based on an estimate of how often the shares will be exchanged. Permitting certain traders to engage in additional trading, especially where the trading strategies involve switching between the funds and cash, imposes unwarranted costs on the other fund investors.

The travails of the managed, diversified mutual fund model led to a market demand for other types of managed funds. This led to the development of a new type of managed fund: the unleveraged, fixed, open-ended exchange traded fund. Though relatively low transaction fee index funds were made available through a few mutual fund companies previously, the first attempt at an exchange traded fund (ETF) was the Index Participation Shares, an S&P 500 proxy, traded briefly on the AMEX and the PHLX. A lawsuit by the CME, which traded a similar futures index, was successful in halting trading. The Toronto Index Participation Shares (TIPS), which commenced trade on the Toronto Stock Exchange in 1990, was the first continuously traded ETF. In January 1993, the AMEX launched the S&P 500 ETF SPDR, known colloquially as "Spiders", now trading as SPY. This particular ETF soon achieved the largest asset value of any ETF. From these early beginnings in index funds, the number and size of ETFs has grown dramatically, to include securities and commodities across geographical boundaries. Table 11.3 illustrates the recent development of exchange-traded funds.

One advantage of the fixed fund model is lower management fees. As such, the incentive for ETF trading to originate in Canada was the highest. Based on a 20-country study by Khorana et al. (2009) and a US/Canada study by

Table 11.3 Number of Equity ETFs by Exchange, June 2015

	Exchange
	Americas
18	BM&FBOVESPA
17	Bolsa de Valores de Colombia
4	Lima SE
555	Mexican Exchange
165	NASDAQ OMX
1,526	NYSE
191	Santiago SE
526	TMX Group
3,002	Total region
	Asia-Pacific
96	Australian SE
39	BSE India
7	Bursa Malaysia
130	Hong Kong Exchanges
8	Indonesia SE
NA	Japan Exchange Group—Osaka
211	Japan Exchange Group—Tokyo
177	Korea Exchange
45	National Stock Exchange India
10	New Zealand Exchange
69	Shanghai SE
42	Shenzhen SE
87	Singapore Exchange
30	Taiwan SE Corp.
21	The Stock Exchange of Thailand
972	Total region
	Europe-Africa-Middle East
3	Athens Exchange
71	BME Spanish Exchanges
14	Borsa Istanbul
1	Budapest SE
1,061	Deutsche Börse
690	Euronext
1	Irish SE

	Exchange
46	Johannesburg SE
151	Luxembourg SE
37	NASDAQ OMX Nordic Exchange
4	Nigerian Stock Exchange
44	Oslo Børs
3	Saudi Stock Exchange—Tadawul
922	SIX Swiss Exchange
18	Wiener Börse
3,066	Total region
7,040	WFE Total

Source: World Federation of Exchanges, Factbook (Equity 1.7)

Ruckman (2003), Canadian investors were saddled with the highest equity security mutual fund fees of any country. Such fees can be broken into: fees paid directly for fund manager services (MGT); total expenses, which when divided by the market value of funds under management gives the management expense ratio (MER); and a load fee adjusted MER (AMER) that adjusts for differences in load fees across funds not included in the MER. Total expenses includes management services, administration, servicing the account, transfer agent fees, audit and legal, and so on. Kohrana et al. (2009, pp.1287–8) provided the following comparison of equity security mutual fund fees (in percent):

Country	MGT	MER	AMER
Australia	1.09	1.17	1.41
Canada	1.96	2.56	3.00
France	1.04	1.22	1.88
Germany	1.05	1.17	1.97
Switzerland	1.47	1.47	2.03
UK	1.07	1.18	2.28
US	0.62	1.11	1.53
20 Country Mean	0.90	1.29	1.80

The incentive to innovative based on shortcomings in the managed, diversified, unleveraged mutual fund has not been limited to ETFs. As Edwards (1999, p.191), observed: "hedge funds are to a large extent the creation of the legal restrictions imposed on mutual funds and other institutional fund managers".

What Is a Hedge Fund?[2]

Hedge funds are a fitting metaphor for the uncertain state of equity markets early in the 21st century. It was a network of feeder hedge funds that Bernard Madoff used to pull off the largest Ponzi scheme in history, lasting from the early 1990s until the collapse in late 2008. It was hedge funds run by Bear Stearns that were implicated in the distribution of the toxic mortgage assets that led to the financial market meltdown of late 2008. Another hedge fund, Amaranth Advisors LLC, lost $6 billion trying to manipulate the natural gas market in Febuary and April 2006, the bankrupt firm eventually being required to pay a $7 million fine to the CFTC for market manipulation. The first hedge fund distributed to Canadian retail investors in 2004 —Portus Alternative Asset Management—was soon discovered to be an intricately designed legal structure aimed at providing the fund manager with unlimited discretion to move capital offshore into a network of hedge funds. The collapse of the fraud in February 2005 resulted in hundreds of millions in losses to investors, some of which were ultimately covered by the investment management companies that directed clients to these products. At least since the collapse of Long Term Capital Management (LTCM), similar red flags to those appearing in the Madoff, Bear Stearns, Amaranth and Portus cases have been apparent in US hedge fund activities.

The term 'hedge fund' is generic, being used to describe a variety of fund strategies that loosely share some characteristics. The term has undergone dramatic change over the last two decades as regulators have adapted to changing equity capital market developments. In the aftermath of the LTCM debacle (Dunbar 2000), the President's Working Group on Financial Markets (PWGFM) (1999, p.40) defined the term "to refer to a variety of pooled investment vehicles that are not registered under the federal securities laws as investment companies, broker-dealers, or public corporations". A similar definition appeared in a 2003 SEC staff report on hedge funds (SEC 2003), with the clarification that a hedge fund "is not registered as an investment company under the Investment Company Act". This recognized ongoing efforts by the SEC to regulate hedge funds under the Investment Advisors Act (1940) (e.g., Pekarek 2007a). The continuing lack of regulatory oversight is not due to vigilance by US regulators. Despite repeated recommendations and attempts to regulate hedge funds dating to the 1960s, the defining characteristic of hedge funds is still "pooled investment vehicles that are not registered under federal securities laws". To achieve this, hedge funds are typically organized as limited partnerships or, in some jurisdictions, limited liability companies with shares that are not publicly traded (Van Berkel 2008). While this seemingly disqualifies a hedge fund from consideration as a tradeable equity security, hedge funds are designed to avoid the restrictions imposed on tradeable securities.

Much is made by finance academics of the different hedge fund categories and that "hedge fund investment strategies provide greater diversification opportunities and may result in higher risk-adjusted returns for investors" (Edwards 2006, p.46). Some even claim: "the hedge fund industry may have played more of a role in creating liquidity and making markets efficient than the mutual fund industry" (Stulz 2007, p.193). On balance, Stulz captured the 'bullish' stance of academics on hedge funds: "regulation should leave alone financial innovators who dream of new strategies and find savvy well-funded investors to bet on them" (p.193). Prior to the market downturn of 2008–2009, and in the aftermath, there has been considerable progress toward allowing 'retailization': retail investors being permitted to directly access 'alternative asset classes' such as hedge funds and private equity funds because such funds "can pursue investment and speculative strategies that are not open to other institutional fund managers, . . . avoid the costs associated with regulatory oversight, and . . . use whatever fee structure they believe to be optimal" (Edwards 1999, p.191).

Viewed as a type of managed fund, the characteristics of classical hedge funds are as follows: actively managed; leveraged; regulatory free rider; and *de facto* investment companies disguised as limited partnerships. Though a hedge fund does not directly issue publicly traded securities, because fund size changes with redemptions and additional investments, hedge funds can also be classified as open-ended funds with restrictions on redemptions. In any case, hedge funds possess essential characteristics of the types of managed funds that the ICA and IAA were designed to stamp out.

There are sound, historically based rationales for restricting highly leveraged speculative trading activities by unregulated entities. The costs associated with regulatory oversight are important to maintaining the stability and integrity of financial markets. Free rider funds that are able to avoid such regulatory costs are at an advantage to funds that do pay such costs. From an historical perspective, permitting unregulated financial entities that operate in securities markets with the sole objective of making speculative profits is ill conceived and reckless and results in increased potential for severe market disruption.

Regulation of Hedge Funds

In order to avoid the registration requirements specified under US securities laws for securities companies, hedge funds have to satisfy a number of conditions. Exemption from the Securities Act (1933) is achieved by having no public offering. This is an issue with using the 'funds of hedge funds' approach as a strategy to bring hedge fund investing to retail accounts. Whether it is possible to issue a tradeable equity security holding assets that would not otherwise be considered tradeable depends on the jurisdiction. Similar regulatory quandaries arise with the exemption from the ICA achieved by being a 'private investment company'. Hedge funds have two possible avenues to qualify as private investment companies: either the '100 person exemption' (Sec.3(c)(1)) or the 'qualified purchaser exemption' (Sec.3(c)(7)) that permits up to 500 qualified investors. While there is often the perception that hedge funds are privately structured and closely held entities qualifying because the primary investors are high net worth individuals, in practice the 100-person exemption is not used because the institutional

investors in hedge funds satisfy the test for 'qualified purchaser'. Each institution, such as a pension fund or investment bank, is counted as a separate
investor. Because such institutions could contain investments from thousands
of investors, the actual 'size' of the hedge fund would be much larger than the
small number of institutions investing in the fund.

Hedge funds have been an ongoing headache for regulators. Since the collapse of LTCM, there has been a parade of hedge-fund-related problems. Still,
a formal legal definition of a hedge fund is lacking: "The term 'hedge fund'
is not defined or used in the federal securities laws" (PWGFM, p.40). For
example, the PWGFM observes that one attractive feature of hedge funds is
the avoidance of certain legalities associated with registration, information filing, taxes and so on; though prior to Dodd-Frank some US hedge funds did
register under the IAA. To achieve exemption from US federal securities regulations, a hedge fund is typically structured as a pooled investment vehicle,
privately organized, closely held among a small number of partners and run
by professional investment managers, typically on an incentive fee basis. The
master-feeder organizational structure of such funds often involves a corporation domiciled outside the US in tax havens such as the British Virgin Islands
or Bermuda (e.g., Greene et al. 2007). The various characteristics of a hedge
fund interact to create a type of managed fund that falls through many of the
cracks in the US securities laws.

One avenue for dealing with hedge funds is enhanced regulation to bring such
funds within the scope of regulatory oversight. As part of the implementation
of the Dodd-Frank Reform Act, some such legislation has appeared, bringing
hedge funds within the scope of the Securities Exchange Act and the Investment
Company Act. This action frustrated efforts that had been waged in federal
court proceedings, especially the Bulldog Investors case upholding the exemption of hedge funds advisors from the IAA (e.g., Pearson and Pearson 2007; Pekarek 2007a, b; Mann 2008). In addition to direct regulation, indirect regulation
of hedge funds occurs through the array of financial institutions which hedge
funds need to conduct business. For example, the SEC imposes capital, margin
and reporting requirements on broker-dealers, which are essential counterparties or clearing members for hedge funds. Included among these requirements
are risk assessment rules specified in the securities laws administered by the
SEC to "establish record keeping and reporting requirements for subject broker-
dealers and their affiliates whose business activities are reasonably likely to have
a material impact on the financial and operational conditions of the broker-
dealer" (PWGFM, p.42).

The SEC website reports on recent changes to hedge fund reporting as follows:

Title IV of the Dodd-Frank Wall Street Reform and Consumer Protection
Act makes numerous changes to the registration and reporting and record-
keeping requirements of the Investment Advisers Act of 1940. Among these
is the requirement that advisers to most private funds (hedge funds and
private equity funds) register with the Commission. Historically, many of
these advisers had been exempt from registration under the so-called "private adviser" exemption. The Dodd-Frank Act replaces this exemption with
several narrower exemptions for advisers that advise exclusively venture

capital funds and advisers solely to private funds with less than $150 million in assets under management in the United States. Foreign private advisers and advisers to licensed small business investment companies also are exempted.

The Dodd-Frank Act provides the Commission with the authority to collect data from registered investment advisers about their private funds for the purposes of the assessment of systemic risk by the Financial Stability Oversight Council. In addition, the Dodd-Frank Act modifies the allocation of responsibility for mid-sized advisers between state regulators and the Commission.

THE MARHEDGE HEDGE FUND CATEGORIES

MARhedge was an important source of information and news about the hedge fund industry. Data available through MARhedge has been thoroughly examined in Ackerman et al. (1999). To provide some organization to the mishmash of hedge fund strategies, MARhedge classified hedge funds into eight broad categories:

Global Macro funds: Take positions on changes in global economic conditions in equity, FX and debt markets. Use derivatives, including index derivatives, and leverage.

Global funds: Similar to macro funds but targeted at specific regions, often involving stock picking.

Long-only (US Opportunistic) funds: Like traditional equity funds but with the hedge fund characteristics of leveraging and incentive fees for managers. Strategies for these funds include Value, Growth and Short-term trading.

Market-neutral funds: The basic objective of these funds is to be long in one group of securities and short in another group, such that market risk is controlled or neutralized. This can be done in a number of ways: By going long one group of stocks and short another group, seeking to benefit from superior stock-picking skills; conversion arbitrages, which are long in underpriced convertibles and short in the underlying stocks; stock index arbitrages; and fixed income arbitrages, which are long, say, off-the-run Treasuries, and short on-the-run Treasuries.

Sectoral hedge funds: Have an industry focus.

Event-driven funds: Target special situations, specifically distressed securities of firms in reorganization or bankruptcy as well as risk trading in takeovers—for example, buying the target and selling the acquirer.

Short Sales funds: Which short sale overvalued securities, investing the balance in indexes or fixed income securities. Such funds are positioned to benefit from market declines. These funds can be index-driven or can be based on stock picking.

Funds of hedge funds: Funds of hedge funds, sometimes leveraged.

Within each of these general groups, a variety of strategies could be pursued. Similarly, some funds may be involved in activities covering more than one fund category.

Hedge Fund Strategies

The situation surrounding regulation of hedge funds is complicated because hedge funds are not the only managed funds which seek such specific exemptions from US securities laws. For example, venture capital pools, private equity funds, venture capital funds, asset securitization vehicles, family estate planning vehicles and investment clubs can receive such treatment. As a consequence, another defining feature of hedge funds is the types of strategies which the funds pursue. Given the restricted scope of other types of funds seeking exemptions, hedge funds can exhibit considerable variation in strategies. "There is no single market strategy or approach pursued by hedge funds as a group. Rather, hedge funds exhibit a wide variety of investment types, some of which use highly quantitative techniques while others employ more subjective factors" (PWGFM 1999).

The diversity of hedge fund strategies extends to the types of securities traded (p.9):

> Many hedge funds trade equity or fixed income securities, taking either long or short positions, or sometimes both simultaneously. A large number of funds also use exchange-traded futures contracts or over-the-counter derivatives, to hedge their portfolios, to exploit market inefficiencies, or to take outright positions. Still others are active participants in foreign exchange markets. In general, hedge funds are more active users of derivatives and of short positions than are mutual funds and many other classes of asset managers.

However, behind all the confusion about hedge fund typology, the basic intuition is relatively clear: Hedge funds combine long positions in certain securities with short positions in other securities. Such 'hedging' strategies can be relatively low-risk, where the securities being traded are highly correlated—for example, the 'on-the-run' 'off-the-run' Treasury security arbitrage run by John Meriwether, first at Salomon Brothers and subsequently at LTCM. Because the price differences involved in achieving a profit are small, substantial leverage is required and warranted. Such hedge fund strategies will, directly or indirectly, involve leveraging. However, many other hedge fund strategies do not have sufficient correspondence between the short and long positions to warrant the degree of leverage that is being partially hidden from public view by the managed funds operating under exemptions from securities laws designed to deter such excessive leveraging.

Hedge funds are not conventional investment vehicles. Investor liquidity is often compromised with "lock-up periods of one year for initial investors and subsequent restrictions on withdrawals to quarterly intervals" (Ackerman et al. 1999, p.834). The regulatory exemption that hedge funds work under restricts the ability of hedge funds to advertise, though this retailization restriction has been gradually eroded. Another atypical feature of hedge funds concerns their management (Ackerman et al. 1999):

> Hedge funds are . . . characterized by strong performance incentives. On average, hedge fund managers receive a 1 percent annual management fee

and 14 percent of the annual profits. For most funds this bonus incentive fee is paid only if the returns surpass some hurdle rate or "high-water mark"—meaning there is no incentive fee until the fund has recovered from past losses. Although incentive fees and high-water marks could lead to excess risk taking under some conditions, there are countervailing forces that may dampen risk. Hedge fund managers often invest a substantial amount of their own money in the fund. Furthermore, the managers of US hedge funds are general partners, so they may incur substantial liability if the fund goes bankrupt.

In contrast to mutual funds, which have a long history that has been intensively studied, hedge funds started to receive academic attention only in the mid-1990s, though work on managed futures funds and commodity pools, which started somewhat earlier, is also applicable (e.g., Cornew 1988; Edwards and Park 1996). As data has accumulated on hedge fund activities, many studies have appeared on various aspects of hedge funds. Among the useful studies directly on hedge funds are Goetzmann et al. (2003), Patton (2009) and Griffin and Xu (2009).

C   SHORT SALES, PROGRAMMED TRADES AND FIDUCIARY CAPITALISM

A Short View of Short Selling

Following Poitras (2002), the renaissance in derivative securities has created an incoherent regulatory environment due to conflict among regulators competing for jurisdiction and different political jurisdictions competing for trading order flow. At the heart of the conflict is the regulation of short selling. By design, derivative security contracts provide the ability to replicate a given cash flow with different combinations of securities. Hence, ignoring transactions costs and other sources of equity market pricing friction, the presence of a functioning options market readily permits the creation of short positions. In practice, these 'replicating positions' may, or may not, have the same settlement date. There are also problems where leverage restrictions on short selling in the derivative security are not the same as the equity security in the cash market. As illustrated by Bris et al. (2007, Table 1, pp.1037–40), restrictions on cash market short selling vary widely across jurisdictions. Most emerging markets do not permit any short selling or lending of securities. Even in developed markets where some form of short selling is usually permitted, a range of restrictions on cash market short selling are in place. Perhaps more importantly, restrictions on short sales have been easing over time.

Replication of cash flows is an essential characteristic of derivative security trading. In a perfect market, combining a written call position with a purchased put at the same exercise price and time to expiration will produce the payoff on a short forward position if the net premium is ignored. In contrast, a short sale position in the cash market typically originates with, say, the stock purchased on margin at a broker-dealer. Such stock is eligible for securities lending. Other sources of stock for short sales are: broker-dealer inventory; stock available for lending from other broker-dealers; specialized firms that locate stock for a fee; and offshore entities. The short sale involves the broker-dealer lending this stock to a short seller who has a margin account with the firm. The stock is then sold in the market and the funds deposited in the short seller's account. The account is then subjected to margin requirements on the value of the stock sold short that depend on a variety of factors such as the exchange the stock is traded on and the particular broker-dealer involved in the short sale.

As Poitras (2012, ch.11) detailed, settlement and margin practices in the equity derivatives markets have created systemically destabilizing risks for accurate price discovery in the cash market for equity capital shares. These risks are exacerbated by the antiquated methods of settlement in the cash market that permit stock that is sold 'regular way' to be 'located prior to settlement', which is two or three days in the future, depending on the national jurisdiction. In effect, it is not necessary for a short seller to have located shares to borrow prior to making the short sale. Shares that cannot be located for delivery result in 'failures to deliver', an overwhelming characteristic of trading during the 2008–2009 equity market collapse. Short trades made in the equity derivatives market generate inter-market arbitrage trades that transmit such sales to the cash market. Such was the case on 6 May 2010, when a single trader was able to place an opportunistically timed short trade of 75,000 E-mini S&P 500 contracts worth about $4.1 billion in the underlying index. The resulting inter-market arbitrage imploded much of the ETF market on the Archipelago exchange (ARCA) and created disturbing pricing in some major stocks.

The ability to short sell is ubiquitous in modern equity capital markets. The following margin requirements for short sales by retail accounts was obtained from a popular US discount brokerage firm:

Short Sales Stock Value	Minimum Margin Required
	(as % of the market value)
$5 & over + Option eligible	130%
$3 & over	150%
Between $1.50 and $2.99	$3 per share
Between 25¢ and $1.493	200%
Under 25¢	100% + 25¢ per share

Precisely how it is determined which non-cash assets are eligible for satisfaction of margin requirements will depend on the particular broker-dealer arranging the short sale. Given this, it is apparent the cash market has rules in place to prevent excessive speculative leveraging using short sales of stocks to generate funds for alternative uses. In order to prevent a replicating strategy using written calls, purchased puts and borrowed money to counteract the cash market restrictions, it is necessary to impose sufficient margin requirements on written option positions. Incoherence emerges when jurisdictions compete and rules needed to deter speculative excesses are relaxed or eliminated as 'no longer necessary to maintain market volatility' or 'contrary to the goal of achieving the lowest possible execution price'.

Short selling being a fundamental feature of trading in equity capital markets is a relatively recent historical development. The Dutch denied the protection of the courts to *in blanco* short selling (i.e., selling for forward delivery an item that was not in possession). Selling an object not owned at the time of the sale had an element of immorality in the 17th century. Over time, short sellers were permitted because of the liquidity provided by market makers quoting both the bid and the offer. In effect, short selling and market liquidity are symbiotic. In modern equity markets, this situation has become convoluted. Evidence indicates that in severe market downswings, honest 'liquidity providers' withdraw from the market due to the instability while other 'liquidity providers' add to the downside pressure. Such destabilizing market activities could be avoided by requiring sales of stock 'regular way' in the cash market to have located stock for delivery at the time the sale is made. This change would be reinforced by shortening the time between the sale and the delivery of shares.

Like other stock market 'crashes', the flash crash of 6 May 2010 involved a severe downside disruption in the price discovery process originating from disruptive speculative short selling originating in the S&P 500 E-mini futures contract. The aftermath of any such discontinuous fall in prices inevitably leads to intense focus on the activities of stock market short sellers. The regulatory response to the flash crash, SEC (2010, 2010a), provides a fascinating glimpse into the stock market at the end of the first decade of the 21st century. Combined with the amendments to Regulation SHO introduced to address short selling during the financial collapse of 2008–2009, the SEC opted to employ a combination of single stock circuit-breakers and restricted price tests to deal with disruptive short selling. While such restrictions on short selling are a decided improvement over unrestricted short selling, the rules appear to have been written by those directly involved in the bulk of short selling. As Poitras (2012) demonstrated, the most effective route to dealing with disruptive cash market short selling originating from futures markets is to significantly tighten the requirements associated with locating stock available for short sale.

The presence of derivative securities, combined with rapid market information transmission and inexpensive trade execution, opens a range of replication trades to hedge traders and other risk arbitrageurs. As is turns out, profitable trades often appear involving portfolios with a short stock position. To satisfy the almost insatiable demand from hedge funds and others seeking speculative profit from trades involving a short stock position, a number of specialist firms have emerged that locate stock available for short sale. Dealers and other trading firms participate in the creation of 'naked' short cash positions. The regulatory response of 2009 was to seek amendment to Rule 201, Regulation SHO, introduced in 2007, which replaced Rule 10a-1, which permitted short sales only on an uptick. Rule 10a-1 had been in place since 1938, and the political role of large investment banks and hedge funds that are seeking to eliminate this rule (for stockjobbing purposes) is a history still to be written. The erratic and volatile market behavior of equity prices since Regulation SHO was introduced produced regulatory response to amend Reg SHO to reintroduce a modified form of uptick rule.

From this, there is at least one conclusion to draw regarding the impact of 'extrinsic regulation' on equity valuation: Do not assume that government will be effective in eliminating stockjobbing practices that distort market pricing. For that matter, it is even possible that regulators will unwittingly change the rules to favour those engaged in 'nefarious' practices that produce 'unnatural' equity market outcomes. Equity capital markets have always attracted participants who seek to gain unfair advantages from weakness in the rules. At times, the volatility and mispricing created by the activities of such participants is sufficiently widespread that profitable equity security trading opportunities can arise. While reasonably successful at eventually identifying problems, legislators and governments typically react in *ad hoc* fashion and only act forcefully in response to market failures. Neither is forward looking—not seeking to adapt in advance to changes, even though sound analysis to guide such adaptation is available. For example, Langevoort (1985) detailed many issues that eventually emerged in the 1990s, and Stout (1988) questioned the dedication to pricing efficiency that now threatens the traditional system of self-regulation with government oversight (e.g., Markham and Harty 2008).

The mechanisms of self-regulation are blunt and often take time to establish. The financial market milieu within which self-regulation takes place also tends to favour the *status quo;* prevent competitive pressures; and resist technological improvements. In particular, the self-regulatory function of exchanges has been under attack in the face of substantial changes in transactions technology. The traditional mutual, non-profit form of national or regional exchange ownership has been 'demutualized' and replaced by international exchange networks that are publicly traded entities. One of the challenges confronting modern equity valuation is to make sense of the implications of such factors, especially the revolution in market trading and communications technology. The universe of equity securities has been increased dramatically, both domestically and internationally. Gradual deregulation of traditional brokerage fees, which began in the 1970s, has significantly reduced the cost of trading equity securities. However, regulatory changes accompanying these developments have substantively increased the systemic uncertainty associated with equity trading.

What Is Programmed Trading?

In a sense, programmed trading could be traced to the 19th-century introduction of the telegraph, the ticker tape and the telephone. These technological advances permitted profitable trading opportunities from inter-exchange arbitrage and increased brokerage and related market making opportunities due to enhanced market liquidity. For example, a 'programmed' inter-exchange arbitrage would be manually executed by clerks paid to monitor the system used to track the prices. When the differential of the same securities in two markets reached a certain point, a trade would be attempted to sell in the expensive market the same security simultaneously purchased in the cheaper market. More than a few firms were engaged in this type of activity, so considerable effort was dedicated to having the most efficient price-gathering network. At various times, exchanges have imposed specific rules to regulate the process. Large firms with a brokerage or dealing business that also made it profitable to maintain a trading unit had a particular advantage in this business.

While interesting, such historical examples only serve to highlight the importance of technological change for the equity trading process. For purposes of practical equity valuation, the trading process determines the market value of the equity claim relative to the unit of account. Whatever the theoretical intrinsic value, it is the market value at which the equity security will be traded that is ultimately of interest. It follows that an assessment of the changes in telecommunications and computing technology that have altered the modern equity trading process is required. The transformation has been nothing short of astounding. In a relatively short time, information and execution costs for virtually all market participants have fallen dramatically. Information flow about market prices and ability to execute trades is almost instantaneous. A range of 'new' and 'innovative' derivative securities were introduced, especially on the lightly regulated OTC markets. All this opened a new range of both speculative and market making trading strategies. Except when confronted by severe market disruption, regulators have reacted to these changes with relative indifference, if not encouragement.

The nomenclature associated with the study of programmed trading is unsettled. As defined here, the class of 'programmed trades' includes: the 'program trades' associated with portfolio insurance strategies; equity index arbitrage and other cash and carry arbitrage trades connecting derivative markets and cash markets; and execution-related cash and derivative security trades, such as interexchange arbitrage and 'flash trades'. The basic element is that the trade can be executed computer to computer, without the need for human intervention. Modern programmed trading can be traced to the NYSE's introduction of an automated order execution system—the Designated Order Turnaround (DOT) system—in 1976, which was upgraded in 1984 to the SuperDOT system for limit orders. Initially intended to automate small orders, the system also was useful to those placing large dollar value orders divided into smaller components, as with index arbitrage and many program trades. The DOT system had the desirable execution feature that market orders were executed by the specialists within three minutes. Initially set at lower share quantity levels, by the time of the 1987 crash orders up to 2,100 shares were eligible for DOT execution. Larger orders were eligible for trade at the opening and, more significantly for program traders, on limit orders.

When a simultaneous order for large number of stocks is combined, as in the case of index arbitrage program trading, then the order size can be considerably larger than intended for a system designed to execute small orders. Prior to the crash of October 1987, combining the maximum number of shares permitted under DOT for each company in the S&P 500, for example, added up to approximately $40 million. At the time of the crash, the number of such trades submitted for DOT execution was so substantial that the execution system could not handle the order flow. It is ironic that the lack of trading system computing power played such a role at the end of the 1980s, whereas the next two decades were characterized by the opposite: a rise in competition among trading platforms due, in part, to an increasing abundance of computing power. As detailed by Markham and Harty (2008), "the ECNs arrived in force in financial markets beginning in the early 1990s in the form of automated trading systems for institutional traders in the third market". The electronic communications network (ECN) and related automated trading system (ATS) have grown from this beginning to engulf the traditional trading practices of equity security markets.

Stock exchanges, in some form, have always been a fundamental component of equity trading. To function effectively, exchanges and those participating in the exchange process, such as exchange members and market makers, have to be a least modestly profitable. ECNs and related systems have revolutionized the ways that profits can be earned from the exchange process. Broadly defined, ECNs encompass a variety of computer-based systems for trading. This includes electronic order routing systems, associated with processes involved in routing a customer's order to a particular trading platform. The legitimate market-making firm associated with the infamous Bernard Madoff pioneered the introduction of a pay-for-order-flow market-making model in which large broker-dealers and other institutions would be provided free execution in exchange for the right to capture order flow. Historically, order routing has been a source of both broker-dealer and exchange member profits. In order to access the trading process, the customer would be assessed a brokerage charge, with negotiated portions paid to the broker-dealer and the exchange. Due to the relentless progress of technology, this model has broken down.

The fatal blow to the traditional brokerage fee model of profit generation at the NYSE was the removal of Rule 390, approved by the SEC in 2000. Similar to Rule 5 on the AMEX, Rule 390 was an NYSE rule associated with the self-regulatory function of exchanges. The rule prohibited off-exchange trading, also referred to as "off-board trading", of listed stocks. At least since the introduction of SEC Rule 19c-3 in 1980 permitting such off-exchange trading, the stock exchanges have resisted the introduction of this rule. The SEC's position is reflected in the lengthy discussion of justifications for rescinding the rule detailed in Release No. 34-42758:

> Off-board trading restrictions such as Rule 390 have long been questioned as attempts by exchanges with dominant market shares to prohibit competition from other market centers. On their face, such restrictions run contrary to the Exchange Act's objectives to assure fair competition among market centers and to eliminate unnecessary burdens on competition. The NYSE has defended Rule 390 on the basis that it was intended to address market fragmentation by promoting interaction of investor orders without the participation of a dealer, which also is a principal objective of the Exchange Act. Even granting the importance of this objective, however, Rule 390 is overbroad as a tool to address market fragmentation— it applies in many situations that do nothing to promote investor order

interaction. In the after-hours context, for example, it creates an artificial incentive for trades to be routed to foreign markets. Rule 390 also effectively restricts the competitive opportunities of electronic communications networks ("ECNs"), which use innovative technology to operate agency markets that offer investors a high degree of order interaction. To avoid the anticompetitive effect of the Rule, some ECNs even have indicated that they would accept the very substantial regulatory responsibilities associated with registering as a national securities exchange, thereby foregoing the streamlined requirements available under Regulation ATS. Rescission of Rule 390 will eliminate these distortions of competition. The Commission will address legitimate concerns about assuring an opportunity for interaction of investor orders in the context of its ongoing review of fragmentation issues.

The drive to achieve an "anticompetitive" solution to equity security trading that produces the cheapest possible price for a particular type of trade fails to recognize the threat to the self-regulatory structure that has historically been responsible for restraining many 'stockjobbing' practices. Reducing these threats to the status of an "ongoing review of fragmentation issues" is inviting yet another regulatory failure.

The decimation of traditional brokerage fees that accompanied the rise of computerized trade execution has produced a number of other initiatives to offset losses of traditional sources of profitability. In particular, given the relatively low cost associated with individual trade execution, exchanges and exchange members are driven to seek higher order volume in order to produce revenue offsets. This change has affected all financial markets, including the derivative exchanges. As Markham and Harty (2008, p.939) observed, the drive to higher-volume trading has produced systemic changes in the marketplace:

> The exchanges' focus on electronic trading highlights the change in their best customers; from smaller volume commercial hedgers and locals, to large volume special investment vehicles. This change ushered in a growing demand for greater electronic access to the marketplace, and trade matching algorithms that are efficient, volume-centered, preserve anonymity, and promote a marketplace where market news is decentralized.

In equity markets, 'special investment vehicles' include high-frequency traders, often operating with or as hedge funds. As in the derivative security markets, the global challenge of increasing volume and inter-exchange competition has been met with an ongoing consolidation of exchanges in the equity markets. Following a conversion of stock exchanges to publicly traded equity securities during the 1990s and later—the NYSE demutualized and become publicly traded only in 2005—this has generated global exchange networks, such as NYSE Euronext, which absorbed the AMEX in 2008. NYSE Euronext was subsequently acquired by the upstart Intercontinental Exchange in November 2013.

Maintenance of the self-regulatory function of exchanges becomes complicated when exchanges are globalized and have publicly traded equity. Because each of the component exchanges is responsible to a national regulatory body, there has been a drive to achieve harmonization of regulations across exchanges. In 2004, the NYSE component of NYSE Euronext created NYSE Regulation, Inc., a not-for-profit corporation with responsibilities to enforce marketplace rules and federal securities laws of the NYSE. NYSE Regulation also oversees NYSE Arca Regulation and NYSE Amex Regulation through regulatory services agreements undertaken when the NYSE merged with Archipelago (ARCA) in March 2006 and with the AMEX in October 2008. In 2007, NASD Regulation merged with NYSE Regulation to form the Financial Industry Regulatory Authority (FINRA). Harmonization of rules in Europe have reached the point where there is a single rulebook governing trading on Euronext's equity security and derivatives markets. Passage of the Markets in Financial Instruments Directive (MiFID) occurred in November 2007. In addition to placing more emphasis on home state supervision, the MiFID abolished the 'concentration rule' that, similar to NYSE Rule 390, permitted member states to require broker-dealers to route client orders through regulated markets.

Even with increased volumes, ECNs still reduce per trade exchange profits from brokerage, a traditional source of exchange revenue. However, it is the automated trade execution feature inherent in ECN trading that poses a greater threat to the lifeblood of exchange floor execution. Specialist trading systems, such as that on the NYSE, or pit trading, as on the Chicago derivative exchanges, are antiquated compared to the anonymous trade-matching algorithms of an ECN. As a consequence, the NYSE-Euronext merger "was followed by a dismantling of a considerable portion of the NYSE floor, and resulted in the layoffs of hundreds of NYSE employees. The number of people employed by specialists on the NYSE floor was cut in half and the number of specialist firms was reduced to seven, down from 40 in the 1990s" (Markham and Harty 2008, p.910). In this process, the cost of trading equity securities has declined dramatically. Offsetting the associated transaction cost gains for equity security trading and valuation is the increased uncertainty associated with the exchange process arising from systemic changes in the marketplace for equity securities.

Path-Independent Portfolio Insurance

By fragmenting trading activity and providing a plethora of platforms for regulatory arbitrage, programmed trading related to the exchange process threatens the centerpiece of the national self-regulatory process: the securities exchanges. In contrast, programmed trading related to 'program trading' involves the implementation of risk-management strategies that fall under the general title of portfolio insurance.[3] Whatever the source, it is likely that significant reductions in execution costs and data transmission times will amplify the equity market pricing implications of program trading. This follows because the associated market-destabilizing trading strategies will be available to a larger group of players. Since the implementation of curbs on program trading following the market crash of October 1987, regulators have slowly moved to ease the ability to execute program trades to the point where, on 7 November 2007, the

NYSE abandoned curbs on program trading, citing ineffectiveness in curbing market volatility.[4] A more likely reason was the drive to increase exchange volume, as program traders and index arbitrageurs can account for as much as 50% of exchange volume on some days. The loss of this business to competing exchanges, ECNs and offshore trading platforms was a substantial threat to the publicly traded NYSE Euronext.

In the context of equity valuation, the elimination of regulatory restraints on program trading supports the expanded use of portfolio insurance schemes based on dynamic trading strategies. This creates a quandary. On one hand, for the individual investor the presence of inexpensive portfolio insurance based on dynamic trading expands the payout universe associated with equity securities. Hopefully, this increases the intrinsic and, eventually, the market value of equity securities. On the other hand, such dynamic trading strategies create systemic uncertainty by increasing the potential for destabilizing or 'unnatural' price volatility that other types of portfolio insurance do not. This follows because dynamic portfolio insurance trading strategies require the sale (purchase) of equity securities as the market is falling (rising). As such, dynamic trading has different cash market implications than other forms of portfolio insurance arising from the replication properties of derivative securities. In turn, concepts from financial engineering can be used to illustrate the different security allocations in portfolios associated with different insurance schemes.

The basic mechanics of "path independent" portfolio insurance can be isolated from the put-call parity arbitrage condition for a non-dividend-paying stock: $S + P = C + X\,e^{-rt^*}$. Following Vaidya et al. (1995), for a warrant bond the call (warrant) is deep in the money, implying that the put is deep out of the money and the warrant bond approximately unbundles the payoff on the stock position. Where the concern is portfolio insurance, S refers to the price of a portfolio of stocks (instead of an individual stock), X is the exercise price (strike price), t^* is the time to expiration measured as the fraction of a year remaining to expiration, P is the price of a put written on the portfolio with exercise price X and time to expiration t^*, C is the call price written on the portfolio with the same X and t^* as the put, and r is the riskless interest rate. Dividends have been ignored for simplicity of exposition. As stated, put-call parity provides two path independent insurance strategies. One strategy is $S + P$, buy puts against the portfolio. If S is an index portfolio, relevant exchange-traded puts may be available. Another strategy is $C + X\,e^{-rt^*}$, buy calls and invest the remainder in appropriately dated bonds. Again, if the portfolio is an index portfolio, exchange-traded calls may be available. One important advantage of this strategy is that transactions costs in bond markets are typically lower than transactions costs for stocks, and the bond portfolio can be actively managed—for example, by riding the yield curve—to earn potentially higher returns than the $S + P$ approach.

While the path-independent strategies have some desirable features, there are some drawbacks. One is the inability to accurately replicate insurance for portfolios that do not track an index for which there are traded options (i.e., the relevant portfolio options are not available). Constructing a portfolio of options using options on the individual stocks will be more expensive, and there is the possibility that not all stocks will have traded options. Using index options as a surrogate for options on the specific portfolio of interest eliminates the potential for gains from individual security selection. Combining index options with options on individual stocks raises the problem of finding the appropriate combination of these options to replicate the payout on the desired portfolio. Another disadvantage is that the maturity dates for options may not be long enough to match the portfolio's investment horizon (i.e., there is insufficient "time invariance"). This requires options positions to be rolled forward, which is more expensive and has pricing risk.

Alternative Paths to Portfolio Insurance

Though portfolio insurance techniques were popularized during the 1980s, heuristic forms of portfolio insurance have been used for decades. For example, a form of portfolio insurance can be achieved with the systematic use of order placement strategies, such as stop-loss and limit orders, which have been acceptable market practice at least since the 19th century. These types of trading-dependent strategies suffer from the defect of being "path dependent", an undesirable property of insurance schemes. In addition to trading-related techniques, option replication strategies using stock/bond combinations were also likely in use, though in the realm of proprietary management practices. These techniques also suffer from the defect of path dependence and, in the absence of 'Greek' information, would probably have been imprecise (Poitras 2002, ch.9). The application of option replication to specifying dynamically traded stock/bond portfolios was not of academic interest until much later, after the development of the Black-Scholes formula.

As for the history of insurance-related financial products, some of the insurance schemes of the late 17th and 18th centuries did offer payouts based on specific outcomes associated with joint-stock performance. Being introduced prior to the development of actuarial science, these insurance schemes were more like gambling than insurance. In more recent history, Benninga and Blume (1985) reported the selling of insurance against investment losses in the UK as early as 1956. In the US, Gatto et al. (1980) reported on portfolio insurance plans offered to individuals by both the Harleysville Mutual Insurance Company and Prudential Insurance Company of America. Brennan and Schwartz (1987) observed that the Harleysville plan was the first without any element of mortality insurance. Academically, Brennan and Schwartz (1976) were the first to make the connection between the potential for integrating insurance and equity returns. Leland, O'Brien, Rubinstein and Associates were important proponents in the marketing of dynamically traded option replication strategies to institutional clients.

The explosion in the use of the various types of portfolio insurance techniques can be traced to the introduction of exchange trading in options. Liquid options markets made possible the implementation of numerous portfolio insurance strategies. Even more strategies were permitted with the development of futures and options markets for stock indices. Analytical contributions based on Black-Scholes resulted in further portfolio insurance strategies being introduced. Many "alternative paths to portfolio insurance" (Rubinstein 1985) were proposed and implemented. The widespread use of dynamically traded portfolio insurance techniques has been identified as an important contributing factor in the October 1987 stock market "crash" (e.g., Tosini 1988). Academic understanding of notions associated with portfolio insurance has expanded considerably since the early work by Leland (1980) and Rubinstein and Leland (1981). The 1987 "crash" provided a textbook illustration of the inadequacies of the academically inspired option replication strategies; investors holding what were expected to be "insured" portfolios experienced sizeable unexpected losses.

One of the factors driving institutions to use dynamic trading strategies, which involve actively trading a portfolio of stocks and bonds seeking to replicate the payoff on a path-independent insured portfolio, was the absence of risk-management products with maturities and other characteristics that captured the time profile of their particular risk exposures. Since the crash, an array of OTC and exchange-traded risk-management products have been introduced which greatly enhance the ability to implement path-independent strategies. Included in the list of such new products are long-dated exchange-traded option products, such as LEAPS for individual stocks and longer-dated index options and equity swaps. Despite these improvements, the bulk of contract liquidity on both the exchanges and OTC is still concentrated in short-dated contracts. The relative absence of strict mark-to-market rules in OTC contracts provides a strong incentive to use short-dated contracts.

An important element in the modern renaissance in derivative securities was the emergence of trading in stock index futures. Sufficient liquidity in these futures contracts has facilitated the trading of futures options on these indexes. The first stock index futures contract, based on the Value Line Index, was introduced in February 1982 on the Kansas City Board of Trade (KCBT). The most important stock index futures contract, the S&P 500 traded on the CME/IMM, was introduced shortly thereafter in April 1982. A raft of stock index futures contracts has appeared since that time, starting with the introduction of the NYSE Composite on the NYSE in May 1982 and the Major Market Index on the CBT in 1984. More recently, there has been the introduction of foreign indexes traded on US exchanges, such as the Nikkei 225 on the CME. This has been accompanied by the trading of domestic equity indexes on futures markets around the world, including markets in Japan, Hong Kong, the Netherlands, Australia, England, France, Germany, Switzerland, and Canada. Another development has been the start of trading in the DJIA index futures in October 1997. The slow pace associated with the introduction of the DJIA was not due to a lack of interest in such a contract. On the contrary, perceiving considerable demand, the CBT had attempted to introduce a DJIA contract as early as 1984. However, these plans were thwarted by Dow Jones and Company, which initiated legal action to prevent trading of the contract. What ensued was a process lasting over a dozen years, ending with the CBT eventually introducing DJIA futures and options contracts.

The following is an excerpt from the testimony given by George Soros to the US House Committee on Banking, Finance and Urban Affairs, 13 April 1994.

I must state at the outset that I am in fundamental disagreement with the prevailing wisdom. The generally accepted theory is that financial markets tend toward equilibrium and, on the whole, discount the future correctly. I operate using a different theory, according to which financial markets cannot possibly discount the future correctly because they do not merely discount the future; they help to shape it. In certain circumstances, financial markets can affect the so-called fundamentals which they are supposed to reflect. When that happens, markets enter into a state of dynamic disequilibrium and behave quite differently from what would be considered normal by the theory of efficient markets. Such boom/bust sequences do not arise very often, but when they do they can be very disruptive, exactly because they affect the fundamentals of the economy . . .

Generally, *hedge funds* do not act as issuers or writers of derivative instruments. They are most likely to be customers. Therefore, they constitute less of a risk to the system than the dynamic hedgers at the derivatives desks of financial intermediaries. Please do not confuse dynamic hedging with hedge funds. They have nothing in common except the word "hedge".

Figure 11.1 CME S&P 500 e-mini futures contract settlement prices, 11 September 2015

The Crash of October 1987

The modern renaissance in derivatives trading started with the launch of the CBOE and the subsequent beginning of trade in selected financial derivatives, both on the exchanges and OTC. As equity markets adopted derivative securities, techniques of financial engineering progressively were adopted to assist in the risk-management activities of institutional investors. Adoption of techniques progressed to the point where delta hedging and portfolio insurance played a central role in the stock market crash of October 1987. Unlike previous market manipulations involving derivative securities, this event was generated not by the desire for unwarranted gains but, rather, as fallout from the desire to innovate, to apply the techniques of financial engineering in pursuit of enhanced portfolio management outcomes. *Ex post,* the equity price volatility related to this event created undervaluations sufficient to provide remarkable trading opportunities. The recent *ex post* re-emergence of these techniques in the slow market crash of 2008–2009 argues for a close inspection of events surrounding the crash of '87.

The causes of the stock market crash of 19–20 October 1987 have been debated *ad nauseum.* The analysis includes: reports by the exchanges (e.g., the CME and the NYSE); the regulators (e.g., reports by the SEC, the GAO, the CFTC and the Brady Commission); and academic studies (e.g., Edwards 1988, Tosini 1988). For sheer attention and regulatory impact, the crash of 1987 could be the disaster of disasters. Incremental reforms were made to market practices, ranging from the introduction of trading circuit-breakers triggered by large market moves to rules impacting the capitalization of specialists on the NYSE trading floor. Physical hardware changes were also made to the execution system for processing orders on the NYSE. As reflected in the comments of George Soros, another fallout from the crash was the drastically reduced use of stock markets for dynamic trading strategies designed to achieve replication of an untraded option payoff. Such schemes had been actively promoted to institutional investors by leading finance academics, including Fischer Black and Mark Rubinstein.[5]

In retrospect, the crash of 1987 still has many lessons for the present, if only these lessons can be adequately understood. Too often, it seems, analysis of the crash has the flavor of an apology for the current method of oversight. Tosini (1988, p.35), a director at the CFTC at the time of the crash, provides an excellent example: "there are many profound, complex and far-reaching issues before the CFTC, as well as other federal agencies and the Congress, concerning stock market and derivative market activities and performance during October . . . the call for 'further research' has hardly ever been more timely". The various reports made some key observations—for example, the Brady Report (1988) (US Dept. of Treasury 1988) recognized that the markets for stocks, stock options and stock index futures were actually one integrated market "linked by financial instruments, trading strategies, market participants and clearing and credit mechanisms". Despite this integration, the regulatory and institutional structure which was designed for separate markets was unable to deal with "inter-market" pressures. The Brady Commission recommended a number of reforms designed to provide for a more integrated approach to market oversight.

The crash of 1987 speaks directly to the problems raised by the systemic change in financial markets brought on by the modern renaissance in derivative securities trading. Various events were replayed in the 1990s because some lessons were not fully understood. This happened because the analysis of the event, on the whole, focused on the specific events and did not adequately account for the singularity of the event. Katzenbach (1987) detailed the chain of events. As measured by the Dow Jones Industrial Average (DJIA), the US equity market had achieved a peak of 2722 in August 1987. P/E ratios for the S&P 500 were averaging 23, relatively high considering the potential for negative market sentiment. In modern parlance, the equity market was due for a correction.

The crash started on 17 October 1987. On Wednesday 15 October there was a news release reporting an unexpectedly large US trade deficit, banks raised prime rates and there was considerable downward pressure on equity prices. The S&P 500 fell from over 314 to below 306. Despite a calming statement by the Treasury secretary on the 16th, the S&P 500 fell again to 298. Significantly, even though things were gloomy, none of this was a shadow of events about to unfold. This leads to a key observation about the crash: It was a severe event which was not associated with a correspondingly severe negative information inflow to the market.

When some negative PPI and industrial production numbers hit the market at the open on Friday the 17th, the stage was set. The DJIA fell a record 108 points. The S&P 500 started the day at 298 and fell to around 282. These were significant market moves that, all things considered, may have presented some buying opportunities. Over the weekend, there was some chatter about a dispute between the US and Germany over interest rates, leading to speculation that the US might let the dollar fall, an event which would be negative for US equities. There was the usual carryover on foreign markets, such as Tokyo and Australia, though the wave of intense selling had not yet hit international markets. The New York market opening was confronted with (incorrect) news that the US had attacked Iranian oil platforms in the Persian Gulf, which almost surely added to the rush of sell orders. At the open the DJIA was down 67 points. The S&P 500 futures contract on the CME fell 18 points at the open. At a time when 100-million-share volumes were uncommon, the NYSE processed 50 million shares in the first half hour. Despite the market turbulence, a 10:00 a.m. meeting of NYSE officials and major brokerage houses did not feel a trading halt was needed.

The sequence of events which was to follow was structured around two institutional procedures. The first concerns the method of executing stocks on the NYSE. Historically, stocks trades on the NYSE involved a floor broker for a member firm to walk the order to the NYSE trading post for that stock and execute the trade directly with the specialist or with another broker using open outcry. At the time of the 1987 crash, this was still the case for block trades involving 10,000 or more shares. This manual method of trading was inefficient and costly for trades involving large bundles of stocks which have to be sold at once. Such trades were being done not only by index arbitrageurs but also by a wide range of market participants. To improve market performance for these traders, the NYSE Designated Order Turnaround (DOT) permitted the computerized execution of small trades. Effectively, brokers with member firms could enter trades into a computerized order system, permitting trades to be entered in brokers' offices. Upon receiving the order, the DOT system would automatically route the trade to the appropriate NYSE specialist, where it would be executed. The whole process takes a matter of minutes.

The new and improved SuperDOT enhanced execution times and access. This remarkable progress in information technology created its own demand from a growing legion of program traders. This category includes a range of trading strategies, including portfolio insurance and index arbitrage. Program traders could enter the exact weights for a portfolio of stocks which could be executed simultaneously by computer entry. Prior DOT and SuperDOT execution risk in such strategies was an important deterrent. Yet, the interaction between the progress in information technology and the ability to introduce new financial engineering products was not well understood at the time. Hints of the crash of October 1987 were observed on 11–12 September 1986 and on 23 January 1987 when 'excessive' stock market volatility was observed. These preliminary tremors attracted some attention, and efforts were made to track the activities of program traders through the DOT system. A poll by NYSE of specialists and floor traders found that, almost without exception, program trading was done through the DOT. On average, in the year leading up to the crash, DOT orders from program traders were found to average around 18% of all DOT trades, with over 28% of all orders on 19 October 1987 being due to program traders.

In addition to the DOT, the other essential institutional feature to consider in evaluating the crash of 1987 is the short sale rule in place at that time. More precisely, the Securities Exchange Act prohibited short selling of securities, except when the short sale took place either: (a) below the last sale price of that security; or (b) at the last price, if that price is above the preceding price. Like the Securities Exchange Act, this rule had origins in the anti-speculator atmosphere of the post-Depression era. The idea is that the rule prevented excessive and accelerating downward pressure on prices during a market downturn. However, there is no such rule on futures markets. As such, dynamic portfolio insurance strategies could be implemented by shorting stock index futures, instead of attempting to short the underlying stocks. Exemptions given to inter-market arbitrageurs effectively transmitted (and still do transmit) shorting in the futures and options market to the cash market. In addition, the single-digit-percentage margins on futures contracts were only a small fraction of the 50% margins on stocks. These substantive differences across markets can be attributed to the regulatory competition between the CFTC, which regulates futures, and the SEC, which regulates securities markets.

Portfolio insurance is a category which includes a range of trading strategies. One important strategy involves dynamically trading stock index futures in order to replicate the payoff on a portfolio composed of the underlying index and a put option. The reason that dynamic trading was used is associated with the relatively limited array of path-independent option products available. Exchange-traded option maturities were a maximum nine months, not all stocks had traded options, index options were relatively illiquid and the OTC market lacked sufficient liquidity to provide options with the exercise price variation and longer-term maturity dates that many institutional investors desired. Even though absence of arbitrage requires that cash-and-carry arbitrage conditions apply to the spot and futures markets, the sheer volume of trading on 19 October meant that a wide spread between the stock index futures and the stock index seemed inevitable. What emerged was much worse: an information technology breakdown. The rush of sell orders effectively crashed the DOT system. At 11:45 a.m. the ticker was approximately one hour behind, and a number of stocks had yet to open because of the lack of an orderly market. By 2:00 p.m., volume had reached 400 million. The final numbers for 19 October were 603 million shares traded, with a drop of 508 points (23%) on the Dow and 80.75 points on the S&P 500, a loss of nearly 30%. At the bell, the ticker was approximately 130 minutes behind.

This slaughter on the stock exchanges led to a flurry of overnight activities. As the US market collapse spread overseas, there were complete or almost complete trading halts on Tokyo and Hong Kong. There was an unprecedented drop on the London FT Index. The opening of the New York market was preceded by reassuring statements and actions from the Federal Reserve Bank, major banks were lowering prime rates and the NYSE shut down the DOT system to prevent the execution of program trades. A temporary and partial trading halt was imposed just after 11:00 a.m. as the market approached 180 on the S&P futures, while the cash market was trading just below 220. This seemed to spell the end of the crash. Prices recovered, and by 2:00 p.m. the spread between cash and futures narrowed close to normal levels, though the spread did widen as the close approached. At the end of the day, the DJIA was up 102 points on volume of 608 million shares. Due to actions taken to combat the crash, there was strong recovery of the dollar and a decline in interest rates. The low prices, combined with the sudden brightening of the economic picture, led to a buying spree, both in the US and offshore. By the close of trading on Thursday 20 October, the market had recovered about half of what had been lost on Monday.

The crash of 1987 was an unprecedented security market event. It exposed serious weaknesses in a regulatory system that was designed to fight the battles arising from old technology. The problems originated from an inability to assess and structure the rapid changes in equity and derivative securities markets. The crash was a debacle that was created by a well-intentioned need to innovate, to improve portfolio management of large financial institutions. As it turns out, the portfolio insurance programs based on dynamic trading were generally unable to deliver the protection *ex post* which was claimed *ex ante*. The situation for which the insurance was most important, the protection of losses in the event of a market collapse, led to preconditions which prevented the outcome from being achieved. The programs could only get so big, and it was not possible for more than a small fraction of market participants to successfully pursue such strategies. In addition, there are numerous untold stories of other strategies, such as delta hedging by option traders, which also contributed to the crash. Undoubtedly, such traders also contributed to the selling via the DOT and floor trading, which only added to the downward pressure on prices.

The Slow-Motion Crash of 2008–2009

The crash of 1987 is a fitting backdrop for the equity market valuation event that began in September 2008 and terminated in March 2009. The Dow Jones

Industrial Average fell 22.6% on 19 October 1987, its steepest one-day decline ever, according to the *Stock Trader's Almanac*. During the final half-hour of trading, program trading represented about 12.2% of total trades, according to the Brady Commission. The slow-motion market crash actually began two decades later in October 2007, with the S&P 500 approaching 1600. Perhaps it was a coincidence that the NYSE dropped curbs on program trading in November 2007. The precipitous market drop, represented by the price of SPY, fell in a matter of months from 1300 in Sept. 2008 until the end of the drop in March 2009 when the S&P 500 dipped below 700 (see Figure 11.2). The majority of the drop happened from September to November 2008, where the price of SPY appears discontinuous in Figure 11.2. It is difficult to shake the suspicion that the wholesale removal of impediments to short selling and enhancement of market technology to facilitate program trading strategies over a relatively short time did play a central role in the unprecedented slow crash of 2008–2009. The dramatic spikes in SPY trading during the slow-motion crash only serve to reinforce suspicions.

In the context of equity security valuation, this raises a number of questions and issues. In a world where the direction of change is left unchecked or allowed to continue, it is difficult to avoid pessimism. Equity security markets have historically imposed a layering of rules aimed at smoothing downside moves in the equity market. Consider the traditional uptick rule for short sales. This rule aims to reduce the volatility of upside moves fuelled through margin buying by increasing the supply of stock available for short sales during such events. Similarly, short sellers are prevented from adding to a general 'rush to the exits' by long-only investors. In addition, it is possible that short sale positions may be liquidated as the supply of stock available for short sale is reduced by margin calls and sales associated with stock purchased on margin. From a vernacular finance perspective, the removal of such rules implies greater market volatility and, over time, a *ceteris paribus* reduction in the value of equity securities due to the removal of the implied real insurance premium provided by the short sales restrictions.

Statistical evidence indicates that "in markets where short selling is either prohibited or not practiced, market returns display a significantly less negative skewness" (Bris et al. 2007, p.1029). The practical implication of such results is "not that extreme returns become more frequent", rather that without short sales restrictions that extreme returns "become more negative" (Bris et al. 2007, p.1032). Not surprisingly, academic reaction to empirical evidence that short sales restrictions "hinder price discovery" is to focus attention on the theoretical connection with market efficiency. An influential early contribution, Diamond and Verrecchia (1987), established a connection between short sales constraints and the speed of adjustment to changes in market information. More precisely, short sales constraints create an asymmetric impact for negative and positive information events. The significantly less negative skewness reported by Bris et al. (2007) is consistent with this theoretical result. Other recent theoretical studies along these lines (e.g., Abreu and Brunnermeier 2002, 2003; Hong and Stein 2003) even claim that short sales constraints can produce bubbles and generate excessive volatility.

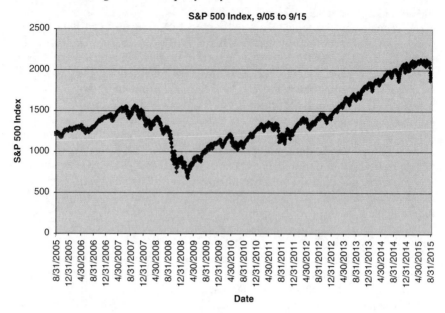

Figure 11.2   S&P 500 Index, September 2005 to September 2015

Academics are generally pleased with results such as Danielsen and Sorescu (2001) that find the reduction of short sales constraints results in statistically negative future returns, in this particular study due to increased short sales using options. "This suggests that negative information is incorporated into price slowly when short selling is constrained . . . Not only do short sales constraints reduce overall price efficiency, but also such an effect is stronger when there is negative information" (Bris et al. 2007, p.1035). Being an "impediment to price discovery", numerous academic studies provide considerable backing for regulators seeking to reduce short sales constraints. However, from an equity security valuation perspective, it is as if J.M. Keynes never wrote anything about the negative impact that the casino element in stock market pricing has on aggregate economic activity. Given revolutionary advances in computer and communications technology, the need for an orderly equity market withdrawal in the face of severe headwinds has been increased, not decreased, as academic studies and the regulatory trend would suggest. Restrictions on cash market short selling are more, not less, necessary.

A useful 'rule of thumb' from vernacular finance regarding the value invest-ing approach to equity valuation is: "Follow the money". Businesses are not nec-essarily run for the shareholders. For example, the car companies, professional sports teams and 'rust belt' industries have found out that present and con-tingent future employee compensation can exhaust shareholder claims against cash flow, even though the business may outwardly appear viable. In this vein, who benefits from an easing of the rules on short selling? At the top of the list is a narrow constituency of hedge funds and related speculative vehicles and speculators that employ trading strategies depending on short sale positions (e.g., Bekaert and Harvey 2000). For example, derivative markets are replete with instances of 'short-the-cash' and carry arbitrage opportunities (e.g., Poitras 2002, esp. ch.4). Another beneficiary is the program traders who are able to use cash market short sales as an alternative route to portfolio insurance, whatever the implications for the aggregate value of equity securities. Finally, the exchanges or ECNs that are able to capture the considerable trading associated with such activities will also benefit.[6] Figure 11.2 illustrates the implications for those unable to follow the money.

Table 11.4 Market Capitalization of Listed Equity Capital Exchanges (millions US$) 14 June 2015

Market Capitalization	Annual % change/ Jun 14 (in USD)	Exchange
		Americas
1,529.4	−6.9%	Bermuda SE
760,225.8	−30.9%	BM&FBOVESPA
122,812.0	−42.3%	Bolsa de Valores de Colombia
67,116.2	19.3%	Buenos Aires SE
73,238.5	−10.5%	Lima SE
463,544.8	−12.5%	Mexican Exchange
7,243,276.1	8.6%	NASDAQ OMX
19,237,429.6	0.3%	NYSE
221,006.7	−14.5%	Santiago SE
2,046,030.4	−12.3%	TMX Group
30,236,209.5	−0.6%	Total region
		Asia-Pacific
1,239,836.2	−15.3%	Australian SE
1,599,630.6	6.7%	BSE India
417,204.6	−22.4%	Bursa Malaysia
22,763.3	11.0%	Colombo SE
50,778.4	6.2%	HoChiMinhSE
3,751,454.3	21.4%	Hong Kong Exchanges
375,523.1	−8.0%	Indonesia SE
NA	–	Japan Exchange Group—Osaka
4,944,150.2	6.9%	Japan Exchange Group—Tokyo
1,334,375.2	1.9%	Korea [Exchange
1,553,246.9	5.5%	National Stock Exchange India
66,471.4	−12.8%	New Zealand Exchange

(*Continued*)

Table 11.4 (Continued)

Market Capitalization	Annual % change/ Jun 14 (in USD)	Exchange
267,011.0	5.0%	Philippine SE
5,694,378.4	136.5%	Shanghai SE
3,907,212.4	156.0%	Shenzhen SE
749,071.6	−7.7%	Singapore Exchange
87,773.2	−7.8%	Taipei Exchange
879,012.7	−2.3%	Taiwan SE Corp.
423,390.9	2.7%	The Stock Exchange of Thailand
25,815,592.7	32.5%	Total region
		Europe-Africa-Middle East
118,924.3	3.1%	Abu Dhabi SE
25,053.9	−5.2%	Amman SE
43,606.3	−54.6%	Athens Exchange
21,518.3	–	Bahrain Bourse
960,331.0	−21.5%	BME Spanish Exchanges
183,943.2	−17.5%	Borsa Istanbul
16,884.1	−8.1%	Budapest SE
50,049.1	−9.9%	Casablanca SE
3,449.8	46.5%	Cyprus SE
1,752,563.7	−9.5%	Deutsche Börse
100,610.8	26.2%	Dubai Financial Market
63,912.0	−4.5%	Egyptian Exchange
3,414,827.8	−10.6%	Euronext
156,173.2	−1.1%	Irish SE
929,021.3	−9.7%	Johannesburg SE
21,417.7	−11.2%	Kazakhstan SE
6,506.3	−27.5%	Ljubljana SE
60,144.4	−19.0%	Luxembourg SE
4,086.1	3.8%	Malta SE
7,859.9	−13.8%	Mauritius SE
492,098.5	−33.0%	Moscow Exchange
39,155.5	1.1%	Muscat Securities Market
1,237,965.1	−4.2%	NASDAQ. OMK Nordic Exchange
57,597.5	–	Nigerian Stock Exchange
226,738.0	−21.4%	Oslo Børs

Market Capitalization	Annual % change/ Jun 14 (in USD)	Exchange
178,270.3	2.7%	Qatar Stock Exchange
537,224.6	3.6%	Saudi Stock Exchange— Tadawul
1,545,736. 2	–3.8%	SIX Swiss Exchange
223,420.0	2.2%	Tel Aviv SE
97,459.2	–20.9%	Wiener Borse
12,577,148.1	–10.5%	Total region
68,628,950.3	7.3%	WFE Total

Source: Adapted from World Federation of Exchanges, Factbook (Equity 1.1)

Equity Capital in the 21st Century

The growth in the depth, extent and influence of equity capital during the 20th century was remarkable and, for some, profoundly disturbing. Michie (2012) observed in 2009 the market capitalization of the 45,328 companies listed on the world's stock exchanges had reached $79 trillion dollars, or 109% of global GDP ($72.5 trillion). These estimates are compared to the 1913 values, using the estimates of Lyndon Moore. Recognizing the difficulties of determining equity capital market estimates prior to World War I, Moore calculated the value of corporate stocks quoted on the world's stock exchanges as $41.1 billion for 1913. Michie adjusted for 2009 prices, producing a value of $918 billion, "indicating an 86 fold increase in the absolute value of quoted corporate stocks in the course of, approximately, 100 years". In relative terms, the market value of corporate common stocks was only 17% of global GDP in 1913, using Angus Maddison's global GDP figure for that date. "This implies a six fold increase in the importance of corporate stocks, which was achieved against the background of an enormous destruction of stock market value during two world wars and successive bouts of government confiscation of privately held assets and the state ownership of many areas of business activity" (Michie 2012, p.30). Such are the fundamental changes in the global macroeconomic importance of equity capital.

Such dramatic change spanning several generations has attracted considerable debate, discussion and criticism in the intellectual attention space. Perhaps the most influential recent contribution has been from Thomas Piketty (2014), *Capital in the Twenty-first Century*. In the search for the inexorable laws of capitalism, Piketty (2014, p.570) observed:

> Without real accounting and financial transparency and sharing of information, there can be no economic democracy. Conversely, without a real right

to intervene in corporate decision-making (including seats for workers on the company's board of directors), transparency is of little use. Information must support democratic institutions; it is not an end in itself. If democracy is someday to regain control of capitalism, it must start by recognizing that the concrete institutions in which democracy and capitalism are embodied need to be reinvented again and again.

Being predicated on the notion that the limited liability corporation with autonomous shares needs, somehow, to be fixed by 'intervening in corporate decision making', such popular impressions ignore the centuries of progress that have produced a legal form that is well adapted to commercial ventures requiring a large and permanent equity capital stock. The advancement of economic democracy and equality of opportunity is aided not by *ad hoc* intervention in commercial decisions but by ensuring that those benefiting from access to the 'public space' pay appropriately.

As Piketty correctly observed, 'real accounting and financial transparency and sharing of information are an essential component of economic democracy'. To this end, various debacles in the first decade of the 21st century—from the collapse of Enron to the implosion of AIG—reveals that uniform rules of financial reporting and corporate conduct have to be fairly and effectively applied. However, improving corporate conduct and financial reporting does not provide a solution to the increasing wealth and income inequality that threatens economic democracy. Reform of corporate conduct is not a reform of tax and fiscal policy. The evolution of the limited liability corporation with autonomous publicly traded shares has taken place against a fiscal backdrop that relies on a concept of 'income' to raise taxes that fails to account for contemporaneous wealth increases associated with the largely untaxed accumulation of capital within publicly traded companies (e.g., Macdonald 2015). For example, instead of taxing individuals on their changes in wealth, in a given tax year, arising from changes in the price of equity capital shares, tax on this 'income' can be: (a) deferred to later years when shares are 'sold'; or (b) avoided entirely by realizing gains from sale in a jurisdiction with favorable tax rates.[7] Such deferring of income associated with wealth changes violates a basic accounting tenet that income and expenses be charged to the period received.

Casual inspection of *Forbes* magazine's list of the wealthiest people in the world reveals the increasing importance of equity capital shares in publicly traded companies. Virtually all the billionaires in the wealthy democracies have an enormous equity capital position in publicly traded corporations. The bulk of this wealth accumulation has not resulted in corresponding tax revenue. The numerous arguments that have been raised to defend the rapid accumulation of wealth without substantial taxation—for example, the double taxation of income at the corporate and individual level—deny the empirical evidence of increasing wealth inequality that Piketty and many others have documented. A transition from a tax system based primarily on wage and salary income to a system that also accurately accounts for wealth accumulation is indicated to promote the advancement of economic democracy and equality of opportunity within national boundaries. Such a transition in fiscal environment is not technically difficult to achieve. Substitution of a portion of the individual income tax with increased property taxes, vehicle registration fees and luxury taxes, combined with taxation of both aggregate wealth and annual mark-to-market increases in equity capital holdings, are achievable changes. The inability of democratic institutions to recognize such initiatives to improve 'the public space' reflects the insidious political strength of the 1%.[8]

Bratton (2001, p.770) provided a fundamental critique of Berle and Means in the modern context:

> The usual argument made . . . is that social demands should be met by external regulation or wealth redistribution through taxation and transfer payments . . . Corporations take advantage of this open territory, using various means of regulatory arbitrage to escape domestic regulation and avoid paying taxes.

While Bratton would be well advised to change "taxation" to "income taxation", the futility of taxing corporate and individual income in a global environment, where funds can be realized and transferred instantaneously across jurisdictions, is identified.[9] Instead of taxing income, which is geographically portable, it is more effective to tax individual physical wealth—houses, boats, automobiles—and changes in the value of equity claims to corporate assets that are physical, hard to disguise and difficult to move. The origins of this approach to taxation stretch back to the trust era and the beginnings of the modern income tax system.[10] "With the ratification of the Sixteenth Amendment to the Constitution, the income tax became a permanent fixture of American life. The passage of the income tax law in 1913 created another 'statistical community' as Americans became members of 'tax brackets' and income (rather than wealth) became the measure of the nation's well-being" (Previts and Merino 1998, p.181). The ability to almost instantaneously monetize an equity claim in a publicly traded limited liability corporation with global reach and simultaneously transfer those funds to other locations on the globe is a challenge that national regulatory and tax authorities are unable and ill-equipped to address. The wealthiest are, once again, treating the 99% like idiots![11]

In addition to a social and political failure to accurately capture a 'fair' amount of payment for use of 'the public space', the statement of Cook (1893, p.7) in *The Corporation Problem*, made during the midst of the social and political reactions to the growth and abuses of the trusts in the US at the end of the 19th century, is revealing of other substantive issues arising in current events:

> [N]ot withstanding all the advantages, material, intellectual and moral, which have been derived from corporations, there is much to be said against them. And they have two peculiarities which have led to these abuses. These are, first, the ease with which all responsibility for bad acts is placed upon the corporation itself, while the real perpetrators are concealed; second, the separation of stockholders from corporate agents, of the investor from the investment, of the principal from the agent, with the expectation on the part

of the investor, the principal, the stockholder, that profits will be made, honestly if possible, but that profits will be made.

While the infamous Bernie Madoff is vilified for defrauding equity capital investors in his hedge fund, this fraudulent violation of fiduciary duty produced a dramatic criminal sentence. Much larger losses created by 'corporations' in the sub-prime mortgage crisis, seemingly based on the 'fraudulent' creation of toxic collateralized mortgage products and other collateralized debt obligations, resulted only in monetary fines. Other recent examples where the perpetrators of parasitic acts are protected by the corporate veil abound (SAC Capital!). In the 21st century, it seems the global search for corporate profits "that will be made, honestly if possible", by agents acting separate from ownership, is under the supervision of national regulators ill-equipped to monitor the activities of corporate management in a global environment. This legal environment is sufficient cover for egregious behavior that, if committed by an individual or partnership, would attract severe sanction.

The disturbing market downturn at the start of the new millennium, referred to as the dot-com bubble, led to passage in the US of the Sarbanes-Oxley Act, ensuring that corporate officers are legally responsible for the validity of financial statements. The dot-com bubble is a poor descriptor of the motivation for Sarbanes-Oxley, because the act was inspired by the collapse of Worldcom and Enron and the perpetration of accounting-related frauds at other firms, such as Tyco. These corporate actors were not 'Internet' firms. The collapse of the major accounting firm Arthur Andersen highlights the cosy relationship between accounting firms and the publicly traded companies that are being externally audited by those same accounting firms. This is a problem that has plagued the accounting profession since early in the 20th century. Sarbanes-Oxley failed to extend liability for inadequate supervision of corporate managers to all but a few directors, permitting the practice of appointing ineffective boards populated by the well connected and entrenched, as opposed to the most competent, to continue unabated.

The next major US effort at equity capital market regulation, the Dodd-Frank Act, was not much more than a request for regulators to design rules addressing specific issues arising from the collapse of securities markets that accompanied 'the Great Recession'. Ineffective legislators were joined by regulators that appeared to be increasingly captured by the entities being regulated: Despite repeated contacts indicating serious impropriety at the Bernie Madoff hedge fund, the SEC failed for years to undercover wrongdoing in the actions of this iconic Wall Street actor. More significantly, the villains of numerous historical 'bubbles and crashes', highly leveraged market participants driven by largely speculative motivations, are present in the expanding universe of hedge funds and other equity capital arrangements that, by design, employ highly leveraged positions to make 'big bets'. Against this backdrop, the fiduciary responsibility of exchange traded fund managers to oversee corporate management on behalf of shareholders is opaque. This complicates any possible resolution to issues arising from the separation of ownership and control confronting modern fiduciary and agency capitalism, detailed by Ireland (2005) and others. This modern quandary provides a fitting end to the rich tapestry that is the history of equity capital.

NOTES

1   This failed perspective reappeared with a vengeance in the 1990s, reaching a peak in the administration of US president George W. Bush in the first decade of the 21st century.
2   Estimates for the size of hedge funds vary, if only because it is difficult to track entities that are not registered. In 2007, PriceWaterhouseCooper estimated hedge funds had $2.17 trillion in assets under management, compared to over $24 trillion for mutual funds (Cumming and Johan 2008, n.1). Given the substantial leverage used by many hedge funds, the actual capital invested would be much less. Poitras (2005, pp.566–8) examined the history of hedge funds, starting with Alfred Jones' (1901–1989) research for a *Fortune* article in March 1949 that led to the creation of the first limited partnership hedge fund in 1952. Evans (1965) is an early contribution to the history and development of certain hedge fund strategies.
3   Prior to the elimination of curbs on program trading, the NYSE defined a "program trade" as the execution of trades involving a basket of at least 15 stocks from the S&P 500 or where the value of the basket is at least $1 million.
4   While NYSE program trading curbs were ended in November 2007, market circuit-breakers have continued in an evolving form. Under the current NYSE Rule 80B, the NYSE sets circuit-breaker levels at 7%, 13%, and 20% of the average closing price of the S&P 500 for the previous trading day. Depending on the point drop and the time of day when it happens, different actions occur automatically. Prior to the program trading rules being removed, the NYSE curb on program trading was imposed for moves in the NYSE Composite Index of greater than 190 points from the previous close. The SEC has also introduced circuit-breaker rules for individual stocks (http://www.sec.gov/investor/alerts/circuitbreakers.htm).
5   Katzenbach (1987) gave a partial listing of key players implementing portfolio insurance strategies for large institutional investors prior to the 1987 crash: Leland O'Brien Rubinstein Associates; Aetna Life and Casualty; Putnam Advisory Co.; Chase Investors Mgmt.; JP Morgan Investment Mgmt.; Wells Fargo Investment Advisors; and Bankers Trust Co. This list does not include the wannabes at Goldman Sachs, Salomon Bros., Nomura and other firms seeking to gain status in this area. Goldman Sachs was the firm which employed Fischer Black at this time.
6   Using a new SEC database started in 2005, Diether et al. (2009) reported that short sales represent 24% of NYSE and 31% of Nasdaq share volume, with most short selling being done by institutions as opposed to individuals. Cohen et al. (2007) discussed the costs of cash short selling, while Diether et al. (2009) overviewed possible short selling trading strategies. Dechow et al. (2001) examined the implications of short selling for fundamental analysis.
7   Numerous anecdotal and academic examples of the disparity of wealth are available. For example, in Canada it is estimated that the wealthiest 86 families and individuals have more combined personal wealth than the combined wealth of more than 11 million Canadians (Macdonald 2015). This number is up from 10 million at the end of the 20th century. As for the reporting of

corporate income, in the UK the total corporate income tax paid by Facebook UK in 2014 was about £1,000 less than the income tax bill of an average individual UK taxpayer.

8   The insurmountable problems involved in advancing such change were accurately captured in the documentary *Inside Job* (2010), directed by Charles Ferguson, available at: http://www.sonyclassics.com/insidejob/.

9   The US Treasury reported that, as of July 2015, the largest holders of US Treasury securities were (in $billions): mainland China (1,240.8); Japan (1,197.5); and, in third place, the Caribbean banking centers (324.5). This holding, in a banking secrecy haven, is larger than the combined holdings of the oil-exporting countries. This illustrates the illusive character of taxation based largely on income instead of wealth. http://www.treasury.gov/ticdata/Publish/mfh.txt

10 Prior to the introduction of the income tax, Henry George (1839–1897) and others argued for taxation based on land holdings, which was the predominant form of aggregate wealth in the largely agrarian economies of the second half of the 19th century. The need to address the colossal wealth that the Vanderbilt, Carnegie and other families were building up using the accumulation of equity capital seems to have eluded this debate.

11 This reference to 'taking us for idiots' is a remembrance of Bernard Maris, who was among the victims of the attack against *Charlie Hebdo* magazine headquarters in Paris on 7 January 2015. Maris was a well-known figure among historians of economics, with several essays on Keynes and economic methodology (in French). His character is reflected in the title of his 1999 book: *Lettre ouverte aux gourous de l'économie qui nous prennent pour des imbeciles* ("Open letter to the gurus of economics who take us for idiots").

References

Abatino, B., G. Dari-Mattiacci, and E. Perotti (2011), "Depersonalization of Business in Ancient Rome", *Oxford Journal of Legal Studies* 31: 365–389.

Abreu, D. and M. Brunnermeier (2003), "Bubbles and Crashes", *Econometrica* 71: 173–204.

Abreu, D. and M. Brunnermeier (2002), "Synchronization Risk and Delayed Arbitrage", *Journal of Financial Economics* 66: 341–360.

Acemoglu, D. and J. Robinson (2015), "The Rise and Decline of General Laws of Capitalism", *Journal of Economic Perspectives* 29: 3–28.

Acheson, G. and J. Turner (2008), "The Death Blow to Unlimited Liability in Victorian Britain: The City of Glasgow Failure", *Explorations in Economic History* 45: 235–253.

Acheson, G., J. Turner, and Q. Ye (2012), "The Character and Denomination of Shares in the Victorian Equity Market", *Economic History Review* 65: 862–886.

Ackerman, C., R. McNally, and D. Ravenscraft (1999), "The Performance of Hedge Funds: Risk, Return and Incentive", *Journal of Finance* 54: 833–874.

Ackerman-Lieberman, P. (2011), "Contractual Partnerships in the Geniza and the Relationship Between Islamic Law and Practice", *Journal of the Economic and Social History of the Orient* 54: 646–676.

Adams, C.F. and H. Adams (1871), *Chapters of Erie and Other Essays*, Boston, MA: James Osgood.

Alborn, T. (1998), *Conceiving Companies: Joint-Stock Politics in Victorian England*, London: Routledge.

Allen, E. (1938), "Study of a Group of American Management-Investment Companies, 1930–36", *Journal of Business of the University of Chicago* 11: 232–257.

Alter, G. and J. Riley (1986), "How to Bet on Lives: A Guide to Life Contingency Contracts in Early Modern Europe", pp. 1–53 in P. Uselding (ed.), *Research in Economic History* (vol. 10), Greenwich: JAI Press.

Amsler, C., R. Bartlett, and C. Bolton (1981), "Thoughts of Some British Economists on Early Limited Liability and Corporate Legislation", *History of Political Economy* 13: 774–793.

Amzallag, N. (2009), "From Metallurgy to Bronze Age Civilizations: The Synthetic Theory", *American Journal of Archaeology* 113: 497–519.

Anderson, A. (1764), *An Historical and Chronological Deduction of the Origin of Commerce*, London: Printed for A. Millar.

Anderson, M., J. Edwards, and R. Chandler (2005), "Constructing the 'Well Qualified' Chartered Accountant in England in Wales", *Accounting Historians Journal* 32: 5–54.

Anonymous (1478), *The Treviso Arithmetic*, reprinted in F. Swetz (1987), *Capitalism and Arithmetic: The New Math of the 15th C. Including the full text of the Treviso Arithmetic* (trans. D.E. Smith), LaSalle: Open Court.

Armstrong, W. (1848), *Stocks and Stock Jobbing in Wall Street, with Sketches of the Brokers and Fancy Stocks*, New York: New York Publishing Company.

Arnold, A. (1997), " 'Publishing Your Private Affairs to the World': Corporate Financial Disclosures in the UK, 1900–1924", *Accounting, Business and Financial History* 7: 143–173.

Arnold, A. and S. McCartney (2011), " 'Veritable Gold Mines Before the Arrival of Railway Competition': But Did Dividends Signal Rates of Return in the English Canal Industry?", *Economic History Review* 64: 214–236.

Arnold, A. and S. McCartney (2008), "The Transition to Financial Capitalism and its Implications for Financial Reporting", *Accounting, Auditing & Accountability* 21: 1185–1209.

Ashton, J. (1899), *The History of Gambling in England*, New York: Burt Franklin; reprint (1968).

Ashtor, E. (1975), "Profits from Trade with the Levant in the Fifteenth Century", *Bulletin of the School of Oriental and African Studies University of London* 38: 250–275.

Attard, B. (2000), "Making a Market. The Jobbers of the London Stock Exchange, 1800–1986", *Financial History Review* 7: 5–24.

Babson, R. (1911), "Factors Affecting Commodity Prices", *Annals of the American Academy of Political and Social Science* 38: 155–188.

Babson, R. (1910a), "Barometric Indices of the Condition of Trade", *Annals of the American Academy of Political and Social Science* 35: 111–134.

Babson, R. (1910b), "Sources of Market News", *Annals of the American Academy of Political and Social Science* 35: 135–144.

Bachelier, L. (1900), 'Theorie de la Speculation', *Annales de l' Ecole Normale superieure*, 17: 21–86; English translation by A. Boness in P. Cootner (ed.) (1967), *The Random Character of Stock Market Prices,* Cambridge, MA: MIT Press.

Backscheider, P. (1989), *Daniel Defoe: His Life*, Baltimore: Johns Hopkins University Press.

Badian, E. (1972), *Publicans and Sinners*, Ithaca, NY: Cornell University Press.

Baker, H., G. Powell, and T. Veit (2001), "Factors Influencing Dividend Policy Decisions of Nasdaq Firms", *Financial Review* 36: 19–38.

Baladouni, V. (1986), "Financial Reporting in the Early Years of the East India Company", *Accounting Historians Journal* 13: 19–30.

Balsdon, J. (1962), "Roman History, 65–50 B.C.: Five Problems", *Journal of Roman Studies* 52: 134–141.

Bang, P. (2008), *The Roman Bazaar: A Comparative Study of Trade and Markets in a Tributary Empire*, Cambridge, UK: Cambridge University Press.

Barbour, V. (1950), *Capitalism in Amsterdam in the 17th Century*, Ann Arbor, MI: University of Michigan Press.

Barnett, W. and R. Solow (2000), "An Interview With Franco Modigliani", *Macroeconomic Dynamics* 4: 222–256.

Bartlett, B. (1992), "Jonathan Swift: Father of Supply-Side Economics", *History of Political Economy* 24: 745–748.

Baskin, J. (1988), "The Development of Corporate Financial Markets in Britain and the United States, 1600–1914: Overcoming Asymmetric Information", *Business History Review* 62 (Summer): 199–237.

Baskin, J. and P. Miranti (1997), *A History of Corporate Finance*, Cambridge, UK: Cambridge University Press.

Begbie, M. (1848), *Partnership "en commandite", or, Partnership with Limited Liabilities (According to the Commercial Practice of the Continent of Europe, and the United States of America), for the Employment of Capital, the Circulation of Wages, and the Revival of Our Home and Colonial Trade*, London: E. Wilson.

Bekaert, G. and C. Harvey (2000), "Foreign Speculators and Emerging Equity Markets", *Journal of Finance* 55: 565–613.

Bellhouse, D. (1988), "Probability in the Sixteenth and Seventeenth Centuries: An Analysis of Puritan Casuistry", *International Statistical Review* 56: 63–74.

Benartzi, S., R. Michaely, and R. Thaler (1997), "Do Changes in Dividends Signal the Future or the Past", *Journal of Finance* 52: 1007–1034.

Benninga, S. and M. Blume (1985), "On the Optimality of Portfolio Insurance", *Journal of Finance* 40 (December): 1341–1352.

Berkshire-Hathaway (2015), *Annual Report 2014*, Obtained from www.berkshire hathaway.com

Berkshire-Hathaway (2003), *Annual Report 2002*, Obtained from www.berkshire hathaway.com.

Berle, A. and G. Means (1932), *The Modern Corporation and Private Property*, New York: Harcourt, Brace & World; 1968 revised reprint.

Bernstein, L. (1993), *Financial Statement Analysis* (5th ed.), Homewood, IL: Irwin.

Bernstein, P. (1992), *Capital Ideas, the Improbable Origins of Modern Wall Street*, New York: Free Press.

Bewes, W. (1923), *The Romance of the Law Merchant*, London: Sweet & Maxwell.

Bhargava, A. (2010), "An Econometric Analysis of Dividends and Share Repurchases by US Firms", *Journal of the Royal Statistical Society: Series A (Statistics in Society)* 173: 631–656.

Bierman, H. (1998), *The Causes of the 1929 Stock Market Crash*, Westport, CT: Greenwood Press.

Bierman, H. (1991), *The Great Myths of 1929 and the Lessons to be Learned*, Westport, CT: Greenwood Press.

Bikai, P., R. Stieglitz, and R. Clifford (1990), "Rich and Glorious Traders of the Levant", *Archaeology* 43: 22–30.

Bindoff, T. (1982), *The House of Commons 1509–1558 (The History of Parliament)* (vols. I–III), London: Seeker and Warburg.

Black, F. (1976), "The Dividend Puzzle", *Journal of Portfolio Management* 2: 5–8.

Black, F. and M. Scholes (1973), "The Pricing of Options and Corporate Liabilities", *Journal of Political Economy* 81: 637–659.

Blanc, J. and L. Desmedt (2014), "In Search of a 'Crude Fancy of Childhood': Deconstructing Mercantilism", *Cambridge Journal of Economics* 38: 585–604.

Boardman, J. (2001), "Aspects of 'Colonization'", *Bulletin of the American Schools of Oriental Research* 322: 33–42.

Böhm-Bawerk, E. von (1891), *Positive Theory of Capital* (trans. W. Stewart), London: Macmillan.

Boockholdt, J.L. (1983), "Historical Perspective on the Auditor's Role: The Early Experience of the American Railroads", *Accounting Historians Journal* 10: 69–86.

Bosher, J.F. (1995), "Huguenot Merchants and the Protestant International in the Seventeenth Century", *William and Mary Quarterly* 52: 77–102.

Bosher, J.F. (1988), "Success and Failure in Trade to New France, 1660–1760", *French Historical Studies* 15: 444–461.

Bosland, C. (1937), *The Common Stock Theory of Investment*, New York: Ronald Press.

Bouchary, J. (1938), "Étienne Clavière d'après sa correspondance financière et politique", *Revus d'historie economique and social* 24 (2, 3, 4): 131–162, 245–281,357–358.

Boyer, C. (1968), *A History of Mathematics*, New York: Wiley.

Boyes, P. (2012), "The King of the Sidonians: Phoenician Ideologies and the Myth of the Kingdom of Tyre-Sidon", *Bulletin of the American Schools of Oriental Research* 365: 33–44.

Bratton, W. (2001), "Berle and Means Reconsidered at the Century's Turn", *Journal of Corporation Law* 26: 737–770.

Bratton, W. and M. Wachter (2008), "Shareholder Primacy's Corporatist Origins: Adolf Berle and the Modern Corporation", *Journal of Corporation Law* 33: 118–152.

Braudel, F. (1982), *Civilization and Capitalism, 15th–18th Century* (vol. 2, trans. from 1979 French ed.), London: Collins.

Brealey, R. (1991), "Harry M. Markowitz's Contributions to Financial Economics; Bibliography of Markowitz's Publications, 1952–1990", *Scandinavian Journal of Economics* 93: 7–21.

Brennan, M. and E. Schwartz (1987), "Time Invariant Portfolio Insurance Strategies", *UCLA Working Paper* (September).

Brennan, M. and E. Schwartz (1976), "The Pricing of Equity-Linked Life Insurance Policies With an Asset Value Guarantee", *Journal of Financial Economics* 3: 195–213.

Brenner, R. (1972), "The Social Basis of English Commercial Expansion, 1550–1650", *Journal of Economic History* 32: 1–32.

Bricker, R. and N. Chandar (2000), "Where Berle and Means Went Wrong: A Reassessment of Capital Market Agency and Financial Reporting", *Accounting, Organizations & Society* 25: 529–554.

Brink, I. and H. Witt (1982), *Modern Internal Auditing: Appraising Operations and Control*, New York: Wiley.

Bris, A., W. Goetzmann, and N. Zhu (2007), "Efficiency and the Bear: Short Sales and Markets Around the World", *Journal of Finance* 62: 1029–1079.

Brown, R. (ed.) (1905), *A History of Accounting and Accountants*, London: Frank Cass, reprint (1968).

Brown, S., W. Goetzmann, and A. Kumar (1998), "The Dow Theory: William Peter Hamilton's Track Record Reconsidered", *Journal of Finance* 53: 1311–1333.

Bryer, R. (1997), "The Mercantile Laws Commission of 1854 and the Political Economy of Limited Liability", *Economic History Review* 50: 37–56.

Bryer, R. (1991), "Accounting for the 'Railway Mania' of 1845—A Great Railway Swindle?", *Accounting, Organisations and Society* 16: 439–486.

Buckland, W. (1963), *A Text-Book of Roman Law from Augustus to Justinian* (3rd ed.), Cambridge, UK: Cambridge University Press.

Buckley, H. (1924), "Sir Thomas Gresham and the Foreign Exchanges", *Economic Journal* 34: 589–601.

Bunting, D. (1986), *The Rise of Large American Corporations, 1889–1919*, New York: Garland Publishing.

Burton, H. and D.C. Corner (1968), *Investment and Unit Trusts in Britain and America*, London: Elek Books.

Butler, H. (1985), "Nineteenth-Century Jurisdictional Competition in the Granting of Corporate Privileges", *Journal of Legal Studies* 14: 129–166.

Byrne, E. (1916), "Commercial Contracts of the Genoese in the Syrian Trade of the Twelfth Century", *Quarterly Journal of Economics* 31: 128–170.

Byrne, R. (2003), "Early Assyrian Contacts With Arabs and the Impact on Levantine Vassal Tribute", *Bulletin of the American Schools of Oriental Research* 331: 11–25.

Campbell, G. (2013), "Deriving the Railway Mania", *Financial History Review* 20: 1–27.

Campbell, G. (2012), "Myopic Rationality in a Mania", *Explorations in Economic History* 49: 75–91.

Campbell, G. and J. Turner (2012), "Dispelling the Myth of the Naive Investor During the British Railway Mania, 1845–1846", *Business History Review* 86: 3–41.

Campbell, G. and J. Turner (2011), "Substitutes for Legal Protection: Corporate Governance and Dividends in Victorian Britain", *Economic History Review* 64: 571–597.

Cangiani, M. (2011), "Karl Polanyi's Institutional Theory: Market Society and Its Disembedded Economy", *Journal of Economic Issues* 45: 177–198.

Cannan, E. (1937), *'Editor's Introduction'* to the *Wealth of Nations*, New York: Modern Library.

Cantillon, R. (1755), *Essai Sur La Nature du Commerce en Général* (trans. Henry Higgs), London: Macmillan (1931); reprinted by New York: Augustus Kelley (1964).

Cardoso, J. (2006), "Joseph de la Vega and the 'Confusion de Confusiones'", chapter 3 in G. Poitras (ed.), *Pioneers of Financial Economics*, Northampton, MA: Edward Elgar.

Carlos, A. and L. Neal (2006), "The Micro-Foundations of the Early London Capital Market: Bank of England Shareholders During and After the South Sea Bubble", *Economic History Review* 59: 498–538.

Carlos, A. and S. Nicholas (1996), "Theory and History: Seventeenth-Century Joint-Stock Chartered Trading Companies", *Journal of Economic History* 56: 916–924.

Carlos, A. and S. Nicholas (1990), "Agency Problems in Early Chartered Companies: The Case of the Hudson's Bay Company", *Journal of Economic History* 50: 853–875.

Carruthers, B. and W. Espeland (1991), "Accounting for Rationality: Double-Entry Bookkeeping and the Rhetoric of Economic Rationality", *American Journal of Sociology* 97: 31–69.

Cassis, Y. (2012), "Capitals of Capital", chapter 1, pp. 15–27 in G. Poitras (ed.), *Stock Market Globalization Research Handbook*, Northampton, MA: Edward Elgar.

Cassis, Y. (2006), *Capitals of Capital: A History of International Financial Centres, 1780–2005* (trans. J. Collier), Cambridge, UK: Cambridge University Press.

Castelli, C. (1877), *The Theory of "Options" in Stocks and Shares*, London: F. Mathieson.

Cawston, G. and A.H. Keane (1896), *The Early Chartered Companies (A.D. 1296–1858)*, London: Edward Arnold.

Chamberlain, L. and W. Hay (1931), *Investment and Speculation; Studies of Modern Movements and Basic Principles*, New York: H. Holt and Co.

Chancellor, E. (1999), *Devil Take the Hindmost: A History of Financial Speculation*, London: Macmillan.

Chandler, A. (1990), *Scale and Scope: The Dynamics of Industrial Capitalism*, Cambridge, MA: Belknap Press.

Chatfield, M. (1974), *A History of Accounting Thought*, Hinsdale, IL: Dryden Press.

Checkland, S. (1975), *Scottish Banking: A History, 1695–1973*, Glasgow, Scotland: Collins.

Cheffins, B. (2008), *Corporate Ownership and Control: British Business Transformed*, Oxford, UK: Oxford University Press.

Cheffins, B. and S. Bank (2009), "Is Berle and Means Really a Myth?", *Business History Review* 83: 443–474.

Christ, C. (1994), "The Cowles Commission's Contributions to Econometrics at Chicago, 1939–1955", *Journal of Economic Literature* 32: 30–59.

Christie, W. (1990), "Dividend Yield and Expected Returns: The Zero-Dividend Puzzle", *Journal of Financial Economics* 28: 95–126.

Chuquet, N. (1484), *The Triparty*, translated and reprinted in Flegg, G., C. Hay and B. Moss (eds.) (1985), *Nicholas Chuquet, Renaissance Mathematician. A Study with Extensive Translation of Chuquet's Mathematical Manuscript Completed in 1484*, Boston: Reidel.

Clapham, J. (1958), *The Bank of England: A History*, Cambridge, UK: Cambridge University Press.

Clark, G. (2007), "A Review of Avner Greif's 'Institutions and the Path to the Modern Economy: Lessons from Medieval Trade Institutions and the Path to the Modern Economy", *Journal of Economic Literature* 45 (3): 725–741.

Clendenin, J. and M. van Greave (1954), "Growth and Common Stock Values", *Journal of Finance* 9: 365–376.

Clews, H. (1908), *Fifty Years in Wall Street. "Twenty-Eight Years in Wall Street" Revised and Enlarged*, New York: Irving.

Clough, S. and R. Rapp (1975), *European Economic History*, New York: McGraw-Hill.

Cohen, J. (1953), "The Element of Lottery in British Government Bonds, 1694–1919", *Economica* 20 (August): 237–246.

Cohen, L., K. Diether, and C. Malloy (2007), "Supply and Demand Shifts in the Shorting Market", *Journal of Finance* 62: 2061–2096.

Cohen, M. (2013), "A Partnership Gone Bad: Business Relationships and the Evolving Law of the Cairo Geniza Period", *Journal of the Economic and Social History of the Orient* 56: 218–263.

Cook, W (1893), *The Corporation Problem: The Public Phases of Corporations, Their Uses, Abuses*, New York: G. Putnam.

Cootner, P. (ed.) (1965), *The. Random Character of Stock Market Prices*, Cambridge, MA: MIT Press.

Cope, S. (1978), "The Stock Exchange Revisited: A New Look at the Market in Securities in London in the Eighteenth Century", *Economica* 45: 1–21.

Copeland, M. (1915), "Statistical Indices of Business Conditions", *Quarterly Journal of Economics* 29: 522–562.

Cornew, R. (1988), "Commodity Pool Operators and their Pools: Expenses and Profitability", *Journal of Futures Markets* 8: 617–637.

Cotton, H. (1986), "A Note on the Organization of Tax-Farming in Asia Minor (Cicero, Fam., XII, 65)", *Latomus* T. 45, Fasc. 2: 367–373.

Coulton, G. (1921), "An Episode in Canon Law", *History* 6: 67–76.

Cowan, B. (2005), *The Social Life of Coffee: The Emergence of the British Coffeehouse*, New Haven, CT: Yale University Press.

Cowan, B. (2004a), "Mr. Spectator and the Coffeehouse Public Sphere", *Eighteenth-Century Studies* 37: 345–366.

Cowan, B. (2004b), "The Rise of the Coffeehouse Reconsidered", *Historical Journal* 47: 21–46.

Cowles, A. (1944), "Stock Market Forecasting", *Econometrica* 12: 206–214.

Cowles, A. (1933), "Can Stock Market Forecasters Forecast?", *Econometrica* 1: 309–324.

Crawford, D. (1950), "Three Accounting Terms of Roman Egypt", *Classical Philology* 45: 185–186.

Crockett, J. and I. Friend (1988). "Dividend Policy in Perspective: Can Theory Explain Behavior?" *Review of Economics and Statistics* 70: 603–613.

Cumming, D. and S. Johan (2008), "Hedge Fund Strategies and Regulation", *Banking and Financial Services Policy Report* 27: 1–15.

Cunningham, L. (ed.) (2002), *The Essays of Warren Buffett: Lessons for Investors and Managers* (revised ed.), New York: John Wiley.

Cunningham, W. (1913), *An Essay on Western Civilization in its Economic Aspects*, Cambridge, UK: Cambridge University Press.

Cushing, B. (1989), "A Kuhnian Interpretation of the Historical Evolution of Accounting", *Accounting Historians Journal* 16: 1–41.

Dale, G. (2013), "'Marketless Trading in Hammurabi's Time': A Re-Appraisal", *Journal of the Economic and Social History of the Orient* 56: 159–188.

Dale, R. (2004), *The First Crash: Lessons from the South Sea Bubble*, Princeton, NJ: Princeton University Press.

Damodaran, V. (1994), *Damodaran on Valuation: Security Analysis for Investment and Corporate Finance*, New York: John Wiley.

Danielsen, B. and S. Sorescu (2001), "Why Do Option Introductions Depress Stock Prices? A Study of Diminishing Short Sales Constraints", *Journal of Financial and Quantitative Analysis* 36: 451–484.

Daston, L. (1988), *Classical Probability in the Enlightenment*, Princeton, NJ: Princeton University Press.

Daube, D. (1944), "The Personality in Roman Private Law by P.W. Duff: Review, Part 2", *Journal of Roman Studies* 34: 125–135.

Daube, D. (1943), "The Personality in Roman Private Law by P.W. Duff: Review, Part 1", *Journal of Roman Studies* 33: 86–93.

Dauverd, C. (2006), "Genoese and Catalans: Trade Diaspora in Early Modern Sicily", *Mediterranean Studies* 15: 42–61.

David, F. (1962), *Games, Gods and Gambling*, London: Charles Griffin.

Davis, J. (1917), *Essays in the Earlier History of American Corporations*, New York: Russell & Russell; reprint (1965).

Davis, N. (1960), "Sixteenth-Century French Arithmetics on the Business Life", *Journal of the History of Ideas* 21: 18–48.

Day, G. (1981), "The Impact of the Third Crusade Upon Trade With the Levant", *International History Review* 3: 159–168.

Dayton, J.E. (1971), "The Problem of Tin in the Ancient World", *World Archaeology* 3: 49–70.

Dechow, P., A. Hutton, L. Meulbroek, and R. Sloan (2001), "Short-Sellers, Fundamental Analysis and Stock Returns", *Journal of Financial Economics* 61: 77–106.

Decock, W. (2009), "Lessius and the Breakdown of the Scholastic Paradigm", *Journal of the History of Economic Thought* 31: 57–78.

Defoe, D. (1719), *The Anatomy of Exchange Alley or a System of Stockjobbing*; reprinted in J. Francis (1850).

Defoe, D. (1701), *The Villany of Stock-Jobbers Detected, and the Causes of the Late Run Upon the Bank and Bankers Discovered and Considered*, London: [s.n.].

Deinzer, H. (1935), "Capital Stock and Surplus: Legal and Accounting Relations", *The Accounting Review* 10: 333–345.

de la Vega, J. (1688), *Confusion de Confusiones*; reprinted in Fridson, M. (ed.) (1996), *Extraordinary Popular Delusions and the Madness of Crowds; and, Confusion de Confusiones* (reprints of classic texts), New York: Wiley.

Deloume, A. (1890), *Les Manieurs d'Argent à Rome*, Paris: Thorin.

De Marchi, N. and P. Harrison (1994), "Trading 'in the Wind' and with Guile: The Troublesome Matter of the Short Selling of Share in Seventeenth-Century Holland", pp. 47–65 in N. de Marchi and M. Morgan (eds.), *Higgling: Transactors and Their Markets in the History of Economics, Annual Supplement to History of Political Economy*. Durhan, NC: Duke University Press.

De Morgan, A. (1846), *Arithmetical Books*; reprinted in D. Smith (ed.) (1970), *Rara Arithmetica* (4th ed.), New York: Chelsea.

Dempsey, B. (1948), *Interest and Usury*, London: Dobson.

Denis, D., D. Denis, and A. Sarin (1994), "The Information Content of Dividend Changes: Cash Flow, Signaling, Overinvestment and Dividend Clienteles", *Journal of Financial and Quantitative Analysis* 29: 567–587.

de Pinto, Isaac (1771), *An Essay on Circulation of Currency and Credit in Four Parts and a Letter on the Jealousy of Commerce*, translated with annotations by S. Baggs (1774), London; reprinted by Gregg International Publishers (1969).

Dercksen, J. (1996), *The Old Assyrian Copper Trade in Anatolia*, Istanbul: NHAI.

de Roover, F.E. (1941), "Partnership Accounts in Twelfth Century Genoa", *Bulletin of the Business Historical Society* 15: 87–92.

de Roover, F.E. (1940), "The Business Records of an Early Genoese Notary, 1190–1192", *Bulletin of the Business Historical Society* 14: 41–46.

de Roover, R. (1974), "Gerard de Malynes as an Economic Writer: From Scholasticism to Mercantilism", reprinted in J. Kirshner (ed.) (1974), *Business, Banking and Economic Thought, Selected Studies of Raymond de Roover,* Chicago: University of Chicago Press.

de Roover, R. (1956), "The Development of Accounting Prior to Luca Pacioli according to the Account Books of Medieval Merchants", reprinted pp.119–180 in J. Kirshner (ed.) (1974), *Business, Banking and Economic Thought, Selected Studies of Raymond de Roover,* Chicago: University of Chicago Press.

de Roover, R. (1955), "Scholastic Economics: Survival and Lasting Influence from the Sixteenth Century to Adam Smith", *Quarterly Journal of Economics* 69: 161–90; reprinted in J. Kirshner (ed.) (1974, ch. 9).

de Roover, R. (1954), "New Interpretations in the History of Banking", *Journal of World History* 4: 38–76; reprinted in J. Kirshner (ed.) (1974, ch. 5).

de Roover, R. (1951), "Monopoly Theory Prior to Adam Smith", *Quarterly Journal of Economics* 65: 492–524; reprinted in J. Kirshner (ed.) (1974, ch. 8).

de Roover, R. (1949), *Gresham on Foreign Exchange*, London: Harvard University Press.

de Roover, R.(1948), *Banking and Credit in Medieval Bruges*, Cambridge, MA: Harvard University Press.

de Roover, R. (1944), "What Is Dry Exchange? A Contribution to the Study of English Mercantilism", *Journal of Political Economy* 52: 250–66; reprinted in J. Kirshner (ed.) (1974, ch. 4).

Derks, H. (2008), "Religion, Capitalism and the Rise of Double-Entry Bookkeeping", *Accounting, Business & Financial History* 18: 187–213.

De Soto, H. (2000), *The Mystery of Capital: Why Capitalism Triumphs in the West and Fails Everywhere Else*, New York: Basic Books.

Dewing, A. (1919), *The Financial Policy of Corporations* (2 vols.), New York: Ronald Press (5th ed. 1953).

Diamond, D. and R. Verrecchia (1987), "Constraints on Short-Selling and Asset Price Adjustment to Private Information", *Journal of Financial Economics* 18: 277–311.

Dickson, P. (1967), *The Financial Revolution in England*, New York: St. Martin's Press.

Diether, K., K. Lee, and I. Werner (2009), "Short-Sale Strategies and Return Predictability", *Review of Financial Studies* 22: 575–607.

Dimand, R. (2009), "The Cowles Commission and Foundation on the Functioning of Financial Markets from Irving Fisher and Alfred Cowles to Harry Markowitz and James Topin", *Revue d'Histoire des Sciences Humaines* 20: 51–78.

Dimand, R. (2007), "Irving Fisher and Financial Economics: The Equity Premium Puzzle, the Predictability of Stock Prices, and Intertemporal Allocation Under Risk", *Journal of the History of Economic Thought* 29: 153–166.

Duff, P. (1938), *Personality in Roman Private Law*, Cambridge, UK: Cambridge University Press.

Dulman, S. (1989), "The Development of Discounted Cash Flow Techniques in U.S. Industry", *Business History Review* 63: 555–587.

Dunbar, N. (2000), *Inventing Money, the Story of Long-Term Capital Management and the Legends Behind It*, New York: Wiley.

Duncan-Jones, R. (1982), *The Economy of the Roman Empire: Quantitative Studies*, Cambridge, UK: Cambridge University Press.

Durand, D. (1992), "What Price Growth? A Paradox Revisited", *Journal of Portfolio Management* 19: 84–91.

Durand, D. (1989), "Afterthoughts on a Controversy with MM, Plus New Thoughts on Growth and the Cost of Capital", *Financial Management* 18: 12–18.

Durand, D. (1968), "State of the Finance Field: Further Comment", *Journal of Finance* 23: 848–852.

Durand, D. (1960), "Portfolio Selection: Efficient Diversification of Investments, Review", *American Economic Review* 50: 234–236.

Durand, D. (1959), "The Cost of Capital, Corporation Finance and the Theory of Investment: Comment", *American Economic Review* 49: 639–655.

Durand, D. (1957a), "Growth Stocks and the Petersburg Paradox", *Journal of Finance* 12: 348–363.

Durand, D. (1957b), *Bank Stock Prices and the Bank Capital Problem*, New York: NBER.

Durand, D. (1937), "Some Thoughts on Marginal Productivity Theory with Special Reference to Professor Douglas", *Journal of Political Economy* 45: 740–58.

Durand, D. and J. Greenwood (1937), "Random Unit Vectors II: Usefulness of Gram-Charlier and Related Series in Approximating Distributions", *Annals of Mathematical Statistics* 28: 978–986.

Eames, F. (1894), *The New York Stock Exchange*, New York: Greenwood Press; reprint (1968).

Easterbrook, F. and D. Fischel (1985), "Limited Liability and the Corporation", *The University of Chicago Law Review* 52: 89–117.

Edwards, F. (2006), "Hedge Funds and Investor Protection Regulation", *Federal Reserve Bank of Atlanta Economic Review,* Quarter 4: 35–48.

Edwards, F. (1999), "Hedge Funds and the Collapse of Long-Term Capital Management", *Journal of Economic Perspectives* 13:189–210.

Edwards, F. (1988), "Futures Trading and Cash Market Volatility: Stock Index and Interest Rate Futures", *Journal of Futures Markets* 8: 421–440.

Edwards, F. and J.M. Park (1996), "Do Managed Futures Make Good Investments?", *Journal of Futures Markets* 16: 475–517.

Edwards, J. and S. Ogilvie (2012), "Contract Enforcement, Institutions, and Social Capital: The Maghribi Traders Reappraised", *Economic History Review* 65: 421–444.

Edwards, J. and A. Warman (1981), "Discounted Cash Flow and Business Valuation in a Nineteenth Century Merger: A Note", *Accounting Historians Journal* 8: 37–50.

Ehrenberg, R. (1928), *Capital and Finance in the Age of the Renaissance* (trans. from the German by H.M. Lucas), London: Jonathan Cape.

Eiteman, W. and F. Smith (1953), *Common Stock Value and Yields*, Ann Arbor, MI: University of Michigan Press.

Ekelund, R., R. Hebert, R. Tollison, G. Anderson, and A. Davidson (1996), *Sacred Trust: The Medieval Church as an Economic Firm*, New York: Oxford University Press.

Ellis, M. (2006), *Eighteenth-Century Coffee-House Culture*, London: Chatto and Pickering.

Emerigon, B. (1811), *An Essay on Maritime Loans*, Baltimore: Philip Nichlin & Co.

Emery, H. (1896), *Speculation on the Stock and Produce Exchanges of the United States*, New York: Columbia University Press; reprinted by AMS Press, New York 1968.

English, H. (1827), *A Complete View of the Joint Stock Companies Formed During the Years 1824 and 1825*, London: Boosey.

Esa-Jussi, V. (2013), "The Discovery of the Faustmann Formula in Natural Resource Economics", *History of Political Economy* 45: 523–548.

Esa-Jussi, V. (2006), "An Early Contribution of Martin Faustmann to Natural Resource Economics", *Journal of Forest Economics* 12: 131–144.

Evans, M. (1965), *Arbitrage in Domestic Securities in the United States*, W. Nyack, NY: Parker.

Ezzamel, M. and K. Hoskin (2002), "Retheorizing Accounting, Writing and Money With Evidence from Mesopotamia and Ancient Egypt", *Critical Perspectives on Accounting* 13: 333–367.

Falcón y Tella, M. (2008), *Equity and Law* (trans. P. Muckley), Leiden: Martinus Nijhoff.

Fama, E. (1976), *Foundations of Finance*, New York: Basic Books.

Fama, E. (1970), "Efficient Capital Markets: A Review of Theory and Empirical Work", *Journal of Finance* 25: 383–417.

Fama, E. (1965), "The Behavior of Stock Market Prices", *Journal of Business* 38: 34–105.

Fama, E., L. Fisher, M. Jensen, and R. Roll (1969), "The Adjustment of Stock Prices to New Information", *International Economic Review* 10: 1–21.

Fama, E. and K. French (2001), "Disappearing Dividends: Changing Firm Characteristics or Lower Propensity to Pay?", *Journal of Financial Economics* 60: 3–43.

Fatemi, A. and R. Bildik (2012), "Yes, Dividends are Disappearing: Worldwide Evidence", *Journal of Banking & Finance* 36: 662–667.

Feaveryear, A. (1931), *The Pound Sterling, A History of English Money*, London: Oxford University Press.

Ferris, S., N. Sen and E. Unlu (2009), "An International Analysis of Dividend Behavior", *Journal of Business Finance & Accounting* 36: 496–522.

Fetter, F.W. (1975), "The Influence of Economists in Parliament on British Legislation from Ricardo to John Stuart Mill", *Journal of Political Economy* 83: 1051–1064.

Fetter, F. (1937), "Reformulation of the Concepts of Capital and Income in Economics and Accounting", *Accounting Review* 12: 3–12.

Fetter, F. (1907), "The Nature of Capital and Income", *Journal of Political Economy* 15: 129–148.

Fetter, F. (1900), "Recent Discussion of the Capital Concept", *Quarterly Journal of Economics* 15: 1–45.

Financial Accounting Standards Board (FASB) (2000), *Accounting for Certain Derivative Instruments and Certain Hedging Activities—An Amendment of FASB Statement No. 133*, Statement of Financial Accounting Standard 138 (June), Stamford, CT: FASB.

Financial Accounting Standards Board (FASB) (1998), *Accounting for Derivatives and Hedging Activities*, Statement of Financial Accounting Standard 133 (June), Stamford, CT: FASB.

Finley, M. (1981), "Debt-Bondage and the Problem of Slavery", pp. 150–166 in B. Shaw and R. Saller (eds.), *Economy and Society in Ancient Greece*, London: Chatto and Windus.

Finley, M. (1973), *The Ancient Economy* (2nd ed. 1985), London: Hogarth.

Finley, M. (1953), "Land, Debt, and the Man of Property in Classical Athens", *Political Science Quarterly* 68: 249–268.

Fisch, J. (2009), "Top Cop or Regulatory Flop? The SEC at 75", *Virginia Law Review* 95: 785–823.

Fisher, I. (1939), "Review of 'Common-Stock Indexes, 1871–1937' by Alfred Cowles", *Journal of Political Economy* 47: 431–433.

Fisher, I. (1930a), *The Theory of Interest: As Determined by Impatience to Spend Income and Opportunity to Invest in It*, New York: Macmillan.

Fisher, I. (1930b), *The Stock Market Crash—and After*, New York: Macmillan.

Fisher, I. (1912), *How to Invest When Prices are Rising*, Scranton, PA: Lynn Sumner.

Fisher, I. (1907), *The Rate of Interest: Its Nature, Determination and Relation to Economic Phenomena*, New York: Macmillan.

Fisher, I. (1906), *The Nature of Capital and Income*, New York: Augustus Kelly; 1965 reprint.

Fisher, I. (1904), "Precedents for Defining Capital", *Quarterly Journal of Economics* 18: 386–408.

Fisher, I. (1896), "What Is Capital?", *Economic Journal* 6: 509–534.

Fisher, P. (1980), *Developing an Investment Philosophy*, Charlottesville, VA: Financial Analysts Research Foundation.

Fisher, P. (1958), *Common Stocks and Uncommon Profits* (revised ed. 1960), New York: Harper and Row.

Fitzpatrick, M. (2011), "Provincializing Rome: The Indian Ocean Trade Network and Roman Imperialism", *Journal of World History* 22: 27–54.

Flegg, G., C. Hay, and B. Moss (eds.) (1985), *Nicholas Chuquet, Renaissance Mathematician. A Study With Extensive Translation of Chuquet's Mathematical Manuscript Completed in 1484*, Boston, MA: Reidel.

Flesher, D.L. (1977), "Modernization of Internal Audit: From Fraud Detection to Operations Auditing", *Accountant*, 177 (August 18): 190–191.

Forbes, K. (1986), "Limited Liability and the Development of the Business Corporation", *Journal of Law, Economics, & Organization* 2: 163–177.

Fortier, M. (2005), *The Culture of Equity in Early Modern England*, Aldershot, Hants, UK: Ashgate.

Fotheringham, J.K. (1910), "Genoa and the Fourth Crusade", *English Historical Review* 25: 26–57.

Franci, R. and T. Rigatelli (1988), "Fourteenth-Century Italian Algebra", pp. 11–29 in C. Hay (ed.), *Mathematics from Manuscript to Print, 1300–1600*, Oxford, UK: Clarendon.

Francis, J. (1850), *Chronicles and Characters of the Stock Exchange* (1st American ed.), Boston, MA: Crosby and Nichols.

Frank, T. (1927), *An Economic History of Rome* (2nd ed.), New York: Cooper Square; 1962 reprint.

Frankfurter, G. (1999), "What Is the Puzzle in the 'Dividend Puzzle'?", *Journal of Portfolio Management* 26 (Summer): 76–85.

Franklin, C. and M. Colberg (1958), "Puts and Calls: A Factual Survey", *Journal of Finance* 13: 21–34.

Freedeman, C. (1965), "Joint-Stock Business Organization in France, 1807–1867", *Business History Review* 39: 184–204.

Frickey, E. (1921), "An Index of Industrial Stock Prices", *Review of Economics and Statistics* 3: 264–277.

Fridson, M. (ed.) (1996), *Extraordinary Popular Delusions and the Madness of Crowds; and, Confusion de Confusiones* (reprints of classic texts), New York: Wiley.

Funnell, W. and J. Robertson (2011), "Capitalist Accounting in Sixteenth Century Holland: Hanseatic Influences and the Sombart Thesis", *Accounting, Auditing and Accountability Journal* 24: 560–586.

Gadamer, H.-G. (1960), *Truth and Method*, New York: Seabury Press; reprint (1975), translation of the second German edition of (1965).

Garbutt, D. (1984), "The Significance of Ancient Mesopotamia in Accounting History", *Accounting Historians Journal* 11: 83–101.

Gasparini, S. (2014), "The Early Civil Statutes: *Codex Marciano Latinus*", *Pax Tibi Marce—Venice: Government, Law, Jurisprudence*, obtained from www.arielcaliban.org/paxtibimarce.html

Gatto, M., R. Geske, R. Litzenberger, and H. Sosin (1980), "Mutual Fund Insurance", *Journal of Financial Economics* 8: 283–317.

Geggus, D. (2001), "The French Slave Trade: An Overview", *William and Mary Quarterly* 58: 119–138.

Geisst, C. (1997), *Wall Street, a History*, New York: Oxford University Press.

Gelderblom, O. (2013), *Cities of Commerce: The Institutional Foundations of International Trade in the Low Countries, 1250–1650*, Princeton, NJ: Princeton University Press.

Gelderblom, O., A. de Jong, and J. Jonker (2013), "The Formative Years of the Modern Corporation: The Dutch East India Company VOC, 1602–1623", *Journal of Economic History* 73: 1050–1076.

Gelderblom, O., A. de Jong, and J. Jonker (2012), "The Formative Years of the Modern Corporation: The Dutch East India Company, 1602–1623", *Mimeo* (June).

Gelderblom, O., A. de Jong, and J. Jonker (2011), "An Admiralty for Asia. Isaac le Maire and Conflicting Conceptions About the Corporate Governance of the VOC", in J. Koppell (ed.), *The Origins of Shareholder Advocacy*, New York: Palgrave Macmillan.

Gelderblom, O. and J. Jonker (2005), "Amsterdam as the Cradle of Modern Futures and Options Trading, 1550–1630", chapter 11 in W. Goetzmann and K. Rouwenhorst (eds.), *The Origins of Value*, Oxford, UK: Oxford University Press.

Gelderblom, O. and J. Jonker (2004), "Completing a Financial Revolution: The Finance of the Dutch East India Trade and the Rise of the Amsterdam Capital Market, 1595–1612", *Journal of Economic History* 64: 641–672.

Ghosh, C. and J. Woolridge (1988), "An Analysis of Shareholder Reaction to Dividend Cuts and Omissions", *Journal of Financial Research* 11: 281–294.

Gibb, D. (1957), *Lloyd's of London, a Study in Individualism*, London: Macmillan.

Giffen, R. (1877), *Stock Exchange Securities: An Essay on the General Causes of Fluctuations in Their Prices*, New York: Augustus M. Kelley Publishers.

Gilboa, A. (2005), "Sea Peoples and Phoenicians Along the Southern Phoenician Coast: A Reconciliation: An Interpretation of Šikila (SKL) Material Culture", *Bulletin of the American Schools of Oriental Research* 337: 47–78.

Gilson, R. and J. Gordon (2013), "The Agency Costs of Agency Capitalism: Activist Investors and the Revaluation of Governance Rights", *Columbia Law Review* 113: 863–927.

Glaeser, E. and J. Scheinkman (1998), "Neither a Borrower Nor a Lender Be: An Economic Analysis of Interest Restrictions and Usury Laws", *Journal of Law & Economics* 41: 1–36.

Goetzmann, W., J. Ingersoll, and S. Ross (2003), "High Water Marks and Hedge Fund Management Contracts", *Journal of Finance* 58: 1685–1718.

Goetzmann, W., L. Li, and K.G. Rouwenhorst (2005), "Long-Term Global Market Correlations", *Journal of Business* 78: 1–38.

Goitein, S. (1964), "Commercial and Family Partnership in the Countries of Medieval Islam", *Islamic Studies* 3: 315–337.

Goitein, S. (1960), "The Documents of the Cairo Geniza as a Source for Mediterranean Social History", *Journal of the American Oriental Society* 80: 91–100.

Goitein, S. (1955), "The Cairo Geniza as a Source for the History of Muslim Civilisation", *Studia Islamica* 3: 75–91.

Goldthwaite, R. (2009), *The Economy of Renaissance Florence*, Baltimore: Johns Hopkins University Press.

Gonzalez de Lara, Y. (2008), "The Secret of Venetian Success: A Public-Order, Reputation-Based Institution", *European Review of Economic History* 12: 247–285.

Gonzalez de Lara, Y. (2002), "Institutions for Contract Enforcement and Risk-Sharing: From the Sea Loan to the '*commenda*' in Late Medieval Venice", *European Review of Economic History* 6: 257–262.

Gordon, J.S. (1999), *The Great Game, the Emergence of Wall Street as a World Power 1653–2000*, New York: Scribner.

Gordon, M. (1962), *The Investment Financing and Valuation of the Corporation*, Homewood, IL: Irwin.

Gordon, W. and O. Robinson (trans.) (1988), *The Institutes of Gaius*, London: Duckworth.

Graham, B. and D. Dodd (1934), *Security Analysis*, New York: McGraw-Hill.

Graham, B., D. Dodd, and S. Cottle (1962), *Security Analysis* (4th ed.), New York: McGraw-Hill.

Green, W. (1930), *History and Survey of Accountancy*, Brooklyn, NY: Standard Text Press; reprinted pp. 39–47 in M. Chatfield, *A History of Accounting Thought*, Hillsdale, IL: Dryden Press (1968).

Greene, K. (2011), "Technological Innovation and Economic Progress in the Ancient World: M.I. Finley Re-Considered", *Economic History Review* 64: 1218–1241.

Greene, N., A. Aziz, and G. Liersaph (2007), "Hedge Fund Organizational Decisions and How They Affect the Sponsor's Compliance Needs", *Journal of Securities Compliance* 1: 247–259.

Greenwald, B., J. Kahn, P. Sonkin, and M. van Biema (2001), *Value Investing, From Graham to Buffett and Beyond*, New York: Wiley.

Greif, A. (2012), "The Maghribi Traders: A Reappraisal?", *Economic History Review* 65: 445–469.

Greif, A. (1994), "On the Political Foundations of the Late Medieval Commercial Revolution: Genoa during the Twelfth and Thirteenth Centuries", *Journal of Economic History* 54: 271–287.

Greif, A. (1991), "The Organization of Long-Distance Trade: Reputation and Coalitions in the Geniza Documents and Genoa During the Eleventh and Twelfth Centuries", *Journal of Economic History* 51: 459–462.

Greif, A. (1989), "Reputation and Coalitions in Medieval Trade: Evidence on the Maghribi Traders' ", *Journal of Economic History* 49: 857–882.

Grice-Hutchinson, M. (1952), *The School of Salamanca, Readings in Spanish Monetary History, 1544–1605*, Oxford, UK: Clarendon Press.

Griffin, J. and J. Xu (2009), "How Smart Are the Smart Guys? A Unique View from Hedge Fund Stock Holdings", *Review of Financial Studies* 22: 2531–2570.

Grullon, G. and R. Michaely (2002), "Dividends. Share Repurchases and the Substitution Hypothesis", *Journal of Finance* 57: 1649–1684.

Guild, S.E. (1931), *Stock Growth and Discount Tables*, Boston, MA: Financial Publishing Company.

Gumbel, E.J., J. Greenwood, and D. Durand (1953), "The Circular Normal Distribution: Theory and Tables", *Journal of the American Statistical Association* 48: 131–152.

Guinnane, T., R. Harris, N.R. Lamoreaux, and J. Rosenthal (2007), "Putting the Corporation in Its Place", *Enterprise and Society* 8: 687–729.

Haar, C. (1941), "Legislative Regulation of New York Industrial Corporations, 1800–1850", *New York History* 22: 191–207.

Habermas, J. (1989), *Structural Transformation of the Public Sphere*, Cambridge, MA: MIT Press.

Hafner, W. and H. Zimmerman (2009), *Vincenz Bronzin's Option Pricing Models: Exposition and Appraisal*, New York: Springer-Verlag.

Hagstrom, R. (2000), *The Warren Buffett Portfolio*, New York: John Wiley.

Hagstrom, R. (1995), *The Warren Buffett Way—Investment Strategies of the World's Greatest Investor*, New York: John Wiley.

Hakluyt, R. (1885), *The Principal Navigations, Voyages, Traffiques and Discoveries of the English Nation, Northern Europe* (vol. 1), E. Goldsmid (ed.), Edinburgh: E & G. Goldsmid.

Hall, P. and D. Soskice (eds.) (2001), *Varieties of Capitalism: The Institutional Foundations of Comparative Advantage*, Oxford, UK: Oxford University Press.

Halpern, P. (1998), "Limited and Extended Liability Regimes", in P. Newman (ed.), *The New Palgrave Dictionary of Economics and Law*, New York: Stockton Press.

Halpern, P., M. Trebilcock, and S. Turnbull (1980), "An Economic Analysis of Limited Liability in Corporation Law", *University of Toronto Law Journal* 30: 117–150.

Hamilton, W. (1922), *The Stock Market Barometer*, New York: Barrons.

Hamilton, W. (1919), "The Institutional Approach to Economic Theory", *American Economic Review* 9: 309–318.

Hamouda, O. and B. Price (1997), "The Justice of the Just Price", *European Journal of the History of Economic Thought* 4: 191–216.

Handlin, O. and M. Handlin (1945), "Origins of the American Business Corporation", *Journal of Economic History* 5: 1–23.

Hannah, L. (2007), "Pioneering Modern Corporate Governance: A View from London in 1900", *Enterprise and Society* 8: 642–646.

Hansmann, H., R. Kraakman, and R. Squire (2006), "Law and the Rise of the Firm", *Harvard Law Review* 119: 1333–1403.

Harling, P. (1995), "Rethinking Old Corruption", *Past & Present* 147: 127–158.

Harold, G. (1934), "A Reconsideration of the Common-Stock Theory", *Journal of Business of the University of Chicago* 7: 42–59.

Harris, R. (2000), *Industrializing English Law: Entrepreneurship and Business Organization, 1720–1844*, Cambridge, UK: Cambridge University Press.

Harris, R. (1994), "The Bubble Act: Its Passage and Its Effects on Business Organization", *Journal of Economic History* 54 (September): 610–627.

Harrison, P. (2001), "Rational Equity Valuation at the Time of the South Sea Bubble", *History of Political Economy* 33: 269–281.

Hattox, R. (1985), *Coffee and Coffeehouses: The Origins of a Social Beverage in the Medieval Near East*, Seattle: University of Washington Press.

Hautcoeur, P. (1997), "Le marche financier entre 1870 et 1900", pp.235–265 in Yves Brenton, Albert Broder and Michel Lutfalla (eds.), *La longue Stagnation en France*, Paris: Economica.

Hautcoeur, P. and M. Petit-Konczyk (2006), "Why and How to Measure Stock Market Fluctuations: The Early History of Stock Market Indices, with Special Reference to the French Case", *Mimeo*.

Hawley, J. and A. Williams (2000), *The Rise of Fiduciary Capitalism: How Institutional Investors Can Make Corporate America More Democratic*, Philadelphia: University of Pennsylvania Press.

Hay, C. (ed.) (1988), *Mathematics from Manuscript to Print, 1300–1600*, Oxford, UK: Clarendon.

Hayes, Richard (1726), *The Money'd Man's Guide: Or. The Purchaser's Pocket Companion*, London: Kress-Goldsmith Microfilm Collection.

Hear, C. (1941), "Legislative Regulation of New York Industrial Corporations, 1800–1850", *New York History* 22: 191–207.

Heaton, H. (1937), "Hecksher on Mercantilism", *Journal of Political Economy* 45: 370–393.

Hecksher, E. (1955), *Mercantilism* (2 vols., 2nd ed.) (ed. E. Soderlund from the trans. M. Shapiro, 1935), London: Allen and Unwin.

Heckscher, E. (1936), "Revisions in Economic History: V. Mercantilism", *Economic History Review* VII (Old Series): 44–54.

Heckscher, E. (1931), *Mercantilism* (2 vols., 1st ed.) (trans. M. Shapiro, 1935), London: Allen and Unwin.

Hein, E. (2012), *The Macroeconomics of Finance-Dominated Capitalism and Its Crisis*, Northampton, MA: Edward Elgar.

Henderson, J. (1986), "Agency or Alienation? Smith, Mill, and Marx on the Joint-Stock Company", *History of Political Economy* 18: 111–131.

Hickson, R., J. Turner, and Q. Ye (2011), "The Rate of Return on Equity Across Industrial Sectors on the British Stock Market, 1825–70", *Economic History Review* 64: 1218–1241.

Hilt, E. (2008), When Did Owndership Separate from Control? Corporate Governance in the Early Nineteenth Century", *Journal of Economic History* 68: 645–685.

Hilt, E. and K. O'Banion (2009), "The Limited Partnership in New York 1822–1858: Partnerships Without Kinship", *Journal of Economic History* 69: 615–645.

Holderness, C. (2008), "The Myth of Diffuse Ownership in the United States", *Review of Financial Studies* 22: 1377–1408.

Homer, S. and R. Sylla (1991), *A History of Interest Rates* (3rd ed.), London: Rutgers University Press.

Hong, H. and J. Stein (2003), "Differences of Opinion, Short Sales Constraints and Market Crashes", *Review of Financial Studies* 16: 487–525.

Hoover, C. (1926), "The Sea Loan in Genoa in the Twelfth Century", *Quarterly Journal of Economics* 40: 495–529.

Houghton, J. (1692–1703), *A Collection for Improvement of Husbandry and Trade*, London: Taylor, Hindmarsh, Clavell, Rogers and Brown; reprinted by Gregg International Publishers (1969).

Howard, S. (1938), "Stockholders' Liability Under the New York Act of March 22, 1811", *Journal of Political Economy* 46: 499–514.

Howard, S. (1934), "The Limited Partnership in New Jersey", *Journal of Business of the University of Chicago* 7: 296–317.

Howard, S. (1932), "Business Partnerships in France Before 1807", *Accounting Review* 7: 242–257.

Hudson, M. and M. van de Mieroop (eds.) (2002), *Debt and Economic Renewal in the Ancient Near East*, Bethesda, MD: CDL Press.

Hunt, B. (1936), *The Development of the British Corporation in England, 1800–1867*, Cambridge, MA: Harvard University Press.

Hunt, B. (1935), "The Joint-Stock Company in England, 1800–1825", *Journal of Political Economy* 43: 1–33.

Hutcheson, A. (1720), *Some computations related to the proposed transferring of eighteen millions of the fund of the South Sea company, to the Bank and East India company*, London. Kress-Goldsmith Microfilm Collection.

Hutchison, T. (1988), *Before Adam Smith, the Emergence of Political Economy, 1662–1776*, New York: Basil Blackwell.

Hutson, E. (2005), "The Early Managed Fund Industry: Investment Trusts in 19th Century Britain", *International Review of Financial Analysis* 14: 439–454.

Ireland, P. (2005), "Shareholder Primacy and the Distribution of Wealth", *Modern Law Review* 68: 49–81.

Ireland, P. (1996), "Capitalism Without the Capitalist: The Joint Stock Company Share and the Emergence of the Modern Doctrine of Separate Corporate Personality", *Journal of Legal History* 17: 41–73.

Ireland, P., I. Grigg-Spall, and D. Kelly (1987), "The Conceptual Foundations of Modern Company Law", *Journal of Law and Society* 14 (Critical Legal Studies): 149–165.

Itzkowitz, D. (2002), "Fair Enterprise or Extravagant Speculation: Investment, Speculation, and Gambling in Victorian England", *Victorian Studies* 45: 121–147.

Jackman, W.T. (1916), *The Development of Transportation in Modern England*, Toronto: Cambridge University Press.

Jacks, D. (2007), "Populists Versus Theorists: Futures Markets and the Volatility of Prices", *Explorations in Economic History* 44: 342–362.

Jagannathan, M., C. Stephens, and M. Weisbach (2000), "Financial Flexibility and the Choice Between Dividends and Stock Repurchases", *Journal of Financial Economics* 57: 355–384.

Jamieson, R. (2001), "The Essence of Commodification: Caffeine Dependencies in the Early Modern World", *Journal of Social History* 35: 269–294.

Johnson, E. (1937), *Predecessors of Adam Smith*, New York: Augustus Kelley; reprint (1960).

Jones, E. (1921), *The Trust Problem in the United States*, New York: Macmillan.

Jones, S. and S. Ville (1996), "Theory and Evidence: Understanding Chartered Trading Companies", *Journal of Economic History* 56: 925–926.

Jovanovic, F. (2006b), "A Nineteenth-Century Random Walk: Jules Regnault and the Origins of Scientific Financial Economics", chapter 8, pp.169–190, in G. Poitras (ed.), *Pioneers of Financial Economics*, (vol 1), Cheltham, UK: Edward Elgar.

Jovanovic, F. (2006), "Economic Instruments and theory in the construction of Henri Lefevre's 'science of the stock market'", chapter 8, pp.169–190, in G. Poitras (ed.), *Pioneers of Financial Economics* (vol. 1), Cheltham, UK: Edward Elgar.

Kahle, K, M. (2002), "When a Buyback Isn't a Buyback; Open Market Repurchases and Employee Options", *Journal of Financial Economics* 63: 235–261.

Katzenbach, N. (1987), "An Overview of Program Trading and It's Impact on Current Market Prices", *New York Stock Exchange Report* (December 21), New York: NYSE.

Kellenbenz, H. (1957), "Introduction" to Confusion of Confusions: Portions Descriptive of the Amsterdam Stock Exchange" as selected and translated by Hermann Kellenbenz., reprinted in Martin Fridson (ed.) (1996), *Extraordinary Popular Delusions and the Madness of Crowds & Confusion of Confusions*, New York: John Wiley & Sons: pp. 125–46.

Kent, C. (1903), "The Recently Discovered Civil Code of Hammurabi", *Biblical World* 21: 175–190.

Kerr, C. (1929), "The Origin and Development of the Law Merchant", *Virginia Law Review* 15: 350–367.

Kessler, A. (2003), "Limited Liability in Context: Lessons from the French Origins of the American Limited Partnership", *Journal of Legal Studies* 32: 511–548.

Kessler, D. and P. Temin (2007), "The Organization of the Grain Trade in the Early Roman Empire", *Economic History Review* 60: 313–332.

Keynes, J.M. (1936), *The General Theory of Employment, Interest and Money*, New York: Harcourt, Brace, Jovanovich/Harbinger; reprint (1964).

Khorana, A., H. Servaes, and P. Tufano (2009), "Mutual Fund Fees Around the World", *Review of Financial Studies* 22: 1279–1310.

Kim, J. (2011), "How Modern Banking Originated: The London Goldsmith-Bankers' Institutionalisation of Trust", *Business History* 53: 939–959.

Kindleberger, C. (1993), *A Financial History of Western Europe* (2nd ed.), New York: Oxford University Press.

Kirshner, J. (ed.) (1974), *Business, Banking and Economic Thought, Selected Studies of Raymond de Roover*, Chicago: University of Chicago Press.

Klapisch-Zuber, C. (1997), "Nobles or Pariahs? The Exclusion of Florentine Magnates from the Thirteenth to the Fifteenth Centuries", *Comparative Studies in Society and History* 39: 215–230.

Kleer, R. (2015), "Riding a Wave: The Company's Role in the South Sea Bubble", *Economic History Review* 68: 264–285.

Kleer, R. (2012), " 'The Folly of Particulars': The Political Economy of the South Sea Bubble", *Financial History Review* 19: 175–197.

Klein, L. (1996), "Coffeehouse Civility, 1660–1714: An Aspect of Post-Courtly Culture in England", *Huntington Library Quarterly* 59: 30–51.

Klein, M. (2001), *Rainbow's End, the Crash of 1929*, New York: Oxford University Press.

Kniep, F. (1896), *Societas Publicanorum* (vol. 1), Jena: Verlag von Gustav Filcher.

Kool, M. (1988), "What Could We Learn from Master Christianus van Varenbraken? A Note on an Arithmetic Manuscript of a Sixteenth Century Flemish Schoolmaster", pp.150–55 in C. Hay (ed.), *Mathematics from Manuscript to Print, 1300–1600*, Oxford, UK: Clarendon Press.

Koopmans, T. (1947), "Measurement Without Theory", *Review of Economics and Statistics* 29: 161–172.

Koyama, M. (2010), "Evading the 'Taint of Usury': The Usury Prohibition as a Barrier to Entry", *Explorations in Economic History* 47: 420–442.

Krueger, H. (1933), "Genoese Trade With Northwest Africa in the Twelfth Century", *Speculum* 8: 385–390.

Langevoort, D. (1985), "Information Technology and the Structure of Securities Regulation", *Harvard Law Review* 98: 747-804.

Langholm, O. (1998), *The Legacy of Scholasticism in Economic Thought. Antecedents of Choice and Power*, Cambridge, UK: Cambridge University Press.

Langholm, O. (1979), *Price and Value in the Aristotelian Tradition. A Study in Scholastic Economic Sources*, Bergen: Universitetsforlaget.

Lapidus, A. (1991), "Information and Risk in the Medieval Doctrine of Usury", chapter 2 in W. Barber (ed.), *Perspectives on the History of Economic Thought* (vol. 5, Themes in Pre-Classical, Classical and Marxian Economics), Aldershot, UK: Edward Elgar.

Larsen, M. (1977), "Partnerships in Old Assyrian Trade", *Iraq* 39: 119–146.

Larsen, M. (1976), *The Old Assyrian City-State and Its Colonies*, Copenhagen: Akademisk Forlag.

Lee, B. and O. Rui (2007), "Time-Series Behavior of Share Repurchases and Dividends", *Journal of Financial and Quantitative Analysis* 42: 119–142.

Lee, G. (1977), "The Coming of Age of Double Entry: The Giovanni Farolfi Ledger of 1299–1300", *Accounting Historians Journal* 4: 79–95.

Lee, R. (1998), *What Is an Exchange?*, Oxford, UK: Oxford University Press.

Lee, T. (1971), "The Historical Development of Internal Control from the Earliest Times to the End of the Seventeenth Century", *Journal of Accounting Research* 8 (Spring): 150–157.

Lefèvre, E. (1923), *Reminiscences of a Stock Operator*, New York: D.H. Doran.

Leland, H. (1980), "Who Should Buy Portfolio Insurance", *Journal of Finance* 35: 581–596.

Letwin, W. (1964), *The Origins of Scientific Economics*, New York: Doubleday.

Levi, M. and P. Sercu (1991), "Erroneous and Valid Reasons for Hedging Foreign Exchange Rate Exposure", *Journal of Multinational Financial Management* 1: 25–37.

Levitt, A. (2006), "The SEC at the Crossroads", *Columbia Law Review, Symposium: Litigation Reform since the PSLRA: A Ten-Year Retrospective*, 106: 1483–1488.

Lewin, C. (2003), *Pensions and Insurance Before 1880: A Social History*, East Lothian, Scotland: Tuckwell Press.

Lewin, C. (1970), "An Early Book on Compound Interest—Richard Witt's Arithmeticall Questions", *Journal of the Institute of Actuaries* 96: 121–132.

Lillywhite, B. (1963), *London Coffee Houses; A Reference Book of Coffee Houses of the Seventeenth, Eighteenth and Nineteenth Centuries*, London: Allen and Unwin.

Lintner, J. (1956), "Distribution of Incomes of Corporations among Dividends, Retained Earnings, and Taxes", *American Economic Review* 46: 97–113.

Livermore, S. (1935), "Unlimited Liability in Early American Corporations", *Journal of Political Economy* 43: 674–687.

512   *References*

Locke, J. (1695), *Further Considerations Concerning Raising the Value of Money. In Several Papers Relating to Money. Interest, and Trade.* London: Printed for A. and J. Churchill at the Black Swan in Pater-Noster-Row; reprints of Economic Classics Series. New York: Kelley (1989).

Locke, J. (1691), *Some Considerations of the Consequences of the Lowering of Interest, and Raising the Value of Money.* London: Printed for A. and J. Churchill at the Black Swan in Pater-Noster-Row; reprints of Economic Classics Series. New York: Kelley (1989).

Loftus, D. (2002), "Capital and Community: Limited Liability and Attempts to Democratize the Market in Mid-Nineteenth-Century England", *Victorian Studies* 45: 93–120.

Love, J.R. (1991), *Antiquity and Capitalism*, New York: Routledge.

Lowenfeld, H. (1909), *Investment an Exact Science* (revised and enlarged 2nd ed., 1st ed. 1907), London: The Investment Registry, Ltd.

Lowenstein, R. (1995), *Buffett*, New York: Random House.

Macaulay, F. (1938), *The Movement of Interest Rates, Bonds, Yields and Stock Prices in the United States Since 1865*, New York: National Bureau of Economic Research.

Macaulay, F. and D. Durand (1951), *Short Selling on the New York Stock Exchange*, New York: Twentieth Century Fund.

Macdonald, D. (2015), *The Wealth Advantage: The Growing Wealth Gap between Canada's Affluent and Middle Class* (June). Ottawa: Canadian Centre for Policy Alternatives.

Machlup, F. (1940), *The Stock Market, Credit and Capital Formation*, New York: Macmillan Company.

Mackay, C. (1852), *Extraordinary Popular Delusions and the Madness of Crowds* (2nd ed.). London: Richard Bentley; reprinted by New York: Bonanza Books (1980); first edition (1841).

Mackay, C. (1841), *Extraordinary Popular Delusions and the Madness of Crowds*, London: Richard Bentley.

Macleod, C. (1986), "The 1690s Patents Boom: Invention or Stock Jobbing?", *Economic History Review* 39: 549–571.

Madden, T. (1993), "Vows and Contracts in the Fourth Crusade: The Treaty of Zara and the Attack on Constantinople in 1204", *International History Review* 15: 441–468.

Maier, P. (1993), "The Revolutionary Origins of the American Corporation", *William and Mary Quarterly, Law and Society in Early America* 50 (1): 51–84.

Malmendier, U. (2009), "Law and Finance 'at the Origin'", *Journal of Economic Literature* 47: 1076–1108.

Maloney, R. (1971), "Usury in Greek, Roman and Rabbinic Thought", *Traditio* 27: 79–109.

Malynes, G. (1622), *Consuetudo, vel Lex Mercatoria or the Ancient Law Merchant Divided Into Three Parts According to the Essential Parts of Trafficke* (1st ed.), London: A. Islip; reprinted by Norwood NJ: Walter Johnson Inc. (1979).

Mann, S. (2008), "Too Far Over the Hedge: Why the SEC's Attempt to Further Regulate Hedge Funds Had to Fail and What, If Any, Alternative Solutions Should be Considered?" *St. John's Law Review* 82: 315–357.

Markham, J. and D. Harty (2008), "For Whom the Bell Tolls: The Demise of Exchange Trading Floors and the Growth of ECNs", *Journal of Corporation Law* 33: 865–939.

Markowitz, H. (1999), "The Early History of Portfolio Theory", *Financial Analysts Journal* 55 (July/August): 5–16.

Markowitz, H. (1959), *Portfolio Selection: Efficient Diversification of Investments*, New York: John Wiley.

Markowitz, H. (1952), "Portfolio Selection", *Journal of Finance* 7: 77–91.

Martinelli, A. (1977), "Business Ventures in Genoa during the Twelfth Century (1156–1158)", *Accounting Historians Journal* 4: 55–68.

Mattessich, R. (1987), "Prehistoric Accounting and the Problem of Representation: On Recent Archeological Evidence of the Middle-East From 8000 B.C. to 3000 B.C.", *Accounting Historians Journal* 14: 71–91.

May, A.W. (1939), "American and European Valuation of Equity Capital: A Comparison", *American Economic Review* 29: 734–745.

McCartney, S. and A.J. Arnold (2003), "The Railway Mania of Market Irrationality or Collusive Swindle Based on Accounting Distortions?" *Accounting, Auditing and Accountability Journal* 16: 821–852.

McCloskey, D. (1997), "Other Things Equal: Polanyi Was Right, and Wrong", *Eastern Economic Journal* 23: 483–487.

McCloskey, D. (1985), *The Rhetoric of Economics*, Maidson, WI: University of Wisconsin Press.

McCraw, T. (1982), "With Consent of the Governed: SEC's Formative Years", *Journal of Policy Analysis and Management* 1: 346–370.

McCusker, J. (1979), *Money and Exchange in Europe and America, 1600–1775*, Chapel Hill, NC: University of North Carolina Press.

McRae, T. (1965), "Accountancy Training in Scotland", *Journal of Accounting Research* 3: 255–260.

Means, G. (1930), "The Diffusion of Stock Ownership in the United States", *Quarterly Journal of Economics* 44: 561–600.

Medbery, J. (1870), *Men and Mysteries of Wall Street*, New York: Greenwood Press; reprint (1968).

Melitz, Jacques (1971), "Some Further Reassessment of the Scholastic Doctrine of Usury", *Kyklos* 24: 473–491.

Melville, L. (1921), *The South Sea Bubble*, London: D. O'Connor; reprinted by New York: Burt Franklin (1968).

Merton, R. (1987), "In Honor of Nobel Laureate, Franco Modigliani", *Journal of Economic Perspectives* 1: 145–155.

Merton, R. (1973a), "The Theory of Rational Option Pricing", *Bell Journal of Economics and Management Science* 3: 141–183.

Merton, R. (1973b), "An Intertemporal Capital Asset Pricing Model", *Econometrica* 41: 867–887.

Merton, R. (1969), "Lifetime Portfolio Selection: The Continuous Time Case", *Review of Economics and Statistics* 51: 247–257.

Michie, R. (2012), "The Stock Market and the Corporate Economy", chapter 2, pp.28–67 in G. Poitras (ed.), *Stock Market Globalization Research Handbook*, Northampton, MA: Edward Elgar.

Michie, R. (1999), *The London Stock Exchange: A History*, Oxford, UK: Oxford University Press.

Michie, R. (1986), "The London and New York Stock Exchanges, 1850–1914", *Journal of Economic History* 46: 171–187.

Miller, M. and F. Modigliani (1961), "Dividend Policy, Growth and the Valuation of Shares", *Journal of Business* 34: 411–433.

Mills, G. (1994), "Early Accounting in Northern Italy: The Role of Commercial Development and the Printing Press in the Expansion of Double-Entry from Genoa, Florence and Venice", *Accounting Historians Journal* 21: 81–96.

Millon, D. (1990), "Theories of the Corporation", *Duke Law Journal* 201: 220–29.

Minton, R. (1975), *John Law, the Father of Paper Money*, New York: Association Press.

Miskimin, H. (1975), *The Economy of Early Renaissance Europe 1300–1460*, London: Cambridge University Press.

Mitchell, W.C. (1916), "A Critique of Index Numbers of the Prices of Stocks", *Journal of Political Economy* 24: 625–693.

Mitchell, W.C. (1910), "The Prices of American Stocks: 1890–1909", *Journal of Political Economy* 18: 345–380.

Mizruchi, M. (2004), "Berle and Means Revisited: The Governance and Power of Large U.S. Corporations", *Theory and Society* 33: 579–617.

Modigliani, F. and M. Miller (1958), "The Cost of Capital, Corporation Finance and the Theory of Investment", *American Economic Review* 48: 261–297.

Monsalve, F. (2014a), "Late Spanish Doctors on Usury, and the Evolving Scholastic Tradition", *Journal of the History of Economic Thought* 36: 215–235.

Monsalve, F. (2014b), "Scholastic Just Price versus Current Market Price: Is It Merely a Matter of Labelling?", *European Journal of the History of Economic Thought* 21: 4–20.

Morgan, V. and W. Thomas (1962), *The Stock Exchange*, New York: St. Martin's.

Mortimer, T. (1761), *Everyman His Own Broker; Or a Guide to Exchange Alley* (2nd ed.) (With the 13th ed. Published 1801), London: S. Hooper.

Most, K. (1976), "How Wrong Was Sombart?", *Accounting Historians Journal* 3: 22–28.

Muhly, J. (1973), *Copper and Tin: The Distribution of Mineral Resources and the Nature of the Metals Trade in the Bronze Age*, Hamden, CT: Connecticut Academy of Arts and Sciences.

Munro, J. (1998), "English 'Backwardness' and Financial Innovations in Commerce With the Low Countries, 14th to 16th Centuries", *University of Toronto Working Paper*, UT-ECIPA-MUNRO5-98–06.

Murphy, A. (2009a), *The Origins of English Financial Markets, Investment and Speculation before the South Sea Bubble*, Cambridge, UK: Cambridge University Press.

Murphy, A. (2009b), "Trading Options Before Black Scholes: A Study of the Market in Late Seventeenth Century London", *Economic History Review* 62 (S1): 8–30.

Murphy, A. (1997), *John Law, Economic Theorist and Policy-Maker*, Oxford, UK: Clarendon Press.

Murphy, A. (1991), "The Evolution of John Law's Theories and Policies 1707–1715", *European Economic Review* 34: 1109–1125.

Murphy, A. (1986), *Richard Cantillon, Entrepreneur and Economist*, Oxford, UK: Clarendon Press.

Murray, D. (1930), *Chapters in the History of Bookkeeping, Accountancy and Commercial Arithmetic*, Glasgow; reprinted by New York: Arno Press (1978).

Musacchio, A. and J. Turner (2013), "Does the Law and Finance Hypothesis Pass the Test of History?", *Business History* 55: 524–542.

Nader, H. (2002), "Desperate Men, Questionable Acts: The Moral Dilemma of Italian Merchants in the Spanish Slave Trade", *Sixteenth Century Journal* 33: 401–422.

Nadri, G. (2007), "The Maritime Merchants of Surat: A Long-Term Perspective", *Journal of the Economic and Social History of the Orient* 50: 235–258.

Neal, L. (2012), *'I am not master of events': The Speculation of John Law and Lord Londonderry in the Mississippi and South Sea Bubbles*, New Haven, CT: Yale University Press.

Neal, L. (1998), "The Financial Crisis of 1825 and the Restructuring of the British Financial System", *Federal Reserve Bank of St. Louis Review* 80 (May/June): 53–77.

Neal, L. (1990a), "How the South Sea Bubble Was Blown Up and Burst: A New Look at Old Data", in E. White (ed.), *Crashes and Panics*, New York: Dow Jones-Irwin.

Neal, L. (1990b), *The Rise of Financial Capitalism: International Capital Markets in the Age of Reason*, Cambridge, UK: Cambridge University Press.

Neal, L. (1988), "The Rise of a Financial Press: London and Amsterdam, 1681–1810", *Business History* 30: 163–179.

Neal, L. and J. Williamson (eds.) (2014), *The Cambridge History of Capitalism*, Cambridge, UK: Cambridge University Press.

Nelli, H. (1972), "The Earliest Insurance Contract. A New Discovery", *Journal of Risk and Insurance* 39: 215–220.

Nelson, H. (1950), "Cato the Younger as a Stoic Orator", *Classical Weekly* 44: 65–69.

Nicolet, C. (1974), *L'ordre equestre d l'epoque republicaine: Prosopographie des chevaliers romains* (vol. 2), Paris: E. de Boccard.

Nicolet, C. (1966), *L'ordre equestre a l'epoque republicaine: Definitions juridiques et structures sociales* (vol. 1), Paris: E. de Boccard.

Nobes, C. and O. Abdullah (2001), "Were Islamic Records Precursors to Accounting Books Based on the Italian Method? A Comment", *Accounting Historians Journal* 28: 207–218.

Noonan, J. (1957), *The Scholastic Analysis of Usury*, Cambridge, MA: Harvard University Press.

North, D.C. (1990), *Institutions, Institutional Change and Economic Performance*, Cambridge, UK: Cambridge University Press.

North, D.C. (1981), *Structure and Change in Economic History*, New York: Norton.

O'Brien, G. (1920), *Essay on Mediaeval Economic Teaching*, London: Longmans, Green, and Co.

Odlyzko, A. (2011), "The Collapse of the Railway Mania, the Development of Capital Markets, and the Forgotten Role of Robert Lucas Nash", *Accounting History Review* 21: 301–345.

Oka, R. and C. Kusimba (2008), "The Archaeology of Trading Systems, Part 1: Towards a New Trade Synthesis", *Journal of Archaeological Research* 16: 339–395.

Oldland, J. (2010), "The Allocation of Merchant Capital in Early Tudor London", *Economic History Review* 63: 1058–1080.

Oldroyd, D. (1995), "The Role of Accounting in Public Expenditure and Monetary Policy in the First Century AD Roman Empire", *Accounting Historians Journal* 22: 117–129.

O'Neill, L. (2013), "Dealing with Newsmongers: News, Trust, and Letters in the British World, ca.1670–1730", *Huntington Library Quarterly* 76: 215–233.

Oppenheim, A.L. (1967), "Essay on Overland Trade in the First Millennium", *Journal of Cuneiform Studies* 21: 236–254.

Oppenheim, A.L. (1954), "The Seafaring Merchants of Ur", *Journal of the American Oriental Society* 74: 6–17.

Origo, Iris. (1957), *The Merchant of Prato: Francesco di Marco Datini*, New York: Penguin.

O'Sullivan, M. (2007), "The Expansion of the U.S. Stock Market, 1885–1930: Historical Facts and Theoretical Fashions", *Enterprise and Society* 8: 489–542.

Ott, J. (2008), "When Wall Street Met Main Street: The Quest for an Investors' Democracy and the Emergence of the Retail Investor in the United States, 1890–1930", *Enterprise and Society* 9: 619–630.

Pacioli, Luca (1494), *Summa de arithmetica, geometria, proportioni, et proportionalita*, Tusculano: Paganino (1523 ed.).

Padgett, J. and P. MacLean (2011), "Economic Credit in Renaissance Florence", *Journal of Modern History* 83: 1–47.

Padgett, J. and P. MacLean (2006), "Organizational Invention and Elite Transformation: The Birth of Partnership Systems in Renaissance Florence", *American Journal of Sociology* 111: 1463–1568.

Parker, G. (1974), "The Emergence of Modern Finance in Europe 1500–1730", chapter 7 in C. Cipolla (ed.), *The Fontana Economic History of Europe*, Glasgow, Scotland: Collins.

Parker, R. (1968), "Discounted Cash Flow in Historical Perspective", *Journal of Accounting Research* 6: 58–71.

Patton, A. (2009), "Are 'Market Neutral' Hedge Funds Really Market Neutral?", *Review of Financial Studies* 22: 2495–2530.

Paulo, S. (2003), "Epistemology, Research Methodology, and Rule 702 of the Federal Rules of Evidence vs. EVA", *Journal of Business Ethics* 44: 327–341.

Pearson, T. and J. Pearson (2007), "Protesting Global Financial Market Stability and Integrity: Strengthening SEC Regulation of Hedge Funds", *North Carolina Journal of International Law and Commercial Regulation* 33: 1–82.

Pegolotti, F. (1936), "La Practica della Mercatura", A. Evans (ed.), Cambridge MA: Medieval Academy of America; reprint n. 24.

Pekarek, E. (2007a), "Hogging the Hedge? 'Bulldog's' 13F Theory May Not Be So So Lucky", *Fordham Journal of Cooperate and Financial Law* 12: 1079–1181.

Pekarek, E. (2007b), "Pruning the Hedge: Who is a 'Client' and Whom Does an Advisor Advise?", *Fordham Journal of Corporate and Financial Law* 12: 913–975.

Perdicas, P. (1939), "On History and Outlines of Greek Maritime Law", *Transactions of the Grotius Society* 25: 33–50.

Peri, G. (1638), *Il Negotiante*, Genova : Appresso Gio (1651 printing; last revised edition 1707)

Piketty, T. (2015), "Putting Distribution Back at the Center of Economics: Reflections on Capital in the Twenty-First Century", *Journal of Economic Perspectives* 29: 67–88.

Piketty, T. (2014), *Capital in the Twenty-First Century*, Cambridge, MA: Harvard University Press.

Pincus, S. (1995), "Coffee Politicians Does Create: Coffeehouses and Restoration Political Culture", *Journal of Modern History* 67: 807–834.

Pitts, M. (2001), "In Praise of the 'other' William Armstrong: A Nineteenth Century British Engineer and Early Management Consultant", *Accounting History* 6: 33–58.

Poitras, G. (ed.) (2012), *Handbook of Research on Stock Market Globalization*, Northampton, MA: Edward Elgar.

Poitras, G. (2011), *Valuation of Equity Securities: History, Theory and Application*, New York: World Scientific Publishing.

Poitras, G. (2009), "The Early History of Option Contracts", chapter 18 in W. Hafner and H. Zimmermann (eds.), *Vincenz Bronzin's Option Pricing Models: Exposition and Appraisal*, New York: Springer-Verlag.

Poitras, G. (2007), "Frederick R. Macaulay, Frank M. Redington and the Emergence of Modern Fixed Income Analysis", chapter 4 in G. Poitras (ed.), *Pioneers of Financial Economics* (vol. 2), Northampton, MA: Edward Elgar Publishing.

Poitras, G. (ed.) (2006–7), *Pioneers of Financial Economics* (2 vols.), Cheltenham, UK: Edward Elgar.

Poitras, G. (2005), *Security Analysis and Investment Strategy*, Oxford, UK: Blackwell Publishing.

Poitras, G. (2002), *Risk Management, Speculation and Derivative Securities*, New York: Academic Press.

Poitras, G. (2000), *The Early History of Financial Economics, 1478–1776*, Aldershot, UK: E. Elgar.

Poitras, G. and M. Geranio (2016), "Trading of Shares in the *Societates Publicanorum*?", *Explorations in Economic History* (forthcoming).

Polanyi, K. (1977), *The Livelihood of Man* (ed. H. Pearson), New York: Academic Press.

Polanyi, K. (1966), *Dahomey and the Slave Trade; An Analysis of an Archaic Economy*, Seattle: University of Washington Press.

Polanyi, K. (1957), "Marketless Trading in Hammurabi's Time", pp. 12–26 in *Trade and Markets in the Early Empires: Economies in History and Theory*, K. Polanyi, C. Arensberg, and H. Pearson (eds.), New York: The Free Press.

Pollins, H. (1954), "The Marketing of Railway Shares in the First Half of the Nineteenth Century", *Economic History Review* 7: 230–239.

Pollitt, R. (1973), "John Hawkins's Troublesome Voyages: Merchants, Bureaucrats, and the Origin of the Slave Trade", *Journal of British Studies* 12: 26–40.

Posthumus, N. (1953), *De Oosterse handle te Amsterdam: Het oudst bewaarde koopmansboek van een Amsterdamse vennootschap betereffende de handle op de Oostzee 1485–1490*, Leiden: Brill.

Postlethwayt, M. (1755), *The Universal Dictionary of Trade and Commerce*; John and Paul Napton, London (4th ed. 1774).

Preda, A. (2007), "Rational Investors, Informative Prices: The Emergence of the 'Science of Financial Investments' and the Random Walk Hypothesis", chapter 7, pp. 149–168 in G. Poitras (ed.), *Pioneers of Financial Economics* (vol. II), Northampton, MA: Edward Elgar Publishing.

Preda, A. (2005), "The Rise of the Popular Investor: Financial Knowledge and Investing in England and France, 1840–1880", *Psychology of World Equity Markets* 1: 387–414.

Preda, A. (2004), "Informative Prices, Rational Investors: The Emergence of the Random Walk Hypothesis and the Nineteenth Century 'Science of Financial Investments' ", *History of Political Economy* 36: 351–386.

Preinreich, G. (1932), "Stock Yields, Stock Dividends and Inflation", *Accounting Review* 7: 237–289.

Presidential Working Group on Financial Markets (1999), *Report: "Hedge Funds, Leverage and the Lessons of Long-Term Capital Management"*, Washington, DC: US Government Printing Office.

Previts, G. and B. Merino (1998), *A History of Accountancy in the United States: The Cultural Significance of Accounting*, Columbus, OH: Ohio State University Press.

Pryor, J. (1977), "The Origins of the Commenda Contract", *Speculum* 52: 5–37.

Queller, D. and G. Day (1976), "Some Arguments in Defense of the Venetians on the Fourth Crusade", *American Historical Review* 81: 717–737.

Rathbone, D. (2000), "The 'Muziris' Papyrus (SB XVIII 13167): Financing Roman Trade with India", *Alexandrian Studies II in Honor of Mostafa el Abbadi, Bulletin of the Society for the Archaeology of Alexandria* 4–6: 39–50.

Rauh, N. (1989a), "Finance and Estate Sales in Republican Rome", *Aevum* Anno 63, Fasc. 1: 45–76.

Rauh, N. (1989b), "Auctioneers and the Roman Economy", *Historia: Zeitschrift für Alte Geschichte* 38: 451–471.

Reed, C.G. and C.T. Bekar (2003), "Religious Prohibitions Against Usury", *Explorations in Economic History* 40: 347.

Reed, M. (1975), *Investment in Railways in Britain, 1820–1844: A Study in the Development of the Capital Market*, London: Oxford University Press.

Ribstein, L. and M. Sargent (1997), "Check-the-Box and Beyond: The Future of Limited Liability Entities", *Business Lawyer* 52: 605–652.

Richardson, J. (1976), "The Spanish Mines and the Development of Provincial Taxation in the Second Century", *Journal of Roman Studies* 66: 139–152.

Riemersma, J. (1950), "Government Influence on Company Organization in Holland and England (1550–1650)", *Journal of Economic History* 10 (Supplement): 31–39.

Ripley, W. (1927), *Main Street and Wall Street*, Boston, MA: Little, Brown, and Company.

Robertson, J. and W. Funnell (2012), "The Dutch East-India Company and Accounting for Social Capital at the Dawn of Modern Capitalism 1602–1623", *Accounting, Organizations and Society* 37: 342–360.

Rogers, J. (2014), "A New Era of Fiduciary Capitalism? Let's Hope So: Guest Editorial", *Financial Analysts Journal* 70 (May–June): 6–12.

Rostovtzeff, M. (1957), *The Social and Economic History of the Roman Empire* (vol. 1), Oxford, UK: Oxford University Press.

Rubinstein, M. (2006), "Bruno de Finetti and Mean-Variance Portfolio Selection", *Journal of Investment Management* 4 (Third Quarter).

Rubinstein, M. (2003), "Great Moments in Financial Economics", *Journal of Investment Management* 1 (Second Quarter).

Rubinstein, M. (2002), "Markowitz's 'Portfolio Selection': A Fifty-Year Retrospective", *Journal of Finance* 57: 1041–1046.

Rubinstein, M. (1985), "Alternative Paths to Portfolio Insurance", *Financial Analysts Journal* 41 (July/August): 42–51.

Rubinstein, R. and H. Leland (1981), "Replicating Options with Positions in Stock and Cash", *Financial Analysts Journal* 37 (July/August): 63–72.

Ruckman, K. (2003), "Expense Ratios in North American Mutual Funds", *Canadian Journal of Economics* 36: 192–223.

Rutherford, M. (2001), "Institutional Economics: Then and Now", *Journal of Economic Perspectives* 15: 173–194.

Rutterford, J. (2009), "Learning from One Another's Mistakes: Investment Trusts in the UK and the US, 1868 to 1940", *Financial History Review* 16: 157–81.

Rutterford, J. (2006), "The World Was Their Oyster: International Diversification Pre-World War I", pp. 5–24 in J. Rutterford, M. Upton and D. Kodwani (eds.), *Financial Strategy: Adding Stakeholder Value* (2nd ed.), Chichester, UK: John Wiley.

Rutterford, J. (2004), "From Dividend Yield to Discounted Cash Flow: A History of UK and US Equity Valuation Techniques", *Accounting, Business & Financial History* 14: 115–149.

Santoni, G. (1987), "The Great Bull Markets of 1924–29 and 1982–87; Speculative Bubbles or Economic Fundamentals?", *Federal Reserve Bank of St. Louis Review* (November): 16–29.

Savary des Bruslons, J. (1730), *Dictionnaire Universel de Commerce* (vol. 3), Paris: Chez Jacques Etienne.

Saville, J. (1956), "Sleeping Partnership and Limited Liability 1850–1856", *Economic History Review* 8: 418–433.

Schaede, U. (1989), "Forwards and Futures in Tokugawa-Period Japan", *Journal of Banking & Finance* 13: 487–513.

Schmitthoff, M. (1939), "The Origin of the Joint-Stock Company", *University of Toronto Law Journal* 3: 74–96.

Schumpeter, J. (1954), *History of Economic Analysis* (ed. E. Schumpeter), New York: Oxford University Press.

Schumpeter, J. (1950), *Capitalism, Socialism and Democracy*, New York: Harper Torchbooks.

Scorgie, M. and J. Kennedy (1996), "Who Discovered the Faustmann Condition?", *History of Political Economy* 28: 77–80.

Scott, W. (1912), *The Constitution and Finance of English, Scottish and Irish Joint Stock Companies to 1720* (vol. 2 of 3), Cambridge, UK: Cambridge University Press; reprint (1968).

Scott, W. (1910), *The Constitution and Finance of English, Scottish and Irish Joint Stock Companies to 1720* (vol. 1 of 3), Cambridg, UK e: Cambridge University Press; reprint (1968).

Scramuzza, V. (1937), "Publican Societies in Sicily in 73–71 B.C.", *Classical Philology* 32: 152–155.

Scratchley, A. (1875), *On Average Investment Trusts*, London: John Wiley and Sons.

Securities and Exchange Commission (2003), *Implications of the Growth of Hedge Funds* Washington, DC: Securities and Exchange Commission (Staff Report).

Securities and Exchange Commission (2010a), "Preliminary Findings Regarding the Market Events of May 6, 2010: Report of the Staffs of the CFTC and SEC to the Joint Advisory Committee on Emerging Regulatory Issues", May 18, 2010, Washington, DC.

Securities and Exchange Commission (2010b), "Findings Regarding the Market Events of May 6, 2010: Report of the Staffs of the CFTC and SEC to the Joint Advisory Committee on Emerging Regulatory Issues", Sept. 30, 2010, Washington, DC.

Shannon, H. (1931), "The Coming of General Limited Liability", *Economic History*; reprinted in Carus-Wilson Carus-Wilson, E. (ed.) (1956), *Essays in Economic History*, NewYork: St. Martin's Press, pp. 358–379.

Sharpe, W. (1964), "Capital Asset Prices: A Theory of Market Equilibrium Under Conditions of Risk", *Journal of Finance*, 425–442.

Sharpe, W. (1963), "A Simplified Model of Portfolio Analysis", *Management Science* 9: 277–293.

Sherratt, S. and A. Sherratt (1993), "The Growth of the Mediterranean Economy in the Early First Millennium BC", *World Archaeology* 24: 361–378.

Sherwin-White, A. (1977), "Roman Involvement in Anatolia, 167–88 B.C.", *Journal of Roman Studies* 67: 62–75.

Shiller, R. (2013), "Capitalism and Financial Innovation", *Financial Analysts Journal* 69 (January/February): 21–25.

Siegel, J. (1998), *Stocks for the Long Run, the Definitive Guide to Financial Market Returns and Long-Term Investment Strategies* (2nd ed.), New York: McGraw-Hill.

Silver, M. (1983), "Karl Polanyi and Markets in the Ancient Near East: The Challenge of the Evidence", *Journal of Economic History* 43: 795–829.

Skaist, A. (1994), *The Old Babylonian Loan Contract: Its History and Geography*, Ramat Gan: Bar-Ilan Press.

Smith, A. (1776), *An Inquiry into the Nature and Causes of Wealth of Nations*, M. Blaug (ed.) with an introduction by E. Cannan; reprinted by New York: Modern Library.

Smith, A. (1763), *Lectures in Justice, Police, Revenue and Arms* with an introduction by E. Cannan (1896); reprinted by New York: Augustus Kelly (1964).

Smith, D.E. (1926), "The First Great Commercial Arithmetic", *Isis* 6:41–49.

Smith, D.E. ([1925], 1958), *History of Mathematics* (2 vols.), New York: Dover.

Smith, E. (1931), "Tests Applied to an Index of the Price Level for Industrial Stocks", *Journal of the American Statistical Association* (Supplement March): 127–135.

Smith, E. (1927), "Market Value of Industrial Equities", *Review of Economics and Statistics* 9: 37–40.

Smith, E. (1924), *Common Stocks as Long-Term Investments*, New York: Macmillan.

Soldofsky, R. (1966), "A Note on the History of Bond Tables and Stock Valuation Models", *Journal of Finance* 21: 103–110.

Spraakman, G. (2001), "Internal Audit at the Historical Hudson's Bay Company: A Challenge to Accepted History", *Accounting Historians Journal* 28: 19–41.

Stech, T. and V. Pigott (1986), "The Metals Trade in Southwest Asia in the Third Millennium B.C.", *Iraq* 48: 39–64.

Steele, F. (1947), "The Lipit-Ishtar Law Code", *American Journal of Archaeology* 51: 158–164.

Steinkeller, P. (2002), "Money-Lending Practices in Ur III Babylonia: The Issue of Economic Motivation", chapter 4 in M. Hudson and M. van de Mieroop (eds.), *Debt and Economic Renewal in the Ancient Near East*, Bethesda, MD: CDL Press.

Stephens, C. and M. Weisbach (1998), "Actual Share Reacquisitions in Open-Market Repurchase Programs", *Journal of Finance* 53: 313–333.

Stern, L.I. (2004), "Politics and Law in Renaissance Florence and Venice", *American Journal of Legal History* 46: 209–234.

Stigler, G. (1965), *Essays in the History of Economics*, Chicago: University of Chicago Press.

Stout, L. (1988), "The Unimportance of Being Efficient: An Economic Analysis of Stock Market Pricing and Securities Regulation", *Michigan Law Review* 87: 613–709.

Stulz, R. (2007), "Hedge Funds: Past, Present and Future", *Journal of Economic Perspectives* 31: 175–194.

Super, J.C. (1979), "Partnership and Profit in the Early Andean Trade: The Experiences of Quito Merchants, 1580–1610", *Journal of Latin American Studies* 11: 265–281.

Sutton, W. (1882), *The Institute of Actuaries Text book of the Principles of Interest, Life Annuities and Assurances*, London: Layton.

Swetz, F. (1987), *Capitalism and Arithmetic: The New Math of the 15th C. Including the Full Text of the Treviso Arithmetic* (trans. D.E. Smith), LaSalle, IL: Open Court.

Swift, J. (1726), *Gulliver's Travels*, edited with a biographical introduction and notes by I. Asimov, New York: Clarkson Potter (1980).

Székely, G. and D. Richards (2004), "The St. Petersburg Paradox and the Crash of High-Tech Stocks in 2000", *American Statistician* 58: 225–231.

Szelely, G. and D. Richards (2005), "Remain Steadfast with the St. Petersburg Paradox to Quantify Irrational Exuberance", mimeo, Penn. State University, Dept. of Statistics, June 27, 2005.

Tawney, R. (1925), *'Introduction' to a Discourse Upon Usury* by T. Wilson (1572); reprinted by London: Frank Cass (1962).

Taylor, G. (1962), "The Paris Bourse on the Eve of the French Revolution", *American Historical Review* 67: 951–977.

Taylor, J. (2006), *Creating Capitalism: Joint-Stock Enterprise in British Politics and Culture, 1800–1870*, Woodbridge, UK: Royal Historical Society/Boydell Press.

Temin, P. (2006), "The Economy of the Early Roman Empire", *Journal of Economic Perspectives* 20: 133–151.

Temin, P. (2004), "Financial Intermediation in the Early Roman Empire", *Journal of Economic History* 64: 705–733.

Temin, P. (2001), "A Market Economy in the Early Roman Empire", *Journal of Roman Studies* 91: 169–181.

Temin, P. and H.-J. Voth (2004), "Riding the South Sea Bubble", *American Economic Review* 94: 1654–1668.

Thomas, W. (1973), *The Provincial Stock Exchanges*, London: Cass.

Thornton, M. (2007), "Richard Cantillon and the Discovery of Opportunity Cost", *History of Political Economy* 39: 97–119.

Tobin, J. (1958), "Liquidity Preference as Behavior Towards Risk", *Review of Economic Studies* 25: 62–85.

Todd, G. (1932), "Some Aspects of Joint Stock Companies, 1844–1900", *Economic History Review* 4: 46–71.

Todhunter, R. (1901), *The Institute of Actuaries Text-Book on Compound Interest and Annuities*, London: Layton.

Toms, S. and J. Wilson (2003), "Scale, Scope and Accountability: Towards a new paradigm of British business history", *Business History* 45: 1–23.

Tosini, P. (1988), "Stock Index Futures and Stock Market Activity in October 1987", *Financial Analysts Journal* 44 (January/February): 28–37.

Tracy, J. (1985), *A Financial Revolution in the Hapsburg Netherlands*, Los Angeles: University of California Press.

Truong, T. and R. Heaney (2007), "Largest Shareholder and Dividend Policy Around the World", *Quarterly Review of Economics & Finance* 47: 667–687.

Tuck, H. (1847), *The Railway Shareholder's Manual, or, Practical Guide to All the Railways in the World, Completed, in Progress, and Projected* (8th ed., carefully rev. and corr.), London: E. Wilson.

Tyerman, C.J. (1995), "Were There Any Crusades in the Twelfth Century?", *English Historical Review* 110: 553–577.

Udovitch, A. (1970), "Theory and Practice of Islamic Law: Some Evidence from the Geniza", *Studia Islamica* 32: 289–303.

Unger, R. (1980), "Dutch Herring, Technology, and International Trade in the Seventeenth Century", *Journal of Economic History* 40: 253–280.

Vaidya, S., G. Poitras, and A. Talib (1995), "International Accounting Implications of Bond-cum-Warrant Issues", *International Journal of Accounting* 30: 25–36.

Van Berkel, K. (1988), "A Note on Rudolf Snellius and the Early History of Mathematics in Leiden", pp. 156–161 in C. Hay (ed.), *Mathematics from Manuscript to Print, 1300–1600*, Oxford, UK: Clarendon.

Van Berkel, S. (2008), "Should Hedge Funds Be Regulated?" *Journal of Banking Regulation* 9: 196–223.

Van de Mieroop, M. (2002), "Credit as a Facilitator of Exchange in Old Babylonian Mespotamia", chapter 6 in M. Hudson and M. van de Mieroop (eds.), *Debt and Economic Renewal in the Ancient Near East*, Bethesda, MD: CDL Press.

van der Wee, H. (1977), "Monetary, Credit and Banking Systems", chapter 5 in Rich and Wilson (eds.), *The Cambridge Economic History of Europe* (vol. 5), London: Cambridge University Press.

van Dillen, J. (1935), "Isaac le Maire et le commerce des actions de la Compagnie de Indes Orientales", *Revue d'Histoire Moderne* 5–21: 121–137.

van Dillen, J. (1930), "Isaac Le Maire en de handel in actien der Oost-Indische Compagnie", *Economisch-Historisch Jaarboek* 16: 1–165.

van Dillen, J. (1927), "Termijnhandel te Amsterdam in de 16de en 17de eeuw", *De Economist* 76: 503–523.

van Dillen, J., G. Poitras, and A. Majithia (2006), "Issac Le Maire and the early trading in Dutch East India Company shares", chapter 2, pp. 45–63 in G. Poitras, (ed.), *Pioneers of Financial Economics* (vol.I), Cheltenham, UK: Edward Elgar.

van Houdt, T. (1998), " 'Lack of money': A Reappraisal of Lessius' Contribution to the Scholastic Analysis of Money-Lending and Interest-Taking", *European Journal of the History of Economic Thought* 5: 1–35.

van Houtte, J. (1966), "The Rise and Decline of the Market of Bruges", *Economic History Review* 29: 29–47.

Veenhof, K. (2010), "Ancient Assur: The City, Its Traders, and Its Commercial Network", *Journal of the Economic and Social History of the Orient* 53: 39–82.

Veenhof, K. (1997), " 'Modern' Features in Old Assyrian Trade", *Journal of the Economic and Social History of the Orient* 40: 336–366.

Velde, F. and D. Weir (1992), "The Financial Market and Government Debt Policy in France, 1746–1793", *Journal of Economic History* 52: 1–39.

Verboven, K. (2002), *The Economy of Friends. Economic Aspects of Amicitia and Patronage in the Late Republic*, Brussels: Editions Latomus.

Verlinden, C. (1953), "Italian Influence in Iberian Colonization", *Hispanic American Historical Review* 33: 199–211.

Viaene, A. (2006), "Les marchés à terme et conditionnels à la Bourse", in G. Gallais-Hamonno (ed.), *Le marché financier français au XIXè siècle: Aspects quantitatifs des acteurs et des instruments à la Bourse de Paris* (vol. 2), Paris: Les Publications de la Sorbonne.

Viner, J. (1937), *Studies in the Theory of International Trade*; reprinted by New York: Augustus Kelley (1965).

Vitala, E.J. (2006), "An Early Contribution of Martin Faustmann to Natural Resource Economics", *Journal of Forest Economics* 12: 131–144.

Vivenza, G. (2004), "Renaissance Cicero. The 'economic' virtues of *De officiis* I, 22 in Some Sixteenth Century Commentaries", *European Journal of the History of Economic Thought* 11: 507–523.

Vollmers, G.L. (2009), "Accounting and Control in the Persepolis Fortification Tablets", *Accounting Historians Journal* 36: 93–111.

Walker, D. (2001), "A Factual Account of the Functioning of the Nineteenth-Century Paris Bourse", *European Journal of the History of Economic Thought* 8: 186–207.

Watson, A. (trans.) (1985), *The Digest of Justinian* (vols.1 and 2), Philadelphia: University of Pennsylvania Press.

Weber, M. (1924), "Commerce on the Stock and Commodity Exchanges", (trans. S. Lestition 2000), *Theory and Society* 29: 339–371.

Weber, M. (1896/1909), *The Agrarian Sociology of Ancient Civilizations*, London: New Left Books edition, 1976.

Weber, M. (1894), "Stock and Commodity Exchanges", (trans. S. Lestition 2000), *Theory and Society* 29: 305–338.

Weber, M. (1891), *Die romishe Agrargeschichte in ihrer Bedrutung fur das Stata- und Privatrecht*, Stuttgart: Enke.

Weinstein, M. (2003), "Share Price Changes and the Arrival of Limited Liability in California", *Journal of Legal Studies* 32: 1–25.

Wellington, A. (1877), *The Economic Theory of the Location of Railways*, New York: John Wiley.

Wendt, L. (1982), *The Wall Street Journal: The Story of the Dow Jones and the Nation's Business Newspaper*, Chicago: Rand McNally.

Williams, H. (ed.) (1958), *The Poems of Jonathan Swift* (vol. 1, 2nd ed.), Oxford, UK: Clarendon Press.

Williams, J.B. (1937), *The Theory of Investment Value*, Cambridge, MA: Harvard University Press.

Williamson, J. (1927), *Sir John Hawkins, the Time and the Man*, Oxford, UK: Clarendon Press.

Wilson, C. (1941), *Anglo-Dutch Commerce and Finance in the Eighteenth Century*, reprinted by London: Cambridge University Press (1966).

Wilson, J. and C. Jones (2002), "An Analysis of the S&P 500 Index and Cowles's Extensions: Price Indexes and Stock Returns, 1870–1999", *Journal of Business* 75: 505–553.

Wilson, T. (1572), *A Discourse Upon Usury* with a Historical Introduction by R. Tawney; reprinted by London: Frank Cass (1962).

Winjum, J. (1971), "Accounting and the Rise of Capitalism: An Accountant's View", *Journal of Accounting Research* 9: 333–350.

Withers, H. (1910), *Stocks and Shares,* London: Smith, Elder and Co. (2nd ed. 1911; 3rd ed. 1914; 4th ed. 1948.)

Witt, R. (1613), *Arithmeticall Questions, Touching the Buying or Exchange of Annuities; Taking of Leases for Fines, or Yearly Rent; Purchase of Fee-Simple*, London: Richard Redmer; with a second edition, edited with supplements by Thomas Fisher (1634).

Witzel, M. (2006), "Early Contributors to Financial Management: Jeremiah Jenks, Edward Meade and William Ripley", mimeo, University of Exeter.

Witzel, M. and G. Poitras (2004), "Thomas Mortimer, 1730–1810", pp. 825–827 in Donald Rutherford (ed.), *Biographical Dictionary of British Economists*, Bristol, UK: Thoemmes Press.

Wordsworth, C. (1845), *The Law of Railway, Banking, Mining and Other Joint Stock Companies* (5th ed.), London: William Benning.

Wright, C. and E. Fayle (1928), *A History of Lloyd's from the Founding of Lloyd's Coffee House to the Present Day*, London: Macmillan.

Wunsch, C. (2002), "Debt, Interest, Pledge and Forfeiture in the Neo-Babylonian and Early Achaemenid Period", chapter 9 in M. Hudson and M. van de Mieroop (eds.), *Debt and Economic Renewal in the Ancient Near East*, Bethesda, MD: CDL Press.

Yamey, B. (2005), "The Historical Significance of Double-Entry Bookkeeping: Some Non-Sombartian Claims", *Accounting, Business and Financial History* 15: 77–88.

Yamey, B. (1980), "Early Views on the Origins and Development of Book-Keeping and Accounting", *Accounting and Business Research* 10: 81–92.

Yamey, B. (1964), "Accounting and the Rise of Capitalism: Further Notes on a Theme by Sombart", *Journal of Accounting Research* 2: 117–136.

Yamey, B. (1949), "Scientific Bookkeeping and the Rise of Capitalism", *Economic History Review* 1: 99–113.

Yener, A., P. Vandiver, and L. Willies (1993), "Reply to J. D. Muhly, 'Early Bronze Age Tin and the Taurus'", *American Journal of Archaeology* 97: 255–264.

Yonay, Y. (1994), "When Black Boxes Clash: Competing Ideas of What Science is in Economics 1924–1939", *Social Studies of Science* 24: 39–80.

Young, J. and B. Gordon (1996), "Distributive Justice as a Normative Criterion in Adam Smith's Political Economy", *History of Political Economy* 28: 1–25.

Zeitland, M. (1974), "Corporate Ownership and Control: The Large Corporation and the Capitalist Class", *American Journal of Sociology* 79: 1073–1119.

Ziskind, J. (1974), "Sea Loans at Ugarit", *Journal of the American Oriental Society* 94: 134–137.

Zook, G.F. (1919), "Early Dutch and English Trade to West Africa", *Journal of Negro History* 4: 136–142.

Index